ANGIE

The Life and Films of Angie Dickinson

James Stratton

Angie: The Life and Films of Angie Dickinson
Copyright © 2020 James Stratton. All Rights Reserved.

No part of this book may be reproduced in any form or by any means, electronic, mechanical, digital, photocopying or recording, except for inclusion in a review, without permission in writing from the publisher.

Published in the USA by:
BearManor Media
1317 Edgewater Dr #110
Orlando, FL 32804
www.bearmanormedia.com

Printed in the United States of America

ISBN   978-1-62933-514-8 (paperback)
        978-1-62933-515-5 (hardback)

Book and cover design by Darlene Swanson • www.van-garde.com

For Angie Dickinson,

Who Inspired This

And Much More

Also by James Stratton

Hitchcock's North by Northwest: The Man Who Had Too Much

A Star Is Born and Born Again: Variations on a Hollywood Archetype

Picture Business: L.A. Stories, Poems and Portraits

100 Guilty Pleasure Movies

Contents

Acknowledgments ix

Prologue xi

Biographical Profile 1

    Starting Out 1

    Stardom 23

    All That Pizzazz 75

    Household Name 113

    Afterglow 149

The Films 213

    Apprenticeship 213

        Lucky Me 213

        Tennessee's Partner 216

        The Return of Jack Slade 220

        Man with the Gun 222

        Down Liberty Road 228

        Hidden Guns 231

        Tension at Table Rock 235

Gun the Man Down 240
The Black Whip 244
Shoot-Out at Medicine Bend. 247
China Gate. 252
Calypso Joe. 261
I Married a Woman. 264
Cry Terror! 269

Stardom. 278
Rio Bravo. 278
I'll Give My Life 291
The Bramble Bush 295
Ocean's Eleven 302
A Fever in the Blood 310
The Sins of Rachel Cade 317
Jessica. 325
Rome Adventure 333
Captain Newman, M. D.. 341
The Killers 349
The Art of Love. 362
The Chase 370
Cast a Giant Shadow 378
The Poppy Is Also a Flower 387
Point Blank. 394
The Last Challenge 404
Sam Whiskey. 410

Some Kind of a Nut 417
Young Billy Young 422
Pretty Maids All in a Row 429
The Resurrection of Zachary Wheeler 437
The Outside Man. 443
Big Bad Mama 450
L'homme en colère 456
Klondike Fever 462
Dressed to Kill 469
Charlie Chan and the Curse of the
Dragon Queen 483
Death Hunt 489
Big Bad Mama II 494

Featured Player 501
Even Cowgirls Get the Blues 501
Sabrina 505
The Maddening 512
The Sun, the Moon and the Stars 517
The Last Producer 520
Duets 523
Pay It Forward 529
Big Bad Love 536
Ocean's Eleven (2001) 543
Elvis Has Left the Building 549

Television Movies and Miniseries Starring
Angie Dickinson 553

Afterword. 559

Notes 571
    Biographical Profile: Starting Out 571
    Biographical Profile: Stardom. 572
    Biographical Profile: All That Pizzazz 575
    Biographical Profile: Household Name 578
    Biographical Profile: Afterglow 580
    The Films. 585

Sources 587

Index 599

Acknowledgments

THIS PROJECT WOULD not have been completed without the help of Robin Cresto, Matt Severson, and Roberto Rangel. Robin prepared and formatted the manuscript, Matt facilitated the gathering of photos, and Roberto offered design ideas. Each of them was supportive of the work at every stage of the process, and I am equally thankful for their encouragement and their contributions.

Ben Ohmart at BearManor Media has also been on board from the beginning, providing direction and support. He and his staff are models of professionalism, and I cannot imagine a better editor. Special thanks to Darlene Swanson for her excellent book and cover design.

This book is intended as a resource and research guide. Therefore, I am extremely grateful to the many sources that provided information and quotations for the biographical profile and to the reviewers who supplied critical commentary for the discussion of individual films.

All photos courtesy the Collections of the Margaret Herrick Library. Sincere thanks to John Damer and all the other supremely talented staff members there. All images are reproduced for the purposes of critical analysis and historical reference only and remain the copyright of the production companies. Special gratitude to each of them for their support of film scholarship. I very much appreciate the assistance of Robin Cresto and Eduardo Rangel in transferring and storing the photos.

A special thank-you as well to the following people for their enthusiastic support and their belief in the value of this particular project: Joanne McGee, Patricia Kondan Davis, Richard Stratton, Marsha Watkins Stratton, Bryan Olivas, Fernando Marquez, Jeanne Broberg, Susan Boyd, Sugano, Barbara Stewart Russell, Wendy Sinnette, Mary Walsten, Corinne Venit, and Mary Irwin. Thanks also to the staff at South Pasadena's Vidéothèque, the world's greatest DVD rental store.

Prologue

It is February 16, 1960, and she is at the Sands Hotel, Jack Entratter's place in the sun. She has been in Las Vegas before but not sitting ringside in the Copa Room and about to be introduced from the stage. The guys call what they are doing the Summit, in reference to the Eisenhower-Khrushchev meeting planned for Paris. Frank Sinatra, Dean Martin, Sammy Davis Jr., Peter Lawford, and Joey Bishop in that order listed on the big neon marquee out front. This is their last night in town before taking a train back to Los Angeles.

Frank she has known since her first TV appearance on *The Colgate Comedy Hour,* Dean is her likable, laid-back co-star from *Rio Bravo,* the hit Western she has just completed for director Howard Hawks. The other three are new acquaintances, part of Frank's always-evolving entourage. Right now they are all making a picture together, a loose crazy thing about eleven former army buddies knocking off five Vegas casinos, including the Sands, on New Year's Eve. She plays Frank's wife and he is the leader, the same title the other four refer to him by in the nightclub act.

If you can label what they are doing on stage an act. It is more like a few noisy friends entertaining each other at a party. They recite off-color limericks, ad-lib mutual putdowns, and occasionally sing some songs. Frank imitates a Japanese tourist, and Dean kids Sammy about being black. Dressed sharply in either suits or tuxes, they joke constantly about booze and broads. "On your way out," Dean tells the audience, "make sure to buy a copy of my new book, *The Power of Positive Drinking*." At one point, a waiter's cart covered in white linen and well stocked with alcohol is wheeled in, and they make cocktails for each other. Dean drinks his from an ice bucket and does a special version of Lerner and Loewe's "Almost Like Being in Love," singing "What a day this has been, what a hole I am in, why it's almost like losing my mind." Lawford smokes a lot and plays straight man to Frank. When the pace slackens, emcee Joey Bishop makes another ethnic crack or Sammy tap dances.

The room is packed with well-known faces and they all seem to be in on the fun. It is exactly the kind of night she enjoys, the kind of celebrity moment she often has imagined for herself. When the nuns back in North Dakota had asked her what she wanted to be after she grew up, she had answered without hesitation, "A movie star." Not a teacher, a nurse, or even an actress, but a movie star. Now with over a dozen screen credits, the John Wayne Western, and a newly signed contract at Warner Bros., she is just about there.

On the opposite side of the room, stage left, Frank is introducing Shirley Jones and her husband Jack Cassidy, declaring them "two of the young bright stars in our industry." As they stand in response, Frank adds, "I nearly made a picture with this girl once," a droll reference to his abrupt departure from the set of *Carousel* in 1956. Down in front, he recognizes columnist Jimmy Starr from the *Los Angeles Herald Express*, Sammy's father and mother, and actress Erin O'Brien, who worked as a featured singer on both his and Eddie Fisher's television variety shows. "A beautiful little girl," he calls the twenty-six-year-old entertainer.

At Angie's table, immediately next to the stage on his right, Frank first singles out her friend and escort Johnny Grant, a KMPC radio personality and the future Honorary Mayor of Los Angeles. "He's the guy causes all the wrecks on the freeway," quips Frank. Then, before moving on to Dodgers relief pitcher Larry Sherry, it is her turn. "Sitting with Mr. Grant is a lovely lady who you saw in *Rio Bravo* with Mr. Martin . . . Tony Martin . . . Irving Martin . . .Sam Martin," he kids. "She is soon to be seen in a picture called *Bramble Bush* and now she is the leading lady in our picture *Ocean's Eleven*, Miss Angie Dickinson, sitting right over there." A spotlight picks her out of the darkness, and she rises slowly in a black sleeveless dress to grasp Dean's hand. He kisses her, steps aside for Lawford's greeting, and then comically returns for a second handshake and a second kiss.

That spotlight will not often leave her in the years to come. She will become a star and a household name. She will marry a famous celebrity husband and give birth to a cherished daughter. There will be soaring highs and crushing lows, both personally and professionally.

But for now, there is just this brief moment at the center of everything the American public considers sophisticated and cool. She smiles, acknowledges the applause, and holds on for the rest of the ride.

Biographical Profile

Starting Out

IN THE INTRODUCTION to her novel *My Antonia*, Willa Cather writes that she and a friend once "were talking about what it is like to spend one's childhood in little towns like these, buried in wheat and corn, under stimulating extremes of climate: burning summers when the world lies green and billowy beneath a brilliant sky, when one is fairly stifled in vegetation, in the color and smell of strong weeds and heavy harvests; blustery winters with little snow, when the whole country is stripped bare and gray as sheet-iron. We agreed that no one who had not grown up in a little prairie town could know anything about it."[1] Angie Dickinson knew about little prairie towns, knew about the boundless open horizons of the Great Plains where you fought the dust and the wind to make a living. She knew about the dreams that reached out for loftier destinies and softer breezes.

She was born Angeline Brown on September 30, 1931, in Kulm, North Dakota, a small rural community founded in 1892 as a railway stop on the Soo Line. Always sleepy, the place today barely hangs on to its identity as a city. Five city council members with day jobs govern the 350 or so residents, making sure they get water, electricity, and garbage pick-up. Many of the old stores and family farms have disappeared, and people drive farther for services that used to be offered nearby. There are roughly 135 students in kindergarten through twelfth grade, and they all attend class in the same building. One teacher covers the middle and high school math classes, another for science, one more for social science. A librarian and Spanish teacher split all of the English classes. To field a football team sanctioned by the North Dakota High School Activities Association, Kulm kids have had to join with students from neighboring schools in Ellendale and Edgeley.

Named after Kulm, Germany, and Kulm, Bessarabia, the town was settled primarily by Germans and South Russians who brought their strict religious beliefs and strong work ethic along with them. Like elsewhere in the southwestern corner of LaMoure County, grain was the main crop and by 1930, a year before Angeline's birth when the town's population peaked at 742, there were seven grain elevators operating at full capacity and filling the Soo freight cars. Kulm's main street included a stretch of two-story brick buildings housing a general merchandise store, a hardware outfit, a bank, café, post office, and other basic businesses. Wedged next to the city hall was a flat-fronted, white box structure (since demolished) occupied by *The Kulm Messenger* (since discontinued), a weekly newspaper printed by Angeline's father, Leo Henry "Bud" Brown.

Depending on the account, the little girl was delivered either in the newspaper office itself or in a farmhouse just outside of town. News of her birth was covered by *The Messenger* along with crop prices and updates on local government. The headline read, "It's a Girl and the Depression Hangs On."[2] The newspaper was a family affair; Bud wrote the stories and his wife, the former Fredrika Hehr, did the type-setting. They never made a lot of money, but in the early days of the Great Depression they counted themselves lucky enough to be earning a steady income.

Not long after Angeline's birth, Bud and Rika, as she was known to friends and family, moved to the nearby town of Edgeley, about fifteen miles northeast of Kulm on state route 13. Here they took over operation of *The Edgeley Mail*, another weekly publication that guided and reflected local social activity. Slightly larger than Kulm by about 100 citizens, it had the same two blocks of commerce, the same mostly all-white population, and the same wide open spaces where kids could play.

Angeline had already become "Angie," and she and her two sisters, Mary Lou the oldest and Janet the youngest, made the most of Edgeley's limited attractions. "Angie was always a lot of fun," remembered Janet. "She was always smiling, liked fun, and was fun."[3] The three girls enjoyed ice cream at the drug store, attended school fairs, romped with their dog Blackie, and looked forward to the movies that Bud screened each week in the city's auditorium. When they got home, they would act out the stories with friends. Mary Lou was considered the most attractive, but Angie was the most out-going. "I was born a flirt," she described herself even then. "I would sell kisses for a nickel" to finance the ice cream treats.[4] She also insisted on "directing" the movie scenes they performed; "ham" and "pain in the ass" is how she described her behavior.[5]

The Brown family lived behind the newspaper office in the center of town. "We knew everybody, everybody knew us," said Janet.[6] Devoutly Roman Catholic, they attended church regularly and the girls also went to catechism classes. With her grandmother living just down the street and plenty of friends who prized her company, Angie struck everyone as happy and content. Photos from the period show a chubby, round-faced toddler growing into a bright-eyed, finely featured little girl. Even then, however, watching Bud's highly anticipated town hall movies, she envisioned a life beyond the stark plains of North Dakota. "In catechism class," she explained, "the nuns would go up and down the row saying 'what do you want to be?' and when they got to me I stood up and said 'I'm going to be a movie star.' Now I didn't say 'I want to be a movie star.' I said 'I'm going to be a movie star.'"[7] The confidence would later come in handy.

Concealed more deeply beneath Angie's carefree exterior was concern about the family. Again, on the surface, everything seemed fine. Popular and handsome, Bud was well received throughout the community, widely respected for his civic involvement. He wrote whimsical columns about the girls and played outside in the yard with them. In a family portrait taken one winter in front of the newspaper office, he looks like a Hollywood star himself. Wearing a dark wool overcoat with the collar turned up and a scarf looped around his neck, he grins boyishly beneath a black fedora tilted to the side, like Clark Gable minus the moustache. Rika, who possessed dark wavy hair, strong cheekbones, and sharp intelligence, was viewed as his ideal companion. But Bud had a problem. He was a serious alcoholic who became a completely different person when drinking. Unable to control his temper, he would lash out angrily at those around him, including his wife and children. Although he tried more than once to quit, he found it hard to get out from under the addiction.

The girls coped as best they could, trying to rationalize the chaos and remember the good times. "We knew it was the alcohol that made my dad do the bad things he was doing," concluded Janet.[8] For Angie, there was something about the prairie itself that explained what was happening: "Like a lot of people in North Dakota before television, you drank, you played cards. It got dark at five o'clock. I can't blame them but he drank a lot, and it was very difficult."[9] The situation continued to get worse. Bud ignored his work, and Rika took over total management of the newspaper. People who had admired Bud's personal success now shook their heads and lamented the effect that drink was having on his personality. The girls were often frightened by his increasingly violent outbursts. "I remember once," said Angie, "he threatened to kill our dog. He was just drunk, but I'll never forget that we ran screaming to our grandmother's house, 'daddy's gonna kill Blackie.'"[10] Not exactly a Disney storybook memory.

Kids process trauma likes this in various ways; Angie seemed to internalize it, even looking to herself for part of the blame. "He was dangerous," she revealed. "It's just so sad, and I feel very guilty because I think I didn't do my part to try to understand him."[11] That acceptance of human weakness, which morphed into a tolerance of male impropriety, would remain with Angie and characterize her relationships with men as important to her as Bud. Finally, the family's patience reached a breaking point when Bud lost the business and became physically abusive toward Rika. She checked him into a state hospital, packed her daughters, her belonging, and Blackie into the car, and set out for her parents' house in Burbank, California.

It was 1942, and they were part of a great wave of people migrating to the Golden State for jobs in the war factories. As historian Carey McWilliams noted, from 1940 to 1947, California "gained 3,000,000 new residents" and "more people moved to California than were living in Los Angeles County before the war."[12] Because of its decentralized, highly dispersed land use patterns, the area could easily accommodate the rapid construction of new housing and manufacturing facilities. Spacious, one-story factories dedicated to war production sprang up in peripheral suburbs all over the county. The federal government, according to McWilliams, "spent more than a billion dollars on the construction of new industrial plants" in these sleepy, blue-collar outposts.[13] One such community was Burbank, home to the huge Lockheed Aircraft corporation, which produced nearly 20,000 combat planes and bombers during the war. Fueled by the labor force growth, Burbank's population more than doubled during the decade, increasing from 34,000 in 1940 to around 80,000 by 1950.

Rika found a house close to her parents and a job as a linotype operator at the *Burbank Daily Review*. Angie and her sisters quickly adapted to their new surroundings. The flatness of the San Fernando Valley suggested the plains, but the sun, the ocean, and the mountains were new delights. They quickly made friends with neighborhood kids who introduced them to southern California food and fads. There was always something to do, whether it was swimming, window shopping, sightseeing, or riding the trolleys that linked Los Angeles to surrounding cities.

Additionally, the war, which seemed so far away in North Dakota, was very much a part of the picture. Men in uniform crowded the streets while airplanes from the assembly lines filled the sky with their test flights and maneuvers. Sirens regularly announced practice air raids and blackouts, both of which carried special significance for the vulnerable Pacific coast factories. In support of the armed forces, families collected scrap metal, cans of cooking grease, old automobile tires, and inner tubes for recycling into war materiel. Ration books were issued for shoes, sugar, meat, and other scarce items, and decals on car windows regulated how often gasoline could be purchased.

Burbank was a particularly busy place. Along with Lockheed, it was home to the Warner Bros. studios, which contributed both personnel and resources to the war effort and had a particularly profitable year in 1942 with patriotic hits such as *Yankee Doodle*

Dandy and *Casablanca*. Jack Warner built a massive bomb shelter on the lot, painted the soundstage roofs in camouflage colors, and lent his set design technicians to Lockheed where they used canvas backdrops, rubber automobiles, and chicken wire shrubbery to disguise the whole plant as a semi-rural neighborhood. The army commandeered the new facility that Walt Disney had just built in Burbank and installed a searchlight battery to protect the adjacent Lockheed property.

Despite the proximity to the studio where she would become a contract player in less than twenty years, Angie concentrated on her education rather than on dreams of movie stardom. Rika enrolled the girls in Catholic school and expected them to take control of their futures just as she had done. Although her job entering text on the big 90 character linotype keyboards could be tedious and exacting, she was never too tired to make dinner or help with homework. Angie and her sisters shared household chores, keenly aware that they were their own best support network. As in North Dakota, they got along well with each other and with their hardworking role model mother. She had enough to worry about, they knew, and didn't need lazy, ungrateful daughters also. To help with expenses, Angie picked up the kinds of part-time jobs available to young girls her age. By the time she was fifteen, she had worked as a babysitter, doughnut shop waitress, and gift store clerk.

Always claiming that Janet effortlessly mastered new information, Angie had to spend more time on her own studies. She took school seriously and stayed up late with her books. Typical of most parochial schools of the day, the curriculum emphasized drills and memorization with little room for creative expression. More than the traditional math, science, and history classes, Angie preferred English. She was a good writer, earning praise for her essays and even thinking at one point of becoming a reporter. Overall, she received good grades and never called attention to herself in the classroom. Although religious studies were an essential part of the school day, neither Angie nor her sisters expressed interest in following the nuns into a life of service. They might act out a religious story from the movies but that was as far as it went.

The Brown girls and their mother settled into a new, less stressful routine until one day, not unexpectedly, Bud showed up on the doorstep. Having checked himself out of the hospital and followed his family to California, he begged Rika to take him back. Like many women of her generation and her religion, who were averse to divorce or to any kind of professional counseling, she agreed. It was not a good decision. Unable or unwilling to change, Bud continued to drink and drifted from one odd job to another. Rika remained the principal bread-winner and now had her husband's erratic, sometimes violent, behavior to contend with as well.

Angie saw what was happening but kept the pain mostly out of sight from others. Her childhood friend Dorothy Howe sensed the damage Bud was causing and later revealed, "I feel that Angie thought she had an absentee father. It was very difficult for her."[14] The most emotionally direct that Angie would ever be was to say, "Love is destroyed in an alcoholic family, and therefore you don't share and you don't become a family because you don't dare talk. The hope that tomorrow is going to be different is always there."[15] Tomorrow wasn't different, however, and the family struggled forward with its unresolved issues. No matter how self-destructive Bud became, Angie always clung to a paternal loyalty that hovered somewhere between denial and forgiveness. "I hate to paint a picture that my dad was only an alcoholic," she told an interviewer many years later. "He was really a fabulous guy. Everybody loved him and everyone who knew him always said, 'What a shame Bud drank.'"[16] Even when he spanked his daughters, Angie believed they probably had deserved it.

As soon as she was old enough, Angie entered the new Bellarmine-Jefferson High School in Burbank. An independent Roman Catholic college preparatory school founded in 1944 by Monsignor Martin Cody Keating, it was located at 465 East Olive Avenue, not far from both Warner Bros. and Lockheed. Still standing today yet struggling to maintain enrollment, the institution's architecture is early colonial, then as now somewhat at odds with the improvised mishmash of styles that characterizes the rest of Burbank. The main building is a replica of Philadelphia's Independence Hall complete with an iconic tower clock frozen on the north and south sides to commemorate the signing times of the Declaration of Independence and the Constitution. Adjacent to this structure is St. Eleanor's Hall, modeled after Thomas Jefferson's design for the library at the University of Virginia. The main entry's thirteen steps are meant to represent the original colonies in the order by which they became states.

Rika scraped for tuition money, and Angie very much appreciated the opportunity she was given. The war had ended, and students had much brighter prospects ahead of them. Perhaps inspired by the school motto "God helping me, I will do my best today," Angie continued to study hard, earning a straight A average in all of her classes. Language and literature remained favorites, and a composition she wrote for a *Herald Examiner* Bill of Rights essay contest took top honors.

As a co-educational school, Bell-Jeff also allowed Angie to pursue her newly-found interest in the opposite sex. "I was so boy crazy," she admitted, "it's embarrassing."[17] She dated frequently and sometimes, according to Janet, saw two guys on the same day, one in the afternoon and another in the evening. "It was always in my diary," she confessed, "which boy walked me home and which boy looked at me in class and which one hasn't called. I went from one to the other to the other."[18] Janet also recalled that even if Angie would turn down a prospective date, she would congratulate the guy on making the effort. Warren Bowen, who was a couple years younger than Angie and went on to become a successful doctor, marveled that she agreed to see him: "Most girls wouldn't be caught dead going out with someone in the grade below them. It meant nothing to Angie. She was always very comfortable with herself. She had a lot of confidence, and if it bothered someone else she could care less."[19] Years later he remembered her with fond admiration.

Angie had grown out of her cute little girl stage and was an attractive young woman. She wore clothes well and had her dark brown hair waved back from her forehead and parted in the middle or on the right. She looked a little like Norma Jean Baker before she became Marilyn Monroe. Family photos show her in beach shorts and straw hat, a short-waisted jacket with matching skirt, an open white blouse under a tailored beige suit. She could have been a model and, in fact, she and her older sister volunteered as practice subjects for the professional photographer who lived next door. Although she appeared briefly in a Metro-Goldwyn-Mayer promotional short titled *Faith and Freedom*, that was just a special diversion arranged by the school, not a serious career move. It was Mary Lou who first experimented with show business, touring for a time as a magician's assistant.

Upon graduation, Angie was offered a full scholarship at Immaculate Heart College, whose campus was situated on a leafy hillside in the upscale neighborhood of Los Feliz, less than ten miles from Burbank. The college is now closed, its old student union building occupied by the American Film Institute, but since 1916 it had been the most prestigious Catholic college for women in southern California (men were admitted later to help with enrollment). Angie knew the offer was part of a bigger plan and noted, "They worked at keeping you in the fold. They were, I think, hoping I would be a nun, hoping I'd be a leader in the religious community, I suppose, because I was somewhat of a leader."[20] Despite the progressive humanities and art classes (some of which were taught by the soon-to-be famous artist Sister Corita Kent), Angie lasted only a semester. The desire to be out in the world, interacting with both men and women in a professional setting, was stronger than the option of staying in school.

"I needed a job," she explained. "I wasn't of the regular thinking of my day where you just assumed you would get married and have babies."[21] To prepare for the workplace, she transferred to Glendale College, a junior college which recently had opened its new campus in the city's upper northeast corner. She enrolled in a series of typing, stenography, and bookkeeping courses and within a couple of semesters had mastered the basic secretarial curriculum. Like the rest of the school population, where men outnumbered women by four to one, she commuted from home and appeared on campus only for class. Still, there were opportunities to meet a wider circle of people, young adults different from the familiar Catholic kids she had spent her life around so far. One of those new acquaintances was Gene Dickinson, a semi-pro football player also picking up some courses at the school. Angie thought he "was a wonderful person. He was cute, quiet, and not pushy, and I was about eighteen when I met him."[22] With his thick black hair, pointed chin, and long arched eyebrows, he had an expressive face to go with his compact, athletic body. They started dating soon after, spending much of their free time with each other.

Angie also pursued her job search, eventually landing a position at Weber Aircraft Corporation, an airplane seat manufacturer located in Burbank. Smart and efficient, she handled her secretarial duties with an ease that proved she would always be able to make a living for herself. Despite this professional advance, her life was still narrowly defined by Burbank, by the seventeen square miles of urban sprawl where she shared a small, one bath bungalow with four other people and where she sat eight hours a day in a factory office. To escape the sense of confinement, she drifted into marriage with Dickinson.

"I knew before I married I was doing the wrong thing," she later admitted. "I realized my real love for Gene was an escape to get out of a two bedroom house with an alcoholic problem."[23] There was also the matter of Angie's very real physical attraction to Gene: "I was Catholic and you didn't have sex unless you were married, so obviously I was eager for that."[24] The wedding took place on June 2, 1952, the bride in a white gown and veil, the groom in a dark suit and white carnation. Both sets of parents attended. A priest officiated at the small, traditional ceremony which was followed by an outdoor reception that included family and friends. For a restless, independent woman, the rush to marry seemed conventional, especially the June bride's young age (20 years old) and the uninterrupted transition from parents' house to husband's house. While the couple settled into their new routine, Angie continued to work and Gene continued to play sports.

As feared, Angie soon became unhappy with her new life. It was not that Gene had drinking problems like her father or was prone to violent mood swings; on the contrary, he was steady and supportive. It was rather that Angie had not yet found what she really wanted for herself. A beauty pageant changed all that. Gene remembered it as his idea whereas Angie claimed that she got the inspiration by seeing an advertisement on her way home from work. In any case, they both agreed that she should enter Jack Rourke's *Beauty Parade*, a televised pageant carried on the local NBC station. "From Hollywood, where you'll find the most beautiful girls in the world," contestants shared the stage with the shiny new Dodge or Cadillac advertised by that week's sponsor, strolled around in one piece bathing suits, and responded to questions from a "guest advisor" panel composed of mid-level celebrities such as Preston Sturges, Katy Jurado, George Jessel, and Margaret O'Brien. It was every regressive sexist cliché possible; the women were judged on their face, figure, and personality. Appearing in a white swim suit, choker necklace, and heels, Angie charmed the audience with a radiant poise that outclassed the tacky studio set. She won the weekly, monthly semi-final, and year-end title competitions, far exceeding her hope to maybe come home with a Wittnauer watch for participation. Comedian Cliff Arquette, one of the judges on her panel, claimed later to know instinctively that she was marked for stardom and took some credit for "discovering" her. Ironically, the questionnaire she completed for entry into the pageant indicated that "if it came push to shove, one or the other, she would prefer to be happily married" rather than successful in a career.[25]

A casting agent for *The Colgate Comedy Hour* had been watching Rourke's program and called Angie soon afterward. The conversation simultaneously confused and clarified her plans for the future.

"Do you want to be in the show Sunday?" asked the agent.

"I can't act," she hesitated.

"Can you walk?"

"Yes."

"So do you want to be in the show or not?"[26]

The epiphanic moment of this autobiographical anecdote, which Angie would tell to almost every reporter who interviewed her over the years, came when she walked into the rehearsal hall and saw Frank Sinatra working on a song for his own appearance on the show. Having idolized the singer since she was eleven, Angie felt comfortable rather than awed and slipped into an easy familiarity with the entire cast and crew. "The camaraderie of that afternoon is indelible," she elaborated. "I just said, 'Wow, this is where I want to be. Now I know where I want to make my life.' And it was in show business.'"[27] A friendship quickly developed with Sinatra that would take on many permutations as she got older.

She worked three days and played a chorus girl in a comedy sketch with host Jimmy Durante that was broadcast on November 8, 1953. With a check for $140.50 and a glimpse of the limelight, she was hooked. Determined to be good not just pretty, she began to take acting classes at Batami Schneider's workshop in Hollywood. Although she had never performed in plays during high school or college, she discovered a natural talent that could be cultivated through training and experience. She drove herself from one audition to another, eventually meeting a casting agent who liked her fresh appeal. He got her small parts on television shows such as *I Led Three Lives*, where she played a Communist agent, and *The Mickey Rooney Show*, where she was a receptionist. During January of 1954, she appeared in three episodes of *Death Valley Days*, a Western anthology series that was sponsored by the Pacific Coast Borax Company (with its trademark 20 mule team wagon) and was hosted from 1952 to 1963 by Stanley Andrews, known on the program as the "Old Ranger." That same year she got her first, albeit uncredited, motion picture role as a party guest in the Doris

Day musical *Lucky Me*. There followed three brief appearances, one of them credited, in the 1955 Western films *Tennessee's Partner*, *The Return of Jack Slade*, and *Man with the Gun*. She went wherever there was work, from Warner Bros. to RKO to United Artists. Additional television work included appearances on *City Detective*, *Buffalo Bill, Jr.*, *Cameo Theatre*, and multiple episodes of *Matinee Theatre*. "I was an achiever," as she put it, adding ominously that Gene "was not."[28]

Angie begins her career in the 50s as a tightly permed brunette.

With Angie spending more and more time with her acting and Gene with his own interests, the marriage suffered. Always supportive of Angie's career, Gene visited some of the locations but "could tell she didn't like me around" and soon "didn't do that anymore."[29] Angie saw the strain as an inevitable consequence of her new lifestyle: "It changes your interests, so you're no longer the person you were, and your other friends just don't fit into your life anymore. And Gene didn't fit into my life at all."[30] There was never any rancor between the two, but Angie had seen too closely what happens when a couple does not confront its issues, and so, in 1955, they decided to separate (they would formally divorce four years later). Gene took the breakup more personally than she did. "To put that kind of pain on someone," Angie realized, "was really the toughest, lowest period of my life."[31] Despite the failure of their marriage, they remained on such good terms that Angie even went camping later with Gene and his new partner. That ability to maintain a friendship after the end of a romance was a quality, a remarkably mature understanding of human nature, that never deserted Angie during all the encounters to come.

On her own, Angie was now free to accept invitations from any of the talented young men she was meeting around town. One of the most interesting of those new acquaintances was songwriter Jimmy Van Heusen, whom she began dating not long after the separation from Gene. She had met him backstage through that same *Colgate Comedy Hour* job that introduced her to Sinatra, with whom the composer maintained a very close friendship. Already an Oscar winner at thirty-one for "Swinging on a Star," Van Heusen had also co-written the hits "Aren't You Glad You're You" and "Moonlight Becomes You" with Sammy Cahn and would go on to create "Come Fly with Me," "Call Me Irresponsible," "High Hopes," "Last Dance," and "September of My Years" for Frank. An avid flier, he shared Sinatra's appetite for women, alcohol, and adventure.

"You would not pick him over Clark Gable any day," admitted Angie, in reference to his sharply drawn features and shaved head, "but his magnetism was irresistible. He was clever and funny. He used to take his hand, spread the fingers, and roll them down a person's arm—naturally a woman—saying 'Beau-tee-ful.'"[32] They made a rather incongruous couple. Tall and extroverted, he loomed over the 5'5" Angie. His obscenity-laced speech seemed at odds with the melodically subtle music he wrote. In contrast to Gene's reserve, she was impressed by the confidence he displayed, an assuredness that stopped just short of aggression. To her, "He had a great swagger. He walked like he thought. I am fascinated by walks. Frank walked great. John Wayne and Robert Mitchum walked great. And Jimmy had an incredible walk."[33]

They hit several of the top Los Angeles nightspots together. When Sinatra chartered a plane in June, 1955, to fly a bunch of his pals up to Las Vegas to catch Noel Coward's opening at the Desert Inn, she was Van Heusen's date. Among the other guests were Humphrey Bogart, Lauren Bacall, David Niven, agent Irving "Swifty" Lazar, restaurateur Mike Romanoff, Judy Garland and her husband Sid Luft, Ernie Kovacs, Joan Fontaine, Zsa Zsa Gabor, Martha Hyer, and Laurence Harvey. According to Bacall, "Looking forward to Noel, we all flew up to Vegas and were met by hotel [the Sands, where Frank had an interest] representatives; luggage was whisked off to appropriate suites filled with booze. Then drinks, dinner, all arranged by Frank, with a hundred dollars worth of chips for each lady. And a front table for the opening . . . Frank forgot nothing."[34] Coward was a major success, and his starry retinue was duly reported in the newspaper reviews and columns.

ANGIE

There were many such celebrity-filled evenings. During the day, Angie remained a working actress trying to catch her big break. In fact, she was an incredibly busy working actress. From January, 1956, through December, 1957, she appeared in nearly twenty different television programs and eight feature films. She did everything from the classic television drama *The Millionaire* to the boarding house sitcom *It's a Great Life*. Several of her TV roles were in dramatic anthologies such as *General Electric Theatre*, *Four Star Playhouse*, *Chevron Hall of Stars*, and *Schlitz Playhouse* while many others were in Westerns, the American viewing public's genre of choice in the mid Fifties. Five of the ten Nielsen top-rated TV shows for the 1957-58 season were Westerns, including *Gunsmoke* (number one), *Have Gun-Will Travel*, *The Restless Gun*, and *The Legend of Wyatt Earp*. Angie had parts in all four as well as in *Broken Arrow*, *Cheyenne*, and *The Gray Ghost*. The film roles were also in Westerns, quickly produced and forgettable ones conventionally titled *Hidden Guns*, *Tension at Table Rock*, *The Black Whip*, and *Shoot-Out at Medicine Bend*. All of it was valuable experience for a newcomer learning the business.

Maybe the most iconic pairing from these early efforts was the work with James Arness. They first appeared together in the film *Gun the Man Down*, a revenge Western made early in 1956 by John Wayne's independent company Batjac, produced by Wayne's brother Robert Morrison, written by Burt Kennedy, and directed by Andrew V. McLaglen, son of actor Victor McLaglen. Both Kennedy and McLaglen would go on to direct much more prestigious pictures that included Kennedy's *The Rounders* (1965) and *The War Wagon* (1967) and McLaglen's *Shenandoah* (1965) and *The Way West* (1967). Shot in less than two weeks on a movie ranch outside of LA and at the Samuel Goldwyn Studios, *Gun the Man Down* (aka *Arizona Mission*) tells the story of a wounded bank robber abandoned by his associates and girlfriend and later released from prison to take both physical and psychological revenge on his betrayers. At six feet, seven inches, Arness towered over Angie, making her look especially petite and delicate. They seemed to physically embody several key generic dualities of the Western: strength and fragility, wilderness and refinement, simplicity and guile, substance and appearance. With her auburn hair swept back from her forehead, she looked every inch the austere Great Plains beauty capable of controlling a man's destiny.

When Arness began his hugely successful twenty year run as Marshal Matt Dillon on CBS's *Gunsmoke*, Angie had one of the earliest guest parts as Rose Daggitt in a 1957 episode titled "Sins of the Father." She played a Native American woman in a story about miscegenation, racial prejudice, sexual assault (suggested), and justifiable homicide, exactly the kinds of narrative elements that made *Gunsmoke* a so-called "adult Western." They were also the kinds of controversial topics and characters that Angie would take on throughout her career.

Another Native American connection brought Angie into contact with legendarily renegade movie director-writer-producer Sam Fuller. Having just completed *Run of the Arrow*, a film about a Civil War veteran who comes West and marries a member of the Sioux tribe, for RKO Pictures, Fuller realized that Sarita Montiel, the young Spanish actress playing the wife, could not be easily understood in the final print. "Sarita Montiel," he recalled, "was gorgeous to look at, but her accent was incomprehensible on the sound mix."[35] It was at this point that he remembered meeting and talking with Angie when she was at the same studio shooting *Tension at Table Rock*. He had a hunch that she could help: "Angie had a great voice, not to mention those gorgeous legs. I told Angie to come over to the editing room when she got off work. She ended up redubbing every word of Montiel's dialogue."[36] As a thank-you, Fuller promised Angie a leading part in a future film.

That picture turned out to be *China Gate*, which both she and Fuller fit into their tight 1957 schedules. Shot on a Twentieth Century-Fox backlot set-decorated to look like French Indochina, it follows the efforts of two American mercenaries (Gene Barry and Nat King Cole) to destroy a Viet Minh ammunition dump during the First Indochina War. Aiding the men is Lucky Legs (played by Angie), a Chinese Eurasian "half caste" whose five-year-old son was fathered by Barry. With typical bravado, Fuller claimed, "There were enough hot topics in this adventure love story to push everybody's buttons. Communism and colonialism. Racism and tolerance. Black markets and capitalism. Abandonment and fidelity."[37] Like Luise Rainer, Myrna Loy, and Katharine Hepburn before her, Angie was made-up and costumed to seem somewhat Asian. Although the "white washing" of an ethnic character would not escape critical comment today, neither Fuller nor Angie believed anything was culturally inappropriate. For Fuller, it was strictly a matter of looks: "With her high cheekbones and slanted eyes, Angie passed for a Eurasian. And those legs of hers stretched all the way across a CinemaScope screen."[38] The main emphasis remained on the action.

Angie played the part straight, minus any stereotypical accent or gesturality. The opportunity to learn from an experienced auteur like Fuller, who made a picture that same year with Barbara Stanwyck, was of great value, and she took direction gratefully. Barry, about to begin his *Bat Masterson* television series, and singer Cole, star of his own variety program on CBS, also were easy to work with, and the shoot went well. "The crew loved her," Fuller observed of his actress. "Warmhearted and caring, Angie was everybody's pal. Angie and I became pals, too. I sang her praises to everyone in Hollywood."39 Released on May 22, 1957, the film did not create much stir either positively or negatively although it is currently much discussed among Fuller fans and scholars. Angie herself, for whatever reason, rarely spoke about *China Gate* when interviewed about her career.

The rest of that year and the following one were packed with additional television work. There were more Westerns, such as *Colt .45*, *Northwest Passage*, and *Tombstone Territory*, of course, but also appearances on the detective show *Mike Hammer*, the police dramas *M-Squad*, *The Lineup*, and *State Trooper*, the courtroom drama *Perry Mason*, and the anthologies *Studio 57* and *Target*. She even did two episodes each of Jackie Cooper's situation comedy *The People's Choice* and Bob Cummings's self-titled comedy series *The Bob Cummings Show*. By 1960, fifty-two million American households, nine out of ten, had television sets, and any one week's viewership for a top-rated program like *Gunsmoke* could be nearly eighteen million people. Angie was getting a lot of exposure, then, but she did not have a recognizable image. One week she might be a suspect in a crime series and the next a pioneer wife in a Western. Coupled with this challenge was the fact that scores of bright young actresses from both New York and Los Angeles were appearing in the same shows.

Angie also had parts in two feature films that were released in 1958. *I Married a Woman* had been completed in 1956 but kept on the shelf while RKO reshot some scenes and tinkered with the final cut. An unsuccessful attempt to make a movie star out of TV comedian George Gobel, it centered around an advertising executive (Gobel) who neglects his beautiful ex-model wife (Diana Dors) just as she learns she is pregnant. During a night out, they see a movie where, by contrast, John Wayne (playing an ideal modern husband) is sweetly attentive to his young, on-screen wife (Angie). It was an amusing little cameo for Wayne and an inadvertent preview of a truly memorable pairing to come.

The other picture, *Cry Terror!*, had a much more immediate impact on Angie. Directed by Andrew L. Stone, who was specializing in low-budget crime thrillers at the time, it featured Rod Steiger as a psychotic gang boss who holds James Mason and his family captive while forcing them to participate in an elaborate bomb-making/ransom scheme. In one of her least sympathetic roles to date, Angie gave a menacing performance as an accomplice who uses a knife to control the family's young daughter. Handily sharing screen time with dramatic heavyweights such as Steiger and Mason convinced her that she was ready to move forward in her career. "It gave me the confidence because I saw that I had 'it,'" she explained in reference to her chemistry with camera and cast. "I saw that I could take over the screen."[40]

It was a bold statement of purpose from the usually self-effacing actress.

Stardom

THE TRANSITION FROM the 1950s to the 60s was auspicious for Angie, a period marked by the major career success of *Rio Bravo* and the cultivation of deep emotional connections to Frank Sinatra and John Kennedy. It was the time during which her image as sultry screen star, Rat Pack sidekick and Democratic Party stalwart became rooted in the public consciousness. It was exactly the kind of life she had dreamed of back in North Dakota.

Among film scholars and historians, *Rio Bravo* will always be the film for which Angie is most fondly remembered. Her casting in the picture came at the end of a long selection process by director Howard Hawks. Highly regarded today for such classics as *Bringing Up Baby* (1938), *Only Angels Have Wings* (1939), *His Girl Friday* (1940), *The Big Sleep* (1946) and *Red River* (1948), Hawks was returning to the United States after a four year hiatus in Europe that had followed the critical and commercial failure of *Land of the Pharaohs* (1955) and was looking for a picture to put him back on top. Initially considering an adult sex comedy by long-time Billy Wilder collaborator I.A.L. Diamond for his "comeback," he eventually settled on the idea of a Western and convinced Warner Bros. to finance it in exchange for the dismissal of Hawks's breach of contract suit against the studio.

Angie in a Warner Bros. publicity photo at the time of *Rio Bravo* (1959).

Written by Jules Furthman and Leigh Brackett with story contributions from Hawks and his daughter Barbara McCampbell, *Rio Bravo* was intended as a direct response to *High Noon* (1952), a film that Hawks hated for the way in which it depicts a small-town marshal (Gary Cooper) appealing to residents for help in confronting a gang of vengeful outlaws. Never, he believed, would a real lawman behave in such a craven manner. Conversely, *Rio Bravo* focuses on the efforts of a sheriff, his alcoholic deputy, a young gunslinger and a game-legged, cantankerous old man to hold a murder suspect in jail as the criminal's cattle baron brother and his henchmen lay siege to the town.

It was always clear that John Wayne, who had worked successfully with Hawks on *Red River* and shared his disdain for *High Noon*, would play Sheriff John T. Chance. For the burnt-out Dude character, Hawks considered Montgomery Clift, James Cagney, William Holden, and nearly twenty other actors before offering the part to Dean Martin. A similarly long list was reviewed for hired gun Colorado until Hawks hit on the clever notion of casting teen heartthrob Ricky Nelson, then starring on his father's hit television show *The Adventures of Ozzie and Harriet* and enjoying a lucrative rock 'n' roll singing career. To play cranky old Stumpy, Hawks selected three-time Academy Award winning character actor Walter Brennan, who was also appearing on a successful TV series, *The Real McCoys*. The television connections, he believed, would pay off at the box office.

Complementing the director's familiar exploration of a tightly bonded male community pledged to the completion of a professional task was the Hawksian woman—vibrant, strong-willed, unconventional and appreciative of personal codes. Like singer Bonnie Lee (Jean Arthur) in *Only Angels Have Wings* and café entertainer Marie "Slim" Browning (Lauren Bacall) in *To Have and Have Not* (1944), wandering saloon girl and gambler Feathers would be *Rio Bravo*'s iteration of the character. She falls in love with Chance and appears at an opportune moment to help him escape an ambush.

Hawks's preference was to groom a complete unknown and mold her into his ideal heroine as he had done with Bacall in *To Have and*

Have Not, but there was not sufficient time for such a laborious process. Instead, he considered several experienced performers as well as a few young actresses who were early in their careers and had not yet established a recognizable "image" with moviegoers. Among the candidates were Mari Blanchard, Diane Brewster, Capucine, Rhonda Fleming, Beverly Garland, Jane Greer, Martha Hyer, Carolyn Jones, Piper Laurie, Julie London, Sheree North, Janis Paige and Donna Reed. As Feldman's girlfriend and client, 30-year-old French fashion model Capucine came close, but Hawks ultimately decided her accent was too heavy (two years later, however, she would make the comedy Western *North to Alaska* with John Wayne). Fleming, Greer, Hyer and Reed had all appeared before in Westerns and would have given Feathers a stronger touch of worldliness yet after extensive deliberation Hawks still was not satisfied.

It was at this point that he took the advice of his friend Christian Nyby, who had directed the science fiction thriller *The Thing from Another World* (1951) for Hawks's independent production company, and screened some of Angie's television work, particularly a *Perry Mason* episode directed by Nyby. Impressed with what he saw, Hawks promptly invited her to his office for a series of meetings. To validate his gut feeling, he shot a test with Angie as Feathers and Frank Gifford as John Chance. That sealed the deal; she was offered the part.

Thrilled with the career opportunity, she explained to Hawks, "I've always been told, if I do a picture with George Cukor or Howard Hawks, I'd be in clover," and he replied, "Do you know why that is? It's because we do all your thinking for you."[1] True to form, he went to work on Angie's look, instructing her to lose weight, talk more slowly, keep her chin tilted downward, and develop a throatier speaking voice. He selected a soft, lacy wardrobe to emphasize her figure and even, briefly and without any follow-through, considered changing her name. It was not the complete make-over he had engineered for Bacall and had planned for Margaret Sheridan (who withdrew from *Red River* to raise a family and then appeared belatedly in *The Thing*), but the sense of control was similar. Hawks signed Angie to a personal contract with his Armada Productions Company and then split the agreement with Warner Bros.; specified "borrowers" included Nyby, Wayne, and Hawks's producer brother William.

Shooting began on May 1, 1958, in Old Tucson, Arizona, a replica of the original adobe walled city built by Columbia Pictures several years earlier. Since almost all of her scenes were interiors, Angie did not report to the location until May 19, by which time temperatures already had surpassed one hundred degrees. Her first day of filming involved a scene, later dropped from the picture, where she arrives in town on a stagecoach. She had trouble feeling natural and getting into the rhythm of her character, and the hot weather did not help. "I hated my costume and I was intimidated in the acting because I felt I didn't look good," she told Hawks biographer Todd McCarthy. "It was a very tough first day, with five or six takes of every shot . . . He (Hawks) didn't want to show me how to do it. If he showed me what he wanted, it wouldn't be my own original approach."[2] Eventually she relaxed, learning how to read Hawks's body language and developing confidence in her interpretation of the role. Much easier was the scene where she throws a flowerpot through a hotel window to distract the outlaws and help Colorado rescue an unarmed Sheriff Chance.

With little on-screen work to do, Angie spent much of her time wandering around the set and exploring the Arizona desert, often in the company of seventeen-year-old Ricky Nelson. As the two "rookies," they felt a professional kinship and gracefully passed the initiation rituals of the older veterans—Nelson getting tossed into a pile of cow manure on his birthday and Angie eating a plate of mountain oysters. So comfortable was she among the mostly all-male cast and crew that she quickly became known as one of the guys, a real-life embodiment of the Hawksian ideal and a flattering reputation that carried over to later productions such as *Ocean's Eleven* (1960) and *Captain Newman, M.D.* (1963).

When the company finished location shooting on May 28, production shifted to Stage 4 of the Warner Bros. studios in Burbank, and Angie became much more directly involved. Because most of her scenes were with Wayne, Hawks concentrated on the dynamic between the two performers, who had actually briefly appeared together a few months earlier as husband and wife in that film within a film cameo from the George Gobel-Diana Dors comedy *I Married a Woman* (1957). Twenty-four years her senior, Wayne was a bit hesitant in the romantic scenes with Angie and Hawks smoothly incorporated the shyness into his character. As Feathers flirts and fusses, Chance reacts with annoyance, frustration and, finally, awkward affection. In a reworking of Bacall's famous "It's even better when you help" response to kissing Bogart in *To Have and Have Not*, Hawks has Feathers announce, "I'm glad we tried it a second time. It's better when two people do it," after she finally kisses Chance.

Aided by Hawks, Angie hit on comic exasperation as the key to Feathers's relationship with Chance. It's there in the moments where Chance accuses her of cheating at cards, scolds her for sitting guard outside his hotel room, and tries to put her on a stage leaving town. For the final scene, after the men have subdued Burdette's gang, Feathers models a skimpy costume she plans to wear for her new singing job at the hotel and Chance threatens to arrest her if she does. Crucially, the gesture tells both Feathers and the audience that the sheriff loves her, but after several takes the interaction was not working. Hawks suggested that Angie start crying midway through her dialogue, and with little other direction she nailed the emotional pay-off.

The sixty-one days of filming wrapped on July 23, only a week over schedule. By December, with Hawks supervising the editing, *Rio Bravo* was ready for release, but Warner Bros. decided to wait until March 18, 1959, when the picture debuted at the Roxy in New York City. Two days later it opened nationally, becoming the number one box office attraction during its first week of release and ultimately totaling $5.2 million in North American rentals on a budget of $1.95 million (plus $100,000 up front for Hawks). The reviews were good if not great with director and cast receiving praise for their competence and professionalism. Over time, however, *Rio Bravo* has grown in reputation, regarded by some critics as one of the best American films ever made. "If I were asked to choose a film that would justify the existence of Hollywood," Robin Wood wrote in his 1968 book on Hawks, "I think it would be *Rio Bravo*."[3] In 2012, the editors of *Sight and Sound* ranked it sixty-third among the top movies of all time, and Guillermo Cabrera Infante summed up its impact by stating simply, "*Rio Bravo* is a masterwork."[4] Of Angie's contribution, David Thomson has argued, "Angie Dickinson took her moment the way Bob Beamon jumped in Mexico City in 1968,"[5] a reference to the track and field athlete's record-breaking long jump at the XIX Olympics.

Based on her personal contract, Angie hoped that moment would lead to more golden opportunities with the newly hot director: "I thought, gosh, I was gonna be molded into this great star by Hawks and do another movie with him." Hawks, however, looking to shore up his own finances, sold the contract outright to Warner Bros. "Which pissed me off," Angie later remembered.[6]

More satisfying was her personal relationship with Richard Brooks, a writer-director nearly twenty years her senior. Responsible for hard-hitting social/political dramas such as *Deadline-USA* (1952), *Battle Circus* (1953), *Blackboard Jungle* (1955), and *Something of Value* (1957), he was lover, mentor, and perhaps even father figure. As an outspoken proponent of civil rights and economic opportunity, he encouraged Angie's growing interest in liberal politics. They were seen around town together at the races and at restaurants, dates which were detailed by Hedda Hopper and other gossip columnists. Sam Fuller recalled, "My close friend Richard Brooks and Angie became a couple. I shot some home movies of the two lovers cavorting in my pool."[7] Known as an "intellectual" filmmaker, he shared Angie's love of books and seemed the ideal companion for her, a man who understood the business but did not allow it to totally define him.

Brooks also had a growing reputation for being difficult on set, prone to angry outbursts when frustrated by cast and crew members or challenged by studio executives over content. Much less social than Angie, he preferred to see a very small circle of friends for dinner or tennis. Brooks would never have jumped aboard a chartered plane with Frank Sinatra and a flock of celebrities to catch Noel Coward's debut in Las Vegas. Eventually personality differences and career priorities drew them apart, yet Angie always remained thankful for the love and support Brooks provided during such an uncertain period in her life. The director went on to marry Jean Simmons, the London-born actress who starred in his award-winning 1960 film *Elmer Gantry*.

Meanwhile, Angie made only three TV appearances between

1959 and 1960, and her film career, rather than building on the *Rio Bravo* momentum, was stalled. Moviegoers' next opportunity to see her on the big screen was in two mediocre films that did little to advance her popularity. *I'll Give My Life*, also known in the United States as *The Unfinished Task*, was shot in 1955 but not distributed nationwide until February 3, 1960. It looks like a catechism film, a strange follow-up to the Hawks picture. Produced by Concordia Films and partly financed by the Lutheran Church, Missouri Synod, it is the story of Jim Bradford, an engineering student who declines to join his father's construction firm and becomes a foreign service minister instead. Angie played Alice Greenway, secretary to the father and wife of the young missionary. Her costumes could not have been further from Feathers's tights and bustiers; she wore high collared dresses, veiled hats with gloves, turtlenecks, and sweaters.

Ironically, the film references much that Angie had left behind, particularly the austere Scandinavian Lutheranism of Kulm and the secretarial job in Burbank. In delivering lines like "Grandma will tuck you in and I'll be in later to hear your prayers" and "You wouldn't wonder if you really knew what the Gospel means to these people," she called on her memories of the proper young women with whom she had attended school. Her performance was credible enough, but the film's limited run drew almost no attention.

Released just three weeks later on February 4, 1960, *The Bramble Bush* was the first picture Angie made under the new Warner Bros. arrangement. Shot entirely on the Warner lot, it kept her in Los Angeles during the first half of 1959. The plot revolves around Dr. Guy Montford (Richard Burton), who returns to his Massachusetts hometown to find a dying childhood friend, a corrupt lawyer running for district attorney, a sympathetic hospital administrator and two willing female admirers. More than one reviewer noticed a close resemblance to Peyton Place, the small New England community of Grace Metalious's 1956 best-selling novel and 20th Century Fox's 1957 movie.

Angie joins Richard Burton and Barbara Rush in *The Bramble Bush*'s steamy love triangle (1960).

"Why do you want to be a nurse? It's so unglamorous,"[8] Angie once told her sister Janet, and now here she was in the part of Fran, a beautiful young nurse involved with the politician but in love with Montford. Both Patricia Crest and Diana Lynn had also tested for the role. For a steamy story involving euthanasia, illicit romance and a climactic courtroom trial, it is not surprising that director Daniel Petrie instructed Angie to emphasize Fran's sexual skills over her medical ones. Clad only in a slip, she did exactly that in a motel scene with Jack Carson and a similar rendezvous with Burton. "I'm not a motel tramp," read her lobby poster tagline, "I don't want you to think I am." Angie was unhappy with her role and later described *The Bramble Bush* as "a rotten movie, just cheap and terrible."[9]

Burton also hated the picture and couldn't wait for it to be finished. One of his biographers, Tom Rubython, has alleged an on-set affair with both Angie and his other female co-star Barbara Rush, but no one else familiar with the actors has confirmed such a claim. Jack Warner had battled Production Code Administrator Geoffrey Shurlock for several months over the film's content and marketed it as an explosive potboiler about people "who hunger for the forbidden fruit of the bramble bush." In competition with similarly sensationalized films such as *Butterfield 8* (1960) and *From the Terrace* (1960), it made a decent enough $3 million. Although she received lower billing after Burton, Rush, and Carson, Angie demonstrated once again that increasing confidence and comfort before the camera, even in her scenes with the formally trained, widely experienced, yet ill-at-ease Burton, that had been building since her *Cry Terror!* self-revelation. In *The New York Times*, Bosley Crowther commented, "As a trained nurse who vainly loves the doctor and has some other gnawing problems of her own, Angie Dickinson is passionate and pretty, a combination that is hard to beat."[10]

Angie's next project, *The Sins of Rachel Cade*, was equally scandalous. Based on a novel by Charles Mercer, the story concerned an unmarried medical missionary who comes to 1930s Belgian Congo and finds herself caught up in tribal rivalries, two clandestine love interests, and an unplanned pregnancy. The fact that she was given such a juicy part over other young Warner Bros. contract actresses like Diane McBain, Carroll Baker, Dorothy Provine, and Connie Stevens testified to the high standing she had with Jack Warner and other studio executives. They envisioned the film as a Protestant version of *The Nun's Story* (1959), complete with the same setting, producer (Henry Blanke), and male co-star (Peter Finch). The hope was that the part of Rachel might do for Angie what *The Nun's Story* did for Audrey Hepburn.

As played out over several years, the picture had a long, laborious path to the screen. RKO first optioned the book in 1956 and then, amidst its ongoing corporate upheaval, sold the rights to Warner Bros. soon afterwards. Edward Anhalt, who with his wife Edna had won an Oscar for the *Panic in the Streets* (1950) screenplay, drafted a script, which lingered in pre-production while various plot and character changes were made. Staffing was strictly an in-house arrangement. Gordon Douglas, having proven himself capable of steering contract players from the Warner Bros. television unit through pictures such as *Fort Dobbs* (1958), *Yellowstone Kelly* (1959), and *Up Periscope* (1959), was selected to direct. Studio veterans J. Peverell Marley, Owen Marks, and Max Steiner, nearing the ends of their remarkable careers, were enlisted for cinematography, editing, and musical score respectively. In addition to Dickinson and Finch, Roger Moore, about to appear in the Warner Bros. television series *The Alaskans* (1959-60) and *Maverick* (1960-61), joined the company as the RAF doctor who fathers Rachel's child. Finally, after all the delays and revisions, Angie reported for wardrobe tests in July and began filming in late August, 1959.

Unlike *The Nun's Story*, *The Sins of Rachel Cade* did not benefit from location shooting but was confined to the studio's backlot and soundstages. Despite the best efforts of art director Leo Kuter and set decorator George James Hopkins, the setting never seemed authentic. Douglas had a good feel for the physical action but not so much for the interior drama of a religious woman torn between her faith and her passion. Realizing that it was up to her to carry the movie, Angie delivered a strong yet restrained performance although early publicity and subsequent advertising focused more on Rachel's sins than on her service. Already by September, the same month that Nikita Khrushchev and his wife visited Los Angeles, the Protestant National Council of Churches was opposing her role as one that "over-emphasized sex for sex's sake."

Playing a nurse for a second time in *The Sins of Rachel Cade* (1961).

Filming continued throughout the autumn with Angie often putting in twelve and fourteen hour days. Certainly she could have used more help from her two British co-stars. Just like Richard Burton before him, Peter Finch disparaged his Warner Bros. assignment, spending most of his time away from the set drinking and carousing. Privately he told friends that the film suffered from "script poisoning," an initial weakness made worse by all the studio meddling.[11] Only thirty-two at the time, Roger Moore was affable and cooperative but much more skilled in light comedies and swashbucklers than adult dramas. With director and cast scheduled for new projects, shooting finally wrapped on November 9, 1959. For unknown reasons, Warner Bros. then sat on the finished film for over a year, ultimately releasing it on April 2, 1961. Angie would have to wait months before learning how critics and audiences were going to respond to her first top-billed part in the kind of "women's picture" usually built around established stars like Susan Hayward and Lana Turner.

At the start of the new decade, Angie found herself in a not-uncommon Hollywood position, that of an aspiring actress with a string of television credits, one hit movie, and a standard studio contract. What made her different, however, was the ongoing presence in her life of Frank Sinatra. She had liked the film and recording star since that first day in 1953 and had begun a romantic involvement with him and Van Heusen at the same time. "I saw both of them alternately," she explained. "I mean, I just adored them both. . . . I was very, very happy with either one, whomever I was with."[12] Frank would have the more lasting influence. "We were lovers on and off for many years," she confided to Australian television host Angela Bishop. "He was the most important man in my life."[13] Theirs was a very loose affair, overlapping with other relationships and mixing periods of intimacy with casual friendship. According to Angie, "We really liked each other, really had a very good relationship. Neither one of us was that hung up on each other, so it was 'hey, want to have dinner.'"[14] They discussed marriage but Frank, after his seven turbulent years with Ava Gardner, didn't want to marry another movie star and that was exactly the goal Angie had set for herself.

In early 1960, the famous Rat Pack movie *Ocean's Eleven* connected the two of them professionally. Director Gilbert Kay had first pitched the story of some World War II army buddies who reunite to simultaneously rob five Las Vegas casinos to Peter Lawford in 1955. Three years later, Lawford purchased the rights for $10,000 and shared the idea with Sinatra, who felt it had the makings of a hit movie and promptly bought into the deal himself. With one picture owed to Warner Bros. as part of an earlier contract, Sinatra offered the project to Jack Warner in July 1958 and the studio boss accepted. The budget was set at just over $2 million.

Once fully on board, Sinatra began to see the film as a holiday excursion, casting his pals in all the major roles. Dean Martin played Sam Harmon, a lounge singer reluctantly involved in the caper; Lawford was playboy Jimmy Foster; Sammy Davis, Jr. was Josh Howard, a former baseball player turned garbage collector; comedian Joey Bishop appeared as ex-boxer Mushy O'Connors. Rounding out the cast were Richard Conte, Henry Silva, Buddy Lester, Richard Benedict, Norman Fell, and Clem Harvey. Sinatra himself played Danny Ocean, mastermind of the eleven man crew, and as uncredited producer he made certain everyone was paid well, from Martin's flat fee of $150,000 to Conte's $8,000 per week. A salaried Warner contract player and Sinatra insider, Angie was an ideal choice to play Ocean's estranged wife Beatrice. She received top billing after Frank, Dean, Sammy, and Peter.

While the ever-evolving script continued to go through a series of revisions, director Lewis Milestone, a sixty-four year old Hollywood veteran who had won an Oscar in 1930 for *All Quiet on the Western Front*, arrived in Las Vegas on January 12, 1960, and began location filming there a few days later. That shoot became the stuff of show business legend. Jack Entratter, general manager of the Sands Hotel and Casino, a key location used in the movie, had hired Sinatra, Martin, and Davis to entertain in the resort's Copa Room for a three week engagement that coincided with the filming schedule. At first they performed individually, two shows a night, until the third night when Sinatra interrupted Davis for going long and carried him off the stage. When Dean did the same thing to Frank, the audience went wild and the guys knew they had something. Soon Lawford and Bishop joined in, and the act became the five of them pouring drinks, horsing around, breaking into each other's songs, and telling a variety of crude, often ethnically tinged, jokes. It was juvenile, it was sloppy, and it was the hottest ticket in town. Paying customers loved the nightly bacchanalia, which quickly attracted visits from Kirk Douglas, Cary Grant, Gregory Peck, Marilyn Monroe, Rosalind Russell, and other Hollywood celebrities. Stories spread in the gossip columns of wild all-night parties and late, hung-over appearances on the set.

Back in the country after a quick three-week holiday USO tour of Japan, Korea, and Taiwan with TV personality Johnny Grant, Angie was there to shoot her own scenes and experienced a somewhat less exaggerated version of the revelry. "It was not as active as one is led to believe," she remembered some years afterward, revealing that the whole group assembled infrequently and did not indulge in twenty-four hour binges. Still, she conceded, the atmosphere was charged with sexual energy and "when you're a single woman you had better know what you're hanging around for or you could get in a lot of trouble."¹⁵ With no desire to "hook up," she concentrated on the work and tried to fit in as one of the boys, just as she had done on the *Rio Bravo* set.

According to Rat Pack chronicler Shawn Levy, the movie's call times may not have been absent but definitely were loose: "Milestone usually got one Rat Packer at a time, occasionally two, having the whole quintet at his disposal only once—to film the closing credits on a workday cut short by high winds. Most days found a single member of the Rat Pack on the set for about three hours, usually from about 3:00 P.M. to 6:00; Sammy and Peter had the most frequent morning calls (9:00 or 10:00 A.M.), with Sammy easily spending the most time in front of the cameras throughout the month."¹⁶ Angie reported whenever Milestone needed her. "It wasn't that it wasn't professional," she explained of the production, "but you'd have to look hard to find a camera to prove to you that they weren't playing. They really had fun together. The director was very easy. He knew exactly who was signing his check."¹⁷

If *Rio Bravo* made Angie Dickinson credible as an actress, *Ocean's Eleven* made her cool. She was introduced in the Copa audience by Frank and photographed smiling broadly from a table right next to the stage. Her role was not large and did not require much effort, but then dramatic impact was not what Frank had in mind. He wanted to have a good time and let viewers have a vicarious taste of his swinging life style. Angie got the point. She looked great, her hair noticeably lightened from the medium brunette she had been in *Rio Bravo*, and she bantered easily with Frank and Dean. "What's wrong with a little hey-hey?" Sinatra asks in one scene and she replies, "Nothing, nothing at all. I'd never knock it as long as there was a little love involved." When Dean makes a reference to mother love, she takes frisky offense: "I'll consider mistress, plaything, toy for a night, but I refuse to be your mother. That's out." The image she projected was that of a savvy and attractive woman of the world, no push-over but willing to have fun with the right guy(s). There was more than just a whiff of misogyny involved (at one point in the film Frank tells her, "Now just sit there and don't interrupt me") and Angie's casual acceptance of her objectification, of her reputation as a naughty sex symbol, would be a defining characteristic over the next many years.

Among the notables who dropped by the Copa Room was the handsome junior Senator from Massachusetts who had just announced a run for the Presidency. "All of us hung out at the bar," recalled Angie, "and Senator John F. Kennedy came up to the table to say hello to Frank and I got introduced to him. And to say the least he was so dynamically charismatic. All of us were keen on him and excited that he might run and he might make it."[18] Sinatra was especially keen on the candidate, partying with him and using his friendship with Kennedy's brother-in-law Lawford to get even closer. Public association with a man who might become President of the United States fueled Sinatra's sense of importance and he encouraged all of his friends, including Angie, to make Kennedy feel at home in Las Vegas.

Location filming finished on February 16, and cast and crew took a train back to Los Angeles where they regrouped two days later at the Warner Bros. studio in Burbank. Discipline did not become much tighter, and the guys continued to make sporadic appearances before the camera. Once again Angie's responsibilities were limited, and she waited expectantly for her next assignment under the Warner contract. Despite the challenges, Milestone wrapped production on March 18, bringing the film in $100,000 under budget and rejuvenating his career. Editor Philip Anderson quickly assembled a final print, which Jack Warner approved for nationwide release in August.

During that spring, Angie participated in two Hollywood ceremonies that further boosted her public profile. On March 10, she accepted the Foreign Press Association's Golden Globe Award for Most Promising Female Newcomer. Discontinued after 1983, the category often had multiple winners and she shared the honor on this occasion with Janet Munro, Stella Stevens, and Tuesday Weld. Past winners had included Shirley MacLaine, Kim Novak, Natalie Wood, Carolyn Jones, Dana Wynter, and *The Bramble Bush* co-star Barbara Rush. Even more of an insider affair than it is now, the event was held at the Ambassador Hotel's Cocoanut Grove and gave Angie the opportunity to mix with the studio executives who might hire her and the international reporters who would be writing about her. Then, on April 4, after being named "Miss April" by *Argosy* magazine, she and *Ocean's Eleven* cast mate Richard Conte appeared at the 32nd Annual Academy Awards to present the Oscars for Best Art Direction to *Ben-Hur* (color) and *The Diary of Anne Frank* (black and white). Hosted by Bob Hope at the Pantages Theatre on Hollywood Boulevard, the ceremony was broadcast by NBC with no commercials and lasted a mere one hour and forty minutes. Although *Rio Bravo* was not nominated in any category, Angie reconnected with John Wayne, who gave the Best Director trophy to *Ben-Hur*'s William Wyler (this was the year of that epic's big 11 awards juggernaut). To be a presenter so early in her career, in the company of stars such as Wayne, Gene Kelly, Doris Day, Gary Cooper, and Susan Hayward, was certainly an indication of the professional interest she was generating. A press report noted that she "was stunning in a fitted gold brocade."

By summer, when the Democratic National Convention convened in Los Angeles on July 11, 1960, Angie, like Sinatra himself, had become an actively involved JFK supporter. The city was buzzing with enthusiasm for the photogenic political star and Angie was caught up in the excitement. "Here was this magnificent, beautiful Senator Kennedy that made us all think it was just a new god on the horizon," she raved.[19] In *The Making of the President 1960*, Theodore H. White wrote that "as the delegates began to gather in the first week of July, Los Angeles gave of its best. Smogless and milk-blue, the skies stretched on day after day, as gentle and pure as they must have been a generation ago, before industry and the automobile fouled the air of the city with their wastes."[20] Against this golden backdrop, Angie showed up for rallies, fund-raisers, and informal gatherings at the Lawfords' Malibu beach house. On the evening of July 10, along with scores of other Hollywood luminaries such as Judy Garland, Tony Curtis, Janet Leigh, Milton Berle, and Shirley MacLaine, she attended a $100-a-plate dinner at the Beverly Hilton. Nominally billed as a money raising event for the entire party, it highlighted the wide support that Senator Kennedy had within the moviemaking community.

Amid the excitement of Presidential politics and Rat Pack socializing, Angie also worked on another film as part of her Warner Bros. contract. Produced by television executive Roy Huggins and directed by Vincent Sherman, *A Fever in the Blood* was one more of those inexpensively produced pictures designed to capitalize on the popularity of the studio's TV performers. Efrem Zimbalist, Jr., then appearing as Stu Bailey in *77 Sunset Strip* (1958-64), and Jack Kelly, known for the role of "Bart Maverick" in *Maverick* (1957-62), starred opposite Angie and veteran actors Don Ameche and Herbert Marshall in a tale of political corruption and murder.

Sherman, who had guided Bette Davis in *Old Acquaintance* (1943) and *Mr. Skeffington* (1944), believed that the story was too dated and the target audience too narrow. In his autobiography, he wrote that "the fact that Zimbalist and Kelly, as the two leads, were known primarily through TV would, I felt, cause audiences to regard the film as merely an enlarged TV program. This, together with the familiarity of the story, despite the good performances of all the actors and a skillful job of producing, writing, and directing, doomed us from the start. Had Roy not been the producer and a friend, I would have refused to make it. The result was that although we worked hard and there were many good scenes of political drama, it was not enough to make it a hit."[21] Angie's role, as the young wife of a senior United States Senator caught up in a bribery scandal, had personal resonance given her very real involvement in national politics. A final scene in which she tells gubernatorial candidate Zimbalist to have faith in the good judgment of nominating convention delegates might have come from any of the speeches delivered that July in Los Angeles.

To help get out the JFK vote in the fall, Angie embarked on a ten-day campaign swing with Curtis, Leigh, and others. "I campaigned for Kennedy the week before the election in seven states across the country," she told *The Hollywood Reporter* many years afterward. "A group of us went out to barnstorm in seven states and we wrapped it up in New York at the Coliseum the Saturday night before the elections were coming on Tuesday, and he came around to thank us all there."[22] Celebrity caravans, a familiar presence on today's political campaigns, were a novelty in the 1960 election, and the group drew large crowds wherever it went. *Ocean's Eleven* was in wide release, having opened on the third of August at a lavish Las Vegas premiere filmed by Jack Paar for his television program, and was doing big business all across the country. Consequently, Angie was a major attraction and one of the troupe's most popular speakers. At every stop, the organizers played the bouncy campaign song that Frank had recorded, a special lyrics version of Sammy Cahn and Jimmy Van Heusen's "High Hopes."

When JFK narrowly defeated Richard Nixon on election day, Angie was delighted, celebrating with friends and conveying congratulations to the President-elect. As a thank-you for all of her hard work during the campaign, he invited her to Washington, D.C. for the Inaugural festivities. Escorted by Kennedy's long-time friend Paul "Red" Fay, Jr., she attended various receptions as well as the big three-hour pre-Inauguration gala organized by Sinatra and where everyone from Frank to Harry Belafonte and Ethel Merman delivered performances. At a private party held afterward in Paul Young's upscale steakhouse, she met JFK's father Joseph P. Kennedy, who noticed her with Fay and remarked loudly, "Why are you wasting your time with a bum like this fellow?" To Fay, the old man commented, "Wait until I tell your wife how you are conducting yourself."[23]

Most Kennedy biographers insist that Jack and Angie were also conducting a months-long romantic relationship. Fay, according to James Kaplan, "had been drafted for the inaugural week to escort Dickinson to various functions—in short to act as a beard for the president-elect, who had commenced a dalliance with the actress months before."[24] No less an authority than Presidential historian Richard Reeves wrote that Fay's "assignment for this night and the next day and night was to escort a twenty-eight-year-old actress named Angie Dickinson, with whom Kennedy slipped away to private rooms a couple of times during the ceremonies."[25] Angie herself never admitted more than friendship and admiration for the President. "He was our hope and our light," she explained, "so

I was thrilled to have campaigned for him and thrilled to have met the family and to say I was a friend."[26] A go-to trope in nearly every biographical profile, the rumor of an affair has dogged her throughout the years and she has referred to it as "kind of like having a broken wrist . . . it's an annoyance but I have to live with it."[27]

What is certain is that just before 1:00 P.M. on Friday, January 20, 1961, when John Kennedy began his Inaugural Address, Angie Dickinson was seated with Fay right below the podium in the VIP Reserved Section 1-A. Shivering in the frigid air, the former small-town North Dakota schoolgirl looked serenely beautiful and perfectly at ease among the nation's political and social elite. During her time in the nation's capital, she also met various current and future government officials. Two favorite acquaintances, about to accept positions in the new administration, were the Harvard professors Arthur Schlesinger, Jr. and John Kenneth Galbraith. Angie became especially friendly with Galbraith and a year later would travel to New Delhi to visit the newly appointed Indian Ambassador and his wife and to tour film studios in the country.

Soon after the Inauguration, Angie returned to southern California and the small but comfortable house she had purchased in Brentwood. For a few brief weeks, she gardened, caught up on her reading, and relaxed in the sun. Sidney Skolsky and other show biz columnists reported dates with Johnny Grant, George Jessel, Edward Byrnes, and most improbably of all, Vincente Minnelli. Although reduced in size from what it had been a couple decades earlier, the studio's publicity department still churned out news releases about the entwined activities of its glamorous young stars. Byrnes, who played the handsome car attendant "Kookie" on the Warner Bros. TV series *77 Sunset Strip*, was a hot property and a favorite of the teen fan magazines. There was no relationship between the two, however, and Angie never took the planted stories seriously. Instead, she worked on losing weight and getting tan in preparation for her next two assignments.

Angie on her Vespa as the independent American midwife of *Jessica* (1962).

By March, she was off to Italy for an independent production with Jean Negulesco. A prolific contract director first for Warner

Bros. and then at Twentieth Century-Fox, Negulesco was now on his own, lured to Europe like so many other American directors to make a personal movie free from studio constraints. Italy, whose own national cinema was enjoying worldwide critical and popular success, was a particular magnet. Already, as of 1960, *Roman Holiday* (1953), *Three Coins in the Fountain* (1954, also Negulesco), *The Barefoot Contessa* (1954), and *It Started in Naples* (1960), among many others, had been shot on location in Italy.

Based on Flora Sandstrom's novel *The Midwife of Pont Clery*, Negulesco's project originally was titled *Apple Pie Bed* and told the story of Jessica, a beautiful American nurse (again) whose husband dies in Sicily on their honeymoon and who decides to remain there as a midwife in the village of Forza d'Agrò. Because the town's men pay so much attention to her, the women devise a Lysistrata-like scheme to withhold sexual favors, cut the birth rate, and thus eliminate the need for a midwife. With the help of the village priest and a handsome aristocrat, she gradually overcomes the hostility. The title was soon changed to *Jessica*.

Negulesco first had offered the title part to Ava Gardner and Marilyn Monroe, with whom he had worked successfully on *How to Marry a Millionaire* (1953). When both stars declined, he turned to Angie, who fixed on several reasons for saying yes. She could see some of Europe for the first time, appear in a film with a contemporary setting and modern dress, experiment more with the comic overtones she had tried in *Rio Bravo*, and learn from another veteran director. Maurice Chevalier signed on for the role of the village priest as did actor/director Vittorio de Sica, then at the height of his international fame for neorealistic masterworks such as *Shoeshine* (1946), *Bicycle Thieves* (1948), and *Umberto D* (1952), to play an aging gardener. When de Sica dropped out because of scheduling conflicts, affable French character actor Noël-Noël stepped in as a last-minute replacement. The supporting cast included handsome leading man Gabriele Ferzetti, Agnes Moorehead, Marcel Dalio, and Sylva Koscina.

Seeking to duplicate the studio publicity effort he knew so well, Negulesco arranged for reporters and photographers to cover Angie's arrival at Rome's Ciampino Airport. While flashbulbs popped, he greeted and welcomed her to the Eternal City. Photos of the director and his star made the papers in Italy as well as in the United States. After a few days of sightseeing and a taste of the famous Via Veneto nightlife, Angie joined the company in Taormina, Sicily, not far from the inland villages where Francis Ford Coppola some years later would shoot scenes for *The Godfather* (1972).

Negulesco efficiently moved the production along, aided by a thoroughly professional cast that needed no special treatment. "Angie Dickinson was a dream," he remembered, impressed by her hard work and dedication to the project.[28] Rather than use a double, she learned to ride a Vespa for shots of the midwife careening along the mountain roads on her daily errands. To emphasize the village men's infatuation with Jessica, Negulesco focused on her rear end bouncing around on the seat, a sexualization that was increasingly defining Angie and one that she herself did not seem to mind. There was also an outdoor shower scene that showed plenty of skin.

One day, while filming, Angie crashed the scooter and sustained a cut left knee, scraped hands, and a bruised right hip. Because she was also in shock, a local doctor ordered her to stay in bed for two days. Angie's willingness to take a few lumps for the team endeared her even more to Negulesco, who hoped to capture her resilient ebullience on film. His affection was expressed so intensely that it sounds somewhat inappropriate today, like a harassment charge waiting to happen. "She has the softest lips I've ever kissed in my life," he raved. "I told her by contract you have to kiss me tenderly and sweetly every morning before we start shooting."[29] Maybe she recalled selling those kisses for a nickel as a kid in Kulm and considered his comments all part of the same innocent fun. Whatever her true reaction, despite the passionate language, there was never anything more than a congenial professional relationship between the director and his star.

The gossip about Angie's romantic life revolved instead around co-star Gabriele Ferzetti, who was going through a much-publicized divorce at the time. Italian newspapers heavily covered their public appearances together, interest which only increased when the company moved to Rome for some interior scenes at Cinecittà, the huge studio complex opened in 1937 at 1055 Via Tuscolana on the edge of the city. Enjoying peak production during the 60s, Cinecittà housed acclaimed productions by de Sica, Federico Fellini, Luchino Visconti, and others along with huge "spectaculars" such as *Ben-Hur* (1959), *Cleopatra* (1963), and *The Fall of the Roman Empire* (1964). Negulesco worked equally fast in the studio, and filming wrapped by the end of May. With the conclusion of the picture so too ended speculation about Angie and Ferzetti, whose "affair" had really consisted of a few amiable social dates. Hopes that *Jessica* would do great things for the personnel involved also faded when it opened about a year later to mostly negative reviews and negligible box office.

As part of her brief Italian period, Angie made a last contracted picture for Warner Bros., a travelogue romance called *Rome Adventure*. Both *The Sins of Rachel Cade* and *A Fever in the Blood* had been released by now and although Angie's performance as Rachel received praise, reviewers felt that neither picture showcased her talent. She agreed, believing that Warner Bros. was not doing much to help her develop as an actress. With predictable regularity, she played wife, mistress, nurse, bad girl, or a combination thereof.

Rome Adventure was more of the same. Following *A Summer Place* (1959), *Parrish* (1961), and *Susan Slade* (1961), it was the final entry in what might be termed director Delmer Daves's "Troy Donahue quartet," pictures featuring the Warner Bros. teen idol in dramas about young love and parental conflict. The handsome blond star of the studio's *Surfside 6* (1960-62) television series, Donahue, like Angie, was under contract and regularly paired with perky, up and coming actresses such as Sandra Dee and Connie Stevens in boy-next-door cum male sex symbol parts. For *Rome Adventure*, he played Don Porter, an American architect living in Italy and torn between a manipulative artist (Angie) and a New England librarian (Suzanne Pleshette). Angie's character was one of her bitchiest to date yet required little more than the narrow-eyed delivery of such lines as "I simply want Bentley to think I'm a tramp and go home."

For once, however, the rumors swirled not around Angie but around her co-stars, Donahue and Pleshette. Involved romantically, they were conducting an affair as tumultuous as the one they enacted on film. After completing this assignment, they would make *A Distant Trumpet* (1964) together, marry on January 5, 1964, and divorce nine months later. Daves, who adapted the script himself from a novel by Irving Fineman, kept the focus on Donahue and Pleshette and on the scenic locations of Lago Maggiore, Florence, Pisa, Orvieto, and Rome. Angie's scenes, all of which were studio interiors, could have been played by any of the Warner contract actresses, Diane McBain or Saundra Edwards for example.

So, after nearly three years and five feature films, Angie obtained a release from the Warner Bros. contract and ventured forth on her own. She would continue to believe that the studio had mishandled her career. In an interview several years later, she revealed, "As a producer, Jack [Warner] didn't have great vision: he could take care of himself and his studio, but he wasn't Arthur Freed. Not long before he died, I saw him and told him, 'Jack, you never knew what to do with me, did you?' And do you know what he said? 'Well, you got an awful lot of red in your hair.'"[30]

Upon her return to Los Angeles, she restarted her social life as well, dating Sinatra, Glenn Ford, producer Arthur Loew, and agent turned producer Charles Feldman. The relationships with Ford and Feldman, both at the height of their professional success, were serious. An early JFK supporter like Angie, Ford shared her interest in Democratic politics (although he later switched parties and supported Ronald Reagan) and Hollywood nightlife. Fifteen years her senior, he had been in pictures since 1939, was recently divorced from actress/dancer Eleanor Powell, and had a young son named Peter. "He's a lovely man," she told *Modern Screen* correspondent Bill Tusher at the time, "but I don't consider Glenn a playboy. I think Glenn cares quite a good deal for somebody he goes out with. Maybe he's not serious to the point of marriage, but I think it's not just to whoop it up every night in a club. I think he genuinely cares for a person."[31] Since both were seeing other people and pursuing busy careers, the affair never became more than a casual one although they remained lifelong friends and were always happy to bump into each other over the years at social events. In addition, there was the probability that Ford actually preferred serial romances. Following his time with Angie, he dated Connie Stevens, Judy Garland, and Hope Lange and then, in fairly rapid succession, married actress Kathryn Hays, Cynthia Hayward, and Jeanne Baus.

Even more significant was Angie's involvement with Charlie Feldman, who had not only founded the Famous Artists talent agency but had also produced such films as *A Streetcar Named Desire* (1951), *The Seven Year Itch* (1955), and *Walk on the Wild Side* (1962). Born just two years after her own father, Feldman was one of those self-made Hollywood power players who knew everybody and had a finger in all kinds of industry pies. He shared a living arrangement with his divorced wife, actress/photographer Jean Howard, boasted over 300 Famous Artists clients, and pioneered the independent production deals that eventually brought an end to long-term studio contracts. Impressed with his self-assurance, the same quality she admired in Sinatra and Van Heusen, Angie was thrilled to be escorted around town by such a handsome, well-connected insider. She admitted to Bill Tusher that "my closest friends wouldn't be entirely shocked if I married Charlie when he is free."[32] Neither romantic partner was very interested in abandoning the single life, and talk of marriage remained just that—talk. Feldman did, however, re-enter Angie's life in a major professional way just a few years later.

As part of her crowded social calendar, Angie happily found time to renew her friendship with President Kennedy. In late autumn of 1961, she attended a luncheon given by Peter and Pat Lawford in his honor at their Spanish-style Malibu beach house. Other guests included Audrey Wilder, Janet Leigh, and Kim Novak. "There were just a few of us—10 or maybe 12," she recalled. "Everyone wanted to talk about politics and what was going to happen. But he laughed and said, 'I don't want to talk about politics, I just want to talk about movies.'"[33] Sinatra himself was not present and a few months later would sever all ties to Lawford when JFK, who had been warned by J. Edgar Hoover of Frank's Mafia connections, chose to stay at Bing Crosby's house during a visit to Palm Springs rather than at Sinatra's. After his extensive campaign efforts, Frank felt devastated by the snub. "If he would only pick up the telephone and call me and say it was politically difficult to have me around, I would understand," he told Angie. "I don't want to hurt him. But he has never called."[34] Lawford claimed that the President did in fact make an explanatory telephone call, but nevertheless the ballyhooed friendship was finished.

With the start of the new year, Angie embarked on several weeks of international travel. During April, she journeyed throughout the Middle East and India. In New Delhi, she was the guest of Ambassador Galbraith and his wife Catherine, whose friendship with her had grown steadily since the Presidential Inauguration. Somewhat star-struck, Galbraith described Angie in his memoir, *Name-Dropping from FDR On*, as "at the summit of her career, combining beauty, intelligence, political interest and general charm."[35] Not just a casual tourist, she was seriously interested in Indian culture and history as well as in a contemporary political scene dominated by controversial Prime Minister Jawaharlal Nehru's efforts to steer a neutral path between Soviet and American regional interests. Spinning a tale for the book, the Ambassador wrote, "As did all visitors to India, many of whom I had to restrain, she wished to see Nehru. One afternoon I sent him a note, saying I knew him to be busy but would he spare a moment for a lovely Hollywood star who would like to meet him? Within an hour I had word back that in great emergencies he could always make time. Could I bring my guest over at once? I found Angie, took her to the Prime Minister's residence, and they talked for nearly two hours." Then, as a kicker, he added, "I remember especially one question from Nehru. 'Miss Dickinson, when you are making a film, you spend some months studying and then creating the character you are playing. Doesn't that have some permanent effect on your personality?' To Nehru's delight, Angie replied, 'I certainly hope not, Mr. Prime Minister. In my last four films I've been a woman of deep ill-repute.'"[36] In addition to charming Nehru, Angie toured the Bollywood film studios and screened a print of *Jessica* that she had brought along on the trip.

By May, she was on the French Riviera for the XVth annual Cannes Film Festival. Begun in 1946 as a low-key movie showcase, it was already transitioning into the glitzy media circus that it is today. Although she had neither an official jury role nor a film in competition, Angie mingled with celebrities and posed for photographers. The participants comprised a who's who of distinguished early 60s cinema. There were films by Luis Bunuel, Satyajit Ray, Michelangelo Antonioni, Robert Bresson, Tony Richardson, Agnes Varda, John Frankenheimer, Li Han Hsiang, and Sidney Lumet. Jury members included Francois Truffaut, Mel Ferrer, and Romain Gary while the various screenings and receptions drew such famous names as Warren Beatty, Natalie Wood, Romy Schneider, Alain Delon, Jeanne Moreau, Sophia Loren, Elke Sommer, and Marcello Mastroianni. Angie's presence on La Croisette, Canne's fabled seaside boulevard, along with stars like these signaled just how far she had come. The actresses gathered on the Riviera that year all projected the same kind of screen image: sleek, modern, stylish women whose beauty was more sharply angled and less elaborately adorned than that of their movie star predecessors.

For someone intensely concerned with advancing her career, Angie did remarkably little studio work in 1962. She made no films and limited her television guest appearances to single episodes of *Checkmate*, *The Alfred Hitchcock Hour*, and *The Dick Powell Show*. Instead, inspired perhaps by the critically lauded actresses she had seen at Cannes, she agreed to do live theatre. Upon her return from Europe, she began rehearsals for a Broadway-bound production of *The Perfect Setup*, a three-act, three-character comedy by Jack Sher about a New York public relations man shuttling between his wife in Westchester and his mistress in Manhattan. Also in the cast were her old *China Gate* co-star Gene Barry as the husband and Jan Sterling, who had appeared with her in *Man with the Gun*, as the wife. Not surprisingly, Angie played the girlfriend.

During out-of-town previews in San Francisco, a newspaper columnist scandalously reported that Angie was involved romantically with the play's producer Martin Melcher. Doris Day's husband and business manager, Melcher was rumored to be having marriage trouble, and so the Angie story quickly gained traction. Accustomed to faulty reporting, she took the unusual step this time of correcting the record. In that same *Modern Screen* interview where she discussed Glenn Ford and Charlie Feldman, she explained, "This columnist happened to see us walking down the street in San Francisco with me hanging on Marty's arm for the very simple reason that I had pins in the skirt of my suit. We had hemmed it up in the store with the pins to walk to the theatre to show Lamont Johnson, the director, for his approval. He couldn't tell with it down to my ankles and we didn't want to buy it (it was an expensive suit) until he said okay. So to hang on and not let the pins cut my stockings, I was taking little bitty steps, hanging onto Marty . . . when we ran into the columnist and he decides that it's a romance."[37]

In a tone somewhere between defiance and defensiveness, she elaborated, "I didn't mind because Marty and I have nothing to hide. I just adore him—we all did. I have a great affection for Marty. I don't care *who* the producer would be—when he came to visit us on the road, after the rehearsal or the show we'd have drinks. After all, when a producer visits his own show two days out of two weeks, you don't *ignore* him."[38] Whatever the truth of the matter, Melcher stayed married to Day until his death in 1968, by which time he had produced six more of her films, squandered her earnings through bad business investments, and left her seriously in debt.

On October 24, 1962, *The Perfect Setup* opened at the Cort Theatre on West 48th Street in midtown Manhattan. Also on Broadway that season were Bert Lahr, Robert Ryan, Joseph Cotten, Anthony Quinn, Margaret Leighton, Charles Boyer, and Rod Steiger. Edward Albee's *Who's Afraid of Virginia Woolf* with Arthur Hill as George and Uta Hagen as Martha was doing big business at the Billy Rose Theatre as was the Anthony Newley/Leslie Bricusse musical *Stop the World–I Want to Get Off* at the Ambassador. Amid such stiff competition, *The Perfect Setup* struggled to find an audience. With simple but effective set design and lighting by Jack McCullagh and Charles Elson, Lamont Johnson staged the proceedings in a well-paced, professional manner, but Sher's flimsy tale of marital turmoil looked archaic compared to what Albee and company were up to just a few blocks away. *The Perfect Setup* closed on October 27 after just five performances, which was two performances more than *The Fun Couple*, another marital comedy starring Jane Fonda and Bradford Dillman that previewed on October 25, opened on October 26, and also closed on October 27. It didn't help either of the two productions to begin their runs at the same time that the Cuban Missile Crisis was playing out on television screens across the country. While President Kennedy spoke to the nation and U.N. Ambassador Adlai Stevenson addressed the Security Council, New Yorkers felt more like locating their nearest nuclear fallout shelter than watching Hollywood stars cavort on stage in light comedies.

Despite the play's failure, the participants all gained valuable experience and a lingering taste for live theatre. Barry returned triumphantly to Broadway twenty-two years later as Georges in the hit musical *La Cage aux Folles*, a role which earned him both Drama Desk and Tony award nominations. Jan Sterling appeared in Joe Masteroff's *The Warm Peninsula* (1971) at the Cape Playhouse in Massachusetts and in two New York regional theatre productions of *Come Back, Little Sheba* (1974). In 2000, Angie was asked to take over for Lauren Bacall in Noel Coward's *Waiting in the Wings* and to star with Phylicia Rashad in a two-week run of *The Vagina Monologues* but had to decline both offers due to scheduling conflicts. Known mostly in proceeding years for his television work, Johnson directed a string of network movies, earning Emmy awards for *Wallenberg: A Hero's Story* (1985) and the NBC mini-series *Lincoln* (1985).

Given her recent disillusionment with Warner Bros., Angie's next professional move was as puzzling as it was unexpected. In early 1963, she signed an exclusive seven-year contract with Universal Pictures, one of the last such long-term arrangements engineered by a Hollywood studio. Half-jokingly, she claimed the deal was her only way to secure the coveted part of Lieutenant Francie Corum in *Captain Newman, M.D.* opposite Gregory Peck: "Universal said I had to sign a long-term contract if I wanted to play Fran. I thought, 'What could be worth that chunk of my life?' Then I thought, Gregory Peck. And I said, 'Oh hell—what's seven years anyhow.'"[39]

Her actual rationale, undoubtedly, was much more complicated than that. Hollywood in the early 60s, with its myriad overlapping deals, was a difficult place to navigate. Being part of a successful independent project meant finding a suitable property, convincing producers to hire you, negotiating a salary, and managing public relations. It was not an easy process to master for a young actress with even the savviest, most experienced of agents. Adding to the uncertainty was the fact that nobody knew exactly what kind of pictures contemporary audiences, buffeted by the decade's social and political upheavals, wanted to see. Released from his contract in 1964 after twenty-two years at M-G-M, director Charles Walters described his own related dilemma: "Where the hell am I gonna find a script? And what do you mean put a package together? Do I go to a bank for financing?"[40]

David Niven congratulates Angie on being named Mayor of Universal City.

So, letting studio executives handle all such strategic details had definite advantages. Moreover, Universal actively courted Angie, promising to shape her career in ways that Warner Bros. had failed to accomplish. Production head Edward Muhl assured her that the studio intended to pair her in a series of pictures with the major male stars of the day. Even with its 1962 takeover by the huge talent agency MCA (Music Corporation of America), Universal still had fewer contract players and a smaller television operation than Warner Bros., and the odds were better that Angie would not get lost among similarly profiled actresses.

Surely, she had all of those factors in mind when she told the *Los Angeles Herald Examiner*, "I want to make films and that's why I signed. Another reason is that I've managed to skyrocket and remain in the star status, but never really have gone into orbit. I feel that a major studio can orbit me." Clarifying her specific goals, she added, "I want to make three films a year. I don't believe in overexposure. Just abundant exposure."[41] More than anything else she wanted the kinds of meaty parts that Jeanne Moreau and Anouk Aimee were getting in Europe.

Universal immediately went to work churning out publicity for its hot new property. Appointing her mayor of Universal City and insuring her legs with Lloyd's of London were just two of the gimmicks cooked up by the PR department. At 415 acres, roughly the size of Monaco, the studio lot had its own fire station, zip code, and business services. The honorary title of "mayor" was bestowed on the hottest star of the moment. Receiving her title from outgoing city executive David Niven, Angie joined a list that included Rock Hudson, Lana Turner, Deanna Durbin, Donald O'Connor, Doris Day, and Janet Leigh. The "swearing in" ceremony was always worth a few photos and a few lines of print in the newspapers. So also was the leg insurance bit, which had been done previously at other studios with Marlene Dietrich and Betty Grable. "It was a publicity gimmick, of course, but I actually signed the policy," she told Hollywood columnist Abe Greenberg.[42] With its $1 million premium, the rate was calculated by publicists to be about $15,000 per limb inch. Her legs were becoming an obsession among the male writers who covered Hollywood. A year earlier, she had received the Golden Garter Award for "the best gams of 1962."

As part of the PR campaign, Angie also gave a series of provocative interviews where she went on at length about being a sex symbol, a swinger, and a party girl. She told *Show* magazine, "I'm a swinger, but I'm very selective. I mean I'm not promiscuous . . . I think I would be further ahead if I were the swinger they think I am, not that they give you the part, but somehow you get lucky more often."[43] In an extensive Q and A with *Pageant*, she revealed, "I hope I have tremendous sex appeal. I believe a full woman thinks of everything and that includes sex. And I ask you why is it so terrible if my sex appeal is my greatest asset? What is so awful about a man wanting a woman . . . but being a Hollywood sex symbol wouldn't destroy me. It's not the sex symbol the audience wants to go to bed with so much as that she makes them want to go to bed with someone else."[44]

For Bob Thomas's Associated Press column, she created an annotated list of Hollywood's ten most eligible bachelors, a ranking that included, among others, Warren Beatty, Alain Delon, Albert Finney, Cary Grant, Rock Hudson, and Sinatra. Of Beatty, she wrote, "Very talented, plays piano, sings . . . impossibly unpredictable, moody . . . devilish . . . sensuous in his entire being."[45] She called Delon "the most gorgeous man I know" and Finney "a tease, but very entertaining on a date."[46] The breathy, elliptical description of Sinatra painted him as "extremely warm and loyal to his friends and his causes . . . generous of his personality and time, and with gifts . . . interesting and unpredictable . . . mad."[47] She concluded with tips on how to land an eligible bachelor and a wink at her own unorthodox behavior.

It was apparent that Angie had decided her sexual identity ("my greatest asset") would be the route to mega-stardom, the celebrity orbit she kept mentioning to reporters. She would distinguish herself from other actresses by sounding hip and looking chic. She would be a new kind of sex symbol, one who was slimmer, smarter, and savvier than the Marilyn wannabes. In reality, the strategy probably worked against her. She was continually cast as a scheming vixen or a sultry girlfriend, characters who were defined solely by their extreme sexuality. Roles where she could have proven her dramatic chops went instead to Gena Rowlands, Jane Fonda, and Faye Dunaway. Still, throughout her career, she clung almost defensively to the sex symbol image, insisting that she was honored to have been embraced as such by the public. As late as 2016, she told Australian TV reporter Angela Bishop that it was "fantastic" to be remembered for her looks.[48]

One of the plum dramatic parts that didn't get away, the role that brought her to Universal, was Francine Corum in *Captain Newman, M.D.* Adapted from a Leo Rosten novel by Richard Breen and the husband and wife writing team of Henry and Phoebe Ephron, the story followed the efforts of nonconformist military doctor Josiah Newman (Gregory Peck) to treat psychologically damaged patients housed toward the end of World War II at Arizona's Colfax Army Air Field Hospital. A precursor to Robert Altman's *MASH* (1970), the film blended comedy and drama in its cynical look at the bureaucratic absurdity and physical havoc of war. True, it was another nurse role for Angie, but she saw 1st

Lieutenant Corum as an equally skilled ally in Newman's struggle to do the right thing for his patients. In her portrayal of the character, she projected a combination of compassion and reason that contrasted with the chaos swirling about her and that became the film's central message of hope.

Angie plays army nurse Francie Corum in *Captain Newman, M.D.* (1963).

Filming occurred throughout the spring of 1963 on location in Arizona and then back at the Universal soundstages. The desert shoot, in and around Fort Huachuca, Arizona, was less than luxurious, but Angie accepted the inconveniences without complaint and once again, as on the *Rio Bravo* set, endeared herself to the mostly all-male cast and crew. Joining her and Peck in front of the camera were Tony Curtis, Bobby Darin, Eddie Albert, Robert Duvall, and James Gregory. Under veteran director David Miller, everyone stayed professionally devoted to the work at hand, particularly Peck, who had invested some of his own money in the film. During production, on May 8, 1963, he won the Best Actor Academy Award for his performance as Atticus Finch in *To Kill a Mockingbird* (1962), and despite celebrating late into the night, he showed up the next morning on time and totally prepared for his scenes. Such commitment bolstered what was already a lofty reputation among his mostly younger on-set colleagues.

A politically active Democrat like his leading lady, Peck forged a friendship with Angie that lasted the rest of his life. Over the years, he and his wife Veronique would share dinners, family events, poker games, and charity drives with her. Their onscreen chemistry in *Captain Newman, M.D.* was warm if not blazing and both were proud of the picture's progressive message. Commercial release later in the decade might have better matched the public's anti-Vietnam War sentiment, but as it was, audiences in December of 1963 were numbed by President Kennedy's assassination and largely unmoved by a World War II era tale of shell-shocked veterans. Although in September Angie had been named "most exciting new star" by the Theatre Owners of America, ticket sales lagged behind those for *How the West Was Won*, *Tom Jones*, and even *Son of Flubber*. Making just over $4 million and coming in 21st at the box office for the year, the movie also managed only mixed reviews, with the *Los Angeles Herald-Examiner* calling it a "remarkable blend of comedy and drama"[49] and *The New York Times* objecting that "it does tend to jump about between solemn and comic situations to the point of monotony."[50] While not delivering the dramatic breakthrough she had hoped for, Angie, relegated too often in the final film to simply admiring Newman rather than assisting him, was praised by *Film Daily* for bringing "charm and warmth to her role as the nurse in love with Peck."[51]

When filming wrapped on May 7, Angie enjoyed a brief but relaxing break before reporting to her next Universal project, a loose adaptation of Ernest Hemingway's short story "The Killers." Previously developed for the big screen in 1946, the plot centers on a man's fatalistic acceptance of his death at the hands of two callous hitmen. Intended as the first made-for-television movie, the production was the result of a deal between NBC and MCA/Universal to create Project 120, a package of TV-ready pictures made under the banner of Revue Studios. As director Don Siegel expanded the film's scope, the budget quickly grew from $250,000 to just shy of $1 million.

In the original story, Hemingway concerns himself only with the gunmen's visit to a shabby Midwestern diner in search of their intended victim, a mysterious loner named Ole Andreson. Both film adaptations pursue the backstory, explaining what motivates Ole's doomed resignation. Robert Siodmak's 1946 version makes him a boxer (Burt Lancaster in his film debut) double-crossed by a girlfriend (Ava Gardner) who involves him in a robbery scheme. Disillusioned by her treachery, he calmly submits to the hitmen sent to keep him quiet. In Siegel's take on the story (written by Gene Coon), Ole has become Johnny North (John Cassavetes), a race car driver whose obsession with a mob boss's mistress marks him as the fall guy in a million dollar mail truck heist. More than faceless assassins, the hitmen (Lee Marvin and Clu Gulager) function as narrative agents who unravel Johnny's past and reveal the multiple betrayals. Angie played Sheila Farr, the evil seductress, and in a truly bizarre bit of casting, Ronald Reagan, about to quit movies and enter politics, appeared as mob boss Jack Browning.

Angie and Ronald Reagan as a treacherous married couple in *The Killers* (1964).

Sheila Farr made Angie's manipulative ice queen in *Rome Adventure* seem like a girl scout. She lies to Johnny, betrays him on more than one occasion, and lures him into an ambush that leaves him for dead. In return, she is manhandled, dangled from an upper floor hotel window, and shot by Lee Marvin. Everything about the film feels unconventional, even transgressive. The violence all occurs in broad daylight, the hitmen enjoy torturing their victims, and by the end of the picture nearly everyone has died.

For a scene in which his character's authority is questioned, Reagan was required to slap Angie hard across the face. Even though the stunt was carefully choreographed, he hesitated doing it for the same reason he disliked his role overall. Jack Browning was the kind of outright villain he had never played before and which contrasted sharply with his cheery public image. "He does not have any maliciousness in him," Angie told a *TV Guide* interviewer toward the end of Reagan's second term as President. "He was very political then, studying all the time" during the shoot. Asked about his charisma, she answered, "He didn't light up a room like John Kennedy. But he is very smart; smart like a fox—not fast and mean, but smart."[52] Although they espoused widely different political beliefs, she and Reagan became friends, and each time they met over the intervening years, he would jokingly apologize for the slap. Upon the fulfillment of this contract obligation, he ran for and won election in 1966 as Governor of California.

On November 22, 1963, while in wardrobe for that morning's scenes, Angie heard the news that President Kennedy had been assassinated in Dallas. Like every other American alive at the time, she forever remembered the exact details of the moment. Director Don Siegel shared the same memory: "I'll never forget the day when she was trying on her wardrobe for a scene and word came over the radio that President Kennedy was dead. She fainted in my arms. She had known the Kennedys socially and it hit her very hard, yet with nerves of steel she pulled herself together and was able to finish the day's work."[53]

The assassination affected the picture in more consequential ways also. Universal executives felt that not only was it too violent for television viewing but that some scenes, especially the one where Reagan shoots Clu Gulager with a rifle from the upper floor of an office building, were too reminiscent of the Dallas tragedy. With a title change from *Johnny North* to *Ernest Hemingway's The Killers*, it was first released in Europe and finally given limited U.S. theatrical distribution during the summer of 1964. Largely ignored at the time, *The Killers* (as it is now simply titled) has grown steadily in critical estimation. Commenting on its 2015 Criterion Blu-ray rerelease, *The New York Times* noted, "The cast is first rate. Thanks to Marvin's sleek, snub-nosed menace and the edgy thrill-seeking projected by Angie Dickinson's moll, the movie exudes a cynical Rat Pack cool,"[54] and Siegel biographer Stuart Kaminsky has argued, "*The Killers* is Siegel at his best, creating a chilling, urban world in which anyone could find himself the next victim of sudden violence."[55]

Angie's next project for Universal, *The Art of Love*, could not have been more different in content and tone. Written by Carl Reiner from a story by Richard Alan Simmons and William Sackheim, it was a comedy about two American art swindlers in Paris fighting with each other over money and girlfriends. James Garner, Dick Van Dyke, and Elke Sommer co-starred with Angie, Ross Hunter produced, and Norman Jewison directed. Although there were some unusually dark overtones involving a murder frame and guillotine sentence, the picture was essentially an example of a very specific, mid-Sixties Universal factory product: the glossy, brightly photographed Technicolor romp where good-looking movie stars in nice clothes talk about sex more than they engage in it and get themselves in and out of romantic entanglements. In fact, Garner, Reiner, Hunter, and Jewison all had collaborated two years earlier on a similar vehicle, *The Thrill of It All*, starring Doris Day.

Directing with the same light touch that had served him well in three previous back-to-back comedies for the studio, Jewison, in the middle of a busy work schedule that also included *The*

Cincinnati Kid, shot quickly and economically throughout the spring of 1964. Like Reiner and the three American co-stars, he was a television veteran used to tight production demands. Convinced that the material worked best as a kind of continental farce, he brought a sense of urgency to the onscreen action, emphasizing delivery and timing. Van Dyke was the increasingly frantic artist who fakes his death to sell more paintings, Angie his rich American fiancée, Sommer the unpredictable girl he saves from drowning, and Garner his equally devious roommate. While not exactly the master farceurs of an Ernst Lubitsch or Preston Sturges comedy, all four actors contributed deft performances.

In her Ray Aghayan gowns and new "sun swept blonde" hair color, Angie looked sensational, more chic and sophisticated than ever. Photographer Russell Metty, who had also shot *Captain Newman, M.D.*, gave her flattering camera angles and close-ups. Known for his lush production values, Ross Hunter made sure the picture reflected the best talent available. Broadway composer Cy Coleman wrote the musical score, Academy Award-winning art director Alexander Golitzen did the sets, studio veteran Milton Carruth edited the movie, and stage legend Ethel Merman appeared as brothel owner Madame Coco La Fontaine, a part that Mae West turned down when she learned that she would not be permitted to write her own dialogue.

To avoid the artificial feel of European stories filmed entirely within a studio soundstage, Jewison shot on location in Paris for two weeks with Van Dyke and Sommer. Angie and Garner were not included for budgetary reasons and did all of their scenes back at Universal. "That gave me two actors on location," explained Jewison in his autobiography, "and I shot them in every scene from the script that featured the two in Paris exteriors. I also shot the French actors, and I shot scenes that gave us Parisian flavor. That was the real Eiffel Tower and the real Arc de Triomphe."[56]

In spite of such care and attention, the movie was not a major hit. At a summer sneak preview in Los Angeles, Jewison and Reiner "couldn't help noticing that no one else in the theatre was laughing." Thinking at first that the audience's indifference was because they preferred to watch Van Dyke for free in his weekly TV sitcom, Jewison soon "realized something more fundamental was wrong. It was the movie's basic premise."[57] The paintings of a mediocre artist would never escalate in value just because he had died. The real problem, however, was more likely a combination of both those factors plus a script that relied too heavily on stale sight gags and strident harangues rather than repartee between the characters. Premiering at the State Lake Theatre in Chicago, *The Art of Love* was released nationwide on June 30, 1965, and did so-so business behind juggernauts like *The Sound of Music* and *Dr. Zhivago*. It finished fourteenth in U.S. box office totals for the year.

Angie's promiscuous onscreen persona continued to stalk her in real life when she was linked romantically with her two male co-stars. A tabloid reported that Van Dyke and Garner, both of whom were happily married at the time, got into a fistfight over her during production. Van Dyke sued, but a judge dismissed the case, asserting that libel laws applied less stringently to public figures. Overcoming their embarrassment, he and Angie stayed friendly throughout their careers, as evidenced many years later by her attendance at a Midnight Mission Golden Heart Award ceremony in Beverly Hills that honored the comic actor.

An early 60s publicity photo conveys a lighter, more natural look for Angie.

After three films, none of which rocketed her into that stellar orbit she envisioned, it was clear to Angie that Universal was not going to do much more for her career than Warner Bros. had. So, by December of 1964, less than two years after first signing on with the studio, she obtained a release from her contract and entered into a representation agreement with Ashley Famous Agency. Like most every other young actor, she was now an independent player, competing for a limited number of top-quality parts.

First to come her way, hopefully a sign of what the future offered, was a role in Sam Spiegel's independent production of *The Chase*. On paper the project looked great, overflowing with an abundance of film and literary pedigrees. The screenwriter was Lillian Hellman, whose script was based on a play by Horton Foote; the director was Arthur Penn, who had won acclaim for the stage and film versions of *The Miracle Worker*; and the cast included Marlon Brando, Robert Redford, Jane Fonda, James Fox, E.G. Marshall, and Robert Duvall. Unapologetically liberal in tone, Hellman's screenplay used a small-town Texas sheriff's attempt to protect a prison escapee from mob hysteria as an indictment of economic inequality, racial prejudice, middle class hypocrisy, and a seriously flawed American justice system.

Bubber Reeves (Redford) and Sheriff Calder (Brando) confront equally daunting challenges as their trajectories converge over a single twenty-four hour time period. Bubber returns to the town where he was framed for a crime he didn't commit and where his best friend (Fox) and wife (Fonda) are having an affair. As he waits for the fugitive to appear, Calder, a principled man of law, fends off interference from a powerful banker (Marshall) and a throng of drunken locals who believe that events are being staged for their

Saturday night entertainment. Calder's ultimate apprehension of Bubber ends violently on the steps of the county jail.

Angie played Calder's supportive wife Ruby, and all of her scenes were with Brando. It is fascinating to watch the two of them on screen together, he the New York Method actor coached by Strasberg and Kazan and she the Hollywood discovery groomed by Fuller and Hawks. Matching Brando's artistry, she delivers what is arguably the film's most restrained and credible performance. Where the others go big, she stays minimalistically simple. For every twist of agony from Brando comes calm resolution from Angie. "Slow it down," Hawks continually told her during *Rio Bravo* and here she does exactly that. The sheriff and his wife represent civilized social standards at odds with the rest of the town. Angie, in that regard, provides the film's clearest exemplar of tolerance and understanding. "Through her," wrote film scholar Robin Wood, "Penn suggests something of what makes it possible for Calder to be what he is."[58]

Director Penn was himself very pleased with the dramatic chemistry between Brando and Angie and encouraged improvisation wherever possible. Known as an "actor's director," he valued the contributions that cast members could bring to what he viewed as a necessarily flexible script. Brando, he declared, "was wonderful in scenes with Angie Dickinson—soft, wonderful little improvisations, but holding the line of the scenes so she never was at a loss."[59] If anything, Angie's grasp of her character's essential humanity was underappreciated in comparison with Brando's showier struggle between rage and control. Backhandedly complimenting her approach, Penn noted, "Angie, you know, is a wonderful girl but [was] not an advanced actress. But in the scenes with Marlon she was responding to the freedom that he was offering, and it was wonderful. A lot of that, unfortunately, never made it into the final cut."[60]

Since Brando, who was often difficult and demanding seemed to be on his best behavior, filming began smoothly at sites throughout southern California. Locations included the Warner Bros., Paramount, and 20th Century-Fox ranches as well as the small towns of Chico and Calabasas. Assuring Penn that he intended to repair the bad reputation he had built during the costly *Mutiny on the Bounty* (1962) delays, he was happy to rehearse, suggest ideas, and feed off-camera lines to the other actors during their close-ups. His relationship with Angie was a playfully flirtatious one. "He'd try to get me to talk about things that were off base—like sex," she remembered. "I'd say, 'Marlon, I'm embarrassed' and he'd say, 'Oh no, don't be, just tell me.'"[61]

As the production stretched from the spring into the summer of 1965, however, the atmosphere changed. Producer Sam Spiegel intruded on Penn's leadership, questioning performances and bringing in three additional writers to reshape the script. Although he had known Spiegel since their days making *On the Waterfront* (1954) together, Brando was particularly offended. He lingered in his dressing room while the film edged behind schedule and over budget. Company tensions were also heightened by the six-day outbreak of civil disorder on August 11 that became known as the Watts Rebellion. While south L.A. neighborhoods went up in flames, the violence depicted within the film seemed only too real. In addition, the climactic Lee Harvey Oswald-like shooting of Bubber outside the jail house reminded Angie and everyone else of November, 1963.

The discord between producer and director reached a peak when Spiegel took possession of all the raw footage and supervised a final edit in London while Penn was busy with other professional commitments in New York. "What happened was that the center of the film moved out of my hands and clearly into Sam Spiegel's hands," Penn told Brando biographer Peter Manso. "When I came to London from New York, I saw eight reels of the picture, finished and scored. It was the performance that Marlon had given, but stripped of all the improvisation."[62] Whether the fault lay in the editing, the rewrites, the original concept, or a combination of each, the film as released was a hot mess of southern Gothic stereotypes. It was as if Tennessee Williams, Truman Capote, and Carson McCullers had gotten drunk together and written a collaborative screenplay in snarky imitation of one another. An oversexed wife cheats on her feckless husband while fat businessmen ogle nubile teenage girls at a neighborhood party. Migrant workers are cheated out of their wages and paid off with broken-down television sets. A group of vigilantes assaults a black prisoner in his cell. Inebriated, white-trash townsfolk set fire to the metaphor-heavy junkyard where Bubber takes refuge.

Opening nationwide on February 17, 1966, *The Chase* drew mostly hostile critical reaction. Pauline Kael called it "perhaps the most uncontrolled liberal sadomasochistic fantasy since *A Face in the Crowd*,"[63] and *Life* magazine reviewer Richard Schickel branded it "a disaster of awesome proportions."[64] Writing for *The New York Times*, Bosley Crowther blasted the film as "a phony, tasteless movie" where "everything is intensely overheated,"[65] and the *New York Herald-Tribune*'s Judith Crist, somewhat less brutally, described it as "a mishmash of Peyton Place sociology, Western mythology, and Deep south psychology."[66] In spite of all its star power, Penn's movie also failed to generate much enthusiasm with audiences; its domestic box office take was barely over $2 million.

All That Pizzazz

Unconcerned about the reviews, Angie had more important things on her mind. She had met the man who was about to become her partner in a celebrity marriage that would play out endlessly on the pages of newspapers and magazines. For the previous few months, she had been seen around town with a variety of escorts, some serious and some just for the hell of it. Hollywood correspondents reported that she attended Tony Bennett's Cocoanut Grove opening with Eddie Fisher, dropped in on department store magnate Tom May's birthday party at PJ's discotheque, surprised Frank Sinatra at his wrap party for *None But the Brave*, performed at Hubert Humphrey's Shrine Auditorium benefit, and enjoyed jazz at Eddie Condon's nightclub with Troy Donahue. She also continued to make public relations appearances whenever possible. On one of her final press junkets for Universal, she met syndicated newspaper columnist Bert Bacharach and struck up a friendship with both him and his wife Irma. Charmed by Angie's grace and intelligence, they suggested that their son Burt, whose single letter deviation from his father's first name allowed him to avoid the "junior" appellation, call her on his next visit to Los Angeles.

Three years older than Angie, Burt had grown up in the Forest Hills neighborhood of New York City, studied classical music at Montreal's McGill University, and served a brief stint in the U.S.

army. As a pianist and conductor, he had worked professionally with singers Vic Damone, Polly Bergen, Steve Lawrence, Joel Grey, and Paula Stewart (to whom he was married from 1953 to 1958). His first major taste of celebrity came when Marlene Dietrich selected him to be the conductor and arranger for her nightclub and concert appearances. "I was on my way to Los Angeles in 1958," Burt told writer Charlotte Chandler, "and my friend Peter Matz, who conducted for various musical acts, as I did, was able to find me in the airport. He had a major conflict in his schedule. He had agreed to accompany Noel Coward at the same time he was supposed to work with Marlene Dietrich. He asked me if I could help him out and work with Miss Dietrich. I said it would be a pleasure."[1]

What started as a temporary gig became a lasting collaboration as the iconic performer came to rely on Burt's musical expertise. "The biggest thing I had to have was her respect," he explained, "and once I got that she would listen intently to everything I said. That didn't mean she just did everything I said. But she listened, and she heard."[2] She also became extremely fond of her young conductor, cooking meals for him on tour and washing his clothes. Tall, slender, and sharply featured, Bacharach was exactly the kind of handsome and well-educated man she admired. "One of the things I liked about Burt," Dietrich confided to Chandler, "was his strength. Nothing wishy-washy about him. He always directed me with certainty in my musical appearances, even in the beginning, when he was only thirty, and I was about twice his age and many times his experience. Actually I like everything about him. He's perfect, the perfect man for me, except for one thing. Too young. Not his fault."[3]

The age discrepancy was probably not the deal-breaker Marlene claimed it to be. Although the star and musician maintained strict discretion over the years, many Dietrich biographers assume the couple shared bedroom as well as rehearsal hall time together. The closest Burt ever came to admitting a sexual liaison was to recount the following incident in his autobiography: "Marlene and I got a little drunk together one night in Vegas and as I was taking her back to her room, she tried to kiss me and said, 'Let's go inside.' But I just didn't want to go there with her. Maybe I was smart enough by then to know I couldn't conduct the orchestra every night behind a woman I was sleeping with, even if I had wanted to sleep with her, which I didn't. It would have been like falling in love with fire."[4]

For several of her most famously successful stage performances, from Las Vegas to Warsaw, he was there to conduct, arrange, and motivate. "I worked with her for more than a decade," Burt recalled. "I would go back and forth from working with her and back to New York. Sometimes we'd be together pretty intensively. Sometimes there'd be longer spaces between our bookings. Looking back, it's hard to say how much time we spent because it was big in my life. It was a great experience seeing so much of the world through her very European eyes."[5] During those breaks in New York, Burt pursued other professional interests.

Since 1957, he and Hal David had been writing songs together, Burt in charge of the music and David handling the lyrics. By 1965, they had created such hits as "Magic Moments," "Only Love Can Break a Heart," "I Just Don't Know What to Do with Myself," and "Reach Out for Me." Their collaborations with singer Dionne Warwick were an essential part of the pop music soundscape: "Don't Make Me Over," "Wishin' and Hopin'," "Anyone Who Had a Heart," "Walk on By," "A House Is Not a Home," and "You'll Never Get to Heaven." Marked by changeable meters, irregular phrasing, unusual chord progressions, and extensive modulation, their music was appreciated by fans, critics, and industry professionals alike. To get just the right effect, Burt arranged and produced most of the recording sessions himself.

So, by the time he remembered his parents' suggestion and telephoned Angie during a February 1965 visit to Los Angeles, Burt Bacharach was almost as successful albeit not as famous as the young actress who agreed to go out with him. They met for drinks at Nickodell's restaurant near Paramount and talked about baseball, family, and show business. When Burt returned to L.A. in February, he called Angie again, and they went out together three times in one week, including romantic dinners at the popular restaurants Chianti and Chez Jay. "After our first date, there were flowers the next day with a note that said, 'It was a wonderful evening. From one penicillin sufferer to another,' because I can't take it either," she remembered. "He oozed charm and he knew it, and it was a seduction."[6] Burt's experience made him seem attractively older than he was. Like Sinatra and Van Heusen, he was a supremely talented musician confident in his own abilities. Like JFK, he was charismatically handsome, and like Feldman, he appreciated her personal career goals. "We had three dates, and I fell, I fell hard," Angie admitted.[7]

Adding to her excitement was a two-episode guest appearance in March on NBC's hugely popular *Dr. Kildare* television series. She played Carol Tredman, a beautiful mystery woman who becomes engaged to Blair General Hospital's most eligible young doctor (portrayed for five successful seasons by heart-throb actor Richard Chamberlain). After surviving a car accident together, the couple plans a wedding that, much to the relief of his legion of female fans, hits a snag when Kildare learns some troubling facts about his elusive fiancée. In accepting the role, Angie joined a distinguished guest star list that over time grew to include Fred Astaire, Lauren

Bacall, Kim Hunter, Celeste Holm, James Mason, Ramon Novarro, Walter Pidgeon, Claude Rains, Gloria Swanson, Robert Young, and many other famous Hollywood names.

With one scene where director Leo Penn kept the camera on her for nearly five minutes of screen time, she was thrilled with the exposure. "That's what I mean about this part," she told the *Los Angeles Time*'s Hal Humphrey. "It's so great. I hope everybody sees it, and that's the first time I've ever been able to say this. In everything else, even my movies, there was something wrong—the way I was photographed or the way they had me act. I've never had a chance to show all that I have to show before."[8] The two episodes scored big ratings and positive notices for Angie.

Other television work for Angie in 1965-66 included appearances on *The Fugitive*, *The Alfred Hitchcock Hour*, and Jack Benny's comedy program. A one-of-a-kind casting decision found her starring along with Hoagy Carmichael, Dolores del Rio, Buster Keaton, Paul Lukas, Cyril Ritchard, Walter Slezak, and Ray Walston in the 1965 TV movie *The Man Who Bought Paradise*. Ralph Nelson, fresh from his *Lilies of the Field* (1963) success, directed.

As soon as she finished her L.A. work commitments, she flew to New York for an appearance on the TV game show *Password* and met Burt for two more dinner dates. About to leave for London and an engagement at the Savoy with Dietrich, he asked her to come along on the trip with him. "I got someone to send me my passport and we went," she declared. "Within six weeks, we had gone out in L.A. three times and gone out in New York three times . . . and it was one of the most romantic courtships ever."[9] Her habit of maintaining friendships with old flames paid off professionally in London when she bumped into Charlie Feldman, who was in England to produce the film comedy *What's New Pussycat?*, written by Woody Allen and starring Peter Sellers, Peter O'Toole, Romy Schneider, Ursula Andress, Capucine, and Allen himself. Informed that Angie's new boyfriend was a songwriter, Feldman asked if he could score a picture and she immediately said that he could. Feldman's first choice, Dudley Moore, had bailed, and John Williams, a possible back-up candidate, was still in Los Angeles. Angie arranged a meeting during which the veteran producer and the young pop composer developed an immediate rapport.

Thus, hired for a job that he'd never done before, Bacharach holed up in a flat on Wilton Row off Belgrave Square for three weeks to write music for a movie whose rough cut he had just seen. Except for a grueling three day back and forth trip to L.A. for an appearance at the Academy Awards, Angie was there with him the entire time, running the Moviola, splicing broken film, preparing sandwiches, and offering feedback. The result was an innovative score that featured the hit title tune by Tom Jones and that initiated a list of film credits ultimately including *After the Fox* (1966), *Casino Royale* (1967, also for Feldman), *Butch Cassidy and the Sundance Kid* (1969), *Lost Horizon* (1972), *Arthur* (1981), *Love Hurts* (1992), and several others.

Reflecting years later on the London adventure, Angie remarked, "We fell harder in love because we felt we had lived through three years instead of three weeks of pressure. It just solidified our relationship."[10] They returned to the states together and several weeks later, while driving on the freeway in L.A., Burt asked Angie to marry him for his thirty-seventh birthday present. The subsequent ceremony had an impromptu, spur-of-the-moment air to it, like the elopement of Norman Maine and Esther Blodgett in *A Star Is Born*. Since Angie did not have to report back to the set of *The Chase* until Tuesday, they caught a 7:00 p.m. Friday flight to Las

Vegas and checked in at the Sands. There was no church and no celebrity guest list, just a simple Silver Bell Wedding Chapel ceremony officiated by the Reverend James Whitehead on May 15, 1965, at 3:45 in the morning, just three days after Burt's birthday. The *Los Angeles Times* reported the next day that the vows were witnessed by actor David Nelson, the brother of Angie's former *Rio Bravo* co-star Ricky Nelson, and his wife June Blair Nelson, an actress/model friend of Angie's who had appeared with her in *A Fever in the Blood*. Burt remembered that since the Nelsons had to get their kids to bed and fly in from L.A., he asked *The Gong Show* host Chuck Barris and his wife Lynn to be ready as stand-ins. Neither the bride's nor the groom's parents attended although Angie called Rika from Las Vegas with the news.

They both had gotten happily drunk early in the evening, but as they waited for the Nelsons to arrive, Burt seemed to sober up to the reality that his much valued independence would no longer be the same. "I think that was the night Burt fell out of love with me," Angie ominously noted, "because here we were sitting and waiting in a casino lounge and it just took the boom [sic] off of it."[11] The next day they returned to L.A., picked up the Chrysler convertible that Angie had on loan from Universal, and drove to Palm Springs for a two-day honeymoon. Afterwards, he flew to New York on business and she went back to the studio.

The early days of the marriage were a whirlwind of adjustment and activity. As soon as Burt joined Angie in Brentwood, they realized that her two-bedroom, one-bath house on North Bundy was too small. The shared living conditions reminded her uncomfortably of the cramped Brown family bungalow in Burbank. To remedy the situation, she promptly put in a half bath as Burt's wedding gift, reasoning "You've got to have two bathrooms."[12]

The newlyweds also purchased a vacation property in the southern California beach town of Del Mar, where they could indulge their mutual passion for horse racing at the "turf meets the surf" track built in 1937 by Bing Crosby and some Hollywood partners. It was here, living next door to trainer Charlie Wittingham, that Burt began his career as race horse owner cum composer. Professionally, Angie had more TV guest appearances to make, and Burt had the commitment to Dietrich plus a solo album called "Hit Maker! Burt Bacharach Plays His Hits" and new singles with Jackie DeShannon and Warwick to push. In addition, they were much in demand on the Hollywood social circuit, attending parties and receptions all over town. "They just had that charisma, that pizzazz," industry insider Johnny Grant said of their popularity among celebrity peers.[13]

By August, Angie was back in Rome filming scenes at Cinecittà for *Cast a Giant Shadow*, a big budget action film based on the life of a Jewish American military officer who participated in the 1948 Arab-Israeli War. Co-financed by the Mirisch Corporation and Kirk Douglas's and John Wayne's independent production companies, the film starred Douglas as the officer and Senta Berger as an Israeli paramilitary agent. Angie played the wife who tries to keep Douglas at home, and Wayne, Yul Brynner, and Frank Sinatra all made cameo appearances. The extensive supporting cast included James Donald, Luther Adler, Michael Hordern, Topol, and Stathis Giallelis. Among such distinguished company and with such a colorless part, it was possible for Angie to have been overlooked, but reviewers appreciated her contributions to the ensemble. Typical was the endorsement from *Variety*: "Miss Dickinson does a good job in a role which calls for her to be a flip, sardonic chick, also an adoring wife."[14]

The action scenes were shot on location in Israel where the Army Chief of Staff Yitzhak Rabin was happy to make available the resources of the military, charging $3.25 per day for each soldier and $66.66 for each tank with full crew. Expensive and complicated, filming took place in the desert during some of the hottest weeks of the year, but since Angie's scenes involved studio interiors, she remained comfortably back in Rome. Her stay this time, however, was much different from when she had been in town for *Jessica*. No late night visits to Via Veneto clubs, no headline-grabbing dates with Italian movie stars. She was married now and anxious to rejoin her husband. As soon as she finished her work late that summer, she flew to London and then on to Scotland, where Bacharach had agreed to conduct the orchestra for Dietrich at the Edinburgh International Festival.

This was to be one of his last concert appearances with the legendary performer. Dealing with Dionne Warwick's jealousy over Angie was difficult enough (Burt claimed she started wearing a blonde wig to needle him), but telling Dietrich about Angie and about his desire to go it alone professionally was much harder. "Marlene had known the day would come," wrote Steven Bach in *Marlene Dietrich: Life and Legend*, "which did not lessen the shock or rage when it did."[15] According to Bach, she exploded, insisting that he was betraying her and ruining his career through marriage to someone who was not a real star. Burt's recollection was similar. On his post-honeymoon trip to London, he went to see Marlene at her suite in the Dorchester and before he could play some new arrangements for her, she came unglued. "You married that cunt! That slut!" he remembered her shouting. "How could you have done such a thing?"[16] As she continued to rant, he made his way out of the room, thinking "It's over between the two of us."[17] It was Marlene at her worst, reminding him of the time on tour in South Africa when she had voodoo dolls made in Angie's image and stuck pins into them.[18]

In her own autobiography, Marlene spun the tale differently, appreciatively blessing Burt's need for career independence. "As for Burt Bacharach," she claimed, "when he became famous, he could no longer accompany me on tour around the world. I understood that very well and have never reproached him in any way. From that fateful day on, I have worked like a robot, trying to recapture the wonderful woman he helped make out of me."[19] Whatever her true feelings, Marlene continued on with replacement conductors Stan Freeman and William Blezard, and Burt returned to the states with Angie. After the initial shock of his departure wore off, the former collaborators re-established their professional relationship to such a degree that Burt briefly signed on to supervise her wildly successful 1967-68 New York engagement at the Lunt-Fontanne Theatre on Broadway.

The friendship, however, was never quite the same. Angie knew what Marlene had said about her but, not a vindictive person by nature, was happy to welcome her over to the Bacharach house for dinner (which often consisted of Kentucky Fried Chicken, potatoes, and cole slaw). "Marlene was nice to me at dinner, but I knew it was a performance on her part," she observed.[20] Sometime later, after Burt had completely stopped conducting for Marlene, Angie bumped into her one day in Beverly Hills and said she was sorry that things with Burt were not as they had been. Grandly quoting the final line of *Pagliacci*, Dietrich said, "Finita la commedia."[21] The two actresses never saw each other again.

The Los Angeles which welcomed the Bacharachs home from Europe had been rocked by the civil disorder in Watts but still felt a lot like the insular industry town it always had been. John Wayne was still starring in Westerns, the studios were still making money with epics like *The Greatest Story Ever Told*, and *The Sound of Music* suggested that musicals might be staging a comeback. The

Beach Boys recorded over a dozen hit singles between 1965-66 that extolled southern California surfing culture, and on October 14, with Sandy Koufax on the mound, the Los Angeles Dodgers beat the Minnesota Twins 2-0 in Game Seven to win the World Series. Flush with the success of *What's New Pussycat?*, Burt and Angie seemed to be the ideal poster couple for the much envied Hollywood lifestyle of the mid-Sixties. "Kind of like Brad Pitt and Angelina," agreed Angie.[22]

Soon after the Christmas holidays, Angie learned that she was pregnant, and both she and Burt were thrilled over the prospect of starting a family. In a subsequent scaling back of her work commitments, she guest-starred on two television series (*The Virginian* and *Bob Hope Presents the Chrysler Theatre*) and accepted a relatively small supporting role in *The Poppy Is Also a Flower*. Based on an idea by James Bond creator Ian Fleming, the film follows a group of narcotics agents as they track an opium shipment from the Afghanistan-Iran border to the main heroin distributor in Europe. It was produced by the United Nations as part of an educational project, first broadcast on the ABC television network, and then released theatrically in the United States by Astral Films. Despite a weak script, the project attracted some major talent including director Terence Young (best known for the first two Bond films as well as *Thunderball*), narrator Grace Kelly, and actors Senta Berger, Stephen Boyd, Yul Brynner, Rita Hayworth, Trevor Howard, Omar Sharif, E.G. Marshall, Marcello Mastroianni, and Eli Wallach. Like the rest of her cast mates, Angie basically donated her time, motivated by a desire to support the U.N.'s anti-drug campaign. Since she was required for only a few days of shooting, the impact on her schedule was minimal.

On July 14, 1966, only six months into her pregnancy, Angie gave premature birth at Cedars of Lebanon Hospital to a baby girl.

ANGIE

Weighing just one pound and thirteen ounces, she hovered precariously near death. "In the first month," remembered Angie, "she stopped breathing three times."[23] A team of doctors worked diligently to save the infant, who remained in an enclosed incubator, a preemie isolette, for three months. Angie later came to believe that being cut off from a mother's voice and touch had lasting impact on her child. Named Lea Nikki by her anxious parents, she narrowly escaped brain damage but developed severe eye problems that required constant attention once she was finally released to go home. The ocular condition, where one eye looked directly at the viewed object while the other turned inward, was known as strabismus and meant that she would always only be able to use one eye at a time. "I would patch an eye and she would rip it off," explained Angie. "The skin would bruise and burn. Oh God! You have a child who is laboring through life, and it is a drain, and when you come close to losing her you hang on."[24]

Hanging on meant major changes in lifestyle. Putting her career on immediate hold, Angie devoted herself to Nikki's care. She made no film or television appearances for several months. Consultations with medical specialists replaced collaborations with directors and producers. Determined that her fragile, undersized daughter lead as normal a life as possible, Angie focused on domestic responsibilities more than she ever had before, nursing Nikki and preparing meals for Burt. Her social life revolved around friends who had young children of their own, old pals like June Nelson. Even in the thick of such hardship, Nelson remembered that Angie's sense of humor kept her resilient. Observing Nelson's own chubby baby boy, Angie remarked, "Well, my baby's long."[25] That strength helped her once again in November when she received the news that her father Bud had died. The emotional undercurrents of families could be treacherous; memories of the past could blend uncomfortably with fears for the future. Having never fully reconciled her conflicted feelings about Bud's alcoholism, she grieved as best she could and then turned the focus back to her daughter.

As Nikki grew into a toddler, it was apparent that she had severe behavioral issues as well, expressing extreme bouts of anger, fear, and anxiety. "She had so many fears, feeling so abandoned when not having the attention she expects," recalled Angie.[26] The usual child development process was seriously askew. She didn't start speaking until she was three years old but played the piano at four like a prodigy, composing strange, incoherent songs. She was good at gymnastics, horseback riding, ballet, and swimming but forced friends and family to sit and watch as she took forever to complete simple tasks. Her compulsiveness could also become aggressively anti-social. "Early on, Nikki started cutting the hair off her dolls and the manes off her toy horses," revealed Angie. "When she was around four years old, Nikki began saving everything—broken toys, pieces of glass, old batteries, and dog poo—in a mound about a foot and a half high on top of a dresser in her closet."[27] Like most children, she occasionally tried to take control by playing her parents off against each other, but her anger when rebuffed was excessive and enduring. "I was playing a lot of concerts," remembered Burt, "and when I'd come back, Nikki didn't want me sleeping with Angie because that was what she had been doing."[28]

With no suitable explanation from the doctors, Angie assumed it was just her own bad parenting. As Nikki's tantrums and obsessions grew in intensity so also did Angie's despair. "She was difficult all the way, but I kept saying, 'oh well, I'll keep working on it,'" she explained. "But I couldn't fix it."[29] Burt believed her efforts to fix Nikki's problems were misguided, remarking "By the time Nikki was eight years old, her relationship with Angie was so symbiotic that it was driving me crazy. Nikki would sit at the dinner table and Angie would feed her."[30] Even more startling, he added, was that his daughter would throw the pet mice Angie bought her against the wall and when they died, Angie would go out and buy more.[31] He believed the situation was out of control.

In reality, Nikki would suffer all her life from a form of Asperger Syndrome, still poorly understood at the time and, in her case, not clearly diagnosed until she was thirty-four. The name comes from Austrian pediatrician Hans Asperger, whose 1944 clinical studies identified children unable to communicate nonverbally and/or unable to interpret social cues. An autism spectrum disorder, Asperger's accounted for Nikki's social deficits and compulsive behaviors. Where treatment now includes various cognitive and physical therapies, the options available to Burt and Angie were not so plentiful. As Nikki grew older, they alternated time at home assisted by a nurse with enrollment at the experimental UCLA Laboratory School which welcomed students from various ethnic groups and backgrounds, including some with disabilities. Relatively happy there, she cultivated a circle of friends who called themselves "Judi's Kids" after the characters in Judi Blume's popular young adolescent novels.

While Angie concerned herself solely with Nikki's care, Burt continued to work. Among the hit songs that he and David produced from 1966 to 1967 were "Alfie," "The Look of Love," "I Say a Little Prayer," and "One Less Bell to Answer." He also wrote an instrumental composition called "Nikki" in honor of his daughter and recorded it as a single in 1966. Having kept his apartment on East Sixty-First Street in New York City, he stayed involved in the music business, traveled often, and appeared on such television shows as *The Hollywood Palace*. There was also the now regular job of scoring for film (*Casino Royale*) and television ("On the Flip Side" episode of *ABC Stage 67*).

Professionally idle for the first time in many years, Angie seemed content with her role as wife and mother. Her public comments focused on the simple pleasures of domestic life. In a guest column written some time later for Sheila Graham, she insisted, "Burt and I are lucky because we are not a team. We never expect to work together. What we have together is our marriage, our daughter, and our racing stable. We both love racing and, while we may not always understand and compare each other's work, we can always get together on such subjects as Hialeah, Hollywood Park, and Churchill Downs."[32] Realizing soon into the marriage that the place on Bundy was inadequate for their needs, they had purchased a bigger, eight-room house with pool in Coldwater Canyon that provided more recreational space for Nikki and what they hoped would be an even larger family (in a 1968 interview with Graham, Angie incidentally remarked that she "lost a baby this summer in England,"[33] but little other reference to a miscarriage has been made over the years, and she and Burt had no other children together).

Angie's inevitable return to moviemaking came in the form of an offer to star again with Lee Marvin in John Boorman's production of *Point Blank*. Since Boorman planned to shoot the film in and around Los Angeles, she was able to report to work each morning and return to Nikki in the evening. Filming began early in 1967 and was completed by the end of April. Even though this was British-born Boorman's first Hollywood picture and only his second feature film overall (he had previously made the pop band comedy *Catch Us if You Can* with The Dave Clark Five), he exuded a confident professionalism that particularly impressed the often difficult Lee Marvin, who ceded all of his contractually specified creative approvals to the young director. From the preparatory rehearsals at Marvin's L.A. home to the grueling location shooting, the production was marked by a highly collaborative, supportive atmosphere.

Based on *The Hunter*, a 1963 crime novel by Donald E. Westlake (writing as Richard Stark), the plot is a fairly familiar revenge tale. Walker (Marvin) pulls off a robbery with the help of a friend who double-crosses him, leaves him for dead, and steals his wife. Recovering, Walker goes after his accomplice and the crime syndicate to which he has handed over all their loot as payment for a debt. Along the way, after his wife has committed suicide with a sleeping pill overdose, he engages in an affair with her sister (Angie), who helps him find the ex-friend. In the climax, Walker squares off against the syndicate superiors in possession of his money.

What makes the film unique is Boorman's innovative visual style. Rather than employ the shadowy, claustrophobic nighttime settings of a film noir, he uses elongated widescreen compositions to isolate characters in vulnerably open spaces. Against an arid, sun-bleached southern California landscape, massive architectural structures seem to crash down on Walker and the others. The dislocation is further heightened by a non-linear time frame, skewed camera angles, and stylized monochromatic color schemes. For added effect, Boorman shot an opening sequence at Alcatraz, the first time the recently closed prison had ever been used as an actual film location.

With a budget of just under $3 million, the film earned three times that cost in its initial release. *Point Blank* also garnered broad critical acclaim, with several reviewers comparing it to a European art film. *Saturday Review*'s Hollis Alpert called it a "quite fascinating visual experience."[34] while *Newsweek*'s Howard Junker described it as a "paradigm of cinematic technique."[35] Writing for the *Los Angeles Times*, Kevin Thomas argued, "British director John Boorman, in an auspicious Hollywood debut, comments through images rather than messages, just as he makes use of the full resources of both camera and soundtrack to allow us to feel the impact of betrayal upon Marvin both physically and emotionally." In regard to the film's generic roots, he concluded, "Like Jean-Luc Godard, Boorman takes gangsters seriously and, also like Godard, makes his audience concentrate hard."[36] Over the years, *Point Blank*'s critical reputation has only increased in stature. Commenting on its rerelease in 1998, *The Sunday Times*'s Tom Shone raved, "John Boorman's masterpiece is rereleased this week, and after all these years it still comes at you with the force of a bullet, leaves you wondering what on earth hit you, but also allows plenty of room for that wonder, what with its cool empty spaces, the studied blankness of its acting, its careful fracturing of time and space. It is like watching a Giacometti sculpture explode in slow motion."[37]

Angie's performance drew equally positive reaction. As Walker's detached sister-in-law, she reluctantly then decidedly helps him take his revenge. With her whispery voice and glacial gaze, she creates a believable character whose frustration at Walker's indifference erupts in spasms of sudden anger. In his biography of Lee Marvin, Robert Lentz remarked, "Dickinson is stunning, whether letting Reese [the double-crosser] paw her or beating herself breathless against Walker's chest. Her vitality is in direct contrast to Walker's lifelessness, and he seems to draw energy from her to keep himself going."[38] *Variety* noted that "Angie Dickinson, playing Miss Archer's sister, provides the right mixture of beauty and bewilderment as she assists Marvin,"[39] and the *Newsweek* review declared, "Angie Dickinson is delectable as an arty, world-worn moll."[40] Other writers commented on how great she looked in the nude scene with Marvin or in the mini-skirts which Boorman was introducing to

American film audiences for one of the first times (a *Life* magazine photo spread also featured Angie and co-star Sharon Acker modeling the film's contemporary fashions against stark Alcatraz backgrounds). In an article for the *Hollywood Citizen-News*, Nadine Edwards succinctly summarized Angie's return to the screen in *Point Blank*: "It's probably her best vehicle to date."[41]

Lee Marvin's Walker keeps his cool against Angie's frenzied physical assault in *Point Blank* (1967).]

Angie herself seemed to agree. She told Kevin Thomas, "I think the director John Boorman could have done more with me in *Point Blank* . . . I would have liked more close-ups. Close-ups are my cup of tea. Still, it's the best part I ever had."[42] She was relieved that her difficult domestic challenges had not dimmed her luster before the camera. While she had never stopped being a favorite subject of celebrity photographers (Ron Galella snapped her in October of 1967 with Judy Garland at the New York Cultural Gala Honoring Stanley Adams), this was a reaffirmation of her screen presence. Not only was she still photogenic, but her acting conveyed a much deeper resonance than the characterizations of Sheila Farr in *The Killers* or of Laurie Gibson in *The Art of Love*. Heartened by the favorable critical reception, she looked forward to additional assignments that would allow her to stay close to home and attend to Nikki's needs. Almost immediately she agreed to star with her old pal Glenn Ford in *The Last Challenge*, a conventional Western about a reformed outlaw cum marshal and the young gunslinger out to test him.

Originally titled *Pistolero's Progress*, it was shot in Arizona and on the MGM lot in Culver City, California. Other than the chance to work with Ford and veteran director Richard Thorpe, who had made everything from entries in the Tarzan and Thin Man franchises to over a half dozen Robert Taylor adventure pictures, it is difficult to understand why Angie accepted the role. Not unfamiliarly, she played the saloon owner in love with Ford and willing to do anything to protect his life. She has a couple of highly charged emotional scenes with both the gunslinger and the marshal, but most of the action is pedestrian. Several reviewers noted similarities to typical television Westerns and to a previous Ford vehicle titled *The Fastest Gun Alive*. The best notice Angie could muster was John Mahoney's comment in *The Hollywood Reporter* that "Miss

Dickinson is both attractive and able as [Ford's] strong-willed ally."[43] With a disappointing take at the box office, *The Last Challenge* is mostly remembered today as being the last film in Thorpe's remarkable forty-three year career, most of which was spent as a contract director at M-G-M.

Not only did the movie do little to stretch Angie's acting skills, it also stalled the buzz generated by *Point Blank*. The issue of audience popularity, the degree of print and public recognition, had always been an important one for both Angie and Burt. When they married, she was the bigger celebrity, but as the decade wore on and he amassed more hit singles and film credits, that position reversed itself. Both were acutely aware of the swing. "You know, I was pretty popular and she was popular, but I probably, when we got married, was a little hotter than she was," Burt concluded.[44] As Angie tried to find a viable career direction, Burt surged ahead with new hit singles ("Do You Know the Way to San Jose?") and, along with David, wrote the score for the Neil Simon/David Merrick musical *Promises, Promises*. The show made its Broadway debut on December 1, 1968, and Angie flew in from Los Angeles to help Burt recover from a bout of pneumonia and to join an opening night crowd that included Burt's parents, Merle Oberon, Ethel Merman, Carol Channing, Sidney Lumet, Tammy Grimes, Milton Berle, Herb Alpert, and other celebrities. During a post-performance party thrown by Merrick at El Morocco nightclub, the entire company celebrated when the early television reviews and Clive Barnes's piece in *The New York Times* indicated that *Promises, Promises* was going to be a hit (it ultimately ran for four years).

"I didn't mind his success," Angie asserted, "I minded losing mine. Of course I hadn't had his success, not as big as his. But I had some. Besides, I loved to work, to act. I hated to lose what I had."[45]

Given that need to work, she co-starred in the TV movie *A Case of Libel*, which aired on February 11, 1968, and was based on the real-life Quentin Reynolds/Westbrook Pegler lawsuit. It was a supporting role, well acted and convincing, but somewhat obscured by the showier performances of Lloyd Bridges, Van Heflin, Jose Ferrer, Anthony Quayle, and E.G. Marshall.

Burt's star power peaked in 1969 when he wrote the music for *Butch Cassidy and the Sundance Kid* and a year later won Academy Awards for Best Score and, along with David, Best Original Song ("Raindrops Keep Fallin' on My Head"). Angie was there by his side at the Dorothy Chandler Pavilion but was not asked to be one of the presenters and was not acknowledged by Burt in his acceptance speech. The skyrocketing "orbit" that Angie coveted seemed now to have been attained by Burt. He starred in his own TV specials, performed in concert, won a Grammy for Best Cast Album for *Promises, Promises*, was nominated for a Tony Award, snagged a *Newsweek* cover story, and continued to produce hit records. Through Angie's acquaintance with Mafia-affiliated lawyer Sidney Korshak, he was also signed to play a week at the Riviera Hotel's Versailles Room in Las Vegas. Angie somewhat ruefully recalled attending one of his concerts soon after the Academy Award ceremony: "I couldn't believe it. The photographers almost ran over me to take pictures of Burt. In the crush, a cameraman said to me, 'Excuse me, miss. Would you mind stepping aside? We want a picture of Mr. Bacharach.'"[46]

Meanwhile, Angie, in addition to singing Burt's "I'll Never Fall in Love Again" on a 1969 Dean Martin television show, appeared in three movies that were forgotten almost as rapidly as the succession in which she made them. Released first, in February of 1969, was *Sam Whiskey*, a comedy Western that also starred Burt Reynolds,

Clint Walker, and Ossie Davis. The project had more than just a passing resemblance to a television program. It was produced by the team of Jules V. Levy, Arthur Gardner, and Arnold Laven, creators of *The Rifleman* (1958-63) and *The Big Valley* (1965-69) TV series and was directed by Laven himself. Both Burt Reynolds and Clint Walker were veterans of TV Westerns (*Gunsmoke* and *Cheyenne* respectively), and screenwriter William V. Norton had written extensively for *The Big Valley*.

The story seemed like a cross between *Maverick* (1957-62) and *The Wild Wild West* (1965-69). Angie is a wealthy widow who seduces Reynolds into returning $250,000 in gold bars to the Denver Mint from which her late husband stole them. Complicating Reynolds's intricate plan is an attempt by a ruthless outlaw gang to procure the gold for itself. There were various clever twists but overshadowing the plot was Angie and Burt's nude scene. By this time, Angie was quite comfortable in various stages of undress before the camera. Burt not so much. Still three years before his breakthrough success in *Deliverance* (1972) and his run of mid-70s comedy hits, he had appeared in only five previous feature films. "It was my first nude scene," he recalled, "and Angie advised me to act as if it was natural to be naked in front of a film crew."[7] Their onscreen chemistry worked, and like most of her male co-stars, he became a lifelong friend, appearing in two more late-career pictures with her. "My God," he said of the scene they finally managed to shoot, "Angie had one of the greatest bodies in the history of the world."[48] In a socially significant postscript, Laven, working under the new Motion Picture Association of America guidelines, was forced to replace a "bare from the waist up" shot of Angie with a tighter "shoulders up" shot to avoid an "R" rating.

Young Billy Young (originally titled *Who Rides with Kane?*) was another Western, another location shoot in Old Tucson, Arizona, and another nude scene. To absolutely no one's surprise, Angie played a dance hall girl, a role she was visiting as often as had Marlene Dietrich before her. The variation this time was that she was appearing opposite Robert Mitchum, a good two decades into his career but still a commanding presence on and off the screen. Reformed gunman Mitchum wanders into a corrupt frontier town, where he confronts outlaws, avenges his son's death, falls for Angie, and mentors a young gunslinger. In the end, he and Angie ride off to get married. Interestingly, the on-set dynamic mirrored the same veteran guiding newcomer theme as the narrative. Director Burt Kennedy, who had already made over a dozen Westerns including *Gun the Man Down* with Angie, steered a cast that featured the offspring of such famous Hollywood names as Robert Walker, John Carradine, and Dean Martin and a crew that included the sons of cinematographer Harry Stradling and sound mixer Al Overton.

The main attraction, the bad boy in chief, was Mitchum. Coaxed into making his next-to-last Western by a co-production deal that gave him $200,000 up front and twenty-seven percent of the gross, he still was unhappy about what he thought was a rote performance in a formulaic picture. He carped, "I'm wearing the same damn hat and the same damn boots I wore in *Five Card Stud*,"[49] drank heavily, and behaved erratically. Reporter Tim Tyler claimed that after one uncomplicated scene shot before a crowd of onlookers, Mitchum exploded, shouting obscenities and prancing around like an effeminate lunatic. Kennedy disputed that account, however, remembering that he "was a great guy, did the job, no problems. He was from the old school, like Duke, Henry Fonda. No problems, no questions, just get the job done."[50]

Angie felt the same way about Mitchum, admiring his craft and enjoying their time together. Her nude takes were accomplished with serious albeit good-natured professionalism all around. Flirtatious bantering characterized her relationship with Mitchum and the once again mostly all-male cast. Apparently, Kennedy took the flirts seriously. In 2008, Angie told Army Archerd, "He was madly in love with me . . . I finally said no."[51]

Among the risqué stories Mitchum liked to tell over the years was one in which an awe-struck female fan approached him on the set of *Young Billy Young* and offered to grant some explicit sexual favors. "Well, that's a great offer, honey," he supposedly replied, "but I see they're right now calling me back to work. Well, gee, Angie's not doing anything, why don't you ask her?"[52] True to form, she and Mitchum would team up again thirteen years later for the TV movie *One Shoe Makes It Murder*.

A contemporary comedy, *Some Kind of a Nut* reunited her with Dick Van Dyke. Written and directed by Garson Kanin, who had penned the Katherine Hepburn-Spencer Tracy pictures *Adam's Rib* (1949) and *Pat and Mike* (1952) with his wife Ruth Gordon, it was the offbeat story of a New York city bank teller (Van Dyke) who grows a conspicuously full beard that alienates his boss, annoys his girlfriend, and impresses his soon-to-be-divorced wife (Angie). This time around, for a change, Angie got to play the sympathetic side of a romantic triangle, supporting her husband as people turn against him and eventually winning him back from his uptight fiancée. Production on the film was marked by a divided shooting schedule; filming began in New York for two weeks during May of 1968, closed down while Van Dyke fulfilled other commitments, and then resumed in January, 1969.

Despite the interruptions, Angie was happy to work again with loyal friend and fellow liberal Democrat Van Dyke, just coming off his hugely popular TV series and pursuing a movie career that would never fully duplicate his small screen success. With references to LSD, Buddhist philosophy, protest marches, and hippies, *Some Kind of a Nut* aimed to be an anti-Establishment farce, but in a year that saw the release of *Alice's Restaurant*, *Bob and Carol and Ted and Alice*, *Easy Rider*, *Goodbye, Columbus*, *Midnight Cowboy*, *Putney Swope*, and *Medium Cool*, its one-note premise of a bank employee's controversial beard seemed hopelessly dated and irrelevant. Typical of the critical reaction was Charles Champlin's assertion in the *Los Angeles Times* that "*Some Kind of a Nut* is a contrivance which never comes coughing and sputtering into life. Its characters don't make it as cartoons or as creatures. Artifice lurks at every turn, ill-concealed."[53]

The movie illustrated Angie's own professional dilemma—how to adjust to the public's changing tastes and interests. She had hoped that this trio of films and her appearance in the politically tinged *A Case of Libel* would showcase her ability to handle comedy, action, and drama with equal agility, but apart from the *Los Angeles Times* calling her a "deftly dizzy comedienne"[54] in *Sam Whiskey*, most reviewers just focused on her looks. David Sutherland praised *Sam Whiskey*'s "picture book photography and the beauty of Angie Dickinson,"[55] Kevin Thomas said she was "delectable and vivacious"[56] in *Young Billy Young*, and a *Motion Picture Exhibitor* correspondent noted that in *Some Kind of a Nut* she "looks great in a bikini."[57] It seemed impossible for her to move beyond the sexy, nude scene-loving glamour girl image that she herself had been working to create since the mid-Fifties.

Beyond its impact on her audiences, the volatile social scene roiling outside the Hollywood movie studios in 1968 touched Angie both politically and personally. On March 31, 1968, amid massive anti-Vietnam War demonstrations and criticism within his own party, President Lyndon Johnson announced that he would not seek another term in the White House. Almost immediately, Robert Kennedy's long-shot candidacy for President, announced only two weeks before, took on a real, legitimate viability. Although some Democratic activists resented RFK for waiting until after lone-wolf candidate Eugene McCarthy of Minnesota had proven in the New Hampshire primary that Johnson was vulnerable, others were happy to come on board. Angie was one of Kennedy's early supporters, stirred by memories of Jack and the campaign of 1960. With the glaring exception of Frank Sinatra, many of JFK's old Hollywood pals joined her in fundraising and vote canvassing. During a frantic two month period, Kennedy won primaries in Indiana and Nebraska, coming up short against McCarthy only in Oregon.

By May, Bobby and his wife Ethel were campaigning intensely in California for its 174 winner-take-all delegates to the nominating convention in Chicago. Concentrating on white working-class neighborhoods, the inner cities, and barrios, Kennedy repeatedly toured the state, drawing huge crowds everywhere he went and dominating news coverage in the three main media markets of Los Angeles, San Diego, and San Francisco. The main campaign headquarters were set up on Wilshire Boulevard in the heart of L.A., where the candidate had time to connect directly with his Hollywood supporters.

One Sunday, several days before the June 4th election, Angie and Burt, along with Warren Beatty, Shirley MacLaine, Jean Seberg, and Seberg's husband, the French novelist Romain Gary, joined Kennedy for lunch at director John Frankenheimer's Malibu beach house. According to journalist David Talbot, amid the pleasantries Gary suddenly told Bobby, "You know, don't you, that somebody's going to try to kill you?" As the group fell silent, "Kennedy, sitting cross-legged in his swim trunks on the floor, simply stared into a glass of orange juice that he was swirling in his hand and answered, 'That's the chance I have to take.'"[58] Although not confirming that exact incident, Angie recalled the afternoon as similarly fraught. "In fact I saw him two weeks before he was killed," she told the *Ladies' Home Journal*. "We were having lunch with some of his other friends at the beach. I had no premonitions. But after I kissed him goodbye, I kissed him again. I don't know why."[59]

She would not see him again. On election day, he captured the state by four percentage points, but following his victory speech in the main ballroom of the Ambassador Hotel in Los Angeles, he was shot while exiting a service pantry by Jordanian immigrant Sirhan Sirhan and died some twenty-six hours later. For Angie, it was truly the end of a golden era. She and Burt stayed friendly with younger brother Ted, taking him out to dinner during L.A. visits, holding a concert to help fund one of his Senatorial campaigns, and playing tennis at the Kennedy family compound in Hyannis Port, Massachusetts, but a sense of loss lingered over everything. The promise of social and economic equality championed by Jack and Bobby seemed to have crashed on the rocks of civil disorder and disillusionment. She would continue to support Democratic Presidential candidates but never again with the same passionate engagement.

Professionally, the decade ended quietly for Angie. With Lloyd Bridges, she starred in *The Love War*, a sci-fi ABC *Movie of the Week* that featured a shot of her as a hideously scarred alien and that aired on March 10, 1970, but no other pictures. A lively audience favorite on *Password*, where she had guested in the mid-60s with Efrem Zimbalist, Jr., Peter Lawford, and Frank Gorshin, she even reduced those kinds of commitments, appearances that required little or no preparation. As was now her custom, she spoke often to the press, telling Abe Greenberg in another of those persistent orbital references, "I keep a stable career. It hasn't gone down, but it hasn't skyrocketed moonward, and I don't mind that either."[60] To Morton Moss, she confided, "Look I think of myself as a liberated woman. But I don't want to be freed from men. Burt—he dictates. Yes, I'm independent. But in the end, you go with him. I acquiesce to my man. But I'm still recognized as a movie star. I'm still hanging in there."[61] The message continued to be that Burt and Nikki came first and that she was okay with the compromises. But occasionally, as in this aside to Moss, there was a tone of professional regret: "When we were married, I was the star. Never the superstar he became, but he was referred to as the husband of Angie Dickinson. I cut out a newspaper clipping that reads that way. I saved it for my bad days. It cheers me up."[62]

Actually, after the high mark of *Butch Cassidy and the Sundance Kid*, Burt's own career had noticeably slowed. He did a television special in 1971 that guest-starred Barbra Streisand but completed no film scores. He and Hal David continued to write songs for Dionne Warwick and B.J. Thomas, but none of them were hits. The best showing was Thomas's "Everybody's Out of Town" at number twenty-six on the *Billboard* Hot 100 list and Warwick's "Let Me Go to Him" at number thirty-two. It was not that American record buyers had lost interest in pop vocals (the *Billboard* top ten for 1971 included tracks by Carole King, John Denver, Rod Stewart, and Donny Osmond), it was that the brilliant team of Bacharach and David seemed to have lost some of its creative synchronicity.

With no hits to her own credit, Angie was also treading water. Given her maternal responsibilities, the conditions for accepting a role remained restrictive. Starring parts almost always needed to be shot in L.A., location work had to be limited, and anything that could be wrapped in two weeks was ideal. "My decisions really are made for me," she explained, "and some of them are tough."63 By "tough," she meant having to say no to a number of plum parts that would have required a prolonged absence from home. "There was a picture that meant six weeks in Toronto. I had to refuse that. It was too long to leave my little girl," she elaborated. "A three-week film trip to Mexico, with part of a weekend free, couldn't work out for the same reason."64 She turned down roles in Jacques Deray's *The Swimming Pool* and Bernard Kowalski's *Stiletto* because the shooting schedules included twelve weeks in the south of France and a month in Puerto Rico respectively. The opportunity to return to Broadway in an historical drama called *Go Home and Tell Your Mother* was rejected for similar logistical reasons.

In the biggest loss of all, she passed on Robert Altman's first big hit. As *People* magazine reported, "Among the parts she had to sacrifice was Hot Lips Houlihan in *MASH*, which helped to establish Sally Kellerman."65 The Deray and Kowalski vehicles were standard fare, but the *MASH* offer could have been a game changer, a role where the frosty bitchiness she had portrayed before could now be played for laughs and for ultimate comic redemption. It would have been a perfect showcase, one that Kellerman herself parlayed into National Society of Film Critics, Golden Globe, and Academy Award nominations for Best Supporting Actress.

A part which promised something of the same comic heft was that of Miss Betty Smith in Roger Vadim's *Pretty Maids All in a Row*. Since this picture was to be shot on location entirely within Los Angeles, it was an offer that Angie could and did accept. Written by *Star Trek* creator Gene Roddenberry, it was a dark comedy about a popular high school football coach/guidance counselor who is mentoring a sexually frustrated male student at the same time he is seducing and murdering a string of aggressively provocative coeds.

Intended as a satire, the film targeted the sexual revolution, law enforcement, educational bureaucrats, and popular culture. Rock Hudson was the coach, Telly Savalas the investigating police captain, Roddy McDowall the principal, and Angie the sexy substitute teacher who helps young John David Carson release his frustrations. With a start date of August 10, 1970, shooting occurred at the Venice Marina, the Santa Monica Pier, Rancho La Cienega Park, West Los Angeles's University High School, and various downtown L.A. locations. Production proceeded smoothly and amicably, but whatever hope there was for *MASH*-like popularity faded when the film opened in the spring of 1971 to lackluster box office and mostly unfavorable reviews. Not even a nine-page photo spread of Angie and some of the "pretty maids" in the April 1971 issue of *Playboy* could drum up much interest.

The problem was tone. Vadim, who had enjoyed some success directing his ex-wives Brigitte Bardot and Jane Fonda in *And God Created Woman* (1956) and *Barbarella* (1968) respectively, did not possess the light touch needed to put over such edgy material. The murders, which should have had the droll whimsicality of an Alec Guiness British comedy, were sleazy and distasteful. The police procedural tropes never jelled with the satire, and most of the actors, unable to keep their tongues firmly lodged in cheek, hovered between solemn and silly in their portrayals.

Much more successful was the ironic, meta-like play on Angie's screen image as a confident, manipulative seductress. Here she is naively unaware of her physical allure, surprised and then delighted by the sexual union with Carson. Their candle-lit nude scenes have an air of innocence at odds with the grating tone of the rest of the film. Hers was a subtle, assured performance that escaped the attention of most critics. She herself dismissed *Pretty Maids All in a Row* as a "bomb."[66]

Another riff on her image, a commodification of her "swinger" reputation, was a television commercial that she and Burt made for Martini and Rossi alcoholic beverages. In the 30-second spot, she is dressed all in white and introduces herself directly to the camera. "Hi, I'm Angie Dickinson, a girl who likes things with character," she says. There's a party in the background, and she pours a glass of Martini and Rossi vermouth, which she recommends "because the taste is light and doesn't overpower you." Holding her drink, she glides over to a baby grand piano where Burt is playing a melody and asks, "Speaking of characters, Burt, what do you say to Martini and Rossi?" Then, as she leans on the piano, Burt sings, "Yes, yes, to Martini and Rossi on the rocks, say yes." In the final two-shot, Angie turns to the camera, smiles, and whispers, "Yeah." Everything about the ad connotes 70s hipness: Burt's white turtleneck and light blue blazer, Angie's pants ensemble, the metallic drink cart, the glass walled house where the party occurs. For the price of a bottle of fortified Italian wine, a typical consumer was offered the chance to sample a little of what made Burt and Angie's celebrity life so glamorous.

The elegant façade, however, concealed deeper cracks within their very public marriage. In addition to the stress associated with Nikki's health and the insecurities over whose career was going stronger, Angie also believed that her husband was seeing other women, a charge which Burt himself denied at the time. "His first affair was the most difficult to deal with,"[67] she confessed many years later to *TV Guide* journalist Mary Murphy. Hurt and humiliated, she mostly kept the anger to herself, unable to process the betrayal. On the one occasion where she did confront him, Burt shrugged off the accusation, saying, "Oh Angie, you've read too many movie magazines."[68] In his autobiography, however, Burt was much more forthcoming about his philandering. He admitted that at the time of Angie's pregnancy he was thinking of returning to his old flame, nightclub singer Slim Brandy, but reconsidered once he learned he was going to be a father. "My relationship with Slim Brandy had begun before I ever knew Angie, but there were also a few others," he wrote, including a violinist who toured with his orchestra.[69]

Always hopeful the marriage would last, Angie dealt with Burt's infidelity the same way her mother had dealt with Bud's alcoholism. She endured it. "I really liked him," she told Murphy. "I was mad about him, so I tolerated it. I tried to close my eyes to it because I knew if I protested, he'd walk."[70] Both of them knew, however, that the marriage was fated. "I don't think we were very happy by the time we were living in Del Mar," admitted Angie. "The marriage was already in trouble before Nikki was born. Very much so."[71] Burt agreed that Nikki was not the decisive factor: "Would our marriage have lasted if not for Nikki? I doubt it."[72]

Partly as solace, she threw herself into a flurry of work projects, none of them particularly memorable. There were four television movies, a couple of features, and some guest appearances on network TV shows. The best of the television work was *Thief*, an ABC *Movie of the Week* entry that starred Richard Crenna as a professional thief who would like to reform but must undertake one last job to pay off a gambling debt. Angie played sympathetic love interest Jean Melville in a cast that also included Cameron Mitchell, Hurd Hatfield, Robert Webber, and Michael Lerner. Initiated in 1969, *Movie of the Week* (or *MotW* as it was known in the trades) was a major success for ABC, never more so than its third season (1971-72) when it ranked fifth in the Nielsen ratings with such hits as *Duel*, Steven Spielberg's feature-length directorial debut about a motorist harassed by a mysterious truck driver, and

Brian's Song, a dramatization of the fated friendship between Brian Piccolo (James Caan) and Gale Sayers (Billy Dee Williams). Made for around $350,000 each, the movies were assigned to various independent production companies and often featured big name actors such as Anthony Perkins, Julie Harris, Barbara Stanwyck, Bing Crosby, Helen Hayes, Myrna Loy, Olivia de Havilland, Susan Hayward, Henry Fonda, Joseph Cotten, Elizabeth Taylor, and Richard Burton. Not bad company for Angie, and one of the reasons, besides the locations, that she was willing to participate. Occasionally, as was the case with *Alias Smith and Jones, Longstreet, The Night Stalker, Kung Fu,* and *The Six Million Dollar Man*, the films also served as pilots for a subsequent TV series.

Airing on October 9, 1971, *Thief* was the seventh offering of *MotW*'s season three, sandwiched between a science fiction thriller with Michael Cole and a Barbara Stanwyck mystery. Written by John D.F. Black and directed by William Graham, the film was Emmy nominated for Outstanding Writing Achievement in Drama and won an Edgar Allan Poe Award for Best Television Feature or Miniseries. Singled out for praise were Crenna's multi-dimensional characterization and the credible rapport between him and Angie.

Not as well received was *See the Man Run*, which paired Angie with Robert Culp and was broadcast as another ABC *MotW* on December 11, 1971. With echoes of *Cry Terror!*, it was a combination kidnap/heist story. Culp played a struggling actor who mistakenly receives a phone call from kidnappers who have made off with a doctor's daughter and are demanding $50,000 in ransom money. At the urging of shrewish wife Angie, he triples that amount, shakes down the doctor, and then plans to give $50,000 to the kidnappers, obtain the girl's release, and keep the rest for himself. But things go wrong with the cops, the kidnappers, and his wife. In an unusual bit of casting, Eddie Albert and June Allyson appeared as the victimized parents, and soap opera actor Charles Cioffi took the police captain part. Sporting the biggest hair of her career, Angie was at her evil best, browbeating the spineless Culp and pushing him further into crime. "You can't make it with reality, can you?" she snarls. "But if you're not playing a part, if someone doesn't assign you a character, you haven't got any." She's like Bette Davis in *Beyond the Forest*, bemoaning the "dump" she lives in, calling her husband a "loser," and insisting, "I hate having nothing." Her anger is visceral. Directed by Corey Allen (James Dean's knife-wielding nemesis in *Rebel Without a Cause*), the picture was marginally noteworthy for marking Allyson's return to acting after a twelve-year absence.

Angie's next TV movie, *The Norliss Tapes*, dealt with vampirism, Egyptian sorcery, and the occult. A cheap pastiche of horror film motifs, it was further evidence that she was willing to accept any part that would take her mind off the problems at home. The narrative frame was clever. Paranormal researcher David Norliss has vanished, leaving behind a cache of audio tapes that explain his recent investigation into wealthy widow Ellen Cort's claim that her dead husband has resurfaced as a blood-draining immortal in league with the Egyptian deity Sargoth. The choice of director, Dan Curtis, was also a good one. Creator of ABC's popular afternoon Gothic serial *Dark Shadows*, Curtis had a feel for macabre material and had already made full-length film versions of the series as well as the highly-rated TV movie *The Night Stalker* (1972). Roy Thinnes, who had starred in the ABC alien visitation series *The Invaders* (1967-68), played Norliss, Angie was Mrs. Cort, Claude Akins was the skeptical sheriff, and television veteran Don Porter appeared as a publisher who listens to the revelatory tapes and sets the narrative in motion.

The finished movie was much less interesting than the concept. To build thrills and compensate for a slow plot with lots of wordy exposition, Curtis ladled in hyper-suspenseful music, camera zooms for shock effect, and visual clichés such as stormy nights and cats jumping unexpectedly into the frame. Angie was required to do a lot of close-up screaming, but she underplayed the campy horror, delivered the dialogue matter-of-factly, and added "woman in supernatural peril" to the list of parts she could make believable. Co-produced by Curtis's independent company and Metromedia Producers Corporation, *The Norliss Tapes* aired on February 21, 1973, as a possible pilot for an NBC series but was not picked up by the network. Angie called it a "wild, ghosty thing."[73]

She guest-starred on an equally bizarre December 15, 1972, episode of NBC's anthology series *Ghost Story* (aka *Circle of Fear*), part of the networks' ongoing effort to entice horror film audiences with such dark-themed series as *Night Gallery* (1969-73) and *Kolchak: The Night Stalker* (1974-75). Preceding Stephen King's *Cujo* by several years, she played a character who is harassed by an evil spirit that has taken possession of a dog. Titled "Creatures of the Canyon," it was written by *Twilight Zone* alum Del Reisman, directed by Walter Doniger, and filmed at night in Los Angeles, a shooting schedule that took her away from Burt and Nikki in the evenings. "We had to shoot then to get more of a feeling of reality into it," she explained. "So I'm working five nights a week and he [Burt] says, 'I can't believe those hours.'"[74] She interpreted the comment not as praise but as rebuke.

Given their less stringent time commitments, she also made appearances on Anthony Quinn's short-lived series *The Man and the City* (1971-72) and Richard Boone's "modern Western" *Hec Ramsey* (1972-74). The last of the television movies she made during this period was *Pray for the Wildcats*, a casting-against-type thriller that was broadcast by ABC on January 23, 1974. Andy Griffith played a psychotic business executive who forces three advertising agency employees to compete for his favor during a grueling dirt bike expedition to Baja, Mexico. Angie was the neglected, unhappy wife of one of the ad men and, along with Janet Margolin and Lorraine Gary, provided backstory to the real point of the film, which was a testosterone-fueled death chase through the Mexican desert. Newspaper critics were not impressed.

The feature film work she squeezed in was diverting if not distinguished. *The Resurrection of Zachary Wheeler* had the same sensationalized tone and content of the TV movies and indeed was shot on videotape before being transferred to film and released theatrically. For once a physician rather than a nurse, she portrayed Dr. Layle Johnson, surgical assistant at a secret hospital where patients receive organ transplants from synthetically developed humans. When a reporter (Leslie Nielsen) and a United States Senator (Bradford Dillman) who has unwittingly received one of the transplants threaten to expose the conspiracy, Dr. Johnson is caught up in the consequences. Although the budget was minimal, the image quality faded, and the distribution limited, the film's cloning theme influenced later movies such as *Coma* (1978), *Parts: The Clonus Horror* (1978), and *The Island* (2005). Angie's scenes, for which she received "Special Guest Appearance" billing, required several days of location shooting in and around Albuquerque, New Mexico.

The Outside Man (*Un homme est mort*) gave her a chance to work with French director Jacques Deray, whose picture *The Swimming Pool* she had been forced to turn down three years earlier. The production values on this project were considerably more lavish than on the other work she had been doing. The script was co-written by Deray, veteran British screenwriter Ian McLellan Hunter, and frequent Luis Bunuel collaborator Jean-Claude Carrière; Michel Legrand contributed the music score; and Angie's co-stars included Jean-Louis Trintignant, Ann-Margret, Roy Scheider, and Michel Constantin. Set in Los Angeles, the plot concerned a French hitman (Trintignant) who bumps off a high-ranking mobster and then is himself tracked by a rival assassin (Scheider). Along the way, he encounters the dead man's girlfriend (Angie) and a beautiful stranger who offers to help him (Ann-Margret).

A long-time fan of Angie's, Deray looked for her to lend his film the iconic weight of her roles in *The Killers* and *Point Blank*. Intending *The Outside Man* as an homage to French gangster films, American film noir, and, like Jacques Demy's *Model Shop* (1969), to L.A. itself, he saw Angie as the embodiment of a very modern, very stylized alienation. She delivered the appropriate characterization, but the picture seemed to leave critics and moviegoers alienated themselves. Released in January, 1973, in both the United States and France, it did little to enhance the reputations of the people involved. Despite a good use of locations (Los Angeles International Airport, the old Venice pier, the Beverly Hilton Hotel) and a well-staged car chase, the rest of the action was plodding and lifeless. For Angie, it was a paycheck and a return to her own house each evening.

And so she drifted along, making the best of inferior parts and trying to keep things on an even keel at home. In only sporadic contact with her sisters and mother, she saw friends infrequently. Motivated by concern over her daughter's health and guilt over her own work absences, she catered to Nikki's constantly changing wishes. Some of them, like the dog and the gymnastics, were expected while others, like the pink flocked Christmas tree, were more unusual. "I held on too tight," she admitted. "I spoiled her."[75]

Burt's reaction continued to be complicated, even contradictory. He shared the worry over Nikki, needed a quiet atmosphere for composing, thought Angie could be too indulgent, and occasionally felt neglected himself. It was a lot for Angie to sort out, and she resented his attitude: "I remember him complimenting somebody else about being a good mother and I remarked, 'I don't understand this thing. Then why do you beat me over the head with it?' That's how people are. All of us are guilty of it. We admire traits in other people and ignore them in our own lives."[76] As Nikki grew older, spending more time in school and functioning to some degree on her own, Angie felt ready for a new direction in her professional and perhaps even personal life as well.

Household Name

IN 1974, SHE accepted a movie role and a television offer that changed everything. The movie was *Big Bad Mama*, a gangster-comedy-action-sexploitation pic produced by the legendary independent master Roger Corman. Capitalizing on films such as *Bonnie and Clyde* (1967), *Boxcar Bertha* (1972), *Badlands* (1973), and *Dillinger* (1973), it was a wild, Depression-era tale of a misfit bank robbing gang led by sexy, gun-toting widow Wilma McClatchie and her equally seductive daughters Polly and Billy Jean. Angie, of course, played Wilma, performing her own machine gun stunts and gleefully tossing off lines such as "Get yer hand off my tit, Barney." Also in the gang, competing for Wilma's affection, were William Shatner and Tom Skerritt. Long on action and short on characterization, it was crude, violent, funny, and also incredibly successful. Shot, as per Corman style, in just 20 days during April of 1974, it was budgeted at significantly less than $1 million and made over four times that amount. To Angie, the film's popularity indicated that audiences still thought of her as a sex symbol and were still willing to buy a ticket to see her perform on the big screen. It validated her "brand" in a way that none of her other recent roles had managed to accomplish.

She accepted the Wilma McClatchie part for the usual pragmatic reasons; the accelerated production schedule and the nearby filming locations in Temecula, El Centro, Malibu, and Elsinore compensated for the B-picture feel of things. Nothing about the movie appeared promising. The story was an R-rated version of *Petticoat Junction* meets the Barrow gang, and the production values were bare-boned at best. No one was likely to confuse *Big Bad Mama* with the classic gangster films of Martin Scorsese and Francis Ford Coppola, both of whom had been given early feature film directing opportunities by Corman.

What made it work were Angie Dickinson's humor, versatility, and beauty. The inevitable nude scene impressed everyone with its forty-two-year-old leading lady's physical resemblance to the young actresses who at roughly half that age were playing her daughters. Co-star William Shatner claimed the nude shoot began as a closed set but that Angie kept making exceptions for crew members around whom she felt comfortable until ultimately just about everybody on the payroll was present. The crew returned her affection. In a press release from Corman's New World Pictures, they labeled her "gorgeous, both physically and creatively, both inside and out."[1] Five years later, in its March 1979 issue, *High Society* magazine printed some of the nude stills with Angie's blessing (conversely, she brought a libel suit against the *L.A. Star* in October of 1974 for printing pictures of her head on a nude woman's body but the case was dismissed three months later). As if to signal her cinematic good fortune, she joined *The Exorcist* star Jason Miller in presenting the Academy Award for Best Adapted Screenplay at the Oscar ceremony held in early April at L.A.'s Dorothy Chandler Pavilion.

Even more momentous was Angie's decision to appear that spring in a first season episode of the popular NBC anthology series *Police Story* (1973-78). Directed by Richard Benedict, who had acted with her in *Ocean's Eleven*, it was called "The Gamble" and like all the installments was set in Los Angeles. She was Lisa Beaumont, a divorced police woman who transfers into a vice unit that is led by Sergeant

Crowley (Bert Convy) and includes officers Styles (Ed Bernard) and Royster (Charles Dierkop). In the opening shot, she drives up to division headquarters in a pink Mustang and matching pink blouse, establishing a pattern of car and costume changes that continues throughout the episode. Her first assignment is to pose as a prostitute in order to bust a madam named Annabelle (former Hal Wallis protégé Corinne Calvet). Then, after a quick lesson by Crowley in card sharking and loaded dice, she infiltrates an illegal gambling operation run out of expensive rented houses. The boss (Joseph Campanella) assigns her the job of escorting high rollers to and from the makeshift casinos, and with the aid of a concealed wire she facilitates a climactic raid on three simultaneously running locations.

There was nothing complex about the story or characters, but the action moved along quickly, and the cast also featured Peter Brown, Jay Adler, John Kerr, and Cesare Danova in supporting parts. Angie was tough, funny, sympathetic, and gorgeous. She was also given a secondary plot thread that had her volunteering at her younger sister's special day school, a facility for emotionally and physically challenged children. For added interest, there were witty insider references to her personal life. When Crowley asks her if she has ever been to Las Vegas, she replies, "I was married there," and Campanella sings a raspy version of Burt's "The Look of Love" to her over cocktails in a hotel bar.

The episode was so well received that producer David Gerber approached her about doing a spin-off series. Occasional guest appearances were one thing, but signing on to a regular weekly TV show was a commitment she had long been reluctant to make. Over a year before, she had told Morton Moss, "A series is too much work and would keep me away from my family too much. It would have to be something really exceptional for me to think of doing a series in my circumstances. I'd have to be a star and the only star."[2] That's exactly what Gerber had in mind. She would be the first woman to anchor an hour-long network action series. Rather than be part of a rotating ensemble as had Barbara Stanwyck in *The Big Valley*, she would appear as the lead in every episode. The program would be a police procedural with her as an undercover officer and would be shot in Los Angeles. Sensing her hesitation, Gerber added, "Don't you want to be a household name?"[3]

Gerber's final pitch is what convinced her—the promise of reaching that mega-orbit of popularity which had long figured in her imagination. To keep the peace at home, she asked Burt to make the final decision, just like Feathers had asked Chance in *Rio Bravo* if she should take the saloon job. Encouraging her to go for it, he reasoned, "I thought she had a gift. I thought she should be working."[4] The more she thought about his advice the more she agreed with him that "this was not only the chance to be a star but to show what I could do as an actress. It wasn't a glamour part—glamour couldn't get in the way. It was a chance as an undercover police woman to play many characters, do many kinds of parts."[5]

Police Woman premiered September 13, 1974, in NBC's 10:00 p.m. Friday time slot. The series was much like the pilot. Angie was now Sergeant Suzanne "Pepper" Anderson (although on a few occasions she was also referred to as "Leanne"), Crowley was played by Earl Holliman, and Bernard and Dierkop were back as Styles and Royster. A member of the LAPD Criminal Conspiracy Unit, she went undercover as a model, airline stewardess, prisoner, nurse, teacher, prostitute, go-go dancer, jewel thief, waitress, bank teller, porn actress, and other colorful character types. The team investigated everything from rape, murder, and drug smuggling to robbery and kidnapping. With the exception of a couple of two-part arcs in seasons two and three, each episode told a self-contained story. After the initial crime was established, Crowley and team would develop a plan that usually put Pepper in jeopardy before a climactic shoot-out or raid apprehended the culprits. There were close-ups for dialogue, zoom-ins for dramatic effect, camera fades to bracket the commercials, and countless shots of big American muscle cars trailing each other through the streets of Los Angeles. While not creating any unique visual style (as would the network's *Miami Vice* in the same time slot ten years later), *Police Woman*, under the guidance of creator Robert Collins, offered up production values that were the equal of any well-made prime time drama of the period. The permanent interior sets, ironically, were housed on various Warner Bros. soundstages.

The opening weeks introduced the mix of sex, violence, pathos, and workplace humor that would define the series. In the premiere episode, a gang of bank robbers pulls a series of heists that involve murder, kidnapping, rape (off camera), home invasion, and a suggested lesbian relationship between two of the gang members. Crowley's team, bantering about who has the worst assignment, stakes out a bank branch, and Pepper fires a fatal shotgun blast to help foil the robbery attempt. For the second episode, Pepper poses as a prostitute and then as a sex ring operator to bring down a crooked model agency owner who provides drugged young women for porn films and foreign flesh markets. While off duty, she and Crowley visit her younger sister Cheryl, brought along from the pilot and now attending the Austin School for Learning Disabilities (a close-to-home allusion to Nikki's own developmental issues and a narrative element that was dropped before the start of the second season). Episode three's plotline has Pepper serving as a decoy in a hospital where someone is raping and slashing the wives of prominent male patients. When the team focuses on the wrong suspect, she is taken prisoner by the real killer and must be rescued from the roof of the high-rise hospital.

Angie sports the look that made her a household name as Sergeant Pepper Anderson in *Police Woman* (1974-78).

For all the references to Pepper's toughness and skill with a firearm, the stories more often than not found her cradling a downed officer or reacting tearfully to the brutalization of an innocent victim. She often expressed reservations about her suitability for the job, but there was always more interest in what she was wearing than what she was thinking. Averaging at least six wardrobe changes per episode, she appeared in low-cut hooker dresses, short skirts, sling tops, denim ensembles, and tight-fitting pantsuits. Apparently there was no dress code at the LAPD. "With a whipped topping of blond hair cascading toward her frequently bare shoulders—the series used any excuse to put her in a halter—the former beauty queen left little wonder why she had been an honorary member of the Rat Pack,"[6] wrote Frank DeCaro in his review of season one for *The New York Times*. And even though the program was all about Angie, Pepper Anderson was not in charge of the department, just as Mary Richards did not run the WJM-TV newsroom on *The Mary Tyler Moore Show*. "She never lost her femininity. Angie was not the boss,"[7] explained Earl Holliman, as if the two conditions were mutually exclusive.

The leader of the Criminal Conspiracy Unit was Crowley, who directed, mentored, and consoled Pepper. "A testosterone-heavy ensemble drama right from the pilot episode"[8] was how DeCaro labeled the show, referring to the fact that it was Crowley, Styles, and Royster who handled the most violent action. They were like three tough brothers who frequently needed to protect their feisty sister from some scrape she'd gotten herself into. More than just familial affection, the professional closeness and good-natured ribbing between Crowley and Pepper also masked an ever deepening romantic attraction that both seemed unwilling to acknowledge. Neither Pepper's reliance on her sex appeal nor her deference to the male detectives won Angie many fans among the women's movement. Her character's behavior seemed to match Angie's own comments about sacrificing career goals for "my man." It didn't help that the eighth episode of season one drew protests for its portrayal of three lesbian friends robbing and murdering the elderly residents of a retirement home they operate. Accurately summarizing her reputation among feminists, she concluded, "I'm not their heroine."[9]

Minus any rousing activist support, Angie's cop show nevertheless became an immediate hit with the viewing public. In a season dominated by CBS's hugely popular comedy *All in the Family* with a 30.2 Nielsen rating, it averaged a solid 22.8, meaning that any given episode attracted just under 16 million viewers. The top-rated show for two separate weeks during the year, it ranked #15 for the 1974-75 season, close behind such powerhouses as *Rhoda*, *Hawaii Five-O*, and *The Mary Tyler Moore Show*. Its popularity in foreign markets, where it was titled everything from *Make-Up und Pistolen* in Germany to *Pepper Anderson agent speciale* in Italy, was equally impressive. "We were a smash from the beginning," boasted Holliman. "We were in 50 countries. And we were number one even in Abu Dabi."[10] There were Pepper Anderson action figures and cartoon story boards. At the end of the first season, Angie was Emmy nominated as Outstanding Lead Actress in a Drama Series and was awarded a Golden Globe for Best Actress in a Television Drama Series. President Gerald Ford once postponed a public appearance in order not to miss *Police Woman*.

David Gerber had kept his promise and then some. Angie had become a household name as well as a celebrity recruiter for police forces all over the nation. "Police departments across the country tell me that applications for police women are way up—because of our show," she commented at the time. "I think it's the easy familiarity Pepper has with Crowley and the other guys and the way they respect her, not because she is a woman but because of the job she does."[11] Daryl Gates, who had been with the LAPD since 1949 and served as Chief from 1978 to 1992, agreed on the scope of Angie's influence: "I've heard a lot of police officers express themselves saying, 'hey, I always wanted to be a police officer since I was a little boy,' but I didn't hear a woman say that until after Angie's series."[12] The show didn't stress forensic detail or procedural verisimilitude, but the locations and the hardware lent a kind of realism to the action. Angie took her responsibilities seriously, maintaining, "I feel like a civil servant. I can't be in a series like *Police Story* [sic] all this time and not have some of it rub off on me. I feel a bit like a cop."[13] Beyond inspiring future women officers, Angie's portrayal of Pepper also made possible the female crime fighters of *Charlie's Angels* (1976-81), *Hill Street Blues* (1981-87), and *Law & Order: Special Victims Unit* (1999-2019).

There were multiple reasons for *Police Woman*'s broad appeal. In his book *The TV-Guided American*, Arthur Asa Berger argued that police shows in general are reassuring because "the criminals are captured and the forces of law and order prevail: this reinforces our commitment to and belief in the justness of the universe, for though the forces of evil may seem to be triumphing, inevitably they will be defeated."[14] Cosmic rectitude might have been the ultimate destination, but the enjoyment of less lofty thrills along the way was very much a part of the attraction. One of those was watching Angie in her sexy costumes with the camera's and the viewer's gaze locked firmly on her breasts, legs, and derriere. Another was getting close, if only vicariously, to the salacious crime stories reported daily in newspapers and on local TV, tales of avarice, cruelty, and perversion that were echoed in the fictional plotlines. Also in play was a hip urban vibe that involved the look of the show. It began with the quick cuts, freeze frames, slow motion, and propulsive Morton Stephens theme music of the opening credits and extended to African American officer Styles's and long haired detective Royster's trendy clothes and use of such now dated street slang as "heavy," "jive," "be cool," and "bread." Finally, right from its inception, *Police Woman* gave fans the chance to see lots of familiar faces as guest stars, many in uncharacteristically villainous parts. Among the TV celebrities making appearances were Edie Adams, Dane Clark, James Darren, Ruby Dee, Patty Duke, Rhonda Fleming, Fernando Lamas, Ida Lupino, Don Meredith, Smokey Robinson, William Shatner, and Robert Vaughn.

Nobody worked harder on the show than Angie. Her days started at 6 AM and lasted until 7 PM, when she would rush home to put dinner on the table. Unlike the ten episodes a season of recent prestige television shows like *Game of Thrones* and *The Crown*, Gerber shot a minimum of twenty-one and as many as twenty-four installments per season with each one running forty-eight to fifty minutes in length. Filming stretched out over eight months and included minimal time off for holidays. Used to grueling location shoots, Angie never complained about the improvised dressing rooms, the bland food, and the sheer physical grind of the action scenes. Willing to promote the show in any way possible, she was well liked and admired among the tightly-knit production company. Holliman, who became a close friend, noted, "Angie and I were together more than she and her husband were together."[15]

That became a problem. Burt had grown increasingly frustrated with Angie's long absences from home and the need for him to pick up more parental responsibilities. On top of that, as his wife's good fortune soared, his own career had foundered. In 1973, Bacharach and David wrote the music for the movie *Lost Horizon*, which turned out to be a critical and commercial disaster. Not only did the score fail to produce a single hit, but their efforts also sounded a bit out of touch with contemporary trends. To make matters worse, the two long-time collaborators decided to split up, a contentious break that resulted in multiple lawsuits. Surprisingly, Dionne Warwick got into the legal blame game herself, suing both the composer and lyricist for alleged professional breaches. On his own, Burt continued to write songs and produced a couple of solo albums, but nothing clicked with the public like it had in the 60s. During a seven year dry spell, he did not have a single record that charted on *Billboard*. Even a brief 1975 reteaming with David came up empty.

Watching from close quarters, Angie could see how frustrated he was, but this was not the London of the *What's New Pussycat?* score. There was no Moviola for her to run, no advice to be given. All she could do was provide the support and space Burt needed for creative inspiration. In her 1975 interview with *Ladies' Home Journal*, Angie remarked, "Burt hasn't been on the tube for more than a year. He decided to stop television appearances, quit his concerts, and forget about a tour of Japan. He is a songwriter, and that's what he had to do—write songs. My guy has written a lot of songs, but the artists didn't accept them. They were either not recorded or not released. Glen Campbell recorded three of Burt's songs, but they just didn't click. Neither Burt nor Hal have written a hit since they split up."[16] It was a concise summary of his dilemma even though Burt may not have appreciated her detailed public disclosure of it.

To friends and fans, the Bacharachs still seemed like Hollywood's golden couple. They invited *People* magazine into the house for a photo shoot and interview, were seen enjoying a day at Magic Mountain amusement park with Nikki, participated in fundraisers for the Reiss-Davis Child Study Center, and circulated on the A-list party circuit. Named *Good Housekeeping* Woman of the Year and *Photoplay* Star of the Year for her work on *Police Woman*, Angie served as chair of the Marine Corps Toys for Tots program and lobbied for increased federal mental health funding. In the most iconic of tinsel town moments, Angie (wearing a Bob Mackie/Ray Aghayan see-through gown like the one Dietrich used for her concerts) and Burt presented the Academy Award for Best Original Song on Monday, March 29, 1976, at the Dorothy Chandler Pavilion. The fact that the Oscar went to actor Keith Carradine for "I'm Easy," a tune he had written to go along with his performance in Robert Altman's *Nashville* (1975), was undoubtedly baffling to Burt; it's simple, folk-like structure was so different from his own complex, sophisticated compositions. Additionally, public appearances like these served only to remind Burt of his fragile celebrity and of how circumstances had been reversed once again. "Angie got very very hot in her career with *Police Woman*, and my career started to dip a little," he admitted, "so we go to the racetrack, and Angie was definitely more popular than me . . . maybe twenty people would ask for her autograph, two would ask for mine."[17]

Ultimately, the work hours, the professional anxiety, and the affairs became too much. In September of 1976, the Bacharachs announced that they were separating. Characteristically, Angie shouldered much of the public blame: "It was impossible. It was horrendous, and I didn't balance it. He flew the coop, and I can't blame him."[18] With Burt staying mostly at their place in Del Mar or his apartment in New York and Angie remaining in the Coldwater Canyon house with Nikki, they referred to their arrangement as "living separately."

The phrase implied an important distinction for Angie, and she reached out to her press contacts to clarify the terms. "Burt and

I are separated," she told the *Los Angeles Times*'s Roderick Mann, "not divorced. Fortunately, we're friends. And that's not as easy as you might think in this town."[19] To a reporter from *People*, she explained, "We are not divorced and we are not separated permanently. At some time in the future one or both of us will decide what to do." The relationship, she continued, was unusual but not an indication of a terminally collapsed marriage: "Burt goes out with women, and I go out with men. But I still consider myself married to Burt Bacharach. I love Burt. I adore him. Today my first choice to go out with would be Burt."[20] Adding other prospective romantic partners to the mix was a dicey proposition, but Angie was defiantly optimistic. She continued to spin the separation as a very modern arrangement that ultimately would lead to reconciliation. "We don't live in the same house," she informed Morton Moss. "We're free to go out with whomever we please. If you go out with a person of the opposite sex and he isn't your husband, people always think you're having an affair. But that isn't true. I just saw Burt in San Diego. We feel married. I'll give odds we'll be back together. I don't know when, but I'll give odds we are."[21] As time went by, however, and Burt showed no signs of regretting his freedom to date, Angie's sunny predictions began to sound more defensive than realistic.

Distracted somewhat by the start of *Police Woman*'s third season, she threw herself into her work, arguing for stronger plots with fewer "hooker of the week" assignments for Pepper. She was earning more than $40,000 per episode and ensuring her financial security, but she also wanted the acting to be respected. Along with a still sizeable portion of prostitute and porn queen roles, she was given stories where Pepper fights a sexual molestation charge, infiltrates a gang of political terrorists, poses as an investigative news reporter, busts a baby-selling operation, and becomes romantically involved with a tennis pro who is himself an undercover police officer. Unfortunately, NBC also tinkered with the show's time slot. During the second season, network execs moved it to Tuesday at nine, where it scored a respectable 20.2 Nielsen and just made it into the top thirty most watched programs. For season three, as it competed in that same slot with *Rich Man, Poor Man Book II* and *Eight is Enough* on ABC, and the popular *M*A*S*H*/*One Day at a Time* block on CBS (numbers four and eight respectively in the Nielsen top ten), it managed only a 17.8 and slid to fifty-fifth place in the rankings. Television viewers were unpredictable during that 1976-77 season. Old pros Mary Tyler Moore, Bob Newhart, Carol Burnett, and James Garner found themselves out of the top thirty while such wildly disparate shows such as *Happy Days, Laverne and Shirley, Baretta, Good Times, The Six Million Dollar Man, The Jeffersons,* and *Little House on the Prairie* worked their way on to the list. Particularly nettlesome to the cast and crew of *Police Woman* was the ascent of *Charlie's Angels*, a series it had made possible, to the nation's fifth most watched hour of television in a 10 p.m. berth that everyone felt was the most appropriate place for an "adult" cop show.

Angie was bothered by the schedule change but knew the call was NBC's to make. "It's their show and they can put it where they want," she complained to Cecil Smith. "But what burns me up is that they move us without telling people about it, without taking out ads to say, hey, *Police Woman* is now on another night."[22] With twenty-four episodes to shoot, however, she settled back into the rigorous work schedule, which definitely kept her mind off separation issues. At home she had a combination nanny/cook/secretary who helped with child care, meals, and other household chores. In her free time, she watched Nikki's gymnastics lessons or took her on shopping expeditions. During two weeks of summer hiatus, they traveled to Fresno and other spots in central California. Encouraged by Nikki's growing independence, she mused, "I guess I've reached the sad part all mothers do—my child does not now need my complete hovering care."[23]

Even minus Burt, there was also no shortage of invitations to Hollywood's most exclusive parties. British theatre critic and writer Kenneth Tynan described one such gathering, a dinner given by super-agent Sue Mengers in his honor, in the November 24, 1976, entry of his published diaries: "Half as good as her word, Mengers strikes back with Streisand (though she arrives too late for the stuffed squab—resembling a scrotum filled with wild rice—which passed for dinner). The supporting cast includes Warren Beatty, Swifty Lazar, Peter Bogdanovich (still nice), Ray Stark, Ryan O'Neal, Tatum O'Neal, Steven Spielberg (who directed *Jaws*), James Coburn, Dudley Moore, Tuesday Weld, Angie Dickinson, Tina Sinatra and introducing Kenneth Tynan, who smoked too much . . . Sue, a nervous hostess to the point of paranoia, buzzed from table to table, anxiously asking whether we were enjoying ourselves. Her hilltop house is like a spacious and virulently modern art gallery without any art in it."[24] Nearly a decade later, Angie would play a thinly disguised version of Mengers in an ABC miniseries adaptation of Jackie Collins's novel *Hollywood Wives*. In another sign of her popularity, she was asked to co-host the 1977 Emmy Awards with Robert Blake at the Pasadena Civic Auditorium.

Although she was unable to control *Police Woman*'s placement in the schedule, she leveraged her dissatisfaction into concessions regarding the production calendar. Specifically, she made sure that filming started earlier in the year and ended in time for her to star in a television movie that director John Newland had been holding for her. It was a project that appealed to her artistically. Speaking to reporter Dorothy Manners, she declared, "When John Newland first brought the story to me, he said, 'Angie, I want to direct you in this even though the man is the title character. But it's a beautiful love story, far removed from your lady cop on TV.' I read the screenplay and loved it. I told John, 'I'd rather be part of this than the solo attraction in a weak story.' The role I play is a sensitive passionate woman who goes all the way to bring her man back from defeat after he falls from big success."[25]

Adapted by Rita Lakin from a book by Barbara Mahoney, the picture was called *A Sensitive, Passionate Man* and starred David Janssen as a successful engineer whose alcoholism is wreaking havoc on his marriage and his career. Playing his wife, Angie was on freighted ground. The themes of alcoholism and marital discord touched on her own personal history, but she saw the film as not only conveying a powerful message but also giving her an opportunity to remind fans that she could be more than just Pepper Anderson. "I insisted on changing my hairstyle, the way I dressed, even to a new cameraman. I wanted a new look," she explained.[26]

With all those changes, she still looked beautiful but beyond that, she and Janssen delivered two exceptional performances. He had the showier part, raging drunkenly in public and suffering physical withdrawal, but she was just as effective in much more subtle ways. When she hears from his secretary that he has been fired or watches him fumble through a career day speech in his son's classroom, the wordless pain in her eyes is palpable. You can see how much she had learned over the years about less is more, about allowing a pause in delivery or a shift in posture to communicate emotion. Even the physical moments where she tries to restrain Janssen are controlled, briefly explosive rather than hysterical.

Especially compelling are the scenes with the two young actors playing her sons. As she tells them, "When a person drinks, he doesn't always drink because he wants to. Sometimes there's something bothering him and he has to drink," she catches the tone of an adult who must reluctantly share hard truths with unsuspecting children (just as she herself had been forced to confront the reason behind Bud's behavior back in Kulm). To the filmmakers' credit, the story stays realistic, unmarred by any twelve-step redemptive return to happiness. Janssen dies in the end and Angie, to the accompaniment of a melancholy title song performed by Melba Moore, walks down a hospital corridor into an uncertain future. Marked by its quality acting and Newland's skillful direction, the movie, which NBC aired on June 6, 1977, was widely praised yet was Emmy nominated only for Outstanding Achievement in Film Sound Mixing. Writing in *The New York Times*, John O'Connor noted that "Angie Dickinson and David Janssen step outside their familiar television images to deliver performances of impressive strength and integrity."[27]

Like Angie, Janssen was experiencing some marital turbulence during the production; he had just separated from his second wife, the actress Dani Crayne Greco. As a result, the two stars spent a great deal of time together, both during and after their work in front of the cameras. "We're both so involved in our roles we had dinner now and then," commented Angie in reference to the friendship that some gossip columnists alleged was actually an affair.[28] Not long after the filming of *A Sensitive, Passionate Man* wrapped, however, Janssen reconciled with Dani, to whom he was still married at the time of his sudden death three years later from a heart attack. Angie was one of many celebrities, including Johnny Carson, Milton Berle, Rod Stewart, Gregory Peck, Jack Lemmon, James Stewart, and eulogist Suzanne Pleshette, who would attend the funeral services at Hillside Memorial Park in Los Angeles.

Newspapers also reported that Angie was dating Dean Martin, divorced now for the third time and dealing with a downturn in his once lofty film/TV/recording career. But these clearly were relaxed get-togethers between two old friends rather than romantic interludes. Loyal and supportive, Angie had known Martin since the *Rio Bravo* days and was close with his second wife Jeanne as well. A guest on his weekly television variety program, she had hung in there with him when the show morphed into a series of loosely conceived specials. She appeared with Ronald Reagan, Nancy Reagan, and Robert Mitchum on his first *Dean's Place* and even agreed to be an "honoree" on the mirthlessly shrill *Dean Martin Celebrity Roast*.

Martin biographer Nick Tosches described the roast spectacle as a "dais of despair" where guests "sat at banquet tables at either side of the podium: the undead of dreamland and the fleeting stars of the television seasons, each rising in turn, at the beckoning of Dean or his bloated sidekick, Orson Welles, to deliver the moribund jokes consigned to him for the occasion."[29] Angie's turn on the spit was no different. Taped at the MGM Las Vegas Grand Hotel's "scintillating" Ziegfeld Room and broadcast on February 8, 1977, the show gathered people she knew well with those she had barely or never met. The men were suited up in black tie and tux, Vegas's de rigeur showbiz uniform of the day, while the women wore various frilly evening gowns. Angie appeared in a white cocktail dress with sparkling sheer lace over the shoulder. On one side of her sat Earl Holliman, Cindy Williams, Jimmy Walker, Cathy Rigby, Rex Reed, Eve Arden, and Scatman Crothers; on the other side were Jimmy Stewart, Juliet Prowse, Red Buttons, LaWanda Page, Ruth Buzzi, Joey Bishop, Foster Brooks, Orson Welles, and, as a seemingly inebriated master of ceremonies, Dean himself. Walker joked, "She plays a cop named Pepper, and she's got a great shaker,"

Holliman quipped, "This is no dumb blonde, I know because I've seen her roots," and Buzzi claimed, "I went jogging with Angie, and when she hung up her sweatshirt, it was still bouncing." For every punchline that connected, ten others fell flatter than a Las Vegas horizon. Most of them concerned Angie's anatomy or her reputation as a playgirl. In between the jokes, there were close-ups of the entertainers guffawing for the camera and cutaways to audience members apparently thrilled to be watching celebrity shenanigans in person. As Tosches wrote, "The jokes were so bad and the canned laughter so false, and that pervading hollow artificiality so funereal, that the shows had the quality of a relentlessly monotonous but vaguely disquieting dream."[30] Much more successful and entertaining was her appearance later that year as a guest (along with George Burns, Don Rickles, Carroll O'Connor, and John Barbour) when Frank Sinatra filled in one evening as host for Johnny Carson on *The Tonight Show*. They flirted and reminisced about *Ocean's Eleven*.

Partly because both Dean's and Angie's shows were carried by NBC, the roast writers had limited their comments about her career to *Police Woman*, but that once-in-a-lifetime gig was coming to an end. Season four would be the last one for Pepper and the guys. Once again the network had changed the time slot, moving the program to Wednesdays at 10 p.m., where it fell to seventy-fourth place in the Nielsens. Angie originally had committed to four seasons, and neither she nor NBC was willing to do more. She talked about the possibility of making two or three *Police Woman* movies of the week each year, but nothing came of that idea. Despite the grind that the series had become, she was forever grateful for the role. "Don't think I'm putting down *Police Woman*," she insisted. "It made me a star, gave me a lot of self-assurance and confidence I'd never had before. I think I'm a better actress now because of the series."[31] Almost anywhere she went in the world, she was recognized as the LAPD's most famous woman officer. On one trip, she remembered, "There was a Russian cruise ship in port, with lots of Australian passengers. I went on board for a visit, and honestly, walking through the dining room was a bit like Rocky going into the ring. It was such a thrill, I can tell you. I knew the show was popular in Australia, but until something like that happens, it's not brought home to you."[32] Gerber's vision had made her a name in households not just in the United States but outside the country as well. Angie Dickinson news, from the silly to the more substantive, was eagerly reported by the press. When Mr. Blackwell ranked her third on his Worst Dressed Women list as the "police woman that has caught everything but fashion,"[33] the *Los Angeles Herald-Examiner* gave the event a special story as did the *Los Angeles Times* when it was rumored that along with Walter Matthau she was part of a six-person syndicate bidding for ownership of the Oakland A's baseball team.

As the years passed, Angie became less sanguine about the time and effort she had devoted to *Police Woman*. "I regret doing the series," she told Mo Rocca during a 2019 interview for *CBS Sunday Morning*. "It just sapped me and four years of my life."[34] Discounting the amount of money she earned, she implied that the commitment may have cost her other, more estimable, parts. When Rocca asked, "Do you think something else better might have happened?" she replied, "Who knows? You never know."[35]

Ironically, one of her first roles beyond the series was playing Pepper Anderson again in *Ringo*, an hour-long TV movie that featured Ringo Starr as himself and as a look-alike nerd with whom, borrowing from *The Prince and the Pauper*, he changes places. Disguised as bullied "maps to the stars" vendor Ognir Rrats, the real Ringo wanders around Los Angeles, experiencing normal life again and getting into trouble. At one point he is mistakenly arrested for grand theft auto by Sergeant Anderson. It was a sixty second cameo that probably took less than half a day to shoot but resulted in top guest star billing along with Art Carney, Mike Douglas, Carrie Fisher, Vincent Price, and John Ritter. There wasn't much plot but there were several songs, Monty Pythonesque animation, and a slew of trippy camera effects. Aired on April 26, 1978, the movie suggested that Angie was as much a pop icon as campy Vincent Price, Princess Leia originator Carrie Fisher, and former Beatle Ringo Starr himself.

After that farewell nod to Pepper, making the most of her newly found geographical freedom, Angie accepted a series of roles that allowed her to travel extensively and take a break from Los Angeles. She went to Tahiti for the television movie *Overboard*, to Hawaii for the miniseries *Pearl*, and to Montreal and British Columbia for the big screen releases *L'homme en colère* and *Klondike Fever*. First up was *Overboard*, a decidedly downbeat tale in which she co-starred with Cliff Robertson as an affluent couple who sail a small 40 foot yacht to Tahiti in an attempt to jump start their routine lives. It was domestic soap opera mixed with high seas adventure.

Four minutes into the movie, after quarreling with her husband, Lindy Garrison (Angie) chases after the boat's pet kitten and falls overboard. Because Mitch Garrison (Robertson) is sleeping below, he does not realize she is missing until the next morning. His attempts to find her alternate with flashbacks that track the deterioration of their marriage (one more uncomfortable real-life parallel for Angie). Mitch is not a happy man. Disillusioned by his legal practice, he buys the sailboat and then seems to grow disappointed with the Tahitian voyage as well. Although he often acts cold to Lindy, he gets jealous when another man takes an interest in her, and by the time she slips into the ocean, they are barely talking to one another. The unexpected ending comes when Mitch finds his wife clinging to a piece of plastic debris but is unable to get her safely aboard. As the boat drifts away, they embrace and sink below the waves, presumably drowning in each other's arms.

Although she received top billing, Angie was not required to do much except look good in a bikini, bob around in the ocean, and argue with Robertson, whose craggy machismo made him as good a foil for her as Janssen had been. Handsome, long-haired actor Lewis Van Bergen provided some steamy moments as Jean-Paul, the French Polynesian sailing enthusiast who falls in love with her. "Quite a few actresses could have played the part I did in *Overboard*," she admitted.[36] Hank Searls adapted the script from his own novel, and John Newland directed again with a leisurely pace that included lots of fuzzy dissolves to announce the flashbacks. It aired on September 25, 1978, the same day that a catastrophic midair collision in San Diego between a Pacific Southwest Airlines jet and a private Cessna dominated television news coverage.

Next was *Pearl*, a six-hour miniseries for ABC set in Hawaii just prior to the attack on Pearl Harbor. "At first I said no to it," revealed Angie. "I felt I needed more work like I needed another separation. But they kept calling and, in the end, I couldn't resist it. It's such a good part. A colonel's wife, pre-Pearl Harbor, who sleeps with everyone but her husband."[37] It was indeed a very good part, an ideal reminder of how thoroughly she could inhabit a character. Like *Rich Man, Poor Man* (1976), *Captains and the Kings* (1976), and *Roots* (1977) before it, *Pearl* was intended as event TV, appointment viewing for those who wanted historical relevance seasoned with sex and spectacle. Written by Academy Award-winning screenwriter Stirling Silliphant, it echoed *From Here to Eternity* (1953) and prefigured both *The Winds of War* (1983) and *War and Remembrance* (1988). Nearly eighty million Americans watched all or part of the three installments televised on November 16, 17, and 19, 1978.

As befitting the genre, there was a large cast in multiple overlapping storylines. Angie played Midge Forrest, whose unhappy marriage to Col. Jason Forrest (Dennis Weaver) leads her into a series of casual affairs, including an ill-fated relationship with her husband's handsome, possibly bisexual driver. The other couples include a cultured southern captain and a widowed doctor, a naval officer and his Japanese-American girlfriend, and a tough yet artistic army private and the prostitute who loves him. Their stories are intercut with preparations by the Japanese Imperial Navy to attack Honolulu. Covering a period of five days, the movie opens on December 4, 1941, and ends on December 8, as the survivors listen to FDR's address to Congress and try to move on with their lives. Much of the miniseries's second and third parts deal with the bombing itself, conveyed through a seamless blend of footage from the film *Tora! Tora! Tora!* and specially photographed action sequences.

Given top billing, Angie ends up with about ten percent of the screen time. Her presence, however, floats over the entire proceeding. At forty-seven and more beautiful than ever, she is a tortured soul whose anger, fragility, sensuality, and fortitude lead her in often conflicting directions. As the counterpoint to her husband's racism and rigidity, she represents free-spirited liberalism. Her promiscuousness masks a much deeper anguish over the death of her four-year-old daughter. The climactic scene in which she reveals the guilt and resentment behind that loss was one of several dramatic moments she was afforded, including the seduction of the driver, a confrontation with a malicious general's wife, and an eye-witness reaction to the destruction at Hickam Air Field. For the first time in her career, she was also given an on-screen confidante and best friend in the person of brothel owner Sally Colton (Katherine Helmond). Their scenes together prove that she didn't always have to become one of the guys but could just as easily communicate intimate female camaraderie.

Along with *Police Woman* and *Wild Palms*, the bizarre Bruce Wagner miniseries she would make fifteen years later, *Pearl* was among the best work she did for television. "It's one of those likable bitch roles," is how she described the Midge Forrest part, but upon further reflection, added, "She's quite beautiful but she's tragic, and because of the tragedy in her life, which comes out in the six hours, you understand why she acts the way she does."[38] Through her nuanced interpretation, the character became more than just a stereotyped wandering wife. Citing Angie's performance, the verisimilitude, and the story, *The New York Times* commented, "*Pearl* is the equivalent of a good read, a good long read. It doesn't strain us; we keep turning pages, and so what if we know early on how it will all turn out? When our attention wanders, *Pearl* reclaims it with another love scene, a sinking battleship or another flight of Zeros."[39]

Almost every review praised the authenticity of the location filming at Schofield Barracks, Iolani Palace, and other places around Honolulu. With Nikki along on the shoot with her, Angie used her free time away from the set for some mother-daughter swimming and sightseeing. One such expedition nearly ended in calamity. While in the water off Diamond Head, they were caught in a riptide that dragged them across a coral reef. "I thought, 'Well this is the end,'" remembered Angie, but she was able to keep Nikki afloat and to save her life.[40] Badly bruised and cut, she took away a permanent eight-inch scar on one of her shapely, previously insured legs as an unpleasant souvenir. "It was a horrifying experience. I'll never get over it," she concluded.[41]

After returning Nikki safely to Los Angeles, she was off to Montreal to make *L'homme en colère* (translated as *The Angry Man* but also known as *Jigsaw* and *Labyrinth*) for French director Claude Pinoteau. Part of a wave of international productions filmed in Canada to take advantage of new tax laws that permitted 100% of investment to be deducted from income, it was the third of four pictures that Pinoteau would build around Lino Ventura, the Italian-born actor extremely popular in France for a series of morally ambiguous tough guy roles. Characteristically, the script, by Pinoteau, Charles Israel, and *The Outside Man* alum Jean-Claude Carrière, featured Ventura as an Air France pilot searching for the estranged adult son who has gotten mixed up in a Quebec mob's drug dealing and immigrant smuggling operation. Angie, an ex-con waitress named Karen, finds herself messily involved in Ventura's hunt and in his life.

This was familiar terrain for her—the gritty, urban worlds of *The Killers* and *Point Blank*. In fact, like *The Outside Man*, it was a salute to classic French and American film noir. With the rumpled trench coat and weathered face of a Jean Gabin or Humphrey Bogart, Ventura slouches through the nightclubs, boxing gyms, and back alleys of Montreal, looking for the truth and willing to take a beating in order to obtain it. Seemingly out of nowhere, Angie appears, like Lauren Bacall in *Dark Passage*, to provide a hideout from his enemies. In the end there is resolution; the mystery of the prodigal son is solved, but not without collateral damage.

Pinoteau oversaw final prints of the film in both French and English, and in the French version, even though Angie had briefly and satisfactorily handled the language in *Overboard*, her dialogue was dubbed. Since her character is an ex-pat living in Quebec, a less than perfect command of the dialect would have been entirely appropriate, but she was given the fluency of a native speaker. Even with a less seductive voice, she perfectly balanced Karen's dual nature, making her one of the most abrasive yet also most sympathetic women she had so far played. Both Pinoteau and Ventura were thrilled to work with her, the latter even making an exception to one of his cardinal acting rules. A profoundly conservative family man, Ventura never kissed actresses on the mouth but agreed to do so for a train platform scene. Pinoteau reported that he prepared as if it were a dangerous stunt, and Angie remembered that on the first take he kissed her so hard she thought she'd lose her breath. On subsequent takes (which Angie didn't seem to mind), Ventura relaxed considerably and the moment became a touching revelation of Dupré's seldom expressed feelings.

While she was in Canada, Angie appeared on a Canadian Broadcasting Corporation interview show where she talked about wanting to reteam with John Wayne for a film and about eliminating sugar from her diet (another of her weight loss tips included using toothpaste to cut hunger pains). Several months later, she returned to Canada, this time British Columbia, to make *Klondike Fever*, an adventure film based on young Jack London's eventful journey from San Francisco to the Klondike Gold Fields in 1898. It co-starred *Run of the Arrow* and *Cry Terror!* partner Rod Steiger along with Lorne Greene, Barry Morse, Canadian actor Gordon Pinsent, and Jeff East as the twenty-year-old London.

Arriving in Skagway on a paddle wheeler, Jack gets into trouble with lawless town boss Steiger, adopts an abused dog named Buck, and sets off for the gold rush town of Dawson. On the way there, he rescues a brothel owner (Angie) and her two beautiful "daughters" and gets attacked by some of Steiger's henchmen. A momentous dog sled race and several other adventures later, Jack returns to San Francisco and begins to write the story of his travels. Angie's role was only a supporting one, but she loved the chance to see some of the Pacific Northwest's most spectacular scenery.

Headquartered in Wells, British Columbia, the company shot from April 2 to May 11, 1979. "There wasn't much to do up there," she recollected, "so watching our dailies provided a little diversion." The entire population of 200 was invited to attend the screenings. "I couldn't face seeing them with all those people present, so I stayed away."[42] As on the *Rio Bravo* set so many years before, she charmed the mostly male cast and crew with her cooperative, uncomplaining attitude. Willing to help the film in any way possible, she also attended its world premiere on March 2, 1980, in Edmonton. Nearly two thousand fans turned out to greet her at the airport, where she gushed, "My gosh, I feel like a rock star."[43] Later that same month, the picture competed for nine Genie (Canadian equivalent of the Oscar) Awards including Best Picture. Gordon Pinsent won for Best Performance by an Actor in a Supporting Role. Despite its wide popularity in both English and French speaking Canada, the film, also known as *Jack London's Klondike Fever*, failed to generate much interest in the states. *Variety* decided that it "tries hard to be story book cinema, but never succeeds in establishing the fascination that kept London's readers turning the pages as fast as they could."[44]

Back in California, Angie signed on to make a third television movie with director John Newland. A fascinating character in his own right, Newland already by this time had acted briefly in movies, hosted and directed all ninety-six episodes of the pioneering paranormal television series *Alcoa Presents: One Step Beyond*, and formed the first of two independent production companies he would co-own. He had also directed thirteen episodes of *Police Woman* and was one of Angie's biggest boosters. More so even than the famous auteurs Hawks and Fuller, he believed in her dramatic talent, in her ability to anchor a film through her own carefully crafted performance. Consequently, he gave her juicy parts with intimate close-ups and weighty dialogue. His impact on her career was significant and has often been overlooked.

The Suicide's Wife was an example of his confidence. As suggested by the title, she portrayed the wife of a college English professor who shoots himself after being denied tenure. In the aftermath of his death, she tries to piece together all the unknown influences that impacted his decision and to reconcile with the teenage son who holds her responsible for the tragedy. There were multiple opportunities for high drama: a romantic interlude with one of her husband's colleagues (played by *Klondike Fever* co-star Gordon Pinsent), a conversation with a gay student befriended by the professor, the denial of an insurance claim, an emotional confrontation between mother and son. Given considerable latitude by Newland, Angie responded instinctively to the situations and offered up a convincing portrait of a survivor working herself through the various stages of grief.

Speaking of his own technique, Newland remarked, "I really don't consider myself a director. That's a pretentious word. Perhaps 'conductor' would be better. I know the actors. I watch them and simply select the best things from their bag of tricks."[45] Nobody knew Angie's arsenal better than Newland. He had seen the silent crying, the quavering voice, the explosive gesture. He knew she could smoothly change the mood mid-scene and encouraged her to stay emotionally raw and open to the moment. The shifts from bewilderment to anger, resentment, sorrow, and resolution stretched her in ways many of her more well-known parts had not. Along with her work in *A Sensitive, Passionate Man*, the performance in *The Suicide's Wife* ranks among her very best.

Critics agreed that she was excellent but were less enthusiastic about the story. Commenting on CBS's November 7, 1979, broadcast, *The New York Times* reviewer Tom Buckley wrote, "Even the capable and attractive Miss Dickinson, every housewife's fantasy of herself, can't make *The Suicide's Wife* bearable."[46] The comment was typical of the reaction she was getting to all of the work (except for *Pearl*) that she had been doing since the end of the TV series. People still liked her a lot but not so much the pictures. She had settled into one of those familiar holding patterns where she worked, made good money, enjoyed the on-set friendships, but failed to generate any major buzz. It was not at all certain there would be any more popular triumphs.

On the other hand, the stalemate in her marriage was resolving itself but not in the way she had hoped and predicted. Burt had met and fallen in love with the singer/songwriter Carole Bayer Sager and was asking for a divorce. While the news was not entirely unexpected, it still left Angie feeling rejected and depressed. She told her sister Janet that Burt casually made the request over dinner in Del Mar but then on Dinah Shore's talk show remembered that "he called for a divorce on the phone," claiming "this will only take a minute."[47] She also remembered that Burt had casually mentioned the possibility of divorce when she appeared as a surprise guest during his co-hosting stint on *The Mike Douglas Show*. The Dinah story, which included Angie leaning into the camera and whispering "you son of a bitch," gets closer to the bitterness she experienced. After all her modern-sounding bromides about being in love but living separately, he had made her look slightly foolish by ending things for good. "I just don't think he respected me," she concluded.[48]

Burt's handling of the divorce underscored some essential differences in their personalities. Supremely talented, he also could be controlling and self-centered. A perfectionist with little patience for others' fallibilities, he was known to have blown up at concert and recording studio technicians. Loved by everybody, Angie was more accommodating and sensitive. Her even-tempered spirit inspired loyalty among friends, co-workers, and former lovers. "What do you want from me?" Burt allegedly once asked Sager. "I'm a selfish guy."[49] Angie seemed instinctively more generous. With little else left to do or say, the divorce papers were filed in 1980 and finalized in 1981. Angie kept the house in Coldwater Canyon and Burt agreed to pay child support. A year later he married Sager and during their ensuing nine year partnership collaborated with her on the highly regarded hits "Arthur's Theme" (co-written with Christopher Cross and Peter Allen and winner of the 1982 Oscar for Best Original song), "Heartlight," "Making Love," and "On My Own."

Meanwhile, Angie was coping with another personal heartbreak—her mother Fredrika's death at age sixty-nine from cancer. Beyond the painful loss, there was also a sense of guilt over not having been more attentive. Unnecessarily concerned with Fredrika's overweight, somewhat dowdy appearance, she had not spent much time together with her in public. "I just wish I'd been a better daughter . . . I didn't respect how great she was," she lamented.[50] Among the now painful memories she regretted was the fact that "I wouldn't go for a walk in the rain with her," a simple pleasure that might have meant a great deal.[51] Added to the second-guessing about her role as wife and daughter was the ongoing challenge of Nikki's always precarious emotional state, compounded now by a rocky entry into her teenage years and a push for greater independence. Tensions at home were high.

Surprisingly, what lifted all of the gloom was a quirky little thriller that Angie had made during the previous summer. *Dressed to Kill* was director Brian De Palma's thirteenth feature film following the breakthrough successes of *Obsession* (1976), *Carrie* (1976), and *The Fury* (1978). An amalgam of Hitchcock's *Rear Window* (1954) and *Psycho* (1960), the story focused on a teenage boy and a high-class prostitute attempting to solve the slasher killing that has savagely uprooted their lives. Veteran actors Michael Caine and Angie teamed with newcomers Nancy Allen, who had just recently married De Palma, and Keith Gordon.

Angie's frustrated housewife in *Dressed to Kill* imagines a sexual fantasy during her morning shower (1980).

The film created a major sensation for a variety of reasons, not the least of which was Angie's sexy and poignant performance. Having just turned forty-eight years old, she looked as chic and gorgeous as always. She engaged in steamy public sex and combined that with an equally erotic nude shower scene. Even more shocking, her character, like Janet Leigh's in *Psycho*, was brutally murdered within the movie's first thirty minutes.

She played Kate Miller, a sexually frustrated New York housewife who allows herself to get picked up during a visit to the Metropolitan Museum of Art. In a series of lush subjective tracking shots, she simultaneously eludes and pursues a handsome stranger through the vast, white-walled galleries (the interiors were actually shot at the Philadelphia Museum of Art). She too is in white—purse, gloves, heels, coat, dress. Just as she thinks the encounter is over, the stalker sweeps her into a taxi outside the museum and begins immediately to undress her. The sequence is a stylistic tour de force, the perfect combination of camera movement, music, and gesture to establish a mood that is both sensual and ominous. Without a single word of dialogue, Angie gets to the complex core of a character whose repressed desire must overcome fear and propriety to find expression.

Angie was all in with the idea of pushing sexual boundaries. She agreed to do the heavy backseat lovemaking on location in a specially rigged car that concealed the camera (she told Johnny Carson that New York City truck drivers looking down on the action would just have nonchalantly figured that Angie Dickinson was having sex in a cab). The scene culminated with Angie and actor Ken Baker in bed together.

She also had no qualms about the opening shower scene in which Kate pictures herself part of a masturbatory rape fantasy. Nude behind the frosted glass door of the shower while her husband shaves, she begins to provocatively soap herself and to imagine being taken by force. The revealing close-ups were done by body double Victoria Lynn Johnson, a former *Penthouse* Pet of the Year, but the profiled establishing shot was all Angie.

The film's violence was another matter. Angie told columnist Marilyn Beck that De Palma's penchant for gore originally caused her to hesitate in accepting the part. When Kate returns to the stranger's apartment to retrieve her forgotten wedding ring, she is slashed to death in an elevator by a tall blonde woman in dark glasses and a black raincoat. About two minutes in length, the scene is so brutal that it had to be severely edited to avoid an "X" rating for the film. Holding a straight razor, the attacker slices away at Kate's hand, face, and neck, splashing blood all across her white clothing and onto the walls and floor of the elevator. De Palma patterned the scene closely on Hitchcock's shower murder in *Psycho*, from the complicated montage of tightly composed individual shots to the aggressive, shrieking string music of the soundtrack. The close-ups of Angie's stunned eyes come directly from *Psycho* as do her sliding slowly down the side of the elevator and reaching lifelessly out into space. De Palma had also decided to shock viewers with the same denial of narrative expectations. The abrupt slaughter of a film's putative star was as audacious in 1980 as it had been when Hitchcock did it with Janet Leigh in 1960.

For some viewers, it was way too much. The Motion Picture Association of America insisted on major changes before letting the picture get away with an "R" rating, and even with that the United States Conference of Catholic Bishops promptly condemned it. Reviews were split between appreciation of the craftsmanship and reservations about the violence toward women. When Kate's son and the call girl who briefly witnessed the killing discover that the murderer is a transsexual psychiatrist (another borrowed element from *Psycho*), that plot point opened up a different controversy. Gay and transgender rights groups strongly protested the false equivalency between sexual difference and psychopathology. Sidestepping the gender issues, Angie overcame her initial hesitations and defended the film's violent content. "People should experience reality at the movies, in this case what violence is really like, not something cleaned up," she told the *Los Angeles Times*. "We may cup our hands to our face, but it's important to know the parts of life that are horror."[52] When questioned about the film over the years, she would continue to defend De Palma's right to his specific artistic vision. To help launch the film, she participated in a New York City panel with over fifty journalists from around the country.

Disagreement over the movie's merits sparked a major smackdown between Pauline Kael and Andrew Sarris, the two most prominent American film critics of the day. Writing in *The New Yorker*, Kael raved that De Palma "has become a true visual storyteller. He knows where to put the camera and how to make every move count, and his timing is so great that when he wants you to feel something he gets you every time. His thriller technique, constantly refined, has become insidious, jeweled." She further argued that the Hitchcock tropes were simply reference points that De Palma had personalized with his own "funky sensuousness" and that the dialogue was "casual, funny, and often good-naturedly off-color."[53] From his perch at *The Village Voice*, Sarris noted that "Kael has rhapsodized over *Dressed to Kill* as if it were a seamless masterpiece" and countered that it was derivative, "unbearably tedious and inept" as well as thoroughly misogynistic. "I do not hold it against De Palma that he imitates Hitchcock," he asserted, "but, rather, that he steals Hitchcock's most privileged moments without performing the drudgery of building up to these moments as thoroughly earned climaxes."[54]

Popular discourse raged on in the press for several weeks and split along similar lines, between those who saw cinematic elegance and well-crafted suspense and those who found smutty mistreatment of women. Some felt De Palma was a visionary auteur and others labeled him a slavish, second-rate imitator. By the time the critical dust settled, a slight majority of reviewers had decided in favor of the film. There was no such debate, however, over Angie's performance, which earned arguably the best reviews of her career. Everyone agreed that she made Kate Miller a touching, sympathetic character. "Angie Dickinson is fabulous,"[55] wrote Michael Sragow in the *Los Angeles Herald Examiner*, and *The Advocate*'s Douglas Edwards concluded simply, "She is stunning."[56] Kenneth Turan's belief, as elaborated in *New West*, was that "Dickinson does her best work since *Point Blank*,"[57] and the *Los Angeles Times* critic Sheila Benson offered the opinion that "Kate is the touching role, perfectly realized by Dickinson."[58]

Commercially, the picture became a major success within the opening days of its release. Made for about $6.5 million (the average cost of a studio movie in 1980 was $9 million), it grossed nearly $3.5 million in its first weekend and then actually increased the take to $3.6 million for the second weekend. After the first seventeen days of release, it had reached $13.7 million and would go on to earn nearly $20 million during its full initial run. Filmways Pictures, the movie's distributor, saw its stock rise dramatically on the New York exchanges, and De Palma, who followed up with *Blow Out* (1981), *Scarface* (1983), and *Body Double* (1984) found himself flush with independent production offers.

Angie reaped publicity rewards as well. She was featured on magazine covers and interviewed by countless reporters. The stories marveled at her ageless beauty and enviable figure. Along with

James Garner, she was signed to host a made-for-TV documentary for ABC called *Sixty Years of Seduction* that charted the careers of Hollywood's all-time most glamorous celebrities and was named one of two stars of the year (Burt Reynolds was the other) by the National Association of Theatre Owners. The Academy of Science Fiction, Fantasy, and Horror Films honored her with a Saturn Award for Best Actress, and the Academy of Motion Picture Arts and Sciences asked her to join Luciano Pavarotti in presenting the Oscar for Best Original Song at its 53rd annual awards ceremony (the year the event was produced by her friend Norman Jewison and postponed for a day because of the assassination attempt on President Ronald Reagan). On her own and without Burt, who surely took notice of the Oscar category, she was red hot once again.

Afterglow

AS HAD HAPPENED so many times before, that attention was not leveraged into something bigger. Her next movie choice was epically ill-conceived. She agreed to appear in Clive Donner's *Charlie Chan and the Curse of the Dragon Queen*. Despite the lessons that should have been learned by then about racial stereotyping in Hollywood movies, British actor Peter Ustinov was cast as Chinese detective Chan complete with eye altering makeup and sing-song accent. A supremely gifted actor, Ustinov gave what he felt was a faithful interpretation of what had always been a broadly sketched character, but certainly he had been much more appropriately made up three years earlier as Agatha Christie's fussy Belgian sleuth Hercule Poirot for *Death on the Nile* (1978). Richard Hatch was cast as Chan's number one grandson. Angie played the Dragon Queen and although it was not completely clear whether she was supposed to be Asian, she sported cheongsams, painted claw-like nails, and an elongated cigarette holder. In her frizzy gray hair and sedge hat, she looked like a dowager drag queen. Having narrowly avoided pushback for her Lucky Legs role in 1957's *China Gate*, Angie in particular should have been alert to the dangers of whitewashing ethnic characters, but for whatever reason she went ahead with the project anyway.

Director Donner attempted to make a romp of it as he had with *What's New Pussycat?* (1965). Angie is the prime suspect in a series of murders related to a rich San Francisco businessman and to this basic plot, Donner added elaborate chases, visual slapstick, stars in quirky supporting roles, and winking references to the original Chan pictures that starred Warner Oland and then Sidney Toler. When the film was released in February of 1981, critics uniformly found the script to be limp and lifeless although a few complimented the cast's hardworking efforts to wring some comedy out of it.

Even this faint praise, however, was overshadowed by the firestorm of protest from Asian-American activists who objected to the racial stereotypes and to the casting of white actors in Asian roles. A group of several dozen demonstrators picketed the movie's premiere at the Hollywood Pacific Theater, chanting "Charlie Chan must not show, racist movies gotta go" and "We don't talk in fortune cookie language."[1] Steve Tatsukawa, a spokesperson for the ad hoc Coalition of Asians to Nix Charlie Chan or "C.A.N. Charlie Chan" argued, "The days when they put black face on actors are long gone. But they still do it with Asians." Citing Ustinov's taped eyes, shuffling walk, and pidgin English, he further claimed, "These are things that don't reflect in any way what Chinese people are really like."[2] Not only did the coalition picket theaters, but it also convinced a number of television stations not to run advertisements for the film. So serious was the backlash that executive producer Alan Belkin wrote a letter to the *Los Angeles Times* in which he countered that *"Charlie Chan* employed more Asian-Americans than any other modern-day film. Several hundred Asian-Americans worked in many capacities on the production staff, the crew and in the cast."[3] In addition, he revealed that several Asian-American actors were offered the part of Charlie Chan but, as "the unfortunate victims of peer pressure," turned it down.[4]

For Angie, it was hardly the kind of notice she had hoped to attract after *Dressed to Kill*. She kept a low profile during the debate and promptly moved on to her next project, another Far North wilderness adventure based loosely on real-life events and titled *Death*

Hunt. Once again it was a controversial production, but this time the notoriety was internal, generated long before filming ever began. Robert Aldrich, whose pictures included *Kiss Me Deadly* (1955), *Whatever Happened to Baby Jane* (1962), and *The Dirty Dozen* (1967), had signed a contract to direct but balked when producers Albert Ruddy and Raymond Chow informed him the budget would be only $10 million rather than the $18 million he himself had calculated. Upon refusing to accept the financial terms, he was fired. Because he had not been provided a top sheet (an executive summary of above and below the line expenses plus post-production and other costs), he took his firing to arbitration and won. In the decision, arbitrator Edward Mosk affirmed that "had the budgetary limitations been clearly and unequivocally communicated to Aldrich from the beginning, the arbitrator is satisfied that Aldrich would have rejected the directorial assignment and all that followed would never have occurred."[5] Aldrich was awarded $25,000, and British-born director Peter Hunt hired as the replacement.

The story concerned Albert Johnson, an actual fur trapper in the Yukon Territory of 1931 who was pursued through the Arctic wilderness by Royal Canadian Mounted Police Sergeant Edward Millen for a murder he may or may not have committed. In the film, Johnson, who is clearly innocent, was played by Charles Bronson, and the Mountie, reluctant to go after a man he respects, was Lee Marvin. Angie accepted what basically amounted to little more than a cameo as a widow who beds Marvin.

"Why the small part in *Death Hunt*?" *Los Angeles Times* reporter Roderick Mann asked her during an interview conducted at her home in Coldwater Canyon.

"Because the script, which was very good, was set in Banff in Canada," she replied, "and I wanted to see Banff."

"You took it for the scenery?" he probed.

"Not just the scenery. I also wanted to work again with two of my favorite actors: Lee Marvin and Charles Bronson. I'd made two films with Lee, and years ago I did the pilot for a TV series Charles starred in . . . As it is, my part is so small it looks as if it's been almost cut out of the picture. It hasn't. That's it. When you see it, you'll realize I probably wouldn't have done it if the film had been set in Lancaster. My agent keeps telling me: Don't be swayed by locations. But how can you help it?"[6]

The film was widely reviewed, with several critics appreciating the reteaming of Angie and Marvin, but was not widely viewed by moviegoers. Sold by Chow to 20th Century Fox for distribution, *Death Hunt* (known originally as *Arctic Rampage*) actually lost money, taking in $5 million less than its production cost. Angie would not make another feature film for six years.

Instead she concentrated again on television, the medium which she had mastered so effectively. One of the first assignments was a made-for-TV remake of Alfred Hitchcock's *Dial M for Murder* (1954), which already had spawned updated television versions in 1958 for NBC and in 1968 for ABC. The by-now familiar plot involved an opportunistic tennis player's framing of his wealthy, possibly unfaithful wife for murder after she foils his plan to kill her. Christopher Plummer was the husband, Anthony Quayle the suspicious police inspector, Michael Parks the former lover, and Angie the wife in peril. She was just as icy, maybe even a few degrees frostier, than Hitchcock's famous blondes. More so than Grace Kelly in the original, she hinted at Margot Wendice's promiscuity and kept the character elusively detached.

When the NBC production aired on April 9, 1981, Janet Maslin wrote in *The New York Times* that "Miss Dickinson's remoteness fits in with the coolly elegant fashion in which the story is told."[7] (Coincidentally, a few months earlier, Angie had played a supporting role in a bizarre real-life police drama when her neighbor, a young independent producer named William Tennant, pounded on her door at 4:30 in the morning, clad only in a pair of shorts and claiming he had been attacked. When police officers arrived, they arrested Tennant himself for having inexplicably trashed another nearby house in the neighborhood. "He was very hysterical," Angie told the *Los Angeles Herald Examiner*[8]).

Just as *Death Hunt* had reteamed her with Lee Marvin, her next TV movie, *One Shoe Makes It Murder*, brought her together again with her *Young Billy Young* co-star Robert Mitchum. The project originated with Mitchum's Santa Barbara neighbor Mel Ferrer, who deposited the script on his driveway one morning along with the day's newspaper. It was a formulaic private detective mystery, the kind of picture that Mitchum could and often did sleepwalk through on his way to the bank. He was a down-and-out gumshoe hired by a gambling boss to find his missing wife, whose subsequent fall from a San Francisco high-rise may have been murder not suicide (since one shoe remained inside the apartment). In an equally proprietary role, Angie played a shady woman from the wife's past who hooks up with Mitchum and helps uncover the truth. Ferrer produced and co-starred as the crime boss, and the company shot on a frantic dawn to late night schedule in the spring of 1982. As Mitchum biographer Lee Server wrote, "It was a sloppy and sleepy B picture, but Mitchum and co-star Angie Dickinson made it something more than watchable—the senior citizen and the old broad were sexier together than most of the 'hot' young couples Hollywood was offering."[9] Confirming the chemistry, Angie confessed during a 1986 appearance on *The Tonight Show*, "One of the most sensuous men I ever worked with is Robert Mitchum." *One Shoe Makes It Murder* (retitled from an equally cumbersome *So Little Cause for Caroline*) aired November 6, 1982, on CBS.

Angie also tended to her brand with quirky ad campaigns and a series of TV guest appearances, in all of which she simply played herself. After separating from Burt, she somewhat defiantly made two solo commercials for Martini & Rossi. In the "red mood" spot, she moves through a house party wearing a red pantsuit and holding a glass of Martini & Rossi Red. After introducing herself to the camera, she says, "When I'm in my red mood, feeling warm and romantic, I don't want an ordinary wine, I want Martini and Rossi Red on the rocks. Luscious. It's a wine, but with a taste all its own. It's perfect at parties, before dinner, anytime." She strolls past a fireplace and a pool table, takes a cue stick from a man in a sports jacket, and blows some chalk off the tip. A red-coated waiter tops off her glass, and she moves into the den, where she sits at a table, toasts the camera, and concludes, "So when I'm in a red mood, I say yes." Voices on the soundtrack sing, "To Martini & Rossi on the rocks say yes," and in close-up she repeats, "Yeah." The pool stick business and the "say yes" refrain shout seductiveness.

The second Martini & Rossi commercial, another "mood" piece, has less inserts of the wine and more shots of Angie having fun. It opens with a long shot of a yacht and then dissolves to the interior where Angie, dressed in another pantsuit, a gauzy white one, takes a seat amid a group of party guests and says, "Hi, I'm Angie, and when I'm in my white mood, feeling light and sunny, I don't want an ordinary wine." A quick montage of Angie running on the beach in a white swimsuit, balancing a bird on her finger, being carried on a surfboard, and playing ping pong is followed by a medium shot of her accepting a drink from a young waiter in a white serving jacket.

"I want a Martini & Rossi Dry on the rocks," she continues, "crisp, refreshing, a wine but with a taste all its own." A second cut-away montage reveals her on a sailboat, holding a flower, standing next to a horse, and playing with balloons. Everything—the clothes and the props and the animals—is in white. Capping off the series of enviably photogenic activities, she clutches her wine, sits down in a captain's chair on the boat, and says, "At parties, before meals, I say yes." Then, in a final close-up reprise of the campaign's tagline, she smiles once more at the camera and murmurs, "Yeah." The subtextual message is that she is single, on her own, and doing just fine, thank you. Her life is full and her attractiveness is undiminished. Both 30-second spots play teasingly with her image as a swinger, consistently using "say yes" as a double entendre that suggests her openness to the wine and to sexual intimacy.

Even more sensational was the multi-format ad campaign she did in 1981-1982 for the California Avocado Commission. In the TV commercial, she is stretched out against a white background like an odalisque, her left elbow propped on the floor at a 90-degree angle and her right knee arched upward. She is wearing strapped silver heels and a sheer white leotard with a white cashmere sweater looped over the shoulders. Slowly, the camera pans up across her legs and torso while she scoops half an avocado with a spoon and explains, "This body needs good nutrition including Vitamins A, B1, C, E, potassium, niacin, iron, and this body gets them all in California avocados for just 153 calories in a luscious half shell." After a quick tip about ripening the fruit in paper bags, there is a return to her full figure in repose, and she asks, "Would this body lie to you?" The piece was slick, clever, and sexy. She was 51 at the time and gobsmackingly beautiful, even more so than she was walking around the beach in a yellow turtleneck and long floral dress for the Sun Country Air Freshener commercial she had made back in the 60s. Billboards and print ads used the same full-length image, which could also be seen on college dorm room walls all over the country. Not surprisingly, sales of the once obscure California agricultural product spiked. The personal meaning was as clear as in the wine "mood" pieces. For as long as she could, Angie intended to embrace and celebrate the sex symbol persona that had shaped her career so significantly.

Circling back again to Burbank, she also maintained a regular presence on several high profile NBC television programs. She worked with Bob Hope and did two Perry Como Christmas specials. By far her most iconic appearances, however, were with Johnny Carson on *The Tonight Show*. Carson's longtime producer Fred De Cordova declared that she was "the ultimate talk show flirt—and possibly every man's secret desire. One of a small group equally popular with men and women, on screen and off."[10] Her approach was to make an elegant entrance and then say something mildly provocative to disconcert Johnny. "So," she asked him once as a greeting, "are you hard at it?" and he replied, "You engender that quality in me." Their conversations were lively and affectionate with Angie professing her infatuation with him and Johnny pushing for details about her love life. Over the course of her many guest appearances, he showed her card tricks, discussed mutual friends, and referenced her career highlights. On a New Year's broadcast devoted primarily to her interview, they flirted madly through two extended segments.

In the profile she did about Angie for *TV Guide*, Mary Murphy wrote, "On the Johnny Carson show, she'll giggle and act coy, spice her conversation with sexual innuendo; when talking to men, she'll turn on the charm and coax them into believing that a complex thought never crosses her mind."[11] What Murphy saw as the "ditzy, breathless side" of her personality was actually a sly, winking nod to public expectations, just a harmless consumer pleasure, like tossing back a Martini & Rossi cocktail or sliding a cracker through the avocado dip. She was not about to reveal personal anguish before 10 million viewers, so she instead used the show as play therapy. When Johnny and Don Rickles both mentioned her daughter on an installment they did together, she quickly turned the conversation back to jokes about her social life. Like any smart show biz professional, she was there mainly to juice the career and to remind her fans why they enjoyed seeing her so much.

Several magazine articles linked her romantically with Carson, and they were photographed in public together on more than one occasion. In her 2019 *CBS Sunday Morning* appearance, she admitted that the two of them dated for a time. De Cordova himself remarked that her frequent appearances on *The Tonight Show* "gave Johnny a chance to pretend to be violently enamored of her. Underneath that pretense was the fact that he was fascinated by her."[12] Only six years apart in age, they shared the same Great Plains background, the same hardworking commitment to career, and the same health-conscious maintenance of their trim, tanned bodies. The bond between them may or may not have been sexual but was so deep that he backed her return to series TV in 1982 with his Carson Productions.

The show was called *Cassie & Company* and lasted for thirteen episodes. Having turned down the part of Krystle Carrington on *Dynasty*, Angie was looking instead for another show where she would be the narrative focus. Originally the idea was for a half hour situation comedy set in a department store, but when that didn't work out, creators returned to familiar territory with an hour long drama about a tough former police officer turned private investigator. As a sign of the times, Angie was now in charge; she played Cassie Holland, the ex-cop who has taken over Lyman Shackleford's detective agency and uses her looks and connections to solve a variety of cases. Also in the cast were John Ireland as Shackleford, Dori Brenner and A. Martinez as her associates, and Alex Cord as the district attorney ex-husband who feeds her valuable information.

The opening credits (split-screen shots of Angie from the knees down accompanied by a jazz-funk theme by Grover Washington Jr.) promised a hip new look, but the stories themselves were predictable. *Cassie & Company* debuted on January 29, 1982, and NBC placed it in *Police Woman*'s old Friday night at 10 p.m. time slot where it competed with *Falcon Crest* on CBS and network movies on ABC. The ratings were low, and within a few weeks NBC executives announced that it would be cancelled, exiting the winter schedule but returning in the spring to finish out its limited production run. Philosophical about what did and didn't click on television, Angie was not resentful toward either the network or the production company for the show's failure.

In contrast to the perceived romance with Carson, there were actually several serious suitors in Angie's life during the 80s. She was reported at various times to be dating newsman Harry Reasoner, handsome Dutch actor and Merle Oberon widower Rob Wolders (who was subsequently involved with Audrey Hepburn and Leslie Caron), TV personality Larry King (again), and singer Julio Iglesias. Although she traveled widely to see Iglesias in concert and appeared with King on his interview show, Reasoner was the leading object of her affections. The February, 1982, issue of *Every Woman* identified him as her "current man."[13] Divorced from his wife of 35 years and back on CBS's popular *Sixty Minutes* after a stint anchoring the ABC evening news broadcast, he was eligible, well-educated, and great company. While nothing permanent came of the relationship, they remained good friends even after Reasoner married insurance executive Lois Weber in 1988. During a January 26, 1983 appearance on *The Tonight Show* with guest host Joan Rivers, Angie admitted that Bacharach was the great love of her life and that she didn't "like to date that much." In the summer of 1984, a London tabloid announced that she was seeing Senator Ted Kennedy, but spokesmen for both insisted that they were old friends simply spending some time together. Certainly their political compatibility was never in doubt. Appropriately and coincidentally, she had once joked to *Variety*, "I've never knowingly dated a Republican," Sinatra's late-in-life decision to campaign for Ronald Reagan notwithstanding.[14]

More important to Angie were ongoing issues with Nikki. She had told Joan Rivers that they got along great, but tensions were high. When Nikki was just fourteen, feeling uncomfortable in regular society, she joined a Sikh religious group. Burt saw it as a sign that his daughter "was getting weirder and weirder,"[15] but Angie tried to be supportive. "The Sikhs were loving and gentle—which Nikki had to have," she believed. "Perhaps the uniformity of dress and the rituals made her feel like one of them, as opposed to an outsider who was always being looked at and stared at."[16]

A major tenet of Sikhism, a monotheistic religion that originated in fifteenth century India, is early morning meditation and prayer recitation. "We would get up at 3:30 a.m. and I would drive her down there for *sadhana*, the devotionals before sunrise," recalled Angie.[17] The early morning travel reflected Angie's willingness to let Nikki find her own way, but Burt was embarrassed by the ashram visits, the headwear, the billowy robes. Not surprisingly, he saw Nikki's behavior as a rejection of the glamorous popular image projected by her parents. For the slightly more than two years of her Sikhism, he brooded over her growing isolation, which Angie once poignantly likened to the scene in *2001: A Space Odyssey* "where the astronaut gets cut off and just floats into space."[18]

It was not the religion, however, but rather an incident at Angie's home that sparked Burt into action. "There were a lot of workmen in the house," she explained, "and one of them took a liking to Nikki." They smoked marijuana and spent time together alone. Since her first impulse was always to defend Nikki's conduct, she stressed the fact that nothing more serious happened: "The workman was forty-two or something, but I don't think there was anything sexual going on between them because Nikki didn't care about that. She just wanted to be loved and to have someone put their arm around her."[19] The Sikhs granted serenity, the marijuana brought peace, the workman provided love. Angie had a rationale for everything, but to Burt it was maternal enabling plain and simple. He lost his patience and threatened to take out a court order if Angie did not agree to admit Nikki to a treatment clinic he had located in Brea, California, an Orange County suburb about thirty miles south of Los Angeles.

"After Nikki went into the clinic in Brea I'd drive down to see her," remembered Burt. "She hated the place because she felt like she was in prison. I was expecting a very uptight therapist, but the man who ran the program was like a street guy who worked with kids all the time."[20] Not surprisingly, Angie disagreed with Burt's sanguine opinion of the program director and felt the whole thing had been a mistake. "Brea was Gestapo in the night. A pound on the door and you're going in and they shoved her into a new world," she claimed.[21]

After about six weeks, Nikki was released but Burt and his new wife Carole Bayer Sager continued to believe she needed additional treatment, preferably far beyond the distractions of Los Angeles. Through research and conversations with medical professionals, they ultimately found the Constance Bultman Wilson Center, a residential psychiatric facility for adolescents in Faribault, Minnesota. "Burt still believed Nikki was not doing well enough when she was a teenager and felt that it would be good to get some distance from me, because I was very symbiotic and too permissive," explained Angie. "And I thought, 'Maybe he's right. Maybe that's what she does need.'"[22] So, bowing to Burt's pressure, she agreed to send her only daughter north to the Great Plains of her own childhood to live in a medical institution for an unspecified period of time. She attempted to explain things by reminding Nikki that adventurous children often left home to attend school on their own. In August of 1983, they got on a plane for Minnesota but Nikki did not stay fooled for long. Within weeks of arriving in Faribault, she called her mother and told her, "It's not a school, Angie. It's a *hospital.*"[23]

Wracked by guilt and regret, Angie talked often with Nikki on the phone and visited four or five times a year. To lessen the loneliness, she flew in for holidays and also got permission to take Nikki on trips to places like the Canadian Rockies, the Tetons, and the Yucatan. Eager for any signs of improvement, she encouraged Nikki's piano lessons, her part time jobs, and the few friendships she was able to make. "She was a natural drummer," remembered Angie. "She played barefoot. She could sit in with the band and keep up with everyone, even if she didn't know what the songs were."[24] On one happy occasion, Burt invited her to join him on stage during a charity concert in Minneapolis and be the drummer on "Heartlight." Afterwards, Hubert Humphrey's widow Muriel, who had been sitting in the audience, presented Nikki with a bouquet of roses.

As Nikki's stay at the Wilson Center stretched on over the decade, Burt continued to hope for major changes even though the doctors never offered a specific treatment regimen nor even a diagnosis. "There was no progress," he admitted, "but I kept thinking that maybe there was."[25] Angie, on the other hand, was only too aware of all the failures and regressions. "When Nikki entered the Wilson Center, she had beautiful thick hair that ran down past her shoulders," she revealed, but because the staff limited her obsessively long time washing it in the shower, "She buzzed if off and kept it that way."[26]

Eye problems continued to plague her as well. When the strain of trying to see notes became too great, she was forced to abandon the piano lessons. According to Angie, "The glasses she wore made her see things smaller than they really were. Try looking through binoculars from the other end—that's how Nikki saw things. Little things became even littler."[27] Despite the sight issues, the staff wanted her to learn to drive so that she could hold down a regular job. "They forced her to drive, which was insane," confirmed Angie. "She totaled one car and wrecked another pretty good. They were trying to make her like everybody else."[28] If her mother knew anything about Nikki, she knew "being like everybody else" was not ever going to be in the cards.

The ultimate blunder for Angie came when one of the psychiatrists there declared, "Nikki, someday your mother is going to die, and then you're going to have to be responsible for your own self."[29] It was a comment, she believed, that "put her into a spiral she never got out of."[30] Despite Angie's firm conviction that the center was completely incapable of helping her, Nikki would remain in Faribault for ten years, a period during which she and her mother's resentment toward Burt grew steadily more pronounced. "The bottom line was that Burt did it to get her away from me," concluded Angie.[31]

Midway through Nikki's residential treatment, another family crisis surfaced; Angie's older sister Mary Lou, who had divorced in 1978 and was living alone, began to show early signs of Alzheimer's disease. Just as she was spending more time with both sisters, taking trips together and meeting for dinner, Angie noticed that Mary Lou would get lost easily or fail to react emotionally to changes and surprises in her life. From there, she progressed to memory lapses and difficulties performing her job as a film permit clerk for the city of Burbank. By 1986, Angie was certain that it was the initial stages of Alzheimer's. "Finally, they had to let her go at work," she recounted. "She just couldn't keep up. She was so frustrated. I felt so sorry for her. But by then I'd made my own diagnosis of Alzheimer's. I'm a news junkie and I read a lot of the medical stories. Also Rita Hayworth had it at the time. Glenn Ford was very close to her and a friend of mine, and he would talk about her. So I was really aware of the disease."[32] A doctor confirmed the suspicions. Only fifty-seven at the time, Mary Lou had been stricken by the progressive dementia which now ranks as the sixth-leading cause of death in the United States.

In an article written contemporaneously for *People* magazine, Angie shared a somber picture of her sister's mental and physical deterioration. Difficulties with physical tasks such as tying a shoelace or hooking a bra had given way to an inability to prepare meals and maneuver about the kitchen. To help with the mental confusion, friends and family posted notes around the house to remind her where things were located. "Her speech has deteriorated steadily," wrote Angie. "She'll use common expressions like 'You bet' or 'You're not kidding,' but putting a new thought into words comes very slowly."[33] When it became clear that Mary Lou could no longer care for herself, Angie and Mary Lou's three grown children hired the sisters' childhood friend Dorothy Howe and two other helpers to provide around-the-clock care. "Mary Lou has lost about 15 lbs. in the last year," Angie noted. "I think she has started to reach the point where there's no enthusiasm, even for eating. Also, she has a hard time finding her fork, and when she does get it, she can't figure out how to maneuver the food to her mouth . . . depressed and sobbing, that's when her anguish is the hardest for all of us to deal with, because then you know what she's going through and that it's painful for her."[34]

Angie's first-hand experience with the disease prompted her to advocate for increased government-funded research. Speaking in Washington, D.C., before two Congressional subcommittees, she also urged that medical costs associated with Alzheimer's, specifically long-term nursing home care, be covered by Medicare and other insurance programs. The token federal support of scientific investigation into possible causes and cures, she argued, was woefully inadequate. On a more personal level, she persuaded Mary Lou's daughter and two sons to enroll in support groups for families of Alzheimer's victims. "Luckily we started planning when we did," she declared. "When the things we thought might happen did, we were prepared."[35]

Even with that preparation, there were inevitable strains within the family, questions about who contributed what, both financially and emotionally. "It's brought us closer together, but it can pull a family apart too," admitted Angie. "'Are you doing enough? Why isn't he here? Where is she?' It's awful and it doesn't end."[36] After lamenting that "many of Mary Lou's friends don't come by unless we solicit," Angie pledged in the conclusion of her *People* article that she would "always take care of her and that she would never have to worry about being abandoned."[37] As often as her jobs allowed, she saw Mary Lou on weekends, going for walks or taking her to the movies and baseball games whose details she could not process but whose ambience she still enjoyed.

It was work, just like it always had been, that offered Angie respite from the various family challenges she was confronting. On a studio set, she could forget about Nikki and Mary Lou for a few hours and concentrate on portraying someone else. Made-for-television movies predominated. Between 1984 and 1989, she appeared in seven of them. For two, *Police Story: The Freeway Killings* (1987) and *Prime Target* (1989), she once again played a police woman. The twist in the first one was that her character, Officer Anne Cavanaugh, also happened to be sleeping with a married division captain (Ben Gazzara). The main plot had her helping detectives Don Meredith and Tony Lo Bianco track down two psychopaths who are murdering young women and dumping their bodies near the freeways of a large, unnamed California city (easily identified as Los Angeles from the location shooting). With multiple characters and overlapping storylines, it was an ambitious attempt to explore the rivalries, political influences, and miscalculations that can impact a large metropolitan police force. Angie's old *Thief* co-star Richard Crenna appeared as a principled deputy chief competing for the chief's job under the glare of the highly publicized freeway killings investigation. Although she received second billing after Crenna, Angie was on screen for only about fifteen of the movie's 140 minutes of running time. One of her best scenes, with dialogue that had to have hit close to home, is when she advises Gazzara not to give up on his drug-addicted daughter. "She'll need you to fight for her life for her," she declares. "She'll always need that."

Much more the central focus of *Prime Target*, she played a New York police detective who discovers she is the possible next victim of a murderer stalking female police officers. The proceedings looked and felt a lot like her old TV series, especially given the fact that *Police Woman* creator Robert Collins wrote and directed the picture. Save for the change in cities, this could have been another Pepper-in-peril drama. Also slightly different was the addition of some familial backstory for her character; Charles Durning played her supportive, Irish-American father. Like the *Police Story* offshoot, *Prime Target* was aired on NBC.

A Touch of Scandal (1984) and *Stillwatch* (1987), both for CBS, were thrillers with political context. Still a government employee, she had advanced to the positions, respectively, of a city councilwoman campaigning for state attorney general and a U.S. Senator hoping to be Vice-President. Both efforts were stymied by past events coming to roost in the present. In *A Touch of Scandal*, she starred as Katherine Gilvey, a local attorney who is trapped in a loveless marriage to her political manager husband Benjamin (Don Murray) and who eventually takes a male prostitute (Stephen Shellen) as her lover. When he is murdered and his body left in her apartment building, she must deal with a variety of threats to her life and career.

There are some steamy bedroom scenes between Angie and Shellen and, before the picture turns into a preposterous one-woman pursuit of the bad guys, a good feel for politics. We see Katherine at TV debates, fundraisers, and press conferences. Smart and independent, she fights for the disenfranchised while resisting the advances of corrupt influence peddlers. Above all else, she is successful in a male-dominated world. "My character definitely feels the pressures facing women in public life," she told a reporter for the *Los Angeles Herald-Examiner*. "I think there is a double standard in society. At least I have never known it to be any other way. It seems pretty much accepted that men can do things like run around with women; it's almost ignored. If a woman cheats on a man, on the other hand, it's big news."³⁸

Female office holder was another new character to add to her resume, and she was quite convincing in the part. Certainly she had been around enough real-life politicians to understand the milieu. From them, she copied the decisiveness, the personal charisma, and also the self-centeredness. To this mix, she added a caustic sense of humor. When a sleazy would-be donor asks her who is fulfilling the amorous duties of her husband, she responds, "The entire UCLA football team. I'm a big Bruins fan." Reviewing the movie for *The New York Times*, critic John J. O'Connor called Angie "one of television's most remarkably preserved veterans" but felt the plot resembled "a story board gone berserk."³⁹

Stillwatch doubled down on the political setting, promoting Angie to a United States Senator angling for the Vice-Presidential job which may soon be available given the precarious health of its incumbent. Lynda Carter co-starred as a TV reporter (Patricia Traymore) assigned to do a profile piece on Virginia's senior Senator Abigail Winslow. Adapted from a Mary Higgins Clark novel, the plot combined political intrigue with psychic mystery and involved two overlapping investigations: Traymore's background research on the Senator and on the residence in Washington, D.C. where she is staying, a house like the one in *The Exorcist* (1973) where twenty-five years earlier a young Congressman murdered his wife and daughter before killing himself.

Inevitably if somewhat incredibly, the two storylines come together when it is revealed that Patricia is the supposedly dead daughter and that Senator Winslow is the Congressman's adulterous ex-lover. There are unexplained break-ins at the house, a nosey psychic across the street, an abrasive Senatorial aide, and several sketchily remembered flashbacks. Nearly everyone, it turns out, was on scene the night of the murders, and although Senator Winslow is not the killer, her political career is sacrificed as part of the collateral damage fallout.

Shot partially on location in Washington, the movie is more successful with the political machinations than with the haunted house tropes. Angie's Senator Winslow is even more ruthless and ambitious than her Councilwoman Gilvey. She barks at staff members, manipulates the media, and constantly jockeys for power. Although no Senator ever looked as stunning as she does, she is equally believable speaking at a Senate subcommittee meeting or schmoozing her way through an embassy ball. When she tells a colleague, "If this budget doesn't get voted on soon, we're going to be in session until Christmas," the moment seems only too real. Interviewed on the steps of the Lincoln Memorial and then whisked away by her driver, she exudes a sense of importance and purpose. It was one of the strongest female roles she had played to date. So often she was asked to be either bitchy or vulnerable, but here she attempts to combine both, an assertive woman whose overbearingness is mitigated by a sympathetic backstory. Similarly, the confrontational scenes between Abigail and Patricia over the affections of Don Murray, along again on this picture as Congressman Sam Kingsley, are not the shrill Wonder Woman vs. Police Woman catfights they could have been but rather narratively significant conflicts of will and intent. Credit belongs to the restraint both actresses brought to their performances.

For hardcore Angie fans, there were also some rich self-referential details included in the story. During an interview with Patricia, Abigail explains that her desire to be appointed to her deceased husband's Senate seat was blocked by the Virginia governor and that "it took a young Senator from Massachusetts to convince him otherwise." As part of her research, Patricia finds a photo of Abigail in a swim suit being congratulated by her mother for winning the Miss New York beauty pageant; in reality, it's a picture of Angie and Rika celebrating the Jack Rourke *Beauty Parade* win. "She was the strongest, most loving woman ever," Abigail says tearfully. Despite the strong performances, solid production values, and political relevance (three years earlier Geraldine Ferraro had been the first female Vice-Presidential candidate of a major national party), the movie was not a huge ratings success.

Two genre pictures, a Western (*Once Upon a Texas Train*, 1988) and an airline disaster docudrama (*Fire and Rain*, 1989), were also part of the television work she did during these years. Both featured large ensemble casts. The former, written and directed by Burt Kennedy, recycled characters from *The Over-the-Hill Gang*, a 1969 ABC made-for-television picture about a former Texas Ranger and three elderly gunfighters uniting to take on a corrupt politician. In the 1989 version, also known as *Texas Guns*, Richard Widmark starred as retired Ranger Captain Oren Hayes, and Willie Nelson appeared as aging outlaw John Henry Lee, just released from prison and bent on successfully repeating the train robbery he botched twenty years earlier. For added narrative interest and audience appeal, pop favorite Shaun Cassidy was cast as the leader of a gang of young gunslingers who interfere with the plans of both Lee and Hayes.

The intended fun was watching a host of familiar Western actors reappear in updated iterations of their younger selves. As Widmark's voice-over explains how tough and professional the veterans are, we see them setting themselves on fire, falling off horses, and wrecking buckboards. Representing hundreds of movie and TV appearances between them were Chuck Connors, Ken Curtis, Royal Dano, Jack Elam, Gene Evans, Hank Worden, Dub Taylor, Kevin McCarthy, and Stuart Whitman. With well over twenty Western credits to his resume by now, Kennedy filled the film with variations on classic genre tropes: a chaotic saloon brawl, a sloppy bottle target practice, a bicycle-riding horseman, a visually challenged tracker. Adding to the nostalgic ambiance was the fact that Kennedy shot much of the movie on location in Old Tucson, site of the Angie Dickinson pictures *Rio Bravo*, *The Last Challenge*, and *Young Billy Young*.

Billed as a guest star, Angie appeared for about eight minutes of screen time. She had three scenes, one with Widmark alone and two with both Nelson and Widmark. Her job was to provide iconic resonance, and in that she fulfilled all of Kennedy's expectations. She enters on a train at night, materializing from the steamy darkness and advancing slowly toward the camera. "Hello, Oren," she whispers. "Been a long time." She is Maggie Hayes, Oren's estranged wife and John Henry's former sweetheart. Looking radiant in a rustling pink and black dress, she echoes Feathers, Lily Beloit, Belinda McNair, and every other frontier siren she had played over the years. In a gauzy flashback, she waltzes with both men, and in the finale, dressed in a light purple gown and matching lavender lip gloss, she salutes John Henry and reconciles with Oren. Given very few lines of dialogue, Angie needed only to thread her arm through Widmark's or smile serenely at Nelson to command the screen. Reacting to the effect, Nelson's character remarks, "What is it about that woman that haunts a man so?" Viewers were also beguiled; airing January 3, 1988, on CBS, *Once Upon a Texas Train* was the third most watched TV movie of the season. It was also Angie's last Western and, in Widmark, her last teaming with an A-list actor from Hollywood's golden age.

Its title borrowed from the James Taylor song, *Fire and Rain* was a reenactment of the crash of Delta Airlines Flight 191 on

August 2, 1985. Originating in Fort Lauderdale and bound for Los Angeles, it encountered wind shear during a stop-over landing in Dallas and went down just short of the runway, bursting into flames and killing 137 of the 163 people onboard. The film attempted to portray events leading to the disaster as well as the emergency response that followed. A large ensemble cast including Charles Haid, Tom Bosley, Dean Jones, Robert Guillaume, Patti Labelle, David Hasselhoff, Susan Ruttan, and Laurence Pressman played the victims, family members, and first responders.

Angie's featured billing misspelled her last name as "Dickenson," and her three minutes of screen time were even less than she received in the Kennedy Western. As hospital administrator Beth Mancini, she bounced in and out of scenes, directing personnel and consoling relatives. Despite being brief in length, there were almost ten of these appearances throughout the picture, giving the impression of a more dominant overall presence. For each one, she was appropriately terse and somber. In its effort to explore both the personal interactions and backstories of the victims as well as specific details of emergency protocol, however, the film ended up doing neither very well. Jerry Jameson, a movie-of-the-week veteran and director of the similarly themed films *Airport '77* (1977) and *Starflight: The Plane That Couldn't Land* (1983), tried to generate the group-jeopardy terror he was known for, but a low budget and awkward technical effects limited what he could accomplish. The picture aired September 13, 1989, on the relatively new USA Network to muted critical response.

Angie's most ambitious project from this period was *Jealousy*, a three-part anthology film like the ones popular in Italy during the 50s and 60s. She played three different characters whose lives are all dramatically affected by the emotion spelled out in the title.

In the first vignette ("Georgia"), she is an elegant divorced mother who grows increasingly jealous of her daughter's interest in the new man of the house. The second episode ("Laura") has her marrying a billionaire in Europe and returning home to compete for his attention with a thirty-year-old pet parrot. In the concluding story ("Ginny"), she is a small-time country and western singer whose jealous boyfriend won't let go as she tries to break up and make a career move to Nashville. Each piece ends with a twist. Unhinged by suspicion, Georgia shoots the young man who turns out to have been the daughter's new husband not hers. Laura accidentally causes the parrot to escape its cage and get trapped in a refrigerator where it freezes to death. Just as she thinks she has the billionaire to herself, he announces that now he can bring back the pet chimpanzee who had been banished for feuding with the bird. Chased down an isolated highway, Ginny finally turns and confronts her stalker, telling him either to shoot her or himself. He pulls out a loaded gun, fires it into a tape deck playing her music, and drives away into the night.

If not quite an artistic tour de force, *Jealousy* allowed her to stretch as an actress in the same way that the work with John Newland had. On screen for most of the picture's 90 minute running time, she moved easily between psychodrama and light comedy. As the increasingly paranoid Georgia, she is cold, detached, and ultimately shattered. Facing off against the parrot, she is both sympathetic and absurd. In one of that vignette's best scenes, she celebrates after getting the bird to approach her and then tries to maintain a touch of dignity when it defecates on her arm. As harassed honky-tonk heroine Ginny, she conveys a very real sense of physical peril and, in a career first, convincingly performs three country and western tunes (with singing voice dubbed by Lynne

Marta). Exceptionally well chosen, the cast included Paul Michael Glaser, Richard Mulligan, and David Carradine as the three male leads and France Nuyen, Bo Svenson, and Susan Tyrrell in supporting roles. ABC broadcast the movie on January 23, 1984.

Overshadowing this performance was Angie's participation a year later in that same network's lavish miniseries *Hollywood Wives*. Having failed to snag her for *Dynasty*, executive producer Aaron Spelling convinced her to play super-agent Sadie LaSalle in this adaptation of Jackie Collins's bestselling novel about Tinsel Town sex and intrigue. It was vintage 80s fashion (big hair and big shoulders) combined with plot clichés from every insider Hollywood picture ever made. There were abrasive studio bosses, fading stars, newcomers with illicit pasts, grasping spouses, alcoholic directors, blackmailers, socialites, star-makers, and the spoiled children of famously spoiled parents. Audiences loved it, ranking each of the three installments among the top-rated shows of the week.

In designer Nolan Miller's expensive haute-couture gowns, Angie looked right at home next to her glamorous, slightly younger co-stars Candice Bergen, Joanna Cassidy, Mary Crosby, Stefanie Powers, Suzanne Sommers, and Catherine Mary Stewart. Working with such a large assemblage of actresses was a first for "one of the guys" Angie, but she seemed to enjoy the experience, talking up the production in a February, 1985, interview with *People* magazine. Her male castmates, sporting as many hairpieces as the women, included Robert Stack, Steve Forrest, Roddy McDowall, and the notorious scenery-chewers Anthony Hopkins and Rod Steiger.

In the *People* article, she confirmed that her character had been reconfigured from the short, fat powerhouse of the novel to someone more chic and elegant. "I was not ready to play caftans and dangling bracelets," she declared.[40] Agent Sue Mengers, who assumed like everyone else in Hollywood that Sadie LaSalle was partially based on her, was pleased with the change. "Sue was the happiest lady in town when Angie was cast," commented author Collins.[41] Although Suzanne Sommers had the best unintentionally hilarious lines ("I play an anthropologist who gets captured by a band of pygmies"), Angie got to scheme, destroy careers, and be menaced at gunpoint by one of the twin sons she thought had both been lost at childbirth. At the conclusion, she drives off in a white Rolls Royce with the other newly found son, her coiffure and straight face perfectly intact.

Except for the extensive use of *Dressed to Kill* footage in *Terror in the Aisles*, a 1984 compilation feature about horror films, Angie's only other big screen appearance at the time was in *Big Bad Mama II*, a sequel to the Roger Corman-produced sleeper hit of the previous decade. Shot in just four weeks during the early summer of 1987, it was not so much a continuation of the original as it was a reworking. With the same Depression Era time frame and the three same main characters, the plot gave new moral purpose to the gun-blazing criminality. Angie returned as Wilma McClatchie, who leads her two winsome daughters Billy Jean and Polly into bank robbing careers when she witnesses her husband shot down by policemen sent to foreclose their farm on the orders of evil banker Morgan Crawford. In revenge, not only does the clan rob Crawford's bank but so also do they discredit his gubernatorial campaign by kidnapping his son and turning him into a willing gang member. Documenting everything for the newspapers is an ambitious journalist (Robert Culp) looking for a professional break himself.

Corman once again served as executive producer, and for his writer/director he hired film school dropout Jim Wynorski, just then at the beginning of a multiple decade schlock film career which ultimately would boast such inventive credits as *The Bare Wench Project* (2000), *The Da Vinci Coed* (2007), *The Breastford Wives* (2007), and *The Devil Wears Nada* (2009). In addition to the standard bank heists and shootouts, Wynorski included striking miners, Hoovervilles, and references to the New Deal. His playfulness came through in the comically staged car crashes and brothel brawls and in a visual style that signaled scene changes with spinning newspaper headlines, montages, wipes, and bullet holes graphically inserted over the image. Angie proved to be a good sport herself, literally winking at the camera and slipping in and out of an ersatz southern accent. She handled the firearms as deftly as the humorously hardboiled dialogue. When Culp tells her that the girls have grown up, she replies, "They've grown out. It's not quite the same thing," and later, faced with an attack from the lawmen, she observes, "If they decide to rush us, we're in deep shit." In a nod to fan expectations, she even agreed to a nude sex scene with Culp, discreetly underlit and covered in the close-ups by a body double.

Surprisingly, reviewers seemed to be in on the joke also, giving the low-budget, R-rated picture almost apologetically good notices. The *Los Angeles Times* called it "a campy romp and a spirited, cheap exercise for ambitious talents,"[42] and *The Hollywood Reporter* complimented the "engaging and nicely silly script."[43] Audiences liked the movie also, their ticket purchases rapidly covering the less than $1.5 million production cost.

At this point in her career, Angie, like her good pals Frank and Dean, didn't much care what anyone thought about the choices she made. She would take a job if she was bored, felt like an adventure, or decided she needed to pack away a little more cash for the golden years. "I don't have my sights set on 'oh I have to have an Academy Award before I die.' I just hope to work," she declared.[44] Instead of an Oscar, she found no shortage of other opportunities and acknowledgements waiting for her to accept them. In September of 1987, she received the 1,853rd terrazzo and brass star on the Hollywood Walk of Fame. During a special ceremony at the plaque's 7000 Hollywood Boulevard location, old friend Johnny Grant summarized her achievements, and she quipped, "If you're near the Hollywood Roosevelt, don't walk on by, come up and step on me sometime."[45] Over the years, she would repay the honor, showing up, as she did in 2007 for writer Jim Bacon, to celebrate other people's induction.

Three months later, she traveled to New York City to host the December 12, 1987, broadcast of *Saturday Night Live*, then as now a recognition of celebrity status. During the opening monologue, dressed in a black skirt and blue floral print sweater, she poked fun at her career, claiming that she often told herself, "You may not play the classics, but you're hot and you're game. And it's working, it's working." In her first sketch, she hosts a Christmas party for Nora Dunn, Phil Hartman, Jon Lovitz, Victoria Jackson, and Dennis Miller. One after another, the guests make innocuous remarks that remind somebody else of a recent traumatic incident. When Victoria Jackson notices a Christmas ornament shaped like a hummingbird, Angie recalls that her husband was recently killed by a hummingbird. "He was standing there in the yard . . . this hummingbird came right at him," she explains. "At his head, and it was going about a hundred miles an hour and he just turned and walked right into it." Other faux pas involve a weatherman fired for a botched hurricane forecast, a woman's parents entombed in a glacier, and Jackson's father sent to prison for embezzlement.

The second sketch has Angie as a flight attendant subtly trying to find out if any of her passengers can land a DC-10 endangered by its unconscious pilot. Informed by Lovitz that he was never in the air force, she asks, "So an emergency landing on a fogged-in runway in about ten or fifteen minutes would be out of the question?" After also checking with Dana Carvey and Kevin Nealon and smothering a hysterical Jan Hooks with a pillow, she strikes gold with Hartman. "I've been a commander in the star fleet for many light years," he assures her. Even though he is obviously crazy, she decides he's the best she's got and takes him into the cockpit anyway. This was another new experience for her, something quite different from the broad routines of a taped Bob Hope or Dean Martin special. She was doing quirky live material with seasoned young performers. Although she was noticeably nervous for the monologue, she relaxed for the sketches, revealing a real gift for ensemble comedy and nailing the airplane bit with her relentlessly cheery stewardess. The week in New York with producer Lorne Michaels and the SNL season 13 cast was a professional high point she was proud to have accomplished.

Stimulated by drifting outside the usual lanes, she took on other projects that caught her fancy. She traveled to Alabama with Dick Clark to co-host the Miss USA Pageant at the Mobile Civic Center and read the religious poem "The Master is Coming" for an Easter Sunrise Service at the Hollywood Bowl. In a particularly ambitious move, she authorized agent Irving "Swifty" Lazar to negotiate a book deal for her. By June of 1987, he had secured a $75,000 advance from G.P. Putnam's Sons for her autobiography. She would write about her family, her career, her marriages, and even some of her affairs. The plan, however, was easier to propose than to realize. Reluctant like so many Midwesterners to talk about herself or to invade the privacy of friends, she made a slow go of it and within two years had returned the money to Putnam.

ANGIE

Friendship would always be more important to her than self advertisement. She took its obligations and responsibilities seriously. When her friend and former co-star Rock Hudson died of AIDS-related complications in 1985, she immediately agreed to join Roddy McDowall, Tab Hunter, Lee Remick, Glenn Ford, Robert Wagner, Elizabeth Taylor, Carol Burnett, Esther Williams, and Susan Saint James in delivering a remembrance during the memorial service held at the Beverly Hills home that Hudson had nicknamed "The Castle." Over the years she could be counted on to be among the mourners at the funerals of almost anyone she had worked with or known, professional acquaintances like Telly Savalas or closer friends like David Janssen. She was also there for the celebrations and honors—Nolan Miller's Couture Fashion Show, the Royal Family of Monaco Tribute to Cary Grant, a National Conference of Christians and Jews Recognition Dinner for Sherry Lansing, the American Society of Composers, Authors, and Publishers "Celebration of Jimmy Van Heusen," Milton Berle's 90th Birthday Party, and the American Film Institute Lifetime Achievement Award Ceremony for Gregory Peck (where she gave one of the tributes).

Just as enjoyable were the small informal gatherings. Once a week, usually on Sunday evening, she played poker with a group that at one time or another included Peck and his wife Veronique, Jack and Felicia Farr Lemmon, Dick and Dolly Martin, the Larry Gelbarts, Dom and Carol Deluise, and Barbara Sinatra. According to the others, she was a formidable player, so skilled and fond of the game that she would later appear on the Bravo TV show *Celebrity Poker*, where she competed in a third season segment with Jeff Gordon, Kathy Griffin, Penn Jillette, and Ron Livingston. "I always liked to sit next to Angie," admitted Peck, "because when

Angie has dropped out of a hand and I'm still in it, I show my cards to her and she tells me what to do."[46]

It was a rich social life, but Angie was not done with film and television. She made a guest appearance on *Empty Nest*, the popular sitcom that her *Jealousy* co-star Richard Mulligan was shooting at NBC, and took a supporting part in *Kojak: Fatal Flaw*, an ABC made-for-television movie based on the Telly Savalas crime drama that aired on CBS from 1973 to 1978. She and Savalas had appeared in only one scene together in *Pretty Maids All in a Row*, but this time they were paired romantically, Angie playing an old flame whom Kojak encounters during a murder investigation. The wife of a writer killed for a Mafia expose he has published, she learns that her husband was not the upright citizen she assumed he was. It would be Savalas's last appearance as the bald, lollipop-loving detective and therefore fitting that he should team up for the finale with the iconic actress whose memorable TV cop show run roughly paralleled his own. When Savalas passed away five years later, Angie attended the Greek Orthodox funeral services along with Frank Sinatra, Don Rickles, and many other stars.

Treacherous Crossing, based on a radio play by John Dickson Carr and a 1953 film starring Jeanne Crain and Michael Rennie, was another television movie that did not require much time on set. Lindsay Wagner starred as a newlywed embarking on a transatlantic voyage to Europe who discovers that her husband has disappeared and that there is no official record he ever existed in the first place. Angie played a free-spirited fellow passenger who is one of the few people onboard who believes the young woman's story. Set in 1947, the picture gave Angie the chance to wear period dresses and brandish matching cigarette holders. Many of her scenes were shot on the *Queen Mary*, which had been permanently moored in Long Beach, California, since 1967, making for another easy commute.

Her other TV movie from 1992 was a return to *Police Woman* territory but with a promotion. She played Angela Martin in the appropriately named *Angie, the Lieutenant*, the story of a Washington, D. C. career officer who becomes the head of an all-male police squad. As part of the déjà-vu, Robert Collins, the creator of *Police Woman*, directed.

Unquestionably, the major work of the decade, however, was her brilliantly realized portrayal of Josie Ito in the six-hour Bruce Wagner mini-series *Wild Palms*, which aired on ABC in May of 1993. Visually stunning and intricately plotted, it dealt with religious cultism, corporate conspiracy, virtual reality, politically controlled media, and domestic terrorism. Underlying the social commentary was a family drama so dark it made the Borgias seem benign.

At the center of everything is the "Fathers," a right-wing political and financial complex led by California Senator Tony Kreutzer, who also directs the Church of Synthiotics and the Wild Palms media group. He controls news through his television network and intends to permanently extend his power by becoming a living hologram. Opposed to the "Fathers" is a guerilla political organization known as the "Friends," whose founder and leader is former college history professor Eli Levitt. Aspiring young attorney Harry Wyckoff, his wife Grace, and their two small children are caught between the two sides in an escalating intrigue that involves undisclosed parentage, attempted suicide, and murder.

There was nothing on network television at the time quite like it. New truths and connections were continuously established, new identities unexpectedly revealed. Children were not necessarily related to the people they thought were their parents; a father's son might actually be his brother. Eerily prescient, it suggested that news could be faked and that Presidential candidates could be totally disinterested in the public good. The startling visual imagery ranged from a rhinoceros in the deep end of an empty swimming pool to a palm tree set ablaze at night. There were references to the Marx Brothers, Zen Buddhism, Walt Whitman, T.S. Eliot, Raymond Chandler, the Mercury Theatre, James Bond, *Rebel Without a Cause*, *The Snake Pit*, the Paramount Consent Decree, Shakespeare, Wallace Stevens, David Hockney, and many other cultural figures and events. The music included selections from Frankie Valli, the Supremes, the Rolling Stones, Wagner, Beethoven, Lou Christie, and the Fifth Dimension. Lounge singer cum Synthiotics acolyte Robert Morse wandered through the episodes singing classics by Irving Berlin and Cole Porter.

As ruthless Josie Ito, Grace's mother and a famous interior designer, Angie gave a fearless, all-stops-out performance, even more willing than she had been in *The Killers* to risk audience alienation with her palpable menace. Early on, Josie is also revealed to be Kreutzer's sister and Levitt's ex-wife, a central figure in the narrative's web of avarice, betrayal, and revenge. Referred to as "that demonic woman," "a dried up monster," and "a pimp with the wings of a bat," she leaves a trail of violence wherever she goes. To help her brother maintain power, she gouges out a man's eyes, gut punches her daughter, threatens to kill her granddaughter, orders Levitt's death by drowning, and ultimately strangles Grace in a murder scene that gets broadcast nationally as a hologram. She herself is slapped, throttled, and bitten on the face. In a final act of revenge the Friends partisan and artist whom she blinded plucks out her own eyes and shoots her as she writhes on the ground in pain. "This sweet woman does these grotesque things," remarked Wagner of the role he had written for Angie.[47] Fabulously costumed in sleekly tailored suits and flamboyant orange, red, and blue gowns, she smiles seductively and then snarls out such lines as "Someone should set him on fire" and "We never meant to kill your mother; what's done is done." Most impressive is her ability to turn on a dime from doting grandmother to queen bitch, often in the same scene. It remains, arguably, the finest achievement of her late career years.

Everything about the project was first-rate. Highly regarded filmmaker Oliver Stone executive produced, and the individual installments were directed by Peter Hewitt, Keith Gordon (who had played Angie's son in *Dressed to Kill*), Kathryn Bigelow, and Phil Joanou. Ryuichi Sakamoto, who had already composed award-winning music for the films *Merry Christmas, Mr. Lawrence* (1983), *The Last Emperor* (1987), and *The Sheltering Sky* (1990), provided the hypnotic, electronically tinged score. Sound, editing, photography, and production design were handled by an assemblage of some of the most talented technicians then working in Hollywood. The cast included Robert Loggia, Dana Delany, Ernie Hudson, Jim Belushi, Kim Cattrall, Bebe Neuwirth, Brad Dourif, and David Warner. Angie was impressed with the celebrated company in front of and behind the cameras, particularly awed by the presence of Stone. "I just bumbled all over the place and blushed," she admitted. "I mean he's sooo magnetic. It was unnerving. I thought, 'Oh God. Now I'm going to have to try and forget you're here so I can get through this scene.'"[48]

Critics were also impressed with the efforts of cast and crew. Writing for *The New York Times*, John O'Connor called the show "a truly wild six-hour mini-series" as "rich and insinuating as a good theatrical film, albeit hard to follow."[49] Author and critic Ken Tucker raved that "in its length, scope, visual tableaux, and over-the-top passion, *Wild Palms* is more like an opera than a TV show."[50] British reviewer Mary Harran agreed with the analogy: "*Wild Palms* should be watched like opera; for its gorgeous images, its emotional set-pieces and its high style."[51] To help viewers untangle the plot, St. Martin's Press published a pre-screening book, *The Wild Palms Reader*, full of time lines, character biographies, and other ancillary material.

Coinciding with the production and broadcast of *Wild Palms* were several important changes in Angie's personal life. Most notably, after ten years of treatment, Nikki was released from the Wilson Center. To ease the transition, Angie encouraged her to think about college. "Nikki wanted to be a geologist," she explained, "so when she was about to leave the Wilson Center in the winter of 1992, I started to look for schools with geology programs. Cal Lutheran in Thousand Oaks had a very good one, and I knew she would like that area."[52] The combination of a fresh start, a realistic goal, and a tangible field of study appealed immensely to Nikki's sense of focus, and she quickly agreed to the plan. "When Nikki was out here on leave, we found an apartment close to the university," remembered Angie, "and from Minnesota that's where the moving truck went."[53]

Cal Lutheran, with its extensive student support services, proved to be a good fit. Since its founding in 1959, the nonsectarian university has provided a diverse liberal arts curriculum to its roughly 3,000 undergraduate and 1,300 graduate students. As Angie had foreseen, the inviting 290-acre campus and the interesting course of study, especially the hands-on laboratory work, validated her daughter in ways the Faribault years never had. With gratitude, she noted, "At Cal Lutheran she had great teachers. She could only handle one class a semester with her poor eyesight. She did great on tests, of course, but writing was difficult. I missed one of her oral presentations, and she always said, 'I wish you could've been there. I was terrific.' I just loved her tenacity and her guts."[54]

Along with the studying, Nikki explored Thousand Oaks and made some new friends. "There was a fantastic karate studio nearby," added Angie, "and Nikki began lessons and got so good, she earned her green belt."[55] Angie often dropped in at the apartment for quick visits, and on weekends Nikki returned to her mother's house in Coldwater Canyon. They went to movies together and had frequent dinners at one of Nikki's favorite restaurants, the Cheesecake Factory in Beverly Hills. Getting to know each other more deeply was part of the adventure; each challenge successfully overcome brought mother and daughter that much closer.

Nikki's connection to her father, however, did not strengthen in the same way. Burt knew only too well that she blamed him for the prolonged treatment at the Wilson Center. "When Nikki was about to turn eighteen," he remembered, "she wrote Carole and me a really loving letter. But then her negative feelings about me began to build and I became her enemy, as did Carole. Nikki thought I had locked her up and imprisoned her and she hated me for having done that to her."[56] Relations between Burt and Angie were equally strained. Although he continued to contribute financially to his daughter's medical care, living expenses, and education, Angie handled all of the daily legwork and tended to Nikki's emotional needs. Quality face time between the three was limited. According to Burt, "I'd go up to where Angie lived about every other month and bring her and Nikki lunch and stay a couple of hours because that was about all I could take. As Nikki got older, all of her problems became bigger and more impossible to deal with. Whenever I visited, I could feel the venom she had toward me for imprisoning her."[57]

At the time of Nikki's return to California, Burt already had divorced Bayer Sager and had married Jane Hanson, a skiing instructor whom he met in Aspen, Colorado. His extended family soon included not only Christopher, the son he and Bayer Sager had together, but also two young children, a boy named Oliver and a girl named Raleigh, with Hanson. His attempts to involve Nikki with her siblings were well intentioned but unsuccessful. "After Jane and I had Oliver and Raleigh," he recalled, "Nikki would come to see us, but she had no patience at all for the kids. For her, they were an interruption, because she wanted to see this beautiful sunset and not be disturbed by them. The language she used was also hard for them to hear because she cursed all the time."[58] He and his first-born child continued to grow further apart.

As Nikki had emerged from institutional care, Mary Lou unfortunately had entered it. In the spring of 1993, she was admitted to a nursing home in Sunland, California, her dementia too severe for the 24-hour, in-home nursing services she had been receiving. "She does not see or speak," reported Angie. "Her eyes are open and she sees something, but we don't know what. She doesn't know you are there, and she doesn't see the food coming to her mouth."[59] Unable to slow the disease, the medical team simply worked to make Mary Lou as physically comfortable as possible. Angie's visits to Thousand Oaks alternated with stops in Sunland, where there was little she could do for her sister beyond staying close and assuring her she was not alone. "When I say, 'I bet you wish you were dancing tonight,' she cries, so I know she is responding," she revealed. "When I say, 'It's Angie,' she might smile or cry."[60] To help influence national policy on Alzheimer's, she continued to speak to physician, scientific, and geriatric care organizations. In June of

1993, *The New York Times* reported that she was scheduled to address the New York Academy of Sciences as part of a program titled "Closing in on Alzheimer's: A Progress Report from the Lab."

Surprisingly, given her intense family commitments, Angie also found time for a new personal relationship, a May-December friendship with handsome 25-year-old Scottish-born singer and actor John Barrowman, whom she had met at a dinner party the previous summer. Already the veteran of such hit London West End productions as *Anything Goes, Miss Saigon, Matador,* and *The Phantom of the Opera,* Barrowman was at the beginning of a career that ultimately would encompass stage, film, music albums, and the iconic role of Captain Jack Harkness on the BBC science fiction dramas *Doctor Who* (2005-10) and *Touchwood* (2006-11). "He's enchanting, funny, sweet—and naughty," Angie told reporters.[61] Linked by a love of animals, theater, and travel, the two of them spent a great deal of time together, often including Nikki in their museum visits and restaurant samplings. "He's such a partier," commented Nikki approvingly on her mother's new pal, "but they're only *friends*. I mean he's younger than *me*."[62]

Although Barrowman later came out publicly and married his longtime partner Scott Gill, there was much speculation at the time that the relationship was also sexual. "Obviously, I'm sleeping alone—most of the time," Angie remarked coyly before also joking, "I'm not embarrassed to be with a younger man, except when I drop him off at school."[63] Barrowman was equally evasive, confirming only, "Getting engaged or married isn't in the forecast, but we're having a sensational time now."[64]

In his autobiography *Anything Goes,* he downplayed the entire relationship. American Cinema Awards producer David Gest, he explained, asked him to escort Angie to a pre-awards dinner. When she picked him up at the Beverly Wilshire Hotel in her Mercedes, he complimented her appearance. "Your legs still look great. I remember when I was eight years old and watched you on *Police Woman*," he clumsily gushed. She waited a beat, smiled, and waved off the faux pas by commenting, "Would you like to put your other foot in your mouth now or wait until later?"[65] Despite the rocky start, they enjoyed each other's company and felt an easy, immediate rapport. Choosing not to elaborate on any additional time together or on his own documented comments to reporters, Barrowman wrote only, "We had a great time at dinner and the next day our 'date' was all over the tabloids with headlines screaming that I was her 'Boy Toy'—which was just rubbish."[66] His failure to say anything more did not necessarily mean there was nothing more to reveal. Their encounter, however brief it may have been, obviously entailed no demands and no drama. "I wouldn't call it a romance," Angie admitted, "but it sure is a nice reminder of one."[67]

Angie was always a good sport and a helpful colleague, but there were limits. She had sung on stage with Burl Ives and Randy Sparks at a cultural center fundraiser in Mt. Vernon, Washington, and had willingly testified for George Panagiotou in his patent suit against GTE Products Corp., asserting under oath that filming with the inventor's cool light system "took less time because I could stay in the scenes longer without needing to be repaired."[68] She had also consented to that distasteful, excruciatingly bad celebrity roast with Dean Martin. She was not, however, about to have intimate details of her private life announced on national television.

This Is Your Life was a popular reality-based variety program that had run on NBC radio from 1948 to 1952 and on NBC television from 1952 to 1966. Host Ralph Edwards would surprise celebrities and then, in front of a live studio audience, guide them through a biographical flashback enlivened with photos, home movies, news footage, and unexpected appearances by family and friends. Among the political, sports, and show business figures who had been profiled were Gloria Swanson, Stan Laurel, Milton Berle, Roy Rogers, Van Heflin, Ted Lewis, Dick Van Dyke, Boris Karloff, Admiral Samuel Fuqua, Jesse Owens, Lowell Thomas, and dozens of others. New iterations of the show were revived in the 70s, 80s, and 90s with hosts who included Joseph Campanella, Pat Sajak, and Edwards himself.

On Tuesday, November 9, 1993, Angie reported to the NBC studios in Burbank thinking that she was there for a tribute to Brian De Palma. When instead she heard the famous tagline, "Angie Dickinson, this is your life," she decided "Hell no, this is not happening," and walked off the set. Left shocked now themselves with nothing to do were the producers, staff, and guests Bob Hope, Earl Holliman, Burt Reynolds, and Jackie Collins, each of whom had prepared an amusing anecdote about the absent star. Angie later apologized, insisting playfully that she would have looked terrible with all the crying and the streaked mascara. The "Morning Report" column of the *Los Angeles Times* noted, "On Wednesday, Dickinson offered no explanation, saying merely that she had 'great regret' that she 'just couldn't do the show.' Dickinson's actions made history: With about 600 *This Is Your Life* shows held since 1952, Tuesday's was the first to be canceled by the honoree."[69] A week later, with Angie in the audience, magician David Copperfield joked on stage at the Wiltern Theater in Los Angeles that it was one of the greatest disappearing acts he had ever seen. In reality, there was not much mystery to the incident; she was just too cool, too skeptical of phony emotionalism, to sit there and listen to people praise her as part of a tacky sideshow ritual. "I didn't want it because I have never been a voyeur," she told *Vanity Fair* columnist George Wayne.[70] Many years later, during her *CBS Sunday Morning* interview with Mo Rocca, she revealed that she finally had flatly insisted to NBC producers that she was not going to do "the fucking show" and that as a result the network curtailed her future *Tonight Show* appearances.

Angie's eternal hipness was also on full display when she appeared on the cover of *Esquire*'s August, 1993, "60 Years of Women We Love" issue and accepted a part in an edgy independent movie. The photo was the one she had done with Frank Bez in 1966 for the magazine. She appears to be wearing nothing more than white stiletto heels and a baby blue sweater, her bare backside turned toward the camera (in reality she's wearing a very sheer, skin-toned leotard-like covering). Recreated for covers by Britney Spears in 2003 and four Victoria's Secret Angels in 2008, it is one of *Esquire*'s and Angie's most iconic images. "It wasn't like a studio shoot," she explained, "where they have a photographer and a set department and a wardrobe department that picks out clothes for you. This was 'Well what should we do? I didn't bring any clothes!' It felt naughty but nice."[71] Both the *Los Angeles Times* and *The Hollywood Reporter* devoted stories to the re-issue. In a thank-you message to *THR*, she noted, "You keep me young, at least for a few moments."[72]

The picture was Gus Van Sant's movie adaptation of the Tim Robbins novel *Even Cowgirls Get the Blues*. She played beauty ranch manager Miss Adrian, a role for which Faye Dunaway had also been considered. It was not much of a part (she appeared a half hour into the picture, had four scenes, then vanished), but Angie was excited about the project. "When I read the script," she revealed, "I was laughing so hard, because it was all fresh to me. It was just clever, and a very different kind of writing than I'm used to."[73] Working with Van Sant, who had recently written and directed the well-received *Drugstore Cowboy* (1989) and *My Own Private Idaho* (1991), was another attraction. "He's marvelous," she raved. "Gus is very fun, very patient, and also very vague about what he wants. He has a way of suggesting, without actually making specific suggestions. Kind of like Howard Hawks: they don't say much, but they get across what they want—or at least what they don't want."[74]

The plot itself, however, was nothing at all like a Hawks picture. Born with hugely oversized thumbs, Sissy Hankshaw (Uma Thurman) becomes an expert hitchhiker known for the ease and scope of her travels. During a stop in New York City, she meets a flamboyant business mogul known as the Countess (John Hurt), who makes her the model/spokesperson for his feminine hygiene products. When she grows tired of urban life, he sends her to his beauty ranch in Oregon where she is caught between strict overseer Miss Adrian and the band of renegade cowgirls who work there. A showdown between the girls and state law enforcement over a flock of peyote-eating whooping cranes quartered at the ranch prompts her to make some major life decisions.

"It's a lot like the 70s" is how Angie described the film. "Imagery is more important than substance, and there's a lot of wandering around and getting nowhere."[75] As part of her story arc, Sissy has a sexual relationship with one of the cowgirls and is politically awakened to the dangers of male privilege. Neither theme was lost on Angie. "The cowgirls are very sexual but there are no men around. Of course that doesn't change their sexual desires. So like everyone in the 70s, they feast on what's there," she maintained, downplaying the idea of preference.[76] Her take on the feminist message was similarly qualified. As always, she liked the concept of female empowerment as long as it did not conflict with the sexy "one of the boys" image she had worked so hard to sustain. "It's feminist, but

I'd say its funky feminist," she argued. "It's not belligerent, which I find a lot of feminist things are nowadays. It's not angry, so that's a relief."[77] Comments such as these continued to cast her as a bit of a throwback in the eyes of progressive activists.

Taking on character parts in the 90s with style and grace.

Given the film's quirkiness, the cast members differed greatly regarding the tone they tried to set. Thurman went for exaggerated innocence, Hurt opted for high camp, and the cowgirls all read their lines as if reciting a manifesto. As she had in *Pretty Maids All in a Row*, Angie played her character straight, assuming rightly that the more she behaved as if nothing bizarre was happening, the funnier the result would be. The picture premiered in September, 1993, at the Toronto Film Festival to a decidedly unenthusiastic reception. Extensively re-edited over the next few months, it was finally released nationwide in May and again failed to win either critical or commercial approval. Budgeted at $8 million, it earned back less than a quarter of that amount during its domestic run.

While *Even Cowgirls Get the Blues* waited on the shelf, Angie did a guest shot on the short-lived Don Rickles/Richard Lewis sitcom *Daddy Dearest* and then finished out the year tending to various family obligations. On January 17, 1994, at 4:30 a.m., like everyone else in the Los Angeles Basin, she was jolted awake by a 6.7 blind thrust earthquake which came to be known as the Northridge earthquake (although the epicenter was subsequently tracked to Reseda, California). Two 6.0 aftershocks followed, one about a minute after the initial event and a second approximately eleven hours later. Nikki was not in nearby Thousand Oaks at the time but safely away on vacation in Hawaii, and that, ironically, became a problem. "Most geology students study earthquakes because they're part of the course work, but earthquakes are what made Nikki want to study geology in the first place. She loved feeling the power of earthquakes, and she always wished they would happen more often but without all the devastation," Angie explained. "When the Northridge quake—the huge one—hit in '94, she was about to come home from vacation in Hawaii, and she missed it by less than 24 hours. She was devastated."[78]

Always attempting to see things from Nikki's perspective, Angie sympathized, listening intently to her daughter's endless discussion of the missed opportunity and her analysis of each smaller aftershock. Nikki's karate instructor was also understanding. "Thank God for her karate master, Mr. Graham," declared Angie. "He helped her through one of the most difficult times of her life."[79] Burt, however, was having none of it. "I called Angie four or five days later and said, 'How's Nikki doing?'" he recalled. "Angie said, 'She's grieving.' I said, 'Really, who died?' Angie said, 'Nikki's grieving because she missed the earthquake.' I thought they were both crazy and I just couldn't deal with it anymore because nothing I had ever tried to do for Nikki had helped her."[80] Where Angie over-engaged, he withdrew.

Burt's sense of Nikki's decline seemed to gain greater validity as the year progressed. In June, Angie sold her Coldwater Canyon home and moved just a short distance away to Trousdale Estates, a hillside community of expensive mid-century modern houses located within the city of Beverly Hills. Her new residence was a spacious, single-story jewel that had belonged since 1966 to Walter Lantz, founder of one of Hollywood's leading independent animation studios and originator of the Woody Woodpecker cartoon series. Neighbors at one time or another included Nancy Sinatra, Swifty Lazar, producer Sherwood Schwartz, Fred De Cordova, and Sid Caesar. As reported in the *Los Angeles Times*, the 5,000 square foot, two-bedroom property with pool was purchased "for just under its $1.25 million asking price."[81] Sadly, Nikki experienced the new address as a vortex of unbearable environmental noise. Angie recounted, "The worst seemed to start when I moved into a new house in '94 and the helicopters drove her crazy. Helicopters, lawnmowers, motorcycles, leaf blowers, and weed whackers were like a drill in her ear. She just really was suffering. She couldn't get rid of the sounds in her head."[82] Scaling back on her professional commitments, Angie accepted no roles in 1994 and spent almost all of her time with Nikki.

"I finally said to myself, 'You know what, Angie? You cannot live your other life,'" she disclosed. "I finally realized that there was only one way to find real peace for Nikki, and that was to stop doing the 'other things.' Don't go to dinners or functions. Don't play poker. Just pretty much give it up, and I did. It helped. Nikki and I did everything together."[83] They traveled, attended movies, visited restaurants in and around Beverly Hills—whatever Nikki seemed interested in doing. People who saw them together at Directors Guild and Academy of Motion Picture Arts and Sciences screenings noticed Angie's friendliness and the upbeat behavior she evinced around Nikki.

There was also a commitment to director Sydney Pollock to fulfill. She had agreed to appear with Richard Crenna as Greg Kinnear's prospective in-laws in Pollock's remake of the Billy Wilder comedy *Sabrina*, the fairy tale story of a chauffeur's daughter in love with the son of a rich industrialist. Shot during the spring of 1995, it was a prestige project with a big budget and a cast that also included Harrison Ford, Julia Ormond, and Nancy Marchand. Angie had four scenes, each with Crenna, in which she mostly looks on disapprovingly as Kinnear appears to lose interest in her successful doctor daughter. As a former flight attendant who longs for the good old days, she tells Harrison Ford, "I'll bet I could still get your seat in the upright position." Although not a box office hit, it was a fun experience and a reminder of what it was like to work on an expensive, A-list production.

Determined as she was to remain optimistic about life in general, Angie soon felt gloom drifting in like morning haze off the

Pacific. Her two best friends from the Rat Pack days, Dean Martin and Frank Sinatra, were both suffering from ill health. A lifelong smoker, Dean had been diagnosed with lung cancer but had rejected surgical treatment. There were other complications as well. "His kidney. His prostate. His liver. One of them fucking things. Whatever it was, it hurt," wrote Martin biographer Nick Tosches.[84] In touch with both Dean and ex-wife Jeanne throughout his illness, Angie was one of the first people to learn of his passing on Christmas Day, 1995, little more than a week after the opening of *Sabrina*. Three days later, she joined Bob Newhart, Jerry Lewis, Robert Stack, Don Rickles, Rosemary Clooney, and dozens of other celebrities for the funeral at Pierce Brothers cemetery in Westwood. Frank, who was too overwrought to attend, had his own serious medical issues. Hospitalized at various times for heart, lung, and bladder problems, he was also diagnosed as having a form of dementia. After 1997, he made no public appearances and remained secluded within the bedroom, den, and garden of his Beverly Hills home. Angie checked in regularly with Barbara but knew there was no hope for recovery.

On May 14, 1998, Frank died at Cedars-Sinai Medical Center after another heart attack. Now, just like that, they were both gone, the impossibly cool older brother and the never-forgotten swinging boyfriend. The halcyon days, when all three were young, trim, and desired, had become the stuff of nostalgia books and newspaper files. There would be no more group excursions to Vegas, no more parties in Palm Springs.

Frank's funeral, held at the Good Shepherd Roman Catholic Church in Beverly Hills, drew over 400 guests, hordes of fans, and at least a half dozen news helicopters hovering overhead. "The roster of mourners," reported *The New York Times*, "was a casting agent's dream."[85] Among the co-stars, friends, and public figures were Quincy Jones, Jack Jones, Jack Lemmon, Jack Nicholson, Steve Lawrence, Eydie Gormé, Kirk Douglas, Liza Minnelli, Betty Garrett, Tony Bennett, Sidney Poitier, Gregory Peck, Robert Stack, Debbie Reynolds, Robert Wagner, Larry King, Milton Berle, Nancy Reagan, former New York Governor Hugh Carey, and, of course, Angie Dickinson. A skywriting plane traced a giant cross, a valentine heart, and the letters "F.S." in the brilliant blue sky above as Roger Cardinal Mahony told the congregation, "Frank Sinatra recognized the great gift that God had given him with such a splendid voice, and developed that gift for the good of others, bringing joy, relaxation, and hope to countless millions of people around the world."[86] Most of the eulogists aimed for humor as they recalled the good times, the late nights, and the jokes. "It was a little laughs, a lot of love," said Pepe Ruiz, a bartender from Chasen's restaurant. "I would not say it was a funeral. It was all of his friends getting together to say goodbye."[87] Angie and the others agreed although the laughter did not make it any easier to admit that something special about their own lives was gone forever.

True to her pledge, Angie accepted only those work projects during these years that could be fitted around her time with Nikki. None of it was a creative challenge. She made two forgettable films in rapid succession, *The Maddening* (1996) and *The Sun, the Moon and the Stars* (1996), neither of which seemed worthy of her talents. The former was a direct-to-video thriller where she and Burt Reynolds played a crazed couple who hold a young woman and her daughter captive on their farm, convinced the two are long-lost relatives. In the second picture, a young Irish girl, distraught at her parents' separation and isolated by her own fantasies, believes a visiting American marine biologist (Angie) is some kind of modern witch. Other than a chance to reunite with Reynolds and to see some of Ireland, the films offered little more than travel money for her and Nikki.

The made-for-television movies she did included a World War II romance (*Remembrance*), a domestic melodrama dealing with abduction, adultery, incest, and murder (*Deep Family Secrets*), a Mafia comedy (*The Don's Analyst*), and a contemporary romantic drama (*Sealed with a Kiss*). In three of them, she had supporting roles as wife or mother, and in *Deep Family Secrets*, where she shared top billing with frequent co-star Richard Crenna, she was a suspicious wife in peril. To stay engaged she found something rewarding about each project. The Mafia picture reteamed her with Robert Loggia and allowed for the brittle comedy she was getting so good at, the modern romance paired her with old friend Robert Stack and hot young TV actor John Stamos, the melodrama was well mounted, and *Remembrance* had the popular cachet of being adapted from a Danielle Steel novel. She certainly had not found that elusive award-winning role that yet might be out there, but at sixty-five she was still working, still pushing the brand, still showing the rookies how it was done. Few of her contemporaries enjoyed the same enduringly iconic presence, especially on television, that she had.

In 1997, she also made several guest appearances on series TV, roles that required little effort even as they stretched her visibility further. On a fifth season episode of Ellen Degeneres's sitcom, she played a librarian who participates in Civil War reenactments with Ellen's father. Assigned the role of field nurse because "they won't even let me be a prostitute anymore," she danced a jig with Ellen and revealed an unrequited passion for the dad. For her old pal Dick Van Dyke, she guested on his *Diagnosis Murder* series as a no-nonsense police captain helping him investigate the possible framing of a city councilman for the murder of his wife. It was familiar territory, much as if Pepper Anderson had been given a nice promotion and was now in charge of the guys. Then, changing the tone again, she appeared on an episode of the single season Bob Newhart/Judd Hirsch comedy *George and Leo* as a possible love interest for Newhart.

The savviest, most inventive guest shot, however, was as herself on the "Artie, Angie, Hank and Hercules" episode of Garry Shandling's landmark meta-comedy *The Larry Sanders Show*. It knowingly echoed her real-life appearance with Shandling back in 1988 when he guest hosted *The Tonight Show*, a night when she went on with laryngitis, declared she didn't have a chest cold, and he replied, "Let me be the judge of that." In the fictional version, Angie replaces a sick Sigourney Weaver and joins Don Rickles as one of the guests on Larry's talk show. During the on-camera chat, she mentions traveling to Ireland for *The Sun, the Moon and the Stars*. Behind the scenes, Larry's producer Artie (Rip Torn), who admits an obsessive attraction to Angie, has sex with her in the dressingroom and then disappears from the show to accompany her to Venice, Italy. For three days, they stay inside her rented villa and party. "All we've done since we got here is drink wine and screw," says Artie happily. When he insists on watching an Italian language version of Larry's show instead of viewing gondolas from the balcony, she explodes. "You're just a gorgeous woman, Angie, but you've got some problems yourself," he responds defensively. "If *Dressed to Kill* were on right now, you'd be humping the set and crying out, 'Mama Mia.'" Back in L.A., Artie claims to be over his obsession, but when he sees her in a backstage hallway, he loses control, informing Larry that they're flying to Mexico for the weekend.

Playing with her image as sex symbol and talk show tease, Angie gamely handled the self-parody and exaggeration. The show-within-a-show segment caught her coquettish TV personality perfectly, and she proved she could be as self-referentially hip as the dozens of younger celebrities who had agreed to appear on Shandling's program. For someone who had debuted on TV in 1954, she seemed completely at ease with the medium's edgier, more daring content.

As a new decade and a new century commenced, her life continued along the steady, more or less routine, course it had adopted. She visited Mary Lou, spent time with Nikki, and gardened, a hobby which focused and relaxed her. During one of her for-real talk show gigs, she had told Shandling all about the begonias she labored over so diligently. She attended charity events, spoke to various groups about Alzheimer's, and collected the occasional honor. She received a Jack Webb Award from the Los Angeles Police Historical Society, and in 2001, the Hollywood Chamber of Commerce presented her with its Mary Pickford Award, bestowed annually on a person who has made a significant difference in the entertainment industry and the Hollywood community. For her ever tightening circle of friends, she could also still be counted on to celebrate the important personal events. When Gregory Peck's daughter Cecilia married Daniel Voll in September of 2001, she was there along with Lauren Bacall, Barbara Sinatra, Jennifer Jones, Larry Gelbart, and other close family friends.

Acutely aware of Nikki's growing discomfort in Los Angeles, she accompanied her daughter on travels all over the map, anywhere she thought they'd find peace and tranquility. "We loved Tahiti," she recalled. "Nikki went 31 times. She counted them in her passports. It's not only warm and hot there, but it's beautiful and peaceful, so her brain could really have a wonderful few days."[88] It could be an effort traveling with Nikki but the rewards were always worth the trouble. Her own mental acuity and ability to manage stress left her grateful and somewhat guilty when she thought about the afflictions that ravaged the brains of her sister and daughter. The least she could do was take care of a few plane and hotel reservations.

She worked only when she felt the urge, mostly for the stimulation of having something different to do each morning. Exploring a new kind of acting, she did voice work for the animated series *Happily Ever After: Fairy Tales for Every Child*. Her character, in another self-referential nod to Pepper Anderson, was a detective. As a favor, she also made a cameo appearance in *The Last Producer* (2000), a film directed by and starring Burt Reynolds as a washed-up movie producer who seeks Mafia help in financing one last project. Not surprisingly, she was a poker player in a game with James Farentino, Alex Rocco, Shelley Berman, and Shecky Greene. Burt was struggling to stay relevant himself and was grateful to have a little help from his friends. "Angie is one of those rare women you can take anywhere, from a prize fight to a presidential dinner," he raved in his autobiography. "She's always the same: she's just Angie. I think we both felt it was unlucky that she and I were never single at the same time. I think we would have been a great couple: We both liked the same things and we could make each other laugh. To me, that's at the top of the list."[89] There was a lot of laughter on the set although the picture itself ended up on TV and home video rather than in wide theatrical release.

She did four other film projects as well from 2000 to 2001. She played Gwyneth Paltrow's grandmother and Helen Hunt's mother in *Duets* (2000) and *Pay It Forward* (2001) respectively. Both were small parts in off-beat, multiple character films with overlapping storylines. Directed by Bruce Paltrow, Gwyneth's father, *Duets* revolved around various pairs of people who perform in karaoke bars across the country during the week prior to a big contest that brings them together, Robert Altman-style, in Omaha, Nebraska. *Pay It Forward* traced the chain of life-changing actions that occur when characters "pay forward" a favor by helping three other people. Portraying someone's mother was the kind of role she used to say she would never accept, but there wasn't much else out there.

"How does it feel after the glamour career to play a grandmother, I mean, really?" Larry King asked her during an interview aired by CNN on September 19, 2000. "Well, the glamour vanished very slowly—I hope very slowly," she replied. "So, I had time to adjust." As King pressed the issue, she added, "I have not fooled myself about my age. I have tried to fool the public, but I have known the glamour roles would end soon, and I wouldn't embarrass myself by playing them past their time."[90]

The age of her characters aside, both movies had other recommending factors. The casts were first-rate, and *Pay It Forward* gave her another opportunity to work with a successful woman director (Mimi Leder) after a career of no one (excepting *Wild Palms*'s Kathryn Bigelow and *The Sun, the Moon and the Stars*'s Geraldine Creed) but men behind the camera. She appreciated the progress.

For Leder, she didn't just play old; she played old, haggard, and homeless. As Hunt's estranged alcoholic mother, she donned a dreary gray wig and shabby clothes to film on location in a run-down area of Las Vegas. "I was apprehensive about the role because it required me to look god-awful," she confessed. "I was telling my friend Gregory Peck about it and he was ashamed of me for thinking I might not want to do it. He really helped me to feel that it would be okay to just look as awful and true to the character as possible. He was right: This role is a great jumping off point for me to be able to play all the good dramatic roles that my glamour-puss image has worked against."⁹¹ Leder was uncertain whether Angie could make audiences forget the still comely star she was. "I made her read two times for it," said the director. "I should be shot. I know she thinks it's because I wanted to see what she looked like, but it was because this was such a different role from anything she'd ever done. Or anything I've ever seen her in."⁹² By the time Angie was slugging vodka straight from the bottle and slouching around a homeless camp, Leder was more than convinced. "She dug deep," reported her new fan. "She is real and honest, just fantastic."⁹³ Although some critics were not buying what they thought of as Angie's slumming act, most were noncommittal. "An initially unrecognizable Angie Dickinson in a rare non-glam role" is how *Variety*'s Todd McCarthy described her contribution.⁹⁴

She had nothing but compliments for everyone involved in the productions. "Oh, I like her [Paltrow] so much," she told King. "She's just wonderful, and she's brilliantly talented, not just good." Questioned about the rest of the cast, she declared, "Who steals the picture for me is Paul Giamatti" and "Maria Bello is fabulous." She was equally thrilled to be working with Hunt, Haley Joel Osment, Jon Bon Jovi, and Kevin Spacey in *Pay It Forward*, which she called "a real do-good movie, it's wonderful." Later in the same interview, she admitted that being in a movie was a tonic for her. She only worked when something interested her, but once on set she felt a familiar electricity. "I like work," she said, "I really enjoy it. You know, work is almost playtime."⁹⁵

The juiciest part from this period was Mrs. Barlow in *Big Bad Love*, actor/writer/producer/director Arliss Howard's slice-of-life tale of an alcoholic Vietnam vet writer dealing with professional rejection and personal loss. Once again she played an aging matriarch, mother of the writer and grandmother of his two young children, but one who is more than just peripheral to the plot. Leon Barlow is understood largely through the effect he has on others, particularly his wife, his best friend, his children, and his mother. Her parental frustration, disappointment, and concern define how lost he has become. Appearing in just seven brief scenes, Angie deftly created a multi-layered character whose resilience masks a deeper emotional vulnerability. Howard was much impressed with the subtlety of her performance. "No, it's not even her stillness or her humor, but it is the diamond-cutter timing," he disclosed. "It is something to be in a scene with her, watching her take it apart and put it back together again; to cut a scene on her rhythm; and so there is a scene totally reincarnated."[96]

She closed out this period of activity by doing a cameo as a boxing match spectator in Steven Soderbergh's 2001 reboot of *Ocean's Eleven*. George Clooney, Matt Damon, Brad Pitt, Casey Affleck, Bernie Mac, and Don Cheadle took on the main Rat Pack roles of ex-con Danny Ocean and his larcenous pals while Julia Roberts had her old part as Danny's disapproving wife Tess. Henry Silva, another actor from the original, shared Angie's cameo. The Las Vegas hotel names were different and the plot more intricate, but the idea was still to rob multiple casinos on a single night. Even more of a success than its predecessor, the Clooney/Soderbergh version drew big audiences and spawned two sequels. The mantle of coolness, it seemed, was being passed to a new generation.

The shift toward cameos and older character parts was prompting Angie to reflect critically on her screen persona and her interaction with the camera. "I'm surprised by every photograph I see of myself, because I don't look like I used to," she told *Life* magazine. "I'm not shocked anymore, just disappointed. Classical beauty, I never had. But I did look pretty good. I was all heart and sexiness, and that came from within. I had beautiful eyes, and unfortunately in trying to help them, I practically destroyed them with plastic surgery. I wish I looked how I looked before, when I was young."[97] She had also admitted the plastic surgery in an interview with *People*. Although she never showed the distorted features of a Joan Rivers or a Priscilla Presley, she did take on a stretched, somewhat puffy look. As she herself remarked, "I've had some. Anybody can look at me and tell. But people can have too much. The trouble is, usually you don't look better. So you're damned if you do and damned if you don't. That's the bottom line."[98]

Angie's analysis stopped short of any indictment of the systemic way Hollywood limits leading roles for women of a certain age. In fact, she often insisted that she herself preferred to see attractive young people making love on the screen. What might come as she advanced to her seventies, she hoped, would be offers to play more of the dramatically challenging character parts. "I've tried for roles that were a bit non-Angie-ish before, but I didn't get them. Shirley MacLaine, Faye Dunaway or Jane Fonda would get them. But I'm older now and ripe, so I can do anything," she declared optimistically.[99]

Those attention-getting, standout roles, however, did not materialize. Instead, in 2004, she appeared on an episode of the CBS legal drama *Judging Amy* and in director Joel Zwick's black comedy *Elvis Has Left the Building*. The film starred Kim Basinger as a cosmetics saleswoman who accidentally kills a chain of Elvis impersonators as they travel to a Las Vegas convention; in keeping with the new trend, Angie played Basinger's mother, a former mechanic for the real Elvis. Funnier in concept than in execution, the picture made little impact, remembered, if at all, by trivia buffs for Tom Hanks's cameo as one of the dead Elvises.

Overshadowing career considerations was the dramatically declining health of both Mary Lou and Nikki. "You don't do well with Alzheimer's," Angie later confided to Larry King. "You just get worse and worse."[100] As she lingered on at the Sunland facility, Mary Lou became almost nonresponsive. "It was horrible to watch her be afflicted. You know, I would sometimes just break down crying," she added.[101] Knowing the ultimate outcome of the disease, Angie and Mary Lou's children wished only for a peaceful end to her suffering. "You pray for the good-bye to come as soon as possible," she said.[102] That farewell came when Mary Lou passed away in December of 2005, more than two decades after she had first been diagnosed with the disease. As was her life, the memorial service was modest. Angie later eulogized her sister to King as "absolutely wonderful. She was gorgeous. She was loving. She was gentle. She was a tender soul."[103] With Mary Lou clearly in mind, Angie would continue to lobby lawmakers on behalf of increased funding for Alzheimer's research and treatment.

When King asked her what advice she would give family members of Alzheimer's patients, she answered, "I would say love them, and I don't mean just love them with your soul and your head, love them with your arms and your company and your touch and whatever pleasure might still be there for them. And don't ever let up. Just stay as close as possible. Comforting them all the way because they're lost."[104] That unconditional love was the wise recommendation she applied to her own relationship with Nikki. Shaken by the loss of her older sister, she clung even more tightly to her daughter. "In 2006, we went to Alaska, Las Vegas, Russia, and Paris," she remarked. "We had melted cheese sandwiches with French fries every night at the top of the Eiffel Tower, and we'd laugh and say, 'This French food is great.'"[105] It was their own private movie, their own travelogue comedy.

Except that Nikki could not shake her dark moods. For some time, she had become worried about what would happen to her if Angie were gone. "Nikki couldn't bear the thought of my death," she remembered. "I asked her once about it when it became so overwhelming for her, and she said, 'When you turned 70, I realized it could happen.' It hit her hard—the realization she could lose me and be left alone without somebody who cared about her or knew her needs."[106] The fear of losing her mother added to the vision and noise problems, making her life a constant agonizing struggle.

Despite Angie's heartfelt attention, she continued on a downward spiral. "She talked a lot about suicide. She was very open about it, even to people she didn't know well," said Angie. "She read *Final Exit*, a book about planning suicide, and she found asphyxiation was the most peaceful way she could do it—like going under anesthesia at the dentist."[107] Clearly, Nikki was serious about taking her own life, and Angie felt powerless to combat her depression. Neither serious discussion nor joking had much impact. In a bantering tone, Angie asked, "Nikki, what would my life be without you in it?" and her daughter replied, "Oh, you will be laughing on the phone and telling jokes and playing poker before you know it."[108] There was a sad yet assured finality to the comment that Angie recognized only too well. It was that single-minded focus on a newly forged idea that Nikki had displayed since childhood. Angie felt unable to convince Nikki how much she was loved and valued.

On Christmas Eve, a year after Mary Lou's passing, she and Nikki went to church services together. "Nikki had always wanted to sing like most people, but she really couldn't, maybe because singing is so much about bringing out what's inside you," Angie explained. That night, however, she noticed that Nikki was singing joyously and without restraint. "I could hardly hear her over everybody else," she added, "but when I looked at her, I smiled at how much gusto she had singing those Christmas songs."[109] Several days later, on Thursday, January 4, 2007, Nikki placed a plastic bag over her head, filled it with nitrous oxide from a tube, and asphyxiated herself. According to Burt Bacharach's assistant and road manager Sue Main, "She basically fell unconscious and died. She suffocated after knocking herself out with the nitrous."[110]

Burt himself was in the hospital recovering from shoulder surgery. As soon as Main told him the news, they drove up to Angie's house, where the two bereaved parents discussed arrangements, newspaper announcements, and donations in Nikki's name. There would be a cremation and no service. To spare Angie the pain, Main went to the mortuary to pick up Nikki's belongings. Among the items was a sealed letter to Burt, which already had been opened by the time Main arrived. "It's a couple of pages long and a very hateful thing," she explained, full of angry recriminations over Nikki's placement at the clinic in Minnesota.[111] Sensing the hurt it would cause, Burt's new wife Jane decided to keep it stashed away out of sight. "I already knew what the letter would say and I didn't want to hear it or read it," Burt said.[112] Despite her later request, he also firmly denied Angie's wish to see the letter.

In lieu of a service, Angie created a memorial booklet with photos and a prose poem. She wrote, "Nikki loved yellow and pink, and bright blue skies with white puffy clouds. She loved scuba diving, and pushing the limits." The conclusion read, "Nikki put on quite a show when she was here on *this* earth. She was not understood by most, but loved and appreciated by a precious few. And now she's finally happy. Her Mom."[113] The notice in the *Los Angeles Times* included a similarly toned statement from the family that Nikki "loved kittens, and earthquakes, glacial calving, meteor showers, and Tahiti. She was one of the most beautiful creatures created on this earth, and she is now in the white light, at peace."[114] Donations in Nikki's name were directed to the non-profit Lange Foundation, a cat rescue organization in West Los Angeles.

Although both the poem and the press release suggested a belief that Nikki had found some kind of afterlife spiritual peace, Angie still felt she could have made things better while she was alive. "In my view," she said, "I could have done so much more but it took me a long time to understand that for Nikki, there were no earthly solutions. Most people can fix what problems they have, but Nikki did not have that gift."[115] Surrounded by photos and mementos, she felt the loss of her daughter intensely. The young woman who had become her nearly constant companion was now gone, not on a quick trip to Tahiti but irrevocably.

"*What greater grief can there be for mortals than to see their children dead?* Euripides said that. *When we talk about mortality we are talking about our children.* I said that," wrote author Joan Didion, whose own daughter Quinta Roo died at age thirty-nine, just a year younger than Nikki.[116] "There is no drawer I can open without seeing something I do not want, on reflection, to see," she continued. "I no longer want reminders of what was, what got broken, what got lost, what got wasted."[117] It was the same for Angie. There were reminders everywhere—the pool where Nikki swam, the room where she slept, the possessions she had stored for safekeeping. The fact that Nikki had been born prematurely and had died prematurely was evidence of everything that Angie herself could not fix, an unspooling of fate beyond her control.

Always a go-to remedy, work held little balm for her now. She would appear in only one more picture, a 2009 Hallmark made-for-television production called *Mending Fences*. It was, fittingly enough, all about mothers and daughters, three generations of women overcoming their differences to pursue a common cause. Accompanied by her teenage daughter, a television reporter returns to the small town where her own mother Ruth (Angie) is fighting a casino development that threatens to destroy the family ranch. By story's end, the reporter has proved that the casino builder is stealing the town's water, has regained her mother's trust, and has decided to remain on the homestead.

In a further connection of personal dots, Angie gave her character the same resilience and strength of the country women she had known as a child in North Dakota. Plagued by failing eyesight, Ruth refuses to sell the ranch but continues, as feisty and independent as ever, to run the operation with the help of a single loyal foreman. There was no attempt to either gild or deglamorize the part; it was Angie the way she looked in real life. With the whispery voice turned hoarse, some puffiness in the face, and a slight hunch to the shoulders, she moved a little more slowly but could still ride a horse and still work magic with her smile. The reviewer for *The New York Times* said, "At 78 she still has an odd and beguiling incongruity—a seductress with an enigmatic, ladylike reserve."[118] The plot may have been entirely predictable but she made Ruth credible and sympathetic. Channeling the same frustration she had witnessed in Mary Lou, she lashes out angrily when her diminished vision makes it impossible for her to find an important document on her desk. Assigned a cane by the doctor, she uses it to slap at various men who get in her way. When the mayor attempts to silence her daughter at a town council meeting, she fires a gun into the air and calmly announces, "I am a blind lady with a gun, so you just need to sit there, be quiet, and listen to what my daughter has to say."

The final scene is particularly poignant. Angie and Laura

Leighton, playing her daughter Kelly, sit on the back porch and gaze into the rolling hills of Thousand Oaks, California, site of the ranch's location filming and home to the university where Nikki had happily studied geology. Angie looks at the sunset, grasps her daughter's hand, and declares, "I love you." It was her last line of dialogue, an affirmation of a mother's enduring love for her daughter that must have served as a kind of personal testament as well.

Earlier in the film, her character Ruth remarks, "Don't let anyone swindle you into thinking growing old is any fun." That was another belief that Angie shared. "A lot of us got older all at once," she told the *Los Angeles Times*'s Susan King that same year.[119] Indeed, friends like Jeanne Martin and Barbara Sinatra were either showing their years or, like Jack Lemmon, Johnny Carson, Gregory Peck, and Larry Gelbart, gone altogether. She saw those who remained as often as she could and also spent time with her sister Janet. There were even occasional dinners with Burt, who claimed in his admirably candid autobiography, "I am now on good terms with all three of my ex-wives."[120] Angie's feelings toward her second husband would remain complicated. As late as 2019, she told Mo Rocca that she had "liked him a lot" but knew that "he never loved me . . . the way one loves" but "loved in his own way, which is not too good."[121]

She neither withdrew into seclusion nor, like Marlene Dietrich in her late seventies, attempted one last glamour shot. She kept doing what she'd always done, just a little less frequently. She attended a Paley Center program on "The Evolution of the Crime Drama" and the "Made in Hollywood Awards," where Los Angeles councilman Tom LaBonge announced, "I asked Angie Dickinson to join me for this occasion because, in addition to her beauty and talents, she exemplifies the determination to bring production back to its home. At her insistence, all episodes of her long-running *Police Woman* series were made locally rather than a previously determined out-of-state location."[122] Never mind that the shooting decision was based on family imperatives, she was still a civic favorite, practically a native, and proud to be recognized. She often appeared at these events wearing dark pants, a dark sweater, and a simple black trilby atop her eternally blond hair.

She also talked freely about the work she had done. This was different from tabloid biography, where her personal life was usually defined by the men she had known—Frank Sinatra's girlfriend, Jack Kennedy's lover, Burt Bacharach's wife. The work was hers. She traveled to Texas to discuss *Rio Bravo* with the Austin Film Society and appeared on stage in San Francisco with Eddie Muller to reminisce about *The Killers*.

She didn't gossip or glorify herself. She had nothing but praise for her directors and co-stars, nothing but accolades for John Wayne, Lee Marvin, Dean Martin, Kirk Douglas, and all the other Hollywood icons with whom she'd shared the screen.

It was, as everyone who knew her had come to expect, the classy thing to do.

The Films

Apprenticeship

Lucky Me

Credits: A Warner Bros. production released on April 9, 1954. WarnerColor and CinemaScope. Running time of 100 minutes. Based on an original idea by James O'Hanlon. **Cast:** Doris Day (Candy Williams), Robert Cummings (Dick Carson), Phil Silvers (Hap Schneider), Eddie Foy, Jr. (Duke McGee), Nancy Walker (Flo Neely), Martha Hyer (Lorraine Thayer), Bill Goodwin (Otis Thayer), Marcel Dalio (Anton), Hayden Rorke (Tommy Arthur), James Burke (Mahoney). **Crew:** Jack Donohue (director), Irving Elinson, Robert O'Brien, and James O'Hanlon (screenwriters), Henry Blanke (producer), Ray Heindorf and Howard Jackson (composers), Wilfrid M. Cline (cinematographer), Owen Marks (editor), John Beckman (art director), William Wallace (set decorator), Moss Mabry (costume designer), Gordon Bau (makeup artist), Check Hansen (assistant director), David Forrest and Oliver S. Garretson (sound).

Plot Synopsis: When entertainers Candy, Flo, Hap, and Duke are stranded in Miami, they must pay for a meal by working in the kitchen of an expensive hotel. Staying at the hotel is a young songwriter named Dick who is developing a new production and looking for a backer. Everyone except Candy realizes who Dick is and hopes to be a part of his show. Prospects look good when Otis Thayer, a wealthy oilman, expresses an interest in sponsoring Dick.

Thinking that Dick is a mechanic employed in the hotel's garage, Candy agrees to go on a date, and the two of them quickly discover a romantic attraction to each other. After Hap reveals Dick's true identity, Candy feels she has been used, but is appeased when offered a leading part in the show. Thayer's spoiled daughter Lorraine becomes jealous and threatens to have her father's money withdrawn if Candy gets the role.

To circumvent Lorraine, the four friends arrange a birthday party for Thayer. In disguise, they perform Dick's new songs and convince Thayer to back the show. Lorraine ends up dunked in the swimming pool, and Dick and Candy end up on their way to Broadway.

Notes and Comments: Angie made her feature film debut as one of the uncredited birthday party guests. Her one line is "Happy Birthday, Otis." Joining her were Lucy Marlow, Dolores Dorn, Perk Lazelle, Gladys Hurlbut, and future *I Dream of Jeannie* co-star Emmaline Henry. Warner Bros. produced the picture but would not be interested enough to offer Angie a long term contract until several years later.

Just as Angie was having her first experience with the studio, star Doris Day was having one of her last. She would make only one more film there under her own multi-year agreement. Although the two actresses had little on-set interaction, they later became friends, with Angie even taping a public service announcement for the Doris Day Animal Foundation in the 80s.

Reminiscent of the Warner Bros. backstage musicals of the 30s (imagine Dick Powell and Ruby Keeler in the Cummings and Day parts), the plot was little more than a vehicle for some forgettable songs by Sammy Fain and Paul Francis Webster.

Reviews:

"*Lucky Me* is a routine musical that will have to depend almost entirely on the name of Doris Day to sell tickets."

"The screenplay by James O'Hanlon, Robert O'Brien and Irving Elinson is a network of rather tired, and often tiresome, gags and situations that display little originality or fresh imagination."

"While the settings take well to the CinemaScope treatment, the players do not and many of the scenes show the principals in an unflattering manner."

—*Daily Variety*, April 9, 1954

"*Lucky Me* is a big, loosely-knit mildly amusing musical with the names of Doris Day, Robert Cummings and Phil Silvers to add box office value."

"Miss Day's stereotyped role calls for little but flouncing around petulantly, every now and then shading the characterization with a pretty scowl. She also has sung better in the past."

"Wilfrid M. Cline's photography is good, attractively embellished by the use of CinemaScope and WarnerColor hues. Sets by John Beckman and musical direction by Ray Heindorf are plus factors."

—Milton Luban, *The Hollywood Reporter*, April 9, 1954

"I was especially pleased to note that Donohue was not unduly awed by the potentially cumbersome dimensions of CinemaScope. He has kept the camera and foreground movement fluid and his backgrounds, mostly of Miami, pictorial."

—Philip K. Scheuer, *Los Angeles Times*, April 22, 1954

"Jack Donohue has come up with a capable directing job, using CinemaScope to its full advantage. Few scenes drag and the over-all package has a nice pace. Teenagers will like this one. They possibly might not identify the story line with a dozen or so musicals out of the past."

—Russ Burton, *Los Angeles Daily News*, April 22, 1954

Tennessee's Partner

Credits: A Filmcrest/Benedict Bogeaus production released by RKO Radio Pictures on September 21, 1955. Technicolor and SuperScope. Running time of 87 minutes. Based on the short story "Tennessee's Pardner" by Bret Harte. **Cast:** John Payne (Tennessee), Ronald Reagan (Cowpoke), Rhonda Fleming (Elizabeth "Duchess" Farnham), Coleen Gray (Goldie Slater), Anthony Caruso (Turner), Morris Ankrum (Judge Parker), Leo Gordon (the sheriff), Chubby Johnson (Grubstake McNiven), Joe Devlin (Prendergast). **Crew:** Allan Dwan (director), Milton Krims, D.D. Beauchamp, Graham Baker, and Teddi Sherman (screenwriters), Benedict Bogeaus (producer), Louis Forbes (composer), John Alton (cinematographer), James Leicester (editor), Van Nest Polglase (art director), Alfred Spencer (set decorator), Gwen Wakeling (costume designer), Mel Berns (makeup artist), Shirley Madden (hair stylist), Nate Watt (assistant director), Terry Kellum and Jean Speak (sound).

Plot Synopsis: Rakish gambler Tennessee is playing high-stakes poker in a bawdy house run by the Duchess. While her girls entertain customers, Tennessee wins the entire roll bet by a prospector names Clifford, who accuses him of cheating and threatens gun play. That same evening, another old-time prospector, Grubstake McNiven, announces that he has found gold and asks wealthy town boss Turner to lend him money for a final stake that will prove his claim. After Turner callously refuses, Tennessee stakes him with money he has won from Turner in the card game.

At dawn the next day, Clifford ambushes Tennessee and is about to shoot him when Cowpoke, a stranger just arriving in town, intervenes and shoots Clifford dead instead. Both Tennessee and Cowpoke are arrested but Duchess and her girls testify as "eyewitnesses" that the killing was in self-defense. Released, Tennessee and Cowpoke become good friends and room together, with Cowpoke confiding that he is on his way to nearby Sacramento to meet and marry a woman named Goldie. Accompanying his new friend to the riverboat dock, Tennessee recognizes Goldie as a duplicitous former flame who admits she is planning another swindle. Cowpoke gives her $5,000 as a token of his commitment, and Tennessee arranges for her to stay with the Duchess, who also realizes she is a gold digging cheat.

To eliminate competition, Turner hires a card-shark named Reynolds to play poker with Tennessee and then shoot him. When Tennessee wins over $50,000 in a masterful bluff, Reynolds accuses him of crooked dealing and pulls his gun. Faster on the draw, Tennessee kills his would-be assassin instead.

To protect Cowpoke, Tennessee pretends to have feelings for Goldie, proposing that they pool their money and elope to San Francisco. At the dock, he abandons her and retrieves Cowpoke's money. Unaware of the truth, Cowpoke is devastated by what he thinks is a betrayal and vows to shoot Tennessee on sight. Now broke, Cowpoke returns to prospecting and helps Grubstake, who has struck gold, to map out his claim on a piece of cloth kept under his shirt.

In town, Grubstake celebrates his discovery, drinks too much champagne, and passes out at Tennessee's house. To square things with his friend, Tennessee rides out to the mine where Cowpoke challenges him to a showdown, and he replies that he is unarmed. Cowpoke attacks with his fists instead but Tennessee refuses to fight back. Badly beaten, he hands over the $5,000, and Cowpoke slowly realizes what his friend has done for him. The two partners are reunited.

Duchess arrives to share the news that Grubstake was murdered and that Tennessee is the prime suspect. Hurrying to Grubstake's claim, they find Turner, the real murderer, trying to steal the rights. Turner shoots and kills Cowpoke, before Tennessee pummels him and hands him over to the sheriff. In the conclusion, Tennessee and Duchess are married and leave town for San Francisco.

Notes and Comments: This was the first of some fifteen feature and made-for-TV Westerns that Angie would make. She is one of the Duchess's girls, essentially a prostitute but referred to vaguely as an in-house escort. Although uncredited, she appears in nine scenes scattered throughout the picture and has four full lines of dialogue. "I haven't seen any man I'd like to marry," she tells the others, and then claims, "I didn't see anything" when the crowd gathers after Clifford's shooting. Outside the jail, she promises "See you tonight, boys" and introduces herself to Goldie with "Hello, I'm Abby Dean." Still a brunette at the time, she is seen mostly in medium long shot with her hands perched on her waist. Even with the smile and the assertive posture, there is little to distinguish her from the rest of the bordello girls.

Directed by silent film veteran Allan Dwan, *Tennessee's Partner* was among the final films released by RKO before the studio finally closed down production in 1957. It was one of seven consecutive pictures that Dwan, producer Benedict Bogeaus, and cinematographer John Alton made together between 1954 and 1956, each noted for vivid Technicolor compositions and atmospheric lighting. It has been cited occasionally as the film where John Payne slaps Rhonda Fleming and she responds, "Big girls don't cry," thus inspiring the hit tune by the Four Seasons. That scene actually appears in *Slightly Scarlet*, another Dwan-Bogeaus-Alton collaboration.

Reviews:

"The Milton Krims-D. D. Beauchamp screenplay from a Harte story, located in a California gold rush boomtown, nicely captures the lusty flavor and atmosphere of the era. Characters and situations are familiar, but director Allan Dwan moves things along at a brisk pace. Of further assistance are the authentic appearing frontier sets and period costumes which cameraman John Alton ably catches in Eastman Color via Tushinsky widescreen SuperScope. (Print is by Technicolor)."

"Payne registers handily as the gambler, Reagan scores as his two-fisted, hard fighting friend, while Miss Fleming is more than decorative as proprietress of the frontier pleasure palace."

—*Daily Variety*, September 28, 1955

"The picture has been beautifully and expensively mounted, shot in Technicolor and SuperScope with the expert direction of an old hand on stories of this type, Allan Dwan, which together with a good cast headed by John Payne and Rhonda Fleming, rounds out a very acceptable piece of film fare."

"Dwan has a grasp on western stories that few other directors possess, resulting in his moving the players and the action most satisfactorily, and the camera work by John Alton is superb as is the musical score and conducting by Louis Forbes and the special song number, 'Heart of Gold,' he authored with Dave Franklin."

—*The Hollywood Reporter*, September 28, 1955

"The settings and costumes are interesting, the photography is good, and easy-to-please patrons of Wester films should find little fault with this filmization of the noted Bret Harte story."

—*Hollywood Citizen-News,* September 29, 1955

The Return of Jack Slade

Credits: A Lindsley Parsons Picture Corporation production released by Allied Artists on October 9, 1955. Black and white and SuperScope. Running time of 79 minutes. **Cast:** John Ericson (Jack Slade, Jr.), Mari Blanchard (Texas Rose), Neville Brand (Harry Sutton), Max Showalter (Billy Wilcox), Jon Shepodd (Johnny Turner), Howard Petrie (Joseph Ryan), John Dennis (Kid Stanley), Angie Dickinson (Polly Logan), Donna Drew (Laughing Sam), Mike Ross (Little Blue Raven), Lyla Graham (Abilene), Alan Wells (George Hagen), Raymond Bailey (Professor). **Crew:** Harold Schuster (director), Warren Douglas (screenwriter), Lindsley Parsons (producer), Paul Dunlap (composer), William Sickner (cinematographer), Maurice Wright (editor), A. Leslie Thomas (art director), Morris Hoffman (set decorator), Pat Whiffing (hair stylist), Glen Alden (makeup artist), Lindsley Parsons Jr. (assistant director), Tom Lambert (sound).

Plot Synopsis: Pinkerton detective Joseph Ryan hires gunslinger Jack Slade, Jr. as a guard for the agency. Adept with a Colt revolver, Slade is the son of a famous hired gun who worked for Wells Fargo. His first assignment is to gather information on a large band of Wyoming outlaws led by Billy Wilcox. Among the 25 gang members are a ruthless killer named Sutton and his loyal friend Little Blue; also in the group are the tough-talking women Texas Rose, Polly, Abilene, and Laughing Sam.

The train Slade is taking to Wyoming is robbed by the outlaws, and Texas Rose manages to steal Slade's prized gun. Re-armed and accompanied by Johnny Turner, a young man who worships him, Slade rides into the gang's mountain hideout, where he challenges Sutton to a gun fight. Although Sutton backs down, he cold-bloodedly murders Johnny. Slade and Texas Rose, who wants to leave the gang, fall in love even as Slade vows revenge against Sutton.

With the help of Ryan, Slade sets a trap for the outlaws. Attempting to pull off a second train robbery, they are surprised and decimated. In a mismatched duel, Slade kills both Sutton and Little Blue. Texas Rose is wounded as she tries to reach Slade. Carrying her on his own horse, Slade rides toward Cheyenne to get medical help.

Notes and Comments: As Polly, Angie had her first credited part and the first of her many bad girl roles. Costumed in jeans, boots, and plaid blouses, she is one of the callous female gang members with no backstory nor character arc to distinguish her from the others. Mari Blanchard, whose abbreviated twelve-year career never progressed far beyond B-pictures, has the more substantial part.

Based on popular lore surrounding Wyoming's Hole in the Wall gang, the film takes the historically inaccurate liberty of adding women outlaws to the mix. Known alternately as *Jack Slade Junior*, the movie is a sequel to *Jack Slade* (1953), which told the father's story and starred Mark Stevens and Dorothy Malone. Both pictures were written by Warren Douglas, produced by Lindsley Parsons, and directed by Harold Schuster.

Reviews:
"Producer Lindsley Parsons came through with a film that will fit well into the intended market. Direction by Harold Schuster concentrates well on the action elements, while Maurice Wright's edit-

ing is smooth. Camera work of William Sickner and other technical contributions are standard."

"Score by Paul Dunlap features 'Yellow Rose of Texas,' a current hit and an exploitable item."

—*Daily Variety*, October 5, 1955

"This is a surprisingly good low-budget western. The kind that sometimes makes the second half of a double bill better than the first. The talent departments of all the major studios should have a look at it, for its leading man, John Ericson, in addition to a fine physique, has a brooding truculence that reminds one of Marlon Brando and James Dean. He injects into even his passive moments, a sense of suspense that makes celluloid come alive."

"The direction by Harold Schuster is much better than usually is found in this sort of production."

"The photography of authentic locations, ably done by William Sickner, presents a refreshing change from over-familiar back-lot western streets."

—Jack Moffitt, *The Hollywood Reporter*, October 5, 1955

Man with the Gun

Credits: A Formosa Productions picture released by United Artists on November 5, 1955. Black and white. Running time of 84 minutes. **Cast:** Robert Mitchum (Clint Tollinger), Jan Sterling (Nelly Bain), Karen Sharpe (Stella Atkins), Henry Hull (Marshal Lee Sims), Emile Meyer (Saul Atkins), John Lupton (Jeff Castle), Barbara Lawrence (Ann Wakefield), Ted de Corsia (Frenchy Lescaux), Leo Gordon (Ed Pinchot), James Westerfield (Mr. Zender), Claude Akins (Jim Reedy, uncredited), Angie Dickinson (Kitty, uncredited). **Crew:**

Richard Wilson (director and screenwriter), N.B. Stone Jr. (screenwriter), Samuel Goldwyn Jr. (producer), Alex North (composer), Lee Garmes (cinematographer), Gene Milford (editor), Hilyard Brown (art director), Edward G. Boyle (set decorator), Jane Romeyn (hair stylist), Don Cash (makeup artist), Sid Sidman (assistant director), Anthony Carras and John Keane (sound).

Plot Synopsis: Cattle baron Dade Holman "owns" Sheridan City, buying up property and allowing his henchmen to terrorize the residents. In the opening scene, a Holman gunslinger named Ed Pinchot rides into town and shoots a little boy's dog for barking at his horse. Another man arriving in Sheridan is Clint Tollinger, who is quickly recognized as a famous "town tamer," a hired gun who cleans up lawless communities.

When Holman's thugs try to burn the property of young farmer Jeff Castle and then wound him in a shooting ambush, the town council, led by blacksmith Saul Atkins, decides it has had enough. Shamed by the town's 14 murders and 31 robberies in the past year and by Marshal Lee Sims's failure to confront Holman, they agree to pay Tollinger $500 to bring some order to the place. Immediately after he is deputized, Tollinger warns two Holman gunmen, wanted for crimes in other territories, to leave town and posts an order that weapons are now prohibited anywhere within the city limits. To prove his point, he takes away the Bowie knife used by Frenchy Lescaux, manager of Holman's Palace Saloon, and fatally shoots one of the outlaws who has ignored his warning to leave town.

Tollinger's relationship with the residents is also rocky. Jeff Castle resents his interference, and Castle's fiancée Stella, the daughter of council leader Atkins, fears that he may be a harmful influence on the town. Tollinger's major interest, however, lies in Nelly Bain, who runs a house for the dancehall girls working at the

Palace. After several unsuccessful efforts, he finally sees her, renewing a previous relationship between the two of them and asking about the welfare of a young girl named Beth.

Testing the new gun law, Holman sends four of his men to town. Pretending to disarm, one of them draws a holstered pistol, and Tollinger shoots him dead. Reedy, the leader, tries to pull a fast one by reaching for a gun hidden in his hat, but Tollinger kills him as well.

At a strawberry festival, Tollinger dances with Stella while Castle continues to insist rudely that he can fight his own battles. One of the town matrons advises the new deputy that he should rid Sheridan of the immoral saloon dancers. Tollinger informs Nelly that she and the girls are subject to the midnight curfew he has imposed, and she says they will be leaving town soon anyway.

Ed Pinchot and a crony ride into town to tell Tollinger they have detained Castle for trespassing and suggest picking him up at Holman's ranch. Instead, Tollinger arrests both men for carrying guns and then exchanges them for a still ungrateful Castle. That night Tollinger again visits Nelly; their conversation reveals that they are married but that Nelly left him because of his profession. She also tells him that their daughter Beth has died of pneumonia. Reacting badly, he burns down the Palace and kills Lescaux when he tries to knife him in the back.

Holman's lawyer Mr. Zender, who has pretended to be a traveling salesman, plans an ambush for Tollinger. Both Pinchot and Holman himself stalk Tollinger through town, waiting for him to be distracted unwittingly by one of the dancehall girls. Having learned of Zender's true identity, Nelly tries to warn her husband. In the end, Tollinger kills Pinchot but is wounded in the shoulder by Holman, who is then shot and killed by Jeff Castle. Nelly and Tollinger, who pledges to change careers, kiss and agree to start a new life together.

Notes and Comments: As in *Tennessee's Partner*, Angie is again one of the saloon girls but with more screen time and more dialogue. Two of her seven scenes are significant, an opening one which establishes the relationship between Nelly and the ladies and a later one where her character Kitty leaves town on the stage. Not mentioned in the credits, she is seen mostly in group compositions and in two-shots or three-shots as photographed by Lee Garmes, one of Marlene Dietrich's favorite cameramen when they both worked at Paramount.

Angie (seated) is one of Nelly Bain's saloon girls in *Man with the Gun* (1955).

Of all the girls, she stands out the most, managing to project a unique and animated personality. She doesn't just unload her lines but directs them as part of a naturally paced interchange she has followed with her eyes and gestures as well. "I'm very fond of Ed Pinchot," she tells the others mischievously. "We had a perfectly divine dance last night except he didn't take off his shoulder holster." In another scene, she does leg stretches while joking that no one is really listening when a pretty blond performer sings. Working the far left side of the chorus line, she does some high kicks and skirt lifts in a credible facsimile of saloon dancing.

The picture was also a qualitative step-up with its strong production values and a talented crew that included Garmes, composer Alex North, producer Goldwyn, and first-time director Wilson, who had been closely associated with Orson Welles and the Mercury Theatre. A stylistic high note is the suspenseful cross-cutting between six different principals during the climax. Above all, it was another money-making vehicle for Robert Mitchum after such earlier successes as *Crossfire* (1947), *Out of the Past* (1947), *River of No Return* (1954), and *Not as a Stranger* (1955).

By all accounts, Mitchum, who was known for his scandalous bad boy behavior, was a model of professionalism during production. "Mitch never gave anyone a bad moment," said director Wilson. "He was never late for work, and he stuck right to his knitting. He worked very hard to bring the picture through on schedule."[1] Mitchum even did his own stunt work during the saloon fire scene, staying inside a bit too long and emerging singed and smoking around the edges.

Reviews:

"As the first directorial effort of writer Richard Wilson (it is also the first production of Samuel Goldwyn, Jr.), *Man With the Gun* struck me as real sharp during the opening sequences—stark photography by Lee Garmes, some clever vignettes of the townsfolk. But it soon

drifted into the talkative type of thing, punctuated too seldom by action, that passes so often today for the off-beat in oaters."
—Philip K. Scheuer, *Los Angeles Times*, December 1, 1955

"Director Richard Wilson has given *Man with the Gun* a brooding, intense solidity akin to *High Noon* and *Shane*. Wilson and N. B. Stone Jr. wrote the screenplay and Alex North did the music."

"Much of the film's dramatic power results from Lee Garmes' splendid photography and a top job of editing by Gene Milford."
—Fred W. Fox, *Mirror-News*, December 1, 1955

"*Man with the Gun* (Goldwyn Jr., United Artists) has all the splendid cardboard heroics of the classic western."
—*Time*, December 5, 1955

"Jan Sterling gives a well sustained characterization as the Madame who was the hero's wife until his way of life and the death of their daughter embittered her. All of the girls in her establishment catch an accurate ring of floozy humor. Henry Hull is good as a downhearted town marshal. And there are a dozen well-drawn minor characters. Alex North's score, conducted by Emile Newman, is another element in a production job that bodes well for all concerned."
—Jack Moffitt, *The Hollywood Reporter*, October 10, 1955

"The story is good, excepting a few pretensions, the acting is exactly right to lift it above the oater level, and Richard Wilson's direction of the screen story he wrote with N. B. Stone, Jr., keeps tension right up to the climax."

"Mitchum portrays the character most effectively, capturing the flavor of an old-time, Max Brand-type of western gunman-hero."

"While it is mainly a male show, the femmes get their opportunities aplenty and do very well by them. Miss Sterling comes over excellently and Karen Sharpe scores in standout fashion as a town girl engaged to hothead John Lupton. Barbara Lawrence, one of the dance girls, counts attractively as the pigeon who abortively sets up Mitchum for a finale kill. There are a number of other lovelies well-seen in the footage."

—*Daily Variety*, October 10, 1955

Down Liberty Road

Credits: A Jerry Fairbanks Productions/Greyhound Lines production released on July 3, 1956. Eastmancolor. Running time of 35 minutes. **Cast:** Marshall Thompson (Mysterious Stranger), Angie Dickinson (Mary), Charles Maxwell (Bill Roberts), Morris Ankrum (Fred Schroder), Tommy Kirk (Jimmy Rollins), Tex Ritter (himself). **Crew:** Arnold Schuster (director), Leo S. Rosencrans and Charles L. Tedford (screenwriters), Jerry Fairbanks (producer), Edward Paul (music supervisor), Jerry Fairbanks (cinematographer), Milton Kleinberg (editor), Theobold Holsopple (art director), Robert Scrivner (assistant director).

Plot Synopsis: As a shiny new Greyhound Scenicruiser bus travels from San Francisco to New York, various passengers interact with each other and with important historical sites along the way. Eagle Scout Jimmy Rollins, headed for a jamboree in Washington, D.C., receives a series of educational mini-lessons from helpful fellow travelers. Among the people sharing information with him are a vacationing married couple, a Philadelphia Eagles football player named Bill Roberts, and a mysterious stranger who seems to know a lot about all the people and all the places. The other passengers include Mary, a pretty young secretary on her way home after visiting family out west, and Fred Schroder, a bitter older man who makes disparaging comments about the government and his fellow citizens. His sorrow, the stranger explains, stems from the loss of his only son in the Korean War.

Excited by what he is seeing from the bus, Jimmy learns about the California Gold Rush, the Pony Express, and the Great Chicago Fire of 1871. At one point, Tex Ritter comes on board and sings "Remember the Alamo" to help explain the Texas Revolution. During the voice-over narrations, there are historical reenactments and documentary travel footage. When the bus reaches Philadelphia, the mysterious stranger gives an extended lesson on the Boston Tea Party, the Continental Congress, and the signing of the Declaration of Independence.

While Jimmy is studying history, Bill Roberts and Mary are falling in love. Even though she is planning to marry Waldo, her successful and straight-laced boss, Bill reminds her that in America a woman is free to change her mind. As the journey continues, the two of them keep realizing how much they have in common. Leaving the bus in Philadelphia, Bill kisses her passionately and she slaps him for his "football manners."

The mysterious stranger also makes a premature departure in Pennsylvania, convincing Schroder to accompany him on a detour to Gettysburg. After a reenactment of Lincoln's famous address, the stranger reveals himself to be the spirit of all Americans who have died for their country. He convinces Schroder that people are still worth the sacrifice both he and Schroder's son have made.

At the same time, Mary has met Waldo at the bus station in New York and realizes she belongs instead with Bill. She travels back to Philadelphia, where the couple reunites and decides to get married.

The final scene finds Schroder and Jimmy at the Tomb of the Unknown Soldier in Arlington Cemetery. As they salute American patriots, the stranger disappears via camera dissolve into the rows of white crosses.

Notes and Comments: *Down Liberty Road* aka *Freedom Highway* is a feature short that functions simultaneously as a travelogue, fiction film, historical documentary, and commercial advertisement for Greyhound Lines, Inc. The filmmakers packed a lot into thirty-five minutes. The narrative itself encompasses both the romantic road trip and supernatural visitation genres (*It Happened One Night* meets *The Bishop's Wife*), and the historical sequences include action staged specifically for the film as well as clips from other movies. In fact, to include footage from a pirate picture, the bus makes an inexplicable detour from Cleveland to Key West, Florida, before returning to the Pennsylvania Turnpike.

For her fifth film, Angie emerges from the background and becomes a featured player with close-ups and sustained dialogue. Although her distinctively sultry voice at this point is still rather flat and toneless, she delivers her lines with confident energy. "Why is it time flies so when you're happy and drags so when you're unhappy?" she asks her new boyfriend plaintively. "Ought to be the other way around."

Financed and co-produced by Greyhound, the movie makes bus travel look elegant. With its split-level layout, the spotless coach offers plush seating and expansive viewing windows. The men all wear sport jackets and the women have hats and gloves. Angie herself makes four costume changes, from a skirt and blouse to sundresses and finally a black dress with matching accessories. There is not a single passenger drinking whiskey from a paper bag or vomiting in the aisles.

Shown as a short subject on a full feature bill, *Down Liberty*

Road also marked the movie debut of future Disney child star Tommy Kirk as Jimmy the precocious Boy Scout.

Review:
"Warners is making a five-reel documentary in Warner-Color, tagged *Down Liberty Road*, due to reception accorded its 33-minute doc *24-Hour Alert* . . . Tex Ritter, appearing in prominent role as a pioneer Texan, will sing 'Remember the Alamo.' Rest of cast includes Marshall Thompson, Angie Dickinson, Charles Maxwell, Morris Ankrum, and Tommy Kirk."
—*Daily Variety*, January 10, 1956

Hidden Guns

Credits: A Republic Pictures production released on January 30, 1956. Black and white. Running time of 66 minutes. **Cast:** Bruce Bennett (Stragg), Richard Arlen (Sheriff Ward Young), Faron Young (Deputy Faron Young), John Carradine (Snipe Harding), Lloyd Corrigan (Judge Wallis), Angie Dickinson (Becky Carter), Damian O'Flynn (Kingsley), Irving Bacon (Doc Carter), Tom Hubbard (Grundy), Ron Gans (Burt Miller), Bill Ward (Joe Miller), Lee Morgan (Emmett Harding), Guinn "Big Boy" Williams (Kingford). **Crew:** Albert Gannaway (director, screenwriter, and producer), Samuel Roeca (screenwriter), Ramey Idriss (composer), Clark Ramsey (cinematographer), Leon Barsha (editor), Erich von Stroheim, Jr. (assistant director), William Brady (sound).

Plot Synopsis: Stragg, owner of Youngstown's Silver Dollar Saloon, cheats people out of land and savings at his gambling tables with the support of hired guns and bribed politicians. When the Miller brothers catch him in the act, he shoots Joe dead and wounds Burt, who hides out in the nearby town of Portersville. Sheriff Ward Young, knowing that neither brother ever carried a gun, investigates but the intimidated witnesses all claim it was self-defense. To seal his control, Stragg also announces that the city council has voted to amend the town character, making the sheriff an appointed rather than an elected official. With only forty-eight hours until the county ratifies his removal, Ward vows to find evidence that will incriminate Stragg. Disgusted by the town's cowardly ingratitude, Ward's son and deputy Faron quits his job and refused to be involved any further.

In Portersville, Ward convinces Burt to return and testify. Stragg, meanwhile, has also sent his hireling Grundy to Portersville to pay gunman Snipe Harding $800 for killing Burt. Seeing Ward, Burt, and Doc Carter's daughter Becky board a stagecoach back to Youngstown, Snipe rides along, planning to signal his sidekick Emmett Harding and Grundy to create a disturbance during which he can shoot Burt. As Becky praises Burt for the testimony that will hang Stragg, Snipe realizes he can hold out for more money and calls off the initial plan.

Back in Youngstown, Snipe informs Stragg that the sheriff has sent for hard-nosed Circuit Judge Parker, thus bypassing the corrupt town judge controlled by Stragg. For $1,000, Snipe sets a trap in which Harding pretends to be an out-of-town killer, diverting Ward and exposing Burt. Although Burt is killed, the sheriff is only knocked unconscious. Demanding an additional payment, Snipe agrees to take care of Ward.

Stragg challenges the sheriff to a shoot-out, and as the two men draw, Snipe fires his rifle from a knothole in the hotel, wounding Ward and clarifying the significance of the title. Incredulous that the sheriff could be outdrawn by the less-skilled Stragg, the townspeople nevertheless conclude it was a fair fight. Doc Carter and Becky tend to Ward's wounds. Faron arrives and notices that the bullet removed from his father is a rifle not a revolver bullet. Understanding what has happened, he goes in search of Stragg, backed by two friends. Snipe and Stragg try the same trick again but Faron changes the line of fire, revealing Snipe's concealed position. Faron unloads several shots in the direction of the hotel, killing Snipe. As Stragg tries to escape, he is surrounded and restrained by the chastened citizens.

Notes and Comments: Of all Angie Dickinson's early films, this is the one with the shabbiest production values. It has all the stylistic markings of a Republic serial—grainy, low-contrast film stock, awkward physical blocking, and erratic sound amplification (the fistfights are more like percussion solos). The story elements have been cribbed from at least a dozen other pictures, and the stock characters are equally familiar.

Another borrowed feature, used to much better dramatic effect in Fritz Lang's *Rancho Notorious* (1952), is the non-diegetic choral music whose lyrics comment directly if inelegantly on the action. "The stagecoach rolls along and the passengers inside / little dreaming that their destiny is coming along for the ride," sings an unseen chorus. "There's one man going to testify and one to enforce the law / but the third man has a hired gun that he's been paid to draw." At the end, the music ties up the narrative and concludes, "There's nothing folks can't do if they're fighting for what's right."

Country singer Faron Young, whose fictional name here is the same as his real one, plays Sheriff Ward Young's son and deputy, occasionally commenting musically on his own behavior ("I'm the man who'll try / I'll win for him or die"). Known as the Hillbilly Heartthrob, he had a hugely successful recording career and made three other low-budget movies after this one. Lean and dark-featured, he is a bit stiff on screen but gives Deputy Young an appealing sense of outrage over the town's ingratitude.

Wearing a bonnet and shawl and carrying a straw basket, Angie is Becky Carter, a passenger on the stagecoach from Portersville to Youngstown. Her line readings are somewhat stilted but then she doesn't have a lot to work with. "Why Burt Miller and Sheriff Young!" she is required to say by way of greeting. Her task is basically to help with the exposition. "I wish you wouldn't be so upset, Burt," she declares. "You're the one person who can put Stragg where he belongs. Your testimony will hang him." She has a brief scene with Faron Young when he helps her down from the stage and says, "Hiya, pigtail." Flashing a smile, she responds, "Is that anyway to treat a lady?" It's not the wittiest of repartee, but they both seem affectionate enough. Angie appears again toward the end when her father, Doc Carter, treats the injured sheriff. Her reaction shots register the requisite surprise as Faron discovers that Ward was shot with a rifle.

Former silent film star Richard Arlen appears as the sheriff and Olympic silver medalist cum prolific character actor Bruce Bennett is the villain. Filming took place at the Republic Pictures Movie Ranch (later sold to Walt Disney) and the Corriganville Movie Ranch, both located in southern California not far from Los Angeles.

Reviews:

"Arlen is excellent as sheriff, while Young, rated one of the top western recording stars, makes a good western-type deputy serving as his father's aide. His singing is heard in the background throughout the production with fine effect."

"John Carradine does better than his usual slick job as the suave but cold-blooded sniper and hired gunman. Bruce Bennett is sufficiently nasty to serve well as the villainous gambler. Lloyd Corrigan makes a sharp bought-up judge, while Angie Dickinson is in briefly for adequate scenic effect. Irving Bacon makes the Doc Carter role realistic."

"Al Gannaway's direction is way above par for a standard western, as is his story and screenplay, on which he worked with Sam Roeca."

—*Daily Variety*, March 5, 1956

Tension at Table Rock

Credits: A Sam Wiesenthal Productions picture released by RKO Radio Pictures on October 3, 1956. Technicolor. Running time of 93 minutes. Based on a novel by Frank Gruber. **Cast:** Richard Egan (Wes Tancred), Dorothy Malone (Lorna Miller), Cameron Mitchell (Sheriff Fred Miller), Billy Chapin (Jody Burrows), Royal Dano (Harry Jameson), Edward Andrews (Kirk), John Dehner (Hampton), DeForest Kelley (Jim Breck), Joe DeSantis (Ed Burrows), Angie Dickinson (Cathy), Paul Richards (Sam Murdock). **Crew:** Charles Marquis Warren (director), Winston Miller (screenwriter), Sam Wiesenthal (producer), Dimitri Tiomkin (composer), Joseph Biroc (cinematographer), Doane Harrison and Harry Marker (editors), Albert S. D'Agostino and John B. Mansbridge (art directors), Glen Daniels (set decorator), Larry Germain (hair stylist), Harry Maret (makeup artist), James E. Casey (assistant director), Terry Kellum and Arthur B. Smith (sound).

Plot Synopsis: Wes Tancred has been a part of Sam Murdock's gang since their Civil War days with William Quantrill. Publicly perceived as a heroic Robin Hood kind of outlaw, Murdock is actually a vicious egotist. When he kills a wounded associate while eluding a posse, Tancred decides to quit. Back at their hideout, he spurns the attentions of Murdock's wife Cathy and explains his disillusionment. As he turns to leave, Murdock pulls a gun but Tancred is faster, shooting him just as the posse arrives. Bitter at her rejection, Cathy lies and says Tancred shot her husband in the back. Tancred is jailed but receives a full pardon and even a $10,000 reward for Murdock, which he rejects.

Wherever he goes, however, he hears "The Ballard of Wes Tancred," which inaccurately paints him as a treacherous coward. Beaten by the citizens of a town after his identity is revealed, he moves on to a stagecoach outpost where Ed Burrows, the crippled caretaker, gives him a job wrangling horses. Using the name John Bailey, he works hard and earns the admiration of Burrow's young son Jody. When three robbers try to hold up a stagecoach, Burrows intervenes and is killed; Tancred grabs his friend's rifle and rapidly shoots down the three outlaws. In the aftermath, he agrees to take Jody to his uncle, the sheriff of Table Rock.

Things are tense in Table Rock because ranch boss Hampton is about to drive a huge Texas cattle herd through the area and Sheriff Fred Miller is uncertain of his ability to control the often lawless cowhands. Badly injured and scarred facially from an earlier incident, he is psychologically averse to confrontation. Tancred/Bailey sympathizes, and although he declines Miller's offer to serve as deputy, he stays in town, bringing Jody home when he follows his idol onto the trail and getting the boy a job with local newspaper editor Harry Jameson. While Jameson advocates law and order, saloon owner Kirk welcomes the money-making cowhands. Faithful to her husband, Miller's wife Lorna observes how helpful Tancred/Bailey is and feels an unavoidable attraction.

Fulfilling Miller's worst fears, Hampton's men drive his herd across a farmer's property, destroying his fences and crops. Although he offers to pay for the damages, Hampton refuses to stop the drives.

That night, one of his cowhands shoots the farmer and puts a gun in his hand to feign self-defense. Both Miller and Tancred/Bailey witness the killing, but in court the next day, only Tancred/Bailey is willing to tell the truth, admitting his real name as part of the testimony. Hampton threatens to return to town with his fifty men to get the prisoner, and Kirk hires a gunfighter to kill the sheriff.

The gunman is Jim Breck, an old Tancred acquaintance, who first agrees to leave the sheriff alone but ultimately is unable to resist the $2,000 payment. In a showdown, Tancred shoots and kills Breck and is about to be shot in the back by Kirk when the sheriff appears and guns down the saloon owner. Hampton and his crew ride into town and are met by Sheriff Miller and Tancred. As the town's citizens materialize with guns in windows and on roofs, Hampton sees he is outnumbered and leaves. Tancred also departs, leaving the hero-worshipping Jody and the grateful Lorna behind.

Richard Egan and Angie feel the stress in *Tension at Table Rock* (1956).

Notes and Comments: The lobby poster for *Tension at Table Rock* is forthright about its thematic influences: "A man like Shane . . . the suspense of *High Noon*." Tancred saves a man's way of life and then rides away from the boy and wife who revere him just as Alan Ladd interacts with the Starrett family in George Steven's classic Western *Shane* (1953). Similarly, the town's armed support of Miller and Tancred is a reversal of the abandonment Gary Cooper faces in *High Noon* (1952).

Angie appears memorably in the opening and then exits the narrative. In a fine, capsulized portrayal of the vengeful, scorned woman, she comes on seductively to Tancred and then betrays him when firmly rejected. With a pink blouse pulled alluringly down over one shoulder, she sidles up beside Tancred and insists, "You've loved me all this time and been afraid to tell me." In a two-shot medium close-up, she spins him toward her, claiming "You can't stand it anymore than I can. You can't stand being near me and you can't stand knowing I want to be near you." Lowering her noticeably breathy voice, she urges, "You're going to take me with you, Wes." After he has pushed her away, she lurks in the background, anxiously watching the mounting conflict between her husband and Tancred. Denied a final time, she lies to the posse. "He did it. His name's Wes Tancred," she glares. "He never gave Sam a chance." It's a look of unadorned hatred, Angie at her evil best.

The rest of the picture belongs to Richard Egan, Dorothy Malone, and Cameron Mitchell, who keep their frontier love triangle free of histrionics. DeForest Kelley, the future Dr. Leonard "Bones" McCoy of the original *Star Trek* TV series and movies (1966-1991), appears as gunslinger Jim Breck.

Reviews:
"Performances are all competent, but the deliberate pacing keeps them from being as colorful as they might have been."

"The Technicolor lensing by Joseph Biroc handles the western settings excellently and Dimitri Tiomkin provides an okay background score."

—*Daily Variety*, October 3, 1956

"These are all good actors and they are interesting to watch, although Egan seems too laconic for sustained sympathy, Mitchell is mentally tormented without clear motivation and Miss Malone is seen too briefly for a clear understanding of her character. Young Chapin is good as the boy; Edward Andrews makes his customary sharp imprint, and Royal Dano, Joe De Santis and Angie Dickinson are good."

"Joseph Biroc's photography and Dimitri Tiomkin's music are important aids to the picture with other credits good."

—James Powers, *The Hollywood Reporter*, October 3, 1956

"The efforts of the principals and a script only lightly infected with standard lines succeed in lifting *Tension* out of the bottom western drawer."

"Mitchell is particularly convincing as so is gorgeous Miss Malone who—believe it or not—is not kissed even once by Egan."

—*Los Angeles Times*, November 8, 1956

"There's an awful lot of shootin' in this one, but it is a western which manages to be just a bit different."

"Our boy Egan is okay as a quick-on-the-draw hero. He should

do more outdoor he-man productions. Cameron Mitchell etches the jellyfish sheriff in expert fashion. Rest of the cast is also good."
—Hazel Flynn, *Beverly Hills Citizen*, November 12, 1956

"Proper charting of the plot, with 'valleys' building and re-building to ever higher 'peaks' of interest, and better revelation of the traits that make each of the central characters stand out as individuals, not 'types' would make for a more engrossing and suspenseful picture."
—*Hollywood Citizen-News*, November 12, 1956

Gun the Man Down

Credits: A Batjac Productions picture released on November 15, 1956, by United Artists. Black and white. Running time of 76 minutes. **Cast:** James Arness (Rem Anderson), Angie Dickinson (Janice), Robert Wilke (Matt Rankin), Emile Meyer (Sheriff Morton), Don Megowan (Ralph Farley), Michael Emmet (Billy Deal), Harry Carey Jr. (Deputy Lee), Pedro Gonzalez Gonzalez (hotel manager). **Crew:** Andrew V. McLaglen (director), Burt Kennedy and Sam Freedle (screenwriters), Robert E. Morrison (producer), Henry Vars (composer), William H. Clothier (cinematographer), Everett Sutherland (editor), Alfred Ybarra (art director), Victor Gangelin (set decorator), Patrick Cummings and Neva Rames (costume designers), Fae M. Smith (hair stylist), Web Overlander (makeup artist), Robert Justman (assistant director), Earl Cain Sr. and Roger Heman Sr. (sound).

Plot Synopsis: To get the money for a ranch, Rem Anderson agrees to join Matt Rankin and Ralph Farley in robbing the Palace City Bank. While Rem's girlfriend Jan, who is worried about the plan, stays behind in a cabin, the three men ride into town. The hold-up goes badly, and although they get away with $40,000, Rem is wounded.

Back at the cabin, Rankin decides that Rem is too weak to travel and intends to leave him behind. Jan at first resists but is eventually taken along as Rankin and Farley escape on horseback. When the sheriff and his posse arrive, they find Rem hiding under the porch. In jail, he refuses to identify the others, intent on exacting his own revenge. He serves a year in jail and is then released.

Out on the trail, he comes across Billy Deal, a hired assassin who tells him that Rankin is in Gunther Wells. Arriving in the dusty, nearly deserted town, he finds his horse tied up outside the Red Dog Saloon and then also finds Farley, whom he thrashes in a fist fight and sends back to Rankin with the message that "they're not gonna have a chance to run out on me this time." Sheriff Morton and his young deputy Lee allow Rem to claim his horse but warn him to obey the law.

Inside the saloon, which Rankin owns, he and Farley decide to send for Billy Deal to eliminate Rem. Having hooked up with Rankin, Jan looks on with disgust as he plots more treachery against the man she still loves. Later, she goes to the hotel to attempt a reconciliation, but Rem rejects her explanations. Before leaving she warns him about Billy Deal and says, "You don't have to believe that either."

Billy arrives the same day, and Rankin pays him $5,000 to kill Rem. Stalking Rem through town, Billy is himself surprised and outdrawn in a gunfight that leaves him dead. The sheriff informs Rankin he's keeping the money for the town and says, "I don't like you, Rankin. I never have. I don't like what you and this saloon stand for." He also releases Rem from temporary custody, cautioning him against any action that is just "plain killing."

That evening Rankin and Farley leave town; after Rankin says she'll always be a saloon girl, Jan reluctantly goes along as well. Rem follows the trio and overtakes them at their campsite. Jan tries to warn Rem and is shot by Rankin. In her dying moments, she tells Rem he is the only man she ever loved. Surrounded by darkness, Rankin mistakenly shoots and kills Farley.

The next morning, Rem tracks Rankin into a box canyon. Rather than kill him, he beats him up and loads him onto a horse for delivery to Sheriff Morton. As Rem rides away into the distance, Morton and Lee comment on what an admirable citizen he will become.

Notes and Comments: Angie is present in the film from the opening moments, a pre-credits scene where she worries about Rem's safety and ominously spills ink across a diagram of the bank's interior. Her role is more complex than any she had played to date. No longer just a provider of background color, she is a featured player here, carrying the main narrative and developing a multi-layered character. Jan is both ally and betrayer, victim and perpetrator, and Angie effectively projects the conflicted emotions that motivate her.

The hotel scene is illustrative. She begins apologetically, claiming "I didn't want to leave you." Faced with Rem's resistance, she goes even further, unabashedly admitting how evil she has been. "I'm every dirty thing you think I am only worse," she exclaims. "I've rolled drunks in every cheap saloon in this territory. I've cheated and lied my way ever since I can remember, and there's not one sin I haven't done at least once." Defiantly, however, she insists, "I loved you. You're the only clean thing that ever happened to me." Then, turning abruptly, she lashes out at Rem for spoiling their dream. "You wanted to settle down, live respectable. You wanted to own your own ranch," she charges. "Then you had to ruin it by throwing in with Rankin and his kind." Finally, aware of how futile her efforts have been, she sadly concludes, "I'm sorry I came up here." It is a challenging speech and Angie gets the shifting flow of it just right.

Along with the big chunks of dialogue, Angie holds the screen solely through gesture and expression as well. Leaving the hotel, she walks across the street followed by a laterally tracking camera; her despair is conveyed through her halting gait and troubled eyes. Similarly, after she thinks Billy Deal has killed Rem, she flashes Rankin a look of unchecked hatred. For Jan's death scene, which could have been melodramatic but remains realistic, she once again correctly interprets the tone. "Rem, hold me," she whispers. "Rem, whatever you think of me, you were the one, the only one. We would have been respectable, wouldn't we, Rem?" After he agrees, she calls his name, cries out softly in pain, and goes silent. As if to signal the emergence of the more experienced performer she was fast becoming, her screen credit read "and introducing Angie Dickinson."

Robert Morrison produced the picture for his brother John Wayne's Batjac Productions. In addition to signing James Arness to play Rem Anderson, Wayne also recommended Arness for the iconic role of Marshal Matt Dillon, which he played from 1955 to 1975 on the CBS television Western *Gunsmoke*. Angie made an appearance on a 1957 episode of the series also directed by *Gun the Man Down*'s Andrew McLaglen, son of film actor and John Ford regular Victor McLaglen.

Reviews:

"*Gun the Man Down* packs enough action and suspense to rate okay for the western market, where name of James Arness should be a potent draw. Film generally is ingrained with the type of ingredients to keep spectators interested."

"First pic to be turned out by team of Robert E. Morrison and Andrew V. McLaglen, story of a manhunt is well sustained through good writing and fast-paced directory by McLaglen. The Burt Kennedy screenplay avoids clichés and offers an opportunity for hard characterization. The usual sugar-coating for a happy romantic windup is passed up for a more realistic climax."

"Star handles his role well and has the benefit of a strong supporting cast. Robert Wilke is quietly menacing as one of the heavies, and Don Megowan qualified as the other. Angie Dickinson registers impressively as the femme, killed finally by Wilke as she tries to warn Arness of his danger during closing sequence."

—*Daily Variety*, February 13, 1957

"Though hardly distinguished, this minor Wester is handled efficiently, and even, with a touch of style. The acting is always competent and Emile Meyer's Sheriff is quietly striking. Largely routine, but by no means an unwatchable supporting Wester."

—*Monthly Film Bulletin*, June, 1957

The Black Whip

Credits: A Regal Films production released by 20th Century Fox in December, 1956. Black and white and Regalscope. Running time of 81 minutes. **Cast:** Hugh Marlowe (Lorn Crawford), Coleen Gray (Jeannie), Adele Mara (Ruthie Dawson), Angie Dickinson (Sally Morrow), Richard Gilden (Dewey Crawford), Paul Richards (John Murdock), John Pickard (Sheriff Persons), Dorothy Schuyler (Delilah Ware), Charles Gray (Chick Hainline), Sheb Wooley (Bill Lassater), Strother Martin (Thorny), Patrick O'Moore (Governor). **Crew:** Charles Marquis Warren (director), Orville Hampton (screenwriter), Robert Stabler (producer), Raoul Kraushaar (composer), Joseph

Biroc (cinematographer), Fred W. Berger (editor), G.W. Berntsen (set decorator), Patti Whiffing (hair stylist), Jack Dusick (makeup artist), Lester Guthrie (assistant director), Lloyd D. Wiler (sound).

Plot Synopsis: After a saloon girl helps spring a prisoner from jail, the sheriff loads her and three other dance hall girls onto a wagon with instructions to dump them in whatever town will have them. Since the prisoner is associated with the Black Legs, a band of notorious post-Civil War Confederate outlaws modeled after Quantrill's Raiders, no place is eager to comply.

Finally, they are deposited at the Star Valley Inn, a ghost town stagecoach station operated by Lorn Crawford and his brother Dewey. Thankful for the rescue, one of the girls (Jeannie) begins to fall for Lorn. Soon, however, the entire gang of Back Legs arrives, virtually holding the brothers and the girls hostage.

The leader is John Murdock, whose weapon of choice is a lethal back whip. A sadistic brute, he enjoys terrorizing the girls and the few remaining residents. He allows his bandits to create chaos in town also. A former Confederate officer, Crawford is well aware of Murdock's past but seems reluctant to confront him.

The stakes become higher when the Black Legs learn that the Governor of Kentucky is scheduled to pass through on the stagecoach. They plan to kidnap him, collect a hefty ransom, and then escape to Mexico.

More resourceful and ultimately a better fighter, Crawford takes a stand, defeating Murdock and foiling the abduction plot. The remaining gang members are apprehended. Jeannie and Crawford resume their romance.

Notes and Comments: Released after her featured role in *Gun the Man Down*, *The Black Whip* finds Angie back in the chorus, once again part of a dance hall group headed by a lead actress, in this case Coleen Gray. Her forward-leaning professional momentum seemed temporarily stalled.

The picture welds the hotel invasion motif of *Key Largo* (1948) and the family hostage/political assassination angle of *Suddenly* (1954) to a Western frontier setting. It is the second film that Angie made with director Charles Marquis Warren. A decorated World War II navy veteran, Warren began his Hollywood career writing such Westerns as *Streets of Laredo* (1949) and *Springfield Rifle* (1952) and later moved on to directing his own pictures. Those efforts included *Hellgate* (1952), and *Flight to Tangier* (1953). In 1955, he joined actor James Arness on his new CBS series *Gunsmoke*, producing the entire first season and directing 26 of the 39 individual episodes. He left in the middle of season two to form his own production company and continued working in both film and television until 1970. Although Warren was one of the earliest men of influence to recognize Angie's potential, the director and actress did not work again on any additional projects.

Warren's cameraman on *The Black Whip* was again Joseph Biroc, who shot 14 films for Robert Aldrich and two each for Mervyn LeRoy, Sam Fuller, and Gordon Douglas. He shared an Academy Award in 1974 with Fred Koenekamp for their collaborative work on *The Towering Inferno*.

Reviews:

"Acting generally is adequate, with Paul Richards, newcomer, making a particularly fine impression. Coleen Gray, Adele Mara and Angie Dickinson are mainly decorative, with the first-named winding up with Marlowe. Richard Gilden is spotted as the latter's brother."

"Charles Marquis Warren's direction of the Robert Stabler production keeps things on the move, and Raoul Kraushaar has provided a good musical backing. Other technical credits are stock."
—*Daily Variety*, December 18, 1956

"There is lots of excitement in Hampton's screenplay and Warren realizes it with interesting performances from Marlowe, Miss Gray, Miss Dickinson, Gilden and Strother Martin. Patrick O'Moore is good as the governor and Paul Richards gives a distinctive and powerful performance as the man with the black whip."

"Joseph Biroc's photography is an aid to the production."
—James Powers, *The Hollywood Reporter*, December 18, 1956

Shoot-Out at Medicine Bend

Credits: A Warner Bros. production released on May 4, 1957. Black and white. Running time of 87 minutes. **Cast:** Randolph Scott (Captain Buck Devlin), James Craig (Ep Clark), Angie Dickinson (Priscilla King), Dani Crayne (Nell Garrison), James Garner (Sgt. John Maitland), Gordon Jones (Pvt. Wilbur "Will" Clegg), Trevor Bardette (Sheriff Bob Massey), Don Beddoe (Mayor Sam Pelley), Myron Healey (Rafe Sanders), John Anderson (Clyde Walters), Harry Harvey (Elam King), Robert Warwick (Brother Abraham). **Crew:** Richard L. Bare (director), John Tucker Battle and D.D. Beauchamp (screenwriters), Richard Whorf (producer), Roy Webb (composer), Carl Guthrie (cinematographer), Clarence Kolster (editor), Stanley Fleischer (art director), Ben Bone (set decorator), Marjorie Best (costume designer), Gordon Bau (makeup artist), William Kissell (assistant director), Francis E. Stahl (sound).

Plot Synopsis: Just released from the army, Captain Buck

ANGIE

Devlin and his two sidekicks, Sergeant John Maitland and Private William Clegg, are on their way to the frontier homestead farmed by Devlin's brother. They arrive to help drive off a band of marauding Indians but not in time to save the brother, whose rifle is loaded with faulty ammunition and fails to fire at a crucial moment. The three men set out for Medicine Bend to find out who sold the bad ammo and to buy supplies for the remaining settlers.

When they stop to bathe in a lake, they are robbed of their horses, uniforms, money, and various possessions (including a locket once belonging to Devlin's mother) that the settlers were hoping to sell. Covered by tree branches, they walk into the camp of a group of Quakers, who give them some of their own simple clothing and reveal that they have recently been robbed as well.

In Medicine Bend, Devlin finds his stolen horse in the possession of Ep Clark who owns the two hotels, saloon, restaurant, and emporium and controls both the mayor and the sheriff. Suspecting that Clark may be responsible for the robberies of pioneers heading west and seeing how he tries to force competitors out of business, the three men stay disguised as Quakers and remain in town. Maitland and Clegg get jobs working in Clark's store and Devlin hires on as a helper for Elam King, an honest merchant with a pretty niece named Priscilla. Convinced of Devlin's trustworthiness, Elam confides that he has ordered a secret wagon train of supplies and guns for several parties of settlers waiting outside of town.

During a visit to the saloon, Devlin notices that Clark's sometime girlfriend Nell Garrison is wearing his mother's locket. That evening, he subdues Clark's henchmen Rafe Sander and Clyde Walters, breaks into the emporium to steal a gun and some clothes, and takes back the locket. Disguised with a mask, he is not recognized. Soon afterwards, Maitland and Clegg discover their uniforms hidden in the storeroom, confirming Clark and gang as the bandits who have been pulling all the robberies.

Suspecting that the three strange Quakers may be responsible for his break-in, Clark forces the mayor and sheriff to post a $1,000 reward. He and Sanders also plan a trap to lure the masked thief back to the store for Clark's moneybox. Knowing it's a trick, Devlin goes anyway and is surprised by Walters. They fight, Walters falls into an abandoned well, and Devlin makes off with the box, whose contents he distributes to the various robbery victims.

Priscilla tends to Devlin's injuries and he tells her of his true identity. She reveals her fondness for him and conceals him from the sheriff. Angered by his losses, Clark orders Nell to get Clegg drunk and find out who the three men really are. Once he discovers they are soldiers, he forces the sheriff to give Maitland and Clegg a rigged one- minute trial and sentence them to hang for the death of Walters. Clark also learns about Elam's secret shipment and sends some thugs to intercept the wagons.

Realizing she is in love with Maitland, Nell convinces the sheriff to redeem himself and release the two prisoners but Sanders shoots him in the back before he can. Nell escapes to a nearby Quaker church where she asks Brother Abraham and his brethren for help.

On the morning of the hanging, Nell, Priscilla, Abraham, and Devlin approach the gallows. While pretending to give a sermon, Abraham cuts Maitland's and Clegg's bonds, and he and the other Quakers put aside their pacifism to fight off Clark's men. In the melee, Devlin shoots Sanders and escapes with his two friends.

Having killed the wagon train drivers, Clark and his gang try to unload the contents at night. The three soldiers, informed of the plan by the dying sheriff, surprise them in the act and a running gun fight ensues. Clark tries to shoot Devlin using his own bad ammo and is instead impaled on a lethal scythe.

Maitland and Nell join Devlin and Priscilla on a journey back to the homestead. Clegg decides to stay in Medicine Bend and become a Quaker for real.

Notes and Comments: Although she receives third billing after Scott and Craig, Angie has a small part and rarely more than a line or two of dialogue at a time. Her best, most extended, scene is the one where she brings Devlin into the kitchen and sponges warm water onto his bruised face. She starts by casually remarking, "I don't suppose I should ask what happened to you" and then probes further with a direct question: "Who are you when you're not masquerading as a brother?" Busying herself with physical tasks, she avoids looking directly in his eyes. As she sits next to him at the table, she dabs gently at his face and gives him a long, sustained gaze. "I've always wanted to go further west, but I'm afraid Uncle Elam wouldn't let me go alone," she says meaningfully. "Of course, if I had a job like teaching school or something, and someone to look out for me . . . ." They are interrupted before she can finish, but the romantic overture is there in the soft voice and the gentle look.

The problem is that she is covered from neck to ankles in a baglike muslin nightgown, an indication of the complete lack of sexual chemistry between her and Randolph Scott. With a thirty-four year age difference between them, the two seem more like relatives than lovers. When Angie climbs up on the wagon to go west with Scott in the end, it's hard to believe they plan to be married. She will confront a similar age differential with John Wayne two years later in *Rio Bravo*, but his muddled shyness and her determined flirtation will make that pairing uniquely credible. Despite a brief scene where she tells Scott not to order her around and takes the reins of a supply wagon, Angie is too passive here to be very interesting. Her fluctuation between good and bad girl parts swings distinctly here in the direction of modest propriety.

Scott's age shows in other ways as well. His action sequences are limited to some minimal horseback riding, dropping a hay bale on an assailant, and firing pistols from behind cover. There is a stunt double for the climatic storeroom fight with Clark. Several moments, such as the three soldiers approaching the Quaker camp in the altogether or drinking buttermilk in the saloon, are played for laughs. Scott, along with Joel McCrea, will use his advancing age to much better thematic effect in Sam Peckinpah's classic 1962 Western *Ride the High Country*.

As Scott was making his last picture for Warner Bros., James Garner was making his second. He plays John Maitland as a randy good old boy, a persona he would adopt for future roles. Although he and Angie appear together in only three brief group scenes, they would team again later in their careers for a Ross Hunter comedy.

Reviews:

"Scott gives one of his more laconic performances although he has some chances for the kinds of repressed humor that he conveys expertly. Craig is forceful heavy and Miss Dickinson is both strong and womanly. Miss Crayne makes her stereotyped dance hall hostess a characterization of more than usual variety and interest and Garner is extremely good."

"The screenplay by John Tucker Battle and D.D. Beauchamp is good and Carl Guthrie's photography helps the action and drama."

—James Powers, *The Hollywood Reporter*, April 10, 1957

"Scott is good as the hero, as are James Garner and Gordon Jones as his sidekicks. A couple of distaff cuties, Angie Dickinson and Dani Crayne, beautify the western setting, pairing with Scott and Garner, respectively, for the fadeout clinch."

—Daily Variety, April 10, 1957

China Gate

Credits: A Globe Enterprises production for 20th Century Fox released on May 22, 1957. Black and white and Cinemascope. Running time of 97 minutes. **Cast:** Gene Barry (Sgt. Brock), Angie Dickinson (Lia "Lucky Legs" Surmer), Nat "King" Cole (Goldie), Paul Dubov (Capt. Caumont) Lee Van Cleef (Maj. Cham), George Givot (Cpl. Pigalle), Gerald Milton (Pvt. Andreades) Neyle Morrow (Leung), Marcel Dalio (Father Paul), Warren Hsieh (Boy), Maurice Marsac (Col. De Sars), Paul Busch (Cpl. Kruger). **Crew:** Samuel Fuller (director, screenwriter, producer), Victor Young (composer, with assistance from Max Steiner), Joseph Biroc (cinematographer), Gene Fowler, Jr. and Doane Harrison (editors), John B. Mansbridge (art director), Glen Daniels (set decorator), Beau Vanden Ecker and Henry West (costume designers), Don Cash (makeup artist), Harold E. Knox (assistant director), Bert Schoenfeld and Jean Speak (sound), Norman Breedlove (special effects).

Plot Synopsis: After a voice-over library footage introduction justifying French imperialism in Indochina, the narrator concludes, "The year 1954, the day Thursday, the time, 10:00 in the morning." In a small northern Vietnamese village, pounded by Communist Viet Minh bombs, a small Asian boy protects his puppy from a starving peasant who wants to kill it for food. As an American plane drops supplies, the villagers run toward the cargo while the boy rushes home to his mother, Lia Surmer, a half-caste saloon keeper known as "Lucky Legs." She too hurries to retrieve some food and is later summoned to a meeting with her friend Colonel De Sars, commander of the local French garrison.

Given Lucky's knowledge of the mountainous China Gate region and the tunnels where the Communists have stashed their vast artillery supplies, he asks her to guide a group of Foreign Legion mercenaries on a search and destroy mission. Her many trips through the jungle to sell cognac have also made her a trusted familiar face to the soldiers and particularly to their commander Major Cham, a mixed race Vietnamese officer in love with Lucky. "As far as I'm concerned, you and the hammer and sickle boys can go fight it out among yourselves," she tells De Sars, who offers her $5,000 and a new bar in Saigon to change her mind. Ultimately, after he accepts her demand that her five-year-old son be sent safely to the United States, she agrees to guide the demolition patrol.

Angie as Lucky Legs in Sam Fuller's *China Gate* (1957).

While assembling the expedition, De Sars introduces Lucky to the American explosives expert Sargent Johnny Brock. When he turns to meet her, she slaps his face, calls off the plan, and walks away into the distance. Brock, it is revealed, is the Korean War vet who married and then abandoned her when she gave birth to an Asian-looking son. To save the mission, Brock asks the local priest who married them, Father Paul, to intervene. Fiercely protective of Lucky for having saved his own life, Father Paul refuses to help Brock and tells him that he is responsible for all of his ex-wife's misfortune. That night, Brock visits Lucky and sees his little boy for the first time. "I shouldn't have slapped you," she confesses. "I should have shot you." Still unable to accept the boy, who smiles shyly at his father and admires his wristwatch, Brock advises Lucky not to jeopardize the child's safety just to spite him. Again, she relents, and the raid is back on.

The team consists of Goldie, an African American vet whom we meet walking along the street with Lucky's son and singing the "*China Gate*" title song; Captain Caumont, the French officer in command; Private Jaszi, a Czech anti-communist patriot; Lucky's Chinese cousin Leung; a Greek soldier of fortune named Andreades; a German mercenary called Kruger; and several French soldiers who wonder why the American armed forces are not more involved. On the first night out, Lucky gets them safely past a guard post and they make camp together in the jungle, sharing backstories and political convictions. "Say, you don't look Chinese," one of the men tells Lucky and she replies, "Everybody doesn't carry their lives in their faces." Jaszi has a nightmare in which he mistakes Goldie for a Russian soldier he killed, and Brock warns him not to endanger the group again.

The next night, further into the jungle, Lucky climbs a watch-tower and distracts the guard while Brock knifes him. Alone together, he admits he has never stopped loving her. "Five years," he says, "is a long time to think about one woman every night." When she realizes that Brock still cannot accept their son, however, she rejects his advances. Aware of his behavior, the rest of the men avoid Brock as day breaks and they continue the journey. Andreades slips down a rocky cliff and breaks his back; before he dies, he too admonishes Brock for spoiling Lucky's life.

That evening's camp goes badly. Brock makes another hamhanded attempt at justifying himself to Lucky, and one of the French legionnaires is killed by a sniper. In the ensuing firefight, other casualties occur before Brock uses some of the explosives to blow up the Communists. Cut off from the others, Goldie steps on a spiked booby-trap and silently endures excruciating pain so as not to give away his position. Rescued and bandaged by Brock, he tells him that his own wife died because she could not conceive the child they wanted and that after the assignment he plans to get Lucky and her son to safety in America. Finally after one more perimeter outpost that Lucky again helps them navigate, the group arrives at China Gate, a walled fortress adorned with posters of Lenin, Stalin, and Mao.

Major Cham happily welcomes Lucky, reminding her of his desire to marry her and adopt her son. A former teacher who used to hate war, he has become a powerful officer being groomed by the Russians for more advanced service. To prove his authority, her shows Lucky the secret tunnel where the armaments are stored. Saying that she needs twenty-four hours to consider his proposal, Lucky reports the tunnel position back to Captain Caumont. In front of the other men, Brock apologies to Lucky and reveals that he is ready to accept his son. When he asks her to marry him again, she announces that they were never formally divorced. After a brief embrace, she leads the group to the tunnel, distracting the guards while Brock wires the explosives.

Just as the detonation is ready, Cham appears and takes Lucky to his nearby headquarters. Proudly sharing the news that he has been offered a position in Moscow, he receives a phone call that informs him of Lucky's betrayal. He asks why and she explains the deal regarding her son's safety. When he tells her that the explosive wire has been cut, she pushes him off a balcony, rushes to the tunnel, and sacrifices herself in setting off the detonation by hand. Lone survivors of the gunfight that follows, Caumont, Brock, and Goldie hijack a plane and escape just as the whole stronghold erupts in flames. Mortally injured, Caumont cannot keep the plane aloft and it crashes into the jungle. Brock and Goldie survive.

In the final scene, Brock receives payment and American travel documents from Col. De Sars. Cradling his son's puppy, he reaches for the boy, proudly wearing his father's wristwatch and they walk hand in hand out of the village. As they pass, Goldie once more sings the "*China Gate*" title song.

Notes and comments: In one of the opening scenes from Jean-Luc Godard's *Pierrot Le Fou*, filmmaker Sam Fuller, playing a gray-haired, cigar chomping version of himself, proclaims, "The film is like a battleground. Love. Hate. Action. Violence. Death. In one word . . . Emotion." As written, produced, and directed by Fuller, *China Gate* is exactly that kind of picture. It fits neatly into his overall body of work.

First, there is the preoccupation with death. Lucky's village is bombed almost daily, the loss of life and property a constant reality. Like the characters in Fuller's *Merrill's Marauders* and *Hell and High Water*, the mercenaries of *China Gate* have voluntarily placed themselves in a war situation where the threat of death is ever present. Often it comes suddenly, absurdly, or, ironically, at the height of physical enjoyment. Andreades breaks his back while scaling a hill and apologizes for "taking so long to die." Saluting the freedom of legionnaire life, Corporal Pigalle exclaims, "I tell you, this is the way to live" and is immediately shot dead by a sniper. Everyone on the mission, except for Brock and Goldie, is killed.

Amid such devastation the sense of self becomes critical. Brock, in the tradition of such Fuller antiheroes as *Forty Guns*'s Griff Bonnell or *House of Bamboo*'s Eddie Kenner, is a true individual motivated not by social norms but by a personal code of behavior. At times that code may seem harsh, as when Brock warns Jaszi that he will be shot if another of his violent nightmares endangers the group, but it also entails a deep sense of loyalty, revealed, for example, when Brock rescues Goldie from the Viet Minh ambush. In addition to physical courage, Brock also displays the trademark Fuller-approved qualities of professionalism, resourcefulness, and resistance to authority.

The individualism helps to explain the virulent anti-Communist sentiment that runs through Fuller's movies. A fight against Communists fuels the plots of *Pickup on South Street*, *Hell and High Water*, *China Gate*, and others. "I have come to finish something we didn't finish in Korea. There are still a lot of live Commies," says Goldie, who has joined with the French out of a personal crusade. For Fuller, Communism is totalitarian by nature, substituting adherence to dogma for self-expression. Rejecting his youthful ideals, Major Cham is willing to kill innocent women and children for the promise of a cushy top job in Moscow. That same notion of hierarchical corruption permeates Fuller's critiques of crime syndicates and corporations.

Captain Caumont's trek through the jungle is one of many journeys pursued by Fuller protagonists. Whether they are searches for a murderer, an enemy encampment, or a new life, the characters' quests often involve much deeper explorations of their hidden personalities. Brock is looking for an ammunition dump but discovers his own true identity as a loving father. Ironically, with such new insights, the films frequently end, as is the case with *China Gate*, in the same physical location where they began.

Even in Fuller's Westerns and crime dramas, the stronger characters are usually the women. Like Candy in *Pickup on South Street*, Jessica Drummond in *Forty Guns*, and Kelly in *The Naked Kiss*, Lucky Legs is both fearless and resilient. She is the one who leads the mercenaries to their objective and who accomplishes the final demolition when all seems lost. Abandoned by Brock, she has struggled successfully to support their child and to keep him safe. Wherever she goes, she's welcomed by both the French and the Viet Minh soldiers and treated as a comrade. Her treachery, another Fuller motif, is motivated not by a desire to punish Major Cham but rather to once again protect her son.

As "little of everything and a lot of nothing," Lucky Legs represents Fuller's notion, expressed even more strongly in *The Crimson Kimono* and *Run of the* Arrow, that the real differences between people are individual rather than racial. She sees no ethnic boundaries and pushes Brock to recognize the irrationality of his own prejudices. "You came here to fight for a Chinese baby, admit it," she tells him. The film's final shot of father and son walking hand in hand is an image of cultural harmony at odds with the political chaos surrounding it.

Stylistically, *China Gate* can also be identified without fail as a Sam Fuller picture. One of the half dozen or so films he made in association with 20th Century Fox, it reflects the special resources available to him, particularly the widescreen Cinemascope cameras that the studio had perfected and been using since 1953. His elongated compositions, with multiple characters carefully balanced throughout the frame, lend visual richness to otherwise conventional action scenes. So too do the lateral tracking shots and the overhead cranes. Among the most impressive Fuller touches are a sustained, one-minute track alongside Goldie as he and Lucky's son walk through the village, the overhead views of the village and of China Gate, and the dolly shots of the men creeping past various enemy encampments. Despite the meagre $150,000 budget, the extensive use of stock footage, and the backlot locations, Joseph Biroc's camera work gives *China Gate* the look of a much more polished film.

Less seamless is the acting. Too often the cast is required to recite dialogue that is pure exposition or that strains for effect. "Soldiering is my business," "I hope there's a heaven or it will kill me to have to come back here again," and "You're the only person who ever made me feel ashamed" are lines that look clever on paper but are hard to deliver convincingly. Gene Barry's attempt to sound like a tough guy from Brooklyn doesn't help.

Still relatively early in her career, Angie is sometimes stiff in the scenes where she needs to project heightened emotion. The cadence of her speech occasionally falters, but she is always engaged with the material, doing her best to make it believable. The unfortunate "white washing" of her Lucky Legs character could have been worse; she does not wear any grotesque makeup designed to alter the shape of her eyes and does not adopt any stereotypical Chinese accent. More than anything else, even here in her mid-twenties, she has screen presence. In those detail-packed Fuller widescreen frames, viewer eyes are almost always focused on Angie. Once again she is a saloon girl doing the right thing, but even more so than in the Westerns she handles the extensive physical action with athletic ease.

Reviews:

"Although the picture reportedly was put together on a tight budget, and brought in on a short schedule it has the look and feel of a major production. The story has meaningful action, a legitimate and hapless romance and some thoughtful and pertinent remarks about the reasons for the conflict in Asia. A better than average title song, sung by Cole, will be an added value in its exploitation."

"The cast is a good one, notably Gene Barry as a somewhat thick-headed but likable soldier, Miss Dickinson as a combination mother and "dance hall hostess" (as they say in the movies), and Cole as a philosophical but hard-bitten soldier of the world."

—James Powers, *The Hollywood Reporter*, May 9, 1957

"*China Gate*" is an overlong but sometimes exciting story of the battle between Vietnamese and Red Chinese, told through the efforts of a small band of French Legionnaires to reach and destroy a hidden Communist munitions dump. Realistic in its action sequences, the effect frequently is dissipated through lengthy scenes of dialog which slow movement to a walk."

"Miss Dickinson does yeoman service with her colorful role and should benefit in further castings. Barry also handles himself well but part sometimes is negative. Cole as the only other American in Legion patrol shows he can act as well as sing."

—*Daily Variety*, May 9, 1957

"Producer-Director-Writer Fuller keeps the action lively during this hazardous march, which includes an assorted group of French Legionnaires from many countries. Some of Fuller's dialogue runs on the wordy side, and the picture seems a bit overlong."

"Miss Dickinson presents a very satisfactory picture of the

Eurasian girl; Barry is okay as the sometimes muddle-headed soldier who doesn't know when he's well off."
—John L. Scott, *Los Angeles Times*, May 10, 1957

"Lucky Legs is played by a new girl, Angie Dickinson, who is beautiful and a very good actress."
—Ruth Waterbury, *Los Angeles Herald-Examiner*, May 10, 1957

"Miss Dickinson, it must be added, is a decorative brunette who makes good one or two opportunities to project genuine emotion. Unfortunately, the rest of the cast do not."
—*The New York Times*, May 23, 1957

Calypso Joe

Credits: A William F. Broidy Pictures Corp. production released by Allied Artists on May 8, 1957. Black and white. Running time of 76 minutes. **Cast:** Herb Jeffries (Calypso Joe), Angie Dickinson (Julie), Edward Kemmer (Lee Darling), Stephen Bekassy (Rico Vargas), Laurie Mitchell (Leah), Claudia Drake (Astra Vargas), Murray Alper (Transfer Man), Linda Terrance (Lady T), Charles Keane (pilot). **Crew:** Edward Dein (director and screenwriter), Mildred Dein (screenwriter), William F. Broidy (producer), Richard Hazard and Herb Jeffries (music supervisors), Stuart Thompson (cinematographer), Thor L. Brooks (editor), Herman N. Schoenbrun (set decorator), Linda Cross (hair stylist), Carlie Taylor (makeup artist), Leo Silver and Ralph Slosser (assistant directors), John Kemp and Al Overton (sound).

Plot Synopsis: Julie, a pretty young airline stewardess, is packing for her last flight before marrying a South American millionaire named Rico Vargas. As she and her roommate Leah, also a stewardess, get ready to leave their apartment, Julie's former boyfriend, television star Lee Darling, arrives and tries to win her back. Despite his pleas and the support of Leah, Julie refuses. In the middle of their discussion, Vargas and his sister Astra show up as well. The men take an immediate dislike to each other, and Astra makes a move on Lee. To make Julie jealous, he responds.

At the airport, Julie and Leah board their plane on assignment as do Vargas and Astra as passengers. Lee suddenly appears and makes another unsuccessful appeal to Julie. Also there and ready to leave on Julie's plane are performer Calypso Joe and his band. All of the musicians are friends of Lee and they smuggle him aboard so he can continue to press his romantic case. During the flight, Lee and the guys serenade Julie, but both she and Vargas are furious with the effort.

When the plane stops in Port-of-Spain, Trinidad, everyone repairs to a swank hotel supper club. Here Vargas's personality grows darker and more domineering, and he begins to give Julie orders. She leaves their table and strolls out onto the patio where Lee, with the help of the moonlight and the music, finally wins her back.

The next morning she and Lee are on a plane back to New York, and Vargas and his sister continue on alone to their home country.

Notes and Comments: Angie received second billing after singer Herb Jeffries, but the film's poster featured only the calypso performers. The slim narrative is little more than a pretext for the dozen or so musical numbers. Besides Herb Jeffries and His Calypsomaniacs, the other entertainers include Lord Flea and His Calypsonians, The Easy Riders, Duke of Iron, and The Lester Horton Dancers. Angie doesn't sing but keeps the action aloft with her emotional vacillation between the two suitors.

The picture was an attempt to capitalize on the calypso music craze that swept the United States following the 1956 release of

Harry Belafonte's version of the "Banana Boat Song." It preceded by a few weeks the similarly themed movies *Calypso Heat Wave* and *Bop Girl Goes Calypso*. Allied Artists released it on an exploitation double-bill along with *Hot Rod Rumble*.

Herb Jeffries, who filled the title role of Calypso Joe, had starred as a singing cowboy in several all black westerns including 1937's *Harlem on the Prairie*. Known as the "Bronze Buckaroo" by his fans, he darkened his skin tone to satisfy producers who felt he was "not black enough." His actual racial profile was probably a mix of Italian, Irish, French, and Moorish roots. William Matons, an entertainer who used the stage names The Calypso Kid and Calypso Joe, was not cast in the film and sued producers for the unauthorized use of his name. He later developed the persona of General Hershy Bar, working as an anti-war street entertainer during the Vietnam War era.

Sal Mineo had initially been announced for the picture but dropped out for undisclosed reasons. His teaming with Angie could have been memorable. Laurie Mitchell, who played Julie's roommate, would appear one year later as the evil, facially scarred queen in the Zsa Zsa Gabor camp classic *Queen of Outer Space*.

Reviews:

"Jeffries is very strong in the musical numbers and pleasant in his acting moments. Miss Dickinson is very pretty, Kemmer amusing with what comedy he has, and Bekassy, Laurie Mitchell, Claudie Drake and others adequate to the story requirements. The Lester Horton dancers spark their scenes and the other musical groups will presumably appeal to calypso enthusiasts."

—James Powers, *The Hollywood Reporter*, May 6, 1957

"In lead roles, Jeffries, Miss Dickinson and Kemmer are adequate to the demands of the script, while Edward Dein's direction of the William F. Broidy production runs along routine lines. Technical credits are stock."

—*Weekly Variety*, May 15, 1957

I Married a Woman

Credits: A Gomalco Productions/RKO Radio Pictures production distributed by Universal Pictures and released on May 14, 1958. Black and white. Running time of 85 minutes. **Cast:** George Gobel (Marshall "Mickey" Briggs), Diana Dors (Janice Blake Briggs), Adolphe Menjou (Fredrick W. Sutton), Jesse Royce Landis (Mrs. Blake), Nita Talbot (Miss Anderson), John Wayne (husband in movie), Angie Dickinson (uncredited, wife in movie), William Redfield (Eddie Benson), Stephen Dunne (Bob Sanders), John McGiver (Girard), Steve Pendleton (photographer). **Crew:** Hal Kanter (director), Goodman Ace (screenwriter), William Bloom (producer), Cyril Mockridge (composer), Lucien Ballard (cinematographer), Kenneth Marstella (editor), Albert S. D'Agostino and Walter E. Keller (art directors), Dorcy Howard and William Stevens (set decorators), Howard Shoup (costume designer), Larry Germain (hair stylist), Harry Maret (makeup artist), John Pommer (assistant director), Terry Kellum and Frank Webster (sound).

Plot Synopsis: Mickey Briggs is a highly successful New York advertising executive whose main account is Luxemberg Beer. When that company decides it is tired of the Miss Luxemberg ad campaign, Mickey's boss Frederick Sutton gives him 48 hours to come up with a new approach. Failing that, Sutton claims he will have to close the agency and fire all the employees dependent on Mickey.

As he tries to concentrate, Mickey is distracted by his sexy wife Janice, a former Miss Luxemberg who feels she is being ignored. Recently told by the doctor that she is pregnant, Janice hesitates in sharing the news with the preoccupied Mickey. Adding to the unrest is Janice's mother who lives with the couple in their swanky apartment and complains about her own sense of neglect.

At Janice's insistence, she and Mickey go to the movies where they see a glossy romantic picture staring John Wayne. On screen, Wayne gives his young wife an expensive necklace and tells her that "just being married to you makes every day an occasion." The sight of the elegantly dressed couple pledging their devotion to each other makes Janice even more depressed. Later, when Mickey offhandedly reminds his ex-model wife that she now is married, he hits on the concept of a "Mrs. Luxemberg Beer" who knows how to please her husband by serving exactly the right beverage.

Sutton loves the campaign idea and sells it to the beer company president. The only problem is all of the former Miss Luxembergs currently are either overweight or divorced except for Janice. Without her knowledge or consent, Sutton has a photographer follow her and Mickey during a night on the town to get pictures for the ad layout. Of course she uncovers the ruse and, believing that Mickey is in on it, sues him for divorce and Sutton for invasion of privacy. The topper comes when she goes out with Mickey's friend Bob Sanders and arranges for the two of them to be photographed enjoying a rival beer.

Everything is finally resolved in an elevator filled with most of the main cast and a couple of lawyers. Mickey learns he is going to be a father, Janice learns that Mickey had nothing to do with the furtive pictures, and Sutton secures the Luxemberg Beer account. In a final scene, Mickey and Janice are on a second honeymoon cruise and see the real John Wayne who is in the middle of a spat with his clearly dissatisfied "real life" wife. Laughing at the irony, Mickey gives Janice a necklace just like the one they saw in the movie.

Notes and comments: Angie appears about ten minutes into the picture and is on screen slightly less than two minutes. As John Wayne's wife Evelyn in the film-within-the-film, she enjoys the kind of idyllic marriage the Diana Dors character would like to have. Alone with Wayne on a nighttime terrace, she receives his compliments and gifts with whispery happiness. "Even after five years it seems we're still on our honeymoon," she gushes as they waltz off the right side of the widened frame.

To emphasize its unrealistic fantasy, the Wayne-Dickinson movie is called *Forever and Forever and Forever* and is shot in color. She is in an evening gown and he wears a tuxedo. By contrast, Mickey and Janice are munching popcorn in their street clothes. When the movie ends, the audience of women sits mesmerized until Mickey whistles loudly to snap them back into their everyday lives. Both Angie and Wayne wisely underplay their parts, never pushing the spoof too far but letting the dialogue deliver the comic effect. They are believable as a couple, and even without close-ups she projects dewy innocence and charm.

Apart from Angie's cameo, *I Married a Woman* is interesting as one more example of the infatuation mid 20th Century American films had with advertising executives. Inspired perhaps by the sociologists who were analyzing conspicuous consumption and consumerism, the Hollywood portraits gave us the ad man as Everyman, a gray flannelled workaholic besieged by creative block, office politics, family chaos, and the pressures of living in the big city. There were dramas such as *The Hucksters* (1947) and *Madison Avenue* (1961) and a whole string of light comedies including

Mr. Blandings Builds His Dream House (1948), *Will Success Spoil Rock Hunter* (1957), *Lover Come Back* (1961), *Good Neighbor Sam* (1964), and *Marriage on the Rocks* (1965). Purporting to be critiques of the ad business's deception and manipulation, most of the films ended up celebrating its energy, glamour, and sophistication.

While not budgeted as generously as most of those pictures, *I Married a Woman* reflects many of the same tropes. Gobel's Mickey Briggs is a mirror image of the besieged, put-upon characters played by Tony Randall in *Rock Hunter* and Jack Lemmon in *Good Neighbor Sam*. Diana Dors looks a lot like Jane Mansfield in *Rock Hunter*, and the romantic discord is similar to that in *Lover Come Back* and *Marriage on the Rocks*. As plot motivator, the illusive Luxemberg Beer account stymies Mickey just as the wham canned meat campaign confounds Jim Blandings in *Mr. Blandings Builds His Dream House*.

To that mix, Gobel added elements from his popular "Lonesome George" television persona such as the slow burn, the wide-stanced loping around the set, and the familiar catch phrases ("You can just bet me"). That television success, however, never translated into the movies. His previous attempt, *The Birds and the Bees* in 1956 with Mitzi Gaynor and David Niven, revealed the same problem; his soft-spoken humor worked well in TV sketches and monologues but was too low-key to sustain a two-hour lead performance on the big screen. Diana Dors had similar difficulty establishing a Hollywood movie career. Well known in her native England for both adult comedies and urban dramas, she was seen by U.S. audiences as an imitation Marilyn Monroe complete with platinum blond hair and breathy voice. Like Gobel, she was on her second try at a big studio success, after the disappointment of *The Unholy Wife* (1957). She and Gobel have an amusing rhumba scene together but otherwise very little chemistry. When *I Married a Woman* failed at the box office, Lonesome George went back to television and Miss Dors returned to England.

Adolphe Menjou is type cast as a manipulative boss, and Jesse Royce Landis shows why Alfred Hitchcock liked her so much in pushy mother parts (1955's *To Catch a Thief* and 1959's *North by Northwest*) A gifted comedienne, Nita Talbot upstages Gobel as his pastry-munching secretary with a penchant for overusing the newspaper's word-of-the-day. Her mistreatment of "misconstrue" is not soon forgotten.

At one point, expectant mother Janice downs a cocktail and remarks, "I'm drinking for two now." That nonchalance over alcohol's effect on an unborn child seems so antiquated now as does the view of women in the workplace. Overall, with its low contrast black and white photography, flat backdrops, and soundstage shooting, the picture comes off like an extended 50s sitcom, an impression reinforced by the presence of television veterans Hal Kanter and Goodman Ace as director and writer respectively.

Reviews:

"It's probably wise that *I Married a Woman* is being released after Easter. Too many people would have been tempted to give it up during Lent. The film's basic flaw lies in Hal Kanter's direction, which seldom gives George Gobel's inarticulate comedy anyone straight to play against."

"The story and script by Goodman Ace contain a number of droll observations on metropolitan life. Nita Talbot, as a secretary trying to use a new word 'every day in every way,' is fairly funny and would be more so if she were doing a single. The same goes for William Redfield as an elevator boy who is studying law. By themselves they are satiric metropolitan types. But from a dramatic standpoint, you just can't believe that Gobel would put up with them."

"Every time the script allows the star to relax, he gets laughs."

—Jack Moffitt, *The Hollywood Reporter*, April 30, 1958

"The Goodman Ace screenplay keeps Gobel in his familiar character, but his type of comedy seems unreal on the theatrical screen. Hall Kanter's direction is leisurely. Biggest laugh in picture is a specially filmed insert of John Wayne, appearing as a 'guest star,' who plays himself in color as a great romantic figure and Miss Dors' favorite star, in some beautifully corny dialog in a love scene."

"Miss Dors handles herself expertly and displays an apt knowledge of comedy timing."

—*Daily Variety*, May 1, 1958

"George Gobel and Britain's pneumatic blonde, Diana Dors, don't make a half-bad comedy team in *I Married a Woman*, but they're not able to do much with some painfully old-fashioned comedy writing by Goodman Ace, whose forte is apparently not movies."

"Gobel extracts a few chuckles with his dead-pan delivery, especially a scene in which he goes on a 'date' with his estranged wife. Nita Talbot also contributes some minor amusement as Gobel's Maisie-like secretary, who spends more time learning a new word for her expanding vocabulary each day than doing her job. But the material is thin and Gobel is pretty subtle for movie comedy."

—Dick Williams, *Mirror-News*, May 16, 1958

Cry Terror!

Credits: An Andrew L. Stone Productions picture released on May 2, 1958. Black and white. Running time of 96 minutes. **Cast:** James Mason (Jim Molner), Inger Stevens (Joan Molner), Rod Steiger (Paul Hoplin), Neville Brand (Steve), Angie Dickinson (Eileen Kelly), Kenneth Tobey (Frank Cole), Jack Klugman (Vince), Jack Kruschen (Charles Pope), Carleton Young (Roger Adams), Barney Phillips (Dan Pringle), Harlan Warde (Bert), Ed Hinton (operative), Chet Huntley (himself), William Schallert (Henderson), Terry Ann Ross (Patty Molner). **Crew:** Andrew L. Stone (director, screenwriter, producer), Virginia L. Stone (producer, editor), Howard Jackson (composer), Walter Strenge (cinematographer), Bernard (costume designer), Richard Maybery (assistant director), Francis J. Scheid (sound).

Plot Synopsis: When Roger Adams, the president of 20th Century Airlines, receives a bomb threat in the mail, he assumes it is just another hoax until details in the letter and a subsequent phone call convince him otherwise. As proof, the caller explains where on Flight 74 from Chicago to New York the bomb can be found. After the pilot discharges the device from the plane, the caller phones again, claiming there is another bomb in the cargo hold timed to go off unless the company pays $500,000. Adams and his security chief Pringle play for time.

Listening to the news coverage in his electronics store, Jim Molner becomes increasingly agitated, especially upon learning that the bomb's main ingredient is an explosive known as RD-X. He rushes home and watches the story unfold on television. Once the plane safely lands in New York and the passengers disembark, Jim tells his wife Joan that he was duped into making the bomb prototype by Paul Hoplin, an enlisted man who served in Jim's demolitions unit during the war. Claiming to have government contacts, Hoplin asked Jim to devise a compact bomb that they could sell to the government, a ruse for what Jim now realizes was an extortion plan all along. In the middle of their discussion, Hoplin, the same man who called the airline company, arrives and forces his way into the house at gunpoint. Arguing that the police will believe Jim is involved, Hoplin waits until the Molners' little daughter Pat gets home from school and then forces the entire family into a car driven by his kidnapping accomplice, an ex-con named Steve.

At the airport, company executives summon the authorities, and FBI agent Frank Cole arrives to lead the investigation. Hoplin calls again and tells Adams to place a coded classified ad in the afternoon paper indicating that the $500,000 will be paid; if not, another bomb will be planted on an unspecified flight. Cole's team determines that the Flight 74 device was stowed in the luggage of a woman who left the Los Angeles to New York itinerary in Chicago. As fellow passengers assemble a sketch of the woman, Adams decides to pay the ransom.

Eileen Kelly, the mystery passenger, and another conspirator named Vince arrive at the rented house where Hoplin and Steve are holding captive the Molners. To leverage further cooperation, Hoplin intends to separate Pat from her parents, but when they challenge him to kill them first, he backs down and changes the plan. Joan, who will collect the ransom money, stays with him and Steve while Jim takes Pat along with Vince and Kelly. Before leaving, Kelly threatens mother and daughter with a lethal-looking shiv.

Away from the house, Hoplin calls Adams with instructions to separate the money into $20 bills from twelve different federal monetary districts. During his absence, Joan is menaced by the Benzedrine-popping Steve, who reveals himself to have been in prison for rape and assault. At the same time, Jim and Pat are hustled into Kelly's penthouse apartment, which is accessible only by a private elevator and a single flight of stairs. The FBI agents, meanwhile, have traced the explosives to Jim's shop and are working to identify the dental imprint on a piece of gum left on the plane by the unknown female suspect.

The next morning, Joan appears at the bank for the money and meets with the authorities, explaining how she and Jim have been forced to participate in the scheme. Although some of the agents are unsure if she's telling the truth, Adams and Cole decide to give her the cash and track her as best they can. Frantic to meet her 1:30 p.m. deadline, Joan gives as many clues and descriptions as possible before departing and following Hoplin's detailed directions which lead her to an unoccupied waiting car. She also reveals that Hoplin, whom she knows only by his first name, has planted another bomb in an unspecified populated area that will detonate if he is not paid.

Shiv-wielding Angie shares the screen with a *Cry Terror!* cast that includes, from left, Neville Brand, Rod Steiger, child actor Terry Ann Ross, James Mason, Inger Stevens, and Jack Klugman (1958).

Cued by an embedded message in the police dispatches on the car radio, Joan races toward the address of Steve's bungalow in the Riverdale neighborhood of the Bronx. When a truck forces her onto the wrong highway, she loses precious time and arrives late, just as Hoplin has telephoned Vince and is about to tell him to kill Jim and Pat. Calling off that murder and revealing that the additional bomb threat was a bluff, Hoplin leaves to stash the money elsewhere. Left alone, Steve makes advances toward Joan at knifepoint and she stabs him with a piece of broken glass. Although she attempts to hide the body, Hoplin suspects the truth upon his return and they both relocate to Vince's apartment.

Fearing that he and his daughter will ultimately be killed, Jim finds his way into the elevator shaft and after some precarious maneuvering there, succeeds in escaping and using a neighbor's phone to call the police, who have also been led to Kelly's penthouse by the FBI's identification of the gum implant. In a brief shootout, Kelly is wounded and taken into custody. Jim uses the shiv to force Vince to tell the address of his apartment.

When he learns of the arrest, Hoplin plans to move once more, but Joan throws hot water in his face and escapes. Running into a subway entrance, she tells a bystander to call the police and jumps into the tunnel to hide. Hoplin pursues her there, but before he can reach the spot where she has fallen on the tracks, he is accidentally electrocuted by the third rail. Alerted by the subway passenger, Cole and Jim arrive to rescue Joan just as an oncoming train approaches the station.

Notes and Comments: On more than one occasion, Angie revealed that upon seeing herself in *Cry Terror!* she realized that after all the years of apprenticeship she had finally developed true screen presence. It is easy to see why she felt that way. As Rod Steiger's coldly seductive moll Kelly, she is mesmerizing. In the scene where all seven principal characters are gathered around the luxurious livingroom of the gang's first hideout, viewer attention is riveted on her. Leaning back on the couch and smirking at the Molners' dilemma, she conveys menace without even speaking. When she does talk, the threat is escalated. Clutching Vince's shiv in one hand and rubbing her fingers along the blade, she snarls, "and the sides are sharp too. They've been ground down and they're like a razor." Edging closer, she suddenly slices off a lock of Joan's hair. "See you hardly felt it, cut it off like it was butter," she observes. "A shiv like this can slip, slip very easily. I'd keep that in mind if I were you." Cradled in her mother's arms, little Pat turns away in terror.

Angie's entrance into the film is equally arresting. As the passengers complete a slide projection sketch of her, there is a cut to the real-life Kelly and Vince arriving at the house where the others await. Having learned to use her entire body as an expressive instrument, Angie thrusts herself purposefully into the setting. Her demeanor is proprietary and dismissive at the same time. Glancing haphazardly at the accommodations, she agrees the place is "classy" but asserts, "I'm more interested in the bar." She is dressed in a gray suit and black pillbox hat yet flops informally onto the furniture. The disparity between her costume and posture emphasizes the casual contempt she directs to the world at large. "Class, huh?" she says again when she leads Vince and Jim Molner into her penthouse and shrugs off the impressive view. "There's Queens over there." As part of the tour, she smugly reminds Jim how impossible it will be for him to escape from the place. That tough talk, coupled with the skillful handling of Vince's shiv, makes her every bit as dangerous as the men. In fact, she later derides Vince's loss of nerve by noting that his "hand shakes like an old woman's" and mocks Hoplin as a "big mastermind" after his plans have to be altered. When the FBI agents break into the apartment, it is Kelly not Vince who instinctively fires a gun and is wounded in return. The evocation of masculine traits by a stylishly dressed woman who also walks down the street like a fashion model is one of the subtle strengths of what Angie rightly regarded as a breakthrough performance.

The film itself was a family project for Andrew and Virginia Stone, married at the time and partners in their own independent production company. For over a decade they made a series of crime thrillers that he wrote and directed and she edited. The usual narrative involved an ordinary person caught up in a dangerous situation partly defined by a race against time.

Cry Terror! demonstrates the strengths and limits of their technique. For starters, it is unnecessarily dense and complicated. The gang continually changes locations for no apparent reason and Hoplin's multiple bomb plantings seem confusingly redundant. There is also a lot of uninteresting procedural minutiae related to bill counting, radio messages, and police signals. The soundtrack's use of a theremin to heighten suspense is stylistic overkill. On the other hand, the action is compelling. Filming occurred at actual locations in and around both New York City and Los Angeles, and cameras mounted in the plane cockpit and on the backseat of Joan's convertible add to the realism. Certain events, covered by reporters (including Chet Huntley as himself) speaking directly into the camera, seem documentary-like in nature.

Above all else, Andrew Stone got excellent performances from the entire cast. James Mason and Inger Stevens capture the Molners' vulnerability, and Steiger fully sells Hoplin's carefully spoken villainy. Neville Brand and Jack Klugman are believable as the jittery accomplices as are Kenneth Tobey and Jack Kruschen (a Stone regular) as by-the-book FBI agents. Angie's ease among such company gives further evidence of her maturing talent.

Reviews:

"In the supporting cast, Angie Dickinson is a standout as a gaily abandoned underworld character who will do anything for a price. Jack Klugman is excellent as a professional thug who shrinks from child murder. Neville Brand makes a moronic masterpiece of the whining, self-pitying degenerate."

—Jack Moffitt, *Daily Variety*, April 15, 1958

"Stone, as director, and Virginia Stone, as editor, keep several scenes boiling simultaneously, cutting sharply from one to another, heightening the effect of each by playing it off against another. The picture, as with other Stone Productions, has the grimy feel of reality through their shooting in actual locations away from any studio. For the kind of story they do, it pays off."

—*Daily Variety*, April 15, 1958

"This quick, threatening cat and mouse thriller gathers its suspense together like strong twine, braiding it in swift, tight loops and following it to an ultimate desperate finale without once faltering."

"Under Mr. Stone's direction everyone has turned in taut, convincing performances. Steiger is a superbly laconic villain, ably abetted by the metallic Miss Dickinson, a nervously cruel Klugman and a decadent, sex–mad Brand. Mason and Miss Stevens are likewise excellent as the terrorized parents."

—Paul V. Beckley, *New York Herald Tribune*, May 15 1958

"Another beauty, Angie Dickinson, talks tough and acts rough as the moll who works with Steiger and Brand. The attack sequences are grim. The pursuit scenes are realistic. The statistical data on bomb explosions (RD-X is the chemical compound) seems very learned. The whole effect is creepy and tingly."

—Irene Thirer, *New York Post*, May 15, 1958

"As the ringleader of the extortionists, Rod Steiger croaks and grins like an old toad, and Neville Brand, Angie Dickinson and Jack Klugman are assorted miscreants in the gang. They, as the uninhibited villains, are the most effective missiles of the Stones."

"But, as so often happens when shocking seems to be the main aim of a film, the flow of events is lightly channeled through a web of implausibilities."

—Bosley Crowther, *The New York Times*, May 15, 1958

"It's the suspense and tension of the plot that carries a movie like this along, and under such circumstances, individual performances may count for very little. Nevertheless, Mason, Miss Stevens and that youngster, Terry Ann Ross, give fairly substantial accounts of themselves as the good people caught up in a web of evil; and Steiger, as the smooth and unctuous extortionist, and Brand and Miss Dickinson as his two assistants, make as horrible a trio as could be desired."

—Leo Mishkin, *Morning Telegraph*, May 15, 1958

"It is a superlative exercise in sheer, unrelenting suspense which moves so fast, with so many constantly unfolding developments, that one has no time to ponder a few loose plot situations. It was produced and directed by Andrew and Virginia Stone, the husband-and-wife team who specialize in this type of story, and it one of their best to date."

—Mirror-News, May 30, 1958

Stardom

Rio Bravo

Credits: An Armada Productions/Warner Bros. production released on April 4, 1959. Technicolor. Running time of 141 minutes. Based on an unpublished short story by B. H. McCampbell. **Cast:** John Wayne (Sheriff John T. Chance), Dean Martin (Dude), Ricky Nelson (Colorado), Angie Dickinson (Feathers), Walter Brennan (Stumpy), Ward Bond (Pat Wheeler), John Russell (Nathan Burdette), Pedro Gonzalez Gonzalez (Carlos Robante), Estelita Rodriguez (Consuela Robante), Claude Akins (Joe Burdette). **Crew:** Howard Hawks (director and producer), Jules Furthman and Leigh Brackett (screenwriters), Dimitri Tiomkin (composer), Russell Harlan (cinematographer), Folmar Blangsted (editor), Leo. K. Kuter (art director), Ralph S. Hurst (set decorator), Marjorie Best (costume designer), Gordon Bau (makeup artist), Paul Helmick (assistant director), Robert B. Lee (sound).

Plot Synopsis: Sheriff John T. Chance keeps order in the town of Rio Bravo with the help of his drunken former deputy Dude and a game-legged old man named Stumpy. One evening Dude enters a saloon jittery and desperate for a drink. Joe Burdette, brother of wealthy land baron Nathan Burdette, tosses a silver dollar into a spittoon and laughs. As Dude reaches to retrieve it, Chance appears and kicks the spittoon away. Shamed by his behavior and his friend's look of disgust, Dude grabs an ax handle and knocks Chance out with it. Burdette's men hold Dude and begin to punch him. When Joe steps in to work him over, a bystander restrains his arm and Joe shoots the man dead at point-blank range.

Joe moves onto his brother's saloon, where a bleeding and dazed Chance arrives to arrest him. One of Burdette's men pulls a pistol, but Dude appears at the door, grabs a gun from another guy's holster, and shoots the weapon out of the gunman's hand. Joe goes for his own gun and Chance knocks him out with his rifle butt. He and Dude drag Joe off to jail.

The next morning, Chance's friend Pat Wheeler arrives in town with his wagon train, which is carrying oil, dynamite, and other supplies. Riding guard for Wheeler is a polite young gunslinger named Colorado. Chance tells Wheeler about the trouble, revealing that since Burdette's men have sealed up the town he will have to wait six days for the marshal to pick up Joe. Over at the jail, Chance has re-deputized Dude and put Stumpy in charge of guarding Joe with instructions to shoot him if his men intervene.

After patrolling the town with Dude, Chance stops at the hotel, where the owner Carlos has warned him that Wheeler is talking too freely about the sheriff needing help and drawing too much attention to his vulnerability. By way of apology, Wheeler suggests that his newly hired gunman could be helpful, but Colorado respectfully declines, preferring to mind his own business and also promising not to start any trouble without first informing the Sheriff, who admires the kid for showing good sense. In the hotel's barroom, Chance again notices an attractive young woman named Feathers, who had previously kidded him and Carlos for discussing a pair of frilly red bloomers that Carlos secretly bought for his wife Consuela. Recently arrived in town on the stage and waiting for its repair, she is the big winner in a card game that also involves Wheeler and Colorado. When Chance notices that the deck they had been using is missing three cards, he follows her upstairs and accuses her of being the gambling cheat referenced on a handbill forwarded from a nearby town. Just then, Colorado enters and claims that another player is the real cheat and that, as promised, he's giving Chance a heads-up before causing trouble. They confront the man and find the three cards. Although he refuses to apologize to Feathers, Chance is no longer so adamant that she leave town.

As Wheeler walks back to the hotel after checking on his wagons, he is shot dead by a Burdette thug hiding in the stable. Colorado wants to help, but Chance tells him, "You had a chance to get in this but you didn't want to. Stay out. We don't need you." He and Dude go after the killer, who escapes from the stable into the Burdette saloon after Dude wounds him. Asking to go in the front door for a change instead of skulking in through the back, Dude checks everyone for the muddy boots he believes the shooter has. All of the patrons have clean ones, and a Burdette man scornfully suggest he needs a drink, tossing a silver dollar into the spittoon. Noticing blood dripping into a glass of beer from above the bar, Dude turns, fires, and kills the gunman overhead on the balcony. Before leaving, he forces the coin tosser to retrieve his money from the spittoon and Chance tells him he can go through the front door anytime he wants.

Feathers is waiting for Chance at the hotel and pours him a drink. "How does a girl get herself on a handbill?" he asks, and she explains that her gambler husband secretly began to cheat at cards once his luck ran out. By the time she found out, it was too late; he had been shot and killed. Chance says he'll have the handbills with her description on them recalled. Unbeknownst to Chance, she stands guard outside his hotel room all night to keep him safe.

Nathan Burdette arrives with a group of newly hired men. Stationed at the edge of town, Dude confiscates their guns and shoots the reins of one guy who resists him. Admitting Nathan to the jail, Chance warns him that Stumpy, still resentful over the Burdettes' seizure of his ranch, will be happy to shoot Joe the minute any stranger tries to come through the door. Carlos interrupts to inform Chance that Feathers has failed to leave on the stage. Hurrying to the hotel, he tells her things might be different if there was no crisis but she kisses him anyway and he responds.

Colorado stops by the jail that night to tell Chance that the tune being played by the mariachi band in Nathan's saloon is the "Deguello" or "Cutthroat Song" which General Santa Anna used at the Alamo to tell the Texans inside that they would receive no mercy in defeat. Seeing how hard Dude is working to stay sober, Chance gives him back the expensive guns and clothes he's been saving ever since Dude was jilted by a treacherous saloon girl and began his non-stop bender. Feathers gives him a shave to complete the transformation.

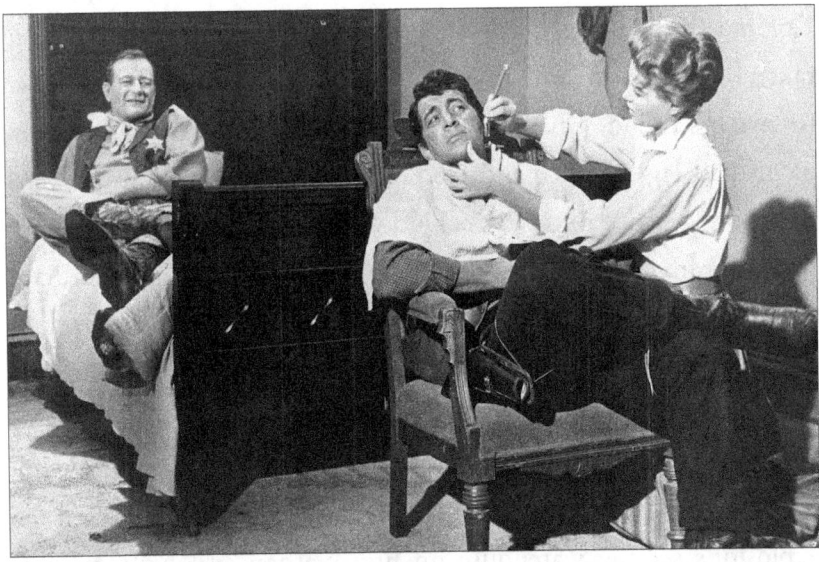

In *Rio Bravo*, Feathers (Angie) shaves Dude (Dean Martin) while Sheriff John T. Chance (John Wayne) looks on (1959).

At his post early the next day, Dude is jumped and tied up by Burdette's men, allowing Chance to be caught by surprise in front of the hotel without his rifle. As instructed by Colorado, Feathers tosses a flower pot through the window while Colorado throws Chance his rifle and shoots two of the gunmen. Chance takes care of another and picks off a fourth man trying to escape on horseback. Realizing he is now fully involved, Colorado becomes deputized.

Chance decides he and his men will hole up in the jail and wait for the marshal. Slightly strung out from the action, Dude almost relapses, but the sound of the "Deguello" pulls him back. He and Chance go to the hotel for supplies. While Dude is having a bath, Burdette's men take Carlos and Consuela captive and use them as a ploy to summon Chance and trip him over some rope tied at the bottom of the stairs. With Dude and Feathers also restrained, Chance is ordered to take the men to jail to free Joe. Knowing how Stumpy will react, Dude urges him to comply.

At the jail, Chance slips out of the line of fire, and Stumpy, with Colorado as back-up, blasts the intruders. Dude, however, has been taken hostage, and Nathan offers to trade him for Joe. Determined to save his friend, Chance agrees. Leaving Stumpy behind because of his bad leg, Chance and Colorado take Joe to Burdette's warehouse on the edge of town. As Dude and Joe are sent out walking in opposite directions, Dude suddenly tackles the younger Burdette, and a gunfight breaks out between the two sides. After knocking out Joe, Dude joins the battle as do Stumpy and Carlos, who have unexpectedly turned up to help. Finding the dynamite from Pat Wheeler's wagons, Stumpy tosses the sticks at the warehouse while Chance and Dude detonate them with their gunshots. After a few explosions set the warehouse on fire, Nathan and his remaining men surrender.

That night, Chance visits Feathers in her hotel room, where she is changing into a skimpy black corset and tights for her new singing job. When he objects and says he'll arrest her, she takes it as proof that he loves her. Walking through town, Stumpy and Dude see the tights fall out of a hotel window, and Dude warns a cackling Stumpy to mind his own business.

Notes and Comments: *Rio Bravo* is not only a classic Western but also one of the best American movies ever made. If Angie had appeared in no other pictures after this one, she would still be a remembered figure in film history.

Before anything else, *Rio Bravo* is also a perfectly achieved example of the consistent personal vision that director/producer Howard Hawks brought to the wide variety of genres in which he worked. A small, tightly bonded group of men comes together to complete a difficult mission. Appreciative of each other's professional skills and tolerant of flaws, they use humor to defuse the danger that threatens their success. As in a club, there are nicknames, running jokes, and initiations. To be called "good" at one's job, whether it's piloting a plane, leading a safari, or shooting a gun, is the highest accolade. Keeping cool under pressure is mandatory.

There is always a much-admired leader in the Hawks picture, and here it is Chance. His organizational style is loose and informal yet also one whose authority is unquestioned. With no family ties of their own, group members are bound to each other by loyalty and love. They are known by the boyish nicknames Dude, Stumpy, and Colorado; Dude refers jokingly to Chance as "papa." Recognition from Chance is sought and valued by everyone. "You were good in there tonight," Chance tells Dude after the saloon balcony shooting. Later, as Chance explains how Colorado helped him take on Burdette's men, Dude asks, "Is he as good as I used to be?"

Making the comparison, Chance replies, "It'd be pretty close. I'd hate to have to live on the difference." Chance's opinion is the only one that counts. Even cantankerous old Stumpy complains that he gets "never a kind word" of appreciation from Chance. "Why are you so goldarned ornery?" he asks. In mock apology, the sheriff declares, "You're a treasure," and kisses him on the head.

Chance's disapproval carries equal importance. Despite the allowances he makes for Dude's drinking and Stumpy's physical limitations, he expects dignity, focus, and self-control. "Sorry don't get it done, Dude," he warns his friend after another show of temper at his own failings. "That's the second time you hit me. Don't ever do it again." When Colorado says he wants to avenge Pat Wheeler's murder, Chance answers, "I wouldn't have let him get shot in the first place." In this tightly connected world of male comradeship, having each other's back takes precedence over almost every other responsibility.

The few women admitted to the club are those who, like Feathers, respect the rituals and make limited demands of their own. Independent and feisty, Feathers wanders into Chance's orbit and decides to stay. "This isn't the first time that handbill has come up. I'd like to know what to do about it," she says when he questions her about the past. "Well, you could quit playing cards, wearing feathers," he suggests. "No, sheriff. No, I'm not going to do that," she argues. "You see, that's what I'd do if I were the kind of girl you think I am." Guided by her own code of conduct, she chooses not to leave town on the stage but to stay and help Chance herself, bravely keeping guard outside his hotel room and tossing the flower pot to distract Burdette's gunmen. Most significantly, she is the one who initiates the romance with Chance. Teasing him about Consuela's red bloomers and gazing intensely at him from the poker table, she makes all the first moves. "I won't get in your way. I'll just be here," she tells him, and he replies, "If I wasn't in this mess, it might be different, but I am." Her immediate response is to say, "That's all I wanted to hear," take hold of his vest, and pull him forward for a kiss.

Angie is the ideal Hawks heroine. After a string of minor roles in lesser Westerns, she was ready, having learned how to make the most of her physical and dramatic assets. On multiple occasions, she angles her body provocatively across a hotel doorway to tease or seduce Chance. The gesture becomes a repeated piece of business, a sign of her assertiveness. Fully inhabiting the playing field, she conveys the same physical expansiveness as the male characters. To show her defiance of Chance, she plants her hands on her hips and leans forward into the frame. For the drinking scene with Colorado, she sits with legs apart and elbows on knees, slurring her words and then missing the first step on the staircase. She even manages the difficult task of mumbling to herself while wandering aimlessly around her hotel room.

At Hawks's suggestion, she has lowered her eyes, her voice, and the speed of her delivery. His intention was to fashion her into the same sharp-witted, accessible siren he had made of Lauren Bacall in *To Have and Have Not* (1944). In fact, some of their dialogue is remarkably similar. "It's even better when you help," says Bacall's character Slim after Humphrey Bogart's Steve returns her kiss, just as Feathers tells Chance, "I'm glad we tried it [the kiss] a second time. It's better when two people do it." Putting their cards on the table, Slim declares, "I'm hard to get, Steve. All you have to do is ask me," and Feathers echoes, "I'm hard to get, John T. You're gonna have to say you want me." In both cases, perhaps a wish fulfillment on Hawks's part, a vibrant young woman expresses unreserved love for an older, more experienced man.

ANGIE

Angie as Feathers tests John Wayne's resistance in *Rio Bravo* (1959).]

Most of Angie's dozen or so big scenes are with John Wayne, and their rapport is notable. Almost twenty-five years his junior, she gives him renewed credibility as a leading man, playfully undercutting his stalwart screen persona with her flirtatiousness. While she chatters away, he hesitates, shrugs, and ultimately carries her upstairs to one of their hotel rooms. She appreciated Wayne's professional patience. "We didn't shoot that many takes, but we rehearsed a lot," she explained. "And never once did Duke say, 'Jesus Christ, can't she just do it?' Never once did he appear to be impatient. And for a star of his caliber, working with a green actress, that was remarkable. Never, not for a second, did I feel he didn't approve of what I was doing."[2]

Rio Bravo accurately has been called a minimalist Western. Except for the pursuit of Wheeler's killer and the final gun battle, not all that much actually happens. The action takes place primarily in the hotel, saloon, and jail, the latter being exclusively reserved space for Chance's fraternity. Characters spend a lot of time just behaving, engaged in what seem like normal, everyday routines. Dude keeps trying to successfully roll a cigarette, Stumpy admits visitors to the jail, Chance walks to and from the hotel. With Stumpy accompanying them on harmonica, Colorado and Dude sing a couple of songs together while hunkered down in the jail. It is the humorous interplay between characters that is entertaining to watch.

Like John Ford, Hawks was never an ostentatious director. Because he moved the camera for function rather than effect, his visual sophistication was often overlooked. Nicely executed here are the parallel tracking shots of Dude and Chance patrolling opposite sides of the street and the moving camera that pulls out in front of Nathan and his men as they ride into town. Additionally, the blood dropping into the beer glass is one of cinema's great revelatory moments.

Rio Bravo received decent reviews at the time of its release and has since become recognized by most film historians as a masterpiece from one of the principal directors of Hollywood's Golden Age. The script was a collaboration between Hawks, Jules Furthman, Leigh Brackett, and Hawks's adult daughter Barbara McCampbell. Hawks himself liked the picture so much that he essentially remade it in 1967 as *El Dorado*. John Wayne again played the leader; Robert Mitchum, James Caan, and Arthur Hunnicutt had the Martin, Nelson, and Brennan parts. Charlene Holt took over for Lauren Bacall and Angie. *Rio Lobo*, Hawks's final film in 1970, again starred John Wayne and presented slightly different characters in a third version of the same basic concept.

Reviews:

"*Rio Bravo* is a big, brawling western with enough action and marquee voltage to assure hefty reception at the boxoffice. Casting of Dean Martin and Ricky Nelson with such vet range stalwarts as John Wayne and Walter Brennan is a smart showmanship move bound to pay off in an expanded market, and performances generally are superior to the average western. While somewhat long, interest is sustained and net effect is one of the better class oaters of the year."

"In for distaff interest and with more legitimate footage than usual in a western is Angie Dickinson, a looker and interesting newcomer fashioned into an important key character who delivers in every way.

—*Daily Variety*, February 17, 1959

"A large, sprawling hulk of a Western has been fashioned by producer-director Howard Hawks in *Rio Bravo*. He has put it together with a power and combustion that should generate mileage at the boxoffice turnstiles."

—*Film Daily*, February 17, 1959

"Here is straightaway, hard-hitting western story adventure, but directed with such accomplished skill, given the benefit of such high level production values, that the film emerges head and shoulders above the routine of its kind. Casting alone should account for a great measure of the success the film appears certain to enjoy among the followers of the Western and they certainly are legion.

—*Motion Picture Herald,* February 21, 1959

"We saw helluva picture the other night, *Rio Bravo,* that had been shaved down from three hours to two hours and 20 minutes, and we'd bet anything that the snipping of an additional 15 or 20 minutes would add a hundred thousand in gross for every foot cut, because the picture gets too draggy at times. But even with this, you are snapped back to the intensity of the story, expertly directed and tremendous cast. (Which reminds us, where did this Angie Dickinson, the girl lead, come from? She's a cinch star with a couple of good vehicles.)"

—*The Hollywood Reporter,* February 26, 1959

"There is excitement, tension, the pleasure of looking at Western landscapes, and the age-old gratification when the good guys beat the bad. The good guys, in this instance, are John Wayne and Dean Martin; and while Wayne swaggers through his role with a contentment bred of familiarity, Martin succeeds in making something quite fresh and fascinating out of his portrait of a gunslinger determined to redeem himself after a two-year bender."

—*Saturday Review,* March 14, 1959

"Miss Dickinson, a tall, shapely brunet with an irresistible Mona Lisa smile, plays it cool in much the same enigmatic but fascinating manner as Lauren Bacall in Hawks' memorable *To Have and Have Not.* And Nelson, with less to do, impresses as quiet but efficient."

"Wayne himself seems more animated than usual, as if he were actually enjoying himself, and both Martin and Brennan deliver highly engaging characterizations—Martin in his struggle with the demon in himself as well as with the enemy, and Brennan gabbling in his best toothless fashion."

—Philip K. Scheuer, *Los Angeles Times*, March 19, 1959

"A surpassing example of this art form is Howard Hawks' *Rio Bravo*. What raises it above most of its kind is that all the conventional ingredients that go into a Western are splashed on the screen with vigor and craftsmanship."

—S.A. Desick, *Los Angeles Examiner*, March 19, 1959

"Sitting on this keg of dynamite for two hours and 20 minutes may prove to be a bit of an endurance contest for the audience, too; but the film's melodramatics are sprinkled with bits of unexpected comedy, a touch of romance, and some solid drama—as well as top-notch color photography. Acting, too, is of the highest order: John Wayne as the sheriff, Dean Martin surprisingly good as the deputy-drunk fighting his way back to sober sanity and self-respect, Walter Brennan as his second deputy. Young crooner Ricky Nelson plays a junior gunfighter neatly enough, and a pretty newcomer named Angie Dickinson has a cute way with her as the gamblin' gal who deals the sheriff in on her hand."

—*Cue*, March 21, 1959

"Q: How do you make a Western movie these days that stands a chance of competing with television?"

"A: First off, you film it in color, Next you hire a big box-office name like John Wayne to play he sheriff. Then you need a gimmick. Alcoholism is in fashion, and Dean Martin did a crackerjack job as a boozer in *Some Came Running*, so you get him to play a deputy. For teenage appeal sign Ricky Nelson and give him a couple of rhythm-and- blues numbers to sing and play on his guitar. Ask Dimitri Tiomkin to dash off the songs (remember that great score he did for *High Noon*?). Don't forget a little love interest for Wayne, just enough for a teaser, say a sexy newcomer called Angie Dickinson, who can be hired just now for peanuts. Then, for a few laughs, throw in Walter Brennan without his teeth."

—*Newsweek*, March 30, 1959

I'll Give My Life

Credits: A Concordia Productions picture released on February 3, 1960. Black and white. Running time of 78 minutes. **Cast:** Ray Collins (John Bradford), John Bryant (James Bradford), Angie Dickinson (Alice Greenway), Katherine Warren (Dora Bradford), Donald Woods (Pastor Goodwin), Jon Shepodd (Bob Conners), Stuart Randall (Rex Barton), Richard Benedict (Cpl. Burr), Sam Flint (Roy Calhoun), Ivan Triesault (Dr. Neuman), Jimmy Baird (Jimmy Bradford), Mimi Gibson (Jodie Bradford). **Crew:** William F. Claxton (director), Herbert Moulton (screenwriter), Sam Hersh (producer), Walter Strenge (cinematographer), Robert Fritch (editor), Bill Ross (art director), Lou Perlof (assistant director), Tom Lambert (sound).

Plot Synopsis: The successful co-owner of a construction engineering firm, John Bradford is looking forward to the graduation party for his son Jim, who has just completed his college degree in engineering. Thinking ahead, he plans to bring Jim into the company and has listed him on a new directory sign that he proudly shows to his partner Rex Barton and his secretary Alice Greenway, who is also Jim's girlfriend of many years.

That evening at the party in the Bradford's penthouse apartment, Jim confides to Alice that he intends to enter the seminary and become a minister rather than an engineer. She is shocked but supportive. After all the guests have departed, Jim also tells his father, who takes the news badly and begins a campaign to change his mind. When a summer working for the company fails to bring Jim back into the fold, John argues that Alice may not be cut out to be a minister's wife. He asks her to pressure Jim but she refuses, and the young man leaves for the seminary.

During his years of study, Jim keeps up a steady correspondence with Alice. Against all indications otherwise, his father continues to hope that he will return to the company as a partner, even deciding not to hire Jim's college engineering friend Bob Conners so that a position will remain open.

Upon graduation, Jim tells Alice that he would like to propose marriage but that he has accepted a foreign mission assignment in New Guinea. His father reacts angrily again, asking "What can you do for a bunch of savages like that?" In a flashback sequence, Jim recounts his World War II army service in the Pacific and explains that he wants to now bring salvation not violence to the native islanders. His parents and Alice see him off at the airport.

Finally abandoning hope that his son ever will join the firm, John hires Bob Conners, who not only takes Jim's old office but also grows attracted to Alice. The Bradfords' fear that Jim and Alice are drifting apart dissipates when Jim sends a cablegram asking her to marry him. Overcome with joy, she leaves for New Guinea.

Settled in at the mission, Jim and Alice befriend the locals and start a family, a son named Jim Junior followed by his younger sister

Jodie. Proud grandfather John keeps friends and associates updated with photos. His peace of mind is interrupted by a cablegram announcing that Jim is suffering from a severe case of tropical fever; John and his wife Dora catch the first available flight to New Guinea.

Although he keeps falling in and out of consciousness, Jim has time to talk with his father about the unfinished work that means so much to him. Just before he dies, he gives his father his diary with the following Biblical inscription: "I must work the works of him that sent me." As she packs to leave, Alice tells John how rewarding it has been to serve a God of love and mercy.

Back in Chicago, Alice and the children slowly adapt to their new life, growing close to the Bradfords and to Bob Conners. Deeply depressed, John continues to read the diary and ponder the meaning of Jim's life. Slowly he realizes that he himself must continue his son's work. Quitting the engineering company, he travels around the country enlisting financial and personnel support for the missions. The film closes with one of his inspirational speeches.

Notes and Comments: Known also as *The Unfinished Task*, *I'll Give My Life* was shot in 1955 but not released until five years later, several months after the premiere of *Rio Bravo*. It is hard to imagine any film more different from the Hawks classic. Financed by the Lutheran Church and staffed with various spiritual advisors, *I'll Give My Life* promotes a kind of Western religious colonialism that is aggressively dismissive of third world culture. Visually, it is flat and lifeless.

As the demure minister's wife, Angie is so "proper" as to be almost unrecognizable. With her tightly permed brown hair and dark winged eyebrows, she never wears anything more daring than a striped blouse opened slightly at the collar. Usually she is seen in hats, gloves, and conservative dresses extending well below the knee. Although she and Jim Bradford have been dating for years, they never kiss or even embrace. Stoically supportive of her husband's grueling ministerial work, she spouts lines such as "The work at the mission becomes your whole life. It's greater than any material reward. It comes from knowing that you've brought these people to their savior." Yet, even given the clichéd part as written, she finds an authentic core to build on, bringing measured yet profound grief to the scenes where she cradles Jim's dead body and discusses his legacy with her father-in-law.

William Claxton directs with a distractingly heavy hand. He consistently uses fades to transition between scenes and tracks in to facial close-ups for dramatic emphasis. The sets, especially the Bradford penthouse apartment, seem to have been borrowed from a low-budget television production. There is an unnatural stillness to terrace scenes that should have had a little air blowing through them.

Ray Collins, best known as Jim Gettys in *Citizen Kane* (1941) and Lieutenant Arthur Tragg on the *Perry Mason* TV series (1957-1964), stars as John Bradford. Ivan Triesault, the evil Eric Mathis in Hitchcock's *Notorious* (1946), appears briefly as the mission doctor who treats Jim Bradford.

Reviews:

"Some names of interest—most notably Ray Collins, long a mainstay of the highly-successful CBS-TV *Perry Mason* series; Angie Dickinson, fast looming as one of the most promising young players, and Donald Woods, easily remembered from his leading man era—people this story of belief in our times. It is a Concordia production and, given the essentials of word-of-mouth buildup, should provide some handsome box office returns."

"Acting values are admirably restrained. Woods contributes a properly somber mood in a religious role."

—*Motion Picture Herald*, February 18, 1961

The Bramble Bush

Credits: A United States Pictures/Warner Bros. production released on February 24, 1960. Technicolor. Running time of 93 minutes. Based on a novel by Charles Mergendahl. **Cast:** Richard Burton (Dr. Guy Montford), Barbara Rush (Margaret "Mar" McFie), Jack Carson (Bert Mosley), Angie Dickinson (Fran), James Dunn (Stew Schaeffer), Henry Jones (Parker Welk), Tom Drake (Larry McFie), Frank Conroy (Dr. Sol Kelsey), Carl Benton Reid (Sam McFie), Patricia Crest (Betsy), William Hansen (Father Bannon), Russ Conway (Sheriff Larson Witt). **Crew:** Daniel Petrie (director), Milton Sperling (screenwriter and producer), Philip Yordan (screenwriter), Leonard Rosenman (composer), Lucien Ballard (cinematographer), Folmar Blangsted (editor), Jack Poplin (art director), Ralph S. Hurst (set decorator), Howard Shoup (costume designer), Gordon Bau (makeup artist), Russell Saunders (assistant director), Robert B. Lee (sound).

Plot Synopsis: Handsome young doctor Guy Montford returns to his hometown, a New England coastal village, to care for his ailing childhood friend Larry McFie. Warmly welcomed by hospital chief Dr. Sol Kelsey and his head nurse Fran, Guy has an unpleasant confrontation with Larry's wealthy father Sam, who does not believe that Guy should be in charge of his son's treatment. Terminally ill from Hodgkin's disease, Larry asks Guy to take care of his wife Margaret. Over an early morning martini, Margaret reveals that Larry is the love of her life and that the thought of losing him has left her sleepless and distraught. Guy prescribes sleeping pills and agrees to entertain Larry's wish that the two of them might marry after he's gone.

When he visits his parents' graves in the town cemetery, Guy pointedly leaves flowers only for his father. He seems equally disturbed to be staying in his boyhood home, where he wanders distractedly through the rooms. An alcoholic elderly man named Stewart Schaeffer shows up there and asks for forgiveness, but Guy angrily ejects him from the premises.

Early one morning, Guy is called to a fire at a nearby motel and finds Fran and Bert Mosley, an unctuous town lawyer running for district attorney, registered there for the night under assumed names. Bert claims they are practically engaged, and Guy covers for Fran when newspaper editor Parker Welk appears on the scene to look for a story. Embarrassed, Fran later tells Bert that she is tired of meeting on the sly.

At Larry's request, Guy tries to take Margaret out sailing but they never get further than the dock. Admitting that Guy confuses her, she once again states how much she misses the passionate relationship she and Larry used to share. At the hospital, Larry is suffering from great pain and begs Guy to do away with him. Telling his friend to hold on in hopes of a cure, Guy also shares with Doctor Kelsey that Larry has asked for a mercy killing.

Fran invites Guy to her room and confesses that she is deeply in love with him. Although they kiss briefly and she offers herself fully to him, Guy gently declines any further involvement. Realizing that he may be in love with someone else, Fran is devastated. Outside the nurses' quarters, Guy encounters Sam McFie, who angrily discharges him from his son's case.

That night, Margaret, no longer under the influence of sleeping pills and alcohol, comes to Guy's house and begs him to stay on the case. During their conversation, Stewart Schaeffer drunkenly barges in again and Guy once more forcibly throws him out. Shocked by the behavior, Margaret listens as Guy reveals that as a child he discovered his mother and Schaeffer were having an affair and that the awareness of it caused his father's suicide. Guy rushes from the house and Margaret follows him to Larry's boat, where they spend the night together.

After church on Sunday, Parker Welk tells Fran he knows about the motel rendezvous and blackmails her into coming to his office. Bert discovers her there posing for racy photos and beats Parker unconscious. Once again Guy covers for Fran by treating Parker, destroying the photos, and threatening to tell Parker's wife if he threatens Fran in the future.

On a visit to Boston, Guy learns from an expert that there is no hope for Larry. In response, he gets roaring drunk and passes out in his hotel room. Margaret finds him there and discloses that she is pregnant with his child.

Returning to the hospital, Guy sees that Larry's pain has become unbearable and injects him with a lethal dose of morphine. After discovering the missing medication, Fran overhears Guy tell Margaret that he has ended Larry's suffering and that he loves her without regret. Uncertain what to do, Fran confides in Bert. Sensing a political opportunity, Bert informs the authorities and then offers to defend Guy in the trial that follows.

Things go badly in the courtroom, especially when Sam McFie lyingly testifies that his son was afraid of Guy. Refused permission from Guy to have Margaret testify on his behalf, Bert calls Dr. Kelsey, who not only confirms that Larry begged Guy to kill him but that Sam McFie has been mentally unbalanced since 1935.

Despite the torrid imagery, Angie's character Fran never manages to win Richard Burton in *The Bramble Bush* (1960).

Guy is acquitted, and Margaret announces that she is leaving town to have the baby by herself. While he accepts the decision, Guy also says that he will live in the hope that they will meet again sometime in the future.

Notes and Comments: "*The Bramble Bush* was written in the blister-heat of feelings and excitations," reads the movie's lobby poster.

"It could come to the screen in no other way." The advertising campaign linked it to a spate of mid-century Hollywood pictures about small town sex and scandal, movies such as *Peyton Place* (1957), *Some Came Running* (1958), *A Summer Place* (1959), and *Splendor in the Grass* (1961). Ironically enough, most of the questionable behavior occurs off screen. Overcome with emotion, Richard Burton recounts how young Guy comes home from school early and finds his mother in bed naked with another man. Slapped by his father for behaving rudely to his mother at dinner, he blurts out the story and runs away. Then, hiding on the beach later that evening, he watches in horror as his father jumps from a cliff to the rocks below. Salacious stuff but all of it in the expository dialogue only. The camera remains on Burton and Barbara Rush in the present. The night of passion between Guy and Margaret is also left to the imagination.

It was up to Angie to sell the steaminess. Barbara Rush gets pregnant but Angie does the cheesecake. When Dr. Montford arrives at the motel fire, he finds Fran stretched out on one twin bed and Bert Mosley somewhat chastely on the other. She is clad only in a slip, however, and tells Montford, "I don't want you to think I'm a tramp." Upon reflection, she adds, "Maybe I am a tramp because I don't love him." Clearly she is meant to be a tragically single woman undone by her own desire. "I'm tired of feeling dirty," she tells Bert later in an attempt at separating from him.

The most explosive scene in the whole picture comes when Fran poses for Parker Welk's smutty photos. She is topless with her back arched toward the camera. When Bert bursts in on the session, she grabs a blanket and covers herself up again. It is the first of Angie's many unclothed scenes to come, the beginning of her reputed willingness to go nude or semi-nude for the sake of a picture. This particular instance serves a clear narrative purpose although not all the future examples will do the same. Some will just celebrate her beauty or cultivate her personally valued image as a sex symbol.

During an eight-year period stretching from 1958 to 1966, Angie appeared on the big screen with Rod Steiger, John Wayne, Richard Burton, Frank Sinatra, Peter Finch, Gregory Peck, Lee Marvin, Marlon Brando, and Kirk Douglas, some of the biggest male stars and/or finest actors of the day. She was overshadowed by none of them. In her work here with Burton, she tries to keep the emotional thermostat on low, matching his outbursts with restrained reaction shots. The confessional love scene where she slides to the floor and clutches his knees pushes the limits but never becomes embarrassing to watch.

This was director Daniel Petrie's first feature film after many years of experience in television. Shooting almost exclusively on the Warner Bros. lot in Burbank with a few days of location work near Newport Beach, California, he creates a convincing facsimile of Cape Cod in the summer. Dr. Montford and the town priest bat around the euthanasia issue although its central morality is never resolved one way or another.

Reviews:

"Angie Dickinson's warmth overcomes some script deficiencies."

—*Daily Variety*, January 20, 1960

"Richard Burton does a smart acting job as the doctor and Barbara Rush is both attractive and effective as the woman of the case. Jack Carson blusters through his role of ambitious attorney and Angie Dickinson is competent as the nurse who is no better than she wants to be. Henry Jones and James Dunn chip in strong characterizations as the editor and drunk respectively."

"Daniel Petrie's direction is strong in places but his pacing is torturous."

—*Harrison's Reports*, January 23, 1960

"Acting under the direction of Daniel Petrie is splendid."

—*Film Daily*, January 24, 1960

"Richard Burton is remarkably substantial and aptly sensitive as the medical man who goes through a deal of personal torment to reach the point of mercy-killing his best friend. His face, his voice and his gestures all speak of person of feeling and depth whose deed seems an act of compassion impelled by a brave philosophy."

"Barbara Rush is likewise substantial and convincing as the wife and Tom Drake is forceful as the husband, even though he has to play his pale role in a bed. As a trained nurse who vainly loves the doctor and has some other gnawing problems of her own, Angie Dickinson is passionate and pretty, a combination that is hard to beat."

—Bosley Crowther, *The New York Times*, February 25, 1960

"Angie Dickinson does a capital job as the nurse in love with Burton."

—*Hollywood Citizen-News*, February 25, 1960

"Another terrific acting job is turned in though by Angie Dickinson as Fran, the promiscuous nurse, who really loves the Doctor but when he can't see her for dust makes other arrangements to assuage her love-hunger . . . Her renunciation scene wherein she first pleads for the Doctor's affection should net her mention among the year's best support as should Drake's work."

—Hazel Flynn, *Beverly Hills Citizen*, February 25, 1960

Ocean's Eleven

Credits: A Dorchester Productions picture released on August 4, 1960. Technicolor. Running time of 127 minutes. **Cast:** Frank Sinatra (Danny Ocean), Dean Martin (Sam Harmon), Sammy Davis Jr. (Josh Howard), Peter Lawford (Jimmy Foster), Angie Dickinson (Beatrice Ocean), Richard Conte (Tony Bergdorf), Cesar Romero (Duke Santos), Joey Bishop ("Mushy" O'Connors), Akim Tamiroff (Spyros Acebos), Henry Silva (Roger Corneal), Ilka Chase (Mrs. Restes), Buddy Lester (Vince Massler), Richard Benedict ("Curly" Steffans), Jean Willes (Mrs. Bergdorf), Norman Fell (Peter Rheimer), Clem Harvey (Louis Jackson), Robert Foulk (Sheriff Wimmer). **Crew:** Lewis Milestone (director and producer), Harry Brown and Charles Lederer (screenwriters), Nelson Riddle (composer), William H. Daniels (cinematographer), Philip W. Anderson (editor), Nicolai Remisoff (art director), Howard Bristol (set decorator), Howard Shoup (costume designer), Gordon Bau (makeup artist), Ray Gosnell Jr. (assistant director), M.A. Merrick (sound).

Plot Synopsis: Fifteen years after the end of World War II, Danny Ocean and Jimmy Foster reassemble their 82nd airborne paratrooper buddies for a peacetime commando raid: the simultaneous robbery on New Year's Eve of the Sahara, Riviera, Desert Inn, Sands and Flamingo casinos in Las Vegas. Irascible criminal mastermind Spyros Acebos provides resources and Danny supplies the organizational skill. Several of the guys take inside jobs to help with the planning. Josh Howard drives a garbage truck that services the casinos, Sam Harmon entertains in one of the lounges, and Vince Massler, Mushy O'Connors, and Curly Steffans work as waiters. The rest of the crew pose as guests.

The idea is that demolitions expert Peter Rheimer will take out a transmission tower and plunge the city into darkness, and master electrician Tony Bergdorf will rewire the control panels so that when the emergency generators kick in they will open the cashier cages instead of turning on the lights. Everybody else will scoop up the cash bags and place them in the trash receptacles that Josh will collect with his truck.

The guys all have different motivations for their involvement in the heist and different plans for what they'll do with their million dollar cuts. Danny wants to take his estranged wife Bea on a reconciliation trip to Rio even though she believes he is too addicted to danger to ever truly settle down. Pampered playboy Jimmy would like to become less dependent on his wealthy mother, especially since she has taken up with a smarmy former crime figure named Duke Santos. Fatally ill Tony wants to leave behind money for his young son's education, and Vince intends to make sure his wife never again has to work as a stripper in a seedy burlesque joint. Despite his reservations, Sam is on board out of loyalty to his pals.

On New Year's Eve, everything proceeds like clockwork. While casino patrons are singing "Auld Lang Syne" at midnight, the tower is blown and Las Vegas goes dark. The cage doors swing open and guided by the illuminated night vision paint tracks they have left, the inside men strong arm the cashiers, clean out the cash, and leave the bags for Josh. When the lights come back on they all stroll nonchalantly out of the five casinos.

Tony, however, has a heart attack and drops dead in the middle of the strip. Responding to the robbery calls, the police wonder if there is any connection. In town with Jimmy's mother, Duke Santos meets with the casino bosses and offers to get their money back for 30% of the take. He follows up with various criminal connections but is told that nobody knows who pulled the job. Informed that Danny and Jimmy are in Las Vegas for some kind of casual reunion with their commando buddies, Santos pieces together the puzzle.

Confronting Danny and Sam in their hotel room, Santos demands half of the loot in return for his silence. To confound Santos and to evade the police roadblocks, the guys wait until night and then transfer the money from the garbage dump to the mortuary in charge of Bergdorf's body. They pack the cash into the coffin, confident that everything will be shipped to San Francisco for burial. At Josh's suggestion, they hold back $10,000 for Bergdorf's wife and son.

In the meantime, the funeral director convinces Bergdorf's widow to save money by having the service in Las Vegas. Alerted to the change, the guys arrive and file into a chapel pew. As an unexplained background noise muffles the voice of the mortician, they gradually discover that the body and the money are being cremated.

Notes and Comments: The hip reputation carried by *Ocean's Eleven* has more to do with the Rat Pack itself than by anything that happens on the screen. In reality, the picture is overly long and tedious. Caper details are needlessly repeated, particularly the rigging of the electrical systems, which is explained during a trial run and then shown again on New Year's Eve. None of it is all that complicated in the first place. Dean Martin even sings bits of the same song, Jimmy Van Heusen and Sammy Cahn's "Ain't That a Kick in the Head," on three separate occasions throughout the movie.

The five pack members (Sinatra, Martin, Lawford, Davis and Bishop) don't really seem to be doing much except sitting around hotel rooms or strolling through the casinos. Especially painful are the scenes where they gather over drinks and trade supposedly cool quips about women, politics, and gambling. The action plays like a cringe-worthy smorgasbord of privileged white male behavior. Sinatra pats two blondes on the rear and says, "All right, girls, time for your nap, beat it" while Martin makes jokes about taking away women's right to vote. A heavily accented Asian houseboy is followed by an equally insensitive bit in which Sinatra, Lawford, and Martin apply camouflage blackface while asking Davis how he gets it off. The only cast member working hard to develop an interesting character is Akim Tamiroff, whose Spyros Acebos is as dyspeptic, easily offended, and hilarious as his Uncle Joe Grandi and his Gerven the cook in *Touch of Evil* (1958) and *Topkapi* (1964) respectively.

Angie on location in Las Vegas for *Ocean's Eleven* (1961).

Simultaneous with location shooting of the picture was the appearance of all five entertainers at the Sands's Copa Room, a wildly popular, free floating spectacle referred to as the Summit. Much as they did in the picture, the boys sang, told crude jokes, and interrupted each other on stage. The nights were long and the drinking heavy. To corral the actors for a few hours of optimal midday filming, director Lewis Milestone made extensive preproduction preparations. As reported at the time by entertainment columnist E.B. Radcliffe, Milestone and several members of the crew carefully scouted locations and created "pencil sketches of every place he has decided to use a camera" along with "typewritten notes on camera angles, dramatic action, and even key dialogue." Then, when the actors arrived at the Las Vegas locations which had been briefly transformed into sets, "he knew what he wanted, what he could get, and how cameras should be placed to obtain results."[3] The outcome was realistic looking casino scenes filled with the same tourist crowds who were also serving as unpaid background in George Sidney's concurrent location shooting of *Pepe* (1960) with Dan Dailey and Cantinflas.

Billed fifth after Sinatra, Martin, Lawford, and Davis and featured in the advertising posters, Angie appears twice, an extended sequence in the first half of the picture and a very brief scene toward the end. By and large, she emerges from the proceedings with her dignity intact. Meant to represent the stability that Danny lacks, she delivers a requisitely sober and low-key performance as Beatrice, the wife who has taken a leave of absence from their chaotic marriage. Her dialogue-heavy segment begins in a hotel room with Martin and concludes in the rooftop lounge with Sinatra.

"I just woke up one morning and realized there was nothing underneath us but thin air," she tells Martin, by way of establishing Danny's impulsiveness. With tears in her eyes, she continues, "I want a life that doesn't depend on the color of a card or the length of a horse's nose." She is neither accusatory nor self-pitying, simply straightforward. Sinatra arrives, hustles her into the elevator, and takes them to the empty skyroom bar. Sitting at a black table with pink vinyl chairs, he asks for another chance and says, "On the morning of January 2nd, I'm going to pick you up and we'll hop down to Rio so you pack a bag." Regretfully, she replies, "Oh, Danny, what a prize you are. The only husband in the world who would proposition his own wife." They continue talking but it is clear that he cannot change and she cannot settle for more of the same. Subtle rather than showy, Angie's performance gets at the combination of love and frustration Beatrice feels for her wayward spouse. Looking elegant in her upswept strawberry blonde hairdo and simple black dress with high white collar, she is the visual correlative of the "class" Danny so admires (his earlier orange alpaca sweater to the contrary). During a very brief scene later on, Angie receives a tell-all phone call from one of Danny's scorned girlfriends and turns the tables. "When I learn Danny has an enemy as venomous as you," she says icily, "it just makes me love him a little more."

Some well-known stars also appear briefly in cameos. Red Skelton plays himself arguing with a cashier to exceed a self-imposed gambling limit. Shirley MacLaine is a tipsy hotel guest who waylays Dean Martin as he attempts to help rig an electricity box, and George Raft is one of the victimized casino bosses. Red Norvo and his quintet accompany Dean Martin during his lounge act. Mildly amusing, these episodes tend to make a seemingly endless picture just that much longer.

Reviews:

"*Ocean's Eleven* is just one dandy of an entertainment, crisp in dialogue, polished in style and deliciously exciting all the way. A glittering marquee cast goes through their acting chores with exuberance under the astute directorial guidance of Lewis Milestone. This melodramatic sundae with comic flavoring takes place largely against a Las Vegas background, and brims over with delight. Mark *Ocean's Eleven* down as a solid box office contender."

—*Film Daily*, August 5, 1960

"A wisecracking script, with plenty of laughs and excitement, Milestone's generally tight and amusing treatment, a bulging fistful of strong stars, a massive promotion campaign; all these add up to strong-to-smash boxoffice."

"In a film devoted to banditry, however, and loaded with some of the top acting pros in the business, it is Cesar Romero who light fingers every scene in which he appears. Perhaps it is because he has a genuine character and lights into it with zeal. Angie Dickinson is lovely and convincing, although her part gets obscured.

—James Powers, *The Hollywood Reporter*, August 5, 1960

"Laboring under the handicaps of a contrived script, and uncertain approach and a cast weighted down with personalities in essence playing themselves, the Lewis Milestone production never quite makes its point, but romps along merrily unconcerned in the process. Where the Warners release no doubt will make the desirable number is at the ticket windows, thanks to the boxoffice magnetism of its cast."

"Likeable, but not very convincing, performances are turned in by Sinatra, Martin, Davis and Lawford. Angie Dickinson is attractively superfluous in a brief scene with Sinatra. Richard Conte gives one of the better portrayals, a heartfelt enactment of the band's ace, but doomed, electrician."

—*Daily Variety*, August 5, 1960

"Richard Conte, also, manages really to turn in a performance that is powerful and touching as, of all things, an electrician. I thought Akim Tamiroff was too broad in his role, and why that lovely thing Angie Dickinson was so wasted in her role, I don't know, except that Frankie seems to be rather wasteful of girls at any time."

—Ruth Waterbury, *Los Angeles Examiner*, August 11, 1960

". . . nothing more than a whopping sick joke in Technicolor . . . It's a completely amoral tale, told for laughs."

—Leo Sullivan, *The Washington Post*, August 13, 1960

"The stars are in top form, particularly Sammy Davis, Jr. with some of the juiciest lines and a good song. Also on hand: Ilka Chase, as Lawford's ultra-chic, much-married mom; Cesar Romero as her current fiancé, an ex-hood who catches on to the amateur bunch fast; Angie Dickinson, as Sinatra's estranged but still-loving wife (this girl *should* find stardom); Akim Tamiroff and Patrice Wymore. Photography is original and exciting, especially in some brassy glimpses of Las Vegas nightlife."

—*Cue*, August 20, 1960

"It is all funny enough when things finally begin to move. But before things do, Sinatra and his chums spend more time than is really necessary punching each other kiddingly, talking tough to dolls, practicing judo chops on waiters and in general playing themselves. The action, when it comes, is fast and foolish enough to make this one of the more entertaining films of a not-too-entertaining summer."

—*Time*, August 22, 1960

A Fever in the Blood

Credits: A Warner Bros. production released on January 28, 1961. Black and white. Running time of 117 minutes. **Cast:** Efrem Zimbalist Jr. (Judge Leland "Lee" Hoffman), Angie Dickinson (Cathy Simon), Jack Kelly (Dan Callahan), Don Ameche (Senator Alex Simon), Ray Danton (Clem Marker), Herbert Marshall (Governor Oliver Thornwall), Andra Martin (Laura Mayberry), Jesse White (Sgt. Mickey Beers), Rhodes Reason (Walter Thornwall), Robert Colbert (Thomas Morley), Carroll O'Connor (Matt Keenan), Parley Baer (Charlie Bosworth), Saundra Edwards (Lucy Callahan), June Blair (Paula Thornwall). **Crew:** Vincent Sherman (director), Harry Kleiner and William Pearson (screenwriters), Roy Huggins (producer and screenwriter), Ernest Gold (composer), J. Peverell Marley (cinematographer), William H. Ziegler (editor), Malcolm C. Bert (art director), George James Hopkins (set decorator), Howard Shoup (costume designer), Jean Burt Reilly (hair stylist), Gordon Bau (makeup artist), Sergei Petschnikoff (assistant director), Robert B. Lee (sound).

Plot Synopsis: A man appears in a woman's bedroom and attempts to take advantage of her. When he is rejected, he smothers her to death with a pillow and starts a fire to make the death look accidental. As he leaves the house, he is spotted by a neighbor lady and hides in the hedges.

In seemingly unrelated action, newspaper publisher Matt

Keenan and district attorney Dan Callahan are enjoying a duck hunting trip at the lakeside cottage of Judge Lee Hoffman. When Hoffman asks Callahan to be his running mate in a possible gubernatorial campaign, the D.A. asks for more time to consider the offer. Early the next morning, Callahan's right-hand man and fixer, police sergeant Mickey Beers, arrives to summon him back to the city. As soon as he learns that Walter Thornwall, the wealthy nephew of a former governor, is the chief suspect in what has now been deemed the murder of his estranged wife Paula, the deeply ambitious Callahan decides to prosecute the case himself, confident that the publicity will propel him rather than Hoffman into the governor's mansion. With a battery of reporters at his side, Callahan personally arrests Thornwall and prepares to steamroll a conviction.

Assigned as presiding judge in the trial, Hoffman resolves to keep his own political goals out of the proceedings. Both he and Callahan seek support from Senator Alex Simon, who surprises them with the news that he plans to resign his United States Senate seat and run for governor himself. Whereas Callahan angrily decides to challenge him anyway, Hoffman graciously steps aside and agrees to consider the suggestion that he run for lieutenant governor on the same ticket. Accompanying Simon is his much younger wife Cathy, who seems to have a long-standing romantic interest in the recently widowed judge.

The trial turns into a media circus with Callahan grabbing headlines through allegations that the murder victim was a sex addict and that Thornwall was having an affair with his pregnant, abortion-seeking secretary. Ex-governor Oliver Thornwall arrives in his wheelchair to testify in defense of his nephew, and the real murderer, a troubled gardener named Thomas Morely, gives nervous testimony about the damaged hedges. At one point, Senator

Simon meets with Hoffman and offers him a recently vacated federal judgeship if he slows down Callahan's political momentum by finding a reason to declare a mistrial. Incorruptible, Hoffman considers exposing the attempted bribe, but Cathy pleads with him to keep it secret, revealing that the stress could cause Simon a second heart attack. She also explains that Simon wants to become governor so that he can control votes at the national convention and have his name placed in nomination for President. Making Cathy first lady, he believes, will win the love she still feels for Hoffman.

Back at the trial, Sergeant Beers unethically divulges on the witness stand that Thornwall had once before threatened his wife. It is inadmissible hearsay evidence and Hoffman must rule on the defense attorney's motion for a mistrial. To show Simon that he has not been influenced by the bribe offer, he denies the motion. Although the evidence is struck from the record, the jury is influenced anyway and ultimately finds Thornwall guilty of murder.

Armed with additional information concerning Callahan's unethical conduct, Hoffman considers exposing him at a public hearing but changes his mind at the last minute. As part of a reopened investigation ordered by Callahan solely for publicity purposes, the police reinterview witnesses, including Morely the gardener. In a panic, he skips town, is apprehended after a car chase, and confesses to murder. Callahan takes credit for the confession and the release of Walter Thornwall.

When Thornwall is inexplicably denied a second trial on appeal, Hoffman's guilty conscience prompts him to go public with the revelation that Senator Simon offered him a bribe. Both Simon and Callahan turn against him and he is threatened with disbarment for not reporting the interference earlier. After arguing with Cathy over how ruthless he has become, Simon dies of heart failure but makes a deathbed confession to reporters confirming Hoffman's version of the quid pro quo.

At the state gubernatorial nominating convention, Callahan fails to win a majority since delegates are suspicious of his many dubious maneuvers. Cathy urges Hoffman to trust the people and appear at the deadlocked convention himself. When he does, Oliver Thornwall places his name in nomination and he wins by acclimation.

Contract players Efrem Zimbalist Jr. and Angie in a publicity still for *A Fever in the Blood* (1961).

Notes and Comments: The plot of *A Fever in the Blood* is impossibly dense and convoluted. Hoffman's unexpectedly called public hearing alone involves Callahan and Beers racing to a TV station to preempt the bribe story, striking a young boy with their car, concocting an official business cover-up story, and having an incriminating phone conversation wiretapped by Hoffman. There are over 100 major and minor characters embroiled in a swirl of schemes, investigations, power struggles, and romances. The players are not so much unique individuals as they are standard pieces on an unnecessarily cluttered gameboard. Focused viewer attention never delivers any commensurate psychological insight.

The odd casting mixes young Warner Bros. television contract actors such as Efrem Zimbalist Jr., Jack Kelly, and Rhodes Reason with old guard Hollywood stars Don Ameche and Herbert Marshall. At times, the combinations strain credibility, as in the marital pairing between fifty-two-year-old Don Ameche and twenty-nine-year-old Angie. Some of the roles are altogether superfluous. Herbert Marshall, for example, is wheeled in like an updated version of his Horrace Giddens from *The Little Foxes* (1941) to say a few positive words about his nephew and later to nominate Judge Hoffman for governor.

Dressed in smartly tailored suits and with her hair pulled back in an elegant French twist, Angie looks like one of Hitchcock's icy blonde heroines. As muse and conscience for both Simon and Hoffman, she has a half dozen big scenes, incrementally developing her role one piece at a time. During a pre-trial dinner with Hoffman and her husband, she nonverbally communicates emotional undercurrents beneath the chatter. Her lowered eyes and forced smiles indicate an attempt to mask the love Cathy still holds for the judge, feelings that are amplified even further when they cross paths in a hotel lobby and she gazes after him with longing. Out of loyalty to her flawed husband, she later begs Hoffman not to expose the bribe attempt and then reacts angrily when Simon ungratefully turns against him. "You saved your political life," she says tearfully, "but you lost something much more important—your self respect." The film's penultimate shot has her standing on the convention floor and looking up proudly at Hoffman as he accepts his party's nomination. Despite some absurd narrative premises, Angie keeps Cathy Simon as credibly motivated a character as possible.

Producer Roy Huggins, creator of the Warner Bros. television dramas *Maverick* (1957-62) and *77 Sunset Strip* (1958-64) among others, approaches the film as another small screen assignment. Visually, the cinematography's shallow depth of field and low contrast lighting result in the flat, gray look of television. The action takes place primarily on the Warner Bros. lot with characters driving around in the big product placement Ford automobiles the studio favored in its detective shows. Director Vincent Sherman, who made pictures in the 40s with both Bette Davis and Joan Crawford, slogs along from one overheated scene to the next without giving special emphasis or nuance to any. Sherman always considered the film a failure, negatively influenced by its roots in television. He would make two more feature films before transitioning into TV work himself.

Sandwiched within the melodrama are some prescient insights into contemporary politics. "This is the day of the celebrity in entertainment, business, politics. Celebrities write their own tickets," says Callahan's campaign manager. "You don't need a machine anymore." The influence of big money and the media on elections is well noted as is the role of personal ambition (referenced in the film's title). Ameche, Zimbalist, and Kelly are fine as the rival candidates although the movie, unlike Franklin Schaffner's *The Best*

Man (1964), spends little time on the actual business of cajoling and wrangling delegates at a political convention.

Carroll O'Connor, a decade away from playing Archie Bunker on TV, makes his credited feature film debut as newspaper publisher Matt Keenan, and Angie's good friend June Blair appears as murder victim Paula Thornwall.

Reviews:
"Miss Dickinson has practically no chance to unleash her acting skills."
—*Limelight,* January 19, 1961

"The beauty of Miss Dickinson will be another plus commercial factor, although she has little to do but look alternately loyal and potentially disloyal. What she does, she does well, however."

"Considering the complexity of the plot, director Vincent Sherman has done a decent job of keeping it all as taut and playable as possible for producer Huggins, who has since ankled his WB post for the top TV niche at 20th-Fox. J. Peverell Marley's busy, tight camera work is similar in technique to TV, with its preponderance of close-ups, a style further reflected in William Ziegler's abrupt editing."

—*Daily Variety,* January 19, 1961

"Some of the wheeling and dealing behind the scenes is interesting. But courtroom arguments take up most of the film and they are long-winded and tiresome."

"The complicated script fails to tie up a lot of loose ends. And since the killer in the murder case is known from the beginning, there isn't much available suspense."

"Angie Dickinson plays the senator's loyal but miserable wife, a shadowy role that never develops into anything, and Ray Danton is persistent as the defense attorney."

—*Los Angeles Mirror*, January 26, 1961

"While the eager politicians are making capital of a crime of passion the hapless defendant is relegated to the sidelines. So is the statuesque Angie Dickinson, whose few scenes as the senator's wife in love with the judge furnish the only excuse for the film's absurd title."

—Eugene Archer, *The New York Times*, April 20, 1961

The Sins of Rachel Cade

Credits: A Warner Bros. production released on April 2, 1961. Technicolor. Running time of 124 minutes. Based on a novel by Charles Mercer. **Cast:** Angie Dickinson (Rachel Cade), Peter Finch (Colonel Henri Derode), Roger Moore (Paul Wilton), Errol John (Kulu), Woody Strode (Muwango), Juano Hernandez (Kalanumu), Frederick O'Neal (Buderga), Mary Wickes (Marie Grieux), Scatman Crothers (Musinga), Rafer Johnson (Kosongo), Charles Wood (Mzimba), Douglas Spencer (Doctor Bikel). **Crew:** Gordon Douglas (director), Edward Anhalt (screenwriter), Henry Blanke (producer), Max Steiner (composer), J. Peverell Marley (cinematographer), Owen Marks (editor), Leo K. Kuter (art director), George James Hopkins (set decorator), Marjorie Best (costume designer), Alice Monte (hair stylist), Gordon Bau and Bill Phillips (make-up artists), William Kissell and Russell Saunders (assistant directors), Francis M. Stahl (sound).

Plot Synopsis: Rachel Cade, a Protestant missionary nurse from Kansas, arrives in the Belgian Congo during the early days of

World War II to help at a remote clinic run by Dr. Bikel. The first two people she meets are Kulu, the young man who will become her most loyal native ally, and Colonel Henri Derode, commander of the nearby colonial outpost. A vocal non-believer, Henri administers local affairs with a wisdom born out of respect for native tradition. Despite their religious differences, he and Rachel develop an immediate respect and fondness for one another.

No sooner has she unpacked her bags at the medical compound in Dibela than Bikel dies suddenly of a heart attack. While attempting to conduct a funeral service, Rachel is interrupted by Muwango the medicine man, who insists that Bikel may not be buried there because he has disrespected the tribal mountain god. Henri arrives to defuse the crisis and force Muwango to back down. Against his advice, Rachel declares that she plans to remain in Dibela and run the clinic herself.

When she learns that Bikel passively accepted the natives' reluctance to visit the mission, she decides to take a more active role. She reads to Kulu from the Bible and rushes into the village when news comes that a young boy is dying from a curse placed on his family. Denied permission by Chief Buderga to intervene, she does so anyway and saves the child with a makeshift appendectomy. In gratitude, the younger, less fearful natives stage a celebration that includes overtly sexual dancing that disturbs Rachel. High priest Kalanumu tries to scare other villagers from seeking medical care, but Henri warns that anyone interfering with Rachel will be punished. At the conclusion of the celebration, Henri tells Rachel he loves her, but after a passionate kiss, she pushes him away.

Over the next several months, activity at the clinic accelerates. As more patients ask for treatment, Rachel must decide which cases she can handle and which ones are beyond her abilities. She is unable to treat the chief's favorite wife's infertility issues, and she loses a young boy to sleeping sickness. Despite the setbacks, the villagers continue to respect her. After he claims to have seen Jesus speaking to God in a vision, Kulu converts and decides to get married by the church. He also says a second vision has revealed that a much needed doctor will arrive soon.

One day a warplane involved in fighting to the north crashes close by, and Rachel treats the injuries of its sole survivor, an RAF captain named Paul Wilton. Diagnosing his own broken leg, he reveals that he is an American doctor who has volunteered with the British to further his medical training. During his extended recovery, he helps in the clinic, performing the surgeries that had been postponed, including a procedure that helps the chief's wife become pregnant. Despite Henri's obvious disapproval, the doctor and Rachel grow close. As the time comes for him to rejoin his unit, Paul makes romantic overtures that Rachel at first rejects. Anxious to leave Dibela and get on with his career, he hastily completes the last of the scheduled surgeries. Giving in to her passion, Rachel sleeps with Paul just before he is transferred.

Several weeks later, Rachel confesses to Henri that she is pregnant and plans to resign. Unable to convince her to tell Paul, he persuades her to stay where she is needed and have the baby at the clinic. Without her knowledge, he also sends a message to mission authorities that he has officially married Rachel and Paul.

Rachel becomes sick, and Kulu fears that Kalanumu's curse is destroying her. On his deathbed, the high priest declares that Rachel is tormenting herself and must apply her own power of forgiveness. More her trusted assistant than ever, Kulu helps Rachel give birth to a healthy baby boy. Still very much in love, Henri offers to marry her and become the child's father, but Rachel declines. In frustration, Henri requests a transfer to the Allied military campaign in North Africa; before he departs, he sends a cable to Paul informing him of his son's birth.

Arriving back in Dibela as a civilian, Paul tells Rachel they will be married and return to a comfortable, well-off life in the United States. For propriety's sake, he also wants to tell everyone there that he is marrying a widow with a young child. Realizing that Paul is motivated more by a sense of responsibility than love and knowing she belongs in Africa, Rachel decides at the last minute to stay at the mission. As Paul drives away, Kulu delivers a sermon referencing the power of forgiveness and praying for the safe return of Colonel Henri. With her son in her arms, Rachel walks through the crowd of villagers and steps back into the clinic.

Note and Comments: The film opens with a steam locomotive chugging through the jungle and then cuts to a shot of Angie riding along inside one of the wooden passenger cars. From then on, except for some scenes between Henri and his staff, the camera follows Angie. She is given the full Warner Bros. star treatment in one of those romantic dramas such as *Susan Lenox: Her Fall and Rise* (1931), *Stella Dallas* (1937), and *Mildred Pierce* (1945), where the name of the female lead character is emphasized as the title of the picture itself. The intention was that *The Sins of Rachel Cade* would bring Angie the same success as *The Nun's Story* (1959) had to Audrey Hepburn. Toward that end, both movies had the same religious framework, the same setting (Belgian Congo), the same producer (Henry Blanke), and the same male co-star (Peter Finch).

For the most part, Angie is up to the task of developing a top-billed character. She makes the conflict between Rachel's physical and spiritual passions a credible dilemma rather than just a plot device. By keeping theatricality to a minimum, she is able to sell the moments of high emotion. Because she has been reserved elsewhere, she can go a bit broader for her agitated reaction to the native dancing and her tearful farewell to the villagers. The pacing of her scenes with the two men vying for Rachel's love is similar—a quiet conversational tone punctuated by spirited outbursts tied to lines such as "I've betrayed every missionary who's ever suffered and died in Africa" (to Henri) and "I wanted you to come back because you wanted to not because you had to" (to Paul). As in *I'll Give My Life*, she is also required to deliver theological insights without sounding sanctimonious. Whether lecturing Kulu on monogamy or telling Henri that "one wooden cross keeps us alive," she is earnest, even hesitant, rather than self-righteous. Highlighting her well-scrubbed, unadorned beauty with flattering close-ups and profile shots is veteran cinematographer J. Peverell Marley, who worked in the 30s and 40s with such stars as Barbara Stanwyck, Joan Crawford, and Loretta Young.

Angie was undermined, however, by a salacious studio ad campaign featuring the tagline "How could it happen to Rachel Cade?" and suggesting that Sadie Thompson had surfaced in the Congo as a promiscuous missionary nurse. The decision to change the title from the novel's *Rachel Cade* to *The Sins of Rachel Cade* was foolishly misconceived. First, there is only one sin not a string of moral transgressions and second, Rachel's concerns are more with running the clinic than finding a man. For most of the picture, she bustles about in her khaki skirts attending to patients and defying the village elders. The scene where she bursts into Paul's hut to the sound of Max Steiner's overwrought score and an equally raging wind is another miscalculation.

Originally scheduled for location shooting in Africa, *The Sins of Rachel Cade* was regrettably confined to the soundstages and backlot of the Warner Bros. studios in Burbank. In place of the gritty authenticity of a film like *The African Queen* (1951) or *The Nun's Story* (1959), there is the obvious artifice of fabricated sets and potted foliage. The hothouse environment tends to further exaggerate Rachel's allegedly torrid romances. The film never opens up visually until a final crane shot where the camera pulls up and away from the villagers as Rachel walks back to the clinic with her infant son.

Peter Finch, Angie, and Errol John on the Warner Bros backlot for a tribal celebration in *The Sins of Rachel Cade* (1961).

Although he hated playing Henri, Peter Finch pairs effectively with Angie, matching her reserve with frank desire. "You're an extraordinarily beautiful woman," he matter-of-factly tells Rachel, "and I think that's something you don't like to face." In one of his best scenes, he and the high priest converse honestly and affably over a tobacco pipe and then appear in public as two seasoned politicians at odds with one another. Roger Moore seems out of place as the American doctor while Errol John and Rafer Johnson are both good as the native villagers who work with Rachel at the clinic. Frederick O'Neal, Juano Hernandez, and Woody Strode bring as much dignity as possible to the stereotypical parts of tribal chief, priest, and medicine man respectively.

Director Gordon Douglas, who got his start with *Our Gang* comedies, keeps the multiple characters and storylines clearly delineated although he and screenwriter Edward Anhalt fail to develop the passing references they make to colonialism, religious hypocrisy, and the ritual mutilation of female genitalia. Douglas's major late-career success would come with a trio of neo-noir detective films he made in the late 60s with Frank Sinatra.

Reviews:
"Enacting *Rachel Cade* is an important assignment for Miss Dickinson, and she is generally persuasive, although a trifle too composed in spots."
—*Daily Variety*, February 27, 1961

"Miss Dickinson gives an interesting performance as the central figure, but she is handicapped by the fact that her role is never fully delineated."
—*The Hollywood Reporter*, February 27, 1961

"It is a demanding performance and Miss Dickinson comes through well."
—*Film Daily*, March 1, 1961

"The title role permits Angie Dickinson, without recourse to cheesecake, to achieve mature stardom by virtue of her own rich talent."
—*Limelight*, March 2, 1961

"Angie Dickinson offers an arresting and fine performance as the purposeful Rachel Cade of the title, who attempts to get the natives to visit the mission hospital, which had been neglected by the doctor, who dies of a heart attack the night of her arrival."

—*Motion Picture Herald*, March 4, 1961

"*The Sins of Rachel Cade* definitely establishes Angie Dickinson as one of the present day screens' top younger performers."

"This actress has depth and a gift for seething emotion seldom encountered among the current crop of rather shallow youngsters who are more often than not all appearance and looks or method with little sincerity in their film work."

"Angie uses her ability to such advantage as 'Rachel Cade' that henceforth she should be much in demand where offbeat dramatic roles are concerned. She apparently is one of the few real recent talent discoveries who show evidence of having lasting qualities."

—Hazel Flynn, *Beverly Hills Citizen*, April 26, 1961

"Angie Dickinson is appealing as the mournful heroine who obviously did not practice what she preached."

—*Los Angeles Mirror*, April 27, 1961

"Angie Dickinson is a most attractive woman and usually a competent performer, but her Rachel Cade seems too much in control of herself. One's sympathies are never swayed greatly by her problems or the manner in which she attempts to meet them."

—Philip Scheuer, *Los Angeles Times*, April 27, 1961

"Under happier circumstances, *The Sins of Rachel Cade* might have been a prime showcase for the talents of Angie Dickinson, who has been buried up to now in secondary roles and second-rate films. Although *Rachel Cade* is no classic, she carries it alone."

—Arthur Knight, *Saturday Review*, April 29, 1961

Jessica

Credits: A Dear Film Produzione/Les Films Ariane production released in March, 1962. Technicolor. Running time of 112 minutes. Based on a novel by Flora Sandstorm. **Cast:** Angie Dickinson (Jessica Brown Visconti), Maurice Chevalier (Father Antonio), Noël-Noël (Old Crupi), Gabriele Ferzetti (Edmondo Raumo), Sylva Koscina (Nunzia Tuffi), Agnes Moorehead (Maria Lombardo), Marcel Dalio (Luigi Tuffi), Danielle De Metz (Nicolina Lombardo), Antonio Cifariello (Gianni Crupi), Kerima (Virginia Toriello), Carlo Croccolo (Beppi Toriello), Georgette Anys (Mamma Parigi), Rossana Rory (Rosa Masudino), Alberto Rabagliati (Pietro Masudino), Marina Berti (Filippella Risino), Angelo Galassi (Antonio Risino), Manuela Rinaldi (Lucia Casabranca), Gianni Musy (Filippo Casabranca), Joe Pollini (Rosario). **Crew:** Jean Negulesco (director and producer), Ennio De Concini and Edith Sommer (screenwriters), Mario Nascimbene (composer), Piero Portalupi (cinematographer), Marie-Sophie Dubus and Renzo Lucidi (editors), Giulio Bongini (art director), Annalisa Nasalli-Rocca (costume designer), Gabriella Borzelli (hair stylist), Amato Garbini (makeup artist), John Kean (sound).

Plot Synopsis: Father Antonio, the old, guitar-playing priest of a small Sicilian village, looks into the camera and explains that "his people" have been disturbed by the presence of an attractive young American named Jessica, a "wisp of a girl" who also happens to be a midwife. As he narrates, Jessica is seen riding around the countryside on her Vespa motorscooter, distracting the men and making the women jealous. She stops to chat with Antonio and shares her backstory: a trained nurse, she married an Italian man in Palermo only to lose him to a fatal car accident on their wedding night. Rather than return home, she responded to a letter from the village requesting a midwife.

Antonio tries to discuss a possible spouse for her, but she is on her way to her first official birthing job. The village women, led by Maria Lombardo, arrive to inspect her work only to find that everything is perfect. She has cleaned the house, fed the family, and delivered the new baby more easily than any of the mother's other eight children. Maria, whose granddaughter Nicolina is going to marry handsome ladies' man Gianni Crupi, is torn between respect for Jessica's skill and concern for the effect she has on the men.

Having flirted with Jessica himself, Gianni asks her to see his uncle Old Crupi, the irascible head gardener for wealthy widower Marchese Edmondo Raumo. A scratch has turned into lead poisoning which Old Crupi refuses to have treated. Pretending to critique the gardens, she distracts him long enough to dress and bandage the wound. Although he realizes he has been tricked, Old Crupi is charmed by Jessica anyway and invites her to come visit the gardens whenever she likes.

After checking on Crupi, Father Antonio meets with Edmondo to present his regular charity wish list. Still embittered over the murder of his young wife by fascists during the war, the Marchese funds individual needs but stays aloof from the affairs of the village. Reluctantly he agrees to attend Gianni's wedding if Crupi himself goes. Afterward, Father Antonio again hears the women complaining about Jessica and plays devil's advocate. Pretending to question her character, he gets them to admit that she is doing an excellent job and is not responsible for the men's behavior. Nevertheless, they continue to feel uneasy about the effect she has on their weak-willed husbands.

Remembering the story of Lysistrata, one wife suggests that they deny sexual favors in retaliation. If there are no babies, the women reason, there will be no need for a midwife, and the problem will be solved. Father Antonio believes it is a bad idea but influenced by the vocal support of the postman's unmarried sister and by Maria's eventual encouragement, they go on strike. Locked out of their bedrooms, the men grow frustrated and irritable. The only woman not participating in the scheme is the beautiful young wife of the mayor, who does not seem interested in her or any other female.

At the wedding of Gianni and Nicolina, Jessica is slighted by the women but proudly escorted by Old Crupi. She also meets Edmondo, who pretends to be a fisherman, and the two are immediately attracted to each other. With their discontent boiling over, the men get into a huge brawl that disrupts the celebration. That evening, against Maria's instructions, Nicolina slips away to the orchard to make love with Gianni. Elsewhere in the village the mayor ravishes his wife and several other husbands also break the strike.

Ultimately Jessica discovers Edmondo's true identity along with details of the women's plot against her. To teach everyone a lesson, she makes them think she is a femme fatale for real. Giving the men rides on her Vespa and chatting them up in the village square, she takes to dressing provocatively in tight sweaters and shorts. Even her friend Nicolina fears she has designs on Gianni.

Events come to a head during a big storm that hits the village. Summoned to the bedside of dying Old Crupi, Jessica impresses Father Antonio and Edmondo with her tender compassion for the man. They both regret ever having considered her an outsider. Viewing the wind-devastated garden, she promises to help replant it. Back at her cottage, a couple of the village women clandestinely appear to ask if she will be their midwife.

With everyone gathered for Old Crupi's funeral, Antonio and Edmondo apologize on behalf of the village and ask Jessica not to leave. Sometime later Father Antonio delivers a sermon giving thanks for a bountiful harvest and mentioning that the mayor's wife has just given birth to two healthy boys. The Marchese and Jessica arrive together to take their place in the Raumo family pew. The camera pans slowly across the church interior as over a dozen very pregnant women stand and receive the priest's blessing.

Notes and Comments: *Jessica's* misogynistic point of view coupled with its appealing observation of everyday village life makes it difficult to embrace yet impossible to dismiss. It is a prime example of how the male gaze traditionally has defined narrative cinema. The camera practically ogles Angie with its close-ups of her backside bumping along on the Vespa and the reaction shots of the excited village men. Often encircled by a group of male spectators, she is admired, groped, and kissed. In scenes that look a lot like pin-up photos, she leans backward across tables to display her short shorts and stiletto heels, the same way that director Jean Negulesco positioned Marilyn Monroe and Betty Grable for the modeling sequence in *How to Marry A Millionaire* (1953). There is also a skinny dipping episode where a partially nude Angie romps in a lagoon and hides behind a flesh-colored towel. For someone supposedly trained to be a midwife, she is only briefly seen involved in the details of her craft or engaged in medical consultation with other women.

More insidious is the celebration of male dominance. Father Antonio speaks repeatedly from the altar on how wives must be subject to the will of their husbands. Female desire is never an issue, only male gratification. The proper order of things, appropriately restored by the film's conclusion, is women in the kitchen or bedroom and men in the workplace. Truly troubling is a sight gag that has a disobedient wife continually showing up in public with a black eye.

At the same time, however, the picture offers an affectionate, more-or-less authentic take on life in the village. Over the opening credits, it features shots of real Sicilians going about typical daily activities. Filmed on location, it places the actors into real streets, cafes, and churches. When not leering at Angie, Negulesco and cinematographer Piero Portalupi capture stunning views of Taormina and Forza d'Agro, used as settings in Francis Ford Coppola's *The Godfather* (1972) as well. Some of the compositions, such as the village women sewing against the backdrop of a ruined Norman castle or Father Antonio and the Marchese speaking together in an ancient Greek amphitheater have the look of plein air painting.

A large international cast adds to the film's many pleasures. Sylva Koscina, Danielle De Metz, and Kerima are excellent as the mayor's wife, Gianni's bride Nicolina, and venomous Virginia Toriello respectively. Adopting a subtle Italian accent, Agnes Moorehead is convincingly stern as Maria Lombardo, and Georgette Anys turns in a boisterously funny performance as Jessica's gossipy housekeeper Mamma Parigi. A popular leading man in Italian cinema, Gabriele Ferzetti looks and acts very much the part of handsome aristocrat Edmondo Raumo. Veteran French character actors Marcel Dalio and Noël-Noël turn Mayor Tuffi and Old Crupi into expertly drawn comic portraits. Finally, as he does in *Gigi* (1958), Maurice Chevalier, playing Father Antonio, directly addresses the camera in musical asides that comment humorously on the action.

For the film to succeed on any level, the Jessica character must be charming, sincere, determined, and flirtatious. Checking all the boxes, Angie deftly balances the role's dramatic and comedic demands, slightly neither in the process. Costumed smartly in light blues, yellows, and pinks, she adds luster to Negulesco's sun-drenched pastel color scheme. With old pros Chevalier and Noël-Noël, she is playfully indulgent and for the love scenes with Ferzetti she turns on the passion. When the village women carp about her "devil-inspired body," she instantly redirects her good-natured civility into righteous indignation. "What quaint words you use for your dirty thoughts, Signorina," she says angrily. "As for stealing your men, I'm innocent and you know it. Still you wanted to get rid of me because you thought I might be trouble. Ladies, you don't know what trouble is." More complex than it seems at first, the part requires frequent shifts in tone and timing. An ambitious follow-up to *The Sins of Rachel Cade*, it provided further proof of Angie's ability to confidently carry a picture's title role.

Angie tends to patient Noël-Noël in *Jessica* (1962).

Jessica was a pet project for director Jean Negulesco. Born in Rumania, he attended art school in Paris and worked as a painter before beginning his Hollywood career. A contract director for Warner Bros. and then 20th Century Fox, he specialized at first in dark melodramas that defined theme and character through the meticulous delineation of place and later in lush CinemaScope romances such as *Three Coins in a Fountain* (1954) and *Boy on a Dolphin* (1957). By the early 60s, he had tired of studio work and had begun planning the independent project that would become *Jessica*. As both the producer and director, he helped to acquire the property, secure financing, and assemble the cast. Having shot on location before, he managed the extensive filming in Sicily with consummate professional ease. The finished movie reveals an artist's eye for color, detail, and composition. His ability to handle large ensembles is evident in the wedding celebration, the comic brawl, and Father Antonio's harvest sermon. The command of space is never in doubt; his expansively framed establishing shots are followed by dynamic cuts into and around the action. The blending of the Sicilian location footage and the soundstage material completed at Cinecittà is seamless, not just between the church exterior and interior scenes but also in the trickier matches of garden and beach long shots with medium-close dialogue filmed on the studio sets.

Negulesco's indie venture was also a family affair. His wife, the former model and actress Dusty Anderson, wrote lyrics for the Marguerite Monnet tunes sung by Chevalier and helped Annalisa Nasalli-Rocca with the wardrobe design. Despite the best efforts of everyone involved, the film was neither a critical nor commercial success. Negulesco directed only three more films, two independently produced and one for 20th Century Fox. Strangely, he makes no mention of *Jessica* in his memoir *Things I Did and Things I Think I Did*.

Reviews:

"It is no strain on Miss Dickinson's histrionic ability to wiggle through this role. Her proportions are admirably tailored to its specifications, and that's about all that's required. Maurice Chevalier breezes through the part of a village priest with that familiar sunny countenance, and pauses occasionally to narrate or tackle one of several listenable, but undistinguished, ditties by Marguerite Monnet (music) and Dusty Negulesco (lyrics)."

—*Daily Variety,* March 19, 1962

"Both Sicily and the star are well chosen for their tasks with the camera catching hillside scenes of a small Italian village as well as some of the most provocative footage ever of the lovely and delectable Angie."

"Her charms and the Negulesco treatment of them are worthy of the assignment for memory fails to bring to mind any star personality creating more of a stir in this field."

—George Jackson, *Los Angeles Herald-Examiner,* March 29, 1962

"*Jessica* has charm, beautiful melodies played by guitars and other stringed instruments. Also offered are some of the most gorgeous views of the Mediterranean ever shown as well as of the Sicilian countryside with Mount Etna towering above the villas, orchards and old Roman ruins."

"All this is painted in vivid color by one of screendom's finest artists where the camera is concerned, Jean Negulesco."

—Hazel Flynn, *Beverly Hills Citizen,* March 30, 1962

"Aside from its truly effective scenic compensations, *Jessica* has not come up with anything really new or exciting for a discerning viewer."

"As the unwitting temptress, Angie Dickinson definitely is a sight to behold. The role, it should be stated for the record, does not require much beyond physical attributes, and the honey-haired Miss Dickinson, in shorts or tight fitting bodices, undulates through her assignment to perfection."
—A.H. Weiler, *The New York Times*, April 20, 1962

"A thoroughly preposterous story about a young American widow who comes to a Sicilian village to serve as a midwife and whose beauty causes all the local males to go mad with desire, it has dialogue that is wooden only when it isn't leaden, and a plot that could have been glued together out of matchsticks by a ten-year-old."
—Brendan Gill, *The New Yorker*, May 19, 1962

Rome Adventure

Credits: A Warner Bros. production released on April 21, 1962. Technicolor. Running time of 118 minutes. Based on a novel by Irving Fineman. **Cast:** Troy Donahue (Don Porter), Suzanne Pleshette (Prudence Bell), Angie Dickinson (Lyda Kent), Rossano Brazzi (Roberto Orlandi), Hampton Fancher (Albert Stillwell), Constance Ford (Daisy Bronson), Al Hirt (Himself), Iphigenie Castiglioni (Contessa), Chad Everett (Young Man), Gertrude Flynn (Mrs. Riggs), Pamela Austin (Agnes Hutton), Lili Valenty (Angelina). **Crew:** Delmer Daves (director, screenwriter, producer), Max Steiner (composer), Charles Lawton (cinematographer), William Ziegler (editor), Leo K. Kuter (art director), John P. Austin (set decorator), Howard Shoup (costume designer), Jean Burt Reilly (hair stylist), Gordon Bau (makeup artist), Russell Llewellyn and Ottavio Oppo (assistant directors), M.A. Merrick (sound).

ANGIE

Plot Synopsis: Called before an administrative hearing panel at Briarcraft College for giving a female student a copy of a banned book, assistant librarian Prudence Bell decides to resign and travel to Italy, "where they really know what love is about." On board her ocean liner, she meets Albert Stillwell, a young student of Etruscan history and the son of a family friend, and Roberto Orlandi, an amorous Italian aristocrat. Although he is several years older, Roberto expresses unabashed romantic interest in the young American. Upon arrival in Rome, he finds both Prudence and Albert rooms in the elegant pensione owned by a countess friend of his.

Also residing at the pensione is Don Porter, a handsome American architecture student who barely takes notice of Prudence. He perfunctorily greets her before rushing off to the train station where his self-centered artist girlfriend Lyda Kent is leaving for Switzerland. Breaking off their relationship, she tells him that she can never be true to just one man. As his friend and confidant, Roberto encourages Don to forget all about Lyda. At the same time, Roberto pursues Prudence, and although they share a kiss on the Castel Sant'Angelo Bridge, she does not hear the bells that will tell her she has met the man of her dreams.

Following a lead from the countess, Prudence gets a job at the American Book Shop, located near the Piazza Barberini and operated by Daisy Bronson and her big affectionate sheepdog. A free-thinking former school teacher, Daisy takes an immediate liking to the young woman whom she sees as a kindred spirit. Running into Don at an outdoor café near the bookstore, Prudence sits down for a glass of Strega and brightens his mood with her enthusiasm for the city. They go sightseeing in a horse-drawn carriage and on his Vespa motorscooter. During a late lunch at Lake Albano overlooking Rome, he buys a candelabra from a peddler. Because of his generosity and the object's gold-like appearance, they refer to it as a symbol of Don's integrity. At dinner later that evening, a singer performs "Al di là" as they hold hands and gaze fondly at each other. Jazz trumpeter Al Hirt, an acquaintance of Don's, invites them to a nightclub, where he plays another version of "Al di là" and starts a fight when a patron muscles in on his girlfriend. Making a quick exit, Prudence and Don ride a carriage back to the pensione and kiss along the way; this time Prudence definitely hears bells.

With the arrival of the summer holidays and the temporary closing of the bookshop, Prudence and Don take a bus tour together of Siena, Florence, and Pisa. When it concludes, they continue on by themselves to Lago Maggiore and northern Italy. In the Italian Alps, they stay in a secluded chalet and in Verona, Don recites Shakespeare at the Romeo and Juliet balcony. Although her love for Don has deepened, good girl Prudence has insisted on separate rooms during the trip. When they bump into Albert and his mother, Prudence worries that their romantic vacation will be inaccurately reported to her family, and they return by train to Rome.

Lyda is waiting for Don at the pensione. One the run from a possessive business tycoon she has gotten involved with, she asks Don to help convince the private detective following her that she is taken. Once she meets Prudence, however, she schemes to get Don back for real. At a dinner in her studio, to which she has invited Prudence and Albert, Lyda keep clutching Don's arm and flaunting the details of their past affair. Convinced Don has not gotten over that relationship, Prudence excuses herself and asks to be taken home.

For the next three days, Don fails to appear at the pensione, an absence which Prudence takes as proof that he has returned to Lyda. In response, she decides to become an experienced woman of the world, showing up at Roberto's villa with a sexy negligee and an intention to spend the night. Agreeing to give her lessons in love, Roberto plays along for a while with the seduction, before stopping to explain that Don had been staying with him during the previous three days to sort through his feelings. Just as he realized he has been in love with Prudence all along, he received an urgent telegram from Lyda asking him to rescue her. Prudence decides she has had enough heartbreak and plans to return to the United States. Arriving at Lyda's expensive lakeside hotel, Don learns that she has married the tycoon and already wants him to help get her out of it. He leaves in disgust as the angry husband walks in on Lyda.

At the train station, Prudence says goodbye to all the friends who have come to see her off. Albert asks her to marry him and she promises only to write. In New York, her parents are at the dock to greet her. Among the crowd, she sees a candelabra and some roses weaving their way toward her. It is Don, who has taken a plane to be there. They embrace as he declares his love and she agrees to marry him.

Notes and Comments: *Rome Adventure* is a lesser example of the "Americans at play in Italy" subgenre, a film type better represented by *Roman Holiday* (1953), *Three Coins in the Fountain* (1954), *Summertime* (1955), *Come September* (1961), and *Light in the Piazza* (1962). Its claim to distinction, however, lies in the fact that it offers more footage of more sights than any of the other pictures. In addition to such standard Rome locations as the Colosseum, the Spanish Steps, the Palatine Hill, and the Vittorio Emanuele II Monument, it takes viewers through Tuscany and into northern Italy. Among the special highlights are Orvieto, Trentino, Arezzo, and Lake Maggiore. So much of the movie is devoted to picturesque vistas that it often seems more like a travelogue than a romantic drama.

This is probably a good thing given the hackneyed nature of the script. Every character is a familiar type, and every narrative development is predictable. At no point is there any doubt but that Don and Prudence will meet cute, fall in love, suffer setbacks, and reunite. Supporting players like the countess and Daisy the bookshop owner are briefly engaging but given far too little screen time. Other characters, namely then popular jazz performer Al Hirt playing himself, seem to show up for no other reason than to attract a few more ticket buyers.

Angie has the most thankless, unsympathetic role of all. Billed second after Troy Donahue, she has only four scenes throughout the picture. As the selfish and manipulative Lyda, she continually takes advantage of Don's good nature and tries to sabotage his relationship with Prudence. Forced to deliver lines such as "I'm no good for you, Don" and "You'll always see something in me that isn't there," she grasps and glares in a scaled-down version of the evil seductress persona she will revisit throughout her career. While the other characters interact with the gorgeous countryside, she is relegated to airless studio interiors, an isolation that emphasizes Lyda's artifice. Three of her scenes are with Donahue only; the fourth is the dinner to which Prudence and Albert also have been invited. Donahue's relative impassivity as an actor makes Angie seem even more like the aggressor.

Despite her limited exposure, Angie looks fantastic in the chic early 60s wardrobe that her frequent costume designer Howard Shoup has provided. For the train station scene, she is in pearls, gloves, and a knit travel suit. When Don finds her waiting at the pensione, she is wearing a mustard brown Chanel-like skirt and jacket. She appears for the dinner at her studio in a silver, Asian-influenced tunic accessorized with slacks, heels, and chandelier earrings. Waiting alone in the hotel room, she is clad in an open blue silk robe that reveals her long, shapely legs. Alternately worn up in a chignon or loosened down into a relaxed bouffant, her light brown hair is streaked with traces of the blond that will become her primary color later in the decade. She has the comportment here of a fashion model.

Troy Donahue is caught between Suzanne Pleshette and Angie in *Rome Adventure* (1962).

The picture belongs to Troy Donahue and Suzanne Pleshette as the appealing young lovers. Romantically involved in real life, they seem to be tightly focused on each other's presence, moving convincingly between quarrels and embraces. In her first major film role, Pleshette, who would memorably play Emily Hartley on *The Bob Newhart Show* from 1972 to 1978, uses her sultry voice to stunning effect. Screen veteran Rossano Brazzi is wasted as the wise Latin lover doling out advice to Don and Prudence.

More troubling than *Rome Adventure's* clichéd storyline is its regressive attitude toward women. In one cringe-worthy scene, Al

Hirt parades his provocatively outfitted girlfriend in front of Don for admiration while panting, "too much, ain't she." Daisy tells Prudence that "every woman competes with every other woman in the world from the day she's born," and Roberto declares, "Women's most important function in life is to anchor men." Prudence takes in all the advice and in the end happily devotes herself to Don, the creator and controller. For a smart, college-educated woman, it's a poorly reasoned choice.

Rome Adventure was Angie's last picture under contract at Warner Bros. as well as the last of the four youth-oriented, sex-splashed romances that Troy Donahue made with writer/director Delmer Daves. Faring better than either of them here was the song "Al di là," which is heard three times and became a big hit for Emilio Percoli (who sings it in the movie), Connie Francis, Jerry Vale, and others.

Reviews:

"*Rome Adventure* is a love story—of young love, brash, bewildered, brave—done in the lush manner that Delmer Daves has now stamped as his own. The romantic melodrama, sparked by a striking performance by a new young actress, Suzanne Pleshette, is an engrossing romantic melodrama."

"Donahue, superficially appealing, never seems to justify all the fuss made about him by the ladies. Angie Dickinson, the female temptress, plays a very small role in the picture, and her characterization is fuzzy and confusing. Rossano Brazzi is charming and manages some depth as a Roman man about town. These two-dimensional characters are redeemed by a glowing performance by Miss Pleshette."

—James Powers, *The Hollywood Reporter*, March 14, 1962

"Pictorial values have their place on the screen, of course, when presented as background. But in this instance the scenic stress is such that the picture in large part comes off as a guided tour and the make believe story frequently gets lost."

"Miss Pleshette is a very pretty gal and talent shows through. But she and the also highly attractive Angie Dickinson are handicapped with dialog that's apparently intended to be frisky, instead is largely banal."

"Daves has given his production an expensive look. Many of the interiors are nicely set and the gals' wardrobes are attractive. Charles Lawton's photography (Technicolor) is a major asset, capturing more adventure out of the Italian sightseeing than the story. Editing is fair enough and Max Steiner's music is firstclass."

—*Weekly Variety*, March 21, 1962

"Until Europe runs out of scenery, I guess we can expect endless variations of the story about the American girl who goes abroad in search of love and finds it against a succession of Romantic old-world backgrounds."

"*Rome Adventure* is another of this genre, and Producer-Director Delmer Daves proves that the formula still hasn't lost its charm."

"The actors mostly are young and good looking—Suzanne Pleshette, Troy Donahue, Angie Dickinson, with a few more mature veterans like Rossano Brazzi and Constance Ford thrown in to add a sophisticated note."

"Donahue already has a proven charm for feminine audiences. Miss Pleshette is a pretty and spirited newcomer, who has a provocative brunette beauty, plus genuine talent. She is one of Hollywood's most promising discoveries in a long time."

—Harrison Carroll, *Los Angeles Herald-Examiner*, May 3, 1962

Captain Newman, M. D.

Credits: A joint production of Universal Pictures, Reynard and Brentwood Productions released on December 25, 1963, by Universal Pictures. Eastman Color by Pathe. Running time of 126 minutes. Based on a novel by Leo Rosten. **Cast:** Gregory Peck (Capt. Josiah J. Newman), Tony Curtis (Cpl. Jackson "Jake" Leibowitz), Angie Dickinson (Lt. Francie Corum), Eddie Albert (Col. Norval Bliss), Bobby Darin (Cpl. Jim Tompkins), James Gregory (Col. Edgar Pyser), Bethel Leslie (Mrs. Helene Winston), Robert Duvall (Capt. Paul Cabot Winston), Jane Withers (Lt. Grace Blodgett), Dick Sargent (Lt. Belden "Barney" Alderson), Larry Storch (Cpl. Gavoni), Robert F. Simon (Lt. Col. M.B. Larrabee), Syl Lamont (Sgt. Kopp), Paul Carr (Arthur Werbel), Vito Scotti (Maj. Alfredo Fortuno), Crahan Denton (Maj. Gen. Snowden), Gregory Walcott (Capt. Howard), Charles Briggs (Gorkow), Ted Bessell, Mike Farrell, Robert Fuca and Ken Swofford (uncredited patients). **Crew:** David Miller (director), Richard L. Breen, Phoebe Ephron and Henry Ephron (screenwriters), Robert Arthur (producer), Russell Garcia and Frank Skinner (composers), Russell Metty (director of photography), Alma Macrorie (editor), Alexander Golitzen and Alfred Sweeney (art directors), Howard Bristol (set decorator), Rosemary Odell (costume designer), Larry Germain (hair stylist), Bud Westmore (makeup artist), Phil Bowles (assistant director), William Russell and Waldon O. Watson (sound) and Albert Whitlock (matte shots).

Plot Synopsis: In 1944, toward the end of World War II, Captain Josiah Newman heads the psychiatric ward at Colfax Army Air Field's military hospital. Ward Seven, as Newman explains to visiting Lieutenant Barney Alderson, whom he first mistakes as an inmate, is short of "beds, doctors, orderlies, nurses, everything—except patients." Among those patients are a fragile young sailor with an imaginary brother, an African American soldier named Bobby who cannot speak, a glib, upbeat serviceman who analyzes Newman, and a husky bully with anger management issues. All of the men like and respect Newman, and he runs the ward with humor, compassion, and a disregard for protocol. That touch of rebelliousness is a constant irritant to the field commander Colonel Pyser, who would like to permanently remove Ward Seven from his base. Watching Newman interact with the patients and the staff, Alderson is immediately impressed with his special talents.

Located in the middle of the Arizona desert, Colfax is considered a less than ideal assignment. There is little entertainment nearby, the work is routine, and a flock of sheep that Newman uses in the medical lab keeps getting in everyone's way. When Corporal Jackson Leibowitz reports for orderly duty, Newman immediately hijacks him for duty in Ward Seven. A fast talking wheeler-dealer from New York, Leibowitz balks at both Arizona and the mental ward but soon becomes indispensable, reading Newman's medical books and offering his own diagnoses.

Newman also tries to convince nurse Francie Corum to join his skeletal staff, whose only other female member is not-so-glamorous 1st Lieutenant Grace Blodgett. Beautiful and gifted, Francie battles Newman over orderly allotments and matches his unconventional approach with her own light-hearted, confident demeanor. During an evening of dinner and dancing, they confess that they have read each other's 201 personnel files out of more than professional interest. "Francie," declares Newman, "you're a good-looking woman . . . one look at your legs and the men would come right up out of the floor." Despite champagne and the gift of an imported Hawaiian lei, Newman awkwardly shows his hand, angering Francie by an obvious plan to get her to change assignments. Their resultant argument is cut short by a phone call informing Newman that a very psychotic Colonel Norval Bliss has forced his way into the ward with a large knife and an intent to harm the doctor for a fitness report blocking Bliss's return to active duty. After watching Newman disarm the Colonel and calm some of his other patients, Francie makes the transfer into Ward Seven.

Bliss is one of three tough cases confounding Newman. The other two are Jim Tompkins, an Air Force corporal whose heavy drinking and insomnia are masking deeper trauma, and Captain Paul Winston, a nearly catatonic patient who had been missing in action for thirteen months. What links all three men is a sense of guilt—Bliss for ordering men into fatal combat, Tompkins for surviving a crash that killed his best friend, and Wilson for hiding in a French basement rather than searching for his unit. Their responses to Newman's treatment are not all the same, however.

Under the influence of sodium pentothal and intense counseling, Tompkins emerges from his emotional turmoil and ultimately returns to service. Bliss resists all efforts to communicate and disassociates from his past. During a fitness hearing called by Pyser, he bolts from the conference room, climbs a water tower, and jumps to his death as Newman tries to coax him off the edge. Through persistent therapy and a visit from his initially uptight, oblivious wife, Winston slowly comes out of his shell and "forgives" himself for a cowardice that never really existed.

Intermixed with the dramatic scenes are a series of comic vignettes that feature Leibowitz pilfering supplies for the ward, feuding with a hot-tempered base corporal, clearing sheep off the runway, and taking charge of a group of Italian POWs who have been sent to Colfax. A second narrative arc traces the developing romance between Newman and Francie. Although they are strongly attracted to each other, he is tempted by an offer to run Colfax as a veterans' hospital after the war and she wants to "get out and have some babies."

The film closes with a Christmas party that Ward Seven has arranged for the entire base. Leibowitz plays Santa, the Italians sing "Hava Nagila," and Pyser forgives the fact that the pine trimmings have been chopped from his own massive Christmas tree. While several of the formerly silent patients, including Winston, join in singing "Jingle Bells," Newman and Francie get a letter saying that young Jim Tompkins has been killed in combat. Amid the celebration, she begins to cry, and he holds her tightly, their future together still unresolved.

Notes and Comments: Prefiguring such films as *MASH* (1970) and *Catch-22* (1970), *Captain Newman, M. D.* tries to capture the comic absurdity of war through an offbeat account of how a rule-breaking military unit uses humor and guile to confront death, bureaucracy, and emotional disorder. Think Newman and Leibowitz as Hawkeye and Radar. The problem is that the comic and the tragic do not intertwine but exist rather as distinctly disparate narrative pieces. It is as if two different movies, one starring Gregory Peck and the other featuring Tony Curtis, have been edited together.

The story also suffers from the same credibility issues that plague *Let There Be Light* (1946), John Huston's famously censored World War II documentary about the hospital care offered returning veterans with post traumatic stress disorder. The psychological breakthroughs in both all come too easily, too quickly. For example, Newman simply has to inject air gunner Jim Tompkins with sodium pentothal (nicknamed "Flak Juice" by the patients) and then steer him through some tough love therapy sessions, and he is ready to report back to duty. Likewise, once Captain Winston's wife sheds her patrician coolness and opens up to her husband, Newman can help him see that hiding in a French cellar for over a year was an unusual albeit completely logical reaction to danger. After a cathartic release, he too is able to communicate and function socially again.

Credit the actors with keeping viewers engaged. Peck, ironically treating the same symptoms that his character Brigadier General Frank Savage suffers from in *Twelve O'Clock High* (1949), provides the right combination of irreverence and gravitas. His Doctor Newman is steady, dedicated, tireless, unorthodox, and tolerant. Although not particularly noted for his light touch, he gamely keeps up with Tony Curtis during the verbal bantering and the chaotic sheep herding. As the resourceful Corporal Jackson Leibowitz, Curtis seems to revisit his role as Lieutenant Nick Holden, the scrounging, slightly crooked supply officer to submarine commander Cary Grant in *Operation Petticoat* (1959), also produced by Universal International. Despite successful dramatic roles in *Sweet Smell of Success* (1957), *The Defiant Ones* (1958), and *Spartacus* (1960), Curtis is most well known for his good looks, fast-talking bravado, and comic assertiveness, all of which are on ample display here.

Two years earlier, Angie had convincingly portrayed a missionary nurse in *The Sins of Rachel Cade*, and she brings a similar touch of empathy to the part of 1st Lieutenant Francie Corum. Seen frequently in reaction shots responding tearfully or supportively to Newman's interventions with the patients, she is there for all of the most severely afflicted cases. Whether helping to restrain Bliss or spoonfeeding Winston, she projects determination tinged with sensitivity. This is another of those occasions, as in *Rio Bravo* and *Ocean's Eleven*, where Angie works deftly with a mostly all-male cast. The object of admiring glances and whistles, she downplays the sexual stereotyping and emphasizes instead her character's resilience and commitment to team.

ANGIE

In *Captain Newman, M.D.,* Angie lends medical and emotional support to Gregory Peck (1963).

In spite of its lack of a resolution, her romance with Peck is also believable. She first appears on screen in a meet-cute scene where she bumps into the distracted Captain in the mess hall and they get into an argument about who will be assigned the newly arrived orderly. The friction continues as Newman takes her to dinner and ruins the mood by prematurely asking her to join his unit. Not unexpectedly, however, soon they are sharing backstories and mutual respect. Angie's rarely utilized skill with physical comedy appears in a scene where Newman gets drunk and she drives him back to the barracks, taking a pratfall onto the floor with him and coolly acknowledging his observation that she has "a beautiful neck." With her stunning smile and glistening eyes radiating out from a wardrobe consisting solely of nurse capes and khaki uniforms,

Angie comes to represent all of the domestic well-being that Peck as Newman is trying to restore. The couple's final Christmas Eve embrace is the film's ultimate note of optimism and hope.

The supporting actors, charged with embodying the psychological damage caused by war, are uniformly good. Singer Bobby Darin, in one of his best film roles, plays Corporal Tompkins as a cocky tough guy barely able to conceal his demons. The scene where he relives the crash of his combat plane is deeply jarring, taking him from mounting anxiety to full-on hysteria in a matter of moments. It is a performance that earned him a best actor award at the Cannes Film Festival and an Academy Award nomination for best supporting actor.

Following his 1962 film debut in *To Kill a Mockingbird*, Robert Duvall offers a continuation of his Boo Radley character, emphasizing Captain Winston's mute, slump-shouldered isolation from his surroundings. Eddie Albert gives Bliss defiant despair, and James Gregory's gravelly voiced petulance seems right for the beleaguered Colonel Pyser. Although they are on screen for limited periods of time, Jane Withers, Larry Storch, and Vito Scotti are amusing as, respectively, Lieutenant Blodgett, Corporal Gavoni, and the captured Major Alfredo Fortuno.

Location shooting took place at Fort Huachuca in southern Arizona, and the exteriors are used for the ceremonial arrival, water tank, and sheep herding scenes. Cinematographer Russell Metty, whose 150 plus credits include *Bringing Up Baby* (1938), *Touch of Evil* (1958), and *The Misfits* (1961), deftly matches the location footage and the studio interiors, working with a color palette that is subdued and slightly faded. He makes particularly effective use of a handheld camera to animate Bliss's climb up the tower and of overhead shots to accent the emotional bond between Newman and Francie.

Paired with *Lonely Are the Brave* (1962), a melancholic reflection on the vanishing of the Western frontier, *Captain Newman, M. D.* constitutes director David Miller's attempt to reach beyond the conventional genre pictures he was regularly assigned for a more profound statement about human perseverance and social fragmentation. The uneven blend of comedy and drama does not obscure his ability to build suspense and choreograph action, evident as well in *Midnight Lace* (1960) and *Sudden Fear* (1952). Miller's origins as an editor at Columbia can be seen in his frequent use of dissolves, cross cuts, and reaction shots to link scenes and punctuate dialogue.

Screenwriters Henry and Phoebe Ephron (parents of writers Nora, Delia, Hallie, and Amy) and Richard Breen received an Academy Award nomination for best adapted screenplay as did Waldon O. Watson for best sound.

Reviews:

"Peck delivers one of his typically low-key performances in which persuasion and power are so subtly projected as to seem accidental."

"Angie Dickinson, as Peck's romantic interest, is warm and sympathetic, but she is out of her milieu among these cannonball pitchers."

"The development of psychiatric treatment is sketchy. Some of the 'cures' are extremely rapid. But some dramatic license may be permitted and this is the justification."

—*The Hollywood Reporter*, October 22, 1963

"Angie Dickinson brings charm and warmth to her role as the nurse in love with Peck, who goes through his chores."

—*Film Daily*, October 22, 1963

"The young and attractive Angie Dickinson, as Peck's nurse ... is good."

—*Motion Picture Herald*, October 30, 1963

"David Miller has made a Gregory Peck picture, subordinating his own style to the actor's and in so doing has turned out a leisurely, affectionate portrait of a man that strives for no large nor spectacular effects but maintains a very pleasant cumulative warmth."

—*Cinema*, Nov/Dec, 1963

"The film is episodic, a loose series of vignettes bearing little relation to each other and failing to build to any sort of solid climax."

—*Our Sunday Visitor*, December 15, 1963

"A remarkable blend of comedy and drama is found in Universal's filmization of Leo Rosten's absorbing novel, *Captain Newman, M. D.*"

—*Los Angeles Herald-Examiner*, December 26, 1963

The Killers

Credits: A Revue Studios production released in the United States by Universal Pictures on July 7, 1964. Eastman color by Pathe. Running time of 93 minutes. Based on a short story by Ernest Hemingway. **Cast:** Lee Marvin (Charlie Strom), Angie Dickinson (Sheila Farr), John Cassavetes (Johnny North), Clu Gulager (Lee), Claude Akins (Earl Sylvester), Ronald Reagan (Jack Browning), Norman Fell (Mickey Farmer), Virginia Christine (Miss Watson), Don Haggerty (mail truck driver), Robert Phillips (George Fleming), Kathleen O'Malley (receptionist), Irvin Mosley (mail truck guard) and Nancy Wilson (nightclub singer). **Crew:** Don Siegel (director and producer),

Gene L. Coon (screenwriter), Richard L. Rawlings (director of photography), Richard Belding (editor), Johnny Williams (composer), Frank Arrigo and George Chan (art directors), John McCarthy and James Redd (set decorators), Helen Colvig (costume designer), Larry Germain (hair stylist), Bud Westmore (makeup artist), Milton Feldman (assistant director) and David H. Moriarty (sound).

Plot Synopsis: Charlie and Lee, two well-dressed hit men in sunglasses, barge into a school for the blind in search of Johnny North, a former race car driver now teaching an auto mechanics class at the school. After roughing up the blind female principal to ascertain Johnny's whereabouts, they pull out their silencer guns and enter Johnny's classroom. Warned of their approach, he calmly faces his killers and takes several fatal rounds to the chest.

Later, on a train out of town, Charlie, the older and more experienced hit man, wonders why "he just stood there and took it" and why they were paid $25,000 for a simple hit. Remembering that Johnny was involved four years earlier in a million dollar mail truck robbery and believing that the money is still missing, they decide to visit Miami to interrogate Johnny's former mechanic Earl Sylvester.

Reluctant to talk until he is gut punched by Lee, Earl begins to share what he knows about Johnny. Drinking whiskey and weeping over the news that his erstwhile friend is dead, Earl introduces the film's first extended flashback. At the top of his game and poised to win a big race, Johnny meets the beautiful, thrill-seeking Sheila Farr. "I can't say I'm impressed," she tells him after watching a practice lap, daring him to drive faster and live more dangerously. During the romance that follows, they spend time in nightclubs and at Sheila's fancy apartment. "You have money written all over you," he observes, but she carefully avoids explaining who pays for everything.

On the day of the race, Sheila visits Johnny in the pit against the wishes of Earl, who believes she is ruining Johnny's health and his future. Watching the activity through binoculars are underworld boss Jack Browning and his associate Mickey Farmer. Leading through much of the race, Johnny suffers a rear wheel mishap and barely survives a fiery crash. In the hospital, Earl explains that Sheila is Browning's mistress and has already had flings with a boxer and a bullfighter. Knowing that Johnny's racing career is over, Earl offers to partner with him in a garage business but Johnny angrily rejects the gesture. When Sheila herself comes to visit, Johnny confronts her with the Browning information and abruptly ends their relationship.

John Cassavetes and Angie share an amorous moment in *The Killers* (1964).

Hearing Earl's story, Charlie and Lee grow even more determined to "find out what makes a man decide not to run." Working from a tip, they journey to New Orleans, where Mickey Farmer operates a gymnasium. Lee, who has become increasingly sadistic and unpredictable, turns up the heat in Mickey's steam cabinet while Charlie extorts the next expository flashback. Reduced to working in a jalopy derby, Johnny is once again approached by Sheila, who suggests she may have a much better job offer for him to consider. Browning is planning to rob a mail delivery truck and needs a fast driver for the pursuit. When Johnny fails to return her calls, Sheila visits his rundown apartment, pledges her love, and convinces him to take the $100,000 job. "I want you to mean this," he says, and she answers, "I've always meant it. I want you."

Johnny makes a successful test run and helps Browning customize the car to make it even faster. Annoyed by the intimacy between Sheila and Johnny, Browning slaps her to assert his dominance and Johnny punches him in the face. Pulled apart by the rest of the crew, they agree to "settle things" after the heist. The plan goes smoothly. Dressed as highway patrol officers, Browning and Johnny put up detour signs and direct the mail truck onto a little-used back road, where they overtake it at a staged accident. While Farmer and another gang member subdue the two mail drivers, Browning and Johnny take off with a million dollars in vacation resort proceeds. Soon after their getaway, Johnny knocks Browning out of the car and continues on with the money himself.

Back in the present, Farmer concludes that Johnny betrayed everyone and simply disappeared. Suspicious about why there was no follow-up ("the only guy who doesn't worry about a million bucks is the guy who has a million bucks"), Charlie and Lee proceed to Los Angeles, where Browning has now become a successful real estate developer. Although he denies any knowledge of the money, Browning agrees to arrange a meeting with Sheila Farr in her hotel. Arriving earlier than scheduled, Charlie and Lee surprise Sheila and pressure her for information. She too insists that Johnny took the stolen cash but after being punched and dangled out of her upper floor window, she relates the film's third and final flashback.

On the night before the robbery, she tells Johnny that Browning plans to double cross him, knowledge which leads to his reversing things and instead dumping Browning from the car. That evening he reunites with Sheila in a rural motel and shows her the bags of money. Browning appears from the shadows and shoots Johnny, who stumbles off into the woods and, after a brief chase, is left wounded and bleeding. Sometime later, Browning tracks down Johnny at the school and hires the hit. Satisfied now that they understand how Sheila manipulated and used Johnny, Charlie remarks, "The only man who's not afraid to die is one who's dead already."

Tipped off by the hotel clerk, Browning ambushes the hit men as they leave the building. Firing a high-powered rifle from a nearby rooftop, he kills Lee and wings Charlie. Browning and Sheila return to their quiet suburban home, scrambling to unload stacks of money from a wall safe. Mortally wounded, Charlie breaks in and shoots Browning. Claiming that she never had anything to do with the scheming, Sheila pleads for mercy, but Charlie calmly replies, "Lady, I don't have the time" and shoots her as well. Stumbling outside, he falls dead on the lawn as money spills out of his suitcase and a police car approaches from the distance.

Notes and Comments: In Ernest Hemingway's 1927 short story "The Killers," which consists almost entirely of clipped, hard-boiled dialogue like the kind Dashiell Hammett had been writing since 1922, two brutish gangsters arrive unexpectedly at a greasy spoon diner in Summit, Illinois. After intimidating the counterman, the cook and Hemingway alter ego Nick Adams, one of the thugs casually remarks that they are going to kill a big Swede named Ole

Andreson. Unable to stay out of it, the counterman asks, "What are you going to kill Ole Andreson for? What did he ever do to you?" and the gangster boasts, "He never had a chance to do anything to us. He never even seen us . . . we're killing him for a friend. Just to oblige a friend, bright boy".[4]

When Andreson fails to show up for his usual evening meal at the diner, the two gunmen leave, and Adams goes to the Swede's rooming house to warn him. "I was up at Henry's," he says, "and two fellows came in and tied up me and the cook, and they said they were going to kill you." Andreson is nonplussed. "There isn't anything I can do about it," he replies.[5] The story ends with Andreson lying in bed, turning his face to the wall and waiting for the hit men.

Both Hollywood film adaptations of "The Killers" have attempted to flesh out a backstory that explains why Andreson seems to passively accept his death. In director Robert Siodmak's 1946 version, the Swede (Burt Lancaster in his movie debut) is an ex-boxer who takes a petty theft rap for and is double crossed by the beautiful but evil Kitty Collins (Ava Gardner). Lured into a payroll robbery planned by Kitty's husband Big Jim Colfax (Albert Dekker), Andreson is the tool by which the couple also betrays the rest of the gang and absconds with the loot. Andreson does not try to evade the killers sent by Colfax to keep him quiet because he is tired of running and disillusioned by Kitty's duplicity. With Woody Bredell's moody black and white photography and Miklós Rózsa's evocative musical score, the picture is regarded as a classic film noir: nocturnal, urban, violent, cynical, and driven narratively by multiple flashbacks. It is an admirable achievement, one of a dozen noirs made by Siodmak between 1944 and 1950, but Don Siegel's somewhat unsavory 1964 version is much more intriguing.

Ole Andreson is now Johnny North, a school for the blind

teacher cum race car driver, whose infatuation with glamorous Sheila Farr leads him into the million dollar mail truck heist. Like Ole, he is warned that two hit men are coming for him but refuses to flee and calmly awaits his death. The two hit men, Charlie and Lee, smarter and more curious than Hemingway's original thugs, wonder at Johnny's behavior and decide to investigate.

It is not the plot, however, that makes the film so fascinating; it is the whacked-out, one of a kind, "only in 60s Hollywood" cast. John Cassavetes is North, Lee Marvin and Clu Gulager play the hit men, Angie is Sheila Farr, and, in his last feature film before entering politics full time, Ronald Reagan is Jack Browning. The future 40th President of the United States bids farewell to pictures as a violent, rifle-toting villain.

And in a strange, slightly creepy way, the casting works. No one, not even Johnny North, is a likable character. Cassavetes plays him as a petulant, abrasive, self-centered jerk. His death is pathetic not tragic. Like Orson Welles, Cassavetes appeared in other people's films in order to finance his own. He always seemed angry to be involved. Watch him here or as Private Franko in *The Dirty Dozen* (1967) or as husband Guy Woodhouse in *Rosemary's Baby* (1968), and the same feral prickliness surfaces. He gives us a Johnny North who callously rejects the advice and friendship of the loyal mechanic who loves him. Ignoring the warning that Sheila is using him, he fritters away his talent and career and then is either so dumb or so arrogant that he comes back for more. A hair shorter than Angie and dwarfed by Reagan, Cassavetes carries resentment in his posture. Whether he is smiling or scowling, the expression is the same—steely eyes fixed, upper lip covered, jaw thrust forward.

As Hemingway knew all along, the story's focus is not on Ole Andreson/Johnny North but on the killers. The film begins and ends with Marvin's Charlie Strom. About to be reborn as existential anti-hero in *The Professionals* (1966), *Point Blank* (1967), and *Prime Cut* (1970), Marvin is in the last of his psychopathic hood roles. Sporting dark sunglasses and a well-cut suit, he calmly pulls out his silencer pistol and dispatches Johnny in the opening scenes. To say that Charlie is brutal is to minimize his capacity for violence. He roughs up a blind woman, whispers a death threat in Earl's ear, and traps a would-be informant in an overheating sauna cabinet. Businesslike and methodical, he continually reminds his victims that they are trying his patience. Dominating everything is the Lee Marvin look: indifferent yet focused, blank but penetrating, cynically aware of every petty human weakness and deceit.

Taking just the slightest edge off Charlie's menace is his teacher-student relationship with junior partner Lee, a jocular camaraderie that influenced the one between hit men John Travolta and Samuel L. Jackson in Quentin Tarantino's *Pulp Fiction* (1994). With Lee, Charlie is more relaxed, mentoring the younger man on strategy and including him equally in every deal. While Lee messes with the people they are trying to question (pouring water on the blind woman's desk to see if she notices, cleaning his sunglasses on the soaked hair of Mickey Farmer in the steam box, picking up a silent phone in Browning's office and talking to no one), Charlie pauses indulgently and waits for the weirdness to pass.

Marvin reportedly said that playing Lee's partner was his favorite movie role. One wonders how aware he was of the homoerotic nature of that relationship. Both men are fastidious dressers and are together continually. Neither has a girlfriend. In the hotel room they share, Charlie washes out a shirt while Lee, who exercises regularly and gives Charlie nutrition advice, does push-ups. Their admiration for each other is terse but obvious. Charlie tells

Lee he is young, good-looking and has a brain. When Charlie explains that they are going to surprise Sheila by showing up several hours early for the meeting, Lee remarks, "You're always on top, aren't you, Charlie?" It is a comment that is both respectful and suggestive. Clu Gulager, as Lee, handles that line and all his dialogue like he's enjoying a joke that very few others can understand. Known mostly at this point in his career for playing Billy the Kid on the television series *The Tall Man* (1960-62), he would go on to co-star in *The Virginian* (1964-68), another TV western, and in Peter Bogdanovich's *The Last Picture Show* (1971). He was always handsome, sleek, and more than a little dangerous.

For all their experience and street smarts, Charlie and Lee still find it hard to understand why Johnny North would wreck his career and life for a "dame" like Sheila Farr. The answer is simple, really; the "dame" is Angie Dickinson. This clearly is one of Angie's iconic "bad girl" parts. Like Jane Greer's famously double-crossing Kathie Moffat in *Out of the Past* (1947), she first appears in all white costumes—a white sleeveless dress with pearls, white slacks and sweater, a white jumpsuit—to reflect Johnny's image of her as a radiant, fresh-faced treasure. Then, as she becomes more scheming and duplicitous, she is clothed in dark colors—a brown suit, a black skirt, a black plaid coat. In several shots, the camera opens on Angie's legs before pulling back to reveal her full figure advancing toward Johnny. Her sensuality is emphasized as the Circean lure that ensnares him. When he takes her for a ride in his race car, she shakes her hair into the wind and opens her mouth with delight. In one especially risqué moment, she grabs his leg and his foot pushes down on the accelerator.

Yet Angie is able to make Sheila somewhat sympathetic as well. There is real concern in her expression when she visits Johnny in the hospital and palpable regret as she watches Browning ambush him in the motel. The soft whispery voice and the shy smile keep us hoping that her better nature will prevail.

Lee Marvin manhandles Angie in a scene from *The Killers* (1964).

Referring to the Sheila Farr part, director Don Siegel told biographer Stuart Kaminsky, "Her role wasn't as clear as I thought it should be. Her motives were ambiguous and in *The Killers* I wanted it to be crystal clear why people do what they do."6 But the ambiguity is what Angie conveys so convincingly. Sheila betrays Johnny yet also seems to want his love. In fact, she wants it all: the passion, the sports car, the luxurious apartment provided by Jack Browning, the dozen or so costume changes, and the thrills. It is not the ambiguity that is problematic but rather the misogynistic brutalizing of Sheila. She is slapped by Browning, punched by Lee, dangled head first out of a seventh floor window, and ultimately shot by Charlie. Fortunately, Angie is spared further *in extremis* indignity; the death itself occurs offscreen.

The film's most bizarre casting choice, of course, is Ronald Reagan as the cold-blooded criminal who "owns" Sheila. He had played one of Bette Davis's sycophantic socialite friends in *Dark Victory* (1939) and Shirley Temple's inappropriately older boyfriend in *That Hagen Girl* (1947), but he had never before been an outright villain. Surprisingly, he is quite good at it. As Jack Carson also repeatedly demonstrated, under many a good-natured but under-appreciated Warner Bros. second string contract player, is a vengeful cad waiting to appear. Watching Sheila play around with Johnny or attempt to sell him out in the end, Reagan arches his eyebrow in a slow burning sneer that he will later dial down and refine as a way to dismiss debate opponents and political adversaries. Ensconced behind the desk of his construction company office, he looks presciently like the Chief Executive to come—projecting power, money, denials, and excuses.

Casting against type is just one of the ways in which *The Killers* upsets genre expectations. Unlike other directors of film noir, Siegel forgoes the dark shadows and shoots all but one scene in the glaring light of day. Among his locations are the sunbelt cities of Miami, New

Orleans, and Los Angeles. The climactic final scene plays out not in a crowded tenement but in a quiet residential neighborhood. There is nothing moody about the color photography; it is vivid, almost garish. In one major respect, however, Siegel remains true to tradition. Everyone, except for Johnny's devoted friend and mechanic Earl, dies.

Among the film's thematic motifs are continual references to passing time and to eyesight. Charlie and Lee race around the country following clues like detectives on a deadline with Charlie continually telling targets that he doesn't "have the time" for their problems. All of the characters don and remove sunglasses, the opening sequence occurs at a school for the blind, and Johnny's accident results in a close-up of an ominously cracked pair of goggles. Such details help to define both the victims and the victimizers, misfits who are all ultimately trapped by tightening options and limited vision.

The Killers was originally intended as the first made-for-television movie. Universal subsidiary Revue Productions made it as part of a proposed *Project 120* series with the tentative title of *Johnny North*. During production, President Kennedy was assassinated and NBC network executives decided that the film was too disturbing for prime time. Instead, it was retitled and released on a limited basis in theatres before disappearing for many years. There are some eerie historical correspondences. Reagan uses a sniper's rifle to shoot Clu Gulager from a multi-storied building like the Dallas schoolbook depository, and that ambush occurs outside a hotel entrance similar to the one where Reagan's own assassination attempt occurred.

Despite a tight budget, the film boasts solid production values: helicopter shots for the mail truck pursuit, location filming for the race scenes, a score by Stephen Spielberg's and George Lucas's future go-to composer John Williams (credited here as Johnny Williams).

The only stylistic blemishes are the obvious rear projections for the vehicle dialogue scenes and the awkward matches between the location footage and the studio interiors (particularly glaring in the race track pit sequences). As a gritty urban thriller, *The Killers* is prelude to Siegel's subsequent work in *Coogan's Bluff* (1968), *Madigan* (1968), and *Dirty Harry* (1971).

Reviews:

"The most positive personality is the most ambiguous one—the femme fatale, invested by Angie Dickinson with an overflowing animal insolence and all the moral qualities that can co-exist with unrelenting egoism. She's largely responsible for the climax being as exciting as it is."

—*Films and Filming*, May 1965

"Miss Dickinson may be overwhelmed by the incongruities of her character because she is personable but not very convincing."

—*The Hollywood Reporter*, May 26, 1964

"The screenplay by Gene L. Coon ably builds and holds and is brilliantly acted out by a fine cast headed by Lee Marvin, Angie Dickinson, and John Cassavetes. Here and there formula touches intrude but in every sense it is an explosive drama that should stir strong box office returns."

—*Film Daily*, June 1, 1964

"Perhaps the sole justification for turning a fine old movie into a just passable new one can be summed up as Angie Dickinson."

—*Time*, July 31, 1964

"The cast is first rate. Thanks to Marvin's sleek, snub-nosed menace and the edgy thrill-seeking projected by Angie Dickinson's classy moll, the movie exudes a cynical Rat Pack cool."

"The movie's small screen origins are apparent in the emphatic cutting and abundant close-ups—vehicles screeching to a halt a foot from the camera—that play to Siegel's strength as an action director and editor."

—*The New York Times*, August 2, 2015
(upon release of Criterion's Blu-ray edition)

"It should be added that Miss Dickinson's demanding role in the picture is probably her best to date—certainly it has increased her dramatic stature to new heights of prestige, and should put her in ever greater demand."

—*Hollywood Citizen-News*, August 22, 1964

The Art of Love

Credits: A Cherokee Productions/Ross Hunter Productions/Universal Pictures production released on June 30, 1965. Technicolor. Running time of 99 minutes. **Cast:** James Garner (Casey Barnett), Dick Van Dyke (Paul Sloane), Elke Sommer (Nikki Dunnay), Angie Dickinson (Laurie Gibson), Ethel Merman (Madame Coco La Fontaine), Carl Reiner (Rodin), Pierre Olaf (Inspector Carnot), Miiko Taka (Chou Chou), Roger C. Carmel (Zorgus), Irving Jacobson (Mr. Fromkis), Jay Novello (janitor), Naomi Stevens (Mrs. Sarah Fromkis), Renzo Cesena (Pepe de Winter), Leon Belasco (Prince), Louis Mercier (magistrate). **Crew:** Norman Jewison (director), Richard Alan Simmons, William Sackheim, and Carl Reiner (screenwriters), Ross Hunter (producer), Cy Coleman (composer), Russell Metty (cinematographer), Milton Carruth (editor), Alexander Golitzen and George Webb (art directors), John Austin and Howard Bristol (set decorators), Ray Aghayan (costume designer), Larry Germain (hair stylist), Bud Westmore (makeup artist), Douglas Green (assistant director), Clarence Self and Waldon O. Watson (sound).

Plot Synopsis: Frustrated by his lack of success as a painter, Paul Sloan, an American artist living in Paris, decides to give up his dream and return home. He picks up his paintings from a gallery whose owner, a man named Zorgus, assures him that collectors are not interested in the work of living artists.

Paul's roommate Casey Barnett, an equally unsuccessful writer whose manuscripts never sell and who sponges off friends, is shocked by Paul's announcement. Without permission, Casey gathers together a bunch of paintings and takes them to a bordello owned by Madame Coco La Fontaine, the subject of his latest book. As an investment, she agrees to give Paul a 5,000-franc credit at the bar in exchange for the paintings. To relay what he thinks is good news, Casey calls and leaves word for Paul at the Paris kosher delicatessen, Chez Fromkis, that serves as the roommates' informal message center. Afterwards, he distributes the paintings among Madame Coco's girls.

An angry Paul arrives and gets in a fight with Casey while trying to retrieve the canvases. With the help of some good French wine, they settle the dispute and end up on a bridge over the Seine. Well under the influence of alcohol, they decide to fake Paul's suicide and thereby increase the value of his paintings. Casey pens an eloquent farewell note which Paul is reading when he sees a girl come out of the fog and jump into the river as part of her own suicide attempt. Taking off his coat and putting aside the note, Paul leaps after her but lands instead on a sand barge passing under the bridge. Cesar the barge owner and his wife Fanny help Paul fish the young woman out of the water. As the barge passes out of sight down the river, Casey assumes that Paul has actually drowned.

Once she is fully revived, the would-be suicide victim, whose name is Nikki Dunnay, responds well to the warm atmosphere aboard the boat. She and Paul grow close to one another. By the time they leave the barge, she has developed a major attraction to him. When he puts her on a bus to her home in Orleans, she declares that she must see him again and he gives her a card with the address of Chez Fromkis on the front and Coco La Fontaine's address scribbled on the back.

Meanwhile, the newspapers have been spreading the story of Paul's "suicide" and his heart-felt final manifesto. After reading the papers, Paul returns to the room above Chez Fromkis and confronts a surprised Casey. Because Paul's work is now selling briskly at inflated prices, they decide to hide him at Madame Coco's and keep him turning out newly discovered paintings. Complicating their efforts is the investigation into Paul's death by Inspector Gustave Carnot.

In disguise, Paul goes to Madame Coco's and meets Nikki, who read the wrong side of the address card and ended up getting a job there as a maid. While they renew their relationship, Casey intercepts a cable from Paul's rich fiancée Laurie, announcing her imminent arrival in Paris. As soon as he meets her at the airport, Casey begins to fall in love, ignoring his loyalty to Paul. Not only does he tell her about Paul's death but so also does he take her on a tour of Paul's hangouts in an attempt to portray him as an unfaithful playboy.

Working away on paintings at Madame Coco's, Paul continues to resist Nikki's romantic overtures. When Laurie appears at the club, jealous Nikki goes along with the story of Paul's infidelity because she herself is so in love with him. Realizing that his friend has betrayed him once again, Paul becomes furious and seeks revenge, which comes courtesy of Inspector Carnot.

Unable to find a body in the Seine, Carnot begins to suspect murder. Paul plants a series of clues that lead to Casey's arrest and trial for murder. Wearing another disguise, Paul sits in the courtroom as Casey's lawyer, Monsieur Rodin, presents an inept defense. Ultimately the judge sentences Casey to death by guillotine.

Despite Nikki's pleas, Paul waits until the day of the execution and then is delayed by a series of interrupts on his way to the prison. In the end, he saves Casey and reunites with Nikki, permitting Casey and Laurie to proceed with their own romance.

Notes and Comments: That Angie Dickinson and Ethel Merman would appear in the same movie is a sign of how desperate and chaotic was Hollywood's mid-60s search for stars and stories that would coax audiences into the theaters. Released in 1965 along with *The Art of Love* was everything from *The Sound of Music* and *Doctor Zhivago* to *Major Dundee* and *The Spy Who Came in from the Cold*. It was also a big year for comedies as different from one other as *Boeing Boeing*, *Cat Ballou*, *Dear Brigitte*, *The Family Jewels*, *Help!*, *How to Murder Your Wife*, *I'll Take Sweden*, *The Loved One*, *What's New Pussycat?*, and *Wild on the Beach*. Among such company, both edgy and familiar, *The Art of Love* finds itself on the conventional side of the spectrum.

As co-written by Carl Reiner and directed by Norman Jewison, the comedy is broadly situational. Both men are television veterans who seem to believe that if their stock characters talk loudly enough and react aggressively enough to each other, then laughs will ensue. To his credit, Jewison skillfully combines some location scenes involving Dick Van Dyke and Elke Sommer with extensive soundstage footage to create the plausible illusion that the whole thing is taking place in Paris. In his fourth consecutive light comedy under contract at Universal, Jewison also shows a commendable sense of timing, never holding the sight gags or the Van Dyke double takes longer than necessary.

Producer Ross Hunter is responsible for first-class talent involved—the Cy Coleman score, the Russell Metty cinematography, the Ray Aghayan wardrobe. Visually the picture has the brightly illuminated, crisply colorful sheen of the melodramas and romantic comedies Hunter produced for Universal, movies such as *Imitation of Life* (1959), *Midnight Lace* (1960), *Back Street* (1961), *Pillow Talk* (1959), and *The Thrill of It All* (1963). His cast reflects the clean-cut, wholesome look he favored so highly and that is epitomized by Rock Hudson and Doris Day in *Pillow Talk*. Although all of the actors in *The Art of Love* perform with the requisite energy and conviction, only Elke Sommer and Angie are truly likable.

As she had in *Rome Adventure* and *A Fever in the Blood*, Angie once again demonstrates that she can play an upper-class character as believably as the working girls she usually portrays. In her expensive Aghayan gowns, she is like Tracy Lord minus the attitude. With regally erect posture and precise speech, she moves through the studio sets as if she really were inhabiting the elegant interiors of Paris. Neither James Garner nor Van Dyke seems in the same league.

Norman Jewison always believed that the reason the movie failed at the box office was because of the flawed premise that a contemporary artist's work would immediately increase in value upon his death. More likely the lack of interest was due to Jewison and Reiner's inability to make the double crossing and backstabbing entertaining enough. The picture might have worked if it had been directed by Ernst Lubitsch in 1940 and had starred Melvyn

Douglas, Fredric March, Claudette Colbert, and Carole Lombard. Author Patricia Highsmith used a similar concept to much better and more appropriately macabre effect five years later in her second Tom Ripley novel, *Ripley Under Ground*.

As an elegant American abroad, Angie captures the attention of co-star James Garner in *The Art of Love* (1965).

Reviews:

"Ross Hunter's *The Art of Love* is a chic comedy, high fashion combined with low farce, a picture that is one of the year's brightest and will light up marquees with immensely saleable razzle dazzle."

"Although *Art of Love* was shot almost entirely on the Universal City lot—with only some long shots of Paris here and there—it gets the Parisian atmosphere in Russell Metty's glowing Technicolor photography."

"Miss Dickinson has her role to date here. Although she comes on somewhat late, her languid grace adds a feline loveliness to the proceedings."

—James Powers, *The Hollywood Reporter*, May 5, 1965

"There is a wealth of talent involved in *The Art of Love*, latest of Ross Hunter's splashy, colorful film fantasies, but that may be where the picture faced its greatest artistic challenge, too. While individual ingredients are often delectable, the whole mixture is not quite as palatable as the recipe seemed to indicate."

"Garner plays like a romantic leading man who shouldn't be doing satire. Elke Sommer and Angie Dickinson are gorgeous to look at and perfect for their roles."

"True to his reputation, Hunter has mounted the production resplendently, particularly with Ray Aghayan's chic costumes, among them a gold trouser-gown worn by Miss Dickinson that will create a reaction from males and femmes alike, but for different reasons. Alexander Golitzen and George Webb's art direction, complemented by Howard Bristol and John Austin's sets, are handsome, and film editor Milton Carruth moves through the abundant material with a frequently-used, but effective, horizontal optical flip."

—*Daily Variety*, May 5, 1965

"Garner, Van Dyke, Miss Sommer, and Miss Dickinson all perform with coordinated effort and smart results under the deft direction of Norman Jewison. Ethel Merman brings a happy burst of melody to the proceedings."
—*Film Daily*, May 6, 1965

"Nobody demands probability from a farce, but this one keeps its hapless actors so busy explaining what is going on that they have no time to stay for laughs."
—*The New York Times*, July 1, 1965

"A kooky screenplay by the talented Carl Reiner; better than average acting under the astute direction of Norman Jewison; plus the presence of two screen lovelies, Angie Dickinson and Elke Sommer, and handsome stalwarts James Garner and Dick Van Dyke, make Ross Hunter's production of *The Art of Love* palatable—if not believable—filmfare."

"Primarily the film belongs to Van Dyke and Garner since they are the pivotal characters. Both have executed their dramatic chores with their usual commendable adeptness. Miss Dickinson has little more to do than display her feline loveliness, enhanced by a wardrobe designed by Ray Aghayan."
—Nadine Edwards, *Hollywood Citizen-News*, July 5, 1965

"On the back lot at Universal City, *The Art of Love* creates a cardboard Paris and fills it with evidence that 1965 is a dull year abroad."
—*Time*, July 16, 1965

The Chase

Credits: A Columbia Pictures Corporation, Horizon Pictures, and Lone Star Pictures production released on February 19, 1966. Technicolor. Running time of 133 minutes. Based on a play by Horton Foote. **Cast:** Marlon Brando (Sheriff Calder), Jane Fonda (Anna Reeves), Robert Redford (Charlie "Bubber" Reeves), Angie Dickinson (Ruby Calder), E.G. Marshall (Val Rogers), Janice Rule (Emily Stewart), Miriam Hopkins (Mrs. Reeves), Martha Hyer (Mary Fuller), Richard Bradford (Damon Fuller), Robert Duvall (Edwin Stewart), James Fox (Jason "Jake" Rogers), Diana Hyland (Elizabeth Rogers), Henry Hull (Briggs), Jocelyn Brando (Mrs. Briggs), Joel Fluellen (Lester Johnson), Paul Williams (Seymour), Malcolm Atterbury (Mr. Reeves). **Crew:** Arthur Penn (director), Lillian Hellman (screenwriter), Sam Spiegel (producer), John Barry (composer), Joseph LaShelle (cinematographer), Gene Milford (editor), Robert Luthardt (art director), Frank Tuttle (set decorator), Donfeld (costume designer), Virginia Jones (hair stylist), Ben Lane (makeup supervisor), Russell Saunders (assistant director), James Flaster and Charles Rice (sound).

Plot Synopsis: The citizens of Tarl County, Texas, are in turmoil. Local bad boy Bubber Reeves has broken out of state prison and several residents have reason for concern. His wife Anna and best friend Jake Rogers, both of whom love him dearly, are having an affair, bank clerk Edwin Stewart is responsible for a petty theft that he blamed on Bubber, and Val Rogers, who owns practically everything in town, wants to protect his estranged son.

There are other issues as well. Edwin's wife Emily flirts boldly with every guy she meets, especially town bully Damon Fuller, whose own wife Mary is indifferent to him. Val Rogers underpays the Hispanic laborers who work for him and upholds the town's ever-present prejudice toward its African American residents.

Bubber's Bible-toting parents have failed him, an elderly couple named Briggs wanders through town spying and commenting on their neighbors, and a group of unsupervised teenagers imitates the bad behavior of the adults. The only admirable characters are Sheriff Calder, who longs to leave law enforcement and return to farming, and his loyal wife Ruby.

Bubber's plight becomes more complicated when the prisoner he escaped with kills a stranger for his car and clothes, leaving Bubber to fend for himself and to face an added charge of murder. Continuing to believe in Bubber's innocence, Calder waits for him to return to Tarl and checks on the people and places he might visit. As Bubber makes his way through the countryside, the film cuts back and forth between his journey and the town's growing sense of expectation.

At a fundraising reception to endow various college buildings, Val tells Calder that he expects rapid apprehension of Bubber. "You owe it to me, Calder," he insists, reminding the sheriff that his job depends on the patriarch's continuing support. Well attended and opulent, the reception has attracted the county's most privileged citizens. Less spectacularly, the Stewarts are throwing their own debauched Saturday night party where a drunken shooting game gets out of hand and requires Calder's intervention to prevent real injury. Bubber, meanwhile, has taken refuge in a junkyard on the edge of town.

Lester Johnson, the black owner of the junkyard, reluctantly agrees to carry a message from Bubber to Anna but is discovered in her upstairs apartment by a group of white thugs and must be escorted to jail by Calder for safekeeping. Fortified by drink, the vigilantes demand additional action from Calder. When he defies them, they beat him to a bloody mess while Ruby tries vainly to help. For good measure, they assault Lester as well.

Aware of Bubber's whereabouts, Anna and Jake reunite with

him and all three reaffirm their feelings. Unfortunately, the rest of the town has followed behind, turning the standoff into a drunken revelry and setting the junkyard on fire. As the three childhood friends scramble through the rubble, a fireworks rocket ignites an explosion that mortally wounds Jake.

Beaten yet determined, Calder manages to locate Bubber and lead him into custody. On the steps of the jail, however, one of the vigilantes shoots and kills Bubber. Finally losing his patience, Calder beats the assailant mercilessly until Ruby pulls him away. Early the next morning, Calder and Ruby remove their belongings from the jail's living quarters, pack the car, and leave town for good.

Notes and Comments: The talent assembled for *The Chase* was remarkable. Sam Spiegel had won Academy Awards for producing *On the Waterfront* (1954), *The Bridge on the River Kwai* (1957), and *Lawrence of Arabia* (1962) while Arthur Penn had built a solid reputation for directing a string of Broadway hits as well as the earnestly conceived pictures *The Left Handed Gun* (1958), *The Miracle Worker* (1962), and *Mickey One* (1965). Lillian Hellman was the reigning doyenne of American dramatists, and the cast of primary and secondary players could not have been more distinguished. It is somewhat surprising then that the film is such a failure. Penn blamed Spiegel for taking the final cut away from him, Hellman blamed the rewriters, and Brando blamed Hollywood in general. There is plenty of blame to go around, however.

Hellman loaded the script with the widest possible spectrum of southern Gothic stereotypes. A corrupt patriarch ruthlessly controls his family and his town, a trashy wife openly cheats on her husband, religious hypocrites judge others, white bigots mistreat African Americans, and vigilantes roam the streets. Adultery, alcoholism, violence, and racism compete for thematic prominence. True to her political convictions, Hellman includes references to class conflict and judicial inequality. As if overwhelmed by the material, Penn directs in a jarringly inconsistent manner. He is quietly retrained in the two-shot conversations, effective with the fragmented spatial compositions of the endowment reception, and completely over-the-top in the symbolic junk yard apocalypse and the Lee Harvey Oswald-like shooting on the steps of the county jail. Noted for the lavish production values of his films with David Lean, Spiegel seems to be skimping on the budget here, using the Warne Bros. lot as an obvious stand-in for Tarl and locations at the Warner Bros., 20th Century Fox, and Paramount ranches for other scenes supposedly set in the Texas countryside.

The acting doesn't help much in establishing a sense of authenticity. Nobody nails the accent, some failing more strikingly than others. Jane Fonda does a sexy finishing school drawl, James Fox modifies his crisp British diction with a sullen mutter, and Robert Redford doesn't even bother to disguise his flat California inflections. Penn seems to encourage his performers' own worst instincts for overacting. Two of the campiest examples: Martha Hyer gnawing on a pearl necklace to signal her frustration and Janice Rule drunkenly spilling out of her dress to show what a tramp she is.

As always, Brando is fascinating to watch. For more than half of the film, he paints Sheriff Calder as a man of principle, stoically enduring the town's veneer of civic order. He is retrained in word and gesture, rarely raising his voice or altering his expression. Then, as the plot spins increasingly out of control, he tumbles along with it. He opts for mannered agony. The movements grow exaggerated, the lines of dialogue overly parsed. The beating scene, often *de rigueur* in a Brando picture, comes off as a grotesquely prolonged sacrifice. The staging is as awkward as the crudely applied makeup. Calder's meltdown on the jail steps has a similar whiff of hysterics to it.

ANGIE

Marlon Brando and Angie as Sheriff Calder and his wife Ruby in *The Chase* (1966).

Consistently, the single most believable actor is Angie Dickinson. She appears in about a dozen scenes, all of them with Brando. Together, they dress for the evening, attend Val's formal reception drive home, discuss events in the jail's office, visit Mrs. Reeves, confront the vigilantes, witness Bubber's shooting, and turn their backs on the feckless residents. Strong willed and supportive, she is the steadying influence that allows Calder to keep going. Playing off Brando's anguish, she remains intentionally simple and direct. Adopting and then abandoning a faint southern accent, she seems hardly to be "acting" at all but rather to be responding to Brando with nearly imperceptible shifts in posture and voice. With Angie, all the emotion is under the surface whereas with the rest of the cast it is front and center.

The reviews for *The Chase* were generally unfavorable, focusing on the lurid content, the overly broad performances, and the sketchy direction. Particular objection was raised to the faux touches of classic drama such as the elderly couple as Greek chorus and the compressed twenty-four hour time scheme. More than one observer also pointed out that, despite the title, there wasn't really a chase.

British film critic Robin Wood, in his 1969 book on Arthur Penn, argued strongly, however, in favor of the picture. Calling it a "masterpiece" and "perhaps Penn's *completest* film,"[7] he attempted to show how a unifying theme of appearance versus reality is used to explore social disintegration, political corruption, and the total failure of conventional morality. Less florid than his overall praise of the film is his clear-eyed assessment of Angie's contribution: "Miss Dickinson is a very considerable presence in every film she graces, but Hollywood has not always put it to the happiest use. Through her, Penn suggests something of what makes it possible for Calder to be what he is."[8]

Reviews:

"Arthur Penn has directed with craftsmanship and theatrical flair. The major roles are powerfully portrayed under Penn's guidance. If one must quibble it can be noted that here and there a subsidiary character takes on stereotyped outlines. The overall effect of the film is a stunning one. Mark it down for major greatness."

—Mandel Herbstman, *Film Daily*, February 2, 1966

"In short, *The Chase* is a melodramatic witch's brew of sinning, and director Penn has kept it boiling at high heat throughout. Fortunately for most of his cast they were able to keep up with the frenzied pace."

"Some people may not like *The Chase*; they will pronounce it lurid and overdone to the point of incredibility. But one thing is certain: Nobody is going to be bored."

—*Motion Picture Herald*, February 2, 1966

"Angie Dickinson, as his wife, by the way, is one of the few members of the cast who manages to give a restrained, reasonable facsimile of a human being through her performance."

—Hollis Alpert, *Saturday Review*, February 19, 1966

"It is a shockingly cheap, sensational film about the crudities of the people in a town in Texas, lacking forcefulness or plausibility, because of the flamboyance of its staging and the abundance of its clichés."

—Bosley Crowther, *The New York Times*, February 20, 1966

"*The Chase* is a conventionally opulent melodrama, over produced by Sam Spiegel, over plotted to the point of incoherence by the author of the screenplay, Lillian Hellman, and over directed by Arthur Penn."

—*The New Yorker*, February 26, 1966

"A few performances are very good: James Fox's wealthy young blade, Brando's sheriff, Redford's lonely long distance runner, Robert Duvall's timorous husband. A few are more or less adequate: Janice Rule's town tease, Angie Dickinson's sheriff's wife. A few are horrid, or horridly directed: Jane Fonda's tart with a sub-deb accent, E.G. Marshall's purblind banker, Martha Hyer's lush and Miriam Hopkins' blubbering Bubber's mother."

"The worst of Miss Hellman's script, in concert with the worst of Penn's direction, yields scene after scene that seems to speak volumes when it is only whispering sour nothings."

—*Newsweek*, February 28, 1966

"*The Chase* is no longer a modest failure. Thanks to the expenditure of a great deal of time, money and talent, it has been transformed into a disaster of awesome proportions."

"A valiant minority of the all-star cast—Miss Fonda, Robert Redford as the escaped con, James Fox as the rich kid, Angie Dickinson as Brando's wife—try to keep their heads while all about them are losing theirs. But their isolated moments of lucidity are no more effective against the fever than cold compresses; they relieve but cannot cure."

—Richard Schickel, *Life*, March 4, 1966

"Everything is farfetched and overdone. The violence is ripely repulsive. The town set is obviously a backlot and the color is washed out. Brando is magnetic, but this role is far beneath him. *The Chase* is no more meaningful than that television potboiler, *The Long Hot Summer*."

—*Cosmopolitan*, April, 1966

"Redford is the luckiest actor in the movie. He spends most of his time skulking around the boondocks outside town and is never subjected to the banalities the rest of the large cast must suffer."

—*Playboy*, April 1966

Cast a Giant Shadow

Credits: A Batjac Productions, Bryna Productions, Llenroc Productions, Mirisch Corporation picture release on March 30, 1966. Technicolor. Running time of 146 minutes. Based on a book by Ted Berkman. **Cast:** Kirk Douglas (Col. David "Mickey" Marcus), Senta Berger (Magda Simon), Angie Dickinson (Emma Marcus), James Donald (Maj. Safir), Stathis Giallelis (Ram Oren), Luther Adler (Jacob Zion), Topol (Abou Ibn Kader), Ruth White (Mrs. Chaison), Gordon Jackson (James MacAfee), Michael Hordern (British Ambassador), Frank Sinatra (Vince Talmadge), Yul Brynner (Asher Gonen), John Wayne (Gen. Mike Randolph), Allan Cuthbertson (Immigration Officer), Jeremy Kent (Senior British Officer) Sean Barrett (Junior British Officer), Rina Ganor (Rana). **Crew:** Melville Shavelson (director, producer, screenwriter). Elmer Bernstein (composer), Aldo Tonti (director of photography), Bert Bates and Gene Ruggiero (editors), Arrigo Equini (art director), Ferdinando Ruffo (set decorator), Margaret Furse (costume designer), Vasco Reggiani (hair stylist), Dave Grayson and Euclide Santoli (makeup artists). Jack Reddish, Charles Scott Jr., and Tim Zinnemann (assistant directors), David Bowen, Church Overhulser, and Clem Portman (sound).

Plot Synopsis: While Christmas shopping at Macy's department store in New York City, Colonel David "Mickey" Marcus, a Reserve Army officer recently released from active duty, is approached by Major Safir, an agent for Haganah, the underground army of the newly declared State of Israel. Safir asks him to help organize Israeli troops into a defense force capable of resisting the Arab Legion. When his argument fails, Safir pleads, "But you're a Jew," and Marcus replies, "I'm an American. That's my religion."

Back home with his wife Emma, he thinks more about the request and reflects on his experiences during the Second World War. A flashback shows him parachuting behind enemy lines prior to the Normandy invasion and running afoul of General Mike Randolph, who respects his courage but not his lack of discipline. Much to Emma's displeasure, he decides to accept the offer and continue a lingering search for meaning in his life. Refused permission by Randolph to travel as a United States Army officer, he flies to Palestine using a flake passport under the name of "Michael Stone."

At customs, he is admitted even though a sympathetic British official recognizes his true identity. His contact is Magda Simon, a beautiful Haganah member to whom he feels an immediate attraction. On their way to defense headquarters, their armored bus is fired on by Arab snipers. Briefed on the opposing Arab forces by Officer Asher Gonen, Marcus goes along on a nighttime mission to receive Jewish refugees arriving by boat from Cypress. The operation is interrupted by British officers, who threaten to open fire but back down when the Israelis refuse to obey. Although Asher is suspicious of Marcus's motives, he is impressed by his steeliness under pressure.

Marcus also is introduced to Ram Oren, the leader of the Palmach, an elite fighting force loosely aligned with the Israeli army. Together they meet with Abou Ibn Kader, an independent-minded Bedouin chief who will side with the Israelis if they can prove some success in fighting the Arab Legion. Spontaneously and without consulting Ram, Marcus announces that they will attack a Syrian ammunition and supply center. In the ensuing raid, the fuel tanks and weapons are destroyed but not before Magda's husband Andre is killed and Ram is wounded. Once again Marcus proves his worth, advising on tactics and rescuing Ram. As thanks, defense minister Jacob Zion, a fictional Ben Gurion-like figure, offers an increased role in the military campaign, but Marcus argues that real success will not be possible until the Haganah, Palmach, and other contingents come together under one unified command. Demurring, Zion suggests that he write an operational manual for the soldiers.

Of immediate concern is the defense of Jerusalem, where the Israelis are surrounded and under siege by hostile Arab forces. As part of a relief convoy to deliver supplies, Magda and Marcus come under attack, and he must save her from a trapped truck. As their relationship intensifies, he is called back to New York, where Emma has suffered a miscarriage. She senses that his mind and perhaps his heart are elsewhere but accompanies him to a medal ceremony at the British embassy where the ambassador honors him for his WWII service and lobbies him about convincing the Israelis to postpone full independence. Also in attendance is General Randolph, who urges him to disregard the Brits and "stand up and be counted and there'll be a lot of us who'll stand up with you."

Resolved, he returns to Israel, where he receives a shipment of weapons from a rogue American pilot named Vince Talmadge. Zion and other government officials, bolstered by the United States's recognition of Israel as an independent state, agree to move ahead with a series of attacks on Arab forces at Latrun and elsewhere. In a decision that has the support of Asher and Ram, Zion also names Marcus "Aluf," the general in unified command of all forces. The subsequent assault is intense and courageous but fails to dislodge the Arabs.

Abou Kader argues that there is another route into Jerusalem besides the road past Latrun fort. Accessing it means scaling steep mountainous terrain but hundreds of volunteers, dubbed by Marcus his army of "shnooks," work round the clock to build a makeshift "Burma Road." Inspired by their example, Marcus proudly recognizes his own Jewish identity and drives the first truck over the route.

That night, in preparation for the relief of Jerusalem, he celebrates with Magda but also tells her that he realizes he is deeply in love with Emma and plans to return to her as soon as possible. Mistaken as an intruder by a young sentry who does not speak English, he is fired on and killed. The next morning, Marcus's body is transported down the mountain in a jeep while rows of supply trucks pass by on their way to Jerusalem.

Notes and Comments: The film has excellent production values. There are several well-orchestrated action sequences including the nighttime landing of the refugee boat, the raid on the Syrian ammunition dump, and the ambush of the Israeli supply convoy. Particularly effective is a five minute sequence depicting the unsuccessful Israeli attacks on the Arab Legion forces hunkered down at Latrun Tegart fort. Thanks to a big assist from the Israeli government, which rented tanks, jeeps, and even soldiers to the company, the military engagements are all realistically depicted. Crowd scenes swell with massive number of extras, and an equally impressive supply of armored vehicles are sacrificed in the artillery explosions. The movie's historical timeline, authenticity, and panoramic sweep are similar to those of Otto Preminger's *Exodus* (1960). The location shooting in Israel centers events close to where they actually happened.

Colonel Mickey Marcus was a real historical figure, and Kirk Douglas plays him as a flippant, protocol-breaking outsider. The tough guy humor is strained at times (e.g., a WWII flashback where Marcus tells General Randolph, "I've been knocking off a lot of guys who've been making soap of my relatives"), but Douglas is more relaxed and less snarling than usual. Most importantly, he convincingly sells Marcus's two crucial epiphanies: his embrace of his Jewish heritage and his realization of his love for Emma.

Like many big-budget action pictures of the 60s, *Cast A Giant*

Shadow boasts an impressive roster of stars in supporting roles, but here they actually contribute more than just glorified audience bait. Topol, almost unrecognizable behind the beard and headscarf, is funny and commanding as the Bedouin chief who ultimately decides to help the Israelis in return for a guarantee that his land rights will be protected. Yul Brynner, a familiar face among star-studded casts, appears throughout as Asher, the Haganah commander whose growing respect for Marcus becomes one of the film's important structural devices. Frank Sinatra shows up fairly late in the proceedings to portray an American pilot who delivers guns and provides some air cover during the siege of Latrun. Feisty and acerbic, he helps to legitimize the validity of the Israeli cause and also gets some of the best lines. When a supply worker hands him a dummy bomb made of seltzer water, he notes, "It screams on the way down," and Frank replies, "Good, that makes two of us." As General Mike Randolph, John Wayne provides a counterbalance at key points to Marcus's impetuousness, representing order, tradition, wisdom, and in the end, basic morality. He also proves once again that he is a much better actor than many have supposed. During one of the flashbacks, he and Douglas are part of the battalion that liberates Dachau. The camera tracks in front of them as they walk into the camp, showing only their faces and none of what they see. The horror of the place is conveyed solely through Wayne's wordless, shocked reaction. Wayne and Douglas both also served on the film as executive producers.

Angie's screen credit reads, "Co-starring Angie Dickinson as Emma Marcus," and she helps to get the movie started. Douglas comes home from the meeting with Major Safer in Macy's and finds her waiting seductively for him in bed. "Hello, my name is Emma, what's yours?" she jokes. It's a tricky role; she is beautiful and supportive but also tries to keep Marcus from following his conscience.

"I guess I'm proud of you," she admits, "but I'm so damn tired of being proud of you." The audience simultaneously admires and resents her, just as to some degree, does Marcus himself.

Angie with John Wayne (far left) and Kirk Douglas (far right) during the medal ceremony scene of *Cast a Giant Shadow* (1966).

She appears in five major sequences, all but one of them with Douglas. In addition to the opening bedroom scene, there are a flashback to a WWII nightclub date, a conversation with her mother where she feels labor pains, a welcome home party for Marcus, and the British medal award ceremony. All of her episodes are interiors, filmed at Cinecittà and away from the location shooting in the desert. The first four are part of an intimate domestic story while the fifth one introduces Emma to the larger historical context. She and Douglas often are filmed in frontal two-shots, placed behind bars, counter tops, and buffet tables. With little action to perform, she is given lots of expository dialogue that explains everything Marcus is leaving behind in New York. She delivers it quietly and convincingly, even lines such as "Don't hate me for loving you so much." One of her best scenes is the award ceremony where, dressed in a well-tailored, gold-colored Chanel suit, she listens with growing concern as the British consul tries to maneuver Marcus into warning the Israelis away from military action. This was her third film with Wayne and second with Sinatra although she appears in no scenes with either.

The film was a matter of political conviction for Melville Shavelson, who produced, directed, and adapted the screenplay from a biography by Ted Berkman. A writer on Bob Hope's radio show, he was known mostly for writing and directing such comedies as *Houseboat* (1955), *On the Double* (1961), and *The Pigeon That Took Rome* (1962). Although this was his first venture into action films, he moves the camera and actors with surprising dexterity. In total command of his technical resources, he shows special visual flair in those moments where he tracks rapidly down a trench line and has soldiers leap successively into the frame or pulls out for a final overhead long shot of Marcus's wooden coffin being transported down the mountain as convoy trucks stream past in the opposite direction. After shooting the blended family comedy *Yours, Mine and Ours* (1965), Shavelson would return to war themes again with the 1979 miniseries *Ike*, based on the WWII experiences of General Dwight Eisenhower.

Reviews:

"Melville Shavelson's overlong pic has some big marquee horsepower, exciting action highlights, fine production values and other assets which spell okay b.o. prospects for United Artists release in general situations."

"Kirk Douglas stars as Marcus in a very good portrayal of a likable, adventurous soldier-of-fortune who cannot get used to domestic inactivity even when wife Angie Dickinson is sitting by the hearth. Miss Dickinson does a good job in a role which calls for her to be a flip, sardonic chick, also an adoring wife."

"Shavelson has obtained effective performances from an unusually large and competent cast, and also shows a neat visual flair, one example of which is a lush, ripe wheat field which becomes, after a highlight skirmish, a blood-sodden pictorial canvas."

"Elmer Bernstein's score adds solid emphasis, while in the technical department all credits are first-rate, main title design, uncredited but executed by Pacific Title, is excellent, utilizing a b&w newsreel montage effect which gradually enlarges to fill the screen."

—*Daily Variety*, March 30, 1966

"It has romance, humor, suspense and some good, big battle sequences. It has its drawbacks, too, and these will mitigate its success. But considered purely as action, *Cast A Giant Shadow* is absorbing and exciting."

"On the credit side, Shavelson's screenplay has some often-good off-hand humor, the hardest kind to write. His characters, especially Douglas as Marcus, seem real and valid. If Douglas, as an American Jew, often seems flippant against the background of incipient tragedy in the emerging Israel, it is likely that this attitude is genuine. It is a characteristic, a combination of American optimism and Jewish chutzpah, that marks many American Jews."

"*Cast a Giant Shadow* has some good battle sequences that provide its climax. It has good performances. Douglas is seen to advantage as the principal character. Three stars play cameos; John Wayne is Douglas' commanding officer over the years, a figure modeled chiefly on Gen. George S. Patton. Yul Brynner is at his best as an Israeli army leader. Frank Sinatra provides some tough-minded humor as an American soldier of fortune who serves with the Israeli army."

"The wife, played by Angie Dickinson with feminne appeal, remains in the United States while her husband is in Israel. This aspect of the story is of dubious value; it is especially difficult to have a hero who is potentially unfaithful to his faithful wife. It is not clear what Shavelson intended to create with this triangle."

—James Powers, *The Hollywood Reporter*, March 30, 1966

"Despite a certain conventionality of script, Melville Shavelson's *Cast A Giant Shadow* manages to convey considerably more of the complexities and crosscurrents attendant upon the birth of Israel some twenty years ago than do most conventional histories or the even more conventional historical novels on the subject."

"And most remarkable of all in a picture of this kind is its constant, and fascinating, explication of military tactics, so that the deployment of men, guns, and tanks is never merely pictorial, but part of the working out of a grand strategy whose logic and necessity have already been grasped."

"While these are all virtues of script, Shavelson has also distinguished himself as a director. His big action scenes have not only scope, but focus; one is never at a loss to understand what is going on. Even better, however, is the restraint of his vignettes."

"In all these actions, Kirk Douglas, as Marcus, is far more than a passive observer. But somehow their sweep is so great that the question of whether he should divorce Angie Dickinson in order to settle in with Senta Berger becomes irrelevant."

—Arthur Knight, *Saturday Review*, April 9, 1966

"As his wife, Miss Dickinson is loyal, affectionate and perhaps, foolhardy when she allows Douglas to believe she is seriously ill in order to bring him home to Brooklyn."

"There is a great amount of action in *Cast A Giant Shadow*; John Wayne, as Marcus' longtime friend and a Pentagon brasshat is merely great."

"Frank Sinatra, looking all of 28 years old, lights up the screen as a soldier-of-fortune flier who loses his life bombing Egyptian tanks with seltzer bottles because he had nothing stronger."
—Clyde Leech, *Los Angeles Herald-Examiner*, May 21, 1966

The Poppy Is Also a Flower

Credits: A Telsun Foundation Inc. production released on October 16, 1966. Eastmancolor. Running time of 100 minutes. Based on an idea by Ian Fleming. **Cast:** E.G. Marshall (Coley Jones), Trevor Howard (Sam Lincoln), Yul Brynner (Colonel Salem), Angie Dickinson (Linda Benson), Gilbert Roland (Serge Marko), Stephen Boyd (Benson), Senta Berger (Maxine), Georges Géret (Superintendent Roche), Hugh Griffith (Salah Rahman Khan), Jack Hawkins (General Bahar), Rita Hayworth (Monique Marko), Harold Sakata (Martin), Omar Sharif (Doctor Rad), Barry Sullivan (Chasen), Eli Wallach ("Happy" Locarno), Marcello Mastroianni (Inspector Mosca), Amedeo Nazzari (Captain Di Nonno), Anthony Quale (Captain Vanderbilt), Trini Lopez (himself). **Crew:** Terence Young (director), Jo Eisinger (screenwriter), Edgar Rosenberg (executive producer), Georges Auric (composer), Henri Alekan (director of photography), Monique Bonnot, Henry Richardson, and Peter Thornton (editors), Maurice Colasson, Eng. Djavaheri, and Tony Roman (art directors), Freda Pearson (set decorator),

Raymonde Ventura (costume designer), Alain (hair stylist), Marie-Madeleine Paris and George Partleton (makeup artists), Hajir Dariush, Richard Jenkins, and Bernard Quatrehomme (assistant directors), Alban Streeter and Jean Monchablon (sound).

Plot Synopsis: After an on-camera introduction by Grace Kelly about "the sickening, deadening pleasures of drug taking" and how "the United Nations and other nations are uniting to stamp out this evil," the film opens in the Iranian desert where U.N. narcotics agent Benson is making a deal with tribal chief Salah Rahman Khan to buy his opium crop. In transit, Benson is ambushed, tortured, and killed by native fighters working for the European drug lord who had intended to purchase the shipment himself. Before it can be unloaded, the booby-trapped opium is detonated. Back in Europe, a group of unhappy Mafia investors tell drug boss Serge Marko that he needs to make good on another shipment. "This time, Marko," they advise, "get there first."

Narcotics agents Jones and Lincoln arrive in Tehran to investigate Benson's death. With local officials Dr. Rad, Colonel Salem, and General Bahar, they come up with a plan to inject a new opium supply with a radioactive element that will allow them to trace it along its Mediterranean distribution route. Jones and Lincoln also become interested in Linda Benson, who has come to Iran to claim the body of her husband. Assured that Benson was not married, Jones searches Linda's hotel room, where she judo trips and holds a gun on him before summoning the police and disappearing.

Following up on the plan, Colonel Salem leads a guerilla force into the mountains and overpowers Khan. Once the opium is irradiated, Salem poses as Khan's lieutenant and engineers a sale to Martin, the assistant Marko personally has sent to Iran. While the shipment is being transported and tracked through the mountain passes, however, Marko has a helicopter intercept the convoy and make off with the opium.

Thinking that the trail is cold, Jones and Lincoln meet Dr. Rad in Geneva and he informs them that the radioactive cargo has been detected in Naples. With the help of two local police officials, they interview deported American gangster Happy Locarno, a "businessman" who manufactures a chemical used in processing heroin. Claiming to be legit, Locarno gives the name of his buyer and other information that helps the agents. In Naples, Jones and Lincoln also again see Linda Benson from a distance and visit a nightclub where one of the performers is a heroin addict. Although she doesn't disclose her supplier, after the agents leave she is knifed by Martin. All the various clues lead to a battered shipping vessel where a Geiger reading indicates that opium had been part of the since offloaded cargo. Vanderbilt, the sleazy ship's captain, pretends to know nothing about the drugs but admits that the boat was commissioned by an export company owned by Serge Marko.

Posing as an airplane parts dealer, Lincoln gets introduced to Marko at a nightclub in Nice, where Trini Lopez is performing and Linda Benson is one of his guests. He joins the entourage when Marko invites them all onto his yacht for a short journey back to Cannes. On board, he meets Marko's drugged wife Monique and snoops around in the radio room. Unfortunately, Vanderbilt remembers him, and his corpse, showing signs of torture, later turns up in the harbor.

A radio message that Lincoln hid in the heel of his shoe directs Jones to a train carrying Marko, his wife, his gangster associates, his henchmen, and Linda Benson. Also recognized from the ship, Jones gets into a fight first with Vanderbilt and then Martin. After pushing Vanderbilt from the train, he takes on Martin in the animal baggage car, where Linda joins him and reveals herself as Benson's sister and an agent for an unnamed but cooperative secret service. They overpower Martin, but Marko escapes when the train comes to a stop. Leaping on a passing train, Jones wrestles with Marko until a group of policemen apprehend him. Linda's says, "at least we got this one wrapped up" while Jones muses that "the answer is miles and miles away in the poppy fields."

Notes and Comments: James Bond creator Ian Fleming conceived of the story idea near the end of his life. The original concept was to narratively follow an opium poppy from a bud in an Iranian field to the raw heroin purchased by a junkie on the streets of New York. After Fleming's death, Terence Young, the director of *Dr. No* (1962) and *From Russia with Love* (1963), took a script based on the idea to the company which controlled the author's assets. Although the executors passed on a production deal, they granted permission to use the credit line "Story based on an idea by Ian Fleming." With financing arranged through United Nations-related foundations, the formidable assemblage of stars essentially donated their time and Terence Young made an early departure from *Thunderball* (1965) to helm the "educational" project.

Reduced in scope, the final film looks much like a conventional crime story. While thrills and action are at a minimum, there are a few surface flourishes that seem left over from a 007 picture. Harold Sakata, the Hawaiian-born professional wrestler famously cast as "Oddjob" in *Goldfinger* (1964), plays the assassin Martin, and the climatic train fight resembles the more famous and better staged one between Bond and "Red" Grant in *From Russia with Love*. The entertainment at the Nice nightclub that Jones and Lincoln visit features a wrestling match between two bikini-clad women similar to the female gypsy fight in *From Russia with Love*, and Lincoln's secret hollowed-out shoe heel and miniature cigarette pack Geiger counter are typical Bond accessories.

More significantly, Angie's Linda Benson character is presented as a conventional "Bond girl." Seen briefly at first from a distance, she flirts with Lincoln over drinks and then, holding a gun and wrapped only in a black towel, confronts Jones when he tries to search her hotel room. Like Pussy Galore in *Goldfinger*, she uses a judo move to take him to the ground. Tough and beautiful, she seems throughout the film to be working against the U.N. agents but then, motivated equally by duty and revenge, reveals herself as an ally who helps to defeat the villain.

Angie gives Linda Benson just the right mixture of sass, threat, and glamour. When Jones asks, "Do all widows carry guns?" she tartly replies, "That's how some of them become windows." Excepting the lead performances by E.G. Marshall and Trevor Howard, she and Yul Brynner receive the most screen time. The film gets a shot of energy each time she appears, and not once does she dissipate her character's air of mystery. So good is she as an international agent that one wonders how she would have fared in an actual Bond film, perhaps as Tracy di Vicenzo in *On Her Majesty's Secret Service* (1969).

The rest of the film is a disappointment. Characters come and go with minimal introduction, unclear connections to the investigation, and little narrative purpose other than to fill one more guest star credit. Halfway through, the radioactive opium angle is abandoned and the cargo ship's contraband ends up being discovered by a drug-sniffing dog. Director Terence Young, whose work ranged from the competently made *Wait Until Dark* (1967) to the disaster that was *The Klansman* (1974), is at his weakest here. His fragmented point of view results in awkward pacing. There are just too many disparate pieces (Princess Grace's prologue, Yul Brynner's commando raid, Jack Hawkins's reprise of his *Lawrence of Arabia* General Allenby routine, Trevor Howard and E.G. Marshall's bromance, Angie's secret agent, Marcello Mastroianni's Mafia takedown) that never coalesce into a narrative or thematic whole. A stronger sense of continuity would help, but Young cuts his expository scenes before the actors have hit all their physical marks and aborts the action sequences prior to any final visual pay-off. To cover defects in staging, he relies on accelerated, choppy editing.

The Poppy Is Also a Flower, known in its DVD release as *The Opium Connection*, remains a curiosity piece noteworthy for its show biz oddities and incongruities. Dedicated to the memory of Adlai Stevenson, it also includes formal "gratitude and thanks" to Shah Mohammed Reza Pahlavi, whose multiple portraits adorn the Tehran office sets. Executive producer Edgar Rosenberg married comedienne Joan Rivers around the time of production and remained her husband until his suicide twenty-two years later. Rita Hayworth insisted on bringing legendary MGM talent manager Kay Thompson along as her vocal coach but then, suffering from the effects of Alzheimer's and alcohol, barely muttered a few lines of dialogue. Eli Wallach shamelessly overplayed his "Happy" Locarno role but ended up with an Emmy for Best Supporting Actor because the film was released on TV as well as in the theaters. Finally, most peculiar of all, is the fact that the producers and director asked viewers to accept E.G. Marshall, the most rigidly postured of American actors, as some kind of jaunty international action hero. There is no suspension of disbelief quite that willing.

Reviews:

"A sizzling adventure thriller, *The Poppy Is Also a Flower* deals with the global efforts of the police of several nations to crack down on international traffic in drugs. The all-star cast, drawn from around the world, is the type to bring a beckoning glow to any showman's marquee."

"Angie Dickinson moves mysteriously in and out of the story. In a climactic scene on a speeding train she proves to be on the side of the law and saves E.G. Marshall from the vengeance of luxury-loving Gilbert Roland who is the iron fist behind the traffic."

—Mandel Herbstman, *Film Daily*, November 1, 1966

"From the opening shot, it is instantly apparent that director Terence Young never intended that this adventure-laden look at the international dope traffic should be limited to the small screen of a TV set."

"The panoramic sweep of the badlands of Iran sets a visual pace that is met, and matched, frequently during the ensuing 100 minutes by cameraman Henry Alekan."

"If an occasional lapse in logic occurs, or a particular character doesn't quite come off, these moments are rare and there's almost no let-up in the suspenseful scenario."

"Fortunately, the big-name cast is uniformly able to restrain individual personalities sufficiently to make their brief roles believable, although the Lucky Luciano type played by Eli Wallach seems overly comic in such serious surroundings. Marshall is amazingly good as the middle-aged agent, even in the obviously hazardous fight scenes, and Trevor Howard provides almost as fine a performance as his British counterpart."

—*Weekly Variety*, November 23, 1966

"*The Poppy Is Also a Flower* is another James Bond movie made without James Bond, and many will wish it had been filmed without film."

"As it is, the picture offers one interesting scene: the screen credits. They reveal that *Poppy* was developed from an idea proposed by author Ian Fleming, who mercifully died before he could see what happened to it: that the man principally responsible for what happened is director Terence Young, who in *Dr. No* struck the first big Bondanza; and that what happened is performed by an awful lot of people who ought to know better."

"By the time heroes get the heroin the customers may find themselves in something of a narcoma. The very best that can be said about this picture is that it's junk, but hardly habit-forming."

—*Time*, December 2, 1966

Point Blank

Credits: An MGM/Winkler Films production released on August 30, 1967. Metrocolor. Running time of 92 minutes. Based on a novel by Donald E. Westlake (writing as Richard Stark). **Cast:** Lee Marvin (Walker), Angie Dickinson (Chris), Keenan Wynn (Yost), Carroll O'Connor (Brewster), Lloyd Bochner (Frederick Carter), Michael Strong (John Stegman), John Vernon (Mal Reese), Sharon Acker (Lynne), James Sikking (hitman), Sandra Warner (waitress), Roberta Haynes (Mrs. Carter), Kathleen Freeman (woman at reception), Lawrence Hauben (car salesman), Susan Holloway (customer), Priscilla Boyd (receptionist). **Crew:** John Boorman (director), Alexander Jacobs, David Newhouse, Rafe Newhouse (screenwriters), Judd Bernard and Robert Chartoff (producers), Johnny Mandel (composer), Philip H. Lathrop (cinematographer), Henry Berman (editor), Albert Brenner and George W. Davis (art director), Henry Grace and F. Keogh Gleason (set decorators), Margo Weintz (costume designer), Sydney Guilaroff (hair stylist), William Tuttle (makeup artist), Al Jennings (assistant director), Franklin Milton (sound).

Plot Synopsis: On deserted Alcatraz Island, two couriers for a crime operation prepare to exchange some kind of contraband for a money drop. A helicopter arrives and the exchange is made. Mal Reese and his friend Walker steal the money, but contrary to the plan, Reese shoots and kills the couriers. After counting the cash, Reese also shoots Walker, leaving him for dead in one of the abandoned prison cells. He takes off with the loot and with Walker's wife Lynne, who has accompanied them on the job. Walker staggers down to the bay and apparently manages to swim back across to San Francisco.

Fully recovered, Walker meets on an Alcatraz sightseeing boat with a mysterious man named Yost, who tells him that Reese used the money to pay off his gambling debts and buy his way back into a criminal enterprise known only as the Organization. Claiming a desire to damage the syndicate, Yost reveals Lynne's address and Walker sets out to recover the $93,000 he is owed as his share of the robbery.

In Los Angeles, Walker bursts into Lynne's apartment and shoots up the bed, only to learn that Reese left her three months earlier. Lynne explains that a messenger brings her money each month to ensure her silence. Depressed at how her life has turned out, she takes a fatal overdose of sleeping pills. After cleaning up the apartment, Walker waits around for the messenger, who confesses that he was sent by car dealer John Stegman.

A low-level associate in the Organization, Stegman refuses to divulge any information until Walker smashes up an expensive car during a test drive. Bruised and battered, Stegman finally says that Reese can be found at the nightclub run by Lynne's sister Chris.

Although Chris is not there when he arrives, Walker gets her address from a waitress friend before fighting off two thugs on his way out.

Shaken out of her sedated sleep by Walker's break-in, Chris acknowledges that Reese is sexually interested in her but insists that "he makes my flesh crawl." While she manages the nightclub for the Organization, she is not beholden to it in any other way and agrees to help get Reese, who has confessed to his superior Frederick Carter that Walker is alive and looking for him.

Under the pretext of a sexual liaison, Chris gains admittance to Reese's heavily guarded penthouse apartment and unbolts a terrace door. Staging a diversion across the street, Walker makes his way inside and surprises Reese in bed with Chris. Holding a gun to his former friend's head, Walker demands the $93,000. Asserting that he doesn't have the money, Reese identifies the Organization higher-ups (Carter, Brewster, Fairfax) who can possibly pay Walker. Wrapped in a towel and forced out onto the balcony, Reese either falls or is pushed to his death.

Yost appears again and tells Walker where to find Carter, who pretends to agree on a payment but plans to double cross Walker instead. Suspecting a trap, Walker has Carter accompany him to a location alongside the cemented Los Angeles River where Stegman is supposed to drop the money. Pushed out into the open to retrieve the cash, Carter is killed by a hitman sniper as is Stegman as he scrambles up the side of the embankment.

Intervening once more, Yost shows Walker a house in the hills above Los Angeles that belongs to Brewster. Because her apartment has been trashed, Walker brings Chris along with him there for safety. In reaction to a perceived insult, she slaps and punches him furiously while he regards her without reaction. Later, they make love interspersed with flashbacks of Lynne.

When Brewster arrives, Walker ambushes him and his bodyguards, once again demanding that someone pay him the money. Under pressure, Brewster calls Fairfax, who refuses to pay for Reese's debt. Fearing for his life, Brewster suggests that they travel to San Francisco, where money will be available through an exchange like the one that started everything in the first place.

At Fort Point, Walker remains hidden as Brewster retrieves a package of cash from another helicopter. The same sniper who eliminated Carter shoots Brewster. Stepping from the shadows, Yost tells Brewster that he arranged the ambush not Walker. "This is Fairfax, Walker. Kill him," Brewster then pleads, revealing Yost's true identity before he dies.

Yost/Fairfax scans the empty building for Walker. "Come on in with me," he shouts, thanking him for killing his rivals and declaring their deal to be finished. Without a word, Walker recedes into the darkness as Yost/Fairfax and the hitman leave the untouched money on the ground and depart.

Notes and Comments: *Point Blank* is a brilliant neo-noir crime thriller whose many virtues have not diminished since its release in 1967. With its sleek visual style and its pared-down acting, it remains one of director John Boorman's finest career achievements, a rarefied reimagining of the gangland betrayal saga.

The plot derives from the Franz Kafka school of fiction. As in *The Trial* and *The Castle*, a detached loner attempts to penetrate a labyrinthianly hostile bureaucracy where identities and allegiances are continuously shifting. The higher Walker progresses up the Organization's hierarchy the further he gets from the $93,000 that was never really his to begin with. "Somebody's got to pay me," he insists while Brewster vacantly replies, "I'm just an officer in an operation." No one takes responsibility for matters that can be passed on to someone else.

The visual design reflects the alienation. Walker passes through a sterile landscape defined by its sharp angles and imposing masses. The buildings are vast and empty, office interiors are barren, and the houses look as if no human has ever lived in them. When Walker strides down one anonymous corridor after another, the sound of his footsteps echo back at him. In Boorman's wide Panavision frames, characters are often obscured by pillars, columns, or shadows.

Time and space are fragmented in a way that compounds the dislocation. The opening, for example, jumps back and forth between the heist, Walker's shooting, and a party where Reese and Walker meet. There are multiple flashbacks and flash forwards. The partners in an extended love scene keep changing into various combinations of Walker, Lynne, Chris, and Reese. Sounds are amplified, distorted, or disconnected from their source. The color scheme is bold, almost glaring. Denied everyday logic, Boorman's camera roams about for linkages of its own, as in the final shot where he zooms out from the dropped money in Fort Point, pans right across the skyline, and then pans back left to reveal Alcatraz Island, the beginning and the end, looming in the distant darkness.

Brutal and impassive, Lee Marvin as Walker is the dark knight of this world. Having already transitioned from the blandly sadistic thugs of his early career to the graying, existential antiheroes of the 60s onward, he gives Walker's relentless pursuit of the $93,000 a sense of purpose. Dispensing and absorbing violence, he keeps moving forward through the collateral damage like a sleepwalker, his eyes focused unblinkingly on the next lead. When he catches up to his disloyal wife, he sits motionless on a couch just staring forward as she tries to explain all the reasons for her betrayal. "He had such a way of looking—gazing, even—when blank hostility faded into hopeless desire: it's a look that Boorman discovered in *Point Blank*," writes David Thomson.⁹ Often silent, Marvin is a coiled spring ready to unwind at any moment. "What do you want, Walker?" the others ask. "My money," he replies simply and obviously.

Angie is an ideal match for Marvin's minimalism. Similarly reactive in style, she plays Chris as the uncomplaining survivor of bad luck and even worse choices. When Walker wakes her from a drug-assisted sleep, she reacts as if seeing him in her bedroom in the middle of the night is perfectly normal. With flat, emotionless intonation, she recounts her dislike of Reese and her willingness to help Walker "get" him. Clothed in a series of startling yellow and orange mini-length dresses, she is a tapped-out siren moving through life as dispassionately as Walker.

Their scene together in Brewster's L.A. home is a tour-de-force. "Forget it," says Marvin, telling Angie that he brought her there for safety not sex. "You forget it," she explodes, flailing at him with her handbag and fists. For nearly a minute, she slaps, punches, grabs his head, and pounds against his chest. As all of her frustrations with Walker pour out, he just stands there taking the punishment. Finally, she collapses to her knees, crawling on the floor and sobbing. Unperturbed, Walker sits down and begins to watch television. Just when the scene appears to have ended, a barrage of sounds erupts from the kitchen, where Chris has turned on every small appliance she can find. Determined to crack Walker's reserve, she leads him around the house by turning on the music system and lighting up the swimming pool. Suddenly Chris's cold, disembodied voice rings out on the intercom: "You're a pathetic sight from where I'm standing, Walker. You're played out. It's over, finished. What would you do with the money if you got it? Wasn't yours in the first place. Why don't you just lie down and die?" When he catches up to her in the billiards room, she cracks him on the head with a cue stick and they wrestle to the floor. The struggle becomes a sexual encounter. Alarming in their intensity, the outbursts come and go like a sudden storm. Chris lashes out and then retreats back inside her own protective shell.

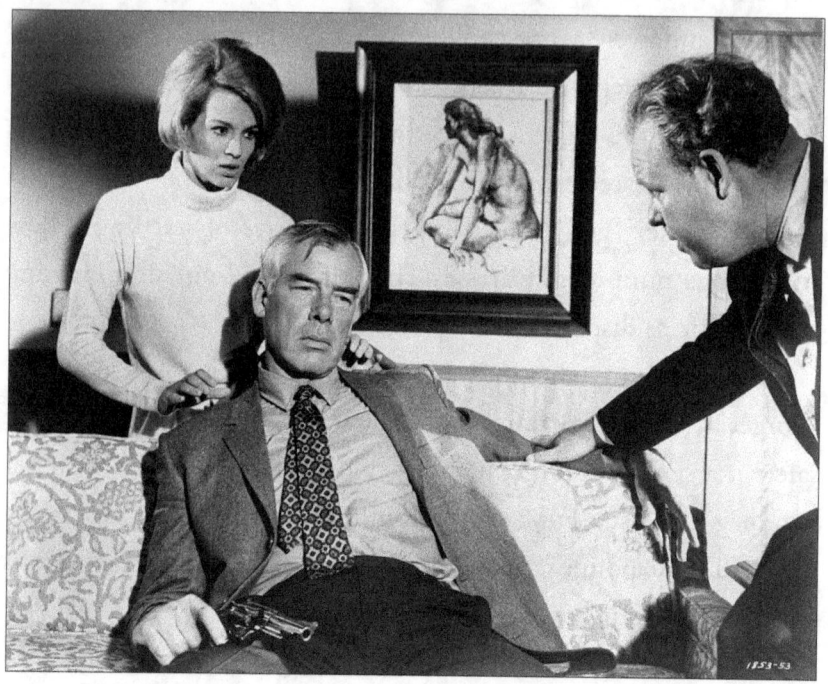

Angie, Lee Marvin, and Carroll O'Connor during a relatively calm moment of *Point Blank* (1967).

There is nothing showy about the acting; it is lean and raw. Chris knows that Walker is empty inside but briefly goes there anyway. "What is my last name?" she asks Walker casually. Unable to tell her, he replies, "What's my first name?" Never before has Angie given any of her characters such a fatalistic acceptance of life's disappointments. It is an outstanding performance, one that should have earned her a Best Supporting Actress Academy Award nomination, replacing either Carol Channing (*Thoroughly Modern*

Millie) or Katharine Ross (*The Graduate*) on a list in 1968 that also included Beah Richards (*Guess Who's Coming to Dinner?*), Mildred Natwick (*Barefoot in the Park*), and eventual winner Estelle Parsons (*Bonnie and Clyde*). Marvin had won a Best Actor Oscar two years earlier for a much less impressive performance in *Cat Ballou*.

The Los Angeles that Walker and Chris navigate is by turns shadowy and blindingly bright. Locations include the Hollywood Hills, the Los Angeles River, West Hollywood, and Culver City. Philip Lathrop's photography places the background details in jarring, hard-edged relief. In one elegantly composed two-shot, Walker and Chris sit on the beach at Santa Monica and discuss the Organization's plans to kill him. Rocky cliffs rise oppressively behind them, completely cutting off the top half of the frame. Even in wide open spaces the characters are trapped.

David Thomson has proposed that the whole picture is a dream, a fading fantasy as Walker lies dying from Reese's gunshots. Like the hanged protagonist of Ambrose Bierce's short story "An Occurrence at Owl Creek Bridge," he imagines everything in the last seconds of his life. It is an interesting suggestion and one that gives additional significance to Boorman's final pan across the San Francisco skyline to Alcatraz.

Reviews:

"Angie Dickinson, playing Miss Archer's sister, provider the right mixture of beauty and bewilderment as she assists Marvin."
—*Daily Variety*, August 31, 1967

"Marvin's performance radiates an animal cunning. As his part time lover, Miss Dickinson looks pretty and effective."
—Mandel Herbstman, *Film Daily*, September 5, 1967

"Construction of the screenplay by Rafe and David Newhouse includes some longish and intricate flashbacks and some split-second reprises of happenings designed to indicate the thoughts of the hero. John Boorman, an English director making his first Hollywood film, has handled these latter and some nude love scenes in such a way as to re-affirm the impression that 'Hiroshima, Mon Amour' still exerts a strong influence on film-makers all over the world."

—*Motion Picture Herald*, September 6, 1967

"There is much ugliness, including the slamming of a gun butt into a man's groin, and a generally distasteful amoral aura. Angie Dickinson has a nude scene to compensate for some of her poor lines, newcomer Sharon Acker adds another dash of sex, and John Vernon, Keenan Wynn, Lloyd Bochner, and others help stir the cauldron of brutality. One frequently forgets what is being viewed and gets lost in the directorial talent."

—*Cue*, September 16, 1967

"Boorman handles his cast with dexterity. Angie Dickinson is delectable as an arty, world-worn moll. Keenan Wynn as a gangland biggie on the way to bigger things is sinister but righteous. And Sharon Acker's Hollywood debut as the doped-up, runaway wife is impressive."

"Such a paradigm of cinematic technique must have a deeper meaning, and *Point Blank* is, finally, a celebration of implacable self-reliance, the story of a lone entrepreneur who will not be kept from his just deserts, not by individual punks, not by the Organization itself."

—Howard Junker, *Newsweek*, September 25, 1967

"Each scene is played as though such scenes have never been played before, and over it all is a hovering sense of menace. The conceptions are always fresh, if the basic material is not, and it is only toward the end that we realize we've been over the same route again. Helpful in keeping this noteworthy exercise in suspense stimulating are Marvin, Angie Dickinson, Keenan Wynn, Carroll O'Connor, and Lloyd Bochner. They're all competent, and contribute to sustain the mood."

—Hollis Alpert, *Saturday Review*, September 30, 1967.

"*Point Blank* is like brass knuckles in the dentistry."

"The rapid pace, the restless camera, the quick cuts, the sudden spurts of violence leave you reeling. And there's no getting steady on the feet before another knockout punch."

"Marvin has in abundance that essential quality of a star, which is that you believe him in all circumstances, and this is what a movie like *Point Blank* must have. To make a one-man attack on a crime syndicate credible an actor must look and act as tough as Marvin."

"Similarly, only a woman as sultry as Angie Dickinson could convincingly tame such a man. Boorman gets the best performance of her career."

—Kevin Thomas, *Los Angeles Times*, October 13, 1967

"Marvin, of course, is excellent as the revengeful man who slugs and loves his way through to the end. A real two-fisted role tailor-made for his special kind of talents. The lovely Miss Dickinson, in a much briefer, but pivotal role, is also excellent as the girl who helps Marvin to attain his ends – fair or foul. It's probably her best vehicle to date."

—Nadine Edwards, *Hollywood Citizen-News*, October 17, 1967

"Angie Dickinson is stunning in, or for that matter out of, her short skirts."

—David Austin, *Films and Filming*, March, 1968

". . . extraordinary editing transforms the film into a Borgesian temporal labyrinth of mirrors and echoes."

—*Time Out London*, June 17, 1998

The Last Challenge

Credits: An MGM production released on December 27, 1967. Metrocolor. Running time of 105 minutes. Based on a novel by John Sherry. **Cast:** Glenn Ford (Marshal Dan Blaine), Angie Dickinson (Lisa Denton), Chad Everett (Lot McGuire), Gary Merrill (Squint Calloway), Jack Elam (Ernest Scarnes), Delphi Lawrence (Marie Webster), Royal Dano (Pretty Horse), Kevin Hagen (Frank Garrison), Florence Sundstrom (Outdoors), Marian Collier (Sadie), John Milford (Turpin), Robert Sorrells (Harry Bell). **Crew:** Richard Thorpe (director and producer), John Sherry and Robert Emmett Ginna (screenwriters), Richard Shore (composer), Ellsworth Fredericks (cinematographer), Richard Farrell (editor), George W. Davis and Urie McCleary (art directors), Henry Grace and Hugh Hunt (set decorators), Mary Keats (hair stylist), William Tuttle (makeup artist), Erich von Stroheim Jr. (assistant director), Franklin Milton (sound).

Plot Synopsis: While having a drink in the town saloon/brothel, Marshal Dan Blaine stops a bully from drawing on an experienced "pistolero" and then shoots the gunfighter dead himself in a fair fight. Looking tired and somber, Blaine retreats upstairs as owner Lisa Denton remarks to the bartender how grueling the lawman's job has become. Blaine and Lisa, who are lovers, banter over breakfast next morning in the saloon's kitchen before he leaves for an overnight fishing trip.

On the trail, Blaine comes across Ernie Scarnes, who has been tied up and left for dead by a band of Indians. Recognizing Scarnes as a treacherous outlaw with whom he previously served time in prison and realizing he probably sold the Indians defective goods, he reluctantly frees him and gives him three days in town to wait for his horse's leg to mend. Riding on, Blaine reaches a secluded stream and begins to fish. A young man approaches on horseback and Blaine invites him to join in; together they catch and fry several fish. Enjoying each other's company over some of Blaine's whiskey, they also recall similar boyhoods in Tennessee. After he deftly shoots a rattlesnake about to strike Blaine, the stranger identifies himself as Lot McGuire, a pistolero who wants to prove he is the fastest gun alive by forcing a duel with the widely renowned Marshal Dan Blaine. When Blaine reveals that he himself is the lawman in question, McGuire packs up his gear and continues on into town.

Upon arrival, McGuire finds a hotel room and gets into a poker game at Lisa's saloon. Caught cheating, card shark Squint Calloway draws his gun but McGuire is faster and shoots him dead. Returning the next day to town, Blaine calls McGuire to his office for some advice. Even though he believes the younger man could have a productive future free of gunfighting, he also warns him that he will kill him if pushed into a showdown. McGuire is still too stubborn to listen.

Lisa and Blaine visit a former saloon girl who has married and also has a new baby. The taste of domestic life makes Lisa even more fearful that she will lose Blaine to violence. In a moment of weakness, she hires Ernie Scarnes to kill McGuire. A failed ambush attempt outside of town results instead in McGuire fatally wounding Scarnes, who asks to be left his own gun to end the suffering. Before dying, Scarnes reveals he was hired by Lisa.

Later that day, McGuire confronts Lisa, who admits that she

acted out of love for Blaine. She also tells him, "He likes you. I don't know, but I guess he sees himself in you when he was your age." Although McGuire pledges not to share Lisa's guilt with Blaine, he also refuses to abandon his desire for a showdown. When he informs Blaine of the ambush attempt, the marshal insists that the two of them ride out to examine and bury the body.

During the journey, they are waylaid by a small group of Indians, and Blaine impresses McGuire with his resourcefulness and presence of mind. Once again they bond and once again McGuire reverts to his old ways when they return to town. Following a restless night, the two men prepare for the inevitable.

Fearing the outcome, Lisa decides to shoot McGuire herself with a Derringer, but a frustrated Blaine takes the gun away. As suspected, he also forces her to admit her involvement in the ambush plan. Rather than meet out on the street, the two men meet in the saloon for the showdown. McGuire draws first and fires but is shot in the chest and dies, eyes open and wordless, on the floor. Blaine suffers a non-lethal wound in the side.

The next day as McGuire's coffin is lowered into the ground, Blaine removes his gun and holster and tosses them into the grave. He then rides out of town while a tearful Lisa watches from the steps of the saloon.

Notes and Comments: Lisa Denton is the apotheosis of all the saloon girls Angie played in the early years of her career. She now owns the business herself. Beyond that, Lisa is much more complicated than the standard frontier beauty. In going to the dark side to save her man, she ends up losing him instead. The violence she solicits is the very thing he ultimately rejects.

Lisa's complexity is also reflected in the dual worlds she inhabits. The saloon is basically a brothel with drinks and gambling. In her low-cut black dresses and high-piled hair, she runs the place like a jaded trail boss, ordering the staff around and mopping up after the occasional gunfight. Nothing seems to penetrate her sleek tough-talking exterior. Upstairs and in the kitchen, however, she is a totally different person. Surrounded by lace curtains and upholstered furniture, she acts more like housewife than madam. This is domesticated feminine space where she plans meals with her maid Sally and indulgently oversees the working girls. Emerging from these private quarters to do her daily shopping, she is dressed conservatively in high-collared pink dresses, hats, and gloves.

The only man admitted entry to Lisa's inner world is Dan Blaine, who shares her bed and her hopes for the future. Except for their professions, they are like any other married couple, comparing schedules over morning coffee. The side trip they take to visit Marie Webster and her husband reinforces Lisa's desire for a more normal life. A former saloon girl whose marriage Lisa helped to arrange and whose past identity she safeguards, Marie seems to have found the happiness Lisa is seeking. After a day spent cooing over the new baby, she is reassured by Blaine that her own life is a full one but replies, "I still feel I've missed out." The fragility of her contentment is made painfully apparent when she violates Blaine's code of honor and cannot prevent him from leaving town.

Angie effectively uses physical signifiers to communicate the two sides of Lisa's personality. In her introductory shot, she stands on a balcony above the saloon, firmly grasping the railing and staring fixedly into the crowd. Her arms are held close to her sides, and her speech is clipped and direct. Whether instructing Lupe the accordionist to "play something a little livelier" or offering a free drink to a new patron, she moves about with the same rigid posture. For Lisa's private moments, she is gesturally more expansive.

The scene where she returns to Glenn Ford/Blaine at rest in the bedroom is a case in point, an example of the remarkable physical dexterity she could bring to character development. Assuming he is asleep in an armchair, she approaches quietly and bends down to check. He pulls her close, and she tumbles onto the chair, lying on top of him and sliding her arms around his neck. As they talk about how beautiful the day is, she nestles against his chest and plants a series of kisses. When he breaks off the caresses to go fishing, she smoothly slides away and feigns indignation. "If you aren't the rudest man I ever saw—and the nicest," she says, leaning up against the wall and watching him gather his hat and holster. At the doorway, she lingers again in the same position before finally kissing him goodbye. The relaxed movements suggest the pliable, sensitive traits that Lisa keeps hidden in public. In the end, as she witnesses Blaine leave town without a word, she returns to the social mask, standing erect on the saloon steps with only a few faint tears seeping from the corners of her eyes.

Glenn Ford, one of Hollywood's top box office draws in the late 50s, is a good choice as the tough but honorable marshal. Having dated some years earlier and having remained good friends, he and Angie generate considerable on-screen chemistry. In the expressive two-shots where they ride side by side on a buckboard or lie next to each other in bed, they bring an easy, mature sexuality to the relationship between Blaine and Lisa.

Longtime MGM contract director Richard Thorpe, who worked extensively on the studio's Robert Taylor pictures, handles the action as effectively as the quieter dramatic moments. The overall effect is engaging, marred only by some unfortunate racism involving drunken Indians and a slow-moving African American maid. *The Last Challenge* was Thorpe's last feature film.

Reviews:

"Ford's laconic blend of concern and quiet anguish is excellent, while Miss Dickinson is both attractive and able as his strong-willed ally. It is in Everett's performance that the film transcends much of its predictability. He invests the character with sufficient complexity and warmth to enlist hope that insight will overtake suicidal ambition, thereby insuring the tension of the final moments."

"Thorpe's direction throughout attends with care to the interrelationship of characters and the exposition and detail by which a sensitive and thorough director elevates the otherwise routine."

—*The Hollywood Reporter*, October 2, 1967

"The acting is good and the romance between Angie Dickinson and Glenn Ford is frank but handled without bedding them down ad nauseam."

—*Boxoffice*, October 9, 1967

"Ford and Everett have their moments as two stoic members of the lawless West. Miss Dickinson is simply very pretty. Richard Shores' background score is a powerful undercurrent for the action."

—Tony Galuzzo, *Motion Picture Herald*, October 11, 1967

"As usual, Ford and Miss Dickinson give dimension to their parts. Everett makes a nice impression but seems altogether too sane to need to be the top gun of the west in order to feel alive. The stars are well-supported by such reliables as Gary Merrill, Jack Elam and Delphi Lawrence."

"With its fine color and authentic-looking settings, *The Last Challenge* is pleasing to the eye and has been written and directed with competence."

—Kevin Thomas, *Los Angeles Times*, November 15, 1967

"For despite the fact two gentlemen, John Sherry and Robert Emmett Ginna, scripted the Robert Thorpe production, *The Last Challenge* remains tedious, dull and so pedestrian-paced that it is almost inconceivable that such astute stars as Ford and Angie Dickinson could have lent the film their talents."

—Nadine M. Edwards, *Hollywood Citizen-News*, November 17, 1967

"The troubles are multiple. There is simply not enough action to justify 105 minutes of wide-screen presentation; the characters are one-dimensional; there are too many rambling discourses of pseudo-western philosophy, most of it lacking in originality or force. Then, too, Ford overplays his tiredness so that he winds up making the viewer tired rather than sympathetic. Perhaps most important, the reason for his liking Everett is never established with any believability. Miss Dickinson is adequate to her role."

—Edward Lipton, *Film Daily*, October 31, 1967

Sam Whiskey

Credits: A Brighton Pictures/Levy-Gardner-Laven production released on April 1, 1969. Color by DeLuxe. Running time of 96 minutes. **Cast:** Burt Reynolds (Sam Whiskey), Angie Dickinson (Laura Breckenridge), Clint Walker (O.W. Bandy), Ossie Davis (Jed Hooker), William Schallert (Mr. Perkins), Woodrow Parfrey (Thorston Bromley), Rick Davis (Fat Henry Hobson), Anthony James (Cousin Leroy), Del Reeves (the fisherman), John Damler (Hank), Robert Adler (Pete), Chubby Johnson (blacksmith), Ayllene Gibbons (Big Annie), Sidney Clute (Clem). **Crew:** Arnold Laven (director and producer), William Norton (screenwriter), Arthur Gardner and Jules Levy (producers), Herschel Burke Gilbert (composer), Robert Moreno (cinematographer), John Woodcock (editor), Loyd S. Papez (art director), Charles Thompson (set decorator), Cherie (hair stylist), Dan Greenway and Frank Griffin (makeup artists), Burt Astor (assistant director), Robert Bertrand (sound).

Plot Synopsis: Through a combination of seduction and a $20,000 fee, beautiful widow Laura Breckenridge convinces Sam Whiskey, a former Union soldier turned gambler and adventurer, to retrieve $250,000 in gold bars from a riverboat that sank in Colorado's Platte River. Her goal is to return the gold, which was stolen from the Denver Mint by her late husband, before the loss is discovered, thus ruining the family name and possibly sending her to jail as an accomplice. Soft-spoken and seemingly guileless, she easily influences the cocky but smitten Sam.

To help with the job, he first secures the help of an African American blacksmith named Jed Hooker. Although he easily sees through Sam's bravado, strong and resourceful Jed agrees to go along on the mission for a share of the $20,000 reward. Together, they next recruit O.W. Bandy, an army friend of Sam's who has since become an inventor. A powerfully built man who wears glasses and quotes Greek philosophy, O.W. at first declines to get involved but ultimately decides that his share of the reward can help finance new inventions.

They set out on horseback for the Platte and along the trail are ambushed by a fat man in thick lensed spectacles who has been observing Sam for some time. Fighting off the fat man's thugs, they finally arrive at the river and locate the sunken boat. Because the gold is fifteen feet underwater, O.W. rigs a diving helmet for Sam out of a bucket, a bellows, and some hosing. Soon after Sam locates the gold, the fat man returns with a larger gang, captures Jed and O.W., and takes over the operation. Assumed by the gang to have been drowned, Sam hides in an air pocket within the riverboat's smokestack. As the intruders drunkenly celebrate their success and prepare to kill their prisoners, Sam resurfaces and uses one of O.W.'s homemade Gatling guns to eliminate the gang members. Once again the fat man himself escapes.

With the gold bars loaded onto a wagon, Sam and his partners start for Denver. At a fork in the road, they are tempted to abscond to Mexico with the treasure, but just at that moment, Laura arrives in her horse-drawn buggy to greet them. Casually mentioning that the fat man is probably the notoriously gold-hungry and vicious Fat Henry Hobson, Laura bolsters the guys' courage with a finely cooked meal and another night of sex for Sam.

Once in Denver, they kidnap U.S. Treasury inspector Thorston Bromley, and while Sam assumes his identity, Laura holds him captive in her hotel room. During his official visit to the mint, Sam intentionally damages a gold-plated bronze bust of George Washington and then hauls it away for repair. At a nearby blacksmith shop, Jed casts a model, melts the gold, and reshapes it into a replica of the statue. After Sam departs with the now valuable duplicate, Fat Henry breaks into the shop and steals the original, believing he has finally seized the missing gold.

That same evening, Sam waits in the mint until Jed and O.W., disguised as plumbers, join him when the building closes. During the next several hours, they melt down the statue, pour the gold into bars, and place the finished product back in the vaults. Interrupted by guards, they make a quick escape and are picked up by a wagon Laura has waiting for them outside.

In a train out of town, Jed and O.W. toast their good fortune while Sam and Laura resume their romantic tryst.

Notes and Comments: Angie is at her comic best opposite Burt Reynolds. Trim and minus the moustache of his later years, Burt plays Sam Whiskey as charming goofball, poking fun at the Western hero archetype and at his own screen persona as tough, young stud. He gives unwanted advice and loses most of his fights but always comes through in the clutch. He is like Cary Grant, whose light comedic touch he continually tried to replicate, in *Gunga Din* (1939). Long before the cockiness turned to schtick, his tendency to shrug and wisecrack through the dialogue still seems endearingly fresh.

Gently mannered and demure, Angie feeds Sam's braggadocio with wide-eyed but calculated admiration. "Oh, Mr. Whiskey," she whispers at crucial moments, "I know you can do it if you put your mind to it." Without ever raising her voice, she apologetically chloroforms the mint inspector as easily as she seduces Sam. She seems to be channeling the Marilyn Monroe of *Gentlemen Prefer Blondes* (1953) and *How to Marry a Millionaire* (1953), a deceptively ditzy naïf who in fact knows exactly what she is doing.

The first scene between Burt and Angie is illustrative. Having arrived in town wearing a lacy pink dress and carrying a bird cage, Angie sounds disoriented when she greets Burt at the entrance to her hotel room. He is there in response to a telegraphed job offer. "Priscilla just died," she says forlornly. "My bird. Would you bury her?" Taken aback, he replies, "Lady, I didn't come 400 miles to bury your bird." She hands him the dead parrot anyway, and as he walks around the room looking for a place to deposit it, she calmly explains the matter of the sunken gold. His belief that the task is too difficult never fazes her nor alters her pleading tone. When he prepares to leave, she asks for one last favor and closes the door onto a momentarily dark frame. Cut to the next shot and they are now in bed together. Each time he tries to disengage, she increases the proposed fee and pushes him down for another round of lovemaking. As Angie keeps chattering away, an exhausted Burt claims that he can't handle things alone and will need two more men. "I'll pay you half the $20,000 now and the other half when you're finished," she offers, and he replies, "I'm damn near finished already." The tone stays playful rather than smutty, and the double entendres land as cleverly as the writer intended. Burt walks gingerly to the door, and Angie purrs, "Mr. Whiskey, it was nice doing business with you."

Burt Reynolds and Angie having fun with each other in a scene from *Sam Whiskey* **(1969).**

Director Arnold Laven had some difficulty getting the sex scenes past the Motion Picture Association of America review board. Not that they were too explicit or concentrated too much on the mechanics instead of the aftermath. There were also no objections to Angie's bare buttocks or Burt's bare chest. The problem was Angie's breasts; a waist-up shot apparently revealed too much. Laven settled for an artfully composed medium close-up where a gauze shawl conceals the nipples. As is, she looks splendid, and Burt apparently kept an enlarged frame from the lovemaking scene prominently displayed in his house for years.

The character interplay, reflected also in the competitive banter between Sam and Jed, is the best thing about the picture. Despite taking too much time on the journey to the riverboat and on the mint heist itself, it moves along briskly in the low-key style of *Butch Cassidy and the Sundance Kid* (1969) as opposed to the broad, gag-filled approach of *Cat Ballou* (1965) and *Blazing Saddles* (1974). Regrettably, Angie and Burt never starred together again in a screen comedy, her brief cameo in *The Last Producer* (2000) notwithstanding.

Reviews:

"Long on cunning and virtually bare of violence, *Sam Whiskey*, the Levy/Gardner/Laven presentation via United Artists, is an amiable western comedy, almost perfectly cast and fulfilling its modest pretensions and budget with handy professionalism."

"Miss Dickinson has been encouraged to play her lines to good effect like a meller school marm, one who might be expected to seduce her way out of a mortgage."

—John Mahoney, *The Hollywood Reporter*, February 3, 1969

ANGIE

"There is a mischievous charm all its own to *Sam Whiskey*, an adventure comedy drama set shortly after the American Civil War. The zany story deals with an attempt to return to the U.S. mint vaults a quarter of a million in stolen gold bars. Novel touches and gentle satire run through the film, rescuing it from what otherwise might have been a formula story."

—*Film Daily*, February 10, 1969

"Miss Dickinson is, as ever, wondrous to see and a deftly dizzy comedienne as well."

—*Los Angeles Times*, March 11, 1969

"*Sam Whiskey* (now playing citywide) is another low-paced cowboy film — this time with a *Goldfinger*-plated plot that offers little more than some travel book photography and the beauty of Angie Dickinson."

"Actually, the only surprise to be found in *Sam Whiskey* is the discovery that its director, Arnold Laven, is the same gentleman who directed the action-packed western *Rough Night In Jericho*."

—David Sutherland, *Hollywood Citizen-News*, March 14, 1969

"The movie, written by William Norton and directed by Arnold Laven, has a kind of clumsy charm, most of it contributed by the performances of Reynolds, who bears a creepy resemblance to Marlon Brando, Miss Dickinson, and Ossie Davis and Clint Walker, who help Reynolds execute a reversal on the usual movie heist."

—Vincent Canby, *The New York Times*, June 12, 1969

Some Kind of a Nut

Credits: A DFI/TFT Productions/Mirisch Corporation production released on October 1, 1969. Color. Running time of 90 minutes. **Cast:** Dick Van Dyke (Fred Amidon), Angie Dickinson (Rachel Amidon), Rosemary Forsyth (Pamela Anderson), Zohra Lampert (Bunny Erickson), Elliott Reid (Gardner Anderson), Steve Roland (Baxter Anderson), Dennis King (Otis Havemeyer), Peter Turgeon (Thomas Allen Defoe), Pippa Scott (Doctor Sara), Heywood Hale Broun (himself), Peter Brocco (Mr. Suzumi), Ben Baker (cabbie), Harry Davis (Dr. Phillip Ball), Roy Roberts (Mr. Burlingame), Robert Ito (George Toyota). **Crew:** Garson Kanin (director and screenwriter), Walter Mirisch (producer), Johnny Mandel (composer), Burnett Guffey and Gerald Hirschfeld (cinematographers), Richard Farrell (editor), Albert Brenner (production designer), Marvin March (set decorator), Anthea Sylbert (costume designer), Cherie (hair stylist), Tom Tuttle (makeup artist), John Chulay (assistant director), Robert Martin (sound).

Plot Synopsis: During a picnic in New York's Central Park, bank teller Fred Amidon and his girlfriend Pamela Anderson are attacked by a bee. Mistaking their gyrations in avoiding the bee as an attempt at public lovemaking, two policewomen arrest them. Fred is also stung painfully on the chin.

At work the next day, he wears a white band-aid over the sting, drawing the objections of his fastidious uptight boss Thomas Defoe, who orders him to replace it with a flesh-colored one. Because he is about to leave on a trip with Pamela, he shrugs off the interference. While on vacation, he discovers that he is unable to shave because of his tender chin, and by the time he returns to the bank he has grown a neatly trimmed beard. Although many people including Pamela, Defoe, and even his doorman and maid dislike the beard, he refuses to shave it. "But Lincoln, Grant, and Freud had one," he tells his boss, who replies, "So did Marx, Lenin, and Castro."

For support, he meets his good friend George at the steam bath. After recommending that Fred visit Zen master Mr. Suzumi for advice, George also mentions that Rachel, the estranged wife whom Fred plans to divorce so that he can marry live-in fiancée Pamela, would like to see him. Two additional meetings do not go as well. After an uncomfortable lunch with Pamela's two narrow-minded brothers, he is ushered in to see bank president Otis Havemeyer. Although the older man has a beard of his own, he freaks out at Fred's refusal to cut his and fires him without further discussion.

Acting on George's suggestion, Fred visits Suzumi's studio, where the master repeatedly throws cups of green tea in his face to stimulate Zen awareness. Also present is free-thinking Bunny Erickson, who proceeds to take him on a whirlwind tour of Manhattan nightspots. Ending the evening in a belly dancing joint called Harry's Harem, Fred drowns his troubles with heavy drink. Back at the apartment, Pamela once again pushes him to shave, and he once again refuses.

Unlike Havemeyer, Fred's coworkers rally to his defense. They organize a protest demonstration outside the bank which draws Bunny, her hippie friends, and several bearded jazz musicians. Newscaster Heywood Hale Broun interviews Fred, and he becomes a media sensation. Pamela and her brothers respond negatively to the coverage as do the bank officials. Rachel on the other hand is thrilled. She had always felt he was too sheepish and had resented having to boss him around. They meet at Fred's favorite swimming pool, a site which allows him to see how great she looks. Not only do they realize that they are still attracted to each other, but they also begin to work out some of their problems.

When he returns home, Pamela drugs him and the brothers

try to shave his beard. Waking up midway through their efforts, he comes unglued and heads for the door. Wearing only his underpants beneath Pamela's coat and brandishing a golf club, he leads the siblings on a wild chase before escaping into the city. Back in Central Park again, he is once more arrested by two police officers and placed under psychiatric observation. The half beard and weird costume make it hard for him to convince doctors that he is normal.

In a show of solidarity, Fred's bank colleagues have all grown beards themselves. Caving to public pressure, Havemeyer offers to reinstate Fred. More in love now than ever, Rachel signs him out of the mental ward and they are greeted by a sign-carrying crowd in support of his heroic stand. Rejecting Pamela, he returns to the apartment that Rachel has completely redecorated and decides to shave the beard that he never intended to keep in the first place.

Notes and Comments: By 1969, Billy Wilder had long since made *One, Two, Three* (1961), Stanley Kubrick had directed *Dr. Strangelove* (1964), and Mike Nichols had recently completed *The Graduate* (1967). It is especially painful, then, to encounter a contemporary comedy as relentlessly and aggressively unfunny as this one. From its decidedly uncool title to its equally outdated premise, *Some Kind of Nut* seems more like a 1950s television variety show sketch than a late 60s feature film.

There are stale topical jokes about hippies, Eastern religion, and social protest. Zohra Lampert plays a stereotypical New York "kook," and the various psychologists are crudely drawn caricatures. Peter Brocco's Zen master offends on multiple levels. Beyond all that, the idea that anyone in 1969 would seriously care about a short, well-maintained beard strains the most generous of credibilities.

This is the second comedy that Angie and Van Dyke made together. They are a sympathetic romantic couple but lack the rakish comic chemistry that she and Burt Reynolds revealed that same year in *Sam Whiskey*. Van Dyke is most appealing when he is at rest, relaxing in bed with Angie or helping her arrange curiosities in her trendy boutique. Unlike the situation in *Rome Adventure*, she is the likable other woman this time around and gets to support rather than manipulate the male lead. Although she has relatively few scenes, she is lovely as always, looking chic in her well-tailored wardrobe and her simple, gently flipped hairdo. She often materializes in Van Dyke's mind, commenting on what he's about to do. One clever bit has Van Dyke watching belly dancers and imaging Angie in place of the main performer, waving scarves and shimmying about in a flattering harem costume. She does equal justice to a bikini swimsuit during the pool scene.

Garson Kanin both wrote and directed *Some Kind of Nut* and thus deserves most of the blame. Achieving early success as director of the hit Cary Grant/Irene Dunne vehicle *My Favorite Wife* (1940) and writer, along with his wife Ruth Gordon, of a string of successful comedies for the likes of Spencer Tracy, Katharine Hepburn, and Judy Holliday, he seems to have run out of gas by the mid-50s. Although he makes good use of the New York exteriors and gets enthusiastic performances from the principals, the picture never goes anywhere fresh or daring. Even the imaginative device of having the first line of a new scene answer the last line of the previous one grows tiresome through overuse.

In his popular *Movie Guide*, Leonard Maltin dismissed the picture as a "bomb", adding, "Pathetic 'contemporary' comedy dates more than Kanin's films of the 30s and 40s."[10]

Reviews:

"There is little to laugh about in this intended comedy of a mild-mannered but high-living bank teller who grows a beard on vacation and finds his life completely changed when he decides to keep it on his return to Manhattan. The timing is irredeemably off, the audience consistently ahead of the film. Even recurring gags, which might have paid off in fast, allusive cuts are tediously set up with a beginning, middle and end. The audience knows what is coming, loses interest before it happens and loses patience as the scene continues beyond its point and its lost laughs."

"Van Dyke looks good in a beard and acts earnestly, to no avail whatsoever. Miss Forsyth looks young and unsure, though the script inspires the uncertainty of her characterization. Miss Dickinson fares best, making credible her patience and understanding with an overgrown clod who barely knows how to shave."

—John Mahoney, *The Hollywood Reporter*, September 22, 1969

"Premise actually is too light and whimsical on which to base a full-length feature, particularly when, as here, there is not sufficient substance in the finished product."

"Van Dyke is mild-mannered personified in an overly-contrived role, but is good for some laughs. Miss Dickinson doesn't stand a chance in a minor part although she's starred, but in what little footage she has, she's mighty visual."

—*Weekly Variety*, September 24, 1969

"Dick Van Dyke, Angie Dickinson and Rosemary Forsyth head the cast of the film which is in DeLuxe color. The pace is breezy and the fun generally pleasant and offbeat. Audiences should find it fresh and diverting even if some sequences are predictable."

—Mandel Herbstman, *Film Daily*, September 25, 1969

"*Some Kind of a Nut* is a contrivance which never comes spluttering and coughing into life. Its characters don't make it as cartoons or as creatures. Artifice lurks at every turn, ill-concealed."

"The consolation prizes include Miss Dickinson, warm and fullblown, and Zohra Lampert as a dizzy hippie; she's a delight. Miss Forsyth is pretty but not very interesting."

—Charles Champlin, *Los Angeles Times*, October 7, 1969

"*Some Kind of a Nut* is a nothing movie. It is neither funny, interesting nor believable. It has nothing to say."

"There is not one good verbal joke and very few visual ones, although Van Dyke flops his long limbs about a lot in a wishy-washy version of his gentle slapstick."

—Bridget Byrne, *Los Angeles Herald-Examiner*, October 10, 1969

Young Billy Young

Credits: A Talbot-Youngstein production released on October 15, 1969. Color by Deluxe. Running time of 89 minutes. Based on a novel by Heck Allen. **Cast:** Robert Mitchum (Ben Kane), Angie Dickinson (Lily Beloit), Robert Walker Jr. (Billy Young), David Carradine (Jesse Boone), Jack Kelly (John Behan), John Anderson (Frank Boone), Paul Fix (Charlie), Willis Bouchey (Doc Cushman), Parley Baer (Bell), Robert Anderson (gambling sheriff), Rodolfo Acosta (Mexican general), Deana Martin (Evvie). **Crew:** Burt Kennedy (director and screenwriter), Max E. Youngstein (producer), Shelly Manne (composer), Harry Stradling Jr. (cinematographer), Otho Lovering (editor), Stan Jolley (art director), Richard Friedman (set decorator), Judy Alexander (hair stylist), Paul Stanhope Jr. (makeup artist), Maxwell O. Henry (assistant director), Frank E. Warner (sound).

Plot Synopsis: Two young hired gunslingers, Billy Young and his friend Jesse, sneak aboard a Mexican troop train to assassinate a corrupt general and his staff. Using a couple of the transported horses to escape, they are pursued through the high desert by soldiers. Thrown from his horse, Billy scrambles for cover as Jesse rides away without him. Later, he finds a semi-wild burro and uses it to reach a river, where a stranger offers him coffee and gives advice about where to cross. Ignoring the warnings, Billy sinks in the mud and the burro scrambles away. The stranger leaves him behind to find his way to the nearby settlement of Bisbee by himself.

In town, Billy gets into a gunfight with a man who cheated him at cards. Because the gambler he shoots and kills is the sheriff, Billy is about to be arrested when the trail stranger, who turns out to be former Dodge city lawman Ben Kane, intervenes in his defense. On his way to Lordsburg, New Mexico, to accept a job as deputy marshal, Kane lets Billy come along with him. Despite Billy's inexperience and hot temper, the older man sees his basic goodness as well. Several miles from Lordsburg, they encounter a stagecoach driven by Kane's old friend Charlie and agree to provide protection. Ambushed by outlaws, they fight off the attack and Billy proves his skill with a gun.

Arriving in Lordsburg, Kane opens up the abandoned jail despite a warning from John Behan, owner of the Gas-Light Saloon, that law enforcement is not welcome. Unimpressed and angered, Kane lays him out with a single punch. At the saloon itself, Billy has met his friend Jesse and gotten into a fistfight over the incident in Mexico. Kane arrives and takes Billy, who has come out on the losing end, to jail for safekeeping. That same evening, Kane meets privately with dance-hall girl and Gas-Light worker Lily Beloit. They flirt heavily, and she tells him that she knows his real reason for accepting the job as Lordsburg's "town tamer" is to settle a grudge with ranch boss Frank Boone. That bad blood seems to be related to a Dodge City shooting that Kane keeps revisiting in flashbacks. Touched by the respect he shows toward her, Lily passes Kane the key to her cabin.

Jealous of the competition, Behan gives Lily a bloody lip. Kane is ready to retaliate, but she talks him out of it, claiming that she needs to protect her job. He prepares a warm bath for her instead, and they draw closer to one another. Although she invites him to spend the night, Kane returns discreetly to the jail.

Realizing that he is outnumbered by Behan and Boone's men, Kane asks Billy if he wants to be a deputy but the younger man chooses not to get involved. The town leaders, led by Doc Cushman, begin to fear that Kane will increase the violence that already plagues them. Unwilling to confront Kane himself, Behan takes out his anger on Lily, slapping her in the face and beating her with his belt. Kane arrives in time to thrash Behan and throw him into the street. More bitter than ever, Behan hires Jesse to shoot Kane.

After treating Lily's injuries, Doc Cushman assures Kane that she is all right and adds another piece to the backstory by revealing that he was the doctor who "worked all night back in Dodge to keep your boy alive." As they are walking through town, Jesse opens fire from a rooftop and kills Cushman by mistake. Kane arrests him and locks him in the jail. When Billy tells him that Jesse is Frank Boone's son, Kane knows he has the bait that will draw his enemy into the open.

As expected, Boone and his men soon ride into town and surround the jail. Preparing to break with Behan and leave Lordsburg, Lily admonishes Billy for not helping Kane and explains it was Boone who murdered Kane's son while the young man watched the Dodge City jail for his father. To prevent Kane from enacting a revenge he will regret, Billy springs Jesse from custody but, realizing that Boone is still unsatisfied, stays to back up Kane in the shoot-out. Jesse tries to stop things, but Behan pulls a gun on him before getting shot and killed himself.

At the height of the battle, Charlie thunders into town on his stagecoach. First knocking out Billy to keep him safe, Kane jumps atop the coach and rides it directly down the main street, picking off shooters from the rooftops. Boone blocks the path and is gunned down.

A few days later, Billy patrols the streets as the new deputy, telling Jesse he will remain locked up until a circuit judge arrives to hear his case. Kane retrieves Lily from the saloon and carries her over his shoulder to the stage, where Charlie prepares to drive them to married life in a new town.

Notes and Comments: For most of her Western films, Angie plays a socially marginalized saloon girl, shaping an overall character arc that connects the individual variations. Throughout the mid-50s, she remains in the background, one of several women dancing in a line on stage or working the saloon floor. As Feathers in *Rio Bravo*, she steps forward to claim the spotlight and the alpha lawman. In *The Last Challenge*, she owns the saloon herself but loses the sheriff and then slides downward even further in *Young Billy Young*, where she is struggling again as an aging saloon performer worried about the future. Always she is caught up in the male power struggles, manipulated by the outlaw or saved, as she is in both *Rio Bravo* and *Young Billy Young*, through marriage to the seasoned authority figure. Her agency is determined by the men.

Angie could be forgiven for thinking the whole project was déjà-vu since *Young Billy Young* is full of similarities to some of her other pictures, particularly *Rio Bravo*. In addition to the ending where her future husband says he doesn't want anyone else seeing her in her revealing saloon tights, both movies feature a young gunslinger (Colorado/Billy) who belatedly comes to the lawman's aid and a cantankerous old coot (Stumpy/Charlie) who appears opportunely in a moment of crisis. Cowardly saloon owner John Behan is much like Stragg in *Hidden Guns*, and Kane's difficult mentorship of Billy resembles the relationship between veteran gunfighter Dan Blaine and stubborn newcomer Lot McGuire in *The Last Challenge*. Most obvious of all is the fact that Mitchum's town-taming Ben Kane is almost a carbon copy of his Clint Tollinger role from *Man with the Gun*.

Robert Mitchum may be the most compatible screen partner Angie ever had. Neither one is showy or mannered but instead mostly intuitive and reactive in approach. The exchanges between them sound like confessional insights from two clear-eyed realists. She tells him that Behan "owns the Gas-Light among other things," and he asks, "Are you one of the other things?" Without a trace of self-pity, she replies, "A girl has to get on." It's like a tennis volley between two old pros. He sets her up with lines such as "When you get that rice powder off you, you aren't bad looking," and she lobs back with "Wantin' a woman is not the same. The wantin' wears off. That happens and there's nothin' left but fightin' and findin' fault. A man could find a lot of that with me bein' who I am." His macho charm and her casual femininity are a fine match despite their fourteen year age difference.

Angie's first appearance in the film is a bit of a shock. She comes out on the steps of the saloon and invites everyone in to see her "act" but is undercut by a badly styled blond wig like the one Mae West will wear a year later in *Myra Breckinridge*. The black glitter leotard doesn't do much for her either. When she finally takes to the stage, the performance consists of nothing more than a couple of high kicks in the center of the dance line.

Equally and more significantly jarring later on is the physical mistreatment her character suffers at the hands of John Behan. Slapped several times, she is also whipped so hard with a leather belt that it leaves wounds requiring a doctor's attention. The abuse, unlike the character-defining violence in *The Killers*, seems gratuitous. Angie herself had reservations, telling Army Archerd "I object to a scene in *Kane* [original title was *Who Rides with Kane?*] where I'm supposed to cringe while I'm being beaten up. No girl is going to cringe—she fights back and that's what I want to do. Sure I'm against violence, but you still have to depict life, without glamorizing the unpleasant. Evil should be punished."[11] In the final film, Lily does not defend herself but is saved by the intervention of Ben Kane.

Also familiar to Angie was writer/director Burt Kennedy, who had written *Gun the Man Down*. Inventive Kennedy touches like the funeral organist playing from the back of a wagon are sometimes overshadowed by scenes such as the opening train ambush where a suspenseful build-up fails to deliver an appropriate pay-off. Noteworthy is Kennedy's embrace of Hollywood's second generation—the sons and daughter of Robert Walker, John Carradine, and Dean Martin in the cast and cinematographer Harry Stradling's son behind the camera. Mitchum's son Christopher appears uncredited as Ben Kane's boy, and Mitchum himself sings the title song.

Reviews:

"United Artists' *Young Billy Young* is an efficiently undistinguished western programmer in the manner and mode of those once turned out by A.C. Lyles at Paramount and Richard and Jerry Thorpe at MGM. If, by chance, it cost no more than that breed, it can eventually show a profit in straight rentals and subsequent television sales."

—John Mahoney, *The Hollywood Reporter*, September 5, 1969

ANGIE

"The acting is surprisingly effective. Robert Mitchum gives another of his easy-going performances that are low on exhibitionism and high in professionalism. Like John Wayne, he plays one role over and over again, but he is always fun to watch, having developed a stereotype that is in some ways more interesting and attractive than 'The Duke's.' Angie Dickinson exhibits her famous legs and supplies the love interest, while Robert Walker turns in a strong performance that augurs an auspicious future for the young actor.

—*Motion Picture Exhibitor*, September 10, 1969

"The film is an immensely likeable, graceful, unpretentious little Western, so agreeable precisely because it refuses to scorn its own conventions."

"Walker and Angie Dickinson, in a nicely-defined love interest role opposite Mitchum, complement the star. All three actors are underrated and overlooked, a misfortune that *Billy Young* is not likely to remedy. The Max Youngstein production achieves its distinction within a limited framework that usually does not provoke comment, even when done this well."

—Barry Glasser, *Motion Picture Herald*, September 10, 196

"Mitchum is quietly effective as the hunter, fast with a gun and accustomed to taking on great odds. Miss Dickinson doesn't have much to do but does it ably, and Walker proves his worth as a young character actor. Nice support is offered."

—*Weekly Variety*, September 10, 1969

"As delectable and vivacious as Miss Dickinson is and as poetic as those legs of hers are—she and Mitchum are not nearly as interesting characters as Walker and Carradine, who perform with energy and individuality."

"True, *Young Billy Young*, with its intersecting, contrasting relationships, has a circularity of structure that can express a philosophical acceptance of life's constant changes, but here Kennedy has drawn it too loosely."

—Kevin Thomas, *Los Angeles Times*, October 17, 1969

"Mitchum is slow and easy as usual, hitting people with great regularity and muttering 'it depends on how you look at it' whenever anyone questions his actions. Angie Dickinson summons all her style to survive some hokey lines about a girl having to make a living. Robert Walker is all right as Young Billy but is neither soft or hard enough to be really endearing."

—Bridget Byrne, *Los Angeles Herald-Examiner*, October 17, 1969

Pretty Maids All in a Row

Credits: A Metro-Goldwyn-Mayer production released on April 28, 1971. Metrocolor. Running time of 91 minutes. Based on a novel by Francis Pollini. **Cast:** Rock Hudson (Michael "Tiger" McDrew), Angie Dickinson (Betty Smith), Telly Savalas (Captain Sam Surcher), John David Carson (Ponce de Leon Harper), Keenan Wynn (Police Chief John Poldaski), Barbara Leigh (Jean McDrew), Roddy McDowall (Principal Proffer), James Doohan (Follo), William Campbell (Grady), Susan Tolsky (Harriet Craymire). **Crew:** Roger Vadim (director), Gene Roddenberry (screenwriter and producer), Lalo Schifrin (composer), Charles Rosher, Jr. (cinematographer), Bill Brame (editor), Preston Ames and George Davis (art directors), Robert Berton and Charles Pierce (set decorators), William Ware Theiss (costume designer), Cherie (hair stylist), Allen Synder (makeup artist), Robert Dijoux and David Silver (assistant directors), Jerry Jost and Hal Watkins (sound).

Plot Synopsis: Ponce de Leon Harper is a sexually frustrated student at Oceanfront High School. Everywhere he looks he sees nothing but beautiful young girls in tight sweaters and mini-skirts. Even his gorgeous substitute teacher Miss Betty Smith seems to be flaunting her décolletage and derriere in his astounded face. To conceal his erection, he asks for permission to use the restroom, where he discovers a strangled female classmate in the stall next to his.

As chain-smoking police captain Sam Surcher and the inept, racist police Chief John Poldaski show up on campus to investigate, Ponce shares his sexual trouble with Michael "Tiger" McDrew, the school's handsome and incredibly popular football coach, guidance counselor, assistant principal, and sometime drama advisor. Ponce becomes Tiger's protégé, assisting him on the football field and taking his advice about the opposite sex. To help Ponce achieve sexual maturity, Tiger convinces Betty Smith to take an extracurricular interest in the boy.

A predator with great outward charm, Tiger has issues of his own. He has been consistently seducing the school's most attractive female students. The flashing red "testing" sign above his office door indicates that inside he has just made another conquest. Befuddled and overwhelmed Principal Proffer has no idea about this or much else that is happening on his watch. Despite his sleazy behavior, Tiger has a beautiful wife and loving little daughter waiting for him at a home near the beach.

Meanwhile, another body has been found and Surcher, who has conducted a series of comically absurd interviews around OHS, begins to suspect Tiger. It seems that once a girl becomes too possessive or demanding, the coach dispatches her with a farewell note pinned to her undergarments. When Poldaski stumbles across the truth, Tiger kills him as well.

Oblivious to all the mayhem, Betty pursues her sexual mission with Ponce. She invites him to her apartment to study, and underneath one of Hieronymus Bosch's feverishly allegorical paintings, they read Milton and drink hot chocolate. Thinking Ponce is impotent, she is pleased to notice his erection, believing she has worked a "cure" and sending him on his way. After a disappointed Tiger demonstrates the kind of sensual session he actually had in mind for Ponce, she invites the boy back for a second evening. This time she greets him in a gauzy white tunic slit high on both sides and follows through on the sex manual information she has gathered. Bathed and bedded by Betty, Ponce happily spends the night.

With events closing in, Tiger struggles to maintain control. He does away with an ex-girlfriend who threatens to expose him but not before she secretly records a tell-all tape message. The big championship football game is held immediately after one of the funerals, and the team plays badly until Tiger gives a demented half-time talk that pushes them to a victory. Hoping for a successor, Tiger encourages Ponce to become a teacher and work at Oceanfront with him just before Ponce listens to the incriminating tape recording. Aware of Surcher's suspicions, Tiger makes a confession to Ponce and drives his car off a pier.

At Tiger's funeral, all the pretty maids are lined up in rows singing hymns. Miss Smith is in attendance along with a new, noticeably older, boyfriend. Ponce, surrounded by girls, has inherited Tiger's big man on campus status. Having kept his conclusions confidential, Surcher watches the service with a wry detachment until he catches sight of a Brazilian airline ticket in Mrs. McDrew's handbag. Tiger, he realizes, probably has faked his death and is waiting for his family in Rio.

Notes and Comments: Roger Vadim's reputation, such as it is, was established through his movies and affairs with Brigitte Bardot, Catherine Deneuve, and Jane Fonda. His cinematic gaze was always intrusive, aggressive, and smarmy. *And God Created Woman*, the 1956 international hit he wrote and directed for Bardot, is illustrative of his nearly fifty year career. As a highly sexual 18-year-old orphan, Bardot is ogled, abused, reviled, and fetishized by a series of possessive men. She is not so much a real character as an embodiment of Vadim's erotic fantasies. The camera leers at her nudity, displayed in mechanically contrived centerfold poses, like a voyeur at a peepshow. "Human realities do not obtrude on his world," wrote David Thomson, "and there are depressing signs of an actual hostility to women as people, rather than the sex object that is possessed in the moment of being seen." Vadim's films, Thomson concluded, "have all the suspended animation of a masturbatory dream."[12]

Pretty Maids All in a Row is no different. In the opening scenes, Vadim zooms in for multiple close-ups of the female students' breasts and bottoms. Angie, as substitute teacher Betty Smith, is introduced at the blackboard shaking her rear along with the erasers and chalk. Bending down to help Ponce, she thrusts the upper half of her body into his field of vision. Tiger's victims are presented as so many sex toys for our amusement, right down to the dismissive notes pinned to their panties.

Vadim and screenwriter Gene Roddenberry, already well-known for his *Star Trek* television series (1966-69), intended the film as a black comedy, a mordant satire about sexual permisssiveness and moral relativity gone too far. Tiger McDrew is to be taken ironically as the guidance counselor in desperate need of counseling himself, the social swinger loved by everybody but who is motivated by the most antisocial of impulses. The humor, however, is stillborn. There is nothing witty about the dialogue, and the visual comedy never gets beyond lame sight gaps such as the one where Angie stops at a gas station and sees a sign that reads, "Put a tiger in your tank." The student murders, which we discover after the fact, are tasteless punchlines. A more accomplished movie might have been able to convincingly make the point that the logical outcome of sexual objectification is the denial of life itself.

Angie seduces high school student John David Carson in *Pretty Maids All in a Row* (1971).

Angie is almost alone among the cast in knowing how to play the material. She is straightforward and innocent as Betty, capturing the character's genuine although misguided wish to help Ponce conquer his sexual problems. Her interaction with nineteen-year-old John David Carson has a charming tentativeness that befits their awkward teacher-student romance. Because she never makes Betty predatory, her semi-nude scenes with Carson are the film's only truly erotic moments, candid-like fulfillments of the young man's desires. The rest of Angie's screen time is spent with Rock Hudson, and she gets that dynamic right also. To show Betty's starry-eyed crush on Tiger she becomes an eager schoolgirl herself, hanging on his every word and obediently carrying out his instructions.

Hudson seems confused by his part. He should have used the light touch on display in his romantic comedies with Doris Day but instead pushes too hard for effect. Neither likable nor threatening, he just looks loud and out of place among all the teenagers. One wonders what the pretty maids found so irresistible about his messy hair, overgrown moustache, and expanding waistline.

The cast and crew are game enough. Telly Savalas seems to be in training for *Kojak*, his CBS cop show which would premiere two years later and overlap with Hudson's (*McMillan & Wife*) and Angie's (*Police Woman*) own police programs. He is sly and cynical, using his cigarette for the same comic effect that Kojak will get out of his lollipop. As the principal, Roddy McDowall goes for bureaucratic fussiness, and Keenan Wynn's irritability is the right tone for his bigoted police chief. Cinematographer Charles Rosher, Jr., son of the well-known early cameraman who photographed Mary Pickford, Janet Gaynor, Constance Bennett, and others, envelopes Vadim's adolescent beauties in a kind of sun-drenched golden haze. Argentine-born composer Lalo Schifrin keeps the action moving along with his percussive, jazz-based soundtrack.

Francois Truffaut journeyed out of France to make a commendable English-language film (*Fahrenheit 451*, 1966), as did

Jacques Remy (*Model Shop*, 1969) and Louis Malle (*Atlantic City*, 1980). Despite the resources of a major Hollywood Studio, Vadim was never able to do the same. It should be noted, however, that Quentin Tarantino once rated *Pretty Maids All in a Row* as one of the top ten films ever made.

Reviews:

"Whatever substance was in the story or screen concept has been plowed under, leaving only superficial, one-joke results. It's hard to believe that Vadim, or any other director with a reputation, could come up with these results. For Hudson, it's another muffed opportunity to crash out of an old mold; but he should keep trying for the break-out part of which he remains capable."

—*Daily Variety*, March 2, 1971

"It is obvious from the beginning that Hudson—who is making time with several girl students at once—will turn out to be the murderer; so since there isn't much tension in the plot, there ought at least to have been some in the performances. Miss Dickinson is a case in point. She still has one of the best figures in the business, but in her make-up, her hair styles and her costuming, she is not well-served; and her development from an understanding teacher into a sex-starved female who initiates Carson into manhood is peculiarly slack."

—Craig Fisher, *The Hollywood Reporter*, March 9, 1971.

"But by comparison, *Pretty Maids* is truly comic relief—a kinky, funny, often on-target satire about libidinous teenagers and their equally eager elders. Director Vadim constantly undercuts himself with the kind of sleazy eroticism (many shots of panties and nubile cleavage) that has made him a cinematic Flo Ziegfeld, but his decidedly black sense of humor has not been so finely honed since he made *Les Liaisons Dangereuses* ten years ago."

—Jay Cocks, *Time*, May 10, 1971

"*Pretty Maids All in a Row* moves fast, evokes laughter even when it is being most serious and boasts unflaggingly zesty dialog and performances. In these show-everything times Vadim remains the master of eroticism by suggesting lots more than he actually reveals."

"The seduction of Carson by Miss Dickinson is a comic gem yet has a powerful sensuality which he uses to involve us in his morality play and thus forces us all the more to ponder the crazy logic that can decree sexual uninhibitedness such a taboo that it must be covered up with murder."

"In a departure even farther out than *Seconds* Rock Hudson, playing at the very edge where satire threatens but isn't allowed to lapse into burlesque, turns in one of the best performances of his career. The same is true of the ever-sultry Miss Dickinson. Carson is most impressive and appealing in his debut."

—Kevin Thomas, *Los Angeles Times*, May 12, 1971

"Angie Dickinson and John David Carson put together the sequences of the film that are most fleshed out and most touching. As the boy with the sexual problem, Carson is wonderfully naïve, hesitant, untouched. As the older woman who initiates him, Miss Dickinson is warm and surprisingly full as a character. Fine performances."

—*Los Angeles Herald-Examiner*, May 12, 1971

"The movie by French director Roger Vadim, working in California, is really an utterly cynical, sometimes clever, and generally merciless comedy-murder tale that comments on preoccupation with sex and rampant insensitivity. The gallows humor is geared to holding up a distortion mirror to distorted life. It succeeds only occasionally, suffers from lack of plot credibility, isn't upsetting enough, and lacks total strength."

—*Cue*, May, 1971

"Angie Dickinson's performance bears the pure stamp of Vadim's direction. As the sensuous and attractive young English teacher with a yen for Tiger, she oddly becomes sidetracked to a teenage student in her class played by newcomer, John David Carson. This misdirection of her intention is beautifully accomplished by the skill of a man who knows the camera and exactly how to handle it. Vadim is a story-teller from the very tips of his fingers."

—Paul Yanitz, *Beverly Hills Courier*, May 28, 1971

"Angie Dickinson blooms in one of her infrequent cinema appearances as a well-stacked teacher (did you think she would unstack for the role?) and does to a fabulously appealing young student, John David Carson, what Rock does to the girls."

—*Cosmopolitan*, July, 1971

The Resurrection of Zachary Wheeler

Credits: A Madison Productions Inc. picture released in November, 1971. Technicolor. Running time of 100 minutes. **Cast:** Leslie Nielsen (Harry Walsh), Bradford Dillman (Senator Zachary Wheeler), James Daly (Dr. Redding), Angie Dickinson (Dr. Layle Johnson), Robert J.

Wilke (Fielding), Jack Carter (Dwight Chiles), Don Haggerty (Jake), Lew Brown (Collins), Richard Schuyler (Bates), Dick Simmons (Adams), William Bryant (Craig Harmon), Ruben Moreno (General Munoz), Peter Mamakos (Premier Mabulla). **Crew:** Bob Wynn (director), Jay Simms and Tom Rolf (screenwriters), Robert Stabler (producer), Marlin Skiles (composer), Bob Boatman (cinematographer), Jerry Greene (editor), Herman Zimmerman (art director), Cherie (hairstylist), Louis LaCava (makeup artist), George Fenaja (assistant director), Robert Post (sound).

Plot Synopsis: When United States Senator Clayton Zachary Wheeler is seriously injured in a car crash, TV reporter Harry Walsh is one of the first witnesses on the scene. After filing a news report, he accompanies Wheeler by ambulance to Bethesda Naval Hospital where the medical team concludes that the injuries are fatal. Dr. Keating, chief of staff, receives a phone call from an unnamed admiral ordering him to stabilize Wheeler, air transport him to a secret medical facility in Alamogordo, New Mexico, and destroy all written evidence that he was ever admitted to Bethesda.

Inquiring about the Senator's condition, Walsh is told that there is no such person in the hospital. When Wheeler is reported to be on a fishing trip to Wyoming, Walsh's editor orders him to retract his story about the accident. Walsh refuses and is fired, vowing to pursue the mystery on his own.

In Alamogordo, Dr. Redding and his assistant Dr. Layle Johnson perform a series of organ transplants that save Wheeler's life. As Wheeler makes a startlingly fast recovery, he becomes romantically attracted to the attractive Dr. Johnson and learns about Redding's special transplantation process. Using synthetically grown human bodies or "somas," Redding injects them with a specific patient's DNA and then harvests the organs in a perfect match that avoids rejection. The somas, equipped only with rudimentary brain function, are destroyed but the patient survives. Confused by the details, Wheeler has lingering misgivings about the ethical questions.

Through determined sleuthing at car rental offices and airports, Walsh traces Wheeler to New Mexico. Arriving in Albuquerque, he is immediately followed by two incompetent agents whom he eludes through a string of comic chases and deceptions. Getting rides with some migrant workers and on a Greyhound bus, he ultimately makes his way to Alamogordo.

The agents have been dispatched by Hugh Fielding, chairman of the Committee, a secret chamber which controls Redding's process. Through a form of medical blackmail, the Committee offers life-saving transplants to powerful world leaders who agree in turn to support the group's business and political interests. As a probable Presidential candidate, Wheeler is an especially valuable client yet, having met one of his barely sentient soma "twins," he refuses to cooperate. Fielding warns him that he will never receive a presidential nomination if the public learns he has had a heart transplant.

With the help of an Alamogordo newspaper friend, Walsh lands at the Los Alamos military site that is being used for the hospital. Discovering the soma which he believes is actually Wheeler, he attempts to free it by hijacking Dr. Johnson and her car. In the ensuing chase through the compound, he swerves to avoid several lost somas and crashes the car. Johnson is critically injured, and Fielding threatens not to okay a transplant for her unless Wheeler plays ball. When Redding announces that Dr. Johnson's injuries are not that serious after all, Walsh and Wheeler decide to fully expose the Committee. Just then word comes that Chinese leader Chou En-lai has suffered his second coronary and will be arriving at the hospital. The film ends as the reporter and the Senator ponder whether the nation may be better served by giving Fielding free reign to go ahead and compromise such an important geopolitical adversary.

Notes and Comments: *The Resurrection of Zachary Wheeler* was one of the first movies to deal with organ harvesting and human cloning. It preceded Robin Cook's similarly themed novel *Coma* by six years. First-time screenwriter Tom Rolf, known more widely in the industry as a film editor, cleverly combined the futuristic medical concept with a secondary plot line involving deep state/shadow government intrigue. Fielding's Committee members are very much like the elite conspirators of *Executive Action* (1973) and *Star Chamber* (1983).

The film is more interesting thematically than it is stylistically. As one of the first movies to use the video-to-film transfer process, it suffers from a somewhat faded image quality. Additionally, Bob Wynn's direction has the look of a daytime drama with its stiff, tightly blocked conversations and its mostly stationary camera. Especially awkward is his habit of unexpectedly reframing the composition and tilting the shot to signal a scene change. The perfunctory music score never captures the suspense of Walsh's pursuit by the agents nor the eeriness of the soma encounter.

The actors all wisely underplay the material's more sensationalistic aspects. James Daly, father of acting siblings Tim and Tyne Daly, portrays Dr. Redding as a variation on the Dr. Paul Lochner role he maintained for seven years on the hit CBS TV show *Medical Center* (1969-76). His gruff, businesslike demeanor obscures the fact that he happens to be dealing in synthetically grown human beings. Known mostly as a villain in film and TV westerns, Robert J. Wilke makes Fielding into a lethal powerbroker who barks commands and computes political odds with absolutely no regard for morality. It is up to Bradford Dillman as Senator Wheeler to surface the ethical issues, and he does this convincingly. Delivering most of his dialogue confined to a hospital bed or a wheelchair, he progresses from confused relief to deep outrage as he learns the reasons behind his miraculous recovery. His best moments are when he confronts the marginally conscious soma that has been cultivated for his benefit and reacts with a mixture of guilt and remorse.

As Doctor Johnson, Angie has perhaps the hardest assignment of anyone in the cast; she is required to convey big chunks of exposition regarding the transplants, the somas, and the Committee. All of her scenes are with either Dr. Redding or Wheeler, asking questions of the former and providing information to the latter. Although her roles is that of physician rather than the by now expected nurse, she mostly takes Wheeler's pulse, checks his blood pressure, and shines a pencil flashlight in his eye. It is one of her most rigid performances, hampered significantly by the narrative demands. Only in the film's second half, as she and Wheeler develop a romantic interest in each other, does she loosen up and become more natural. "Everything is flat in New Mexico," she tells Wheeler at one point and, darting a look at her lab coat, he responds, "Not everything." She smiles and suddenly the tone is lighter. Unfortunately, after the car accident, Angie's character disappears from the film and her romance with Wheeler is one of several unresolved story threads.

In his dramatic parts, Leslie Nielsen always runs the risk of inadvertently reminding viewers of how he later spoofed himself in movies such as *Airplane!* (1980) and *The Naked Gun* trilogy (1988, 91, and 93). There's a little of the hyper-intense Lt. Frank Drebin in his Harry Walsh, but generally he makes Walsh's search for Wheeler compelling and even suspenseful. That pursuit, which keeps him isolated from the events at Alamogordo until the last few minutes of the film, constitutes a separate story, a conscious imitation of Hitchcock's *North by Northwest* (1959). Like Roger Thornhill in that film, Walsh witnesses an event disbelieved by others and races across the country pursued by two henchmen who, among other assaults, lock him into the back seat of a car. Wearing the same matching suit and tie throughout, he even steps onto (rather than off) a Greyhound bus that appears mysteriously in the middle of a vast, empty wasteland.

What *The Resurrection of Zachary Wheeler* does best is to suggest how commerce steers scientific research and how corporate decision making typically ignores ethical considerations. In one extended scene, the Committee, which is composed of eight old men, meets to consider which candidates are deserving of a transplant. Those who are too independent or too liberal are rejected. A scientist who is working on a substitute for oil-based fuels is deemed particularly objectionable. To be "good for the country" is to maximize capital return. Anyone who ignores profit is expendable. Dr. Redding's and Dr. Johnson's acceptance of this reality is as troubling s the soma process itself.

Reviews:

"The ending is the only minor flaw in an otherwise intelligently planned work. One senses that perhaps the story was concluded too abruptly with its one-line revelation of a new patient in the secret medical center."

"But *Zachary Wheeler* as a whole is a fine achievement, due in no small part to Wynn's crisp direction. He had versatile actors to work with and all performed smoothly, making the story a seamless artistic whole. Nielsen is especially convincing as the determined newsman, and Bradford Dillman in dual role as senator and cadaver, contributes a tight, solid performance. James Daly, Angie Dickinson, and Carter are also very good."

—*Daily Variety*, November 12, 1971

"Unfortunately, *The Resurrection of Zachary Wheeler* is a rather disappointing movie. The production values are all okay and the script idea is potentially an exciting one. The final effect, however, is one of general blandness. The film seems much more suitable for television entertainment than for theatrical release."

"The problems seem to be in a lack of a definite point of view, thin character developments, and a weakly constructed script."

"Bradford Dillman as the Senator, and James Daly and Angie Dickinson as the doctors, give smooth and intelligent performances which are lost on the material. Director Robert Wynn keeps the film moving at a brisk pace, substituting action for interest."

—Ron Pennington, *The Hollywood Reporter*, November 15, 1971

The Outside Man

Credits: A Cité Films and General Production Company production released in January, 1973. Technicolor. Running time of 104 minutes. **Cast:** Jean-Louis Trintignant (Lucien Bellon), Ann-Margret (Nancy Robson), Roy Scheider (Lenny), Angie Dickinson (Jackie Kovacs), Georgia Engel (Mrs. Barnes), Felice Orlandi (Anderson), Carlo De Mejo (Karl), Michel Constantin (Antoine), Umberto Orsini (Alex), Rico Cattani (butler), Ted de Corsia (Victor), Edward Greenberg (hitchhiker), Jackie Earle Haley (Eric), Alex Rocco (Miller), John Hillerman (department store manager). **Crew:** Jacques Deray (director and screenwriter), Jean-Claude Carrière and Ian McLellan Hunter (screenwriters), Jacques Bar (producer), Michel Legrand (composer), Silvano Ippoliti and Terry K. Meade (cinematographers), William K. Chulack and Henri Lanoë (editors), Kenneth A. Reid (art director), Marvin March (set decorator), Cherie (hair stylist), Robert Norin (makeup artist), Georges Pellegrin and Robert Rosenbaum (assistant directors), Jacques Maumont (sound).

Plot Synopsis: French hitman Lucien Bellon arrives in Los Angeles to kill mob boss Victor Kovacs. He successfully completes the job at Kovacs's Beverly Hills mansion and is spotted by the gangster's adult son Alex and wife Jackie, who misreport his physical description to the police. Back at his hotel, he learns that he has been checked out and that all of his belongings, including passport, have been removed. A target now himself, Lucien first finds the tires of his rental car flattened and then is fired upon by a second hitman. Escaping from the hotel parking structure, he runs to a nearby supermarket and forces a single mother named Mrs. Barnes to drive him to her apartment.

He spends part of the evening there, watching TV with her bratty son Eric and placing a phone call to his friend Antoine back in Paris. The man who got him the hit job in the first place, Antoine now tells Lucien that a woman named Nancy Robson, working in downtown L.A. at the Aces High Club, may be able to help. Taking Mrs. Barnes's car, he leaves and is followed by the hitman, known only as Lenny.

To show him how to get downtown, Lucien picks up a Jesus freak hitchhiker, who begins an impromptu front-seat sermon. Pulling up alongside, Lenny aims at Lucien but instead shoots the hitchhiker in the head. A car chase ensues, and Lenny is left behind when he spins out on a freeway curve. Lucien locates cocktail waitress and former hooker Nancy, and she reluctantly agrees to help. They visit her cab driver friend Karl, who lends them his apartment for the night and makes a deal to obtain a fake French passport for Lucien.

Following a lead from Mrs. Barnes, Lenny surprises Nancy the next morning when she returns home and forces her to divulge Lucien's whereabouts. After a failed ambush attempt at the apartment, Lenny chases Lucien onto an abandoned pier, where their running gun battle attracts the attention of the police. Just as he is about to be caught, Lenny shoots a cop and drives off in a patrol car; Lucien uses the confusion to make his own exit.

Later that day, Lucien meets Karl at a roller derby game and collects the newly made passport. Nancy drives him to the airport to catch a flight for Paris, but at the last minute he decides to stay in L.A., partly to discover who has set him up and partly to be with Nancy. The two of them check in to a motel and take two adjoining rooms. Lenny, in the meantime, has returned to Karl's apartment and learns about the passport. After shooting Karl point-blank, he calls Alex Kovacs and reports that Lucien has left the country, thus revealing Alex and the widow Jackie as the adulterous schemers behind Victor's death.

Having figured out Alex's probable involvement himself, Lucien follows Jackie and intentionally lets her see the name and address of the motel. When, as expected, Lenny shows up, Lucien disarms him and together they drive to the Kovacs mansion. At the last minute, Lenny pulls a hidden gun and Lucien shoots him dead against the entrance gates. A police lieutenant arrives and tells Alex the only reason he is not in custody is because the city prefers the crime world's status quo.

Antoine and a friend arrive from Paris to help Lucien. Together they all go to Victor's funeral to confront Alex. In a climactic shoot-out there, nearly everyone, including Alex and the two Frenchmen, is killed. Lucien escapes behind the wheel of a hearse but later dies of his wounds. Jackie is arrested, and Nancy waits futilely for Lucien at the airport.

Note and Comments: Like many other European film directors in love with Los Angeles, Jacques Deray makes a character of the city itself, a sprawling maze as confounding to Lucien as the double cross. Among the glamorous as well as grimy locations used in the picture are the Beverly Hilton Hotel, Los Angeles International Airport, Sunset Boulevard, the Olympic Auditorium, Beverly Hills, and Venice Beach. In an inspired bit of dark humor, Deray sets the final gun battle at Forest Lawn Cemetery. While an embalmed Victor Kovacs sits upright in a throne-like chair, the guests begin firing on each other. Alex is shot to death while hiding in a coffin, Antoine rushes outside only to be dragged behind a hearse, and Lucien makes a tire-screeching getaway across the cemetery lawn. The sequence ends with the hearse parked next to a dry, cemented stretch of the Los Angeles River and Lucien dying slowly of a gunshot wound. The settings here as elsewhere tend to make the action more realistic, but they also contextualize *The Outside Man* within a recognizable framework of familiar images and locations from movie history.

Deray uses his other major asset, the four lead actors, in the same way. They each bring iconic resonance to their parts. As the dueling hitmen, Roy Scheider is just one year out from his tough guy cop in *The French Connection* (1971), and Jean-Louis Trintignant plays the strong loner he perfected in *A Man and a Woman* (1966) and *Z* (1969). Ann-Margret and Angie come to the roles of Nancy and Jackie with similar reputations as two of the most sexually provocative leading ladies of the 1960s. Thus, the actors' presence legitimates the picture much as the settings do. Yet, with the strong advantages of persons and place, there is an occasional awkwardness to the proceedings. It is as if Deray never got fully comfortable working in English. The actors move stiffly at times, and Trintignant delivers his lines without inflection or affect. His character is alienated to be sure, but that fact doesn't fully explain the inertia. Even the action scenes are less dynamic than they could be. Only Ann-Margret seems totally at ease, turning in a well-rounded performance as vulnerable, hard-luck Nancy.

The fourth billed star, Angie appears intermittently throughout the picture as Jackie Kovacs, usually alongside stepson Alex. She also has two scenes with Trintignant but none with either Scheider or Ann-Margret. Working with relatively little dialogue, she gives Jackie a steely veneer that makes the romance with Alex seem more like a business arrangement than an affair of the heart. Sleek and stylish, she greets houseguests and store clerks with the same curt disinterest. Her best scenes are the ones with Trintignant. In the first, she offers his Lucien character a drink while he waits to see her husband. Dressed in a short white beach wrap, she pretends to be just another polite wife and then exits for the pool, where she strips to a floral bikini and telegraphs her link to Alex by casually ruffling his hair. In the second, Lucien follows her as she drives her Rolls Royce convertible to a Beverly Hills department store. While she is slipping out of her dress in the changing room, he suddenly pulls open the curtain to purposefully let himself be recognized. A sudden look of panic flashes across her face and is held for a few seconds in medium close-up. The encounter and her subsequent search for Lucien through the store are without dialogue, providing evidence again of how easily Angie could hold the screen through movement and expression only. Assured moments like these alternate with more awkward blockings (e.g., the police interview in her home) where she seems unsure how to stand and what to do with her hands. Overall, it is an uneven, underdeveloped performance. She might have been better served in the more challenging and more likable role of Nancy.

A former film and stage actor, Jacques Deray specialized in crime thrillers that were heavily influenced by American film noir. He made several pictures each with Alain Delon and Jean-Paul Belmondo, including 1970's *Borsalino* where they famously appeared together. *The Outside Man* marked his second attempt to work with Angie; she had been offered a part in *La Piscine* (1969) but was unable to fit it into her schedule. Known in France as *Un homme est mort*, *The Outside Man* was filmed in 1972 and received a staggered distribution in the United States throughout 1973. The scenes between Lucien and Antoine take place in French without subtitles and show how effective and at-ease Deray could be when working in his native language. The picture's X-rating stems from some full frontal nudity at a strip club.

Reviews:
"It could be used for playoff Stateside but would need hard sell for more demanding firstruns. Names of Roy (*French Connection*) Scheider and Angie Dickinson will help with a fine cameo bit by Georgia Engel as a woman Trintignant uses for a hideout who wants to be on TV. Well made, technically."

—*Weekly Variety*, February 14, 1973

"Aside from its intriguing cast, none of whom has much chance to make anything of his or her role, *The Outside Man* has almost nothing going for it. There is a modicum of humor, no sex (Trintignant and Ann-Margret share separate rooms at a motel), and there is only a smattering of suspense. As for Deray's direction—well, the hero may be on the lam, but the movie drags."

—*Product Digest*, October 17, 1973

"A picture with both Ann-Margret and Angie Dickinson in it is ahead right there. The by now familiar story of a hit-man being gunned down himself gets entertaining results due to a good cast and direction."

"Director Jacques Deray uses the Los Angeles milieu with superior results. Although the material is strictly routine fodder, it gets the kind of classy look and slick action treatment that keeps one entertained."

—*Cue*, November 22, 1973

"For the action market, a French-American co-production made entirely in Los Angeles and suburbs with a good international cast, *The Outside Man* has enough action to sustain itself. A minimum of French is spoken (with English titles) and some dubbing is evident. Screenplay by Jean-Claude Carrière, Jacques Deray and Ian McLellan Hunter, from a Carrière-Deray story, brings in a new character or locale whenever the story threatens to intrude too much upon the action."

—*Boxoffice*, November 29, 1973

"This early color noir shows the city from the perspective of a complete outsider—a French hit man (Jean-Louis Trintignant), awkward with English, abandoned and on the run from both the cops and his employers. I can't say it's a great film, but it captures *something*—if nothing else, a cranked-up version of the alienation I experienced back then."

—Andy Klein, *L.A. City Beat*, May 20, 2004

"Director Jacques Deray and cinematographers Meade and Ippoliti consciously capture the city's endless network of asphalt streets, concrete and glass boxes, and underground parking lots. *The Outside Man* is a perfect time-capsule of 1970s Los Angeles; rarely have the city's urban spaces been captured so precisely—from LAX to West Hollywood to Skid Row."

—*UCLA Archive Program Notes,* May 22, 2004

Big Bad Mama

Credits: A New World Pictures production released on September 19, 1974. Metrocolor. Running time of 83 minutes. **Cast:** Angie Dickinson (Wilma McClatchie), William Shatner (William J. Baxter), Tom Skerritt (Fred Diller), Susan Sennett (Billy Jean), Robbie Lee (Polly), Noble Willingham (Uncle Barney), Dick Miller (Bonney), Tom Signorelli (Dodds), Joan Prather (Jane Kinston), Royal Dano (Reverend Johnson), William O'Connell (crusade preacher), John Wheeler (lawyer), Sally Kirkland (Barney's customer). **Crew:** Steve Carver (director), William Norton and Frances Doel (screenwriters), Roger Corman (producer), David Grisman (composer), Bruce Logan (cinematographer), Tina Hirsch (editor), Peter Jamison (art director), Coke Willis (set decorator), Jac McAnelly (costume designer), Ray Forman and Edith Lindon (hair stylists), Alan Fama and Harry Maret (makeup artists), Richard Franchot and Teri Schwartz (assistant directors), Robert Gravenor (sound).

Plot Synopsis: A dirt-poor East Texas widow in 1932, Wilma McClatchie is struggling to provide for her sexually adventurous teenage daughters Billy Jean and Polly. Reluctantly, she accompanies Polly to the country church where she intends to marry an equally destitute farm boy. Unable to contain her disapproval, Wilma disrupts the ceremony and hustles Polly away before the vows are completed. Wilma's bootlegger boyfriend Barney barricades the groom's family inside the church and provides an escape car for her and the girls. Later, with Wilma behind the wheel, two federal agents who have been looking for Barney give chase. Pretending not to understand, Wilma forces their car off the road but not before one of the feds shoots and kills Barney.

To make some much needed money, Wilma takes over Barney's business. When Polly gets caught making a delivery, Wilma has to pay off a corrupt sheriff with all of their earnings. Moving on, they arrive in a small town that is hosting a July 4th veterans' reunion. Unbeknownst to Wilma, the girls get a job as strippers at one of the receptions. In the middle of their awkward act, Wilma barges in and robs all of the veterans at gunpoint. "We ain't ever gonna be poor again," affirms Wilma in a vow that will be repeated throughout the film.

The bootleg-chasing feds, named Bonney and Dodds, follow up on the robbery and begin a comically inept pursuit of Wilma. They find her broken-down car, but Wilma and the girls give them the slip by mingling with a busload of weird Christian crusaders. Pretending to help, the phony preacher fails in an attempt to steal their veterans' money and suffers the theft of his own car in return. Eluding both the feds and the crusaders, Wilma and her daughters splurge on new clothes and a night at a fancy hotel.

Resolved to make it to California, Wilma tries to earn more money by cashing a fake check. While she is negotiating with a bank teller, Fred Diller and an accomplice enter the building and pull a hold-up. In the melee that follows, the accomplice is shot by a guard as Wilma, Billy Jean, and Polly grab money bags from behind the counter and flee. Thinking fast, Diller jumps on the running board of their car and they all escape together. That evening Wilma and Diller become lovers as well as partners.

In celebration, they attend a horse race, where Wilma meets a well-dressed, refined grifter named William J. Baxter, who gives her a couple of winning tips. Excited by the easy money, Wilma decides to rob the betting office as well, enlisting Baxter, Diller, and the girls in the effort. There is another machine-gunning car chase ending in another close getaway. Baxter becomes Wilma's new bedmate while Billy Jean and then Polly seduce Diller.

Arriving in California, the gang simmers with tension. Diller is jealous of Baxter, and Polly announces that she is pregnant. True to her rule of never pulling the same job twice, Wilma engineers the successful robbery of an oil refinery. Afterwards, she and Diller argue and nearly separate. Despite the conflicts, everyone comes together for an even more inspired Wilma scheme. Disguised as invitees and servants, they crash a high society party and rob all of the rich guests. While mingling with the crowd, Wilma meets a lawyer who unintentionally gives her the idea for one last job that will make them all "set for life."

They kidnap an heiress and hold her for a million dollar ransom. Diller nearly allows the snobbish young woman to escape and Baxter bails from a lack of nerve, but Wilma and Diller reconcile, spending one last night together. The money is delivered the following day; Bonney and Dodds, however, have been tipped off by Baxter and arrive with a huge force of police officers. As a gun battle rages, Diller shoots Baxter and stays behind to give Wilma and the girls cover enough to escape by car. "We ain't ever gonna be poor again," says Wilma once again, and with blood streaming down her arm she slumps against Polly and dies.

Notes and Comments: Any film that is billed as an action-crime-sexploitation comedy has a tricky road to navigate. One wrong turn and the whole thing becomes a sick joke. That *Big Bad Mama* succeeds so adroitly is due in large part to Angie's fearlessly inventive performance. On screen for most of the film's eighty plus minutes of running time, she plays Wilma as a cross between mother hen and femme fatale.

We first see her ushering her sassy daughters into the family jalopy. "I try to teach you girls manners," she tells Polly, "and look at you sittin' there with your underpants showin' and holdin' a damn doll." When Billy Jean boasts that she is going to marry a rich old husband and wait for him to die, Angie snaps, "Keep your legs together, Billy Jean, and shut up. I'll tell you when to get married." The comic timing is masterful, the dialogue delivered with the same rapid-fire precision as the machine gun bursts that come later. When Barney leers over the wedding night gift Polly is about to receive, Wilma/Angie replies, "That's more than you're going to get." In shaping Wilma's character, Angie could have opted for some of the menace she had successfully evoked in previous roles (compare *Cry Terror!* and *The Killers*) but goes with sarcasm and determination instead. She moves deliberately through space, never hesitant or tentative, giving Wilma a sense of control rather than cruelty.

Like the screen's most gifted physical comediennes, she also uses her body to get laughs. At somewhere around 5 feet, 5 inches and 115 pounds, she moves with the agility of an athlete. Some of the film's best moments are watching her struggle with a prohibitionist over a bottle of hooch, stand in the back seat of a moving convertible and fire a machine gun, sprint into getaway cars, or roll around on a hotel bed with her daughters.

ANGIE

The cast of *Big Bad Mama* includes, from left, William Shatner, Angie, Susan Sennett, Tom Skerritt, and Robbie Lee (1974).

Then, of course, there are also the legendary nude scenes. Unlike *Dressed to Kill* and *Big Bad Mama II* later in her career, Angie uses no body doubles here but does all of the undressing herself, twice with Tom Skerritt and once with William Shatner. Shadows and discreet camera angles partially obscure the lovemaking, but her second bedroom scene with Skerritt features full frontal nudity. Simply put, Angie looks stunning.

Fabled filmmaker Roger Corman produced with his usual penchant for economy and speed. The picture hurtles along from one exciting set piece to another. Director Steve Carver handles the action skillfully, keeping the violence more cartoon-like than visceral. He even throws in some nods to Arthur Penn's *Bonnie and Clyde* (1967), for example the lively bluegrass music to accompany the car chases and the crosscutting between close-ups of Wilma and Diller during the fatal climax. Budgeted at less than one million dollars, *Big Bad Mama* more than tripled its investment at the box office.

Reviews:

"Dickinson's energy almost saves the day. It's a delight to watch her open, accessible and witty performance. She may well be the most sensuous woman in American film, and only the male-dominated movies of the Sixties prevented her from becoming the superstar she promised to be in Howard Hawk's *Rio Bravo*."

"Visually, *Big Bad Mama* has the handsome precision one associates with the resources of major studios and comfortable budgets. The art direction of Peter Jamison not only brings the depression stunningly to life but also transforms entire streets into bright, vividly colorful comic fantasies."

"Jac McAnelly's costumes are both flattering to the performers and historically sophisticated. Bruce Logan's photography is nothing less than a tour de force, given the time restrictions of low-budget production."

—Alan R. Howard, *The Hollywood Reporter*, July 2, 1974

"Miss Dickinson plays with enthusiasm the mother of two teenage daughters who yearns so strongly to escape back-roads poverty that she recently develops a violent career of crime with sexual sidelights. Miss Dickinson and Tom Skerritt, as her partner in crime, have the best defined roles and do right by them, while Shatner's niche as the Kentucky conman is less distinct."

—*Boxoffice*, August 19, 1974

"The plotline is flimsy at best, opening circa 1932 with Angie Dickinson posturing as a hard-bitten mother, rum runner, bank robber, jewel thief, kidnapper and queen bee in the sack. Both Corman and director Steve Carver make a feeble attempt at social import of having Mama and true-blue lover Tom Skerritt martyr themselves so that the children may live and spend their ill-got gains."

—*Daily Variety*, August 27, 1974

"Carver plays William Norton's and Frances Doel's serviceable script very broadly, yet the film retains an unobtrusive underlying level of social protest. Spirited and sexy, Miss Dickinson gives a vivid, sympathetic performance as a woman motivated by mother love above all else, but who is not averse to having some fun for herself."

—Kevin Thomas, *Los Angeles Times*, October 16, 1974

"But with mother love in her favor—she's just after the best for her two teenage daughters—Ms. Dickinson develops an unexpectedly sympathetic and raucous performance."

—Ray Loynd, *Los Angeles Herald-Examiner*, October 19, 1974

L'homme en colère

Credits: A Cinévidéo, France 3 Cinémas, Les Films Ariane production released on March 14, 1979. Eastmancolor. Running time of 97 minutes. **Cast:** Lino Ventura (Romain Dupré), Angie Dickinson (Karen), Laurent Malet (Julien Dupré), Hollis McLaren (Nancy), Donald Pleasence (Albert Rumpelmayer), Lisa Pelikan (Anne), Chris Wiggins (MacKenzie), R.H. Thomson (Borke), Peter Hicks (Lentini), Olivier Guespin (young Julien). **Crew:** Claude Pinoteau (director, screenwriter), Jean-Claude Carrière and Charles Israel (screenwriters), Joseph Beaubien and David Patterson (executive producers), Claude Bolling (composer), Jean Boffety (cinematographer), Marie-Josèphe Yoyotte (editor), Earl Preston (production designer), Blanche-Danielle Boileau (costume designer), Joan

Isaacson (makeup artist), Richard Lightstone, Harald Maury, Alex Pront, and Claude Villand (sound).

Plot Synopsis: After a border patrol helicopter passes overhead, a man dressed in a suit and carrying a valise emerges from the woods outside of Montreal and follows a young man who is there to meet him. Obscured by darkness and heavy undergrowth, the young man shoots the stranger, steals the valise, and flees in a blue Jeep station wagon driven by a third shadowy figure. On the trip back into Montreal, they are pulled over by two cops for an irregular license. As he exits the car, the passenger shoots the younger cop dead and is himself killed by the cop's partner. The driver of the blue Jeep slams into some stopped cars and makes a successful escape.

Romain Dupré, a former Air France pilot, appears in Montreal to identify his dead son, the shooter from the woods. Inspecting the body in the coroner's locker, he turns to the officials and says, "Ce nèst pas mon fils" ("This is not my son"). Apparently, the dead man was using his son Julien's passport and identity.

That evening, back at his hotel, Dupré recalls via flashback the defining tragedy of his family life. Many years earlier, Julien and his mother were trapped by a forest fire. As they attempted to escape, their vehicle overturned, pinning the mother before exploding into flames. Dupré arrived too late and was able to save only Julien. As the boy grew older, he and his father drifted apart, his mother's piano lessons replaced by Dupré's boxing instruction. Looking out over the Montreal skyline, he decides to search for Julien himself.

The next day Inspector MacKenzie shows him the retrieved blue Jeep and suggests that Julien himself was involved in criminal activity. On his own, he searches through the boxing gyms where he guesses Julien may have earned some money as a sparring partner. In one of them, a young black fighter gives him a lead which takes him to a pregnant friend of Julien's and a video arcade operator he also knew. After a brief fight, the arcade operator reluctantly explains that Julien ran afoul of the mob and had his hands broken. The girl mentions that he used to work at a nightclub called The Musical.

Although he gets admitted to the private club, the bartender and bouncer refuse to give him any information about Julien. The owner and his goons also deny knowing anything and kick him out of the place. Waiting outside, Dupré follows the boss but is ambushed, roughed up, and thrown into a car whose parking brake is released and sent crashing down a steep city street.

Back at police headquarters, MacKenzie gives him some history of the mob's involvement in dealing drugs and smuggling immigrants. Their conversation is interrupted by the loud complaints of Karen, the woman whose car was used in Dupré's assault. She and Dupré leave headquarters at the same time and are forced by a rainstorm onto the same bus. Still angry about her car, she refuses to speak to him, but he follows her into a cheap, crowded restaurant anyway. When he sees that she is a waitress there, he tries to keep a low profile, but she gets rattled, spills a tray of food, and ends up quitting her job. Outside, he asks if she is hungry and takes her to a cafeteria. Over lunch, she tells him a convoluted story about travel and study; he says only that he is looking for his son. During the cab ride home, she admits that she really has been in a women's correctional institute for the last two years. They part on friendly terms.

Waiting for him at the hotel is Albert Rumpelmayer, who returns some of Julien's unclaimed dry cleaning and mentions a girlfriend named Anne. Tracing her to a volleyball club and then to a hockey stadium, he finds her working as a food vendor during the game. She ultimately tells him how to get in touch with Julien, but before he can follow up, Rumpelmayer confronts him again, offering to act as a go-between for the return of the valise and then setting him up for another ambush. Although he flees into an abandoned power plant and overpowers two of his attackers, he is badly beaten by the rest of the gang.

With nowhere else to turn, he telephones Karen, and she not only tends to his injuries but also hides him in a motel on the edge of town. Together, they arrange to meet Julien but their first attempt is interrupted by the cop following Dupré. After speaking again with MacKenzie and buying time, Dupré finally reunites with Julien outside of a theatre. Via flashback, Julien admits that he was the driver of the Jeep and that he intends to cross the border into the states with the valise full of mob money. His father begs him to turn himself in, but he ignores the advice.

Meanwhile, Anne has been severely beaten up by mob thugs and is hospitalized. Both Dupré and Karen visit her on their way to a rail station where she puts him on a train to Magog, Quebec. Before parting Karen says, "I bet you're not the kind of man who kisses a woman on a train platform," and, shaking his head no, he holds her by the back of the head and kisses her passionately. On her way out of the station, she is first strong-armed by a mob lieutenant and then rescued by the cops assigned by MacKenzie to follow her.

In Magog, Dupré drives off in a van with Julien. Their ensuing argument results in a physical fight that ends with Julien walking away into the woods. As a mob gunman wounds Dupré, police officers close in and arrest the entire gang. Hearing the gunfire, Julien returns to help his father and turn himself in. Updated on the news, MacKenzie steps outside his office and tells a waiting Karen that Dupré will be all right.

Notes and Comments: The film works the way a detective story works. Although he is a former pilot and not a gumshoe, Dupré proceeds from one clue to the next as he ultimately tracks down his missing son. He is like Robert Mitchum as Philip Marlowe in *Farewell, My Lovely* on the hunt for Moose Malloy's girlfriend. Physically, he also resembles the Mitchum of that picture or the aged, jowly DeNiro of *Heist* (2015). Adjusting his oversized glasses and shrinking into his trench coat, he has the look of a man who has faced one too many disappointments.

Along with its themes of entrapment, double cross, isolation, and betrayal, *L'homme en colère* also has the visual style of a classic film noir. The wet nocturnal streets, the mirrored reflections, and the shabby urban settings enhance the sense of gloom and confusion. Dupré's trek through the city's boxing gyms and bars is a journey made by countless antiheros before him. Symbolic and universal, the mise-en-scène is also distinctly Canadian. Shot entirely on location, the film functions at times as quirky travelogue for Montreal, giving glimpses of Rue St. Denis, a Canadians hockey game, urban parks, and cityscape vistas. Famous French Canadian professional wrestler Édouard Carpentier even appears in a brief cameo as the bouncer at a nightclub.

Angie's character, the tough but vulnerable woman accidentally plunged into danger, is also familiar. She appears thirty-five minutes into the film, provides brief company for Dupré, and then seems to vanish. When she re-emerges later on, she becomes his major ally, tending to his wounds and helping to arrange the meetings with Julien. She risks a great deal by assisting him but does it because of his decency and her own moral compass. Cinematic counterparts include Lauren Bacall in *Dark Passage* (1947), Gloria Grahame in *The Big Heat* (1953), and more recently Faye Dunaway in *Three Days of the Condor* (1975).

Her performance as Karen hits all the right notes. She is hard-edged yet sympathetic, a woman who has been in prison but has not surrendered her humanity. When she is futilely questioning the police about her damaged car or arguing with the restaurant manager over being late, she gives us a beleaguered victim plagued by bad luck but then during lunch with Dupré she blossoms into a warm, affectionate survivor in control of her options. Always effective when playing against strong, laconic men, Angie matches Ventura's silent intensity with her own ability to listen closely and act decisively. Even in the French version, where her dialogue is dubbed, she commands attention. Whether in an off-the-rack black raincoat or a waitress uniform, she needs only her fabulous blond hair and smile to look beautiful. Having surfaced as the film's emotional anchor, she is wisely given its final ambiguously optimistic close-up.

Director Pinoteau keeps things moving at a quick pace. Exposition and dialogue are alternated with the pursuits and confrontations. Generally dark in tone, there are occasional moments of dry humor. In one scene, Dupré looks over at the ham and potato dinner a fellow restaurant guest is eating, and the man wordlessly shakes his head in discouragement.

Barely noticed upon release in the United States, the film did much better in France, where Pinoteau and Ventura were highly regarded for their previous work together in *Le Silencieux* (1973) and *La Gifle* (1974). It remains noteworthy for containing one of Angie's best, though least well-known, performances.

Reviews:

"Claude Pinoteau's *L'homme en colère* is a competent but conventional psychological thriller with the kind of story and craftsmanship that shows up fairly frequently on TV these days."

"Script is neatly constructed but, wholly predictable. One

knows reels in advance that Ventura is going to bloody and be bloodied and one suspects (rightfully) that the stubborn father and equally stubborn son will try to resolve the impasse of their relationship with blows."

"Still, film is moderately interesting with some fine taut moments and scenes. And, of course, there is Lino Ventura, who in action or immobility is an always fascinating camera subject. He is ably supported by Angie Dickinson, Laurent Malet as the son and Donald Pleasence in one of his typically unpleasant roles."

—*Weekly Variety*, April 11, 1979

"*L'homme en colère* is a harsh and hectic crime thriller but one with a beating heart. Though it refers to American crime dramas of the early 70s, it also evokes French policiers and Italian poliziotteschi of the time, due in part to the film being set in Montreal and its distinctive international milieu. Only French jazz composer Claude Bolling's mawkish score and the film's fabricated ending bring it down a level."

"It's the '70s and there's no way around it. There is also no way around Angie Dickinson in *L'homme en colère*, who at age 48 is as beautiful and as sexual a presence as ever."

—Gary Deane, noirworthwatching.blogspot.com, posted November 24, 2017

Klondike Fever

Credits: A CFI Investments production released on January 12, 1980. Color. Running time of 119 minutes. Based on a novel by Jack London. **Cast:** Jeff East (Jack London), Rod Steiger (Soapy Smith), Angie Dickinson (Belinda McNair), Lorne Greene (Sam Steele), Barry Morse (John Thornton), Gordon Pinsent (Swiftwater

Bill), Robin Gammell (Merritt Sloper), Lisa Langlois (Diamond Tooth Gertie), Michael Hogan (Will Ryan), Sharon Lewis (Louise), John Curtis (Ed Burns), Bill Mankuma (Hopkins), Buck (the dog). **Crew:** Peter Carter (director), R.J. Dryer and Martin Lager (screenwriters), Gilbert W. Taylor (producer), Hagood Hardy (composer), Albert J. Dunk (cinematographer), Stan Cole (editor), Seamus Flannery (production designer), Kimberley Richardson (set decorator), David McLeod (assistant director), Andy Malcolm, Larry Sutton, and Don White (sound).

Plot Synopsis: In August of 1897, future author Jack London and his partner Merritt Sloper disembark from a paddle wheeler in Skagway, Alaska, on their way to the Klondike Gold Fields. Almost immediately Jack gets in trouble when he saves a dog named Buck from a brutal beating by villainous Will Ryan, chief enforcer for Soapy Smith, a former priest turned lawless gang boss who runs the town. After friendly dog trainer and outfitter John Thornton tends to Buck's wounds, Jack approaches Smith and offers to buy the dog. Knowing the rash twenty-year-old man can't afford it, Smith sets the price at $500. Undaunted, Jack bets his stake money in a series of high card cuts with gambler Swiftwater Bill. He loses the first cut but recovers to eventually win enough to buy Buck. When Smith welshes and refuses to sell, Jack calls him a liar and leaves. In the street, he is attacked by Ryan and another of Smith's henchmen but fights off both of them. Thornton tells him of an alternate way out of Skagway and he and Sloper leave with Buck. Appearing unexpectedly, Swiftwater Bill asks to come along with them to ease Smith's control over him, but the two partners decline his request.

Making their way through Chulkoot Pass, Jack and Sloper come to the Canadian border, where they must be cleared to enter by the notoriously strict Inspector Sam Steele ("he kept Sittin' Bull sittin"). Despite Jack's confrontational attitude to what he sees as one more authoritarian cop, Steele, recognizes Jack's basic morality and allows him and Sloper to cross the border. Finally free of civilization, they travel through a pristine wilderness of blue skies, forests, and waterfalls before arriving at Lake Lindeman. As they begin to build a boat that will take them to Dawson, Ryan and his thugs once again stage an assault that the two partners and Buck overcome. "If you don't kill me, one day I'm gonna kill both of you," threatens Ryan before Jack sends him on his way. After much bickering, he and Sloper finish their sturdy wooden boat.

Arriving out of nowhere on a stagecoach, Swiftwater Bill shows up in the company of a beautiful madam named Belinda McNair and her two "daughters" Gertie and Louise. Anxious to get to Dawson City, Belinda offers to buy the boat, but even after both she and Gertie sleep with him, Jack refuses. Instead, Belinda pays Ryan to take her, the girls, and Swiftwater down the Yukon River on his own boat. Sometime later, Jack and Sloper find the three women stranded on the river's edge. Ryan, explains Belinda, cast them ashore after he got paid and Swiftwater set out to find help. Jack takes them on board, and he and Sloper steer the boat through some treacherous rapids. As they make camp that evening, Swiftwater materializes from out of nowhere to rejoin the group.

Upstream from Dawson, Jack and Sloper prepare to leave so that they can travel inland and prospect for gold. At the last minute, Sloper, frustrated by Jack's headstrong refusal to ever take advice, declares that he is breaking up the partnership and continuing on with the others. Surprised and chastised, Jack admits how much he needs his friend, and a grumbling Sloper changes his mind again. Swiftwater and the three women leave on the boat, and the reunited partners travel on foot to the gold fields.

Panning the water at Stewart Creek, Jack discovers gold, but bad weather forces him and Sloper inside for an extended period of time. Overcome by cabin fever, they begin a quarrel that soon escalates into a physical brawl. At the height of their fight, they are once again attacked by Ryan and his goons, who surround the cabin and pepper it with gunfire. John Thornton and his dog sled arrive unexpectedly to help defeat the intruders but not before Sloper is seriously wounded.

Jack and Thornton take him into Dawson City only to find that the doctor has died in an accidental fire. No one else, neither Belinda nor Swiftwater, who now are partners in the Eldorado Saloon, will even help to find a warm room for Sloper. Denied assistance, Sloper passes away in a cold hut on the edge of town, his death announced by Buck's mournful howling. On his way to inflict revenge on Ryan, Jack meets Inspector Steele, who listens sympathetically and reminds him of the law. "What about a town that is so cold and greedy and heartless that no one in it would lift a finger to save a man's life?" asks Jack. "There's no humanity, no pity, no love," he says. "Just the great blind law."

To make matters worse, Soapy Smith arrives in town and demands the return of his dog. Refusing to take payment, he proposes a sled dog race against Ryan; Jack keeps Buck and $2,000 if he wins and forfeits Buck and signs on to work for Smith if he loses. Thornton offers the use of his team, and Jack accepts.

On the morning of the race, Belinda apologizes for her behavior and wishes Jack well. As soon as the dog sleds are out of sight, Ryan begins to cheat, whipping Jack and taking the lead. While waiting in town near the finish line, Soapy also insists that Swiftwater clear his debt by playing high card cut with the saloon as part of the stakes. When Soapy tries to use his own deck of cards, Steele steps in to make sure a fresh deck is provided. Unable to intimidate Steele, Soapy welshes on the deal once again, agreeing instead to settle things through the race results.

As they near town, Ryan tries to push Jack from his sled. In the ensuing fight, Ryan is knocked down a cliff and killed. Jack and the dogs struggle across the finish line to win the race and all of the bets. Smith is kicked out of town by Steele, and Swiftwater and Belinda decide to get married.

In the final shot, Jack and Buck wonder off down the snowy streets on their journey back to San Francisco, where, according to a voice-over narration, Jack will begin to write the stories of his adventures.

Notes and Comments: Angie received second billing after Rod Steiger and figured prominently in the advertising posters. Her entrance into the film is a fanfared big event. A shuttered, well-appointed stagecoach appears, Swiftwater mentions the famous musical hall artist inside, and out steps Angie in a ruffled blue dress and fur-trimmed blue coat. Once introduced to the story, she becomes a dominant figure, appearing throughout the river sequences and most of the Dawson City action. To Jack, she is a consistently surprising combination of grace and greed.

Belinda McNair was a slightly different kind of character for Angie to play. She has a familiar duplicity about her but also an apologetic awareness of her shortcomings. Her performance exists in a sweet spot between drama and comedy. She can coldly evaluate how to manipulate somebody and then move on with a smile, a shrug, and a *mea culpa* when her plan collapses. Her seduction of the much younger Jack is thoroughly credible given the silky voice and the ageless beauty. Each time Belinda seems to have exited the picture she unexpectedly re-emerges to spice up the action all over again.

The way in which characters suddenly appear at narratively

convenient moments is one of the film's most glaring problems. Ryan is the major offender. He comes out of the shadows to assault Jack in Skagway, interferes with the boat building at Lake Lindeman, and most improbably of all, descends on the cabin at Stewart Creek to attack Jack and Sloper in the middle of their quarrel. That same scene also features the inexplicable appearance of John Thornton swooping in on a dog sled to drive away the villains. It is not at all clear what has motivated him to suddenly set out for the gold fields nor is it logical that Soapy Smith should decide to leave his Skagway fiefdom to reclaim a dog hundreds of miles away in Dawson City. Inspector Steele's own unexpected presence in Dawson City is equally mystifying.

Writers Charles Israel and Martin Lager have similar difficulty weaving together the various plot threads. There is a sense of several different movies competing for dominance: the buddy story of Jack and Sloper, the coming of age tale, the gold rush saga, the Belinda/Swiftwater romance, and the dog adventure borrowed from *The Call of the Wild*. Much is made in the introduction of London's socialism, a political angle that is then abandoned. Although the segments never coalesce, some of the individual set pieces are quite good. The arrival in Skagway, directed by Peter Carter as a dark, claustrophobic muddle, captures the chaos of a lawless frontier town. Extras pack the frame, a brawl bursts through a window into the mud-clogged street, a captive bear is forced to fight a man for entertainment, and another man is suddenly shot dead. Carter's handheld camera jostles along with Jack as he plows his way through the teeming crowd. Similarly well photographed are the whitewater rapids and the dog race sequences. Carter seamlessly matches long shots of the stunt doubles with close-ups of the lead actors to keep the action compelling and convincing.

The diverse cast is also good. As London, Jeff East summons up the brashness, naiveté, and moral outrage that characterize any likable young hero. Athletic and photogenic, he shifts easily between tough guy and lover. Robin Gammell invests muttering comic sidekick Sloper with dignity and purpose, and Barry Morse is reassuringly wise as the dog trainer who acknowledges young Jack's decency. Almost unrecognizable behind his moustache and accent, Ottawa-born Lorne Greene returns to his roots in the part of Inspector Green, a stalwart man of firm convictions and few words. Canadian actor/writer/director Gordon Pinsent takes what could have been a second-string heavy in Swiftwater Bill and makes him a surprisingly sympathetic character unable to consistently follow his own moral convictions. He and Angie play their romance like the courtship between two well-matched con artists of a Preston Sturges comedy. Appearing at the beginning and end of the picture as Soapy Smith, Rod Steiger exudes menace with his usual snarling intensity.

Klondike Fever was widely popular throughout Canada. It was nominated for nine Academy of Canadian Cinema and Television Genie Awards, including Best Picture, Director, Adapted Screenplay, Actor (Gammell), and Foreign Actor (Steiger). Pinsent won the Genie for Best Supporting Actor, the first of three such awards he would ultimately receive.

Reviews:

"Although he was known as a novelist, American writer Jack London was basically a yarn-spinner. Peter Carter's *Klondike Fever*, based on London's own exploits during the Klondike gold rush, tries hard to be story book cinema, but never succeeds in establishing the fascination that kept London's readers turning the pages as fast as they could."

"Angie Dickinson looks slightly silly playing one of those heart-of-gold saloon madams; Lorne Greene, almost unrecognizable in a black mustache, stands for Canada's idea of law and order and Barry Morse is a good-guy vet who takes kindly to London's reckless mistakes."

"The film is jerkily edited with some jarring transitions. Director Carter keeps losing track of the dog, leaving him out entirely in an unexciting scene in which London and company shoot some angry white-water rapids."

—*Weekly Variety*, February 13, 1980

Dressed to Kill

Credits: A Filmways Pictures/Cinema 77 Films production released on July 25, 1980. Technicolor. Running time of 104 minutes. **Cast:** Michael Caine (Doctor Robert Elliott), Angie Dickinson (Kate Miller), Nancy Allen (Liz Blake), Keith Gordon (Peter Miller), Dennis Franz (Detective Marino), David Margulies (Dr. Levy), Ken Baker (Warren Lockman), Susanna Clemm (Betty Luce), Brandon Maggart (Sam), Amalie Collier (cleaning woman), Mary Davenport (woman in restaurant), Anneka De Lorenzo (nurse), Norman Evans (Ted), Robbie L. McDermott (man in shower), Bill Randolph (chase cabbie), Fred Weber (Mike Miller), Samm-Art Williams (subway cop). **Crew:** Brian De Palma (director and screenwriter), George Litto (producer), Pino Donaggio (composer), Ralf Bode (cinematographer), Jerry Greenberg (editor), Gary Weist (art director), Gary Brink (set decorator), Gary Jones and Ann Roth (costume designers), Robert Grimaldi (hair stylist), Joseph Cranzano (makeup artist), Michael Rauch (assistant director), Dan Sable (sound).

Plot Synopsis: While taking a shower, Kate Miller, an attractive but sexually frustrated New York City housewife, fantasizes that a stranger is raping her as her husband Mike stands at the sink shaving. In reality, she and Mike share some mechanical, early morning sex that leaves her angry and unfulfilled. Disappointed that her teenage, science-whiz son is cancelling their museum visit and lunch, she kisses him goodbye and leaves for the day. During her therapy session with psychiatrist Dr. Robert Elliott, Kate discusses the resentment she feels toward Mike. Unsure of her own self-worth, she asks Elliott if he finds her sexually attractive. He says that he does but that professional ethics prevent him from acting on his desire.

Kate goes to the Metropolitan Museum of Art where she flirts with a handsome stranger wearing a black blazer and sunglasses. Pursuing each other through the various gallery rooms, they play a seductive game of cat-and-mouse. Outside on the steps, she approaches a taxi from which he is dangling a glove she dropped inside the museum. As she leans forward, he pulls her into the cab to begin a torrid sexual encounter that continues back at his apartment. When she wakens in his bed, it is already late in the evening. Hurrying to get dressed, she realizes she has left her panties in the cab. Then, after she writes a goodbye note, she discovers a notice from the health department informing her partner that he has contracted a venereal disease. Appalled, she rushes from the apartment only to remember she has forgotten to retrieve her wedding ring from the nightstand.

She rides back up in the elevator. When the doors open, a tall blond woman in a dark raincoat and sunglasses brandishes a straight razor. Unable to defend herself, Kate is violently slashed to death. A few floors below, call girl Liz Blake and a client wait for the elevator, and when it arrives they see what has happened. Although the client immediately flees, Liz catches a quick mirrored glimpse of the killers as she picks up the dropped razor. Consequently, she becomes a police suspect and the killer's next target.

Dr. Elliott listens to an answering machine message from Bobbi, a transsexual patient who is preparing for sex reassignment surgery. After berating Elliott for not supporting her wishes, she implicates herself in Kate's murder and threatens to kill the witness also. Summoned to police headquarters, Elliott meets with Detective Marino but neglects to mention anything about Bobbi. Skeptical of Liz's story, Marino gives her forty-eight hours to produce corroboration from her client or be arrested herself. Using a homemade listening device, Kate's son Peter eavesdrops on all of the police station conversations and resolves to catch the killer himself. His first step is to rig a time-lapse camera outside Elliott's office that will record all patients leaving the building.

Elsewhere in the city, Liz is being followed by a tall blonde in sunglasses. Thinking to have eluded her, she rushes onto a subway train and is pursued not only by Bobbi but also by a group of five African American thugs. Running through the cars, she ends up trapped and overpowered by the razor-wielding Bobbi. Just then, Peter, who has been trailing Bobbi from Elliott's office, appears on the scene to spray her with homemade mace and force her to flee at the next stop.

Liz and Peter join forces. Reviewing photos from Peter's camera, they come up with a plan to get inside Elliott's office in order to match the time of Bobbi's departure with a birth name and address in the appointment book. Meanwhile, Elliott has met with Bobbi's new therapist, Dr. Levy, to warn him of Bobbi's increasingly violent and unstable condition.

Pretending to be suffering from post-traumatic stress, Liz goes to see Elliott and flirts aggressively with him during the consultation. Stripped down to her sexy lingerie, she tells him to get comfortable and excuses herself long enough to flip through his appointment book. Watching outside in the rain with binoculars, Peter is suddenly pulled away by a tall blonde in a raincoat. Simultaneously, Bobbi appears in the office and comes at Liz with the razor. The blonde outside, who is actually an undercover policewoman, shoots Bobbi. As she collapses on the floor, Bobbi loses her wig, revealing herself to be Dr. Elliott.

At the police station, Dr. Levy explains that the male and female sides of Elliott's personality were at war with one another. Whenever a woman sexually attracted Robert, who resisted the sex change operation, murderously vindictive Bobbi would take over. As soon as he realized what was happening, Levy called Marino, who had the policewoman already trailing Liz step up surveillance.

Since his stepfather Mike is out of town, Peter invites Liz to spend a few days at his house. Escaping from the mental hospital where he has been confined, Elliott surprises Liz in the bathroom and slashes her throat. She wakes up screaming, comforted by Peter and realizing the assault was just a dream.

Notes and Comments: The ideological underpinnings of *Dressed to Kill*'s violence toward women certainly can be questioned, but what should not be disputed is the brilliance of Angie's performance.

Her Kate Miller is warm, touching, and ultimately tragic. She dominates the first part of the picture and then, like Janet Leigh in *Psycho* (1960), is brutally eliminated from the narrative. Her abrupt, almost incomprehensible, removal reverberates poignantly through the remainder of the film.

Much of her performance is silent, conveyed solely through expression and gesture. She makes extraordinarily expressive use of her eyes, whether in the masturbatory pleasure of the shower scene or the sudden fear of the elevator. The centerpiece, a triumph for both her and director De Palma, is the extended ten-minute Metropolitan Museum of Art sequence, which actually was shot inside the Philadelphia Museum of Art. A slightly elevated camera tracks in on Angie as she sits on a bench looking at a large red and yellow portrait of a woman. Dressed stylishly in a white dress and matching white coat, she also watches two couples and a young Asian family. Cross-cutting links her gaze with those of the portrait subject and a gorilla odalisque. Her expression is pensive yet unreadable. She makes notes in a date book, which are later revealed to be items for a grocery list. A handsome stranger sits next to her and she seems shocked. Nervously, she removes a glove to unintentionally reveal her wedding ring. When the stranger moves away, she looks offended. Dropping the glove, she follows after him as a fluid subjective tracking camera (a Panavision adaptation of the Steadicam) records her passage through the galleries. Having momentarily vanished, he reappears and follows her. Somewhat alarmed, she hurries away, with the camera now tracking along in front of her and the stranger looming behind. Just as she turns around with a decisive smile, he veers off again into a side gallery. Disappointed and back where she started, she lingers momentarily next to a sculpture until his hand, encased in the dropped glove, reaches into the frame to grasp her shoulder. The contact is too aggressive, however, and she retreats in annoyance verging on fear before realizing the stranger now has her glove. Her pursuit and the accompanying subjective tracking shots repeat themselves. He leads her through the museum and out onto the front steps, where the dangling glove lures her toward the open window of a taxi.

Up to this point, the entire sequence has been wordless, accompanied only by languorous instrumental music and the sound of

Angie's high heels clicking across the floor. She has expressed an entire range of emotions, from desire to regret, almost exclusively through her eyes. Approaching the cab, she barely utters, "I'm sorry. I shouldn't have been so rude. Thank you for picking up . . . ," before the stranger pulls her inside and silences her with a kiss. Nothing further is spoken between the two of them, neither in the cab nor the apartment. In fact, except for the brief conversations with Peter and Dr. Elliott, all of Angie's scenes are without dialogue.

Waking up late in the stranger's apartment, she is seized by escalating panic. After she hurriedly dresses, she calls home but hangs up at the sound of her husband's voice. When she inadvertently learns that she may have been exposed to a sexually transmitted disease, her look of alarm conveys the enormity of what this casual tryst has cost her. During the ride down and then back up in the elevator, as a little girl stares almost accusingly at her and she discovers that she has left her wedding ring behind, her eyes cloud up with tears. The hopelessness of her expression binds the audience to her more tightly than the subjective camera does.

It is that identification which makes the murder so devastating. Having invested so much emotional capital, we resist seeing narrative expectations ripped abruptly from under us. Killing off the second-billed star so early in the picture just doesn't seem possible, even after it has happened. The elevator slashing looks and feels a lot like the shower scene in *Psycho*. Lasting just over two minutes of screen time, it has the same rapidly edited montage, shrill music, and graphic violence. There are more than sixty separate pieces of film, medium shots of the characters intercut with close-ups of eyes, hands, and mouths. The razor flashes in the light before slicing across Kate's palm and neck. Blood splashes against the walls and streams down over her all-white wardrobe. As actor, Angie performs a wrenching pantomime of death—staring in wide-eyed terror, flailing at her attacker, slumping lifelessly to the floor while she reaches out to Liz. It is the kind of meticulously choreographed action that took days to block and to shoot.

Kate Miller (Angie) faces her assailant in *Dressed to Kill*'s bloody elevator scene (1980).

Professional gossip has claimed that De Palma first offered the part to Liv Ullmann, but it is hard to imagine anyone but Angie as Kate Miller. Projecting a vulnerability far removed from her *Police Woman* persona, she makes Kate an achingly sympathetic victim. The performance should have gained her an Academy Award for Best Supporting Actress, but the prize went instead to Mary Steenburgen for *Melvin and Howard* (1980). Angie's body double for the masturbatory shower scene is former *Penthouse* model Victoria Lynn Johnson; the unrated version of the film shows full frontal nudity, including pubic hair.

Ill-suited to the role of Elliott, Michael Caine makes for a disinterested doctor and an unconvincing transsexual. Despite Dr. Levy's psychobabble, the Robert/Bobbi concept never becomes more than a plot contrivance, a clumsy way of introducing the requisite slasher. Complicating the credibility issue is the fact that De Palma cheats viewers by substituting another actor for Caine during most if not all of the fleeting glimpses of Bobbi prior to the climax. As outspoken call girl Liz Blake, Nancy Allen effectively sells the menace of her many perilous situations. Her best scenes are with Keith Gordon as Kate's appealingly geeky son Peter. Dennis Franz's mouthy Detective Marino will become his mouthy Detective Sipowicz on *NYPD Blue* (1993-2005).

De Palma's stories and themes come largely from Alfred Hitchcock. As mentioned before, the elevator murder, narrative rupture, and transsexual killer are borrowed from *Psycho*. The art gallery pursuit is inspired by *Vertigo* (1958) while Kate's dropped glove and Liz's incriminating retrieval of the razor have their source in *North by Northwest* (1959). The spying on Elliott is a direct reference to *Rear Window* (1954). De Palma's visual style is also influenced by Hitchcock, especially the elevated camera and the sustained subjective tracking shots. Composer Pino Donaggio's alternately romantic and frenetic stringed music quotes directly from several of the scores that Bernard Herrmann wrote for Hitchcock. To this repertoire, De Palma adds his own innovative touches, such as the split-screen character linkages and the superimposed flashbacks. His command of technique is never in doubt.

More suspect are his politics. Tired of having her own pleasure considered an afterthought by her husband, Kate experiences sexual gratification with a stranger. Almost as a consequence of that expanded agency, she is immediately punished. Not only does she learn that she may have contracted a venereal disease, she is also viciously slashed to death while attempting, significantly enough, to recover her wedding ring. The violence is prolonged and excessive. Similarly, Liz's provocatively fetishized appearance in black lingerie provokes another grisly assault. By ascribing the attacks to Bobbi, De Palma suggests that transsexuality is some kind of pathological rather than biological condition. His phobia surfaces again as Liz squeamishly explains to Peter the details of male to female sex reassignment surgery. Also disturbing is the casual racism of having Liz sexually harassed in the subway by five young black men.

Dressed to Kill initiated a fierce critical debate between those who saw De Palma as a daring visual stylist and those who believed he was a derivative misogynist. Despite or perhaps because of the notoriety, *Dressed to Kill* became one of his greatest commercial successes, along with *Carrie* (1976), *Scarface* (1983), and *The Untouchables* (1987).

Reviews:
"Brian De Palma goes right for the audience jugular in *Dressed to Kill*, the director's latest stylish exercise in ersatz-Hitchcock suspense-terror. Despite some major structural weaknesses, the cannily manipulated combination of mystery, gore and kinky sex adds up to a slick commercial package that stands to draw some rich blood money."

—*Weekly Variety*, July 23, 1980

"Director Brian De Palma's growing reputation as the poor man's Alfred Hitchcock should receive a healthy boost with *Dressed to Kill*, a mystery adventure film that bears more than a passing resemblance to the Master's *Psycho*. Indeed, if only he had some of Hitch's urbane humor, De Palma might be ready to inherit his mantle today."

"*Dressed to Kill* (the title is wholly apropos) marks the first time that De Palma has worked with anything like a star cast, and he reveals an expert proficiency in drawing first-rate performances from all of them. Outstanding is Angie Dickinson's portrait of a libidinous suburban housewife, eagerly on the make for just about anything in pants. Her sudden, unanticipated demise after an afternoon's *dolce far niente* leaves a hole in the film for quite a while, so vivid and intense is her portrayal."

—Arthur Knight, *The Hollywood Reporter*, July 24, 1980

"*Dressed to Kill* is one succeeding spectacular effect after another. The fun is not in logic but watching how Mr. De Palma successfully tops himself as he goes along, and the fun lasts from the sexy, comic opening sequence right through to the film's several endings."

"The performers are excellent, especially Miss Dickinson whose drawn, taut beauty says as much about her character as anything she actually does. Mr. Caine, after the disaster *The Island*, is in top form, and Miss Allen and Mr. Gordon are most appealing as strictly 1980's versions of what used to be called the ingénue and the juvenile."

"Even the title is good."

—Vincent Canby, *The New York Times*, July 25, 1980

"Angie Dickinson is fabulous—touching and sexy—as a frustrated Manhattan housewife. The repression of Dickinson's character, Kate Miller, begins to settle on her like a brittle glaze, but the actress' own vibrancy shines through."

"As shot by De Palma and photographer Ralf Bode (who helps make the movie's virtuosity look easy), the museum sequence is a killer. They register every shift in Kate's changeable mood with camera moves as poetic as the paintings on the walls."

—Michael Sragow, *Los Angeles Herald-Examiner*, July 25, 1980

"The brilliance of *Dressed to Kill* is apparent within seconds of its opening gliding shot; it is a sustained work of terror—elegant, sensual, erotic, bloody, and a directorial tour de force."
—Sheila Benson, *Los Angeles Times*, July 25, 1980

"*Dressed to Kill* is such an inadequate film in genre terms that it would hardly be worth discussing but for the obviously personal implication of De Palma in the material. It's loaded with clever ideas, some of them quite good, but virtually all are undermined by an apparently insatiable desire to play sadistic jokes on his characters and on his audience."
—Myron Meisel, *Los Angeles Reader*, July 25, 1980

"De Palma's movies no longer explore these tensions; they have become exhibitions of a master puppeteer pulling high-tension strings. In *Dressed to Kill*, the marionettes on-screen still respond to De Palma's manipulations. Moviegoers may not, especially those who hoped that De Palma would become the heir to Hitchcock's throne rather than the scavenger of his vaults."
—Richard Corliss, *Time*, July 28, 1980

"*Dressed to Kill*, the new thriller directed by Brian De Palma, is the first great American movie of the eighties. Violent, erotic, and wickedly funny, *Dressed to Kill* is propelled forward by scenes so juicily sensational that they pass over into absurdity. De Palma releases terror in laughter: even at his most outrageous, Hitchcock could not have been as entertaining as this."

"Angie Dickinson is so sad and sweet in this movie! She has the symmetrical bone structure of a classic beauty—the kind of bone structure that implies breeding and control and dignity in old age. Yet Kate is a woman churning around inside and falling into rapt fantasies, and De Palma, with his teenager's dirty-mindedness and entertainer's instinct working in tandem, can't help seeing her tremulous longings as funny."

—David Denby, *New York*, July 28, 1980

"Brian De Palma's *Dressed to Kill* is the 13th feature film he has directed since his debut in 1968 with *Murder a la Mode*, but he still seems to be scrambling for a personal style that he can truly call his own. He seems at one and the same time vulnerable and manipulative, sentimental and cynical, overwrought and flippant. Even in terms of De Palma's muddled, almost schizophrenic oeuvre to date, however, *Dressed to Kill* is an unusually disconcerting experience."

—Andrew Sarris, *The Village Voice*, July 29, 1980

"Brian De Palma's *Dressed to Kill* contains many of the same ingredients found in a McDonald's hamburger: chopped meat (mostly Angie Dickinson's), sweet flavoring (primarily from Pino Donaggio's sugary score), and, of course, lots and lots of blood-red ketchup. To argue that such a concoction has its merits as filmic junk food is one thing; to confuse *Dressed to Kill* with cinematic *haute cuisine* is quite another."

"My own view is that women have every right to hate *Dressed to Kill* if they can take it seriously enough. In the course of a second viewing the film struck me as almost unbearably tedious and inept. The acting is B-picturish in its banality, and the dialogue is flat, crude, witless, and vulgar beyond belief."

"I do not hold it against De Palma that he imitates Hitchcock, but, rather, that he steals Hitchcock's most privileged moments

without performing the drudgery of building up to these moments as thoroughly earned climaxes."
—Andrew Sarris, *The Village Voice*, September 23, 1980

"*Dressed to Kill* is the most voluptuously crafted, formally dazzling movie to come out of Hollywood since *Apocalypse Now*, but unlike that flawed epic it's a tightly wrought, near-perfect mechanism."
—J. Hoberman, *The Village Voice*, July 29, 1980

"It is decadent filmmaking in full flower: a hothouse demonstration of style for style's sake. Yet as much as I enjoyed its cheap thrills and its exquisite craft, *Dressed to Kill* left me wanting something more from De Palma."
—*Newsweek*, August 4, 1980

"The apprehensive moods are stretched out voluptuously, satirically—De Palma primes you for what's going to happen and for a lot that doesn't happen. He sustains moods for so long that you feel emotionally encircled. He pulls you in and draws the wires taut or relaxes them; he practically controls your breathing."

"The desperation in Kate's sexual loneliness makes it possible for Angie Dickinson to show a much warmer expressive range than might be expected—you can read every nuance of desire, embarrassment, and trepidation on her face."

"De Palma's sense of humor makes him the least respectable of the front-rank American directors. He presents extreme fantasies and pulls the audience into them with such apparent ease that the pleasure of the suspense becomes aphrodisiacal."

"This picture is such a unified, confident piece of work that De

Palma can even make the image hazy and provide a stylized chorus of observers out of Bedlam—giving it away that something isn't really happening—and still you're terrified."

—Pauline Kael, *The New Yorker*, August 4, 1980

"De Palma is also very well served by his cast. Caine is appropriately icy yet controlled as the psychiatrist, Dickinson does her best work since *Point Blank*, and even the minor roles—Keith Gordon as Kate Miller's boy-genius son and Dennis Franz as a strident police detective—are just right. Best of all, however, is Nancy Allen as Liz Blake, a high-class call girl who gets involved in murder."

—Kenneth Turan, *New West*, August 11, 1980

"It is a well-made, occasionally brilliant, thoroughly terrifying whodunit. As they say in the trade, it works. It's also, to twist the razor blade about 180 degrees, an absolute mess, and in many ways a terrible embarrassment. How can *Dress to Kill* be in two mutually exclusive places at the same time? Actually, it's quite easy; all it takes is a completely irresponsible approach to filmmaking."

—*Los Angeles Magazine*, September, 1980

"But what *Dressed to Kill* most decidedly is *not* is sleazy. Rather, it is cool and gleaming, as polished, precise and sharply honed as a new straight razor. It represents the full sharpening of De Palma's skill and artistry as a filmmaker."

"But there is much more, not the least of which is Dickinson's performance throughout. She is stunning. Caine, too, is superb in a smaller but essential role; and Allen more than holds her own as the plucky, resilient survivor of Bobbi's brutal attacks."

—Douglas W. Edwards, *The Advocate*, September 4, 1980

Charlie Chan and the Curse of the Dragon Queen

Credits: An American Cinema Productions/Jerry Sherlock Productions picture released on February 13, 1981. Color. Running time of 95 minutes. **Cast:** Peter Ustinov (Charlie Chan), Lee Grant (Mrs. Lupowitz), Angie Dickinson (Dragon Queen), Richard Hatch (Lee Chan, Jr.), Brian Keith (Police Chief), Roddy McDowall (Gillespie), Rachel Roberts (Mrs. Dangers), Michelle Pfeiffer (Cordelia), Paul Ryan (Masten), Johnny Sekka (Stefan), Bennett Ohta (Hawaiian police chief). **Crew:** Clive Donner (director), Stan Burns and David Axelrod (screenwriters), Jerry Sherlock (producer), Patrick Williams (composer), Paul Lohmann (cinematographer), Walter Hannemann and Phil Tucker (editors), Sam Jones and Anne McCulley (set decorators), Jocelyn Rickards (costume designer), Mary Keats and Joy Zapata (hair stylists), Charles Schram and Fred Williams (makeup artists), Richard Luke Rothschild (assistant director), Bruce Bisenz (sound).

Plot Synopsis: In an opening flashback to a past case set in Hawaii, master detective Charlie Chan interrogates a group of people regarding the death of rich industrialist Bernie Lupowitz. Prominent among the suspects is a mysterious woman known only as the Dragon Queen.

Back in present day San Francisco, Chan's grandson and wannabe sleuth Lee begins another gaffe-prone day at the estate of his maternal grandmother Sylvia Lupowitz, Bernie's widow. Assisting both of them is a household staff comprised of paranoid housekeeper Mrs. Dangers, wheelchair-bound butler Gillespie, and African prince cum chauffeur Stefan. On the way to his office, Lee startles the horse of his fiancée Cordelia and causes a chain of water-related accidents in Chinatown.

ANGIE

Accompanied by the San Francisco Chief of Police, Lee greets his grandfather Charlie, who has been summoned to the city to investigate a series of bizarre killings that include one man baked with a potato on his chest in a sauna and another pierced to death at an acupuncture salon. As the older Chan lands in a helicopter, Lee gets tangled in electronic cables and pulls all of the reporters into the bay. Later, at a downtown hotel, Chan meets Cordelia and is reunited with Sylvia and her staff. Cordelia asks how Chan solved the murder of Sylvia's husband, and another flashback reveals him explaining a poisoned cup of tea and faked suicide engineered by the Dragon Queen. As she is taken into custody, she puts a three-generation curse on Chan.

The Dragon Queen, who has been listening to all this in the present, walks through the hotel lobby and disappears. Soon afterwards an elevator opens, disgorging a flood of water and several drowned occupants. Another killing almost occurs when Sylvia is attacked in her home and nearly strangled with a knotted purple scarf.

Lee receives a note saying the next murder will occur in Golden Gate Park. He, Cordelia, and Chan arrive and are attacked by the Dragon Queen brandishing a blow dart. A long, chaotic chase involving horse-drawn carriages and police cars ensues before the Dragon Queen escapes along the beach.

While preparing the next day for his wedding, Lee gets a phone call from the Dragon Queen claiming that his grandfather is being held captive at a theater in Chinatown. When he and Cordelia, dressed in their wedding clothes, arrive, they are chloroformed and taken hostage. Learning of the trick, Chan, Sylvia, and the entire staff follow behind. With everyone gathered at the theater, the Dragon Queen points a revolver at Chan, but Lee tackles her before she can fire.

The police chief arrests her, but Chan announces she is not

responsible for Bernie's death or the recent bizarre killings. She has only been trying to enact her curse and get revenge for Chan's faulty accusation. The real murderer is Sylvia, also seeking retribution for Charlie having exposed her husband's infidelity and making her a social outcast. Her plan was to ruin Charlie's career and reputation by plotting murders he could never solve.

Sylvia tries to escape through the theater, which is showing a Charlie Chan film starring Peter Ustinov, but is ultimately apprehended. Back at the mansion Lee and Cordelia are married. Driving away on their honeymoon, they are followed by the police chief's car taking Sylvia to jail.

In one of her least well-chosen parts, Angie plays the title villain in *Charlie Chan and the Curse of the Dragon Queen* (1981).

Notes and Comments: The real mystery here is how so many talented people got involved with such a terrible movie. Everyone is miscast beginning, most egregiously, with Peter Ustinov as the

Chinese detective. His eyes are cosmetically altered, and his speech is stereotypically sing-song. He drops inscrutable epigrams like so many precious pearls. Earl Derr Biggers's fictional character was never a model of ethnic correctness, but by continuing the Hollywood practice of white actors playing Chan in "yellow face," Ustinov is never able to elevate his portrayal beyond anachronistic embarrassment.

Since he is only half Chinese, Richard Hatch's Lee is spared a similar fate. He gets away with just a Bruce Lee haircut and bumbling boyishness. Clearly no Peter Sellers, he awkwardly navigates the Clouseau-like pratfalls. The rest of the cast is stuck repeating the same single note. Lee Grant's shrillness, Roddy McDowall's haughtiness, Rachel Roberts's confusion, and Michelle Pfeiffer's cluelessness never shift into anything unexpected or nuanced.

It is not clear what Angie's identity is supposed to be. Outfitted in elaborate headwear, elongated nails, and flowing silk gowns, she suggests a touch of the Far East but stays clear of any obvious eye work or accent. Glimpsed fleetingly throughout the film, she never remains on screen long enough for a full deconstruction of her appearance. Her gesturality is more studied than usual; she continually flourishes ornamental cigarette holders and drags her nails across the scenery during exits. However, as usual with her comic roles, she avoids full-on caricature. There's always some core of authenticity. Even when she snarls, "Chan, I curse you. I curse you and your descendants to the third generation," the approach is more indignation than it is camp.

Director Clive Donner never seems able to sustain an appropriately comic tone or pace. When all else fails, he plunges the cast into one of those frantic group chases so popular in such 1960s British comedies as *The Wrong Box* (1966) and Donner's own *What's*

New Pussycat? (1965). The dash through Golden Gate Park, accompanied by the overture from Louis Herold's 1831 opera *Zampa*, gives Angie a nice opportunity through editing and stunt doubles to appear to be handling the reins of a speeding horse carriage, but the whole sequence ultimately runs out of gas before reaching a suitable payoff.

The funniest moment in the film is also one of the quietest. After introducing a young Chinese neighbor as a girl scout, Lee exits his office to discuss a case with her. Through the frosted glass of his door, we see her physically abusing him for failing to retrieve the cat she has hired him to find. When he re-enters, Cordelia casts a glance at his disheveled clothes and quips, "Darling, I think you should have bought the cookies."

Reviews:
"Unfortunately the efforts of the director and his cast can't hide the fact that *Charlie Chan and the Curse of the Dragon Queen* has no real plot. Writers Stan Burns and David Axelrod have whipped up a situation involving Lee Grant (in a surprisingly forced performance) as a rich widow menaced by a sinister mass-murderess, the Dragon Queen (an equally uncomfortable Angie Dickinson). There's the potential for a mystery spoof somewhere in all this, but when the action stops dead for a lengthy comic chase scene through San Francisco's Golden Gate Park, you know the filmmakers haven't been able to find it."
—David Ehrenstein, *Los Angeles Herald-Examiner*, February 13, 1981

Angie takes the reigns of a horse-drawn getaway carriage in *Charlie Chan and the Curse of the Dragon Queen* (1981).

"It's a movie that is utterly devoid of charm, style or humor. All that it has going for it is a minor galaxy of hard-working stars—Ustinov, Lee Grant, Angie Dickinson, Brian Keith, Roddy McDowall, and Rachel Roberts—who strive like fiends to extract some comedy from a pedestrian screenplay by Stan Burns and David Axelrod. Producer-writer Jerry Sherlock has provided an awful lot of plot, but it's singularly lacking in fun."

—Arthur Knight, *The Hollywood Reporter*, February 13, 1981

"Not helping matters is that *Charlie Chan and the Curse of the Dragon Queen* (selected theaters) is thoroughly dreary, the familiar instance of a group of proven talents struggling to wring laughs from hopelessly unfunny and uninspired material. As is usually the case, the more they struggle the grimmer the film becomes."
—Kevin Thomas, *Los Angeles Times*, February 14, 1981

"A perfect mixture of screwball comedy, mystery, slapstick and camp parody, Clive Donner's *Charlie Chan* is a fine example of how to recycle a half-forgotten film genre."
—Karen Kreps, *Boxoffice*, April, 1981

Death Hunt

Credits: A Golden Harvest production released on May 21, 1981. Color. Running time of 97 minutes. **Cast:** Charles Bronson (Albert Johnson), Lee Marvin (Millen), Andrew Stevens (Alvin), Carl Weathers (Sundog), Ed Lauter (Hazel), Scott Hylands (the pilot), Angie Dickinson (Vanessa McBride), Henry Beckman (Bill Luce), William Sanderson (Ned Warren), Jon Cedar (Hawkins), James O'Connell (Hurley), Len Lesser (Lewis), Richard Davalos (Beeler), Maury Chaykin (Clarence), August Schellenberg (Deak De Bleargue). **Crew:** Peter Hunt (director), Michael Grais and Mark Victor (screenwriters), Murray Shostak (producer), Jerrold Immel (composer), James Devis (cinematographer), John F. Burnett and Allan Jacobs (editors), Ted Haworth (production designer), Bob Benton (set decorator), Olga Dimitrov (costume designer), Paul LeBlanc (hairstylist), Bill Morgan (makeup artist), Frank Ernst (assistant director), Ray Alba (sound).

Plot Synopsis: It is the Yukon Territory of 1931. A solitary American trapper named Albert Johnson observes a dog fight and forcibly rescues a white German shepherd injured in the spectacle. He pays $200 to its owner Hazel, a mean-spirited bully who also makes a living by trapping. Insisting that the dog was stolen, Hazel complains to Sergeant Edgar Millen, commander of the local Royal Canadian Mounted Police bureau. Aware of Hazel's vices, Millen refuses to act and returns to the outpost, where he helps Vanessa McBride process some business related to the recent death of her husband. Along with young constable Alvin Adams and veteran tracker Sundog Brown, Millen and Vanessa spend the evening getting drunk, before also going to bed together.

Still resentful, Hazel and some associates descend on Johnson's isolated cabin and open up with gunfire. After the dog is shot, Johnson fatally wounds one of the attackers, a thug named Jimmy Tom. Hazel rushes back to the Mounties, interrupting Millen's romance and demanding that something be done about Tom's death. Reluctantly, Millen says good-bye to Vanessa and agrees to investigate.

Because it is learned that Johnson has bought a sizable cache of ammunition with large bills, some of the locals also assume that he is the "mad trapper," a much feared bogeyman who murders trappers and extracts their gold teeth. A strange old trapper named Bill Luce warns Johnson that the authorities are coming for him and he barricades his cabin.

With the help of Adams and Brown, Millen leads a group of Mounties and trappers to the property. Despite Millen's respect for Johnson and belief that the matter can be easily cleared up, things turn deadly when one of the trappers starts shooting. Several men, including a Mountie, are killed and Johnson narrowly escapes the dynamiting of his cabin. In the public frenzy that follows, newspapers run front page stories on the case and the government places a $1,000 bounty on Johnson's life.

Millen, Adams, and Brown set off into the frigid wilderness to search for Johnson. They are followed by Hazel and his tracking dogs, assorted civilians attracted by the bounty, and a Royal Canadian Air Force pilot named Hank Tucker, who has been dispatched by jittery national officials. A former member of a special United States Army intelligence unit during World War I, Johnson deftly eludes his pursuers. Millen begins to feel a stronger bond to Johnson than to the annoying outsiders.

On his own, Luce encounters two trappers camping in the snow, shoots them dead, and pulls out their teeth, thus revealing himself as the mad trapper. Due to superior technology, the searchers finally overtake Johnson. Tucker strafes the ground with his plane's machine gun, killing Brown. In anger, Millen and Adams shoot down the aircraft with their rifles; it crashes into a canyon wall, killing Tucker. In a final confrontation, Johnson kills Hazel and escapes once again.

Driven by the reward money, Luce finds Johnson but is tricked and captured. When Millen sights Johnson in the distance, he fires a bullet that strikes the fugitive in his head. Examining the body, Adams and Millen realize it is actually Luce, who had been forced to change clothes with Johnson. Realizing that everything Johnson did was in self-defense, they allow him to escape into Alaska.

When the rest of the posse arrives, Adams tells them that Millen has killed Johnson. A trapper finds gold teeth in the pocket of the dead man whose face has been all but obliterated and everyone hails the demise of the mad trapper.

Notes and Comments: Angie's sudden appearance in the film and equally quick departure would become an increasingly familiar pattern in several of her later projects. She is the less-than-grieving widow who takes up with Millen. As they become intimate during a night of social drinking, she rides a raft of somewhat conflicting emotions. First, she is the indifferent wife who announces that "it wasn't until now that I fully realized how little I cared for the man, that I will not miss him." Then, under the influence of too much whiskey, she responds dim-wittedly as Sundog Brown explains how being African American kept him out of major league baseball. Finally, after they sleep together, she becomes a needy lover, asking Millen "didn't it mean anything?" and "would it make any difference if I waited?" It is a curious portrayal that never fully congeals into a realistic characterization. What is much more credible is the undeniable chemistry between Angie and Lee Marvin. In their third film together, they make an extended slow dance as sexy a bit of foreplay as ever performed in public.

The lovemaking provides a brief interlude in what is otherwise an all-male action picture. After the contentious departure of Robert Aldrich over budget issues, Peter Hunt was the perfect choice to direct the enterprise. Involved in the first five James Bond films as editor and second unit director, he scored his first solo directing credit with *On Her Majesty's Secret Service* (1969), which despite the absence of Sean Connery contains some of the best action sequences in the early days of the 007 franchise. Noteworthy in *Death Hunt* are the aerial photography, the handheld camera chase scenes, and the expert orchestration of actors and animals in challenging outdoor situations.

The movie was shot entirely on location in Banff, Canada (the reason why Angie accepted her limited part), and based very loosely on the real-life Mountie manhunt for a trapper named Albert Johnson. Its original title was *Arctic Rampage*.

Reviews:

"Beware of any film like *Death Hunt* that claims to be based on real-life and stars Charles Bronson and Lee Marvin, since real-life isn't grand enough for either one of them, much less together. But exaggeration should be appealing to action fans."

"While, they're out chasing around in the snow, Angie Dickinson waits back in the warmth of Mountie headquarters, hoping for a few more brief scenes bedded with Marvin."

—*Daily Variety*, April 15, 1981

"I liked the grudging admiration that develops between hunter and hunted, and director Peter Hunt's skilled use of forbidding terrain to underscore the deadliness of their encounter. Snow-clad forests, swift-running streams, sheer precipices add their own menace to the pursued and his pursuers."

"The supporting roles are also well cast, although Angie Dickinson, listed as a costar, has little more than a walk-on as Marvin's lady for a night. More substantial are Carl Weathers as Marvin's good buddy and companion in arms . . . and of course, Lauter's single-minded, spite-ridden gambler, the driving force behind the action."

—*The Hollywood Reporter*, April 17, 1981

"Mr. Bronson and Mr. Marvin are such old hands at this sort of movie that each can create a character with ease, out of thin, cold air. Everyone else acts up a storm, especially Ed Lauter, the principal villain, the transparency of whose lies goes unnoticed by Sergeant Millen, a decent man if not a very bright one. Early in the movie Angie Dickinson shows up at the remote Mountie headquarters looking not like a character within the movie but more like an actress whose agent plays nasty practical jokes."

—Vincent Canby, *The New York Times*, May 22, 1981

"Angie Dickinson is on hand for love interest purposes as a far from bereaved widow who takes up with Marvin until he has to take after Bronson. Dickinson's role is a bald, obtrusive contrivance that doesn't belong in the film, yet it's fun to see her and Marvin together again for the first time since *Point Blank*."

—Kevin Thomas, *Los Angeles Times*, May 25, 1981

Big Bad Mama II

Credits: A New Horizons production released in October, 1987. Color. Running time of 82 minutes. Based on characters created by William Norton and Francis Doel. **Cast:** Angie Dickinson (Wilma McClatchie), Robert Culp (Daryl Pearson), Danielle Brisebois (Billie Jean McClatchie), Julie McCullough (Polly McClatchie), Jeff Yagher (Jordan Crawford), Bruce Glover (Morgan Crawford), Ebbe Roe Smith (Lucas Stroud), Jacque Lynn Colton (Alma), Charles Cyphers (Stark), Nick LaTour (Doc Robey), John Dresden (Aaron McClatchie), Frank Schuller (Sheriff). **Crew:** Jim Wynorski (director and writer), R.J. Robertson (writer), Roger Corman (producer), Chuck Cirino (composer), Robert C. New (cinematographer), Noah Blough and Nancy Nuttall (editors), Billie Greenbaum (art director), Archie D'Amico (set decorator), Vicki Graef (costume designer), Mike Snyder (assistant director), Chat Gunter and Lee Milliner (sound).

Plot Synopsis: Aaron McClatchie, his wife Wilma, and their two teen daughters Billie Jean and Polly are tending to chores around their Texas farm. Banker and land baron Morgan Crawford and his hand-picked sheriff Lucas Stroud arrive with some deputies to enforce a foreclosure notice. In an ensuing gun fight initiated by the lawmen, Aaron is killed and Stroud tosses the notice on his dead body. "Come on Mrs. McClatchie, gather up your girls," he says. "It's over." Staring directly at the camera, Wilma replies, "You're wrong sheriff. It ain't over at all."

Abandoning their homestead, Wilma and the girls set out for revenge. Under the cover of a striking miners' demonstration, they rob one of Crawford's banks. As she brandishes her machine gun, Billie Jean announces, "Mr. Thompson here would love ya all to raise your arms." Observing the getaway, reporter Daryl Pearson believes the women will provide a good story and follows them out of town. "I just saw next year's Pulitzer rob a bank," he tells his editor. Caught two days later spying on the girls while they skinny dip in a river, Pearson tells Wilma he only wants to report on their exploits but she forces him to strip off all his clothes and stay behind, not, however, before giving him an encouraging wink. To make the girls appreciate what they now have, Wilma detours through a Great Depression Hoovertown.

Their next target is a fancy fundraising event for Crawford's gubernatorial campaign. Before Stroud can stop them, they rob the guests, shoot up the banquet room, and kidnap Crawford's son Jordan. Pearson is present and his subsequent news story helps to build Wilma's popular reputation as a modern day Robin Hood. To ruin Crawford's election chances, Wilma includes Jordan in an armored car robbery. Since he and Polly have fallen for each other, Jordan seems willing to disgrace the father he doesn't like much anyway. Pearson appears again to convince Wilma that she needs his stories to keep the public on her side. Impressed with his brashness, she allows Pearson to accompany the clan to the Jackson County Fair where they disrupt a Crawford campaign rally and he gets a picture of Jordan holding up a ticket vendor. In the rapid-fire montage that follows, they rob more banks, crash more cars, and gun down more cops.

Pearson takes everyone to his friend Alma's bawdy house to hide out and celebrate. He and Wilma spend a night together before the place is raided. During the escape, Wilma is wounded and recovers under the care of a black doctor who lives in one of the Texas Hoovertowns. In gratitude, she gives him a big cache of stolen jewelry, and Pearson pledges to document the lives of people pushed into poverty by the Depression. Billie Jean, who has been chafing under mama's authority, decides to strike out on her own.

The rest of the group travels back to Wilma's old farm, where she visits her husband's grave and says goodbye. During a trip into town for supplies, Polly is captured by the police. Stroud comes out to see Wilma and offers to exchange Polly for Jordan. In the meantime, Crawford schemes to kill the McClatchies after the trade and Pearson goes on the radio to cover the story. With everyone gathered at the farm house, Polly and Jordan are sent walking toward each other. Realizing how much he loves her, Jordan tries to pull Polly to safety but is shot in the leg by his father. In return, Wilma kills Crawford, sparking a pitched gun fight between both sides. At the height of the battle, Billie Jean comes riding in on a truck and blasting away with her Thompson machine gun. Bringing along dynamite, she joins her family and explains that she heard about their situation on the radio. As Stroud lobs a Molotov cocktail into the house, Wilma shoots him dead and the three women apparently die in the huge explosion that follows.

In a final scene, Jordan tells Pearson about the house's rock-solid cyclone cellar, built to withstand any calamity. Printed postscripts update the characters' biographies. Jordan marries Polly and is elected Senator; Pearson wins an Emmy for a documentary about the homeless; Billie Jean buys the largest casino in Las Vegas. Wilma and her great granddaughter "Willie" Crawford are seen speeding down the highway in a red convertible pursued by a police car. "How am I doing, gran?" the blond girl asks. "Just fine, darling," answers Wilma, giving a thumbs up and winking at the camera.

Notes and Comments: This was Jim Wynorski's fourth film as writer-director. Like the McClatchies, he would have a robust career, going on to make over 75 low-budget features that included erotic thrillers, as well as horror, action, creature, parody, and family pictures.

The violence of *Big Bad Mama II* is more comic book than graphic. Wilma and her girls rack up a huge body count, but the killings are usually pictured quickly in long shot. There are blood squibs for some splatter effects, but the images never include maimed or disfigured close-ups. The sex scenes are similarly restrained. More is suggested than shown. While Julie McCullough bares her breasts with Danielle Brisebois for the skinny dip and again when she ties Jeff Yagher to the bed, the steamier aspects of that bondage scene are left to the imagination. Similarly, Angie appears in a bubble bath and in bed with Robert Culp, but we see only her exposed shoulders. The body doubled flashes of skin during the lovemaking are dimly lit and softly focused.

From start to finish, Angie anchors the picture. She is its *raison d'être*, embodying the title and dominating the screen time. Aware that it's all a joke, she is almost never without a grin, a chuckle, or a smile. Realizing as well that the mother-daughter relationships give the film its emotional core, she plays Wilma as a comically solicitous matriarch constantly trying to teach the girls how to get along in the world. "Polly is the dearest thing in my life," she realistically admits, "but she ain't too terribly bright." Watching Billie Jean clumsily shoot up a bank, she takes the Thompson and models proper technique for her. "Honey," she says, "you still don't have the hang of it yet." The iconic shots of Angie in an evening gown with that machine gun as accessory would be copied over twenty years later by Dame Helen Mirren in *RED* (2010). The scenes with previous co-star Culp are equally droll, enlivened by low-key banter between two seasoned professionals who have been to the country fair many times before.

Operating on a budget of less than $1.5 million, Wynorski shows what can be done with imagination and creative flair. Setting his story in a parallel time frame with the original, he includes editing devices from the 30s, historical references, and allusions to other movies (at one point Wilma threatens to put a bullet through Pearson's brain and quoting *Casablanca's* Captain Renault, he replies, "That's my least vulnerable spot.") The West Texas towns may be obvious sets from the Paramount Ranch outside Los Angeles, but the lightly subversive spirit is authentic.

Reviews:

"When not straining for idiotic 'socially redeeming values' in having Dickinson show solidarity with striking miners and Hoovertown denizens, pic is one long rehash with endless machinegun fire, exploding squibs and period car chases."

"Its main thrust is to provide some skin for those successors to the drive-in: homevid and paycable."

"The Peter Principle has former Corman publicist and writer for *Castle of Frankenstein* magazine Jim Wynorski directing this mess, which falls into the 'no retake' school of cinema. Actors' readings suffer accordingly and sense of rip off is underscored by Chick

Cirino's music which draws heavily (and without credit) upon the work of Ennio Morricone, particularly his *The Good, the Bad and the Ugly* score. Idiotic ending features Dickinson in a white wig in 1987 with great-granddaughter Willie (played by Kelli Maroney) to carry on the family tradition."

—*Weekly Variety*, October 21, 1987

"*Big Bad Mama II* (citywide) ranks as one of the strangest sequels ever to crash through a roadblock."

"While other tales of America's lawless 30s have played the action with a wry smile, *Big Bad Mama II* is the first genuine moral fairy tale of the genre. Robin Hood would play like a clinical document next to this film."

"Director and co-writer Jim Wynorski is an apt purveyor for this chock-a-block entertainment. Although apparently strapped with a minuscule budget, he has thrown caution to the wind and piled on as much action and humor as possible to misdirect our attention from the implausible, improbable and illogical that permeates every page of his script."

"*Big Bad Mama II* is a campy romp and a spirited, cheap exercise for ambitious talents. One's memory may be fading but it feels like the *Mama II* film makers have created twice the fun with only half the resources of the original at their disposal."

—*Los Angeles Times*, February 13, 1988

"Fourteen years after Roger Corman produced *Big Bad Mama's* first adventure, he's back with a better sequel, once again featuring Angie Dickinson and two teen daughters as gun-toting cop-slaying outlaws who manage to get rich and righteous at the same time. As actioners go, this one works, if you don't think about it, and don't bother."

"Characters could all be cartoons, and script unfolds like it was made up in a hurry, but it's fast and silly enough to hold interest."

"Filmmaker's best trick is the twisting of morality to suit film's purposes—even though mama and the girls have blown away enough cops to man a precinct, they're described as 'courageous women fighting for their lives' by newscaster Culp in the final shootout."

—*Daily Variety*, February 17, 1988

"Appropriately, in this unpretentious, tongue-in-cheek ditty, the players marvelously keep straight faces throughout, especially Robert Culp who plays an easygoing muckraker who works for the *Philadelphia Eagle*, as opposed to, say, the *Philadelphia 76-er*."

"While no one ever accused Roger Corman of making socially conscious films, he has exceeded himself on a production level in this latest opus."

—Duane Byrge, *The Hollywood Reporter*, February 19, 1988

"But with the fuzzy B-film stock, dreadful cinematography, awful costumes and all, *Big Bad Mama II* doesn't pretend to be one whit more than tongue-in-cheek tackiness. Robert Culp's in here too, by the way, as a devilishly charming newspaper reporter, and he's held up well."

—*L.A. Weekly*, February 19, 1988

Featured Player

Even Cowgirls Get the Blues

Credits: A Fourth Vision production screened at the Toronto International Film Festival on September 13, 1993, and released on May 20, 1994. Color. Running time of 95 minutes. Based on a novel by Tom Robbins. **Cast:** Uma Thurman (Sissy Hankshaw), Lorraine Bracco (Delores Del Ruby), Pat Morita (The Chink), Angie Dickinson (Miss Adrian), Keanu Reeves (Julian Gitche), John Hurt (The Countess), Rain Phoenix (Bonanza Jellybean), Ed Begley Jr. (Rupert), Carol Kane (Carla), Sean Young (Marie Barth), Crispin Glover (Howard Barth), Roseanne Barr (Madame Zoe), Buck Henry (Dr. Dreyfus), Grace Zabriskie (Mrs. Hankshaw), Treva Jeffryes (Young Sissy). **Crew:** Gus Van Sant (director and screenwriter), Laurie Parker (producer), Ben Mink and k.d.lang (composers), John Campbell and Eric Alan Edwards (cinematographers), Curtiss Clayton (editor, with Van Sant), Dan Self (art director), Nina Bradford (set decorator), Beatrix Aruna Pasztor (costume designer), Anne Morgan (hair stylist), Gina Monaci (makeup artist), Phillip Christon (assistant director), Kelley Baker (sound).

Plot Summary: Sissy Hankshaw is born with enormously elongated thumbs and uses that physical oddity to become a master hitchhiker. Stopping in New York City on one of her many cross-country treks, she meets the Countess, an outrageously effeminate entrepreneur who makes her the spokesperson/model for his line of feminine hygiene products. He also plays matchmaker, introducing her to Julian Gitche, a wealthy, asthmatic Mohawk Indian and his clique of artsy New York sophisticates. Soon tiring of Manhattan, she decides to go back out on the road, but the Countess convinces her instead to film a commercial at his Rubber Rose Ranch for some new deodorant sprays.

Located in Oregon, the ranch is a women's beauty spa managed by elegant Miss Adrian and staffed by a group of rebellious cowgirls. Two of the most vocal dissidents are Delores Del Ruby, a peyote-using visionary, and Bonanza Jellybean, a gunslinger with a longtime crush on Sissy. As part of her orientation, Sissy learns that the ranch is losing clients to Elizabeth Arden's spa and that the property is also home to a flock of endangered whooping cranes. Almost immediately, she and Bonanza begin a sexual relationship.

One day, while Sissy is filming the commercial dressed as a giant crane herself, the cowgirls revolt, stripping down to expose their unwashed genitalia and chasing off the guests. Torn between her loyalty to the Countess and her friendship with the cowgirls, Sissy takes refuge in the mountains with a religious mystic known as the Chink. A believer in the philosophy of "Ha, ha, ho, ho, hee, hee," he has surrounded himself with rocks bearing hand-painted self-help messages. Before she hitchhikes away, he and Sissy sleep together.

Back east again, she reunites with the Countess, but they almost immediately begin to argue. He slaps her, and her return blow is so strong that it knocks out his false teeth and leaves him unconscious. Fearing the Countess has died, she leaves quickly and ends up in Virginia, where she convinces her childhood doctor to surgically shorten one of her thumbs, a decision she soon regrets when she see how it lessens her ability to hitchhike.

Meanwhile, the cowgirls are in a stand-off with federal authorities over the whooping cranes. Having been fed a diet of brown rice, worms, and peyote, the birds are content to stay on the ranch whereas the feds want them to resume their migratory patterns. Bonanza gives a televised speech in which she declares the cranes will be better cared for by the cowgirls than by the patriarchal forces who endangered them in the first place. Once she hears the speech, Sissy hitchhikes back to the ranch and restarts her affair with Bonanza.

Inspired by one of Delores's visions, the cowgirls decide to release the cranes, but when Bonanza approaches the heavily armed state troopers with the news, she is shot and killed by a nervous young cop. The Chink is also wounded in the gun battle which follows and which prompts the flock to take off into the sky.

Mostly recovered from his head wound, the Countess deeds the ranch to the cowgirls. After a memorial service for Bonanza, Sissy burns her love letters and rides into the hills, leaving us to wonder if she will stay at the ranch as leader or take to the road once again.

Notes and Comments: As Miss Adrian, Angie struggles to keep the cowgirls in line and to protect the status of the Rubber Rose Ranch. She commands four scenes a third of the way into the film and then disappears. In a suitably dramatic entrance, she pulls up next to Sissy in a chauffeured Lincoln Continental and tells the startled hitchhiker that she's been expected. Showing Sissy around the property, she bemoans the loss of clients to Elizabeth Arden and refers to the girls as "those crazy bitches." Ignoring the looming threat of rebellion, she dresses chicly, sips cocktails, and dances cumbia with the Countess right up until the moment she is lassoed and apparently deposed.

Gus Van Sant's biographer James Robert Parish has written that Angie "seemed bewildered by the chaotic plotline and seemed awkward on-screen."[13] On the contrary, she knew exactly what she was doing. While John Hurt overplayed, Uma Thurman underplayed, and the cowgirls seemed to recite political text, she gave a controlled, straightforward performance. Whatever humor the script contained, she knew it would need to flow from how the characters responded to their absurd circumstances. She was funny because she acted unaware that the world was falling apart around her. "Miss Adrian is kind of oblivious to her own inadequacies," she told a reporter. "The world is changing, and she just goes along her merry way and doesn't notice anything. I found that very endearing."[14] Such insight turned what would have been a villain into a weirdly sympathetic victim.

Director Van Sant himself was less certain of an own overall vision for the picture. Unable to mold the episodic vignettes and multiple characters into anything resembling a unified whole, he remained content to let the k.d. lang soundtrack, the trippy scenes, the celebrity cast, and the quirky cameos (authors William Burroughs and Ken Kesey, Edward James Olmos, River Phoenix) speak for themselves. In the end it was like a New Age Stanley Kramer picture, filled with lots of guest stars and uneven set pieces. Neither critics nor audiences cared much for the result, and the film (dedicated to River Phoenix, who had died a few months before its ultimate release) lost money.

Reviews:
"Missing from *Cowgirls* is the poetry of yearning and desperation running through Van Sant's *My Own Private Idaho*. Pic stays on the surface without attempting any exploration of painful depths. Result is at best amusing; at worst, uninvolving, often confusing and sometimes a little boring."

—Deborah Young, *Weekly Variety*, September 20, 1993

"This miscasting in the major roles is particularly disappointing because the supporting cast is so devilishly good. In addition to terrific performances from Dickinson and Hurt, Roseanne Arnold, Crispin Glover, and Sean Young turn in great cameos, as do Buck Henry and Ed Begley, Jr."

—Cathy Thompson-Georges, *Entertainment Today*, May 20, 1994

"One of the many problems with Gus Van Sant's tortured, worked-over *Even Cowgirls Get the Blues* is that Sissy Hankshaw talks like a novel, and a dated one at that."

—Caryn James, *The New York Times*, May 20, 1994

"The eclectic casting doesn't help much either. Thurman is appealing as Hankshaw, with an innocence contrasting nicely with the lurid caricatures around her. But Hurt, Lorraine Bracco, and Pat Morita are simply freakish as her various influences. The cameos supplied by the likes of Keanu Reeves and Sean Young are fun but completely inconsequential. The actors just remain adrift in symbols and bizarre imagery, attempting to interpret roles with no basis at all in reality. Even viewers get the blues."

—Tom Crow, *Los Angeles Village View*, May 20-26, 1994

"Only Angie Dickinson seems absolutely right as Miss Adrian, the pre-feminist beauty-ranch manager appalled by the unladylike habits of her rowdy ranch hands."

"The sole bright spot in the movie is the dreamily countrified musical score written and performed by Canadian cowgirl k.d. lang. The soundtrack outshines the movie, and there are blues to be sung all around."

—Russell Smith, *Dallas Morning News*, May 22, 1994

Sabrina

Credits: A Paramount Pictures production released on December 15, 1995. Color. Running time of 127 minutes. Based on a play by Samuel Taylor and a screenplay by Taylor, Billy Wilder, and Ernest Lehman. **Cast:** Harrison Ford (Linus Larrabee), Julia Ormond

(Sabrina Fairchild), Greg Kinnear (David Larrabee), Nancy Marchand (Maude Larrabee), John Wood (Fairchild), Richard Crenna (Patrick Tyson), Angie Dickinson (Ingrid Tyson), Lauren Holly (Elizabeth Tyson), Dana Ivey (Mack), Meriam Colon (Rosa), Elizabeth Franz (Joanna), Fanny Ardant (Irene), Paul Giamatti (Scott), Patrick Bruel (Louis). **Crew:** Sydney Pollack (director), Barbara Benedek and David Rayfiel (screenwriters), Lindsay Doran and Ronald Schwary (executive producers), John Williams (composer), Giuseppe Rotunno (cinematographer), Fredric Steinkamp (editor), John Kasarda (art director), George DeTitta, Jr. and Amy Marshall (set decorators), Gary Jones and Ann Roth (costume designers), Stephen Bishop (hair stylist), Bernadette Mazur (makeup artist), Tom Reilly (assistant director).

Plot Synopsis: Chauffeur's daughter Sabrina Fairchild has spent her life watching the glamourous activities of the Larrabee family. Matriarch Maude Larrabee and older son Linus run the powerful family business and younger son David enjoys life as a carefree playboy. Sabrina, in her baggy clothes and owlish glasses, has a major crush on David and secretly tracks his every move. On the night before she is to leave for Paris on a coming-of-age trip, she sneaks into David's room and confesses her love only to discover that she mistakenly has been talking to Linus instead.

In Paris, she gets a job at *Vogue* and gradually becomes a beautiful, stylish, and cultured woman of the world. Magazine photographer Louis becomes romantically interested in her and teaches her about fashion photography as well. Meanwhile, back in New York, David has become engaged to Elizabeth Tyson, an attractive young doctor and daughter of electronics mogul Patrick Tyson. Both Maude and Linus are pleased with the idea of a billion dollar merger between the two family companies.

Returning home to see her father, Sabrina learns about the wedding and feels more attracted to David than ever. Although he fails at first to recognize her, David soon becomes smitten and falls in love. At his engagement party, they dance closely together, much to the chagrin of the Tysons and Larrabees. Linus tells Mr. Tyson that the two are like brother and sister, and the skeptical father of the bride-to-be responds, "I have a sister. That isn't how we dance."

David arranges a rendezvous with Sabrina for later that evening, but Linus tricks him into sitting on champagne glasses and suffering a delicate injury that takes him out of action. To stop the budding romance and save the meager, Linus first unsuccessfully offers Sabrina two million dollars if she will return to Paris and then convinces her to visit Martha's Vineyard with him under the pretense of photographing a summer "cottage" that the Larrabees want to sell. During that trip and a subsequent night on the town in New York, Linus, despite having been described as "the world's only living heart donor," begins to fall in love with Sabrina himself. Surprisingly, she returns the affection.

Still motivated by business, he devises a plan to take Sabrina to Paris and force David back into the marriage. Rebuked by his mother and ashamed of his treachery, Linus confesses to Sabrina, who decides to return alone to Paris. Her father reveals that he has steadily made over two million dollars investing in stock tips from the late Mr. Larrabee and that she can use that money for anything she wants. When David learns of Linus's deception, he confronts his older brother and punches him in the face. Repentant, Linus says he doesn't care about the merger and gives David a ticket for Paris.

The next day, during a meeting between the Tysons and Larrabees, David surprises everyone with his hitherto unknown knowledge of the two family businesses and his sincere intention to marry Elizabeth.

He convinces Linus to find his own happiness with Sabrina. Taking the Concorde, Linus arrives in Paris before Sabrina and greets her with his declaration of love. They reconcile and embrace.

Notes and Comments: It is not immediately obvious why anyone in 1995 would greenlight this project, why any Paramount executive would feel a compelling need to remake Billy Wilder's less than classic *Sabrina* (1954). In a year where *Toy Story*, *Batman Forever*, and *Ace Ventura: When Nature Calls* were among the five highest grossing films, the idea that an old-fashioned, dialogue laden romance was going to draw large audiences was a stretch at best.

Even with Humphry Bogart, William Holden, and Audrey Hepburn, the original relied more on the real-life affair between Holden and Hepburn and the off-beat casting of Bogie than on its narrative to generate audience interest. Cinderella meets Prince Charming's materialistic older brother was always going to be a plot in need of actors adept at the difficult art of light comedy, performers who could breathe life into stock characters. Despite their best efforts, Harrison Ford, Greg Kinnear, and Julia Ormond are not those actors. Minus Indiana Jones's fedora and Hans Solo's uniform, Ford seems lost, capturing Linus's hardness but not his vulnerability. In his film debut, Kinnear gives us little evidence of what Sabrina finds so charming in this dull and spoiled man-child. As the chauffeur's daughter, Julia Ormond is much too cerebral to be a convincingly impressionable gamine. Nancy Marchand is the outspoken Larrabee matriarch, a part she handles with ease.

Angie appears in four brief scenes, each time in the company of Richard Crenna. As the Tysons, they look on disapprovingly while David becomes increasingly infatuated with Sabrina. They mostly interact with Linus and/or his mother, discussing wedding and merger details. A seasoned television and film veteran like Angie,

Crenna has her same ability to quickly establish character with a withering glance and a lowered tone of voice. They are credible as nouveau riche parents looking out for their daughter's best interests.

Former co-stars Richard Crenna and Angie reunite to play the in-laws in *Sabrina* (1995).

Angie's scenes pass quickly although the rest of the film drags. It is at least a half hour too long. Director Sydney Pollack, whose uneven career includes both the fast-paced *Three Days of the Condor* (1975) and the plodding *Bobby Deerfield* (1977), lets things meander here. Despite the misfire, the production values and behind-the-camera talent are impressive. John Williams provided the music, and frequent Fellini collaborator Giuseppe Rotunno did the cinematography.

Ultimately, the film never addresses some of its most basic premises: inherited versus earned wealth, economic disparity, class prejudice, and male privilege. More importantly, it never persuades us to care about any of these people, neither the self-absorbed rich nor the interchangeable working stiffs foolish enough to admire them. By the end of the picture, the underserving billionaire brothers have landed both their business deal and their future brides, a resolution that we in the audience are supposed to find satisfying. The closest we get to an entertaining character is probably Angie's Ingrid Tyson, the former flight attendant who longs for her less-uptight glory days. "I'll bet I could still get your seat in the upright position," she tells Linus. Indeed she could.

Reviews:
"Richard Crenna, as the earthy head of Tyson Industries, and Angie Dickinson as his nouveau-riche, looker wife are well cast."
—Duane Byrge, *The Hollywood Reporter*, December 11, 1995

"This is a genuinely funny romantic comedy, one which never feels forced or frantic but relies on razor-sharp dialogue and all-too-recognizable characters to make its mark. Nor does it stint on old-fashioned romanticism, which it plays completely straight and pulls off splendidly."
—Cathy Thompson-Georges, *Entertainment Today*, December 15, 1995

"Mr. Pollack's new film runs straight up against a snobbish and dated story, Billy Wilder's status as a national treasure and Audrey Hepburn's heart-stopping way of purring the word 'Paris' with music in her voice."

"Mr. Pollack's film runs into these obstacles so hard, in fact, that it runs right over them without difficulty. His *Sabrina* succeeds as a breezy, lighthearted throwback, made without benefit of the Hepburn magic but with much else in its favor. Blossoming into radiant color, this film has picture-postcard charms that the black-and-white earlier version could only hint at. It has also been improved by a newly sharpened sense of humor."
—Janet Maslin, *The New York Times*, December 15, 1995

"If you've been pining for faithful remakes, you're going to love Sydney Pollack's *Sabrina*: it's every bit as dull as the original."

"In struggling to make something better than a generic romantic comedy, Pollack has made something worse. *Sabrina* doesn't have nearly enough light or air."
—Jeff Giles, *Newsweek*, December 18, 1995

"Watching *Sabrina* is like leafing through the perfumed pages of a house, garden, and celebrity mag while under sedation."
—J. Hoberman, *The Village Voice*, December 19, 1995

"Richard Crenna is suitably tough and Angie Dickinson projects engaging optimism as the prospective Larrabee in-laws."
—Abbie Bernstein, *Drama-Logue*, January 4-10, 1996

"I am really sick of people going easy on this dud remake, which was based on the argument that the 1954 Billy Wilder original wasn't that good anyway. Rent the video and wake up."
—Peter Travers, *Rolling Stone*, January 25, 1996

The Maddening

Credits: A Thinkfactory Media production released on September 8, 1995. Color. Running time of 93 minutes. Based on a novel by Andrew Neiderman. **Cast:** Burt Reynolds (Roy Scudder), Angie Dickinson (Georgina Scudder), Mia Sara (Cassie Osborne), Brain Wimmer (David Osborne), Josh Mostel (Chicky Ross), William Hickey (Daddy), Kayla Buglewicz (Samantha Osborne), Candace Hutson (Jill Scudder), Angela Bomford (Mrs. Plummer), Darrell Fetty (Truman), Rett Wedding (Conrad), Bobby Amor (Jake), Marie Debrey (Joanne). **Crew:** Danny Huston (director), Leslie Greif (screenwriter and producer), Henry Slesar (screenwriter), Peter Manning Robinson (composer), Nick McLean (cinematographer), Eric L. Beason and Roberto Silvi (editors), Bobby Amor (production designer), Mike Daniel (set decorator), Howard Sussman (costume designer), Lynda Kyle Walker (hair stylist), Brain McManus (makeup artist), Randy Carter (assistant director), Elmo Weber (sound).

Plot Synopsis: After an argument over her husband David's frequent business trips, Cassie Osborne takes the couple's young daughter Samantha to visit her sister Joanne in Tampa, Florida. They stop at a rundown gas station where Roy Scudder, the owner, tells her about a shortcut and also secretly sabotages the water pump. When her vintage red Thunderbird breaks down, Roy appears and tows them to his isolated house in the woods.

Upon arrival, they are greeted by Roy's unbalanced wife Georgina, who mistakes the Osbornes for Marlena and Donna, the widowed sister and niece she hasn't seen in a while. Almost immediately, Georgina introduces her own daughter Jill and sends the two girls upstairs to play. Hearing a cry, Cassie follows after and is locked into a boarded-up room by Georgina.

The Scudders make plans to hold mother and daughter captive

indefinitely. Roy destroys Cassie's phone and begins to dismantle the Thunderbird. Convinced that Marlena has actually returned, Georgina gives Cassie long baths and talks about the death of her chronically-ill, brain-damaged infant son Arthur, implying ominously that Roy was somehow responsible for the tragedy. Short-tempered Jill bullies little Samantha and leads her around with a rope.

Panicked over Cassie's no-show, Joanne reports her as missing to the police. A cop named Chicky Ross interviews David, who leaves immediately for his sister-in-law's house. He and Joanne argue about involving the authorities before he takes her Volkswagen Microbus and begins a backtracking search from Tampa. Informed by a gossipy neighbor that the Osbornes had recently argued and discovering blood that David dropped in the kitchen after cutting himself on a broken plate, Ross begins to suspect that Cassie's husband may have had something to do with her disappearance.

Within the Scudder house, Roy has grown increasingly violent and deranged. He browbeats Georgina for mentioning Arthur, abuses his daughter, and makes sexual advances toward Cassie. In moments of high stress, he has angry conversations with an old man who taunts him from a wheelchair and turns out to be his unreal, long-dead father.

Stopping by chance at the Scudder gas station and receiving a tip from Truman the attendant, David makes his way to the house, where Roy denies having seen his family. On his way out, he recognizes a doll that Jill drops from a window as the one he recently bought for Samantha and realizes that she and her mother are inside. Before he can do anything, Roy strangles him with a chain and throws him into a dry water well.

In a shadowy flashback, Roy relives how he smothered little Arthur to stop his crying. Goaded by the hallucinations of his father, he drugs Cassie and makes her put on Marlena's nightgown. Using one of Roy's misplaced wrenches to remove the door hinges and escape her room, Cassie tumbles down the stairs and is knocked unconscious. Roy carries her back, chains her to the bed, and rapes her.

Injured but alive, David climbs out of the well and briefly reunites with both Samantha and Cassie before fleeing the house and hiding from Roy in the swamp. Having tricked Jill into taking her to the woods, Samantha watches the older girl dig up Arthur's mummified remains to scare her and then makes a quick escape. At the same time, Chicky Ross, who has spotted the Osbornes' Thunderbird medallion at the gas station and gotten directions from Truman, arrives and also finds the Volkswagen. He phones in his discovery but has his throat cut by Roy and dies.

Back in the house, Cassie tells Georgina about the rape but she refuses to believe her. Completely unhinged, Georgina mentions that Marlena had intended to tell the police that Roy killed little Arthur. Sitting in the wheelchair, she watches as David arrives and uses a hacksaw to file away Cassie's chains. Roy suddenly interrupts the proceedings and starts to fight with David and Cassie. In the confusion, he throws a hurricane lamp at the wall and starts a fire. After revealing that Marlena and Donna were killed to prevent them from going to the cops, Roy shoots at the hallucination of his father but kills Georgina instead. As Roy shouts "I love you Marlena," Cassie grabs the rifle and shoots him dead. The following morning, she and David are reunited with Samantha.

Notes and Comments: This convoluted, unseemly nonsense marked a low point in the careers of everyone involved. The acting of the supporting cast is so shrill and amateurish that Burt and Angie don't look too bad in comparison. The two old pros try to give viewers some authentic chills, but even they cannot produce much more than derisive groans.

As poor demented Georgina, Angie wanders about in a catatonic haze, speaking as softly and slowly as possible. The cadence is meant to suggest Georgina's confused state of mind. When she first comes out from behind a dingy screen door, she looks like a faded southern beauty, Blanche DuBois at sixty-four. "Marlena is that really you?" she asks distractedly, projecting the bewilderment that will intensify throughout the film. Costumer Howard Sussman has not done her any favors, clothing her in shapeless sack dresses, nightshirts, and bathrobes to conceal an expanding waistline, but the perfect hair and inviting eyes hint at the possibly well-adjusted, happy young woman she once was.

Angie could always be counted on to handle big chunks of expository dialogue, and she delivers here as well. "Then came my little boy. Of course, that was even worse, poor little Arthur," she tells Cassie. "Roy didn't mean to do what he did. He just wanted Arthur to stop crying, that's all. The doctors weren't sure he'd live anyway. He was in so much pain." It's purely plot information but she makes the speech sound like an emotional revelation. The sudden tears midway through help to humanize the character a bit as well.

Burt has no similarly redeeming moments. He appears to have located the dark doppelganger of the good old boy persona he perfected in films such as *Smokey and the Bandit* (1977) but keeps the portrayal at full throttle throughout. With moustache and rug firmly in place, he uses his swaggering physicality to intimidate the women and brutalize the men. He is creepy but not all that believable.

John Huston's son Danny, ultimately more well-known as an actor than a director, is at the helm here of his third feature film.

Shot in and around the studio facilities Burt Reynolds built for himself in Jupiter, Florida, *The Maddening* makes good use of its swampy rural locations. Huston also gets some dramatic mileage out of the little girl in peril theme but is so desperate for frights that he relies on such horror film clichés as nighttime thunder and otherworldly voices on the soundtrack. When it comes to scaring audiences, he would be much more effective playing the brutish vampire in *30 Days of Night* (2007) or the depraved gangster boss in the TV series *Magic City* (2012-13). After a limited theatrical run, *The Maddening* went directly to video.

Reviews:
"*The Maddening* is an average, conventional psycho-thriller that works but does little more. Talent and production values are all up to par and the story is exciting enough, but its longest life looks to be on video."

"Writers Henry Slesar and Leslie Greif, and director Danny Huston, seem afraid to really set the audience's hair on end, though the script sports good dialogue and moves swiftly. Huston's direction is fine, but neither he nor the script or performances provide the movie with any real edge."

"Film's best asset is the teaming of Dickinson and Reynolds as the isolated crazies. But acting the heavy for once hasn't inspired either of them, and Reynolds could have given a much bigger, fuller, Southern-man spin to his role."

—Eric Hansen, *Weekly Variety*, August 14, 1995

"Reynolds and Dickinson . . . manage to maintain a degree of dignity and wit throughout this inferior suspense tale, whose artless script alternates stupid comic relief (two Bill-and-Ted buttheads at the gas station) with waiflike Mia Sara's agony in tearing off a fingernail trying to pry up a door's hinge."

—*TV Guide*, November 3, 2007

The Sun, the Moon and the Stars

Credits: A Blue Light Productions picture released on October 25, 1996. Color. Running time of 93 minutes. Based on a short story by Geraldine Creed. **Cast:** Angie Dickinson (Abbie McGee), Jason Donovan (Pat), Gina Moxley (Monica), Elaine Cassidy (Shelley), Aisling Corcoran (Dee), David Murray (Danny), Vinny Murphy (Tom), Patrick Dawson (Larry), Eamonn Hunt (Jack), Dawn Bradfield (Blaise), Kieran Hurley (Billy), Robbie Doolin (Mike). **Crew:** Geraldine Creed (director and screenwriter), Brendan McCarthy (producer), Noel Eccles (composer), Cieran Tanham (cinematographer), Catherine Creed (editor), Eleanor Wood (production designer), Kieran Hennessy (assistant director), Nuala Roche (sound).

Plot Synopsis: Morose, disagreeable teenager Shelley and her precocious, know-it-all younger sister Dee are in a shared custody arrangement with their divorced parents Monica (Mo) and Tom. When her boss chooses not to promote her because of her family commitments, Mo resigns from her bank job and hastily departs Dublin for a vacation in a seaside Irish village. Before leaving, Shelley leaves a message for her father to join them as always.

Upon arrival, they learn that their usual accommodation, a glorified Quonset hut with add-ons, has been given to an American marine biologist named Abbie McGee. Assigned a smaller, rougher unit in the "resort," Mo makes the best of the situation while Shelley sulks and complains even more. As the days pass, Mo strikes up a romance with Pat, the property's laid-back young caretaker, and becomes friendly with Abbie, who encourages her to loosen up and live more freely for herself.

Frustrated by the collapse of her plan to reunite her parents and by the ongoing presence of Pat, Shelley sinks more deeply into her angry depression. One day, she sneaks into Abbie's quarters and rifles through her possessions. The various sea specimen jars and tarot deck with the sun, moon, and stars cards on top convince her that Abbie is a witch responsible for all the unhappiness in her life. Out of revenge, she begins sticking pins into an effigy of the woman.

At Dunphy's Bar, the village's social center, Dee convinces Shelley to perform a karaoke version of Madonna's "Holiday," much to the delight of a young local boy named Danny. Although she is not interested at first, Danny's knowledge of where to find hallucinatory mushrooms wins her over. A nighttime rowboat adventure at sea goes badly and Danny, Shelley, and Dee must be rescued by Abbie.

A near drowning and a different look at life help Shelley to mature. By the film's end, she has grown closer to the people around her.

Notes and Comments: Angie's choice of film roles was often based on location, and this small independent production gave her the opportunity to visit Ireland for the first time. It was also her first experience working with a crew whose members, from director and editor to clapper loader and third assistant director, were predominantly female. For an actress who always had prided herself on being one of the guys on many mostly male film sets, it was a fun change of pace. She meshed easily with director Geraldine Creed and her company.

The Sun, the Moon and the Stars was Creed's first feature film following the production in Ireland of three short fiction pieces.

Directing her own screenplay, she keeps the action and camera work simple, opting for flashy visuals in a couple of dream and hallucination sequences only. Wisely she lets the setting establish the atmosphere, not the dramatically grand western Irish seascapes of *Ryan's Daughter* (1970) but a more tranquil coastline in keeping with the reduced emotional tone of her story.

Angie is introduced into the film by way of that scenery. A small green sedan packed with scientific gear drives along the shore. It proceeds down a dirt road and stops on the front lawn of a remote dwelling. Dressed in a flowing magenta jacket, matching scarf, and dangling gold earrings, Angie steps out and looks around the place. With her hair blowing in the breeze, she smiles and says, "Perfect." The most beautiful marine biologist ever to have stained a microscope slide, she also seems in synch with her surroundings. Everything she does here looks authentic, from handling scuba diving equipment to negotiating with a bureaucrat on the phone over a fish farming license. The scenes where she and Gina Moxley (as Mo) confide in each other capture the magic of two sympathetic strangers becoming friends. They are so good together that the time spent with pubescent drama queen Shelley becomes even more painful than it already is.

Reviews:

"Though the elements take a while to cohere, there's an easygoing, likable quality to *The Sun the Moon and the Stars*, a light character comedy that signals first-time writer-director Geraldine Creed as a name to watch. Neatly cast and relaxedly played, this part rites-of-passage, part divorcee-on-the-move pic is too small to make much theatrical impact but has a bigheartedness that should click with festgoers."

"Donovan, almost unrecognizable under stubble, and long locks, is good as Monica's entree to another life, and Dickinson brings some dignity to an initially out-of-place role. Spicing the whole pie with some terrific comic timing is young Corcoran, as Shelley's bratty sis."

"Editing and dialogue are admirably lean, but pic does take time to work its magic and is basic at some tech levels."

—*Daily Variety*, September 23, 1996

"Creed's flamboyant use of color and the everyday humor of the piece evoke the winsome Australian comedies of the 70s, and Moxley in an impressively measured performance gives the picture its dramatic heart. But the film fails to deliver on some of the more promising situations in which the characters find themselves. The subtle simplicity of the script demands more than the one-note performances that the younger cast delivers, imbuing the climatic reel with a somewhat awkward resolution."

—*Screen International*, November 8, 1996

The Last Producer

Credits: A Bigel/Mailer Films and LP Productions Inc. picture released on February 9, 2000. Color. Running time of 90 minutes. **Cast:** Burt Reynolds (Sonny Wexler), Rod Steiger (Sheri Ganse), Benjamin Bratt (Damon Black), Ann-Margret (Mira Wexler), Lauren Holly (Frances Chadway), Sean Astin (Bo Pomerantz), Kim Chase (Teddy), Charles Durning (Syd Wolf), Robert Goulet (Henry Moore), Erin Gray (Dee Freeman), E.J. Peaker (Rosie), Greg Germann (Rueben Tallridge), Arthur Darbinyan (Nidal), Paul McCrane (Austin Green), Angie Dickinson (poker player). **Crew:**

Burt Reynolds (director), Clyde Hayes (screenwriter), Daniel Bigel and Michael Mailer (producers), Peter Manning Robinson (composer), Nick McLean (cinematographer), Jennifer Jean Cacavas and Tod Feuerman (editors), Suzette Ervin (production designer), Elizabeth Zdansky (set decorator), Warden Neil (costume designer), Leslie Anne Anderson (hair stylist), Isabel Harkins (makeup artist), Maria Melograne (assistant director), Chuck Michael (sound).

Plot Synopsis: After 43 years in the moviemaking business, producer Sonny Wexler finds himself washed up and ignored by the new Hollywood elite. A past Oscar nominee, he now lives in Torrance and drives an old, beat-up convertible. Feeling that he is soon going to die and be forgotten, he decides to commit all his energy to one last project, the production of a movie by promising young screenwriter Bo Pomerantz. He has one week to come up with the $50,000 that will renew his option on Pomerantz's script or it will become the property of Damon Black, an unctuous young studio executive who harbors a barely-disguised contempt for old-timers like Sonny.

With time running out, Sonny pitches the idea to a weird array of connections: his equally forgotten former producing partner Syd Wolf; his ex-showgirl wife who isolates herself in what she calls a "cocoon" of pills and alcohol; a rich but selfish actor friend; his feckless son-in-law Rueben; a dodgy detective incongruously named Sheri Ganse; and an Armenian arms-dealer living in the Hollywood Hills with his marginally talented actress girlfriend Frances Chadway.

Despite multiple rejections, he ultimately puts together a deal that may or may not involve insurance fraud. With the money in hand, Sonny rushes to meet Black, who smugly declares that he has missed the deadline by a few precious seconds. At the same moment, Syd Wolf appears and shoots Black for having fired him from his own final-curtain position at the studio. Only slightly wounded, Black is loaded into an ambulance as he admits a grudging respect for Sonny, who decides to get out of the business and give the money to Rueben so he can cover his gambling debts. In the final scene, Sonny and Ganse walk down Sunset Boulevard, bickering with each other about what to do next.

Notes and Comments: Angie appears about 20 minutes into the film as a player in a poker game where Sonny is trying to raise some cash. The other gamblers include James Farentino, Shecky Greene, Alex Rocco, Anthony Denison, and Shelley Berman. As the game proceeds, Greene tells a story about how Frank Sinatra saved his life in front of the Miami Beach Fontainebleau Hotel. Five guys, he says, were beating him up and Sinatra ordered, "That's enough." Everyone laughs while drawing cards and laying down chips. It is less than a cameo even, just a slight glimpse of Angie on screen for a few seconds as the camera pans rapidly around the table. A boost to the cast list, her appearance was also a winking acknowledgment of her friendship with Reynolds and her fondness for poker. The Sinatra reference provided additional self-referential humor.

The Last Producer was the final picture that Reynolds would direct although he acted in several more films before his death in 2018, including a critically acclaimed performance in the ironically titled *The Last Movie Star* (2017). Like *The Player* (1992), *Get Shorty* (1995), and *Bowfinger* (1999), *The Last Producer* is a satirical look at contemporary Hollywood deal making coupled with a nostalgic celebration of the past: "We used to have guys drilled in story," says Sonny, "guys who had a love for making motion pictures—a breed who learned how to make films through sweat and blood, not some goddamn film school or a $300 weekend seminar offering some kind of cinematic magic bullet." The sentiment is one that

Reynolds, Angie, and Rod Steiger, who had worked often with each other in the good old days, could easily comprehend.

Reviews:
"Reynolds clearly wants to present Sonny as a real guy—he's not a comic fraud, nor is he a tragically neglected genius. The character isn't drawn with the sharpest clarity, and at times the portrayal becomes just a touch self-pitying, but overall this is an honest, caring view of a Hollywood has-been, and it reaches moments of true poignancy."

—Steven Oxman, *Daily Variety*, February 6, 2001

"*The Last Producer* offers little in terms of industry insight or character development, though its quips often strike right to the heart of a film colony that is obsessed with youth and the repackaging of proven successes. Story lines involving the women in Sonny's life are developed tangentially and then dropped."

—Marjorie Baumgarten, *The Hollywood Reporter*, June 1, 2000

Duets

Credits: A Hollywood Pictures production released on September 9, 2000. Technicolor. Running time of 112 minutes. **Cast:** Gwyneth Paltrow (Liv Dean), Huey Lewis (Ricky Dean), Maria Bello (Suzi Loomis), Paul Giamatti (Todd Woods), Andre Braugher (Reggie Kane), Scott Speedman (Billy Hannan), Angie Dickinson (Blair), Kiersten Warren (Candy Woods), Locklyn Munro (Ronny Jackson). **Crew:** Bruce Paltrow (director and producer), John Byrum (screenwriter and producer), Kevin Jones (producer),

David Newman (composer), Paul Sarossy (cinematographer), Jerry Greenberg (editor), William Heslup (art director), Lesley Beale (set decorator), Mary Claire Hannan (costume designer), Ian Ballard and Kay Georgiou (hair stylists), Tina Earnshaw and Joann Fowler (makeup artists), Jim Brebner (assistant director), Adam Kopald and Piero Mura (sound).

Plot Synopsis: The film cuts back and forth between three unlikely pairs of strangers making their way across the country to a karaoke contest in Omaha, Nebraska.

Ricky Dean is a talented singer/hustler who travels from town to town, pretending ignorance of karaoke and then winning both the contests and side bets with unsuspecting contestants. Summoned to Las Vegas for the funeral of an ex-flame, he crosses paths with her mother Blair, who introduces him to his long-forgotten daughter Liv. Against his wishes, she follows him out onto the karaoke circuit even performing some solo numbers herself. In one city, his betting hustle is exposed, starting a bar fight that involves both of them. Although she pushes to build an emotional connection, he resists her efforts to see him as a father figure.

Todd Woods is a hardworking sales rep so exhausted by his job that he gives a presentation to poultry association members in Houston thinking he is speaking to theme park investors in Florida. When he returns to his suburban California home, a sterile box filled with plastic floor runners, his wife Candy and two young children completely ignore him. Pushed over the edge, he abandons his family and sets out on an aimless road trip. In New Mexico, he ends up in a karaoke joint, where a pretty female contestant gives him some anxiety-reducing beta blockers and shoves him on stage to perform a well-received version of "Hello, It's Me." Hooked on a combo of the blockers and stimulants, he continues driving recklessly around the interstates. In Utah, he picks up an African American hitchhiker named Reggie Kane, who turns out to be a fugitive convict who has already robbed a truck driver at gunpoint. They become friends with Reggie joining Todd on stage during one of their karaoke stops to sing a fantastic duet of "Try a Little Tenderness" and Todd teaching his new buddy how to drive. The tone darkens when Todd uses Reggie's gun to shoot up the lobby of a hotel that won't accept his frequent flyer miles and to later exchange gunfire with a service station clerk. Although the shooting takes place off camera, we assume that Todd has either killed or seriously wounded the attendant.

Finally, there is Billy Hannan, a kind-hearted, handsome taxi driver from Cincinnati who learns that the co-owner of his cab has been sleeping with his girlfriend. Setting out on a drinking binge, he meets Suzi Loomis, a singer who is trying to get to California by winning karaoke contests and granting sexual favors. They spend the night together and she convinces him to take the cab, repaint it a bright lavender pink (paid for with one of her favors), and drive her westward. The journey is argumentative. She thinks he is an underachieving loser and as a former seminary student, he believes she is a callous misanthrope. During one of their stops, however, he sees her perform a touching rendition of "I Can't Make You Love Me" and recognizes how sensitive she really is.

Ultimately, all three pairs end up in Omaha for a karaoke contest with a $5,000 grand prize. Ready now to be a father, Ricky invites Liv on stage to perform a duet of her mother's favorite song, "Cruisin.'" Billy finds Suzi vomiting from stage fright in the restroom and helps her summon the confidence to perform. Noticing that the police have arrived, Reggie sings a stirring a cappella version of "Free Bird" and then pulls out his gun, prompting the police to shoot him and diverting blame away from Todd for the service station incident.

The next morning, Billy and Suzi get ready to leave but not before he asks Liv, to whom he has become attracted, to join them. She and Ricky agree, and all four set out for California, planning a detour through Sparks, Nevada, for a $2,000 grand prize karaoke contest. Candy Woods, who was called to Omaha by Reggie, tells Todd she loves him, and they pledge to try building a new, less restricted life together.

Notes and Comments: Angie has two back-to-back scenes early in the picture. As Liv's grandmother Blair, she introduces father and daughter at a Las Vegas mortuary and then has lunch with them in the mobile home that Liv shared with her mother. Dressed conservatively in a black blazer, charcoal gray sweater, and dark skirt, she still exhibits the demeanor of the brassy, much-traveled chorus girl she used to be. "I enjoyed the gypsy life," she explains, "but when Mr. Sinatra got me my job at the Dunes, the roots began to sprout. The dynasty was born." Barely able to contain her anger at Ricky, she chatters on about Paul Newman ("I must have rented *Sweet Bird of Youth* a hundred times") and then lets loose as soon as Liv leaves to use the bathroom. "Listen you no good son of a bitch," she rails, "you knock up my daughter like she's some bitch in heat and then you disappear without so much as a backwards glance. Well it's time to pay up." Fiercely protective, she doesn't swing wildly but attacks with controlled, laser-like fury. For Liv's well-being, she argues, "You may not be much, but what she needs now is a father." It is one more example of Angie's ability to step briefly into a picture, economically develop a character, and make an indelible impression that lasts long after she has exited the narrative.

All of the actors turn in strong performances. Paltrow gives Liv an endearing innocence, rock singer Lewis looks like a natural on screen, Braugher manages to be both menacing and sympathetic, and, as Angie stated during an interview at the time, Giamatti's erratically wired salesman practically steals the movie. Two unexpected joys are Marion Seldes as a cranky, foul-mouthed passenger in Billy's cab and Maya Rudolph as the bubbly Omaha karaoke emcee. Michael Bublé and director James Cameron make brief cameo appearances as karaoke contestants. All of the musical performances are good with everyone except Braugher (whose voice is dubbed by Arnold McCuller) doing his/her own singing.

Duets tries for the ensemble sprawl of Robert Altman's *Nashville* but misses that movie's complex originality. The plot resolutions are predictable and in many cases somewhat implausible as well. Gwyneth Paltrow's father Bruce directed from an original script by John Byrum.

Reviews:

"This character piece is an ensemble of outstanding performances, moving yet unimposing storylines and damn good singing. Even the father-daughter stuff, which at times can feel typical, still has a unique and satisfying resolution."

"Bruce Paltrow keeps all the stories balanced and gives them equal weight in the script. Some stand out naturally more than others, but all are worth watching."

—Fred Topel, *Entertainment Today*, September 15, 2000

""*Duets* is six characters in search of a movie. Any movie will do, and a lot are tried: a tedious road picture, a joyless comedy, a toothless social satire, to name a few. The only aspect of *Duets* that is successful is its singing, which not only sounds good but keeps all that other nonsense off the screen."

"In addition to its other shortcomings, *Duets* is awfully slow in getting going, and it seems like forever before all six characters—quasi-losers and lovable misfits every one—are introduced and tidily matched off into nonromantic pairs."

—Kenneth Turan, *Los Angeles Times*, September 15, 2000

"As long as it stays with the music and in a larky, serio-comic vein, *Duets* takes the audience for a jaunty spin. A cross-country road movie about three twosomes headed for a karaoke contest in Omaha, TV vet Bruce Paltrow's second big screen feature displays good reflexes for unpredictable humor and gives several of its actors chances to have fun in ways that are agreeably contagious."

"By far the most engaging of the duos, however, is Giamatti and Braugher. Latter is solid, as always, but Giamatti all but steals the movie as the meek little pushover who becomes a liberated monster of risk and freedom, a self-declared terrorist against the homogeneity of America as represented by the strip malls and chains which are the film's principal settings."

—Todd McCarthy, *Weekly Variety*, September 18, 200

"Do we really need a movie that uses the karaoke-bar scene as a metaphor for life? *Duets* interweaves the disparate stories of three couples chasing the American Dream, and it's woozy with its own windy philosophizing."

"Paltrow does her own singing, and she has a pleasing voice that goes well with Lewis's mellifluous rasp, but she's playing a character of such bemused innocence that she seems stunted. She's insufferably dewy."

—Peter Rainer, *New York*, September 25, 2000

"Karaoke represents liberation in *Duets*—far more than a train-wreck by-product of oblivious drunkenness, it's a transformative escape for the wounded souls here, who stumble upon true meaning in the act of belting out some moldy oldie that we haven't heard nearly often enough. A more interesting movie would have positioned karaoke, with its sad, cruel sense of repetition and predestination, not as a cure but a metaphor for the deadening treadmill routineness of modern life."

"*Duets* is, broadly speaking, a road movie, though there's a decided lack of forward motion in the way it ushers together three odd couples for a climatic amateur night in Omaha."

—Dennis Lim, *The Village Voice*, September 28, 2000

Pay It Forward

Credits: A Bel-Air Entertainment, Tapestry Films, Pathé production released on October 20, 2000. Color. Running time of 123 minutes. Based on a novel by Catherine Ryan Hyde. **Cast:** Kevin Spacey (Eugene Simonet), Helen Hunt (Arlene McKinney), Haley Joel Osment (Trevor McKinney), Jay Mohr (Chris Chandler), Jim Caviezel (Jerry), Jon Bon Jovi (Ricky McKinney), Angie Dickinson (Grace), David Ramsey (Sidney Parker), Gary Werntz (Mr. Thorsen), Colleen Flynn (woman on bridge), Marc Donato (Adam), Kathleen Wilhoite (Bonnie). **Crew:** Mimi Leder (director), Leslie Dixon (screenwriter), Peter Abrams, Robert L. Levy, and Steven Reuther (producers), Thomas Newman (composer), Oliver Stapleton (cinematographer), David Rosenbloom (editor), Lawrence A. Hubbs (art director), Peg Cummings (set decorator), Renee Ehrlich Kalfus (costume designer), Waldo Sanchez (hair stylist), Vivian McAteer (makeup artist), Steve Danton (assistant director), Christopher S. Aud (sound).

Plot Synopsis: Two seemingly unrelated storylines operating in different time frames ultimately converge. In one, a freelance journalist named Chris Chandler attempts to learn what motivated a relative stranger to give him a new Jaguar, and in the other, Trevor McKinney, a seventh grader living in Las Vegas with his recovering alcoholic mother Arlene, devises a charitable program for his social studies class.

When Trevor's unconventional teacher Eugene Simonet challenges the students "to think of an idea to change our world and put it into action," he comes up with the "pay it forward" concept—doing a major favor for three people who will each repay the deed by doing favors for three other people. His first beneficiary is a homeless man named Jerry, whom he brings home to stay in the garage. Angered by the intrusion, Arlene goes to school to confront Simonet over what she feels is a reckless assignment, but he dismisses her concerns.

Back home, she finds Jerry repairing her car and is impressed by the apparent effect Trevor has had on his life. However, when Jerry slips back into drugs, Trevor feels he has failed and chooses Mr. Simonet himself for the second favor. Heavily scarred on his face and neck, Simonet lives by himself with no social contacts beyond school. Although Trevor successfully tricks Simonet and Arlene into a romantic dinner, the evening ends prematurely with more misunderstandings. Later, as Trevor and Arlene argue over her attachment to her abusive, alcoholic ex-husband Ricky, she slaps him in the face and he runs away. With nowhere else to turn, she asks Simonet for help and they find Trevor at the bus station and bring him home, all three now closely bonded.

Chandler, meanwhile, has learned from his car donor that he was paying forward a black gang member named Sidney who helped save his daughter from an asthma attack. Despite initially claiming that the idea was all his, Sidney explains that he was repaying an old homeless woman who helped him escape from the police. Chandler travels to Las Vegas to pursue the lead.

After a series of false starts, Eugene and Arlene become involved romantically. In bed together, she sees that his entire body is scarred but assures him that the physical disfiguration does not matter. The sense of family is disrupted when Ricky reappears and Arlene decides to give him another chance. In anger, Eugene accuses her of behaving just like his own mother, who continued to put up for years with an abusive husband. He also explains that it was his father, incensed by his son's physical defiance and protection of the mother, who doused him with gasoline and set him on fire. As Ricky returns to his old behavior, Arlene realizes she has made a huge mistake and kicks him out of the house.

Having arrived in Las Vegas, Chandler identifies Grace, an older alcoholic woman living out of her beat-up station wagon, as the person who touched Sidney's life. Over a shared bottle of vodka, she reveals that she was repaying a favor from her daughter Arlene, who found her in a homeless camp, forgave her for being a failed mother, and invited her to be a part of Trevor's life as long as she remained sober.

With this final piece of the puzzle, Chandler appears at Arlene's house during Trevor's birthday party and convinces her to allow him to be interviewed on television. During the taping, which occurs at school, Simonet realizes he does not want to be one of the lost people described by Trevor and reconciles with Arlene. All appears to end happily as Trevor sees his often bullied friend Adam, the third favor on his list, being threatened by some gang kids. In his attempt to help, Trevor is stabbed in the abdomen by one of the bullies. Rushed to the hospital, Trevor dies later that night from his wounds.

ANGIE

Devastated by the loss, Arlene and Eugene comfort each other at home as hundreds of people, hearing about the story on television, gather outside in a candlelight vigil to pay their final respects to Trevor.

Notes and Comments: *Pay It Forward* was a much hyped, highly anticipated project that consequently received critical pushback upon its release. Many reviewers argued that in spite of the solid performances the story itself was overly sentimental. Given time, distance, and perspective, the film actually holds up well, effectively balancing the gritty working class milieu and the emotional messaging.

Particularly good are the number of one-on-one scenes between Osment and Hunt, Osment and Spacey, and Hunt and Spacey. Intense yet restrained, they surface the psychological need that motivates the broader action. Only twelve years old at the time, Osment is thoroughly convincing as a little boy with an old soul and an extraordinary capacity for empathy.

Three of Angie's five scenes are also charged two-character interchanges. In the first, she drives by in her station wagon cum shelter to help street thief Sidney evade the police. Barely recognizable in a ratty blond/gray wig and dirty face, she wears a tattered poncho over baggy pants and a sweatshirt. Her features are somewhat bloated and the famous voice has gone more throaty than whispery. When Sidney asks provocatively what she expects in return, she answers, "Don't matter 'cause you ain't gonna do it." Upset that she may have bungled the first favor she is granting, she mutters, "I paid it forward for a hop head son of a bitch."

The second scene has her sitting in a freight car with Chandler and explaining her involvement in the movement. That conversation leads via flashback to her third and most powerful appearance in the film, the reunion with her daughter. Arlene has found her crouched in front of a homeless encampment fire and declares that she forgives her for all the alcohol-fueled danger she subjected her to as a child. Angie slowly tears up, swallows hard, and asks if she can see her grandson Trevor. Told that she has to be sober during those visits, she resolutely responds, "I can do that." It's a fine dramatic exchange between two highly talented actresses. Hunt reaches out hesitantly and Angie responds with a blend of surprise, relief, regret, and gratitude. With the tone seemingly fixed on anguish, Angie then shifts to humor when Hunt says they can't live together and she answers, "Who would want to?" Only a pro could seize and release an audience so smoothly.

Angie's final two scenes are ensemble pieces; she's part of the group celebrating Trevor's birthday and the crowd assembling outside Arlene's house for the candlelight vigil. In addition to the emotional contribution, Angie's character is also pivotal in connecting the two seemingly independent storylines, Chandler's investigation and Trevor's fulfillment of the class assignment.

Among the interesting supporting cast members are director Mimi Leder's real-life husband as the car donor and rock singer Jon Bon Jovi as Arlene's handsome but abusive ex-husband. James Caviezel, who would go on to star in Mel Gibson's *The Passion of the Christ* (2004), is excellent as the drug-addicted homeless man who seems to be totally irredeemable but then justifies Trevor's belief in him by later in the story saving a would-be suicide victim from jumping off a bridge in Oregon.

Reviews:

"An inherently inspirational, issue-driven drama centered on three emotionally battered people who challenge their personal limitations and in the process develop the possibility of changing society itself, *Pay It Forward* is an unusual film that intelligently avoids numerous potential pitfalls even if its central earnestness is ultimately inescapable. With a top-flight cast led by recent Oscar winners Kevin Spacey and Helen Hunt, along with Haley Joel Osment, again outstanding, in his first feature since *The Sixth Sense*, Warner Bros. has everything it needs to promote this serious-minded, well-acted picture as one of the major prestige releases in the fall."

—Todd McCarthy, *Weekly Variety*, October 9, 2000

"To put it mildly, it is uncomfortable and embarrassing to have one's cynical ass whipped by a huge, hulking Hallmark card, and this is exactly the sensation one takes away from Mimi Leder's *Pay It Forward*."

"It's a little bit sickening to be sounding the Oscar trumpet so far in advance, but the performances—purposefully clunky, junky, and funky—are by far this production's strongest suit. As if it weren't enough to receive fine supporting work from Jon Bon Jovi in a wife-beater shirt as Trevor's deranged father, and Angie Dickinson as an absentee, alcoholic grandmother (looking for all the world like some extra out of *Ironweed*), the other adults arrive far above expectations."

—Gregory Weinkauf, *New Times Los Angeles*, October 19-25, 2000

"*Pay It Forward* is as notable for where it doesn't go as where it does, for avoiding the missteps of bathos and piling on that almost invariably mar these kinds of three-hankie productions."

"Without the quality of acting *Pay It Forward* attracted, this would not have been possible. Cast by Geraldine Leder, the film is strong through its main supporting roles, which include Jay Mohr as a curious journalist, James Caviezel as a homeless man with a drug problem, Jon Bon Jovi as an absent husband and Angie Dickinson as a decidedly unglamorous street person."

—Kenneth Turan, *Los Angeles Times*, October 20, 2000

"Ms. Leder's staging, stiff at best, mangles several big moments, including the shameless climax. Bent on doing good, *Pay It Forward* doesn't do well at all."

—Joe Morgenstern, *Wall Street Journal*, October 20, 2000

"That it succeeds at all—that the film elicits moments of genuine feeling, rather than the derisive laughter it deserves—is largely thanks to the three principal actors."

"Plausibility and character are sacrificed in what the movie congratulates itself is a good cause. And it would be a tolerably hokey bit of uplift—a special two-hour episode of *Touched by an Angel*, perhaps—if not for its ending, which the people at Warner Brothers have asked reviewers to refrain from divulging, I'd like to think because they were ashamed of themselves for stooping to gratuitous spiritual pornography."

—A.O. Scott, *The New York Times*, October 20, 2000

"*Pay It Forward*, which was written by Leslie Dixon (from Catherine Ryan Hyde's novel) and directed by Mimi Leder, is mostly an embarrassment, but the movie is still worth seeing for Hunt, who gives it a first-rate performance as an alcoholic Las Vegas cocktail waitress and single mom—a woman with lousy judgement who wants to do the right thing but doesn't know how."

"Not a single scene devoted to the central idea feels convincing, and the movie is inept in a variety of commonplace ways. The filmmakers employ a complicated past-and-present time structure that doesn't pay forward or backward (it's merely confusing)."

—David Denby, *The New Yorker*, November 6, 2000

"Not since *Gump* has there been such a pandering, faux-virtuous package of populist pap for Hollywood to shove in the faces of electioneering politicos and say: Look, we don't just market unwholesome swill to families, we market wholesome swill, too."

"Man, oh, man, is this a lousy movie. And it comes from smart people who should know better."

—Peter Travers, *Rolling Stone*, November 9, 2000

Big Bad Love

Credits: An IFC Films production released on February 22, 2002. Technicolor. Running time of 111 minutes. Based on stories by Larry Brown. **Cast:** Arliss Howard (Leon Barlow), Debra Winger (Marilyn), Paul Le Mat (Monroe), Rosanna Arquette (Velma), Angie Dickinson (Mrs. Barlow), Michael Parks (Mr. Aaron), Alex Van (deputy), Zachary Moody (Alan), Olivia Kersey (Alisha), Kevin Mitchell (twin #1), Matt Mitchell (twin #2), Michael Williamson (young Barlow). **Crew:** Arliss Howard (director, co-writer, producer), James Howard (co-writer), Bob Johnston and Debra Winger (producers), Joe Mulherin (music supervisor), Paul Ryan (cinematographer), Jay Rabinowitz (editor), Patricia Norris (production designer and costume designer), Leslie Morales (set decorator), Terri Ewton (hair stylist), Gloria Belz (makeup artist), Karen Estelle Collins (assistant director), Steve Aaron and Dave Patterson (sound).

Plot Synopsis: Leon Barlow is a struggling alcoholic writer who lives by himself on the outskirts of a small southern town. Engulfed by a steady flow of rejection letters and returned manuscripts, he frequently slides into sexual fantasies involving his ex-wife Marilyn, assorted childhood memories, and flashbacks to his combat service in Vietnam. Behind on child support payments and in need of quick cash, he accepts a house painting job along with his best friend and drinking buddy Monroe.

With the money earned, Leon squares his debts and is granted legal permission to see his children. When Marilyn drops off their son Alan and daughter Alisha for the weekend, it is evident that Leon has forgotten the cleared financial obligation and is totally unprepared for the visit. Thinking fast, he sets up a tent outside and entertains the kid with stories invented on the spot. All three also continue painting a mural on a freight car that has been diverted into the tracks behind Leon's house.

Leon's efforts at being a dad and at writing alternate with binge drinking spells where he and Monroe carouse around town, get in fights, and pass out. During her frequent visits to check on him, Leon's wealthy, socially respectable mother reminds him of what a disappointment he has become. "You have no vocation," she says, promising that she will give the grandchildren "all the mam-ma they can stand" but arguing also that they need a responsible father. Despite the candor, it is clear that she very much loves Leon as well.

Good news of sorts arrives in the form of a letter from literary editor Betti DeLoreo. Although she is declining to accept his story, she believes he has real talent and asks him to send other submissions. Leon retrieves the typewriter he has thrown into the weeds and gets to work.

ANGIE

Monroe and Leon spend a night drinking and cruising around town with local hottie Velma and her mostly silent twin brothers. Soon afterwards, Monroe and Velma get married in Vegas. Choosing not to attend the reception, Leon writes a story for the couple and all is forgiven.

In their own private celebration, Leon and Monroe get roaring drunk one night and drive off in Monroe's truck. When it runs out of gas, Leon stops in the middle of the road and perches on the window. Practically invisible in the darkness, they are struck from behind by an army reserve truck, and Monroe is seriously injured.

More tragedy strikes when Leon's daughter Alisha, who suffers from congenital respiratory problems, has an attack that prevents her from breathing. Although Mrs. Barlow rushes her to the hospital, the little girl dies upon arrival. At her funeral, Leon gets drunk, relives memories of his father's death, and participates in a clumsy, slow-motion fight with a seriously brain-damaged Monroe.

Afterwards, Leon is sent to jail coupled with daytime community service for thirty days. Upon release, he receives another letter from Betti DeLoreo accepting a story and asking to see his book. He and Velma take Monroe for a ride in the couple's new truck and she asks him to write affectionately about Monroe.

In lieu of a happy ending, Leon's life partially resolves itself. Still resisting his reconciliation overtures, Marilyn reveals that their son wants to tell stories, and Leon confronts the reality of his own father's drinking related death. The painted boxcar is finally removed and Leon sends his book to DeLoreo. Its title is *Big Bad Love*.

Notes and Comments: *Big Bad Love* is a heartfelt personal collaboration between filmmaker Arliss Howard and writer Larry Brown, an attempt to visually realize the sleepy yet character-rich rural south of Brown's stories. Shot on location in Holly Spring,

Mississippi, the film alternates between the gritty reality of Leon's daily life and the feverish imagery of his imagination. Some of those dreamlike segments are particularly striking—a home-movie wedding run backwards, a cow grazing next to Leon's desk, mortar explosions as he approaches Marilyn's house with a stuffed animal, Marilyn tied to railroad tracks on a red velvet sofa.

In his directorial debut, Howard has gone the Orson Welles route, filling the roles of producer, writer, director, and actor himself. As such, there is a tinge of self-indulgence to the picture, a few too many scenes of Leon stumbling drunk around his house or reciting long passages of florid prose. Moments that could serve as the climax of a short story, for example Alan's revelation that he wants to be a storyteller or the removal of the painted freight car, don't generate much emotional or thematic heft here.

As director, Howard has gotten uniformly fine performances from his cast, especially Angie, Paul Le Mat, Rosanna Arquette, and his real-life spouse Debra Winger, who also co-produced. Each actor brings restraint and authentic detail to what could have been a collection of stock Southern Gothic caricatures. An unexpected pleasure is Sigourney Weaver as Betti DeLoreo in the voice-overs.

Angie first appears when she drives up to Leon's house in a white Mercedes SLS coupe and is confronted by his dog. "Leon, are you gonna get this beast away from me or not?" she shouts. Unlike the exaggerated dialect she sporadically adopted as Wilma McClatchie in the *Big Bad Mama* pictures, her accent is subtle, precise, and refined. Throughout the movie she reflects the pain that Leon has caused others, her eyes touched with sadness and regret. Two of her best scenes are nearly wordless. In one, she is telling a sotto voce story at her granddaughter's funeral about a Portuguese waiter who sliced lemons for her tea when Leon stumbles into the room. Breaking off the anecdote, she watches silently and apprehensively as he approaches Marilyn. In the other, she walks outside on the porch to see Leon and Monroe fighting foolishly on her lawn. She gazes at them for a few seconds, almost imperceptibly shakes her head, and then goes back inside the house. Arliss Howard raved that her timing was flawless.

Although it screened at Cannes, *Big Bad Love* failed to garner much attention there or in its limited theatrical release and ended up losing money at the box office.

Reviews:

"Women characters, including Rosanna Arquette as Monroe's sweetheart, generally are less satisfyingly drawn. But Winger takes on richer dimensions in the final stretch; and Dickinson has her moments as the faded beauty for whom her son's troubles represent a painful reminder of the loss of her husband."

"Paul Ryan's graceful widescreen lensing, bold use of color and unconventional framing, homing in on odd but telling details, give the indie production an accomplished look. Jay Rabinowitz's fluid editing also impresses, and bluesy vocals by Tom Waits enhance the melancholy mood."

—David Rooney, *Weekly Variety*, May 21, 2001

"As a director, Mr. Howard is intoxicated with the lean lyricism of Mr. Brown's writing, to which he adds poetic flourishes of his own. He prefers lush, dreamy imagery and free-associative editing to linear narration, and the movie's look and rhythm is, like Leon himself, alternately charming and annoying."

—A.O. Scott, *The New York Times*, February 22, 2002

"A smashing directorial debut by actor Arliss Howard in which he also plays the chronically smashed lead character, *Big Bad Love* is an underdog IFC Films release that opened Friday in New York and March 9 in Los Angeles."
—David Hunter, *The Hollywood Reporter*, February 25, 2002

"Directed by and starring Arliss Howard, Winger's husband, as struggling Mississippi writer Leon Barlow, it's a slow slog through the perfervid consciousness of a self-destructive artist—a southern-fried cross between Pollock and the Charles Bukowski booze-a-thon *Barfly*, although not nearly as strong as either. Larry Brown's story collection *Big Bad Love* is the basis for a string of alcoholic jags intended to mimic the writer's sordid life, but the only cosmic question that arises from watching this film is, why should we care about any of these people?"

"We should care about Winger, though. As Leon's estranged wife, she brings the movie its only whiff of genuine emotion."
—Peter Rainer, *New York*, March 4, 2002

"Howard has a weakness for cornball surrealism—a wedding scene run backward quickly grates, and a woman on a white horse seems to have ridden straight in from a David Hamilton photo shoot. But the rest of it is just fine, and sometimes better than that. There's Howard himself, who, with his stringy muscles, his melancholy and his voice-over, takes you deep into Barlow's shame and folly. There's Angie Dickinson, weirdly perfect as the writer's patrician mother, and Paul Le Mat as his best friend and foil, Monroe. And there's Howard's own wife, Debra Winger, who, though out of place as a small-town muse, doesn't take up much room even as she makes the most out of a few tender moments."

"Held together by the blues (wailed by, among others, R.L. Burnside, T-Model Ford and Junior Kimbrough), Brown's prose and Howard's performance, *Big Bad Love* is a mess, but it's a sincere mess, beautifully shot by Paul Ryan and faithfully adapted by screenwriter James Howard (the director's brother)."

—Manohla Dargis, *Los Angeles Weekly*, March 8, 2002

"Barlow's war buddy and best friend, Monroe (*American Graffiti*'s Paul Le Mat, doing a wonderfully sincere job here), does his best to keep his pal in fix-it work and drunken good times, even as Barlow's mother (a regal Angie Dickinson) and ex tend to question his every move as irresponsible—and not without good reason."

"But, again, it's not the big picture story that's important here. Instead, it's Arliss' simple directorial touches that do the best talking."

—Aaron M. Fontana, *Entertainment Today*, March 8, 2002

"*Big Bad Love* is a calculated risk that succeeds in evoking what it means to be a fiction writer as few films have. Shot through with beauty, pain and humor, this complex and intimate film is drawn from the short story collection of the same name by Mississippi writer Larry Brown. It stars Arliss Howard as Brown alter ego Leon Barlow."

"Fine ensemble support is supplied by Dickinson, Arquette, Le Mat and Michael Parks as the philosophical proprietor of the local grocery and gas station."

—Kevin Thomas, *Los Angeles Times*, March 8, 2002

Ocean's Eleven (2001)

Credits: A Village Roadshow Pictures and Warner Bros. production released on December 7, 2001. Color. Running time of 116 minutes. Based on a 1960 screenplay by Harry Brown and Charles Lederer. **Cast:** George Clooney (Danny Ocean), Brad Pitt (Rusty Ryan), Bernie Mac (Frank Catton), Elliott Gould (Reuben Tishkoff), Casey Affleck (Virgil Malloy), Scott Caan (Turk Malloy), Eddie Jemison (Livingston Dell), Don Cheadle (Basher Tarr), Shaobo Qin ("The Amazing" Yen), Carl Reiner (Saul Bloom), Matt Damon (Linus Caldwell), Andy Garcia (Terry Benedict), Julia Roberts (Tess Ocean). **Crew:** Steven Soderbergh (director and cinematographer), Ted Griffin (screenwriter), Jerry Weintraub (producer), David Holmes (composer), Stephen Mirrione (editor), Keith P. Cunningham (art director), Kristen Toscano Messina (set decorator), Jeffrey Kurland (costume designer), Katherine Gordon (hair stylist), Julie Hewett (makeup artist), Gregory Jacobs (assistant director), David E. Stone (sound).

Plot Synopsis: Released after four years in prison, Danny Ocean reconnects with his former partner and friend Rusty Ryan to propose a simultaneous heist of the Bellagio, Mirage, and MGM Grand casinos in Las Vegas, all owned by ruthless magnate Terry Benedict. Once they convince wealthy Reuben Tishkoff, who was squeezed out of his own hotel by Benedict, to finance the operation, they begin to assemble the team. Among the specialists are casino worker Frank Cotton, mechanic brothers Virgil and Turk Malloy, electronic surveillance expert Livingston Dell, explosives master Basher Tarr, acrobat Yen, elderly con man Saul Bloom and pickpocket Linus Caldwell.

The plan is to break into the impenetrable Bellagio vault, which serves all three casinos, on the night of an upcoming Lennox Lewis-

Wladimir Klitschko championship fight and steal the approximately $160 million that the Nevada Gaming Commission will require the establishments to have on hand to cover all their patrons' bets. In preparation, several team members study the Bellagio security routines and staff procedures while others build an exact replica of the vault itself to practice how to crack it. When Rusty learns that Benedict's art gallery curator and girlfriend is Danny's ex-wife Tess, he questions whether Danny can keep his emotions from interfering with the job. Despite some lingering doubts, he and the others accept Danny's assurances. On his part, Danny appears to also take Tess's rejections as final.

On fight night, Linus poses as a gaming commission official and fakes an altercation with Catton that gains him entry to the Bellagio inner sanctum. Easily visible on the casino floor, Danny also gets himself restrained by two Benedict thugs and confined to a backroom, where an even bigger goon he has planted there pretends to beat him up while he escapes into the ductwork and joins Linus at the vault. While Saul, Rusty, and the Malloys distract staff members in security headquarters, Livingston taps into the computer system and switches the monitors to an image of the duplicate vault.

With everything ready to go, Basher cuts power across Vegas by setting off a "pinch," a scientific device stolen earlier by the team that fries circuitry with a huge electromagnetic pulse. Danny and Linus break into the vault with inside help from Yen, who has been stuffed in a money bin and wheeled into the vault on a cashier cart. Rusty calls Benedict on a cell phone that Danny surreptitiously dropped in Tess's coat and tells him that unless he agrees to let them have half the money in the vault they will blow up all of it. The monitors switch to a feed from the real vault and Benedict sees footage of the robbers inside. He agrees and has security officers load duffel bags of money into a remote-controlled van waiting outside the casino. When Benedict calls in a SWAT team to regain the vault, the remaining cash is detonated. Stopping the van, his men discover that the money bags are filled with fliers for hookers.

In reality, after rerouting the emergency phone call, Danny's team disguised themselves as the SWAT squad, walking out of the Bellagio with all the money in their gear bags. Viewing the footage again, Benedict notices that the vault floor is missing a recently added Bellagio logo and realizes that the "normal" video was faked. Even though Danny has returned to the locked detention room, Benedict suspects his involvement. While Tess watches on closed-circuit television, Danny denies pulling the job but tricks Benedict into admitting he would give up Tess in exchange for his money. Unimpressed with Danny's idea for getting the cash back, Benedict informs the police that he is violating his parole by being in Las Vegas.

Tess leaves Benedict and says goodbye to Danny as he is being arrested for the parole violation. Millions of dollars richer, the rest of the team watches the water fountain display outside the Bellagio, before silently going their separate ways. Several months later, Rusty and Tess greet Danny as he is released again from prison. The three of them drive off together, well aware that they are being followed by two of Benedict's bodyguards.

Notes and Comments: In the briefest feature film role of her career, Angie makes a don't-blink-or-you'll miss-it cameo appearance just prior to the heist. Accompanied by Henry Silva, another star of the original *Ocean's Eleven*, she plays herself as a celebrity spectator at the Lewis-Klitschko fight. On screen for only a few seconds, she air kisses Eydie Gormé and smiles into the crowd. It's a packed medium close-up without any dialogue, but she looks stunning in a black evening dress and silver earrings. Also seated at ringside are then Las Vegas mayor Oscar Goodman and entertainers Danny Gains, Wayne Newton, and Siegfried and Roy. Joey Bishop, who is to the Rat Pack as Zeppo is to the Marx Brothers, was also invited to do the scene but turned down the offer, apparently in the belief that he should have been given one of the beefier supporting roles.

Director Steven Soderbergh shot the fight crowd sequence himself at the MGM Grand Garden Arena on Thursday evening, April 5, 2001. The tightly framed cameos were then combined with more expansive crowd footage taken two days later during a match between Marco Antonio Barrera and Prince Naseem Hamed. The altercation between Lewis and Klitschko, exacerbated by the heist's power blackout, was also staged on April 5th.

Julia Roberts, present at ringside with Andy Garcia, was anxious to meet Angie. Unbeknownst to one another, the two stars asked producer Jerry Weintraub to arrange an introduction, which resulted in a flurry of mutual compliments. In the role of Danny's wife, Julia was playing the same part that Angie had performed forty years earlier. With a credit that jokingly read "and introducing Julia Roberts as Tess," she was actually given more to say and do than had Angie in the original.

The expanded participation of Tess is one of many ways in which the 2001 version improves upon its predecessor. Several minutes shorter in length, the pace is quicker, the high-tech heist is more inventive, and the bantering between Clooney and Pitt is actually funny. With its clever use of split screens and wipes, Soderbergh's direction is both light-handed and assured. All of the supporting characters have uniquely interesting backstories and personalities, and the actors portraying them are excellent, notably Casey Affleck and

Scott Caan as the quarrelsome, scene-stealing Malloy brothers. By the time the camera pans leftward across the guys' faces in a penultimate scene reminiscent of the original, we have come to like Danny Ocean's eleven way more than we ever did the first time around.

Reviews:

"An all-star remake of an all-star original, *Ocean's Eleven* is a lark for everyone concerned, including the audience. Breezy, nonchalant and without a thing on its mind except having a little fun, this lightweight caper doesn't take itself seriously and hardly expects the viewer to do either, which itself sets it apart from any other mainstream film Steven Soderbergh has ever made."

"Original pic is repped by Dickinson and Henry Silva, who fleetingly appear in the crowd for the Lennox-Wladimir Klitschko prizefight that occurs the night of the robbery."

—Todd McCarthy, *Weekly Variety*, December 3, 2001

"A suspense-free caper, it really does fit the director's own description of a 'two-hour commercial for Las Vegas.' Too bad it commits the crime of being so intensely average, because what could have been sensational turns out to be merely this week's heist movie."

—Gregory Weinkauf, *New Times Los Angeles*, December 6, 2001

"*Ocean's Eleven* is one smoothie of a movie, a self-assured action adventure about a mostly self-assured crew of con men who pull off an epic trifecta in Las Vega—a three casino heist."

—Joseph Morgenstern, *Wall Street Journal*, December 7, 2001

"*Ocean's Eleven* is the most purely entertaining movie to come out of Hollywood so far this year, and if that doesn't seem worthy of

Soderbergh's talents, it's worthy enough for a night's amusement. The plot may be flimsy, but screenwriter Ted Griffin's dialogue has the snap of classic screwball comedy, with the occasional hiccup of Soderbergh's own puckish humor."

—Manohla Dargis, *L.A. Weekly*, December 7, 2001

"The movie, in a very real sense, is about the privilege, the sexiness, of being a movie star. Certainly it isn't about the heist; never was a McGuffin more of a McGuffin. If there is any incentive to see this film, it's for the same reason many people saw the original, 1960 version with Frank Sinatra and Dean Martin and Sammy Davis Jr. We want to watch celebs acting real cool."

—Peter Rainer, *New York*, December 10, 2001

"Most of Lewis Milestone's direction of the original was poky and flat—the Rat Pack stood around in a group waiting for something to happen. This is a much more attentive and intricate job of moviemaking, with lines of terse narrative winging on and off the screen and perfectly fitted together."

—David Denby, *The New Yorker*, December 10, 2001

"The actors look as if they're having a good time, and their playfulness is contagious (though some of the aren't-we-cool banter is too self-conscious by half)."

—David Ansen, *Newsweek*, December 17, 2001

"Performed, choreographed, shot and directed with deceptive ease, this wholly enjoyable entertainment sees Soderbergh setting himself a new challenge—the high-tech robbery procedural—and relishing the clichés even as he freshens them with a dab of polish, wit, pace and just the right light touch of irony. His familiar play with film syntax here translates into a delight in ingenious confidence trickery and connivance; seldom has escapist fare felt so civilized."

—*Time Out London*, February 13, 2002

Elvis Has Left the Building

Credits: A Capitol Films production released on August 27, 2004. Color. Running time of 90 minutes. **Cast:** Kim Basinger (Harmony Jones), John Corbett (Miles Taylor), Annie Potts (Shirl), Sean Astin (Aaron), Mike Starr (Sal), Phil Lewis (Charlie), Denise Richards (Belinda), Philip Charles MacKenzie (Darren Swirl), Angie Dickinson (Bobette), Gil McKinney (young Elvis), Madison McReynolds (young Harmony), Jenny Gabrielle (young Bobette), Richard Kind (burning Elvis), David Leisure (hole in the head Elvis), Tom Hanks (mailbox Elvis), Joel Zwick (squashed Elvis), Pat Morita (man in turban). **Crew:** Joel Zwick (director), Mitchell Ganem and Adam-Michael Garber (screenwriters), Sharon Harel and Tova Laiter (producers), David Kitay (composer), Paul Elliott (cinematographer), Heather Persons (editor), James Oberlander (art director), Wendy Barnes (set decorator), Nancy Mayer Allan (costume designer), Katie Douthit (hair stylist), Jane Galli (makeup artist), Alex Gayner (assistant director), Paul Timothy Carden (sound).

Plot Synopsis: A successful sales rep for Pink Lady Cosmetics, Harmony Jones travels around the southwest giving motivational speeches to new recruits. Although she is revered by her associates, she feels stuck in a routine. Her best friend Shirl suggests the need for a romance, but she remains skeptical. Before she can figure out a solution, a string of bizarre accidents turns her dissatisfaction into panic. First, a lecherous Elvis impersonator drunkenly incinerates himself before she can help, and then two more Elvises are killed in her presence. One is hit by an engine projectile when she stops to fix his broken-down car and the other is decapitated by a flying mailbox she has bumped into. Convinced that she will cause the death of any Elvis impersonator who gets too close, she rushes from one training seminar to another.

The Elvis connection has deep roots. Her mother Bobette, a mechanic with her own garage in Memphis, used to service Elvis's Cadillac. Harmony continually flashes back to the childhood moment when she met the singing idol and he gave her a ride home. Their conversation, including a pledge of mutual support, has never left her memory. In honor of Elvis, she drives a vintage pink Cadillac convertible.

Ad executive Miles Taylor's backstory overlaps with Harmony's. His father also owned a garage in Memphis, he drives a classic Pontiac GTO, his agency is working on a lipstick account, and he is connected to Elvis. His estranged wife is insisting that she will sign divorce papers only if he hand delivers her own Elvis costume to a Las Vegas convention, and additionally his GTO is involved in a freak accident that squashes a particularly obnoxious impersonator.

Harmony and Miles eventually meet at a roadside hotel and are immediately attracted to each other. Fearing that he is an Elvis impersonator, she flees before she can inflict any unintended harm. Miles sets out to find her.

Because Richard Nixon named Elvis an honorary agent, the FBI is conducting a search of its own for whomever is bumping off all the impersonators. Sal and Charlie, two squabbling, mismatched field agents, pursue a series of high tech clues that threaten to identify Harmony, who has been making frantic calls to Shirl and has taken a detour to visit her mother.

By chance, Miles finds Harmony once again out on the highway and they agree to rendezvous at a nearby roadhouse. She changes from her standard pink ensemble to a black evening dress but before they can reunite, he hides in the trunk of her car to evade policemen who are tracking the GTO. Thinking she has been stood up, Harmony drives off in despair.

Ultimately everyone ends up in Las Vegas, which is hosting an international convention of Elvis performers. Disguised as impersonators themselves, Sal and Charlie are about to break open the case when a rumor that Elvis is alive and on the hotel roof drives the entire crowd to the top of the building. An Elvis constellation lowers from the sky, and a celestial blast flattens the throng of impersonators. The agents realize that everything has happened by cosmic design, freeing Harmony and Miles to pursue their preordained romance.

Notes and Comments: The single authentic moment in this ridiculous picture comes when Angie, playing Harmony's mother Bobette, shares a barbecue lunch with her daughter and breaks into tears as the jukebox plays "Love Me Tender." It is the only reminder of the emotionally powerful rapport Elvis had with his fans. "I remember where I was, the exact spot," she explains. "I had just jacked up the car, and I was singing this song like I always did when I was doing a brake job and then your daddy came in with the news that Elvis had died." In the straightforward way she always understood the character she was playing, she sincerely projects Bobette's grief. Everything else in the movie is a condescending joke, but this is genuine.

Angie has two scenes, one where she greets Harmony outside the restaurant and the other inside at the table. It is not clear why Harmony has come to see her mother and she never appears again in the story. Despite the lack of narrative purpose, the scenes between mother and daughter have the same quirky familial humor that director Joel Zwick did so well in *My Big Fat Greek Wedding* (2002).

It was the huge financial success of that film, in fact, that gave Zwick the clout to make another offbeat, independent comedy. Unfortunately, he was not able to duplicate the achievement, settling here for surprise cameos (himself as squashed Elvis, Tom Hanks as mailbox Elvis, Wayne Newton as Wayne Newton) and pratfalls in place of a well-developed script. Far from being a moneymaker, the picture went quickly to video after a very limited theatrical release.

Elvis Has Left the Building constituted Angie's last big screen feature film appearance. Luckily, however, she accepted a major role five years later in the made-for-television movie *Mending Fences*. Her portrayal in that project of an independent woman struggling to reconcile with her adult daughter and to protect her ranch from a casino development is a much stronger showcase for her talent and a much more poignant farewell.

Reviews:

"*Elvis* is one continuous groaner of a comedy, a one-note eye-roller whose sharpest idea is to play 'Burning Love' on the soundtrack when something accidentally catches on fire. Once that starts playing, get comfy: it's going to be a long, hard slog from here."

—David Cornelius, *eFilmCritic.com*, August 2, 2005

"*Elvis Has Left the Building* is undoubtedly far more effective as a romance than as a comedy, thanks to the genuine chemistry between Basinger and Corbett. Both actors deliver charismatic engaging performances, to the extent that it's hard not to wish that they were in a better movie."

—David Nusair, *Reel Film Reviews*, August 2, 2005

Television Movies and Miniseries Starring Angie Dickinson

The Man Who Bought Paradise (1965)
A fugitive hides out in a foreign country. Role: Ruth Paris, an international traveler.

A Case of Libel (1968)
Drama based on Quintin Reynold's lawsuit against Westbrook Pegler for defamation. Role: Plaintiff Lloyd Bridges's supportive wife Anita Corcoran.

The Love War (1970)
Science fiction thriller in which two warring planets battle to take over earth. Role: Sandy, an alien humanoid posing as an attractive earthling.

Thief (1971)
A professional thief looking to reform must complete one last job to square a gambling debt. Role: thief Richard Crenna's love interest Jean Melville.

See the Man Run (1971)
A struggling actor gets involved in a botched kidnapping plot. Role: the actor's shrewish wife Joanne Taylor.

The Norliss Tapes (1973)
Paranormal researcher investigates the possibility that a recently deceased man of wealth has resurfaced as an all-powerful vampire. Role: the vampire's widow Ellen Sterns Cort.

Pray for the Wildcats (1974)
A crazed business tycoon forces three ad men to compete in deadly wilderness ordeals for his business. Role: Nancy McIlvain, wife of one of the competitors.

A Sensitive, Passionate Man (1977)
Successful engineer loses his company, marriage, and life to alcoholism. Role: the man's long-suffering wife Marjorie Delaney.

Ringo (1978)
Ringo Starr changes places with a look-alike nerd and wanders around Los Angeles. Role: a cameo as the Sergeant Pepper Anderson character from *Police Woman*.

Overboard (1978)
An affluent couple's attempt to repair their troubled marriage with an around-the-world yacht voyage is interrupted when the wife is lost at sea. Role: wife in peril Lindy Garrison.

Pearl (1978)
Set in Hawaii just prior to the bombing of Pearl Harbor, this three-part miniseries alternates between overlapping romantic storylines and Japanese preparations for the attack. Role: unhappy, promiscuous colonel's wife Midge Forrest.

The Suicide's Wife (1979)
College English professor shoots himself and his wife tries to understand why. Role: bereaved widow Diana Harrington.

Dial M for Murder (1981)
Television remake of Hitchcock film about gold digging husband who frames wife for murder after she foils his plot to kill her. Role: victimized wife Margot Wendice.

One Shoe Makes It Murder (1982)
Detective is hired by crime boss to find missing and possibly murdered wife. Role: wife's hardboiled friend Fay Reid.

Jealousy (1984)
Three-part anthology film in which three different female characters have their lives impacted by jealousy. Roles: Georgia, divorced mother increasingly jealous of daughter's interest in new man of the house; Laura, newly married billionaire's wife who competes with the man's pet parrot; Ginny, a country-western singer stalked by jealous boyfriend.

A Touch of Scandal (1984)
A city councilwoman running for state attorney general is involved in a murder scandal. Role: councilwoman Katherine Gilvey.

Hollywood Wives (1984)
Three-part TV miniseries adaptation of Jackie Collins's novel about sex, scandal, and power struggles in the movie business. Role: influential super-agent Sadie LaSalle.

Stillwatch (1987)
Television reporter investigates old Washington, D.C. murder mystery as well as the career of powerful U.S. Senator. Role: Senator and possible Vice-President Abigail Winslow.

Police Story: The Freeway Killings (1987)
Police detectives track down two serial killers who are murdering young women and dumping their bodies next to the L.A. freeways. Role: assisting officer Anne Cavanaugh.

ANGIE

Once upon a Texas Train (1988)
Retired Texas Ranger goes after aging outlaw bent on successfully completing failed train robbery that sent him to prison years earlier. Role: Maggie Hayes, the woman who is loved by both men.

Fire and Rain (1989)
Docudrama about 1985 crash of Delta Airlines Flight 191 in Dallas. Role: hospital administrator Beth Mancini.

Prime Target (1989)
New York police detective discovers she is possible next victim of murderer stalking female police officers. Role: targeted police sergeant Kelly Mulcahaney.

Kojak: Fatal Flaw (1991)
Iconic TV detective Lieutenant Theo Kojak investigates murder of writer who published incriminating Mafia story. Role: writer's widow and former Kojak flame Carolyn Payton.

Treacherous Crossing (1992)
Newlywed on a 1947 transatlantic voyage discovers that her husband has disappeared and that there is no official record of his existence. Role: sympathetic fellow passenger Beverly Thomas.

Angie, the Lieutenant (1992)
A woman takes over as lieutenant of an all-male police squad in Washington, D.C. Role: Lieutenant Angela Martin.

Wild Palms (1993)
Five-part futuristic Bruce Wagner miniseries about a right-wing political and financial organization headed by cult leader and U.S. Senator Tony Kreutzer. Role: Kreutzer's diabolical sister and enforcer Josie Ito.

Remembrance (1996)
Danielle Steel potboiler about beautiful aristocrat who marries American officer in post-World War II Italy and is shunned by his stateside family. Role: evil mother-in-law Margaret Fullerton.

Deep Family Secrets (1997)
Young woman uncovers family history full of adultery, abduction, incest, and murder. Role: the heroine's menaced yet suspicious mother Renee Chadway.

The Don's Analyst (1997)
Comedy about Mafia family arranging psychotherapy for godfather who wants to go legit. Role: the don's wife Victoria Leoni.

Sealed with a Kiss (1999)
Young business exec reevaluates his life after meeting beautiful woman attempting to save museum dedicated to poet Henry Wadsworth Longfellow. Role: Lucille Ethridge, wife of the exec's uptight boss.

Mending Fences (2009)
Television reporter returns to her small Nevada hometown and helps to fight casino development threatening water supply. Role: reporter's aging but independent mother Ruth Hanson.

Afterword

IN THE 1954 version of *A Star Is Born*, Norman Maine tells Esther Blodgett, "A career is a curious thing. Talent isn't always enough. You need a sense of timing—an eye for seeing the turning point, of recognizing the big chance when it comes along and grabbing it." So it was with Angie Dickinson. She seemed always to find the right opportunity at the right time. The beauty pageant and *The Colgate Comedy Hour* got her started, the early Westerns gave her experience, and *Rio Bravo* made her a star. Whenever that stardom seemed to slip over the years, she came roaring back with such projects as *Point Blank*, *Big Bad Mama*, *Police Woman*, *Dressed to Kill*, and *Wild Palms*. There was rarely a time when she was not working, was not taking new professional chances.

What stands out immediately about her career is the sheer scope of it. During the fifty-five years between 1954 and 2009, she made over fifty feature films, appeared in nearly thirty made-for-television movies, starred in two network television series, and made over 70 guest appearances on other people's TV shows. She worked in a variety of genres—Western, crime thriller, film noir, action adventure, romantic comedy, drama—and always tailored her performance to the demands of the narrative, never the other way around. One does not speak, therefore, of an Angie Dickinson vehicle the way one would reference a Bette Davis, a Greer Garson, or, for that matter, a Grace Kelly picture. Even when given top billing, she was always an ensemble player.

In his book *Acting in the Cinema*, James Naremore distinguishes between two kinds of film performance: presentational and representational. The former is more theatrical and mannered, given to broad gestures, declamation, and emotional display. Bette Davis and Marlene Dietrich, especially when they are playing versions of themselves, are often presentational. Performances-within-performances are by their nature ostensive. Representational acting, in contrast, is naturalistic and restrained, attempting to approximate the tones and rhythms of everyday conversation. Physical movement is similarly intended to look like the way people carry themselves in real life. Among Hollywood's Golden Age performers, Myrna Loy, Irene Dunne, Spencer Tracy, and Cary Grant provide clear-cut examples of representational acting.

Even at her most flamboyant, extravagantly outfitted as the eponymous villain in *Charlie Chan and the Curse of the Dragon Queen*, Angie is representational in approach, identifying the motivational through line of a scene and following it as realistically as possible. She doesn't pose or preen; she portrays the dragon lady as a believable albeit extreme character just as she straightforwardly plays the sexually transgressive teacher in *Pretty Maids All in a Row*, the gun-toting matriarch of *Big Bad Mama*, and the embattled beauty ranch manager of *Even Cowgirls Get the Blues*. Her decision to handle farce with a straight face was always the right choice.

Like Dietrich, Angie was often cast in the early films as a saloon girl, but even these portrayals are devoid of theatricality. Her characters are seen off the stage more frequently than on, holding interest through their narrative function more than through any innate showmanship. In fact, except for some high kicking chorus line steps in *Man with the Gun* and *Young Billy Young* and some lip-synching in *Jealousy*, she never actually performs at all. She deftly appropriates the body language of a music hall entertainer and then moves on to other levels of the characterization, never lingering too long on the theatrical illusion itself. Her approximation of performance, as with the country-western singer she plays in the third vignette of *Jealousy*, leaves audiences wanting to see more, desiring to see what kind of cabaret act she might really be able to deliver.

Angie tends to husband Marlon Brando's injuries in *The Chase* (1966).

Despite the formal classes with Batami Schneider, Angie's acting is essentially intuitive. It is neither overly analytical nor technique-driven, but there is always a sense that she knows exactly how a character will move, talk, and react in any given situation. She does not dazzle with foreign accents or physical disguises. There are no Russian doll performances where she reveals one emotion to the actors in the scene and then signals something entirely different to the viewer. She tends rather to maintain a singular expressive focus but within that direct disclosure, the acting, as in *Dressed to Kill*'s wordless cat-and-mouse art gallery pursuit, is often superb.

Among her major assets are her distinctive voice, luminous eyes, and trimly athletic body. Soft-spoken and whispery, she can sound playful, seductive, or malicious. The piercing glance can invite and threaten in equal measure. Having learned by the time of *Cry Terror!* to fully inhabit the cinematic frame, she moves through the subsequent films with a physical assurance that enriches her increasingly diverse characterizations.

Those parts fall along a spectrum that ranges from the noble missionary nurse of *The Sins of Rachel Cade* to the murderously sadistic power broker of *Wild Palms*. The support providers of *Jessica, Captain Newman, M.D., The Chase,* and *The Last Challenge* alternate over and over again with what she jokingly called the "bitch" roles—the shiv-wielding kidnapper of *Cry Terror!*, the manipulative man-eater of *Rome Adventure*, the treacherous gun moll in *The Killers*, and the disloyal gangster's wife in *The Outside Man*. No major actress since Bette Davis has been as willing to portray such dislikable characters and to embrace them as fully as the more virtuous ones.

Angie joins director Howard Hawks on the set of *Rio Bravo* (1959).

It is also difficult to find any contemporary of Angie's who equals her ability to play women from the wide range of social classes she has covered. She is a dirt-poor Depression farm wife in the *Big Bad Mama* pictures, a working class waitress in *The Angry Man*, and an alcoholic bag lady living out of a station wagon in *Pay It Forward*.

Conversely, dressed in elegant designer clothes, she appears as a patrician Hitchcock-like blonde in *A Fever in the Blood*, a wealthy American abroad in *The Art of Love*, and a nouveau-riche industrialist's wife in *Sabrina*. Combining money with politics and channeling her inner Kennedy, she becomes an ambitious elected official herself in the made-for-TV movies *A Touch of Scandal* and *Stillwatch*. The range is surprisingly broad, especially for an actress often considered to have played the same sexual siren throughout her career.

Another way she distinguishes among the many characters is in the amount of physical agency she assigns them. She can be either forceful or fragile. In *China Gate*, she guides a guerrilla fighting unit; in *Jessica*, she zooms around Sicily on a Vespa; in *Sam Whiskey*, she drives a team of horses; and in *Big Bad Mama*, she stands and fires a machine gun from a speeding car. Based largely on her stunt work as Sergeant Pepper Anderson, *Police Woman* is remembered more today as an action series than a drama. By contrast, her women in peril can seem almost mystifyingly helpless. Kate Miller doesn't even try to defend herself from *Dressed to Kill*'s elevator razor attack, and *Overboard*'s Lindy Garrison gets carelessly lost at sea. Less victimized but equally restrained are the characters who spend much of their time either admiring powerful men (*Captain Newman, M.D.*, *Cast a Giant Shadow*, *The Last Challenge*) or waiting to be rescued by them (*Klondike Fever*).

The actors playing opposite her in these parts are top of the line. She worked three times with Robert Mitchum, Burt Reynolds, Lee Marvin, Rod Steiger, Richard Crenna, and John Wayne; twice with Dean Martin; and once each with James Mason, Richard Burton, Peter Finch, Gregory Peck, Marlon Brando, Kirk Douglas, Glenn Ford, Rock Hudson, Randolph Scott, Michael Caine, and Richard Widmark. She meshes well with all of them. Counterbalancing the emotional ferocity of Burton and Brando, she is steady and contained, the calm center around which they reverberate. For the more physically anchored styles of Wayne, Ford, and Widmark, she lets her effortlessly graceful body do much of the communicating. If there is an ideal screen partner, it may very well be Mitchum, whose laid-back delivery and casually concealed intelligence she could parry quip pro quip. In films as dissimilar from one another as *China Gate*, *Rio Bravo*, *The Sins of Rachel Cade*, and *Captain Newman, M.D.*, Angie seems, despite the presence of some briefly glimpsed female secondary players, to be the only woman in an all-male cast. Being one of the guys is an image she cultivated both on the screen and on the set.

Her directors, united in their praise of her collegial professionalism, ranged from silent film pioneer Allan Dwan to indie arthouse auteur Gus Van Sant. In Howard Hawks and Brian De Palma, she enjoyed major success with two of the most celebrated directors of their respective generations. As Lucky Legs in *China Gate*, she embodied the ideal Samuel Fuller heroine, a strong woman of action who is often wiser and more resourceful than the hero. She did the same for Hawks, transforming *Rio Bravo*'s Feathers into the kind of uniquely independent female who is granted admittance to his tightly bonded all-male fraternity. Along the way, there were also pictures with Vincent Sherman, Jean Negulesco, Don Siegel, Arthur Penn, John Boorman, Roger Vadim, Jacques Deray, Sydney Pollack, and Mimi Leder.

The key career achievements, the work for which Angie will long be remembered, are the films *Rio Bravo*, *The Killers*, *Point Blank*, and *Dressed to Kill*, the network television series *Police Woman*, and the audacious miniseries *Wild Palms*. Each in its distinct way showcases her technical skill, emotional versatility, and deference to the narrative. Also noteworthy is the trio of made-for-television movies (*A Sensitive, Passionate Man, Overboard, The Suicide's Wife*) that she made for director John Newland. Minor little gems, these stories of alcoholism, suicide, and infidelity harken back to the days of the women's picture and afford multiple opportunities for the kind of high drama that could have fallen flat with a less disciplined actress.

Angie confers with director Brian De Palma while shooting *Dressed to Kill*'s brilliant art gallery sequence (1980).

Not everything Angie made, however, is first-rate. Some of it, in fact, is quite the opposite: the dreadfully inept horror picture *The Maddening*, the grotesque supernatural vampire TV movie *The Norliss Tapes*, the lead-footed counterculture comedy *Some Kind of a Nut*. In her quest to always be working, she sometimes made unwise decisions, like playing Asian in *Charlie Chan and the Curse of the Dragon Queen* or agreeing to be the recipient of a Dean Martin celebrity roast. Still, to have participated in only a handful of rank embarrassments during more than five decades of work is a professional benchmark to be admired.

Throughout her long career, Angie's resilient beauty worked both for and against her. The stunning looks and figure are what got her noticed in the first place, propelled her from the chorus lines, and earned her the important early roles. In pictures like *Jessica* and *The Killers*, the idea of her physical allure is central to the narrative, the prime motivator behind much of the action. Never was she cast as a bookish ugly duckling. Once the publicity departments at Warner Bros. and Universal went to work on her backstory, they leaned heavily on the sex symbol angle. There were the cheesecake photos, the million dollar insurance policy for her legs, the spicy comments about Hollywood's eligible bachelors.

When she took over her own public relations, she continued talking to reporters about the qualities she found appealing in her dates and her co-stars. Playful and provocative, she always gave good copy. Fans loved her sauciness, just as they did the steamy nude scenes which she was increasingly willing to perform whether, as in *Sam Whiskey*, they were germane to the plot, or, as in *Big Bad Mama*, they seemed gratuitously voyeuristic. The TV persona she cultivated during her perennially hip appearances with Dean Martin, Johnny Carson, and Garry Shandling furthered the notion that she was a slightly ditzy, sexually adventurous swinger. To the audience's delight, she flirted madly and made risqué double entendres that she gigglingly pretended not to understand. She seemed always to be defined by the male gaze fixed upon her. Critics, unfortunately, conflated fiction and reality, often failing to take her seriously enough as an actress. The default critical stance was to overlook the subtleties of her performance and comment instead on how beautiful she appeared. Few observers understood how purposefully she used the spectator's pleasured look to build character.

Consider again Norman Maine's theory about the role of chance in building a career. Imagine what might have happened if Angie had met Michelangelo Antonioni while in Italy for *Jessica* and been given the Monica Vitti part in either *L'Eclisse* (1962) or *Red Desert* (1964). Or if John Cassavetes, her old co-star from *The Killers*, had been unable to cast his wife Gena Rowlands in *A Woman Under the Influence* (1974) and had convinced Angie to appear as the troubled lead instead. Roughly the same age as both actresses, she easily could have projected the haunted beauty and emotional alienation that characterize each of those iconic roles. Or, closer to reality, think how she might have handled the Hot Lips Houlihan part that Robert Altman offered her in *MASH* (1970). Any one of those hypotheticals would have dramatically altered her professional trajectory and left critics with an even more favorable assessment of her talents.

Apart from such speculation, her place in film history is secure. Like Barbara Stanwyck before her, she enjoyed a run of stardom distinguished by its longevity and scope. One of the last of the studio contract players, she also succeeded as an independent actress who never lacked for major roles in both television and film. Emblematically American, she has been a 60s party girl, an arguably liberated 70s police officer, and a late century veteran of the sexual revolution. She has played Frank Sinatra's wife and Gwyneth Paltrow's grandmother. Blessed with an ideal top of the marquee name, she worked hard at being a movie star, constantly burnishing her image through talk show appearances, ad campaigns, and all the actual performances. Yet, she never talked much about the details of her craft, the assured technique that could make even her bad girls seem vulnerable. Perhaps she found such analysis difficult or perhaps she believed it would sound pretentious. In the end, it doesn't matter because the movies and television shows speak for themselves. They give us an actress whose authenticity illuminated even the dimmest of parts. "I'm hard to get, John T.," she tells John Wayne in *Rio Bravo*. "You're gonna have to say you want me." For over half a century, audiences have been doing exactly that

Notes

Biographical Profile: Starting Out

1. Willa Cather, *My Antonia*, p. 3.
2. *Headliners and Legends: Angie Dickinson*, televised MSNBC documentary hosted by Matt Lauer, originally aired 2000.
3. *Lifetime Intimate Portrait: Angie Dickinson*, televised documentary hosted by Meredith Vieira, originally aired 2002.
4. Ibid.
5. *Headliners and Legends* documentary.
6. *Lifetime Intimate Portrait* documentary.
7. *A&E Biography: Angie Dickinson*, televised documentary hosted by Harry Smith, originally aired October 26, 1999.
8. *Lifetime intimate Portrait* documentary.
9. Ibid.
10. Ibid.
11. Ibid.
12. Carey McWilliams, *California: The Great Exception*, p. 8.
13. Ibid, p. 233.
14. *Headliners and Legends* documentary.
15. Ibid.
16. Ibid.
17. *A&E Biography* documentary.
18. *Headliners and Legends* documentary.
19. *A&E Biography* documentary.
20. Ibid.
21. *Lifetime Intimate Portrait* documentary.
22. Ibid.

23. Ibid.
24. *A&E Biography* documentary.
25. Ibid.
26. Ibid.
27. *Lifetime Intimate Portrait* documentary.
28. *Headliners and Legends* documentary.
29. *A&E Biography* documentary.
30. *Lifetime Intimate Portrait* documentary.
31. *A&E Biography* documentary.
32. James Kaplan, "The King of Ring-A-Ding-Ding," *Vanity Fair*, November, 2007.
33. Ibid.
34. Lauren Bacall, *By Myself*, p. 222.
35. Samuel Fuller, *A Third Face: My Tale of Writing, Fighting and Filmmaking*, p. 340.
36. Ibid
37. Ibid, p. 345.
38. Ibid, p 348.
39. Ibid.
40. *Lifetime Intimate Portrait* documentary.

Biographical Profile: Stardom
1. Todd McCarthy, *Howard Hawks: The Grey Fox of Hollywood*, p. 556.
2. Ibid, p. 562.
3. Robin Wood, *Howard Hawks*, p. 35.
4. Guillermo Cabrera Infante, "Cowboy Cop," in Hillier and Wollen, *Howard Hawks American Artist*, p. 46.
5. David Thomson, *"Have You Seen . . . ?"*, p. 728.
6. Nick Tosches, *Dino: Living High in the Dirty Business of Dreams*, p. 312.
7. Fuller, *A Third Face*, p. 348.
8. *A&E Biography* documentary.
9. *Lifetime Intimate Portrait* documentary.
10. Bosley Crowther, "Screen: 'Bramble Bush,'" *The New York Times*, February 25, 1960.

11. Elaine Dundy, *Finch, Bloody Finch*, p. 238.
12. Kaplan, "The King of Ring-A-Ding-Ding," *Vanity Fair*.
13. *Studio Ten* television interview with Angie Dickinson, conducted by Angela Bishop, originally aired August 30, 2016.
14. *Lifetime Intimate Portrait* documentary.
15. *Studio Ten* interview.
16. Shawn Levy, *Rat Pack Confidential*, p. 108.
17. Tosches, *Dino*, p. 326.
18. *Lifetime Intimate Portrait* documentary.
19. *A&E Biography* documentary.
20. Theodore H. White, *The Making of the President 1960*, p. 164.
21. Vincent Sherman, *Studio Affairs: My Life As a Film Director*, p. 274.
22. Aaron Crouch and Erik Hayden, "'I Want You to Meet This Fella Jack Kennedy': Hollywood Remembers JFK," *The Hollywood Reporter*, November 22, 2013.
23. James Kaplan, *Sinatra: The Chairman*, p. 371.
24. Ibid.
25. Richard Reeves, *President Kennedy: Profile of Power*, p. 35.
26. *A&E Biography* documentary.
27. Sam Kashner, "A Legend with Legs," *Vanity Fair*, January, 2008.
28. Michelangelo Capua, *Jean Negulesco: The Life and Films*, p. 117.
29. Ibid.
30. Scot Eyman, *John Wayne: The Life and Legend*, p. 284.
31. Bill Tusher, "Angie," *Modern Screen*, October, 1963.
32. Ibid
33. Mary Murphy, "Unlike Marilyn Monroe, 'I'm Strong . . . I'm Sturdy,'" *TV Guide*, May 2, 1987.
34. Kaplan, *Sinatra: The Chairman*, p. 441.
35. John Kenneth Galbraith, *Name-Dropping from FDR On*, p. 133.
36. Ibid.
37. Tusher, "Angie," *Modern Screen*.
38. Ibid.
39. Lynn Haney, *Gregory Peck: A Charmed Life*, p. 324.
40. Brent Phillips, *Charles Walters: The Director Who Made Hollywood Dance*, p. 236.

41. Dean Gautschy, "Angie Dickinson New Title Holder," *Los Angeles Herald-Examiner*, March 9, 1963.
42. Abe Greenberg, "Wife and Mother First, Then Actress, Sez Angie," *Hollywood Citizen-News*, October 8, 1969.
43. *Show* magazine interview with Angie Dickinson, *Show*, November, 1963.
44. "Why Men over 35 Have Sexual Magic and Other Important Matters," *Pageant*, March, 1964.
45. Bob Thomas, "Hollywood's Most Eligible," *Associated Press*, January 27, 1964.
46. Ibid.
47. Ibid.
48. *Studio Ten* interview.
49. Review of *Captain Newman, M.D.*, *Los Angeles Herald-Examiner*, December 26, 1963.
50. Review of *Captain Newman, M.D.*, *The New York Times*, February 24, 1964.
51. Review of *Captain Newman, M.D.*, *Film Daily*, October 22, 1963.
52. Murphy, "Unlike Marilyn Monroe, 'I'm Strong . . . I'm Sturdy,'" *TV Guide*.
53. Stuart Kaminsky, *Don Siegel: Director*, p. 172.
54. Review of Criterion Blu-Ray release of *The Killers*, *The New York Times*, August 2, 2015.
55. Kaminsky, *Don Siegel: Director*, p. 169.
56. Norman Jewison, *This Terrible Business Has Been Good to Me*, p. 89.
57. Ibid, pp. 91-92.
58. Robin Wood, *Arthur Penn*, p. 61.
59. Nat Segaloff, *Arthur Penn: American Director*, p. 132.
60. Ibid.
61. Murphy, "Unlike Marilyn Monroe, 'I'm Strong . . . I'm Sturdy,'" *TV Guide*.
62. Peter Manso, *Brando: The Biography*, p. 595.
63. Pauline Kael, *Kiss Kiss Bang Bang*, p. 186.
64. Richard Schickel, review of *The Chase*, *Life*, March 4, 1966.
65. Bosley Crowther, review of *The Chase*, *The New York Times*, February 19, 1966.
66. As quoted in Jeff Stafford, www.tcm.com/thismonth/article/The Chase.

Biographical Profile: All That Pizzazz

1. Charlotte Chandler, *Marlene*, p. 193.
2. Ibid, p. 194.
3. Ibid, p. 193.
4. Burt Bacharach with Robert Greenfield, *Anyone Who Had A Heart: My Life and Music*, p. 53.
5. Chandler, *Marlene*, p. 195.
6. Bacharach, *Anyone Who Had A Heart*, p. 93.
7. *Lifetime Intimate Portrait* documentary.
8. Hal Humphrey, "Angie Not Cool to Being A Girl," *Los Angeles Times*, March 18, 1965.
9. Bacharach, *Anyone Who Had A Heart*, pp. 93-94.
10. *Lifetime Intimate Portrait* documentary.
11. Bacharach, *Anyone Who Had A Heart*, p. 108.
12. Ibid, p. 110.
13. *A&E Biography* documentary.
14. *Daily Variety* review of *Cast A Giant Shadow*, *Daily Variety*, March 30, 1966.
15. Steven Bach, *Marlene Dietrich: Life and Legend*, p. 416.
16. Bacharach, *Anyone Who Had A Heart*, p. 108
17. Ibid, p. 109.
18. Ibid, p. 106.
19. Marlene Dietrich, *Marlene*, p. 241.
20. Bacharach, *Anyone Who Had A Heart*, p. 110.
21. Ibid, p. 111.
22. Ibid, p. 113.
23. Murphy, "Unlike Marilyn Monroe, 'I'm Strong . . . I'm Sturdy,'" *TV Guide*.
24. Ibid.
25. *A&E Biography* documentary.
26. *Lifetime Intimate Portrait* documentary.
27. Ed Leibowitz, "Autism: A Struggle in Black and White, Nikki Bacharach's Story As Told by Her Mother, Actress Angie Dickinson," *Los Angeles*, September, 2010.
28. Bacharach, *Anyone Who Had A Heart*, p. 163.

29. *Lifetime Intimate Portrait* documentary.
30. Bacharach, *Anyone Who Had A Heart*, pp. 163-64.
31. Ibid, p. 164.
32. Angie Dickinson, "Actress Tells Why Marriages Go Sour," *Hollywood Citizen-News*, May 15, 1969.
33. Sheila Graham, "Angie's Marriage 'A Happy Thing,'" *Hollywood Citizen-News*, May 15, 1969.
34. Hollis Alpert, "Fun and Games," *Saturday Review*, September 30, 1967.
35. Howard Junker, "Doublecrossfires," *Newsweek*, September 25, 1967.
36. Kevin Thomas, "*Point Blank* on Paramount Screen," *Los Angeles Times*, October 13, 1967.
37. Tom Shone, review of *Point Blank* rerelease, *The Sunday Times*, June 1, 1998.
38. Robert J. Lentz, *Lee Marvin: His Films and Career*, p. 118.
39. *Daily Variety* review of *Point Blank*, *Daily Variety*, August 31, 1967.
40. Junker, "Doublecrossfires," *Newsweek*.
41. Nadine Edwards, "Emotionally Charged Two-Fisted Picture," *Hollywood Citizen-News*, October 17, 1967.
42. Kevin Thomas, *Point Blank* interview with Angie Dickinson, *Los Angeles Times*, July 14, 1967.
43. John Mahoney, review of *The Last Challenge*, *The Hollywood Reporter*, October 2, 1967.
44. *Lifetime Intimate Portrait* biography.
45. Morton Moss, "Marriage À La Angie," *Los Angeles Herald-Examiner*, June 2, 1977.
46. D.L. Lyons, "JFK and Me," *Ladies' Home Journal*, June, 1975.
47. "Old Flames, Hot Stuff," *People*, August 1, 1994.
48. Burt Reynolds and Jon Winokur, *But Enough About Me*, p. 240.
49. George Eells, *Robert Mitchum*, p. 239.
50. Lee Server, *Robert Mitchum: "Baby, I Don't Care,"* p. 426.
51. Army Archerd, "Good Morning," *Daily Variety*, August 22, 2008.
52. Server, *Robert Mitchum: "Baby, I Don't Care,"* p. 477.
53. Charles Champlin, "'Kind of Nut' Comedy with Credibility Gap," *Los Angeles Times*, October 7, 1969.

54. *Los Angeles Times* review of *Sam Whiskey*, *Los Angeles Times*, March 11, 1969.
55. David Sutherland, "Beauty Highlights Slow-Paced Film," *Hollywood Citizen-News*, March 14, 1969.
56. Kevin Thomas, "Mitchum Stars in 'Young Billy Young,'" *Los Angeles Times*, October 17, 1969.
57. "Some Kind of Nut: The Showmen's Trade Reviews," *Motion Picture Exhibitor*, September 17, 1969.
58. David Talbot, *Brothers: The Hidden History of the Kennedy Years*, pp. 363-64.
59. Lyons, "JFK and Me," *Ladies' Home Journal*.
60. Greenberg, "Wife and Mother First, then Actress, Sez Angie," *Hollywood Citizen-News*.
61. Morton Moss, "She Hangs in There," *Los Angeles Herald-Examiner*, December 14, 1972.
62. Ibid.
63. Ibid.
64. Ibid.
65. Mark Goodman, "Angie and Burt Bacharach: He's the Family Star Now," *People*, June 10, 1974.
66. Moss, "She Hangs in There," *Los Angeles Herald-Examiner*.
67. Murphy, "Unlike Marilyn Monroe, 'I'm Strong . . . I'm Sturdy,'" *TV Guide*.
68. Ibid.
69. Bacharach, *Anyone Who Had A Heart*, p. 167.
70. Murphy, "Unlike Marilyn Monroe, 'I'm Strong . . . I'm Sturdy,'" *TV Guide*.
71. Bacharach, *Anyone Who Had A Heart*, p. 165.
72. Ibid, p. 167.
73. Moss, "She Hangs in There," *Los Angeles Herald-Examiner*.
74. Ibid.
75. Murphy, "Unlike Marilyn Monroe, 'I'm Strong . . . I'm Sturdy,'" *TV Guide*.
76. Moss, "Marriage À La Angie," *Los Angeles Herald-Examiner*.

Biographical Profile: Household Name

1. *Big Bad Mama* production notes housed at Margaret Herrick Library, Academy of Motion Picture Arts and Sciences, Beverly Hills, CA.
2. Moss, "She Hangs in There," *Los Angeles Herald-Examiner.*
3. *Headliners and Legends* documentary.
4. *Lifetime Intimate Portrait* documentary.
5. Cecil Smith, "Angie Dickinson's Ticket to Stardom," *Los Angeles Times*, June 25, 1976.
6. Frank DeCaro, "Angie Dickinson Wasn't So Tough in 'Police Woman,' But She Sure Looked Good," *The New York Times*, April 16, 2006.
7. *Headliners and Legends* documentary.
8. DeCaro, "Angie Dickinson Wasn't So Tough in 'Police Woman,' But She Sure Looked Good," *The New York Times.*
9. Scott Haller, "Sex and The Single Star," *People*, February 17, 1985.
10. *A&E Biography* documentary.
11. Smith, "Angie Dickinson's Ticket to Stardom," *Los Angeles Times.*
12. *A&E Biography* documentary.
13. Moss, "Marriage À La Angie," *Los Angeles Herald-Examiner.*
14. Arthur Asa Berger, *The TV-Guided American*, p. 106.
15. *Lifetime Intimate Portrait* documentary.
16. Lyons, "JFK and Me," *Ladies' Home Journal.*
17. *A&E Biography* documentary.
18. Ibid.
19. Roderick Mann, "Angie Dickinson: Now She Can Sleep In," *Los Angeles Times*, May 28, 1978.
20. Wilmer Ames, "Solo, Vulnerable, Angie Dickinson, 47, Finds Her Career Still Has Legs But Does Her Marriage?," *People,* November 24, 1978.
21. Moss, "Marriage À La Angie," *Los Angeles Herald-Examiner.*
22. Smith, "Angie Dickinson's Ticket to Stardom," *Los Angeles Times.*
23. Dorothy Manners, "Angie Dickinson: Not Your Average Cop," *Los Angeles Herald-Examiner*, April 10, 1977.
24. Kenneth Tynan, *The Diaries of Kenneth Tynan*, p. 355.

25. Manners, "Angie Dickinson: Not Your Average Cop," *Los Angeles Herald-Examiner*.
26. Ibid.
27. John O'Connor, review of *A Sensitive, Passionate Man*, *The New York Times*, June 6, 1977.
28. Manners, "Angie Dickinson: Not Your Average Cop," *Los Angeles Herald-Examiner*.
29. Tosches, *Dino: Living High in the Dirty Business of Dreams*, p. 414.
30. Ibid.
31. Manners, "Angie Dickinson: Not Your Average Cop," *Los Angeles Herald-Examiner*.
32. Mann, "Angie Dickinson: Now She Can Sleep In," *Los Angeles Times*.
33. "Mr. Blackwell Names Worst Dressed List," *Los Angeles Herald-Examiner*, January 5, 1977.
34. *CBS Sunday Morning Profile: Angie Dickinson*, televised interview with Angie Dickinson, conducted by Mo Rocca, originally aired February 24, 2019.
35. Ibid.
36. Mann, "Angie Dickinson: Now She Can Sleep In," *Los Angeles Times*.
37. Ibid.
38. David Moore, interview with Angie Dickinson for Bakersfield, CA, ABC-TV Affiliate, 1978, posted December 8, 2016.
39. John Corry, "*Pearl*, Mini-Series on Attack," *The New York Times*, August 21, 1985.
40. Ames, "Solo, Vulnerable, Angie Dickinson, 47, Finds Her Career Still Has Legs But Does Her Marriage?," *People*.
41. Ibid.
42. "Full House," *Los Angeles Times*, May 31, 1979.
43. *Klondike Fever* location filming field report, *The Hollywood Reporter*, March 3, 1980.
44. *Weekly Variety* review of *Klondike Fever*, *Weekly Variety*, February 13, 1980.
45. John Newland obituary, *Los Angeles Times*, January 17, 2000.

46. Tom Buckley, "TV: *The Suicide's Wife* Has Strong Guilt Feelings," *The New York Times*, November 7, 1979.
47. As quoted in *People* interview, August 28, 1989.
48. Murphy, "Unlike Marilyn Monroe, 'I'm Strong . . . I'm Sturdy,'" *TV Guide*.
49. Bacharach, *Anyone Who Had A Heart*, p. 202.
50. *Headliners and Legends* documentary.
51. Ibid.
52. Marilyn Beck, *Dressed to Kill* interview with Angie Dickinson, *Los Angeles Times*, September 12, 1980.
53. Pauline Kael, "Master Spy, Master Seducer," *The New Yorker*, August 4, 1980.
54. Andrew Sarris, "Dreck to Kill," *The Village Voice*, September 23, 1980.
55. Michael Sragow, "A Chiller to Steam up the Summer," *Los Angeles Herald-Examiner*, July 25, 1980.
56. Douglas Edwards, "The Film Ticket," *The Advocate*, September 4, 1980.
57. Kenneth Turan, "Blood and Guts," *New West*, August 11, 1980.
58. Sheila Benson, "'Dressed to Kill': The Terror Is Stunning," *Los Angeles Times*, July 25, 1980.

Biographical Profile: Afterglow

1. Nicole Szulc, "50 Picket Opening of 'Charlie Chan' Film," *Los Angeles Herald-Examiner*, February 14, 1981.
2. Ibid.
3. Alan Belkin, "Asians in the News," *Los Angeles Times*, March 8, 1981.
4. Ibid.
5. Jim Harwood, "Failure to Inform Director Aldrich of 'Arctic' Budget Costs Ruddy and Chow 45 G," *Daily Variety*, April 18, 1980.
6. Roderick Mann, "Angie Dickinson," *Los Angeles Times*, May 7, 1981.
7. Janet Maslin, "TV: 'Dial M for Murder' in Remake," *The New York Times*, April 9, 1981.

8. Richard Turner, "Angie's 'Real Drama': A Crazy Night of Crime," *Los Angeles Herald-Examiner*, October 14, 1980.
9. Server, *Robert Mitchum: "Baby, I Don't Care,"* p. 489.
10. Fred De Cordova, *Johnny Came Lately*, p. 98.
11. Murphy, "Unlike Marilyn Monroe, 'I'm Strong . . . I'm Sturdy,'" *TV Guide*.
12. *A&E Biography* documentary.
13. *Every Woman* profile of Angie Dickinson, *Every Woman*, February, 1982.
14. *Daily Variety* interview with Angie Dickinson, *Daily Variety*, September 28, 1981.
15. Bacharach, *Anyone Who Had A Heart*, p. 193.
16. Leibowitz, "Autism: A Struggle in Black and White," *Los Angeles*.
17. Ibid.
18. Ibid.
19. Bacharach, *Anyone Who Had A Heart*, p. 194.
20. Ibid, p. 196.
21. Ibid.
22. Leibowitz, "Autism: A Portrait in Black and White," *Los Angeles*.
23. Ibid.
24. Ibid.
25. Bacharach, *Anyone Who Had A Heart*, p. 197.
26. Leibowitz, "Autism: A Portrait in Black and White," *Los Angeles*.
27. Ibid.
28. Ibid.
29. Ibid.
30. Ibid.
31. Bacharach, *Anyone Who Had A Heart*, p. 197.
32. Angie Dickinson, "Helpless to Save Her Sister from Alzheimer's, An Anguished Actress Provides what Comfort She Can," *People*, November 12, 1990.
33. Ibid.
34. Ibid.
35. Ibid.
36. Ibid.

37. Ibid.
38. Eirik Knutzen, "Angie Dickinson Knows What She Wants," *Los Angeles Herald-Examiner*, November 25, 1984.
39. John O'Connor, review of *A Touch of Scandal*, *The New York Times*, November 27, 1984.
40. Scott Haller, "Sex and the Single Star," *People*, February 17, 1985.
41. Ibid.
42. *Los Angeles Times* review of *Big Bad Mama II*, *Los Angeles Times*, February 13, 1988.
43. *The Hollywood Reporter* review of *Big Bad Mama II*, *The Hollywood Reporter*, February 19, 1988.
44. *Headliners and Legends* documentary.
45. *A&E Biography* documentary.
46. Ibid.
47. J.D. Reed and Kristina Johnson, "Still Sexy After All These Years," *People*, May 24, 1993.
48. Ibid.
49. John O'Connor, "The Sunshiny Menace of 'Wild Palms,'" *The New York Times*, May 16, 1993.
50. Ken Tucker, review of *Wild Palms*, *Entertainment Weekly*, May 14, 1993.
51. Mary Harron, "Television: Never Mind Reality Just Revel in the Kitsch," *The Independent*, November 7, 1993.
52. Leibowitz, "Autism: A Portrait in Black and White," *Los Angeles*.
53. Ibid.
54. Ibid.
55. Ibid.
56. Bacharach, *Anyone Who Had A Heart*, p. 198.
57. Ibid, p. 199.
58. Ibid, p. 243.
59. "Angie Dickinson . . . to make an appearance today at the New York Academy of Sciences," *The New York Times*, June 10, 1993.
60. Ibid.
61. Reed and Johnson, "Still Sexy After All These Years," *People*.
62. Ibid.

63. Ibid.
64. Ibid.
65. John Barrowman, *Anything Goes*, p. 92.
66. Ibid.
67. Reed and Johnson, "Still Sexy After All These Years," *People*.
68. "Actress Angie Dickinson . . . testified in a Boston court on behalf of a man . . . ," *The Hollywood Reporter*, May 18, 1990.
69. "Morning Report: It's Not Angie Dickinson's Life," *Los Angeles Times*, November 11, 1993.
70. George Wayne, "Thoroughly Modern Angie," *Vanity Fair*, April, 1995.
71. Julia Black, note on March 1966 cover photo, *Esquire*, October, 2015.
72. Ibid.
73. Jeff Schwager, "Back in the Saddle," *Boxoffice*, February, 1994.
74. Ibid.
75. Ibid.
76. Ibid.
77. Ibid.
78. Leibowitz, "Autism: A Struggle in Black and White," *Los Angeles*.
79. Ibid.
80. Bacharach, *Anyone Who Had A Heart*, p. 200.
81. Ruth Ryon, "Angie Dickinson Buys Home of Cartoonist Walter Lantz," *Los Angeles Times*, June 26, 1994.
82. Leibowitz, "Autism: A Struggle in Black and White," *Los Angeles*.
83. Ibid.
84. Tosches, *Dino: Living High in the Dirty Business of Dream*, p. 441.
85. Todd Purdum, "Family and Friends Bid Sinatra Farewell," *The New York Times*, May 21, 1998.
86. Ibid.
87. Ibid.
88. Leibowitz, "Autism: A Struggle in Black and White," *Los Angeles*.
89. Reynolds and Winokur, *But Enough About Me*, p. 240.
90. Larry King, "Angie Dickinson Discusses Her Role in 'Duets'," *CNN Larry King Live* telecast, September 19, 2000.

91. *Pay It Forward* production notes housed at Margaret Herrick Library, Academy of Motion Picture Arts and Sciences, Beverly Hills, CA.
92. Ibid.
93. Ibid.
94. Todd McCarthy, review of *Pay It Forward*, *Weekly Variety*, October 9, 2000.
95. King, "Angie Dickinson Discusses Her Role in 'Duets'," *CNN Larry King Live*.
96. Arliss Howard, *Big Bad Love* IFC production notes housed at Margaret Herrick Library, Academy of Motion Picture Arts and Sciences, Beverly Hills, CA.
97. *Life* magazine interview with Angie Dickinson, *Life*, May, 2000.
98. *People* magazine interview with Angie Dickinson, *People*, April 21, 1997.
99. *Pay It Forward* production notes.
100. Larry King, "Unthinkable: The Alzheimer's Epidemic," *CNN Larry King Live* telecast, May 1, 2011.
101. Ibid.
102. Ibid.
103. Ibid.
104. Ibid.
105. Leibowitz, "Autism: A Struggle in Black and White," *Los Angeles*.
106. Ibid.
107. Ibid.
108. Ibid.
109. Ibid.
110. Bacharach, *Anyone Who Had A Heart*, p. 245.
111. Ibid, p. 247.
112. Ibid.
113. Ibid, p. 246.
114. Lea Nikki Bacharach obituary, *Los Angeles Times*, January 7, 2007.
115. Bacharach, *Anyone Who Had A Heart*, p. 246.
116. Joan Didion, *Blue Nights*, p. 13.
117. Ibid, p. 44.

118. Alessandra Stanley, "What to Expect When You're Lying (and other television reviews)," *The New York Times*, July 17, 2009.
119. Susan King, "A Memory Maker," *Los Angeles Times*, July 15, 2009.
120. Bacharach, *Anyone Who Had A Heart*, p. 264.
121. *CBS Sunday Morning Profile: Angie Dickinson*.
122. "Made in Hollywood Awards," *Daily Variety*, August 16, 2013.

The Films

1. Server, *Robert Mitchum: "Baby, I Don't Care,"* p. 285.
2. Eyman, *John Wayne: The Life and Legend*, p. 303.
3. E.B. Radcliffe, "A Milestone," *Cincinnati Enquirer*, February 7, 1960.
4. Ernest Hemingway, *The Short Stories of Ernest Hemingway*, p. 283.
5. Ibid, p. 287.
6. Kaminsky, *Don Siegel: Director*, p. 172.
7. Wood, *Arthur Penn*, p. 52.
8. Ibid, p. 61.
9. David Thomson, *The New Biographical Dictionary of Film*, p. 568.
10. Leonard Maltin, *Leonard Maltin's 2015 Movie Guide*, p. 1304.
11. Archerd, "Good Morning," *Daily Variety*.
12. Thomson, *The New Biographical Dictionary of Film*, p. 889.
13. James Robert Parish, *Gus Van Sant: An Unauthorized Biography*, p. 189.
14. Schwager, "Back in the Saddle," *Boxoffice*.

Sources

"Actress Angie Dickinson ... testified in a Boston court on behalf of a man ...." *The Hollywood Reporter*, May 18, 1990.

A & E Biography: Angie Dickinson. Televised documentary hosted by Harry Smith, originally aired October 26, 1999.

Alpert, Hollis. "Fun and Games." *Saturday Review*, September 30, 1967.

Ames, Wilmer. "Solo, Vulnerable, Angie Dickinson, 47, Finds Her Career Still Has Legs But Does Her Marriage?" *People*, November 24, 1978.

"Angie Dickinson ... to make an appearance today at the New York Academy of Sciences." *The New York Times*, June 10, 1993.

Archerd, Army. "Good Morning." *Daily Variety*, August 22, 2008.

_____ "Just for Variety." *Daily Variety*, June 9, 1999.

Bacall, Lauren. *By Myself.* New York: Alfred A. Knopf, 1979.

Bach, Steven. *Marlene Dietrich: Life and Legend.* New York: William Morrow and Company, Inc., 1992.

Bacharach, Burt with Robert Greenfield. *Anyone Who Had a Heart: My Life and Music.* New York: Harper, 2013.

Bacharach, Lea Nikki obituary. *Los Angeles Times*, January 7, 2007.

Barrowman, John. *Anything Goes.* London: Michael O'Mara Books Limited, 2008.

Beck, Marilyn. *Dressed to Kill* interview with Angie Dickinson. *Los Angeles Times*, September 12, 1980.

Belkin, Alan. "Asians in the News." *Los Angeles Times*, March 8, 1981.

Benson, Sheila. "Dressed to Kill: The Terror Is Stunning." *Los Angeles Times*, July 25, 1980.

Berger, Arthur Asa. *The TV-Guided American*. New York: Walker and Company, 1976.

Big Bad Mama production files housed at Margaret Herrick Library, Academy Of Motion Picture Arts and Sciences, Beverly Hills, CA.

Black, Julia. Note on March 1966 cover photo. *Esquire*, October, 2015.

Bragg, Melvyn. *Richard Burton: A Life*. New York: Little, Brown and Company, 1988.

Buckley, Tom. "TV: *The Suicide's Wife* Has Strong Guilt Feelings." *The New York Times*, November 7, 1979.

Capua, Michelangelo. *Jean Negulesco: The Life and Films*. Jefferson, NC: McFarland and Company, Inc., Publishers, 2017.

Cather, Willa. *My Antonia*. New York: Penguin Books, 1994.

CBS Sunday Morning Profile: Angie Dickinson. Televised interview conducted by Mo Rocca, originally aired February 24, 2019.

Champlin, Charles. "'Kind of Nut' Comedy with Credibility Gap." *Los Angeles Times*, October 7, 1969.

Chandler, Charlotte. *Marlene*. Milwaukee, Wisconsin: Applause Theatre and Cinema Books, 2011.

Corry, John. "*Pearl*, Mini-Series on Attack." *The New York Times*, August 21, 1985.

Crouch, Aaron and Erik Hayden. "'I Want You to Meet This Fella, Jack Kennedy': Hollywood Remembers JKF." *The Hollywood Reporter*, November 22, 2013.

Crowther, Bosley. Review of *The Chase*. *The New York Times*, February 19, 1966

———. "Screen: 'Bramble Bush.'" *The New York Times*, February 25, 1960.

Daily Variety interview with Angie Dickinson. *Daily Variety*, September 28, 1981.

DeCaro, Frank. "Angie Dickinson Wasn't So Tough in 'Police Woman,' But She Sure Looked Good." *The New York Times*, April 16, 2006.

De Cordova, Fred. *Johnny Came Lately*. New York: Simon and Schuster, 1988.

Dickinson, Angie. "Actress Tells Why Marriages Go Sour." *Hollywood Citizen-News*, May 15, 1969.

———. "Helpless to Save Her Sister from Alzheimer's, An Anguished Actress Provides What Comfort She Can." *People*, November 12, 1990.

Didion, Joan. *Blue Nights*. New York: Alfred A. Knopf, 2011.

Dietrich, Marlene. *Marlene*. New York: Grove Press, 1989.

Dundy, Elaine. *Finch, Bloody Finch: A Life of Peter Finch*. New York: Holt, Rinehart and Winston, 1980.

Edwards, Douglas. "The Film Ticket." *The Advocate*, September 4, 1980.

Edwards, Nadine. "Emotionally Charged Two-Fisted Picture." *Hollywood Citizen-News*, October 17, 1967

Eells, George. *Robert Mitchum*. New York: Franklin Watts, 1984.

Every Woman profile of Angie Dickinson. *Every Woman*, February, 1982.

Eyman, Scott. *John Wayne: The Life and Legend*. New York: Simon and Schuster, 2014.

Fuller, Samuel. *A Third Face: My Tale of Writing, Fighting and Filmmaking*. New York: Alfred A. Knopf, 2002.

"Full House." *Los Angeles Times*, May 31, 1979.

Galbraith, John Kenneth. *Name-Dropping from FDR On*. New York: Houghton Mifflin Harcourt, 1999.

Garnham, Nicholas. *Samuel Fuller*. New York: The Viking Press, 1971.

Gautschy, Dean. "Angie Dickinson New Title Holder." *Los Angeles Herald-Examiner*, March 9, 1963.

Goodman, Mark. "Angie and Burt Bacharach: He's the Family Star Now." *People*, June 10, 1974.

Graham, Sheila. "Angie's Marriage 'A Happy Thing.'" *Hollywood Citizen-News*, January 22, 1968.

Greenberg, Abe. "Wife and Mother First, Then Actress, Sez Angie." *Hollywood-Citizen-News*, October 8, 1969.

Haller, Scot. "Sex and the Single Star." *People*, February 17, 1985.

Haney, Lynn. *Gregory Peck: A Charmed Life*. New York: Carroll and Grant, Publishers, 2004.

Harron, Mary. "Television: Never Mind Reality Just Revel in the Kitsch." *The Independent*, November 7, 1993.

Harwood, Jim. "Failure to Inform Director Aldrich of 'Arctic' Budget Costs Ruddy and Chow 45G." *Daily Variety*, April 18, 1980.

Headliners and Legends: Angie Dickinson. Televised MSNBC documentary hosted by Matt Lauer, originally aired 2000.

Higgins, Bill. "Pre-Kardashian, Angie Dickinson Dared to Bare." *The Hollywood Reporter*, November 28, 2014.

Howard, Arliss. *Big Bad Love* IFC production notes housed at Margaret Herrick Library, Academy of Motion Picture Arts and Sciences, Beverly Hills, CA.

Humphrey, Hal. "Angie Not Cool to Being a Girl." *Los Angeles Times*, March 18, 1965.

Infante, Guillermo Cabrera. "Cowboy Cop," in Jim Hillier and Peter Wollen, eds., *Howard Hawks American Artist*. London: British Film Institute, 1996.

Jewison, Norman. *This Terrible Business Has Been Good to Me*. New York: Thomas Dunne Books, 2004.

Junker, Howard. "Doublecrossfires." *Newsweek*, September 25, 1967.

Kael, Pauline. *Kiss Kiss Bang Bang*. New York: Bantam Books, 1969.

_____"Master Spy, Master Seducer." *The New Yorker*, August 4, 1980.

Kaminsky, Stuart. *Don Siegel: Director*. New York: Curtis Books, 1974.

Kaplan, James. *Sinatra: The Chairman*. New York: Doubleday, 2015.

_____"The King of Ring-A-Ding-Ding." *Vanity Fair*, November, 2007.

Kashner, Sam. "A Legend with Legs." *Vanity Fair*, January, 2008.

Keesey, Douglas. *Brian De Palma's Split-Screen*. Jackson, Mississippi: University Press of Mississippi, 2015.

Kilday, Gregg. "Dressing Down." *Los Angeles Herald-Examiner*, August 18, 1980.

King, Larry. "Angie Dickinson Discusses Her Role in 'Duets.'" *CNN Larry King Live* telecast, September 19, 2000.

_____"Unthinkable: The Alzheimer's Epidemic." *CNN Larry King Live* telecast, May 1, 2011.

King, Susan. "A Memory Maker." *Los Angeles Times*, July 15, 2009

Klondike Fever location filming field report. *The Hollywood Reporter*, March 3, 1980.

Knutzen, Eirik. "Angie Dickinson Knows What She Wants." *Los Angeles Herald-Examiner*, November 25, 1984.

Langer, Carole video interview with Angie Dickinson. October 17, 1998.

Lehman, Katherine J. *Those Girls: Women in Sixties and Seventies Popular Culture*. Lawrence, Kansas: University Press of Kansas, 2011.

Leibowitz, Ed. "Autism: A Struggle in Black and White, Nikki Bacharach's Story As Told by Her Mother, Actress Angie Dickinson." *Los Angeles*, September 1, 2010.

Lentz, Robert J. *Lee Marvin: His Films and Career*. Jefferson, North Carolina: McFarland and Company, Inc., Publishers, 2000.

Levy, Shawn. *Rat Pack Confidential*. New York: Doubleday, 1988.

Life magazine interview with Angie Dickinson. *Life*, May, 2000.

Lifetime Intimate Portrait: Angie Dickinson. Televised documentary hosted by Meredith Vieira, originally aired 2002.

Lyons, D.L. "JFK and Me." *Ladies' Home Journal*, June, 1975.

"Made in Hollywood Awards." *Daily Variety*, August 16, 2013.

Magill, Frank, ed. *Magill's Survey of Cinema*. Englewood Cliffs, NJ: Salem Press, 1981.

Mahoney, John. Review of *The Last Challenge*. *The Hollywood Reporter*, October 2, 1967.

Maltin, Leonard. *Leonard Maltin's 2015 Movie Guide*. New York: Signet, 2014.

Mann, Roderick. "Angie Dickinson." *Los Angeles Times*, May 7, 1986.

_____"Angie Dickinson: Now She Can Sleep In." *Los Angeles Times*, May 28, 1978.

Manners, Dorothy. "Angie Dickinson: Not Your Average Cop." *Los Angeles Herald Examiner*, April 10, 1977.

Manso, Peter. *Brando: The Biography*. New York: Hyperion, 1994.

Maslin, Janet. "TV: 'Dial M for Murder' in Remake." *The New York Times*, April 9, 1981.

Mast, Gerald. *Howard Hawks, Storyteller*. Oxford: Oxford University Press, 1982.

McBride, Joseph. *Focus on Howard Hawks*. Englewood Cliffs, NJ: Prentice-Hall, Inc., 1972.

_____*Hawks on Hawks*. Berkeley: University of California Press, 1982.

McCarthy, Todd. *Howard Hawks: The Grey Fox of Hollywood*. New York: Grove Press, 1997.

_____Review of *Pay It Forward*. *Weekly Variety*, October 9, 2000.

McWilliams, Carey. *California: The Great Exception*. Santa Barbara, CA: Peregrine Smith, Inc., 1976.

Moore, David. Interview with Angie Dickinson. Bakersfield, CA, ABC Affiliate, 1978, posted December 8, 2016.

"Morning Report: It's Not Angie Dickinson's Life." *Los Angeles Times*, November 11, 1993.

Moss, Morton. "Marriage À La Angie." *Los Angeles Herald-Examiner*, June 2, 1977.

_____"She Hangs in There." *Los Angeles Herald-Examiner*, December 14, 1972.

"Mr. Blackwell Names Worst Dressed List." *Los Angeles Herald-Examiner*, January 5, 1977.

Murphy, Mary. "Unlike Marilyn Monroe, 'I'm Strong . . . I'm Sturdy.'" *TV Guide*, May 2, 1987.

Naremore, James. *Acting in the Cinema*. Los Angeles: University of California Press, 1988.

Newland, John obituary. *Los Angeles Times*, January 17, 2000.

"Old Flames, Hot Stuff," *People*, August 1, 1994.

O'Connor, John. Review of *A Sensitive, Passionate Man*. *The New York Times*, June 6, 1977.

_____Review of *A Touch of Scandal*. *The New York Times*, November 27, 1984.

_____"The Sunshiny Menace of 'Wild Palms.'" *The New York Times*, May 16, 1993.

Oppenheimer, Jerry and Jack Vitek. *Idol, Rock Hudson: The True Story of an American Film Hero*. New York: Villard Books, 1986.

Parish, James Robert. *Gus Van Sant: An Unauthorized Biography*. New York: Thunder's Mouth Press, 2001.

Pay It Forward production notes housed at Margaret Herrick Library, Academy of Motion Picture Arts and Sciences, Beverly Hills, CA.

People magazine interview with Angie Dickinson. *People*, April 21, 1997.

Phillips, Brent. *Charles Walters: The Director Who Made Hollywood Dance*. Lexington, Kentucky: The University Press of Kentucky, 2014.

Purdum, Todd. "Family and Friends Bid Sinatra Farewell." *The New York Times*, May 21, 1998.

Radcliffe, E.B. "A Milestone." *Cincinnati Enquirer*, February 7, 1960.

Redelings, Lowell E. "The Hollywood Scene: Producers at Work." *Hollywood Citizen-News*, May 7, 1958.

Reed, J.D., and Kristina Johnson. "Still Sexy After All These Years." *People*, May 24, 1993.

Reeves, Richard. *President Kennedy: Profile of Power*. New York: Simon and Schuster, 1993.

Reynolds, Burt and Jon Winokur. *But Enough About Me*. New York: G.P. Putnam's Sons, 2015.

Ryon, Ruth. "Angie Dickinson Buys Home of Cartoonist Walter Lantz." *Los Angeles Times*, June 26, 1994.

Sarris, Andrew. "Derivative." *The Village Voice*, July 29, 1980.

_____"Dreck to Kill." *The Village Voice*, September 23, 1980.

Schickel, Richard. Review of *The Chase*. *Life*, March 4, 1966.

Schwager, Jeff. "Back in the Saddle." *Boxoffice*, February, 1994.

Segaloff, Nat. *Arthur Penn: American Director*. Lexington: University Press of Kentucky, 2011.

Server, Lee. *Robert Mitchum: "Baby, I Don't Care."* New York: St. Martin's Griffin, 2001.

Sherman, Vincent. *Studio Affairs: My Life as a Film Director*. Lexington, Kentucky: The University Press of Kentucky, 1996.

Shone, Tom. Review of *Point Blank* rerelease. *The Sunday Times*, June 1, 1998.

Show magazine interview with Angie Dickson. *Show*, November, 1963.

Smith, Cecil. "Angie Dickinson's Ticket to Stardom." *Los Angeles Times*, June 25, 1976.

"Some Kind of Nut: The Showmen's Trade Reviews." *Motion Picture Exhibitor*, September 17, 1969.

Sragow, Michael. "A Chiller to Steam up the Summer." *Los Angeles Herald Examiner*, July 25, 1980.

Stanley, Alessandra. "What to Expect When You're Lying (and other television reviews)." *The New York Times*, July 17, 2009.

Studio 10. Australian television interview with Angie Dickinson. Conducted by Angela Bishop, originally aired August 30, 2016.

Sutherland, David. "Beauty Highlights Slow-Paced Film." *Hollywood Citizen-News*, March 14, 1969.

Szulc, Nicole. "50 Picket Opening of 'Charlie Chan' Film." *Los Angeles Herald-Examiner*, February 14, 1981.

Talbot, David. *Brothers: The Hidden History of the Kennedy Years*. New York: Free Press, 2007.

Thomas, Bob. "Hollywood's Most Eligible." Associated Press column, January 27, 1964.

Thomas, Kevin. "Mitchum Stars in 'Young Billy Young.'" *Los Angeles Times*, October 17, 1969.

_____*Point Blank* interview with Angie Dickinson. *Los Angeles Times*, July 14, 1967.

_____"'Point Blank' on Paramount Screen." *Los Angeles Times*, October 13, 1967.

Thomson, David. "*Have You Seen . . . ?*". New York: Alfred A. Knopf, 2009.

_____*The New Biographical Dictionary of Film*. New York: Alfred A. Knopf, 2002.

Tosches, Nick. *Dino: Living High in the Dirty Business of Dreams*. New York: Doubleday, 1992.

Tucker, Ken. Review of *Wild Palms*. *Entertainment Weekly*, May 14, 1993.

Turan, Kenneth. "Blood and Guts." *New West*, August 11, 1980.

Turner, Richard. "Angie's 'Real Drama': A Crazy Night of Crime." *Los Angeles Herald-Examiner*, October 14, 1980.

Tusher, Bill. "Angie." *Modern Screen*, October, 1963.

Tynan, Kenneth. *The Diaries of Kenneth Tynan*, ed. John Lahr. London: Bloomsbury, 2001.

US Weekly magazine interview with Angie Dickinson. *US Weekly*, February 20, 1979.

Vadim, Roger. *Pretty Maids All in a Row* production notes housed at Margaret Herrick Library, Academy of Motion Picture Arts and Sciences, Beverly Hills, CA.

Wayne, George. "Thoroughly Modern Angie." *Vanity Fair*, April, 1995.

White, Theodore H. *The Making of the President 1960*. New York: Atheneum Publishers, 1961.

"Why Men Over 35 Have Sexual Magic and Other Important Matters." *Pageant*, March, 1964.

Wood, Robin. *Arthur Penn*. New York: Frederick A. Praeger, Inc., Publishers, 1969.

_____ *Howard Hawks*. London: British Film Institute, 1981.

Zehme, Bill. *The Way You Wear Your Hat: Frank Sinatra and the Lost Art of Livin'*. New York: Harper Collins, 1997.

Index

Academy Awards, 41, 80, 95, 114, 124, 134, 175-76, 372, 400-01, 475
Ace, Goodman, 264, 268-69
Acker, Sharon, 92, 394, 402
Affleck, Casey, 203, 543, 546
Aghayan, Ray, 68, 124, 363, 366, 368-69
Akins, Claude, 108, 222, 278, 349
Albert, Eddie, 63, 108, 341, 347
Aldrich, Robert, 151, 246, 492
Allen, Corey, 108
Allen, Nancy, 143, 469, 476, 482
Allyson, June, 108
Altman, Robert, 61, 103, 124, 201, 527, 568
Alzheimer's disease, 163-164, 185-86, 199, 205, 392
Ameche, Don, 42, 310, 314-15
Andrews, Stanley, 14
Angie, the Lieutenant (TV movie), 180, 556
Ann-Margret, 111, 443, 446-49, 520
Antonioni, Michelangelo, 54, 568
Archerd, Army, 98, 427
Arness, James, 18-19, 240, 243-44, 246
Arquette, Cliff, 13
Art of Love, The (film), 67, 69, 93, 362, 365-69, 564
Asperger Syndrome, 88

Bacall, Lauren, 17, 25, 27-28, 57, 79, 137, 199, 285, 288-89, 460
Bach, Steven, 83
Bacharach, Bert, 75
Bacharach, Burt, 75, 210-11
  career achievements of, 76-80, 82, 88-89, 94-95, 102, 122-24, 142

  daughter Nikki and, 86-88, 112, 159-63, 183-85, 193, 207
  Marlene Dietrich and, 76-77, 79, 83-84
  marriage to Angie, 80-89, 94-95, 102, 105-06, 122-25
  relationships of, 105-06, 141, 184-85
Bacharach, Lea Nikki, 136, 142, 159, 192, 194, 199, 204
  birth of, 85-86
  childhood of, 87-88
  death of, 206-08
  health challenges of, 86-88, 162, 193
  mother's care for, 126-27, 136, 194
  schooling of, 88, 112, 126, 160-62, 183-84
Barris, Chuck, 81
Barrowman, John, 186-87
Barry, Gene, 20, 55, 57, 252, 259-61
Basinger, Kim, 204, 549, 552
Beatty, Warren, 54, 60, 100, 127
Belafonte, Harry, 44, 263
Belkin, Alan, 150
Bellarmine-Jefferson High School, 9-10
Bello, Maria, 202
Belushi, Jim, 182
Benedict, Richard, 37, 114, 291, 302
Ben-Hur (film), 41, 49
Bennett, Bruce, 231, 234
Bergen, Candice, 173
Berger, Arthur Asa, 121
Berger, Senta, 82, 85, 378, 386-87,

Berle, Milton, 42, 94, 129, 178, 188, 196
Bernard, Ed, 115-16
Bez, Frank, 189
Big Bad Love (film), 202, 536, 538, 540-42
Big Bad Mama (film), 113-14, 450, 453-55, 499, 539, 559-60, 563-64, 567
Big Bad Mama II (film), 174, 454, 494, 497, 499-500
Big Valley, The (TV show), 96, 116
Bigelow, Kathryn, 182, 201
Biroc, Joseph, 235, 239, 245-47, 252, 259
Bishop, Angela, 36, 61
Bishop, Joey, xi-xii, 37-38, 130, 302, 304, 546
Black Whip, The (film), 18, 244-46
Blackwell, Mr., 132
Bogart, Humphrey, 17, 28, 137, 285, 508
Bon Jovi, Jon, 202, 529, 533-35
Boone, Richard, 109
Boorman, John, 89-91, 93, 394, 397-398, 401-03, 565
Bowen, Warren, 10
Bramble Bush, The (film), xiii, 31-33, 41, 295, 298
Brand, Neville, 220, 270, 272, 275-77
Brando, Marlon, 71-74, 222, 300, 370, 372-77, 416, 561, 564-65
Brandy, Slim, 106
Bratt, Benjamin, 520
Braugher, Andre, 523, 527-28
Brazzi, Rossano, 333, 338-40
Breen, Richard, 61, 341, 348
Brennan, Walter, 25, 278, 288, 290-91
Bridges, Lloyd, 95, 101, 553
Bronson, Charles, 151-52, 489, 493-94
Brooks, Richard, 30
Brown, Leo "Bud" (father), 2-5, 8-9, 12, 86-87, 106, 129
Brown, Fredrika Hehr (mother), 2, 4-9, 12, 81, 142, 169
Brown, Janet (sister), 3-8, 10, 32
Brown, Mary Lou (sister), 3-8, 10, 163-65, 185, 199, 205
Brynner, Yul, 82, 85, 378, 382, 386-87, 391-92

Burnett, Carol, 126, 178
Burton, Richard, 31-33, 36, 107, 295, 298-301, 564-65, 588
Butch Cassidy and the Sundance Kid (film), 80, 95, 102, 415
Buzzi, Ruth, 130-131
Byrnes, Edward, 45

Cahn, Sammy, 16, 44, 304
Caine, Michael, 143, 469, 475, 478, 482, 564
Cal Lutheran University, 183-84
Calvet, Corinne, 115
Calypso Joe (film), 261-62
Campanella, Joseph, 115, 188
Canby, Vincent, 416, 478, 494
Cannes Film Festival, 54, 347
Captain Newman, M.D. (film), 28, 57, 61-63, 68, 341, 344, 346, 348-49, 562, 564-65
Capucine, 26, 80
Carradine, David, 173, 422, 429
Carrière, Jean-Claude, 111, 137, 443, 449, 456
Carson, Jack, 32-33, 295, 300, 359
Carson, John David, 104, 429, 433-37
Carson, Johnny, 129, 131, 144, 156-58, 210, 567
Carter, Lynda, 167
Carter, Peter, 463, 467-69
Carvey, Dana, 177
Case of Libel, A (TV movie), 95, 99, 553
Cassavetes, John, 64, 349, 351, 355, 361, 568
Cassidy, Joanna, 173
Cassie & Company (TV show), 157-58
Cast a Giant Shadow (film), 82, 378, 383, 385-87, 564
Cather, Willa, 1
Caviezel, James, 529, 533-34
Chamberlain, Richard, 78
Chandler, Charlotte, 76
Charlie Chan and the Curse of the Dragon Queen (film), 149, 483, 485, 487-89, 560, 566

Chase, The (film), 71, 74, 80, 370, 372, 374-77, 561-562
Cheadle, Don, 203, 543
Chevalier, Maurice, 47, 325, 329-332
China Gate (film), 20, 21, 55, 149, 252-60, 564-65
Chow, Raymond, 151-52,
Cinecittà, 49, 82, 331, 383
Clark, Dick, 177
Clooney, George, 203, 543, 546
Cole, Nat "King," 20, 252, 260,
Coleman, Cy, 68, 363, 366
Colgate Comedy Hour, The (TV show), xi, 13, 16, 559
Collins, Jackie, 127, 173-174, 188, 555
Collins, Ray, 294
Collins, Robert, 117, 166, 180
Columbia Pictures, 27, 370
Como, Perry, 156
Constance Bultman Wilson Center, 161-63
Conte, Richard, 37, 41, 302, 309
Convy, Bert, 115
Cooper, Gary, 24, 41, 238
Corman, Roger, 113-14, 174, 450, 454-55, 494, 498-500
Coward, Noel, 17, 30, 57, 76
Creed, Geraldine, 201, 517-20
Crenna, Richard, 106-07, 165, 194, 197, 506, 508-11, 553, 564
Crosby, Bing, 53, 82, 107
Crowther, Bosley, 33, 74, 277, 301, 376
Cry Terror! (film), 22, 33, 107, 138, 270, 272-73, 275, 453, 562
Culp, Robert, 107-08, 174-75, 494, 497-98, 500
Curtis, Dan, 108-09
Curtis, Tony, 42-43, 63, 341, 344-45

Dalio, Marcel, 48, 213, 252, 325, 329
Daly, James, 437, 440, 443
Damon, Matt, 203, 543
Darin, Bobby, 63, 341, 347
Daves, Delmer, 50, 333, 339-40
David, Hal, 77, 88, 94-95, 102, 123
Davis, Bette, 43, 108, 315, 359, 559-60, 562

Davis, Ossie, 96, 410, 416
Davis, Sammy Jr., xi-xii, 37-38, 302-06, 308-09, 548
Day, Doris, 15, 41, 55-56, 59, 67, 213-15, 366, 434
De Cordova, Fred, 156, 157, 193
De Palma, Brian, 142-43, 145-47, 188, 469, 473, 475-82, 565-66
De Sica, Vittorio, 47
Death Hunt (film), 150-52, 489, 492-93
Death Valley Days (TV show), 14
DeCaro, Frank, 119
Deep Family Secrets (TV movie), 197
DeGeneres, Ellen, 197
Delany, Dana, 182
Delon, Alain, 54, 60, 448
Deluise, Dom, 178
Democratic National Convention, 42
Deray, Jacques, 103, 110-11, 443, 446, 448-50, 565
Dial M for Murder (TV movie), 152, 153, 554
Dickinson, Angie, 35, 38, 55-57, 61, 65, 90, 97, 103, 113, 144-46, 150, 174, 187-89, 211, 214, 217, 220-21, 222, 228, 231, 240, 245-46, 262, 270, 272, 278, 281, 291, 295, 302, 310, 325, 328, 333, 341, 365, 370, 378, 387, 394, 410, 417, 450, 483, 489, 501, 506, 512, 517, 520, 522-23, 529, 536, 545-46, 549
    acting talent of, 13-14, 20, 22, 27-29, 34, 62, 72, 93, 104, 128-29, 135-36, 138, 140, 167-68, 170-72, 175, 177, 181-82, 192, 198-99, 202-03, 209-10, 225-26, 230, 234, 238, 242-43, 250-51, 259, 266, 273-76, 285-87, 294, 299-300, 306-07, 315, 320-21, 329-30, 345-47, 357-59, 374-75, 382-84, 391, 399-401, 406-08, 412-14, 419, 425-27, 433-34, 441, 446-47, 453-54, 460-61, 466, 472-75, 486, 491-92, 497-98, 503-04, 508-10, 514-15, 519, 526, 532-33, 539-40, 551-52, 560-66, 568-69

ANGIE

advertising campaigns fronted by, 105, 154-56

Charlie Feldman and, 51-52, 78-80

childhood of, 1-9

critical assessment of performances, 29, 33, 49-50, 64, 67, 91-92, 94, 99, 129, 141, 147, 152-53, 167, 202, 209, 235, 244, 246-47, 251-52, 260-61, 263-64, 276-77, 288-91, 294, 300-01, 308-09, 316-17, 323-25, 332-33, 339-40, 348-49, 361-62, 368-69, 375-77, 385-87, 393, 401-04, 409-10, 415-16, 421-22, 428-29, 435-37, 443, 448-49, 455-56, 462, 468-69, 478-82, 487-88, 493-94, 498-99, 504-05, 510-11, 516, 520, 534-35, 540-42, 547

daughter Nikki and, 85-89, 93, 11-12, 142, 159-63, 183-85, 192-94, 199, 204, 205-08

early career of, 13-15, 17-22

education of, 3-4, 7-11

female friendships and, 8, 86, 130, 164, 178-79, 195, 210

Frank Sinatra and, xi-xiii, 14, 16, 36-37, 39, 51, 53, 78, 100, 131, 159, 175, 194-96, 211, 305, 382, 568

Glenn Ford and, 51, 93, 163

houses owned by, 45, 81-82, 89, 142, 184, 193

Howard Hawks and, xi, 26-30, 139, 190, 285, 563, 565

Jimmy Van Heusen and, 16-17, 52, 78, 178

Kennedys and, 40, 42-45, 52, 66, 73, 100-01, 211

late career of, 189-92, 194, 196-98, 200-04, 208-10, 503-04, 508-10, 514-15, 519, 522, 526, 532-33, 539-40, 545-46, 551-52

male friendships and, 49, 63, 66, 69, 95-96, 98, 122, 129-31, 158-59, 178-79, 186-87, 194-95, 199, 210

marriage (first) to Gene Dickinson, 12-13, 15-16

marriage (second) to Burt Bacharach, 75, 80-89, 94-95, 102, 105-06, 122-25, 141

parenting shared with ex-husband Bacharach, 159-63, 184

parents of, 2-9, 12, 86, 141-42, 169

personality of, 3-5, 16, 21, 28, 114, 122, 211

physical appearance of, 3, 10, 15, 26, 39, 41, 68, 70, 96, 99, 114, 118-19, 128, 135, 143, 149, 155-56, 170, 173, 181-82, 191, 201-02, 203-04, 209, 211, 237, 253, 293, 298, 305, 313-14, 322, 337-38, 346, 351, 357, 358, 366-67, 415, 420, 433, 454, 475, 485-86, 509, 519, 546, 567

popularity of, 3, 6, 20-21, 28, 131-32, 139, 147-48, 156, 170, 173, 199, 569

Richard Brooks and, 30

sister Janet and, 3-8, 10, 32, 111, 141

sister Mary Lou and, 3-8, 10, 11, 111, 163-65, 185, 199, 204-05

socializing of, 16-18, 30, 52, 75, 82, 111, 127, 178-79, 199, 210

studio contracts of, 30-31, 33, 37, 40, 42, 49-51, 57-60, 67, 71

television career of, 13-15, 18-19, 21, 30, 54, 78-79, 95, 99, 101, 106-10, 114-22, 125-36, 147-48, 152-54, 156-58, 165-74, 176-83, 192, 197-99, 208-10, 553-57, 559

travels of, 46-48, 53-54, 79-80, 126, 132, 133-34, 137-39, 151-52, 161, 176, 194, 199, 205

Dickinson, Gene, 11-13, 15-17
Didion, Joan, 208, 584, 589
Dierkop, Charles, 115-16
Dietrich, Marlene, 60, 76, 79, 82-84, 97, 124, 210, 225, 560
Dillman, Bradford, 56, 110, 437, 440, 442-43
Don's Analyst, The (TV movie), 197, 557
Donahue, Troy, 50, 75, 333, 337-40
Donner, Clive, 149, 483, 486, 489
Dors, Diana, 21, 28, 264, 266-69
Douglas, Gordon, 34, 246, 317, 323
Douglas, Kirk, 38, 82, 196, 211, 300, 378, 381-83, 385-87, 564
Douglas, Mike, 133, 141
Dourif, Brad, 182
Down Liberty Road (film), 228, 230-31
Dr. Kildare (TV show), 78
Dressed to Kill (film), 142-43, 146, 150, 174, 182, 198, 454, 469, 472, 475, 477-82, 559, 562, 564-66
Duets (film), 200, 523, 527-29
Dunaway, Faye, 61, 189, 204, 460
Dunn, Nora, 176
Durante, Jimmy, 14
Durning, Charles, 166, 520
Duvall, Robert, 63, 71, 341, 347, 370, 376
Dwan, Allan, 216, 218-19, 565
Dynasty (TV show), 157, 173

East, Jeff, 138, 462, 468
Edgeley, North Dakota, 3-5
Edwards, Nadine, 92, 369, 403
Edwards, Ralph, 187-88
Egan, Richard, 235, 237-39
Elam, Jack, 169, 404, 409
Elvis Has Left the Building (film), 204, 549, 552
Emmy Awards, 57, 107, 120, 129
Entratter, Jack, xi, 38
Ephron, Henry, 61, 341, 348
Ephron, Phoebe, 61, 341, 348
Even Cowgirls Get the Blues (film), 189, 192, 501, 505, 560

Fay, Paul "Red" Jr., 44-45
Ferrer, Mel, 54, 153
Ferzetti, Gabriele, 48-49, 325, 329-30
Fever in the Blood, A (film), 42, 49, 81, 310, 313-14, 366, 564
Finch, Peter, 34, 36, 300, 317, 320, 322, 564
Finney, Albert, 60
Fire and Rain (TV movie), 169-70, 556
Fisher, Eddie, xii, 75
Fleming, Ian, 85, 387, 390, 394
Fonda, Jane, 56, 61, 71, 104, 204, 370, 373, 377, 432
Ford, Gerald, 120
Ford, Glenn, 51, 55, 93, 94, 163, 178, 404, 408-10, 564-65
Ford, Harrison, 194, 505, 508
Ford, John, 243, 287
Forrest, Steve, 173
Fox, James, 71, 370, 373, 376-77
Frankenheimer, John, 54, 100
Fuller, Sam, 19, 20-21, 30, 72, 139, 246, 252-53, 256-60, 565

Galbraith, John Kenneth, 45, 53
Gammell, Robin, 463, 468
Gardner, Ava, 37, 47, 64, 354
Garland, Judy, 17, 42, 51, 93
Garmes, Lee, 223, 225-27
Garner, James, 67-69, 126, 148, 247, 251-52, 362, 366-69
Gary, Romain, 54, 100
Gates, Daryl, 121
Gazzara, Ben, 165
Gelbart, Larry, 178, 199, 210
Genie Awards, 468
Gerber, David, 115-16, 120, 122, 132
Ghost Story (TV show), 109
Giamatti, Paul, 202, 506, 523, 527-28
Glaser, Paul Michael, 173
Glendale College, 11
Gobel, George, 21, 28, 264, 267-69
Golden Globe Awards, 41, 103, 120
Gordon, Keith, 143, 182, 469, 476, 478, 482

Gormé, Eydie, 196, 545
Grable, Betty, 60, 328
Graham, Sheila, 89
Grant, Cary, 38, 60, 178, 345, 413, 420, 560
Grant, Johnny, xii-xiii, 38, 45, 82, 176
Grant, Lee, 483, 486-88
Greco, Dani Crayne, 129, 247, 252
Greenberg, Abe, 60, 102
Greene, Lorne, 138, 462, 468-69
Greene, Shecky, 200, 522
Gregory, James, 63, 341
Griffith, Andy, 110
Gulager, Clu, 65, 66, 349, 355, 357, 360
Gun the Man Down (film), 18, 97, 240, 243, 245, 427
Gunsmoke (TV show), 18-19, 21, 96, 243, 246

Hanks, Tom, 204, 549, 552
Hanson, Jane, 85
Hartman, Phil, 176-77
Hatch, Richard, 149, 483, 486
Hawks, Howard, xi, 23-29, 31, 72, 139, 190, 278, 283, 285, 287-90, 293, 563, 565
Hayward, Susan, 36, 41, 107
Hayworth, Rita, 85, 163, 387, 392
Hellman, Lillian, 71, 370, 372-73, 376-77
Helmond, Katherine, 136
Hemingway, Ernest, 64, 67, 349, 353, 355
Hepburn, Audrey, 34, 158, 320, 508, 510-11
Hewitt, Peter, 182
Hidden Guns (film), 18, 231, 426
High Noon (film), 24-25, 227, 238, 291
Hirsch, Judd, 198
Hitchcock, Alfred, iv, 54, 79, 143, 145-46, 152, 268, 294, 314, 442, 476-77, 479-80, 554, 564
Holden, William, 25, 508
Holliman, Earl, 116, 119, 120, 122, 130-31, 188
Hopkins, Anthony, 173

Hollywood Wives (TV miniseries), 127, 173, 555
Hooks, Jan, 177
Hope, Bob, 41, 85, 156, 177, 188, 384
Hopper, Hedda, 30
Howard, Arliss, 202-03, 536, 538-42
Howard, Trevor, 85, 387, 391-93
Howe, Dorothy, 8, 164
Hudson, Ernie, 182
Hudson, Rock, 59, 60, 104, 178, 366, 429, 434-36, 564
Huggins, Roy, 42, 310, 315-16
Humphrey, Hal, 79
Humphrey, Hubert, 75, 161
Hunt, Helen, 200-02, 529, 532-35
Hunt, Peter, 151, 489, 492, 493
Hunter, Ross, 67-68, 251, 362, 366, 368-69
Hurt, John, 190, 192, 501, 503-05
Huston, Danny, 512, 516

I Married a Woman (film), 21, 28, 264, 266-69
I'll Give My Life (film), 31, 291, 293, 321
Iglesias, Julio, 158
Immaculate Heart College, 10-11

Jackson, Victoria, 176
Jameson, Jerry, 171
Janssen, David, 128-29, 134, 178
Jealousy (TV movie), 171-72, 179, 555, 561
Jeffries, Herb, 261-64
Jessica (film), 46-49, 54, 83, 325-32, 562, 564, 567-68
Jewison, Norman, 67-69, 148, 362, 365-66, 369
Joanou, Phil, 182
Johnson, Lamont, 55-57
Johnson, Victoria Lynn, 145, 475

Kael, Pauline, 74, 146, 482
Kaminsky, Stuart, 67, 358
Kanin, Garson, 98, 417, 420
Kanter, Hal, 264, 268-269
Kaplan, James, 44

Keith, Brian, 483, 488
Kelly, Grace, 85, 152, 388, 392, 560
Kelly, Jack, 42-43, 310, 314-315, 422
Kennedy, Burt, 18, 97, 169, 240, 244, 422, 427, 429
Kennedy, John F., 23, 40, 42-45, 52, 56, 63, 66, 100, 211, 360
Kennedy, Robert (Bobby), 100-101
Kennedy, Ted, 101, 159
Killers, The (film), 65, 67, 93, 111, 137, 181, 211, 349, 351, 358-361, 427, 453, 562, 565-568
"Killers, The" (short story), 64, 353, 354
King, Larry, 158, 196, 201-202, 205
Kinnear, Greg, 194, 506, 508
Klondike Fever (film), 133, 138-140, 462, 468, 564
Klugman, Jack, 270, 272, 275-277
Kojak: Fatal Flaw (TV movie), 179, 556
Koscina, Sylva, 48, 325, 329
Kruschen, Jack, 270, 275
Kulm, North Dakota, 1-3, 31, 49, 129

LaBonge, Tom, 210
Lampert, Zohra, 417, 419, 422
Lancaster, Burt, 64, 354
Lantz, Walter, 193, 583, 594
Last Challenge, The (film), 93-94, 170, 404, 408-10, 425-26, 562, 564
Last Producer, The (film), 200, 415, 520, 522-23
Lauter, Ed, 489, 493
Laven, Arnold, 96, 410, 415-16
Lawford, Peter, xi-xiii, 37-38, 40, 42, 52-53, 101, 302, 304-06, 308-09
Lazar, Irving "Swifty," 17, 127, 177, 193
Leder, Mimi, 201-02, 529, 533-35, 565
Leigh, Janet, 42-43, 52, 59, 144-45, 209-10, 472
Leighton, Laura, 209-10
Lemmon, Jack, 129, 196, 210, 267
Lentz, Robert, 91
Lewis, Huey, 523, 527-28
L'homme en colère (film), 133, 137, 456, 460-62

Lo Bianco, Tony, 165
Loggia, Robert, 182, 197
Love War, The (TV movie), 101, 553
Lovitz, Jon, 176-77
Loy, Myrna, 20, 107, 560
Lucky Me (film), 15, 213, 215

Mac, Bernie, 203, 543
Mackie, Bob, 124
MacLaine, Shirley, 41-42, 100, 204, 307
Maddening, The (film), 196, 512, 516, 566
Mahony, Roger Cardinal, 196
Main, Sue, 207
Malone, Dorothy, 221, 235, 238-39
Man with the Gun (film), 15, 55, 222, 225, 227, 426, 561
Mann, Roderick, 125, 151
Manners, Dorothy, 128
Marchand, Nancy, 194, 506, 508
Marcus, Mickey, 378, 381
Marshall, E.G., 71, 85, 95, 370, 377, 387, 391-93
Marshall, Herbert, 42, 310, 314
Martin, Dean, xi-xiii, 25, 37-38, 175, 278, 302, 308-10, 548
    Angie's friendship with, 129-30
    Angie career connections with, 39-40, 95, 129-31, 177, 211, 281, 288-91, 304-07
Martin, Jeanne, 210
Marvin, Lee, 65, 67, 89-92, 151-53, 211, 300, 349, 355-56, 358, 361-62, 394, 398-401, 403, 417, 444, 489, 492-94, 564
*M*A*S*H* (TV show), 126
MASH (film), 61, 103-04, 344, 568
Maslin, Janet, 152, 511
Mason, James, 22, 79, 270, 272, 275-77, 564
Mastroianni, Marcello, 54, 85, 387, 392
McBain, Diane, 33, 50
McDowall, Roddy, 104, 173, 178, 429, 434, 483, 486, 488
McLaglen, Andrew V., 18, 240, 243-44
McWilliams, Carey, 5

Melcher, Martin, 55-56
Mending Fences (TV movie), 208, 552, 557
Mengers, Sue, 127, 173
Meredith, Don, 122, 165
Merman, Ethel, 44, 68, 94, 362, 365, 369
Merrick, David, 94
Metty, Russell, 68, 341, 347, 363, 366, 368
Milestone, Lewis, 38-40, 302, 306, 308, 548
Miller, David, 63, 341, 348-49
Miller, Dennis, 176
Miller, Nolan, 173, 178
Mitchell, Cameron, 106, 235, 238-40
Mitchum, Robert, 17, 97-98, 130, 153-54, 222, 226-28, 288, 422, 426-29, 460, 564-65
Monroe, Marilyn, 10, 38, 47, 267, 328, 413
Montiel, Sarita, 19-20
Moore, Mary Tyler, 119-20, 126
Moore, Roger, 34, 36, 317, 322
Moorehead, Agnes, 48, 325, 329
Moreau, Jeanne, 54, 59
Morse, Barry, 138, 462, 468-69
Morse, Robert, 181
Moss, Morton, 102, 115, 125
Muhl, Edward, 59
Mulligan, Richard, 173, 179
Murphy, Mary, 105-06, 156-57
Murray, Don, 166, 168

Naremore, James, 560
Nealon, Kevin, 177
Negulesco, Jean, 46-49, 325, 328-32, 565
Nehru, Jawaharlal, 53-54
Nelson, David, 81
Nelson, June Blair, 81, 86
Nelson, Ralph, 79
Nelson, Ricky, 25, 27-28, 81, 278, 288-91
Nelson, Willie, 169-70
Neuwirth, Bebe, 182
Newhart, Bob, 126, 195, 198, 338
Newland, John, 127-29, 134, 139-40, 172, 566
Nielsen, Leslie, 110, 437, 441-42
Niven, David, 17, 58-59, 267
Noel-Noel, 48, 325, 329-30

Norliss Tapes, The (TV movie), 108-109, 553, 566
Nun's Story, The (film), 33-34, 320, 322
Nuyen, France, 173
Nyby, Christian, 26-27

O'Connor, Carroll, 131, 310, 316, 394, 400, 403
O'Connor, John J., 129, 167, 182
Ocean's Eleven (1961 film), xiii, 28, 37, 39, 41, 43, 114, 131, 302, 304-05, 308, 345
Ocean's Eleven (2001 film), 203, 543, 545, 547
Old Tucson, Arizona, 27, 97, 170
Once Upon a Texas Train (TV movie), 169-70
One Shoe Makes It Murder (TV movie), 98, 153-54, 555
Ormond, Julia, 194, 505, 508
Osment, Haley Joel, 202, 529, 532, 534
Outside Man, The (film), 110-11, 137, 443, 446, 448-50, 562
Overboard (TV movie), 133-34, 137, 554, 564, 566

Paltrow, Bruce, 200, 523, 527-28
Paltrow, Gwyneth, 200, 202, 523, 526, 528, 568
Parish, James Robert, 503
Parks, Michael, 152, 536, 542
Password (TV show), 79, 101
Pay It Forward (film), 200-02, 529, 532-35, 563
Pearl (TV miniseries), 133-34, 136, 141, 554
Peck, Gregory, 38, 57, 61, 63-64, 129, 178, 196, 199, 201, 210, 300, 341, 344-49, 564
Penn, Arthur, 71-74, 370, 372-73, 375-77, 454, 565
Penn, Leo, 79
Perfect Setup, The (play), 55-56
Petrie, Daniel, 32, 295, 300, 301
Pfeiffer, Michelle, 483, 486
Pinoteau, Claude, 137-38, 456, 461

Pinsent, Gordon, 138-40, 462, 468
Pitt, Brad, 85, 203, 543, 546
Pleshette, Suzanne, 50, 129, 333, 338-340
Plummer, Christopher, 152
Point Blank (film), 89-94, 111, 137, 147, 356, 394, 397-398, 400, 402-03, 482, 494, 559, 565
Police Story (TV show), 114, 121
Police Story: The Freeway Killings (TV movie), 165, 555
Police Woman (TV show), 116-18, 120-22, 124-27, 131-32, 136, 139, 158, 166, 168, 180, 187, 211, 434, 475, 554, 559, 564-65
Pollack, Sydney, 506, 509-11, 565
Poppy Is Also a Flower, The (film), 85, 387, 392-94
Porter, Don, 50, 108, 333-34
Powers, Stefanie, 173
Pray for the Wildcats (TV movie), 110, 554
Pretty Maids All in a Row (film), 103-04, 179, 192, 429, 432-33, 435-36, 560
Prime Target (TV movie), 165-66, 556
Promises, Promises (play), 94-95
Psycho (film), 143-45, 472, 474, 476-77

Quayle, Anthony, 95, 152
Quinn, Anthony, 56, 109

Rat Pack, 23, 37, 39, 42, 67, 119, 195, 203, 304, 362, 546, 548
Reagan, Nancy, 130, 196
Reagan, Ronald, 51, 65-66, 130, 148, 159, 216, 219, 349, 355, 359-60
Reasoner, Harry, 158-59
Redford, Robert, 71, 370, 373, 376-77
Reeves, Richard, 44
Reiner, Carl, 67-69, 362, 365-66, 369, 543
Resurrection of Zachary Wheeler, The (film), 110, 437, 440, 442-43
Return of Jack Slade, The (film), 15, 220
Reynolds, Burt, 95-96, 148, 188, 196, 200, 217, 410, 412, 414, 416, 420, 512, 516, 520-23, 564
Rickles, Don, 131, 157, 179, 192, 195, 198
Ringo (TV movie), 132, 554

Rio Bravo (film), xi, xiii, 23-25, 29, 31, 39, 41, 47, 63, 72, 81, 116, 130, 139, 170, 211, 250, 278, 281, 283, 286-90, 293, 345, 425, 455, 559, 563, 565, 569
Ritter, Tex, 228-29, 231
Rivers, Joan, 159, 204, 392
RKO Pictures, 15, 19, 21, 34, 216, 218, 235, 264
Roberts, Julia, 203, 543, 546
Roberts, Rachel, 483, 486, 488
Robertson, Cliff, 133, 134
Rocca, Mo, 132, 189, 210
Roddenberry, Gene, 103, 429, 432
Rolf, Tom, 438, 440
Rome Adventure (film), 49-50, 65, 333, 336, 338-40, 366, 420, 562
Rourke, Jack, 13, 169
Rowlands, Gena, 61, 568
Run of the Arrow (film), 19, 138, 258
Rush, Barbara, 32-33, 41, 295, 299-01

Sabrina (film), 194-95, 505-09, 511, 564
Sager, Carole Bayer, 141-42, 160, 185
Sam Whiskey (film), 95, 99, 410-11, 413-16, 420, 564, 567
Sands Hotel and Casino, xi, 17, 38, 81, 302, 306
Sarris, Andrew, 146, 480-81
Saturday Night Live (TV show), 176-77
Savalas, Telly, 104, 178-79, 429, 434
Scheider, Roy, 111, 443, 446-448
Schickel, Richard, 74, 377
Schlesinger, Arthur Jr., 45
Schneider, Batami, 14, 562
Schneider, Romy, 54, 80
Schuster, Harold, 220-222
Scott, Randolph, 247, 250-252, 564
Sealed with a Kiss (TV movie), 197, 557
See the Man Run (TV movie), 107, 553
Sensitive, Passionate Man, A (TV movie), 128-29, 140, 554, 566
Server, Lee, 153
77 Sunset Strip (TV show), 42, 45, 315
Shandling, Garry, 198-99, 567

Shatner, William, 113-14, 122, 450, 454-55
Shavelson, Melville, 378, 384-86
Sher, Jack, 55-56
Sherman, Vincent, 42-43, 310, 315-16, 565
Shoot-Out at Medicine Bend (film), 18, 247
Shoup, Howard, 264, 295, 302, 310, 333, 337
Siegel, Don, 64, 66, 67, 349, 354, 358-62, 565
Silva, Henry, 37, 203, 302, 545, 547
Simon, Neil, 94
Sinatra, Barbara, 178, 195, 199, 210
Sinatra, Frank, xi-xiii, 16-17, 175, 194-96, 302, 308-10, 378, 386-87, 522, 548
    Angie career connections with, 14, 37, 39, 40, 131, 304-07, 382
    Angie's relationship with, 36-37, 51, 131, 211
    John Kennedy and, 40, 44, 52-53
Sins of Rachel Cade, The (film), 33-35, 49, 317, 320-22, 324, 330, 345, 562, 565
Siodmak, Robert, 64, 354
Skerritt, Tom, 113, 450, 454-56
Soderbergh, Steven, 203, 543, 546-48
Some Kind of a Nut (film), 98-99, 417, 419-20, 422, 566
Sommer, Elke, 54, 67-68, 362, 365-66, 368-69
Sommers, Suzanne, 173-74
Spacey, Kevin, 202, 529, 532, 534
Spelling, Aaron, 173
Spiegel, Sam, 71, 73-74 370, 372-73, 376
Stack, Robert, 173, 195-97
Stanwyck, Barbara, 20, 107, 116, 321, 568
Starr, Ringo, 132-33, 554
Steiger, Rod, 22, 56, 138, 173, 270, 272-73, 275-77, 300, 462, 466, 468, 520, 523, 564
Steiner, Max, 34, 252, 317, 321, 333, 340
Sterling, Jan, 55, 57, 222, 227-28
Stevens, Andrew, 489
Stevens, Connie, 33, 50-51
Stevens, Inger, 270, 272, 275-77
Stewart, Catherine Mary, 173

Stewart, Jimmy, 129-30
Stewart, Paula, 76
Stillwatch (TV movie), 166-67, 555, 564
Stone, Andrew, 22, 270, 275-77
Stone, Oliver, 182
Stone, Virginia, 275-77
Sturges, Preston, 13, 68, 468
Suicide's Wife, The (TV movie), 140-41, 554, 566
Sun, the Moon and the Stars, The (film), 196, 198, 201, 517-18
Svenson, Bo, 173

Talbot, Nita, 264, 268-69
Tamiroff, Akim, 302, 305, 309
Tarantino, Quentin, 356, 435
Taylor, Elizabeth, 107, 178
Tennant, William, 153
Tennessee's Partner (film), 15, 216, 218, 225
Tension at Table Rock (film), 18-19, 235, 237
Thief (TV movie), 106-07, 165, 553
Thinnes, Roy, 108
This Is Your Life (TV show), 187-89
Thomas, Kevin, 90, 93, 99, 403, 409, 429, 436, 456, 489, 494, 542
Thomas, Bob, 60
Thomson, David, 29, 399, 401, 432
Thorpe, Richard, 93-94, 404, 408-09
Thurman, Uma, 190-92, 501, 503, 505
Tobey, Kenneth, 270, 275
Tonight Show, The (TV show), 131, 153, 156-57, 159, 189, 198
Torn, Rip, 198
Tosches, Nick, 130-31, 195
Touch of Scandal, A (TV movie), 166, 555, 564
Treacherous Crossing (TV movie), 179, 556
Trintignant, Jean-Louis, 111, 443, 446-49
20th Century Fox, 32, 73, 152, 244, 252, 258, 316, 331, 373
Tynan, Kenneth, 127
Tyrrell, Susan, 173

Universal Pictures, 57-59, 61, 63-64, 66-68, 71, 264, 341, 349, 362, 366, 567
Ustinov, Peter, 149-50, 483, 485-86, 488

Vadim, Roger, 103-04, 429, 432, 434-37, 565
Van Dyke, Dick, 67-69, 98, 188, 197, 362, 365-66, 369, 417, 419-21, 422
Van Heusen, Jimmy, 16-17, 36, 44, 52, 78, 178, 304
Van Sant, Gus, 189, 501, 503-05, 565
Ventura, Lino, 137-38, 456, 461-62
Vitti, Monica, 568

Wagner, Bruce, 136, 180-81, 556
Wagner, Lindsay, 179
Walker, Clint, 96, 410, 416
Walker, Jimmy, 130
Walker, Robert Jr., 422, 428, 429
Wallach, Eli, 85, 387, 392-93
Walters, Charles, 58
Warner Bros., xii, 6, 9, 15, 23-24, 27-31, 33-34, 36-37, 40, 42, 45, 49-51, 57, 59, 71, 73, 117, 213-14, 247, 251, 278, 295, 300, 310, 314-15, 317, 320, 322, 331, 333, 339, 359, 373, 534, 543, 567
Warner, David, 182
Warner, Jack, 7, 33, 37, 41, 51
Warren, Charles Marquis, 235, 244, 246-47
Warwick, Dionne, 77, 82-83, 102, 123

Wayne, John, xii, 17-18, 22, 25-28, 41, 82, 84, 138, 211, 243, 250, 264-66, 269, 278, 281, 286, 288-91, 300, 378, 382-85, 387, 428, 564, 569
Weaver, Dennis, 135
Welles, Orson, 130, 226, 355, 539
West, Mae, 68, 426
What's New Pussycat? (film), 79, 85, 123, 149, 365
White, Theodore H., 42
Widmark, Richard, 169-70, 564-65
Wild Palms (TV miniseries), 136, 180-83, 201, 556, 559, 562, 565, 582, 596
Wilder, Billy, 23, 194, 419, 505, 508, 510-11
Williams, John, 80, 350, 360, 506, 510
Winger, Debra, 536, 539-41
Wolders, Rob, 158
Wood, Natalie, 41, 54
Wood, Robin, 29, 72, 375
Wynn, Keenan, 394, 402-03, 429, 434
Wynorski, Jim, 174-75, 494, 497-99

Young Billy Young (film), 96, 98-99, 153, 170, 422, 425, 427-29, 561
Young, Faron, 231, 233-34
Young, Terence, 85, 387, 390-94

Zimbalist, Efrem Jr., 42-43, 101, 310, 313-15
Zwick, Joel, 204, 549, 552

www.ingramcontent.com/pod-product-compliance
Lightning Source LLC
Chambersburg PA
CBHW060906300426
44112CB00011B/1362